Innovative Applications and Changing Framework in Digital Broadcasting

Nursel Bolat
Ondokuz Mayis University, Turkey

IGI Global
Scientific Publishing
Publishing Tomorrow's Research Today

Vice President of Editorial Melissa Wagner
Director of Acquisitions Mikaela Felty
Director of Book Development Jocelynn Hessler
Production Manager Mike Brehm
Cover Design Jose Rosado

Published in the United States of America by
IGI Global Scientific Publishing
701 East Chocolate Avenue
Hershey, PA, 17033, USA
Tel: 717-533-8845
Fax: 717-533-7115
Website: https://www.igi-global.com E-mail: cust@igi-global.com

Library of Congress Cataloging-in-Publication Data

Names: Bolat, Nursel, 1968- editor
Title: Innovative applications and changing framework in digital broadcasting / edited by Nursel Bolat.
Description: Hershey, PA : IGI Global Scientific Publishing, [2025] | Includes bibliographical references and index. | Summary: "The book aims to comprehend the developments and changes in the field of digital publishing in a multidimensional way in the digitalizing world"-- Provided by publisher.
Identifiers: LCCN 2025009730 (print) | LCCN 2025009731 (ebook) | ISBN 9798337319575 h/c | ISBN 9798337319582 s/c | ISBN 9798337319599 ebook
Subjects: LCSH: Online journalism | Webcasting | Information behavior | Digital media
Classification: LCC PN4784.O62 I45 2025 (print) | LCC PN4784.O62 (ebook) | DDC 302.23/1--dc23/eng/20250509
LC record available at https://lccn.loc.gov/2025009730
LC ebook record available at https://lccn.loc.gov/2025009731

British Cataloguing in Publication Data
A Cataloguing in Publication record for this book is available from the British Library.

Editorial Advisory Board

Table of Contents

Transformation of Reality and Space

Detailed Table of Contents

In addition to providing high-quality images and sound in the field of broadcasting, digitalization has also greatly changed content production processes. With this transformation, analog broadcasting was replaced by the digital coding system. Digital platforms interacting with new media have created significant changes in both content production and audience habits. The main purpose of the study is to analyze the transition process of television broadcasting from traditional to digital and to evaluate the functionality of digital broadcast platforms that emerged in this process. Additionally, the transformation in audience habits is also addressed with these platforms. As a result, with the effect of digitalization, television broadcasting has become a versatile and interactive communication tool rather than just a broadcasting medium.

The present study aims to explore and discuss the transformation of movie and TV series viewing experiences in the digital age. The study sought to address the following research questions: why are digital platforms preferred over traditional channels, and how do internet-based digital viewing platforms transform viewing habits? The study adopted a qualitative research model, conducting in-depth interviews with ten participants who expressed a preference for digital platforms over traditional ones. The data set obtained was subjected to content analysis. The analysis yielded several key reasons for the preference for digital platforms over traditional platforms, including independence from time and space, the presence of original storylines

The study examines the binge-watching habits popularized with the rise of digital media platforms and the effects of these habits on media consumption habits. Platforms such as Netflix, Amazon Prime Video and Hulu have encouraged binge-watching by making content instantly accessible, offering viewers a seamless viewing experience. Thanks to technological innovations, personalized content recommendations and advanced algorithms, these habits may deepen in the future. AI-powered systems can reinforce binge-watching behaviors by recommending content based on viewers' moods and viewing history.

This study examines the role of the TRT-established digital platform Tabii in the representation and promotion of Turkish culture in response to the growing cultural hegemony imposed by international streaming services, particularly Netflix. Drawing upon theoretical frameworks such as Antonio Gramsci's concept of cultural hegemony and Adorno and Horkheimer's culture industry, the article investigates how digital platforms have become central to the transmission of cultural narratives. The study focuses on TRT's international digital platform "Tabii" and this platform's historical dramas available exclusively on the platform and utilizes Roland Barthes' semiotic approach to analyze cultural representations embedded in these narratives. The selected sample includes five series—Mahsusa Trablusgarb, Kızıl Elma, Akif, Rumi, and Hay Sultan—which span various epochs of Turkish history and foreground themes central to Turkish identity.

This study examines the evolution of radio audience interaction from the early days of letter writing and radio magazines to contemporary engagement through social media platforms such as Instagram, Facebook, and X. Using the netnography method, it analyzes audience behavior toward Turkey's most listened-to radio stations and prominent presenters. The findings reveal a shift in audience loyalty from radio institutions to individual broadcasters, driven by the immediacy and accessibility

As digital publishing platforms undergo a significant transformation in content production, AI-themed films have become central to this shift. These platforms present such content through varying strategies—some focus on popular and accessible productions, while others prioritize philosophical and niche themes. This study examines how AI-themed films are represented on digital publishing platforms and how these narratives shape the broader media ecosystem. Through a comparative analysis of Netflix's JUNG_E and Apple TV+'s Swan Song, the study finds that while JUNG_E offers a critique of class exploitation and gender through an action-driven and dystopian narrative, Swan Song explores themes of individual consciousness through ethical and existential questions. In both films, the representation of the body and the boundaries between humans and artificial intelligence are addressed through cultural and ideological codes. Moreover, the content strategies of the platforms significantly influence the form and presentation of the films.

Cinema, with its use of virtual technologies that immerse the audience in the narrative and present reality in new ways, reinvokes Siegfried Kracauer's concept of the 'found story'. Kracauer states that everyday reality can be captured through cinema and defines this as the 'found story'. This study aims to explore that concept within the framework of VR film technology. The research focuses on National Geographic's 360-degree VR series Plastic on the Ganges, which addresses social reality. The series depicts how plastic waste pollutes oceans and drinking water, affecting both human health and ecosystems. Its impact comes not only from what it tells but also from how it allows the audience to experience the story in an immersive way. The audience becomes part of the scene, among real individuals whose health is at risk. Thus, the 'found story' does not express the spectacle of a reality, but its experience.

At the intersection of postmodernism and cinema, digital platforms offer an innovative context that redefines the concept of space. In this way, space becomes not only a physical background but also a narrative element enriched with aesthetic, cultural and ideological elements. The Hannibal series is a powerful example of how space design is integrated with postmodern aesthetics and how it leaves an impact on the audience. The spaces used in the series are not only the movement spaces of the characters, but also metaphorical reflections of their psychological states, ideological conflicts and the narrative. The grotesque murder scenes shaped by aesthetics both disturb the viewer and prompt a deep questioning process on ethics and aesthetics. The viewer is confronted with simulations that manipulate their spatial perceptions and encourage them to get lost in the fictional world.

Spaces are essential elements of visual narratives and act as a supporting force for storytelling. As cinema and television broadcasting rapidly integrate with evolving technology, they are taking a leading role in creating innovative spaces. Virtual Production, a combination of virtual reality (VR), augmented reality (AR), and advanced computer graphics, offers a revolutionary method for film and television production. Virtual Production stands out as an approach that merges virtual environments with physical shooting processes, enhancing both creative freedom and production efficiency. By joining the realm of spaces created in virtual environments, Virtual Production opens up new and fascinating horizons for the cinema and television industries. Through the technological integration of footage shot at different times and locations, new virtual spaces are brought to life.

Foreword

In an era profoundly marked by digital transformation, broadcasting stands as a compelling testament to technology's potential to reshape culture, society, and everyday life. The book, *Innovative Applications and Changing Framework in Digital Broadcasting*, skillfully edited by Nursel Bolat, presents a comprehensive exploration into how digitalization has fundamentally altered not only the media landscape but also the very nature of content production, audience interaction, and narrative engagement.

Under Bolat's meticulous guidance, chapters authored by scholars from diverse academic backgrounds systematically address the transformative influence of digital platforms on traditional broadcasting paradigms. Her editorial expertise ensures an insightful investigation of profound shifts in viewing habits, content consumption, and audience preferences triggered by the ascendancy of digital media. Topics such as binge-watching behaviors, personalized content delivery through artificial intelligence, and the interactive dynamics fostered by social media platforms are carefully examined to uncover their implications for viewers and media producers alike. Additionally, the volume delves into critical ethical considerations emerging from technological advancements in broadcasting. Issues around data privacy, misinformation, and algorithmic bias are thoughtfully explored, emphasizing the need for ethical frameworks and accountability in digital media practices.

Further enhancing its richness, the book engages with the international dimensions of digital broadcasting, highlighting cultural strategies such as TRT's "Tabii" platform, which actively counters global cultural hegemony through historically grounded narratives. Furthermore, the interplay between traditional mediums and emerging technologies, including virtual production and artificial intelligence, is scrutinized to reveal their revolutionary potential and challenges within contemporary broadcasting.

Ultimately, this publication, expertly curated by Nursel Bolat, not only captures the essence of digital broadcasting's current state but also anticipates future trends and ethical challenges, providing invaluable insights for academics, media professionals, policymakers, and students seeking to understand and navigate the ever-evolving digital media landscape.

Recep Yılmaz
Ondokuz Mayıs University, Turkey

Preface

INTRODUCTION

The rapid development of digital technologies has revolutionized the broadcasting landscape, reshaping not only the way content is produced, distributed, and consumed but also how audiences engage with media. Traditional broadcasting models, once dominated by linear programming and passive audiences, are now giving way to on-demand, personalized, and interactive experiences. This edited volume, *Innovative Applications and Changing Framework in Digital Broadcasting*, brings together a diverse range of perspectives from scholars and researchers across Turkey, India, and Ethiopia to examine the evolution, impact, and future of broadcasting in a digital era.

The chapters in this book reflect a rich interdisciplinary approach—encompassing media studies, communication theory, cultural studies, ethics, technology, and audience analysis—to investigate the significant shifts that define contemporary digital broadcasting. From the influence of artificial intelligence and virtual reality to the cultural narratives promoted through streaming platforms, this book aims to offer readers a comprehensive understanding of the transformative forces at play.

CHAPTER OVERVIEW

Chapter 1 by *Nursel Bolat* examines the transformation of traditional television broadcasting with the advent of digital platforms. It explores how audience habits have shifted toward more interactive and diversified consumption.

Chapter 2 by *Rabiya Saltik Duvan* delves into the new TV and movie watching behaviors shaped by digital platforms, highlighting preferences such as binge-watching, genre-based selection, and ad-free viewing.

Chapter 3 by *Damla Saylan* and *Ömer Çakin* compares traditional Turkish television series with digital series, analyzing how the structure and content have evolved to meet the expectations of an increasingly active audience.

Chapter 4 by *Prof. Rashid Hashmi* presents a critical look at ethical considerations in digital broadcasting, particularly focusing on AI integration, algorithmic bias, and data privacy in an increasingly automated environment.

Chapter 5 by *Serhat Erdem* investigates the rise of binge-watching as a central behavior in digital media consumption, identifying its technological, psychological, and social underpinnings.

Chapter 6 by *Aysegul Akaydin Aydin* offers an in-depth analysis of the TRT digital platform "Tabii" and how it serves as a tool for cultural preservation and international promotion of Turkish historical narratives.

Chapter 7 by *Ufuk Inal* tracks the evolution of audience interaction in radio broadcasting, from letters and magazines to real-time engagement via social media.

Chapter 8 by *Shashi Kant* et al. examines personalized broadcasting in the Horn of Africa, introducing the concept of "Pop-cast" and how tailored digital content boosts audience engagement.

Chapter 9 by *Yagmur Kiliç* explores virtual universe narratives in series like *Upload* and *Black Mirror*, comparing how different platforms construct digital immortality and virtual consciousness.

Chapter 10 by *Mert Gürer*, *Gözde Islamoglu*, and *Emel Ateşçi* discusses Netflix's venture into gaming, analyzing how interactive gaming strategies enrich user experiences and reinforce platform loyalty.

Chapter 11 by *Volkan Cetin* presents a comparative analysis between traditional and AI-powered broadcasting, highlighting improvements in production efficiency, quality, and audience interaction.

Chapter 12 by *Fahrettin Kayan* tackles the modern dilemma of smartphone dependency, evaluating its effects on social behavior, attention span, and digital well-being through a multidisciplinary lens.

Chapter 13 by *Abdulkadir Cabuk* and *Esennur Sirer* explores the participatory culture around television series on social media, showing how fan-driven content creation blurs the line between producer and consumer.

Chapter 14 by *Tugçe Karaca Özdemir* compares AI-themed films on different platforms, revealing how content strategies and narrative techniques vary between popular appeal and philosophical depth.

Chapter 15 by *Ummuhan Molo* and *Kubra Nisanoglu* analyzes the use of 360-degree VR films in conveying social reality, drawing from Kracauer's notion of the "found story" to explore immersive storytelling.

Chapter 16 by *Esennur Sirer* highlights how artificial intelligence is integrated across all stages of television production, from scriptwriting to audience targeting, and what this means for the future of broadcasting.

Chapter 17 by *Cem Tutar* applies Henri Lefebvre's theory to digital television broadcasting, focusing on how it intersects with the temporal and spatial rhythms of everyday life in urban environments.

Chapter 18 by *Can Murat Demir* and *Yeter Demir* investigates the construction of narrative space in digital publishing through postmodernist aesthetics, using the *Hannibal* series as a case study.

Chapter 19 by *Arzu Çelik* and *Nursel Bolat* explores the use of Virtual Production in broadcasting, revealing how digital and physical environments merge to create immersive and efficient storytelling spaces.

CONCLUSION

This book provides an essential resource for scholars, practitioners, and students interested in understanding the dynamic and multifaceted world of digital broadcasting. Each chapter offers a unique lens, collectively mapping out the innovations, challenges, and future directions of an industry in constant flux. As we move deeper into a digitally mediated society, the insights offered in this volume become increasingly vital for navigating and shaping the future of media and communication.

Nursel Bolat
Ondokuz Mayıs University, Turkey

Section 1
Current Views of Television and Radio Broadcasting

Chapter 1
The Transformation of the Viewer With Digital Platforms in Television Broadcasting

Nursel Bolat
https://orcid.org/0000-0002-3986-7408
Ondokuz Mayıs Universty, Turkey

ABSTRACT

In addition to providing high-quality images and sound in the field of broadcasting, digitalization has also greatly changed content production processes. With this transformation, analog broadcasting was replaced by the digital coding system. Digital platforms interacting with new media have created significant changes in both content production and audience habits. The main purpose of the study is to analyze the transition process of television broadcasting from traditional to digital and to evaluate the functionality of digital broadcast platforms that emerged in this process. Additionally, the transformation in audience habits is also addressed with these platforms. As a result, with the effect of digitalization, television broadcasting has become a versatile and interactive communication tool rather than just a broadcasting medium.

INTRODUCTION

Television has reached the remotest corners of the world reflecting its Latin origin meaning "to see far away". Throughout the broadcasting process, television has made great progress in terms of both program and broadcasting and has taken

DOI: 10.4018/979-8-3373-1957-5.ch001

its place in the first place among mass media in terms of prevalence and influence. Developments in communication technologies have begun to change television viewing areas and digital platforms have come to the fore. In connection with digitalization, television broadcasting has gone beyond its basic functions and turned into platforms where different elements come together. Television itself, as a tool, connects to the internet, offers an environment for listening to radio, and functions as an environment where photos and videos are projected on tablets and phones.

Although traditional broadcasting is considered within the scope of analog broadcasting technologies, it continues to exist in the digital era by digitalizing with developing technologies. Traditional broadcasting shows a different structure with the use of new devices with technological developments depending on the content production process, program presentation styles as well as the changes experienced in terms of the audience. Despite all the changes, it continues its understanding of broadcasting. Technological developments continue to increase rapidly day by day. This process of change makes itself visible in life and in connection with this, traditional broadcasting is changing its form (Erdem & Akmeşe, 2015, p. 1297). Technological innovations enable more people to interact within the society. When developing and changing communication tools are combined with the internet, their usage areas become widespread. These technologies, which are used intensively in all areas of life, are effective in many dimensions, from the way individuals communicate to the shaping of their lives. This new technology makes the viewer a participant, changing the passive viewer structure specific to traditional media and activating it. Traditional television broadcasting covers very large audiences.

The most important distinguishing feature of traditional television broadcasting is that it presents its content to the audience unilaterally and the audience consumes this content. In this type of broadcasting system, the viewer cannot intervene in the content, such as making any changes or sharing the content. Since there is no direct connection between the viewer and the broadcast channel, one-sided broadcasting is practiced. One of the most important features of traditional television broadcasting is the weak understanding that the results are always clear.

Traditional television broadcasting is facing a new competitive environment with developing technologies. With the new media included in the broadcasting process, broadcasting is moving towards a new field. With this process of change and the transformation to in message sharing between individuals that started with digitalization, the time and space compression specific to traditional broadcasting replaced by fluid time and virtual spaces. This fluidity changes the meaning of communication, broadcasting and, more importantly, the socialization process. In connection with these emerging needs, the importance of social media and its impact on television broadcasting is increasing with new tools, namely social media (Çakın & Bolat, 2018, p. 176). The change experienced with digitalization not only brings many innovations and services to the traditional broadcasting field, but also makes change in itself inevitable. Digital television broadcasting brings much higher quality image transmission and sound use to the field of broadcasting by using developing technology. Accordingly, as in every field of communication, content production through digital processes has become widespread in the field of broadcasting. In television broadcasting, analog broadcasting, which has been used for a long time since the first period, has now been replaced by digital codes.

With the developments in communication technologies in the historical process and the use of computer and network technologies, the digital era in communication technologies begins. The basis of digitalization is based on numbers. Therefore, digitalization is seen as the most important feature that distinguishes today's media from traditional media. With digitalization, new concepts have emerged and the names "digital media" or "digital new media" have started to be used. With the new understanding of broadcasting, the process of content transfer in the media is based on digital transfer rather than physical media (Van Dijk, 2006, p. 9). Today, with the developments in digital media, traditional media is also taking its place in the digitalization process. In connection with this expansion process, the ease of use in digital storage and display, as well as the interactive publishing structure, which is at the basis of this expansion, made this change necessary (Neuman, 2018, p. 96).

Digital television broadcasting refers to the transition to a broadcasting system that provides broadcasting through digital media, that is, different from the previously used analog broadcasting, by converting sound and images into bits over 0s and 1s and to receivers. With digital broadcasting, it is possible to obtain and transmit much better quality images and sound in the field of television broadcasting. In addition, the number of channels and diversification in channel options are increasing. Digital broadcasting also provides easy and trouble-free access to broadcasts for the audience. In addition to the diversification in the field of broadcasting with the developments and digitalization, it also contributes positively to the change in content and quality. Among the most important changes seen in the field of television broadcasting with digitalization digital television platforms.

With digitalization in television broadcasting, digital codes are sent from the transmitter to the receiver. In the process of transition to digital broadcasting, it is necessary to prepare the technical infrastructure for the transfer of these codes. As in the world, digital broadcasting was initiated in Turkey with the establishment of the technical infrastructure. broadcasting platforms have been activated in television broadcasting in order to provide quality broadcasts for the audience as well as channel diversity due to the increasing broadcast quality with digitalization in television programs.

Audience defines the audience that has an important place in determining the form and content of the messages transmitted through television. The reaction of the audience is important for the program to be watched or taken off the air (Kars, 2003, p. 9). Each broadcasting organization defines the concept of audience in line with its own goals and interests. In connection with technological developments, it is seen that the audience is not only a consumer of media products but also a receiver and user. As consumers of television, viewers are interested in programs that will meet their preferences and needs (Çaplı, 2002, p. 168). This viewer understanding that emerged in the traditional broadcasting understanding has started to transform with digital broadcasting platforms and interactive broadcasting. Television programs, which are structured depending on interaction options, create a structure in which individual preferences come to the fore for users. In the developing process, on the one hand, the transformative effect of technology on the audience is seen, and on the other hand, with this new audience emerging, transformations are also taking place in terms of content demand.

In this study, it is attempted to address the new understanding of broadcasting that is shifting towards new-looking and digital platforms, which are experiencing an interactive transformation with new media along with technological developments and digitalization that have emerged in the world of television. The study aims to discuss the use of these new broadcasting platforms that emerged with the transition from traditional broadcasting to digital broadcasting in terms of broadcasting. In addition, one of the most important transformations brought about by new broadcasting platforms is experienced in terms of viewers. Digital broadcasting platforms, which are new broadcasting systems emerging with the changes experienced, and the transforming viewer understanding constitute the aim of the study.

The Evolution of Television Broadcasting and Digitalization

Television rapidly gained an important place in people's lives both visually and audibly in the 1940s. Television, which started broadcasting in analog form depending on the technology of the time, continued to broadcast as a one-sided mass communication tool for many years. From the late 20th century and 1970s onwards, a new understanding of media began to emerge with the developments in the technological field. With the rapid process of change and the developments in electronic communication technologies, the introduction of the computer into the world of communication and the increasing prevalence of its use have begun to eliminate the boundaries between communication systems.

Mass media, which were previously characterized as quite different from each other, have entered a process of convergence with telecommunication and computer-based unity (Uğur, 2003, p. 95). In recent years, the Internet has become accessible to billions of people and has entered every aspect of life through networks. In terms of convergence, the combination of mobile communication and the Internet has offered new environments (Castells, 2008b, p. 246). All these are now visualizations of the great changes that will begin to take place in the field of broadcasting. Internet technology, which will fundamentally shake the field of broadcasting, has now become a part of broadcasting.

By the 1990s, the concepts of time and space were also changing in terms of mass communication. With technological developments, mobile devices, tablets and smartphones have entered people's lives. Along with technological tools, the services offered by the use of the internet by combining computers with traditional tools come to the fore. As a result, audiences are significantly divided and diversified. Therefore, the audience is changing its form (Sorice, 2009, pp. 14-15). The Internet creates complex communication platforms in broadcasting as well as in many other areas of the media. In addition to storing and changing information with the Internet, the interaction process brings mergers in terms of communication in terms of reproduction and changes in communication channels (Pavlik, 1998, p. 80). One of the most effective areas where the changes in this field are most effective is in digital television broadcasting. Within the scope of digital broadcasting, broadcasting over the internet and with the internet protocol has become possible.

Digital television broadcasting began to increase rapidly after satellite broadcasting was first introduced in 1994. In 2000 and afterwards, satellite broadcasts are largely transformed into digital broadcasting. Later, cable television broadcasting and then terrestrial broadcasting switched to digital technology (Morgül, 2011, p. 20). Thus, digital broadcasting, which started to be used with satellite broadcasting, offers a great change environment by covering all broadcasting areas. Higher image quality and more effective use of broadcasting compared to analog broadcasting have accelerated the spread of digital broadcasting.

Kandemir states that through the compression techniques used in digital television broadcasting, the transmission capacity has increased and it offers multimedia and interaction features with certain features. In addition, he states that its limited capacity in terms of transmission, its streamed structure in terms of programs, and its generally one-way and non-interactive traditional television broadcasting have brought great changes in economic, cultural and social terms (2013, pp. 16-17). Digital television broadcasting increases the resolution in terms of converting sound and images into computer language and image quality. Television, which has an important function in terms of social life, increases quality and viewing pleasure due to digital transformation (Atar, 2017, p. 355). Television, which has an important place in terms of social life, expands and changes its audience network with the transformation. With the widespread use of digital television broadcasting, the audience is introduced to a higher quality and interactive broadcasting.

The most important share in the evolution of digital television broadcasting towards an interactive broadcasting approach stems from its convergence with the Internet. In connection with this convergence process that emerged with the Internet technology, the features of newspapers, radio and television bring integration in a single environment. Therefore, in the internet environment, many media formats such as text, graphics, video and audio etc. can be brought together and transmitted simultaneously on a single area (Aktaş, 2007, p. 62). With the emergence of the digital broadcasting concept, one of the most frequently heard concepts is the concept of convergence as mentioned by Aktaş. In the new understanding of broadcasting, convergence provides the connection of communication channels with each other and is also seen in the television broadcasting process.

Henry Jenkins calls the process of technological and cultural change in media culture observed in the last two decades "convergence culture". According to Jenkins, rather than replacing each other in the process of development, media technologies reveal new and different cultural practices through the combination of new and old media systems in different ways. In this framework, Jenkins discusses convergence culture in three interrelated ways. The displacement of a text between various media platforms occurs through the convergence of different communication functions (2006, p. 2). This shows that the operations performed with different devices can be realized through a single device in connection with the developing technology. With the developments in communication technologies, the ability to connect television to the internet and watching videos on phones are the most obvious visuals of convergence.

Internet television, which has an important place in the spread of digital broadcasting, also has its own unique features. These features are as follows: Television broadcasts can be streamed from the Internet in the form of streaming video and can be watched in real time, and the viewer can watch different types of programs as well as traditional broadcasts on his/her computer. In addition, the way of accessing television programs and watching television is similar to browsing through videos on the Internet. It also offers the chance to view all additional information when desired during the television viewing process and to watch interactively. At the same time, the convergence of televisions with computers brings televisions into a position connected to the Internet. Therefore, it makes it possible to access television broadcasts from the internet in addition to traditional television broadcasts (Uluoğlakçı, 2011). Every change and development in communication technologies provides an environment for changes in the media sector. Obtaining, storing and sharing information becomes easier. Digital technologies and especially the Internet have caused significant changes in television as in other media sectors. Concepts such as audience, television and broadcasting have moved to different dimensions compared to traditional broadcasting. New television viewing platforms that have emerged with digital change have inevitably brought about changes in viewing habits and audience concepts.

The content determined by traditional media is presented to the viewer/listener/reader from a certain place with a certain content. In traditional broadcasting, users do not have the power to intervene in the content. In traditional television broadcasting, broadcasts are transmitted from a certain point, i.e. the television station, to a large number of receivers at the same time. At the same time, the viewer or listener's involvement or intervention in the content in traditional broadcasting is very limited. The people involved in the production and consumption process of the content have quite different characteristics and positions (Alemdar & Kaya, 1983, p. 11). In addition, for the traditional television viewer, the television device comes before the content of the television. In traditional broadcasting, the viewer's connection with television is limited to turning the television on, changing the channel or turning it off. Therefore, the viewer's connection with television is in the form of a weak relationship. Due to one-way communication in traditional broadcasting, it is seen that the viewer is a passive viewer instead of active participation.

The fact that the audience is an interactive subject rather than a passive one, which Castells particularly emphasizes, has led to the emergence of changes in the audience. In connection with this change, with the disappearance of the efforts to prevent this in terms of mass media technology, companies and institutions, it has paved the way for a fragmentation and individualization in the mass communication process, as well as bespoke production (2008a, p. 451). The environment that has emerged with the changes that have taken place has brought about social, economic and cultural changes by diversifying the flow of information. With the development and change in communication technologies, the internet entered human life and transformed the information process of the information age into a "network society".

When examined in terms of the impact of technological transformation in broadcasting on the viewer, with the changing viewer structure, the viewer has the chance to record the program he/she wants, stop the broadcast or resume it later from where he/she left off. Thus, the structure of traditional broadcasting that condemns the viewer to the television, such as waiting for the program time, watching the broadcast on time, and missing the program they cannot watch, is completely changing. Therefore, the obligation of the viewer to be in a certain place at certain times is eliminated. In addition, interactive broadcasting creates an environment of interaction between the viewer and the broadcaster, and viewing habits are differentiated depending on the change in the concepts of time and space. In addition, internet technology and the tools developed in connection with it take the viewer out of the position of merely watching and put him/her in a position of producing content. The viewer is now involved in the content according to its place and offers content according to its place. The stereotypical one-way message flow is also being destroyed.

The Rise of Digital Platforms and Their Impact on Audience Habits

Most of traditional television broadcasting consists of linear broadcasts and content is broadcast in a certain order according to scheduled time slots. Unlike traditional broadcasting, online platforms have an interactive and multi-directional communication structure without time constraints. In this context, with the effective use of social media platforms in new generation television broadcasting; it is possible to say that an interactive social TV broadcasting has emerged (Dikmen, 2022, p. 33). With the transition from linear broadcasting to demand-based content consumption with digital platforms, nonlinear broadcasting is being introduced.

With the developments in digitalization and internet-related television broadcasting and broadband internet infrastructure, different types of broadcasting such as IPTV, OTT, internet TV have started. According to Van Dijk, digitalization is one of the elements of the network society and has gained importance in the communication infrastructure of data transmission and computer technology (2006, p. 79). With digitalization, digital television platforms are rapidly increasing and traditional broadcasting organizations are also moving their broadcasts to these platforms. This process of change also brings about changes in viewer habits, exhibits quality broadcasting and updates its programs in the context of viewer expectations.

In the fast pace of Internet technologies, the impact of traditional television broadcasting, which adopts a linear broadcasting flow, is decreasing day by day. Today, viewers do not want to have to wait for a certain day of the week or a certain time of the day to watch the programs they want. Platforms are working with this desire in mind. At this point, it has been seen that platforms broadcasting over the internet can meet consumer expectations in the right way. It has been determined that digital platforms allow viewers to create their own broadcast streams and have an ad-free viewing experience. In addition, viewers spend time on the platform in a faster and more enjoyable way with the recommended productions.

The increase in viewing rates on digital platforms cannot be analyzed independently of social developments and indicates that there is an orientation towards digital platforms to escape from the negativities of daily life and social developments. It is possible to say that this situation has emerged as a factor that increases the viewing time on digital platforms. It can be said that the use of digital platforms such as Netflix, Amazon Prime Video and Disney+ has changed traditional television viewing habits and has become more popular, especially among young viewers. However, the original content and ease of use of digital platforms are becoming attractive not only for young viewers but also for viewers in all age groups (Başer & Söğütlüer, 2023, p. 3). Despite the increasing prevalence and importance of digital broadcasting, there is a limited number of studies examining usage habits and reasons for preference on these platforms (Dan, 2024, p. 199). Despite all these, according to the data on audience growth on digital platforms, there has been a significant increase in the number of viewers. The increase in the number of viewers has also led to transformations in viewer habits.

At Netflix, members can watch the broadcasts as much as they want, whenever they want, wherever they want, on almost any device connected to the internet; they can play, pause and continue watching their entire broadcasts ad-free and without any commitment. In this context, Netflix has created a model that places the user at the center of decisions for less than two decades (Manzano & Neira, 2016, p. 569). In addition to Netflix, many platforms such as Amazon Prime Video and Disney+ have an impact on content consumption patterns as well as viewers' viewing preferences. These platforms attract viewers' attention by offering original content, which causes viewers to consume more content in certain genres or categories (Başer & Söğütlüer, 2023, p. 4).

Digital platforms such as Netflix, Amazon Prime Video and Disney+ started out with the hope that they could replace linear television and offer a better, more entertaining viewing experience. Their first goal is to give their subscribers the ability to access any content they like, anytime, anywhere, any way they want. It strives to ensure that everyone can access the kind of content they want on the platform. To this end, they try to put examples of adult animations, children's TV series or any other kind of content imaginable. By working with the best people in the world, they strive to produce content for every taste and taste and bring them to the audience.

Transforming Audience Behavior

In traditional television broadcasting, the viewer is defined as the person or persons who consume the broadcasts in front of a screen. It is possible to say that the viewer, who is said to be far from interaction, is in an interaction even in traditional television broadcasting. This is because the viewer's emotional participation or reaction to the content, such as changing the channel, turning the television on or off, shows that the viewer is in an interaction (Kandemir, 2013: 78). However, with digital platforms, different approaches have emerged in the position of the audience.

With the emphasis on the fact that a significant change has taken place from audience to users, from content consumers to producing consumers, it is thought that the ongoing audience discussions and studies in the field of new media are technological in one aspect and social and cultural in another (Özsoy, 2011, pp. 113-114).

Although Web TV was primarily created for viewing on computers, today, content has started to be transferred to televisions due to the compatibility of devices such as tablets, phones, etc. with each other. In this broadcasting system, individuals can watch the content they want on their portable devices, wherever they are, if they have internet access. In this context, internet television, which simulates traditional television, tries to collect the contents of traditional television broadcasting within its own structure and offers them in a virtual environment (Demirkıran, 2010 p. 76). In order to determine audience practices on such broadcasting platforms, unlike the rating system in traditional television broadcasting, the program data watched by users over IP signals are accessed, and according to the viewing figures, both the most popular programs are determined and subscriber habits are determined and content selections are made according to this information.

It emerges as a feature in digital broadcasting where content is provided by the broadcaster to anyone who requests it and the audience can purchase broadcasts by contacting the broadcaster by phone, electronic program guide or live customer service. The difference of this feature is that instead of subscribing to the channel for a certain period of time, charges are made according to the time viewed (Uluoğlakçı, 2011, p. 76). In addition to changing viewing habits, this process not only changed the viewing measurements in the traditional broadcasting system, but also brought along the concept of personal time management instead of prime-time in traditional broadcasting.

Another prominent feature of digital platforms in terms of the viewer's relationship with time is that they have broken the time-based hierarchy of traditional television. In the digital age, the viewer no longer has to be present in front of the television at the predetermined broadcast time to access a television content. Almost all television channels have their own official websites and make their program archives available on their websites. Viewers who do not find traditional television satisfactory, especially in terms of quality, turn to digital platforms and can access the content they want at any time.

The most important feature that activates users who watch television over the Internet is the package broadcasting approach of television broadcasting over the Internet. Within the framework of this approach, the viewer has the opportunity to watch TV series, movies, documentaries or news programs at any time. In addition to accessing television broadcasts over the Internet anytime and anywhere, the viewer can pause, rewind or fast forward the package programs at any time, or select information about the features of the programs. The viewer can even change the colors of the objects on the stage to see how they will look (Metin, 2004, p. 96). Therefore, in these new broadcasting platforms, viewers can watch the program they want in line with their own wishes and expectations, and leave the screen without time problems.

Although one of the primary applications of digital platforms to save their viewers from the fatigue of choosing is to offer recommendation lists using various algorithms, the domestic digital platform Blu TV, which started broadcasting in Turkey in the same year as Netf lix, draws attention with a different user experience.

Blu TV, which produces its own content in addition to local and foreign TV series and movies, offers an interface that includes local thematic channels such as news, sports and music in addition to the mainstream channels of traditional television with its 'Live TV' option. Among all these channels, two in-platform channels, Blu TV Action and Blu TV Comedy, stand out. In these channels, action and comedy productions, which are among the licensed content of the platform, are broadcast in a stream throughout the day, serving users who do not want to take responsibility for making choices about content (Yıldırım, 2021, p. 79). This situation shows that culturally, each country produces program types and content in line with the expectations of its viewers within the framework of its own audience profile.

Netflix eliminates the need to watch the same credits over and over again before each episode by including the 'jskip intro' icon at the beginning of the series, preventing the user from wasting time even by fast-forwarding the series for a few minutes and allowing them to access new content immediately. In this way, the viewer gets the impression that they are watching a long-term movie divided into episodes. Netflix's other streaming strategy is its fixed day preference for the timing of the release of new series. By always releasing new series on Fridays, it allows viewers to engage in binge-watching activities that can completely fill the weekend (Jenner, 2018, pp. 222-223).

In 1996, Thomson defined the concept of quality television as a broadcast stream that enriches and enriches the viewers with the content it broadcasts, enlightens them, includes them in the content they watch, touches their emotions, and should be followed carefully (1996, p. 16). Another concept is 'binge watching', which is conceptualized as the consumption of many episodes of a series or program by watching them one after another (Dikkol, 2020, p. 493). The spread of binge-watching culture comes to the fore with digital platforms and reveals a new viewing habit in the audience.

This concept of binge-watching on digital platforms, which started with Netflix, is a combination of the verbs 'binge' for overeating and 'watching' for television. However, as noted in studies on binge-watching behavior, there is no common definition of the concept despite the large number of academic publications on the subject. However, it is generally defined as the self-determined consumption of multiple episodes of a serialized production consecutively. The fact that there is no common criterion for the duration of binge-watching, for example, there is no definite limit to how many consecutive episodes of a series can be considered as binge-watching behavior, makes a common definition of the concept problematic. Nevertheless, there is a consensus that binge-watching behavior refers to the uninterrupted viewing of multiple episodes of a serialized program at once (Ersin, 2023, pp. 42-43). The term binge watching is used in the sense of unhealthy behavior that refers to a period of uncontrollable excess (Steiner & Xu, 2018, p. 94).

The term binge-viewing can be used instead of binge-watching, and the binge-watching experience can also be expressed with the concept of marathon watching. In this regard, Netflix management has stated that they prefer the term marathon, which has healthier and more positive connotations, due to the negative connotations of binge. On the other hand, they have accepted the concept because of the established use of binge-watching among viewers and in the media. For adult viewers, spending an evening or a weekend glued to the screen, watching multiple episodes or an entire season of a series in a row, is characterized as a 'guilty pleasure' or a 'dirty secret' similar to snacking on junk food (Ateşalp & Başlar, 2020, pp. 115-116). Thanks to technological developments, it is clearly seen that cultural changes have opened the doors to important changes today and that the television industry is going through a process. In this process, one of the points that started with Netflix and differed from traditional television in terms of the audience's viewing and behavior is the new viewing practices developed by the audience.

Personalized Content and Audience Experience

Personalization can be considered as a way to improve the user experience, to show that you know and remember the user. User experience is important in terms of trying to meet the needs of the user. Netflix, a digital platform, has prominent features for its subscribers in terms of personalization and user experience. It is an important issue that needs to be investigated what kind of importance these features have for users and how they have an impact on becoming a subscriber and continuing the subscription. In sustainable subscription, user experience and personalization are important, despite the importance of personalization, this may cause privacy concerns in some users, the trial period has an active role in the process of establishing a bond with Netflix and understanding how the user experience is, and binge watching as a consumption phenomenon makes Netflix attractive (Başer & Akıncı, 2020, pp. 868-869).

The concept of personalization is defined as obtaining data from the user's past experiences by new media systems and adapting the system interface to the user with this data (Sundar & Sampada, 2010, p. 301-302). The process of personalization involves the software and algorithms of new media technologies recognizing and remembering the user based on the user's behavior or personal information and rearranging the content according to the individual's preferences or needs. The fact that digital platforms offer personalized content and similar movies is another element added to the habits of the audience as a feature that has not been experienced before.

The role of algorithms and artificial intelligence in content recommendations is also increasing in the process of change based on audience characteristics. Today, all corporate and private companies have started to use machine learning and digital platforms have made significant breakthroughs in this field. Platforms such as Netflix, Amazon, Hulu, Applei Spotify and Puhu can be counted among these companies. Every time users log in to the platforms they subscribe to, they create their own data with their own choices and likes, while companies store this data according to them with machine learning. In addition, a data can be processed into the company's database and personal data can be determined according to their preferences.

Every time the play button is pressed and a series or movie is watched on Netflix, the algorithm is notified and updated data is collected. The more the viewer watches, the more up-to-date the algorithm remains (Özcan, 2020). As Netflix states on its own page, it categorizes the recommendation system factors in three areas. These include information about the viewer's viewing history, other members with similar tastes, genres, categories, actors, and year of release. In addition, the individual's personalized system also records the time of day they watch, the devices they watch Netflix on, and how often they watch. All of this data becomes the data that Netflix processes and the recommendation system is included in the decision-making process. In the context of this data obtained on digital platforms, personalized content based on audience preferences is offered.

With the introduction of new products and the personalization of these products, individuals' motivations for using communication tools are also changing. According to Yüksel (2005), media content reveals 'consumer preference' for people to watch and buy a television program and opens the concepts of 'customer' oriented broadcasting to discussion.

The conveniences provided by technology also affect people's consumption patterns. Consumers can listen to the songs they want with Spotify, YouTube, Apple Music with the help of a smart phone, and the viewer who buys a video player or goes to the cinema to watch a movie can watch movies, series, programs or documentaries whenever and wherever they want with digital platforms such as Netflix, YouTube, Puhu, Blue Tv, Hulu and Exxen with phones and similar technological products. It can also be seen that all these developments and technologies are renewed day by day by the companies that offer products/content in line with the specific needs of individuals, in a way, they have to use the innovations of technology. This process also increases the viewer's control over the content and brings the viewer into an interactive position.

The production process in new media involves a user-oriented interactive relationship, and thanks to technological possibilities, the consumption of new media has also become independent of time and space and transformed into personalized consumption. The concept of personalization generally refers to the process of reshaping digital media content in line with the user's behavior or personal information (Sundar & Sampada, 2010, pp. 300-301). Therefore, this process includes the collection and use of information about the user by systems that provide personalized services.

Thanks to interaction, the individual takes part in the digital environment as a participant, thus individualizing the content, increasing the options offered to the individual and encouraging the individual's participation. In this direction, interaction enables the individual to come together with the content, which activates the individual in the process and increases his/her participation in the content. Interaction in new media brings the source and the receiver together (Akyol & Ünlü, 2022, p. 208). Television viewers can also be involved in the process by giving feedback to the receiving source through this interaction. As a result, the content is individualized and can be accessed interactively thanks to the opportunity to interact individually.

In interactive television, the viewer has two roles in the activism process. One of them is to witness the story and the second is to participate in the story (Çakır, 2006). With digital platforms, the concepts of participant and user show that the individual is not only a consumer of what is presented, but also a participant in the process, moving the individual away from the concepts of watching and watching what is presented to him.

Changing Audience Demographics and New Generations

The digital age, data mining and cable broadcasting have caused mass marketing to be replaced by personalized marketing (Yılmaz, 2017, p. 263). The viewing habits of Generations X, Y and Z are differentiating with the developments in communication technologies. Today, individuals who make up a significant majority of the world's total population are defined as 'digital natives'. This generation, which likes to balance its social life with technology, prefers long-term relationships in business and private life, is partially open to innovations but does not like to take risks, is defined as Generation X and this generation is the generation that raised Generations Y and Z (Erdem, 2018, p. 220). This generation is defined as 'digital immigrants' who joined digital platforms and the digital world later, but they also participate in digital technologies quickly.

Millennials adapt to technology very easily. They are inquisitive, express their thoughts openly and are always open to innovations. Their consumption habits and self-centeredness are negative characteristics of this generation. The moment Generation Z was born, computers and the internet have been a natural part of their lives. For this reason, they have tablets in their hands instead of toys, they watch viral videos on Youtube instead of puppet shows. Growing up in this way, Generation Z refers to a much more creative, self-confident and communicative generation (Erdem, 2018, p. 221). These generations are also insistent on using their own technological devices to watch programs. These users prefer video-on-demand platforms, online streaming services that allow users to choose and watch video content such as movies, series, documentaries and TV shows whenever they want, rather than watching at a scheduled broadcast time, which is a common approach.

With the younger generation's shift towards digital platforms and the abandonment of traditional television, new accessibility has not only allowed for a more personalized viewing experience, but has also changed the physical and psychological spaces surrounding today's television consumption experience. Today, watching television no longer means sitting in front of a television to access broadcast and cable network programming, as online streaming services offer new distribution platform alternatives for TV content (McCreery & Krugman, 2017, pp. 197-199). This situation leads to changes in viewing tools in terms of digital natives' use of mobile devices for television viewing.

With the widespread use of smartphones and tablets, especially in the 2010s, television viewing habits have become widespread in the direction of watching content on mobile devices. People can now watch content even on buses and during travel, thanks to the opportunity to continue where they left off without having to watch for a long time (Çağıl & Kara, 2019, p. 11). Today, mobile phones serve as an intermediary for individuals to use the internet and provide the opportunity to use the internet anytime and anywhere, facilitating communication and access to information for the masses with this feature. Mobile devices also provide an increase in viewing rates.

In addition to portable devices that change the spatial concept of television viewing, wireless television broadcasting gives television viewers the chance to watch the programs they want through personal televisions, in addition to catching them wherever they want. This brings an important social change to the forefront and individualizes television viewing behavior, which is a collective viewing activity. With smartphones, the viewer is no longer dependent on the home or the television device to watch television. Anyone with a smartphone and internet access can follow television broadcasts. The internet has changed every aspect of life, from politics and social relations production and consumption habits.

All this process has shown that technological developments seem to have shifted the control of time in terms of television viewing the viewer. The one-way viewing option characteristic of traditional television broadcasting has been transformed, leading to multiple platforms, websites and portals to choose from. In conjunction the convergence of computer technology with television, new television offers much more choice than traditional television and brings with it a more interactive approach to broadcasting. This qualitative growth in communication options is mainly due to the presentation structure that has developed due to broadband technology (Van Dijk, 2018, p. 27; Sirer, 2020, p. 51). In this way, the most important problem of television broadcasting, the inability to access broadcasts at the desired timeis eliminated. In addition to the viewer's dependence on the day and time specified for television programs, the obligation to be physically present is meaningless in terms of this new broadcasting approach.

In the context of rapid changes in communication technologies and internet-based digital possibilities, the concept of 'audience' is also changing. Accordingly, the concept of audience has expanded include the definitions of the concepts of user and content consumer. The audience now plays a more active role in the communication process and the opportunity to become a source (Özsoy, 2011, p. 105). This new audience structure begins to manifest itself much more with the convergence of television and the Internet and the integration of the flow of media content in different media.

Looking at the factors that will shape audience habits in the future, the rapid progress of digitalization is radically changing audience habits. One of the most important factors that will shape these habits in the future will be artificial intelligence-supported content recommendation systems. Today, platforms such as Netflix, YouTube and Disney+ offer personalized recommendations based on users' viewing history. With the development of AI, these systems will become more precise and offer content tailored to viewers' preferences, enhancing the individual experience. This will lead us to move away from traditional broadcasting and towards a fully personalized viewing model (Karataş, 2023). With the developments in artificial intelligence technologies and their active use on digital platforms, the concept of television may be replaced by experiences where the viewer is a part of the content. In addition, with the development of metaverse universes, virtual movie theaters or personalized series-film experiences may come to the agenda (Karataş, 2023). Apart from this, it is likely to see many innovations between participants and channels in connection with the changes in technologies.

CONCLUSION AND EVALUATION

The Internet is one of the main factors that have made recent years stand out in terms of communication technology and characterize them as a new era in terms of communication and technology. This process creates transformations in classical methods and leaves its place to the new by creating transformations in classical methods, with each new technology being fed on the basis of the same technological infrastructure as a continuation of the previous one. The understanding of broadcasting based on new communication technologies also abandons the classical methods in the traditional understanding of broadcasting and replaces them with new approaches.

The transition from analog broadcasting to digital broadcasting brings with it new forms of broadcasting. Television broadcasting has entered a significant transformation process with the rise of digital platforms. While the traditional understanding of television has been built on certain broadcast streams and mass communication models for many years, the spread of digital platforms has led to radical changes in audience habits. This transformation has not only been limited to viewing practices, but has also profoundly affected many elements from content production to distribution strategies.

This process, together with technological transformation, leads to changes at every stage of the television sector. With the developments in digitalization and computer technologies, all types of data can be transmitted through the same infrastructure. Thus, convergence with a transformation between infrastructures. In addition, with digitalization, content can be transmitted over different infrastructures and different data services can also be provided. With this transformation process, television is no longer just a means of watching programs, but is transformed into an area where many operations such as accessing the internet and watching videos can be performed.

With the digital transformation, television broadcasting has shifted to an internet-based broadcasting approach, and one of the most important changes has been realized in terms of viewers. With the digital platforms entering the broadcasting process, viewers purchase the packages they want from the platforms that broadcast in line with their own interests, and move from the position of passive viewers to the identity of active viewers. In addition to this, one of the most important transformations is that the active audience, which emerged in a timely manner, has the opportunity to watch the program they want from wherever they want with mobile devices without being dependent on television. Here, the process of transforming different devices into a single device with a new approach also provides an environment for the concept of convergence. With the change in communication technologies, not only the concept of time is transformed, but also the concept of space. The audience has the opportunity to watch television programs with mobile devices in any location they want. Another change seen in terms of the audience with digital broadcasting and digital broadcasting platforms is the introduction of features such as recording, stopping, forwarding or rewinding, and re-watching at any time, as well as watching the program anywhere at any time. This the viewer's obligation to be in front of the television at the time of the program as in traditional broadcasting.

In addition, the widespread use of mobile devices and smart televisions for content consumption together with digital platforms has opened the doors to a new era in television broadcasting. While traditional television used to be a media tool that was located in a certain corner of the house and supported a collective viewing practice, today the role of television has changed thanks to individualized viewing habits. Content that can be accessed from anywhere via mobile devices has changed viewers' expectations and forced television channels to develop new strategies.

Digital platforms have transcended the boundaries of traditional television broadcasting by offering viewers the freedom to consume content regardless of time and space. Platforms such as Netflix, Amazon Prime Video, Disney+, BluTV and Exxen have reshaped viewers' expectations by offering personalized content recommendations, ad-free viewing experience and a wide range of content. This has transformed viewers from passive consumers to active individuals who have a say over content. Viewers are now able to create their own viewing schedules and shape their preferences according to their personal tastes, without being dependent on the flow determined by broadcasters.

Changing audience habits have also affected the way television content is produced. While traditional television programs offer generic content that appeals to a wide audience, digital platforms focus on niche content tailored to audience segments. While this has made viewers feel more represented, it has also given content producers the opportunity to develop more original and creative formats.

Developments and transformations in the field of broadcasting also show changes in the expectations of the audience in terms of television. One of these expectations is interactive broadcasting. With interactive television broadcasting, the viewer, who takes an active position, can participate in the program content and send feedback to the television organization very easily. Therefore, with digital broadcasting platforms, television viewing habits as well as the television broadcasting concept undergo a radical transformation and broadcasting becomes a two-way structure with interactive technology. Thus, the traditional perception of television is changing and personalized broadcasting is gaining importance.

In conclusion, the interaction between television broadcasting and digital platforms has changed the position of the viewer and profoundly transformed media consumption habits. The personalized experiences and free viewing environment offered by digital platforms have shaken the dominance of traditional television, but this process has also led to the digitalization of television channels. In the future, television broadcasting is expected to evolve further with artificial intelligence-supported recommendation systems, interactive content and augmented reality applications. Instead of the complete disappearance of traditional television, new broadcasting models blended with digitalization are expected to emerge.

This transformation process shows that a new media ecosystem is being built where the viewer is no longer just a consumer, but plays an active role in content selection, interacts and even contributes to content production. Therefore, the future success of television broadcasters and the media sector will be directly related to their ability to adapt to this new audience profile.

REFERENCES

Aktaş, C. (2007). *Comparison of New Media with Traditional Media, Medya Studies on*. IstanbulBeta Publication.

Akyol, O., & Ünlü, T. T. (2022). Interactive Television Broadcasting and Audience Reception Black Mirror: Bandersnatch Example. In Mavnacıoğlu, K. (Ed.), *Digital Transformation New Media and Communication*. Çizgi Publication.

Alemdar, K., & Kaya, R. (1983). *Basic Approaches in Mass Communication*. War Publication.

Atar, Ö. G. (2017). Transformation of Television Audience in the Digital Age, *SOBIDER Social Journal of Social Science / The Journal of Social Science* / Year: 4, Issue: 15, 350-379.

Ateşalp, S. T., & Başlar, G. (2020). Transformation of Series Watching Practices on the Internet: Extreme A Research on Binge-watching. *Galatasaray University Communication Dergisi*, (32), 108–136. DOI: 10.16878/gsuilet.560832

Bagdikian, B. H. (2016). *The New Media Monopoly*. Akıl Çelen Publication.

Başer, E., & Söğütlüer, T. (2023). Digital Platforms and Digital Platforms within the Framework of Changing Monitoring Trends A Review on Content Advertisements. *Akdeniz İletişim*, (41), 1–26. DOI: 10.31123/akil.1303391

Çağıl, F., & Kara, F. M. (2019). The TV Series Sector in Turkey in the Context of Digital Transformation and The Future. *Arts*, (1), 8–18.

Çakın, Ö., & Bolat, N. (2018). *Social Media Advertising and Digital Media Interactions, Digital Culture and Communication* (Çakmak, V., & Çavuş, S., Eds.). Literatürk Publication.

Çaplı, B. (2002). *Medya ve Etik*. İmge Publication.

Castells, M. (2008a). *The Rise of the Network Society* (Kılıç, E., Trans.). Bilgi Universty Publication.

Castells, M. (2008b). *The Information Age: Economy, Society and Culture. Network Society Rise*. Istanbul Bilgi Universty Publication.

Dan, İ. M. (2024). Digital Platforms in Turkey in the Context of New Media: Usage Analysis of Habits and Reasons for Preference. *Journal of Social, Humanities Administrative Sciences, 10*(2), 198–212. DOI: 10.5281/zenodo.10897924

Demirkıran, C. (2010). Web TV as a Virtual Model of Traditional Television and TV Management in Livestream Portal. *Journal of Akdeniz University Faculty of Communication, 14*, 73–85.

Dikkol, S. (2020). Reading Blu TV Experience in Turkey in the Context of Economic and Symbolic Capital. *Gümüşhane University Faculty of Communication Electronic Journal*, 8, (1). 478-502, DOI: 10.19145/e-gifder.671271

Dikmen, E. Ş. (2022). The Changing Face of Television: Twitch TV and New Generation Broadcasting. *Selçuk İletişim, 15*(1), 27–55. DOI: 10.18094/josc.987200

Erdem, M. N. (2018). Brands in the Game! A Product/Brand Placement Space in Digital As Game-Vertising. In Bolat, N. (Ed.), *Product Placement Applications*. Konya Literatürk Publication.

Erdem, Serhat and Akmeşe, Zuhal (2015). New Communication Technologies: Social

Ersin, N. (2023). Motivations for Binge-Watching Netflix Series in Turkey A Research on. *Journal of Communication Theory and Research*. Spring, (61). 40-64. https://doi.org/ (2023)DOI: 78436443/90439323-STOCK-2021

Jenkins, H. (2006). *Convergence Culture: Where Old and New Media Collide*. New York University Press.

Jenner, M. (2018). *Netflix and the Re-invention of Television*. Palgrave Macmillan. DOI: 10.1007/978-3-319-94316-9

Kandemir, C. (2013). *Problems and Future of IPTV Broadcasting*. Derin.

Karataş, A. (2023). *Digital Media and Future Publishing Trends*. Beta Publication.

Kars, N. (2003). *Television Program Yapalım Herkes İzlesin*. Derin Publication.

Manzano, E. P., & Neira, E. (2016). Data Managment in Audiovisiual Business: Netflix as a Case Study. *El Profesional de la Información, 25*(4), 568–576. DOI: 10.3145/epi.2016.jul.06

McCreery, S., & Krugman, D. M. (2017). Tablets and TV Advertising: Understanding the Viewing Experience. *Journal of Current Issues and Research in Advertising, 38*(2), 197–211. DOI: 10.1080/10641734.2017.1291386

Metin, A. (2004). "MPEG-4 and Efficiency", Broadcasterinfo Monthly Television, Radio. *Journal of Cinema Technologies*, *6*, 124–127.

Morgül, A. (2011). *Sayısal TV Tekniği*. İstanbulPapatya Publication.

Networks Social Effects on Life: The Case of Facebook, *YBS 2nd National Management InformationSystems Congress*, Erzurum, Turkey, October 8 - 10, 2015, pp.1297-1301.

Neuman, W. R. (2018). *The Digital Difference: Digitalization and Media Effects in Everyday Life Theory* (Metin, G., Trans.). The Kitap Publication.

Özcan, G. (2020). *The Surprising Power of Netflix Algorithm*, medium.com https://medium.com/sirkhet/netflixalgoritm

Özsoy, A. (2011). *Television and Audience: Transforming Television Culture and Audience*. Ütopya Publication.

Pavlik, J. (1998). *New Media Technology: Cultural and Commercial Perspectives*. Ally and Bacon.

Sirer, E. (2020). The Spirit of Time: Asynchronicity. In Sirer, E. (Ed.), *In the Era of Television 4.0 Society 5.0 Yeni İzlence Yeni İzlerkitle*. Literaturk Publication.

Sorice, M. (2009). *Mobile Audiences.* Rome: CMCS Working Papers.

Steiner, E. & Xu, K. (2018). Binge-watching Motivates Change: Uses and Gratifications of Streaming Video Viewers Challenge Traditional TV Research. *Convergence: The International Journal of Research intoNew Media Technologies*, 26(1), 82-101.

Sundar, S., & Sampada, M. (2010). Personalization Versus Customization: Importance of Agency, Privacy, and Power Usage. *Human Communication Research*, *36*(6), 298–322. DOI: 10.1111/j.1468-2958.2010.01377.x

Thomson, R. (1996). *From Hill Street Blues to ER: Television's Second Golden Age*. Continuum.

Uğur, A. (2003). *Culture Continent Atlas.* Yapı Kredi Publication.

Uluoğlakçı, C. (2011), From Media Economy to Business Model: New Broadcasting Technologies, *Expertise Thesis*, Radio and Television Supreme Council, Ankara.

Van Dijk, J. (2006). *The Network Society Social Aspects of New Media* (2nd ed.). SAGE Publications Ltd.

Van Dijk, J. (2018). *Network Society* (Sakin, Ö., Trans.). Epsilon Publication.

Yildirim, N. (2021). Skip the Credits: Changing Time and Audience Relationship in the Digital Age. *NewJournal of Communication Studies in the Century*, *3*, 71–83.

Yılmaz, R. (2017). Structural Transformation of Advertising Narrative in Turkey in the Digital Age. *1st International Conference on New Trends in Communication*. Istanbul: Ticaret Universty.

ADDITIONAL READING

Altuntas, Z., & Onay Durdu, P. (2020). Website Accessibility Assessment: A Barrier Navigation Study. *Journal of Social Policy Studies*, *1*, 119–144.

Anderson, K. E. (2018). Getting Acquainted With Social Networks And Apps: Streaming Video Games on Twitch.tv. *Library Hi Tech News*, *35*(9), 7–10. DOI: 10.1108/LHTN-08-2018-0054

Arifoğlu, A., Demirer, M., & Şengül, G. (2006). *Glossary of Informatics Terms*. Turkish Standards Institute.

Baik, S. (2010). Rethinking QR Code: Analog Portal to Digital World. *Multimedia Tools and Applications*, •••, 427–434.

Beuscart, J. S. (2012). La fin de la télévision? *Resaux*, *5*, 43–82.

Bolter, J. D., & Richard, G. (2000). *Remediation: Understanding New Media*. The MIT Press.

Castells, M. (2004). Informationalism, Networks, and the Network Society: A Theoretical Blueprint. In Castells, M. (Ed.), *The Network Society A Cross-cultural Perspective*. Edward Elgar Publishing. DOI: 10.4337/9781845421663.00010

Hammar, P. (1994). *Charles P. Ginsburg 1920-1992. Memorial Tributes*. The National Academies Press.

Katz, E. (2009). The End of Television? *The Annals of the American Academy of Political and Social Science*, *625*(1), 6–18. DOI: 10.1177/0002716209337796

Kocurek, C. A. (2015). *Coin-Operated Americans: Rebooting Boyhood at the Video Game Arcade*. University of Minnesota Press. DOI: 10.5749/minnesota/9780816691821.001.0001

Pertierra, A. C., & Turner, G. (2013). *Locating Television: Zones of C onsumption*. Routledge.

Shove, E., Pantzar, M., & Watson, M. (2012). The dynamics of social practice: Theorizing. *European Journal of Social Theory*, *5*(2), 243–263.

KEY TERMS AND DEFINITIONS

Digitalization: Digitalization means the digitization of various information and content in parallel with technological developments along with the expansion of the use of the internet. Digitalization, which includes the storage and transfer of data as well as technological transformation, has an impact on many areas.

Digital Broadcasting: With digitalization, television broadcasting has brought much higher quality image transfer and sound usage to the broadcasting field by taking the developing technology with it. Accordingly, content production through digital processes has become widespread in the broadcasting field as in every field of communication.

Digital Platforms: Digital television platforms stand out as the most important indicators for preference, as they offer viewers a variety of content, are always ready to be watched, and do not have commercials between broadcasts. Among the reasons for preference for digital platforms is that the viewer can access the program they want to watch from any device with an internet connection, at any time, in any environment.

Digital Audience: The changing broadcasting approach with digitalization also brings about changes in viewing habits, and the viewer can record any program they want, pause the broadcast or continue watching from where they left off freely. Thus, the structure that binds the viewer to the television, such as the viewer waiting for the program time, watching the broadcast on time, and missing the program they cannot watch in traditional broadcasting, is completely changing.

Personalized Content: Personalization, as a newly emerging concept, describes the production of user-specific content based on viewer behavior or personal information through software and algorithms in a manner related to technology. With personalized content, personalized content is offered on digital platforms and similar movies according to the viewer's tastes, sending movies or series with features that the viewer has previously experienced.

Changes in Audience Demographics: With digitalization, demographic changes are seen in the audience characteristics, and the viewing habits of generations X, Y and Z are also different. Generation X, who like to balance their social life with technology, prefer long-term relationships in their business and private lives, are partially open to innovations but like to take risks, while Generation Y adapts to technology very easily. Generation Y is more questioning, expresses their thoughts openly and is open to innovations. From the moment Generation Z was born, computers and the internet have become a natural part of their lives.

Binge-Watching: The concept of binge-watching on digital platforms is defined as the consumption method determined by the viewer in succession of many episodes of productions, usually produced in series, which is translated as excessive watching. There is a certain criterion for binge-watching time, and watching many episodes of a series in succession is considered binge-watching.

Chapter 2
Transformation of Television and Movie Watching Experiences in the Age of Digital Platforms

Rabiya Saltik Duvan
https://orcid.org/0000-0003-4378-3490
İstanbul Gelişim Üniversitesi, Turkey

ABSTRACT

The present study aims to explore and discuss the transformation of movie and TV series viewing experiences in the digital age. The study sought to address the following research questions: why are digital platforms preferred over traditional channels, and how do internet-based digital viewing platforms transform viewing habits? The study adopted a qualitative research model, conducting in-depth interviews with ten participants who expressed a preference for digital platforms over traditional ones. The data set obtained was subjected to content analysis. The analysis yielded several key reasons for the preference for digital platforms over traditional platforms, including independence from time and space, the presence of original storylines and non-clichéd content, the absence of advertisements, and content diversity and personalised options. Furthermore, it was determined that viewing behaviours in the digital age encompass individual viewing, multi-screen viewing, binge viewing, genre-oriented selective viewing and content-driven viewing focused on new content.

DOI: 10.4018/979-8-3373-1957-5.ch002

INTRODUCTION

Television has been among the most effective means of communication since its advent. As a cultural apparatus, television is a mass communication tool that is ubiquitous in every home, functioning as an ordinary part of individuals' lives. However, the organisation of this communication tool is currently undergoing a transformation. The advent of the digital age has precipitated a paradigm shift in our cultural and social experiences, with viewing experiences being profoundly impacted by this transformation. Conventional forms of viewing, such as cinema and television, have undergone substantial changes with the advent of digital platforms, and these new conditions have reshaped the manner in which audiences approach content, interact with it, and derive meaning. The present study aims to analyse how traditional viewing habits have evolved and how audiences develop interactive experiences in digital media, thereby examining the impact of digital technologies on viewing experiences.

The advent of novel communication technologies has engendered a plethora of new debates within the field of communication. A salient example of this is the advent of televised political debates, a phenomenon that has been catalyzed by the advent of digital broadcasting. The advent of novel communication technologies and the increasing popularity of digital broadcasting since the 2000s have precipitated a reinterpretation of the television viewing experience. As is the case in all areas of social life, digitalisation has initiated a transformation in the field of viewing practices. Following the advent of viewing practices such as CDs and DVDs, internet-based viewing options have become popular through various platforms, with digital broadcasting becoming an integral part of viewing experiences. Television, with its capacity to engage both visual and auditory senses, is now predominantly experienced through internet-based digital platforms, thereby expanding its reach to a global audience. The numerous possibilities offered by new media platforms, including asynchronous viewing, genre selection and serialised viewing, have rendered digital viewing experiences more attractive than traditional viewing options.

In recent years, a multitude of global and domestic digital platforms, including Netflix, Amazon Prime, Puhu Tv, Blu Tv, Exxen, and Disney+, have witnessed a notable expansion in their operational scope. This development has resulted in the emergence of an active viewer profile, characterised by viewer choices rather than the viewer having to adapt to the linear television flow. The viewer, no longer bound by the linear broadcast schedule of traditional television, now has the autonomy to select content according to their preferences, at their own pace, and to the extent they desire, from any location equipped with computers, tablets, or mobile devices. Furthermore, an audience profile that aligns with genres and content that cater to their individual preferences and demands is emerging. This transformation has led to the emergence of a new audience profile, characterised by a return to self-regulation, driven by individual desires and expectations. Consequently, the concept of personalised viewing experiences has come to the fore. Consequently, it becomes imperative to deliberate on the ramifications of this transformation in viewing experiences, and to undertake a thorough analysis of audience habits in the digital age. The present study seeks to explore the impact of internet-based digital viewing platforms on viewer habits. The study will address the following research question:

Firstly, how have internet-based digital viewing platforms (e.g. Netflix, Disney+, Blu Tv, Tabi, Exxen) transformed viewing habits? Secondly, what are the determinants of the preference for digital platforms over traditional channels? Finally, the study will explore how digital viewing experiences positively or negatively affect audience habits.

The research model employed in this study was qualitative in nature, as guided by the specific research questions that formed the study's foundation. It was planned to interview 10 participants who stated that they preferred digital platforms to traditional platforms for watching television series and movies. The data obtained from the interviews was analysed by content analysis method. The findings obtained within the scope of the research are discussed in the conclusion section.

The rapid change in media consumption habits in the digital age has radically transformed audience behaviour and viewing experiences. The traditional television viewing habits of the past have been superseded by the flexible, personalised and accessible content experiences offered by internet-based digital platforms. This transformation necessitates a novel industrial organisation, which in turn profoundly impacts not only individual viewing practices but also content production and distribution processes. Consequently, analysing this transformation is imperative to comprehend audience needs and expectations, and to unravel the dynamics of cultural consumption. This study aims to contribute to the understanding of current transformations in the field of media by examining the effects of the possibilities offered by digital platforms on the audience.

Theoretical Framework

Television, a medium with a long-established presence in the domain of visual media, has undergone a radical transformation in the wake of technological developments and digitalisation. The transition from a conventional broadcasting model to internet-based content platforms has significantly impacted audience habits and media consumption patterns. The advent of smart TVs, online streaming services and personalised content offerings has precipitated the evolution of television from a mere entertainment medium to a multidimensional interaction and communication platform. This transformation has had profound effects on the competitive balance in the media industry and on cultural and social dynamics.

The advent of new media platforms has precipitated a paradigm shift in the realm of viewing experiences, which have consequently begun to be analysed through a variety of theoretical frameworks. New forms of viewing, including asynchronous viewing, pause viewing, episodic viewing, multi-screen use, on-the-go viewing, individual viewing, personalised screen preferences and serial viewing, have transformed users' habits. These transformations have resulted in more flexible, controllable and unique experiences in media consumption. Analyses of these new media experiences of users make it possible to better understand audience behaviour and reshape media content accordingly.

Digital technology has precipitated a significant transformation in the realm of media consumption, wherein the medium of television is no longer the exclusive purveyor of content. Consequently, smartphones, tablets and computers have emerged as viable alternatives for accessing content, enabling users to enjoy viewing experiences from any location with an internet connection. This development has led to the widespread adoption of mobile television viewing options. Mobile broadcasting has thus rendered the "anytime, anywhere" viewing experience a reality for the viewer. In the traditional linear broadcasting model, content was consumed within a specific time period, from a designated device, and the broadcast stream was determined by the broadcaster. However, mobile broadcasting has introduced greater flexibility into the relationship between audience and content, thereby strengthening the interactive broadcasting approach through the use of new media tools and giving rise to a content-oriented broadcasting model. This transformation has placed content and audience interaction at the centre of broadcasting by empowering viewers with greater control over content (Altın, 2021, p. 42). The advent of digital platforms such as IPTV (Internet Protocol Television), OTT (Over The Top), Smart TV (Smart Television), Mobile TV and Web TV has further transformed television, enabling it to evolve into an individual experience. This evolution has eliminated the time limitation previously associated with watching television and has empowered viewers to create their own broadcast stream.

Contrary to conventional media, novel communication technologies are characterised by their interactive nature and individualised approach (Castells, 2008, p. 441). Since the 1970s, the evolution of emerging technologies has led to a shift in viewer behaviour, from communal viewing in the living room to individual viewing in private spaces, and subsequently to mobile devices (Turner & Tay, 2009, pp. 1-2). This shift in communication patterns has led to a reversion to a more individualised viewing experience. The advent of technological developments, the decline in media production costs, and the rapid proliferation of the mobile media sector have collectively contributed to an escalation in individual media consumption. The paradigm shift from the traditional concept of "family television" to the contemporary notion of "individual television" signifies a paradigm shift in which each member of the household possesses their own personal television set (Hepkon, 2011, p. 126). In the contemporary context, the advent of advanced media algorithms has led to the emergence of personalised screening experiences, catering to the diverse preferences of individual users. This paradigm shift has also given rise to a demand-driven broadcasting approach, where content providers are compelled to align their offerings with the expectations and desires of the users. The logic of the algorithm is such that it personalises the entire video catalogue for each member profile. The video similarity algorithm, termed "sims", directs recommendations based on previous viewings (Gomez-Uribe & Hunt, 2015, pp. 2-4). The advent of on-demand broadcasting has transformed the traditional passive viewer into an active participant in an interactive environment. Conversely, platforms offering on-demand broadcasting services are intricately linked to the marketing strategies of contemporary capitalism, with their utilisation of personalised algorithms. The concept of hyper-personalisation is employed in the context of on-demand broadcasting platforms, whereby content is tailored to the individual viewer. Zengin (2021, p. 707) defines hyper-personalisation as "a new artificial intelligence-based phase of relational digital marketing that includes a series of one-to-one marketing, customisation, customerisation, and especially personalisation". In this sense, it is observed that individual viewing experiences on hyper-personalised screens support a new viewer model that is self-contained and believes that it is in control, with the illusion of "free choice".

A further significant transformation in viewing habits in the new media age is the multiscreen experience, which is defined as the practice of viewers engaging with multiple screens concurrently. This phenomenon can be attributed to the necessity to augment the screen space available for the display of information (Neate et al., 2019, p. 392). The advent of second screen use can be traced back to the emergence of the second screen itself, thus signifying its status as a by-product of the digital age and the ubiquity of mobile technology. The tendency to interact with digital platforms while watching television has become an increasingly common behaviour that shapes modern media dynamics. While traditional television is passive, interacting with content often requires minimal effort. This stands in marked opposition to other activities, such as reading, which requires greater cognitive effort and in-depth conceptual analysis. Reading demands a mental effort to carefully examine words, grasp their meaning, and construct meaning as a whole. In contrast, the experience of television viewing is frequently marred by distractions, prompting viewers to engage with mobile devices or seek information via digital content (Neate et al., 2019, p. 393).

The prevalence of the second screen experience in contemporary living rooms has become a common phenomenon. Second screen or multi-screen experiences encompass a spectrum of behaviours, ranging from the search for specific information related to the program being viewed, to activities that are entirely unrelated (Neate et al., 2019, p. 391). The practice of watching television has evolved from a traditional focus on a single screen in a room to a social platform that enables interaction between viewers. These interactions frequently occur through social media applications such as Facebook, Twitter and Instagram. The advent of rating systems, buttons, chat rooms, viewer comment sections on TV series and movie websites, and image-uploading applications on news websites has further facilitated this transformation by expanding the use of second screens. Consequently, conventional mass and individual viewing habits of television have begun to yield to an understanding of virtual massiveness based on interaction in the digital environment (Bilginer Kucur, 2022, p. 1364). However, it is noteworthy that in most cases, the utilisation of second screens is not directly associated with television content (D'heer et al., 2012, pp. 195-198). Indeed, users are typically distant from the content of the program they are watching or a second screen interaction related to that content. Instead, the focus of second screen experiences is on content that is not related to the text being watched. Consequently, the phenomenon of unrelated screen experiences is predominantly associated with attention needs that are not being met by television (Neate et al., 2019, p. 391).

The migration of television channels and programmes to the YouTube platform is indicative of a significant transformation in media consumption. Historically, the traditional television screen was regarded as the primary screen, with new media devices such as smartphones and tablets being considered the secondary screen. However, contemporary evidence suggests a paradigm shift towards a more integrated approach, wherein the traditional television screen now functions as the primary screen, while new media devices are increasingly recognised as the secondary screen. The transition of the primary screen from traditional TV channels to digital platforms such as YouTube is indicative of this shift in viewing habits (Çelik, 2023, p. 3).

A seminal shift in viewing habits in the new media age is undoubtedly the transition from the reserved viewing of traditional media to the serialised viewing experiences of new media. It is therefore worthwhile to address and expand this change, which can be seen as an implication of the consumption habits of postmodern capitalism at the media level, under a separate heading.

From 'Reserved Viewing' to 'Binge-Watching Experience'

In the contemporary era of digital platforms, television has evolved to become a medium that can exert a global impact, catering to diverse cultural sensibilities and empowering viewers through interactive experiences. In the 21st century era of digital platforms, television has both technically transcended traditional broadcasting standards and its identity as a representative of mainstream culture, referred to as the "idiot box" (Steiner & Xu, 2018, pp. 2-3), has become controversial. In Marxist theory, television was defined as a mediator for the dissemination of the ideology of corporate capitalism (Adorno & Horkheimer, 2007) and the audience factor was completely ignored. In contrast to the passive viewer theory of the Marxist perspective, cultural theorists began to focus on the question "what do viewers do with television?" in the 1960s. Theorists such as Elihu Katz emphasised that the manner and purpose for which television is used by the audience is of greater significance than the impact of television on the audience itself (Erdoğan & Alemdar, 2010, p. 154). The "passive viewer" approach, which was also opposed by theorists such as David Morley (2003) and Raymond Williams (1989), has become a paradox in today's new media age. In the current era of digital platforms, the question of viewer behaviour has become increasingly salient. The concept of the "active viewer" has gained traction in this era, where viewers have the capacity to select content that aligns with their expectations from a myriad of movies or television series, and to engage with them through diverse viewing practices such as pause-watching or binge-watching.

Notwithstanding the active viewer thesis, which is espoused more vigorously in the context of new media platforms, it remains unfeasible to assert that viewers possess a comprehensive control mechanism. The studies undertaken have indicated that the user-centric nature of these platforms is open to discussion. In accordance with the self-organisation possibilities supported by the directive strategies of service providers, it is observed that viewers find themselves in a position between controlling and being controlled (Lüders, 2022, pp. 2-3).

In the contemporary era of new media, the advent of digital platforms has precipitated a paradigm shift in the realm of media consumption, offering an alternative to conventional forms of entertainment such as mainstream television and cinemas. This transformation has been predominantly interpreted within the ambit of liberal ideology, with its emphasis on "freedom" as a fundamental principle. The potential for experiencing a viewing event "wherever, whenever, whatever" held the promise of a remarkably democratic and libertarian impression (Steiner & Xu, 2018, p. 2). Furthermore, the content available on digital platforms typically encompassed the entire season at once, a development that was viewed as particularly significant. Conversely, traditional television programming was constrained by the linear timeline of a calendar (Alimoradi et al., 2022, p. 1). Viewers on traditional broadcast platforms had to wait a week for new episodes, enabling them to watch the entire season in a short period of time without the need to wait on digital platforms. Consequently, the concept of the viewer who must wait a week for the new episode, as was the case on traditional broadcast platforms, has begun to lose its significance. This has led to the emergence of a more "selective" viewer profile on digital streaming platforms, who can watch multiple episodes simultaneously and who must be convinced to watch a production from among many options. It was observed that streaming platforms, which initially appeared to be very libertarian, had in fact led to the development of binge-watching behaviour among viewers (Trouleau et al., 2016, p. 1215).

Media critic Mary McNamara defined binge-watching in 2012 to describe situations in which "more than three episodes of a one-hour drama or six episodes of a half-hour comedy are consumed at once" (Steiner & Xu, 2018, p. 3). The binge-watching theory draws parallels with the concepts of binge eating and overeating in the literature on eating disorders, and this concept refers to the excess in television viewing behaviour, just like the excess in eating behaviour.

The affordability of digital streaming platforms, coupled with their accessibility from any device with internet access and their multi-choice content libraries that respond to users' demands, has been observed to initiate a cultural transformation in viewing habits as a whole (Flayelle et al., 2020, p. 44). Researchers working on the concept of binge-watching, which can be interpreted as a consequence of this cultural transformation, state that binge-watching behaviour is manifested by binge-watching several episodes in a row, but they also define this behaviour as an end result of on-demand streaming platforms (Ulusoy et al., 2024, p. 2). Digital platforms, which are capable of meeting individual demands according to the characteristics of the content (series or movie) and genre (comedy, romance, crime, thriller, action, fantasy, etc.), leave control to the viewers in one aspect and turn them into loyal followers in another. In this context, broadcast platforms benefit from the excessive viewing behaviour of consumers based on audience loyalty (Anghelcev et al., 2021, pp. 132-133). Indeed, a significant number of digital broadcasting platforms opt to make the initial episode of their latest content available free of charge on ad-centred platforms such as YouTube. Subsequent episodes are then made available to view on a subscription basis. Song et al. (2022) posit that content immersion is more effective in the realization of impulsive paid subscriptions. It can be posited that domestic digital platforms in Turkey have adopted this tactic.

An examination of the motivations for binge-watching, as indicated by data published by Netflix, reveals that the predominant reason for viewer engagement is the desire to enhance their enjoyment of the content. Curiosity about the subsequent episode constitutes the second most prevalent motivation (Erickson et al., 2019, p. 2). In a separate study, it was posited that the pursuit of binge-watching can be attributed to a multifaceted array of motivations, including the desire to disengage from the vicissitudes of daily life, to regulate negative emotions, and to attain instantaneous gratification (Starosta & Izydorczyk, 2020, p. 13).

In the current age of digital viewing, where binge-watching has become a prevalent practice, users frequently characterise it as a leisure activity. Nevertheless, numerous studies have demonstrated that binge-watching or marathon viewing can result in both physical and psychological health complications (Alimoradi et al., 2022, p. 2):

> *"...For instance, excessive viewing can result in sedentary behaviour due to prolonged sitting, which can contribute to an unhealthy lifestyle. Repetitive binge-watching has been demonstrated to result in sleep disturbances due to disruption of circadian rhythms. Furthermore, the practice can have a detrimental effect on an individual's social relationships, as it can result in the neglect of important social activities and a reduction in social interactions. Consequently, there is a mounting interest among healthcare providers and researchers in comprehending the repercussions of excessive monitoring."*

The term "binge-watching" has been employed to denote the consumption of television programming in excess of recommended amounts, with such behaviour often being likened to the consumption of junk food. This phenomenon has been designated a "guilty pleasure" or a "dirty secret". Critics of binge-watching have likened popular television programmes such as Breaking Bad and Orange is the New Black, which have been identified as worthy of binge-watching, to a snack like potato chips. These highly palatable snacks have the potential to induce physical discomfort in viewers when consumed in excess (Matrix, 2014, pp. 124-125). Research on the cultural transformation in viewing habits in the age of digital platforms has identified that excessive viewing can lead to physical problems such as obesity and sleep disturbances (Saeed, 2024) and mental health issues such as depression and loneliness (Tefertiller & Maxwell, 2018; Steins-Lober et al., 2020). A study by Vaterlaus et al. (2019, pp. 470-479) highlighted the alarming rise of binge-watching, which is characterised by increased social isolation as it leads to prolonged periods spent in solitude. When binge-watching persists for several hours, it can lead to behavioural disorders, emotional avoidance, and health risks (Thakur et al., 2025, p. 31). A further study by Anozie (2020, p. 1) concluded that individuals engaging in binge-watching reported experiencing more negative emotions, such as a sense of loss of control and addiction, while those who binge-watch less reported experiencing more positive emotions.

In a study conducted by Starosta and Izydorczyk (2020, pp. 1-16), the objective was to present the current understanding and psychological conditions of excessive monitoring in research articles published between 2013 and 2020. To this end, a systematic review of 28 articles was conducted. The study's findings revealed two distinct perspectives on the concept of binge watching. The first perspective pertains to the domains of entertainment, positive emotions and leisure, while the second one elucidates the adverse consequences of binge watching and the symptoms of addiction. The study identified that binge-watching patterns are associated with symptoms of addiction, including a lack of control, adverse health and social effects, feelings of guilt, and the neglect of tasks. Notwithstanding the plethora of studies that have identified negative consequences associated with binge-watching, another study found that binge-watching of television series was generally only associated with low levels of problematic use. The study concluded that regular binge-watching cannot be considered a problematic behaviour or even an addiction, as the frequency of binge-watching sessions did not increase (Ort et al., 2021, p. 5).

The preponderance of studies in this field indicates that individuals who engage in excessive viewing experiences frequently encounter adverse health consequences. In this regard, it can be posited that digital platforms, which function as content libraries, are perceived by users as a form of "addiction library" due to the extensive repository of content they offer. While libraries are typically institutions that promote education, broaden the mind, and expose individuals to new information, digital monitoring libraries have been shown to have the opposite effect. Users have become addicted to these platforms, constantly anticipating new content, and their expectation from the addiction library is to regularly upload an archive of content that will soothe them. This phenomenon can be interpreted as a strategic marketing tactic employed by new media platforms, whereby the concept of "user control" is effectively repackaged as a marketing strategy. In essence, there is a conspicuous absence of mechanisms that genuinely promote user autonomy within the context of digital monitoring platforms.

The practice of binge-watching, or the consumption of large quantities of media content in a short period of time, fits neatly into the structure of postmodern capitalism, where consumer habits and identity overlap. In this regard, Jeffrey T. Nealon has drawn parallels between the emergent media environment, characterised by a focus on individual preferences, and the postmodern economic paradigm (Jenner, 2014, p. 11). Digital viewing platforms are equipped with algorithms that act in accordance with personal tastes. The resultant phenomenon of monotonous dissatisfaction with the content consumed is attributable to individual usage and personalised screen experiences (Mazıcı & Can, 2021, p. 841). In this context, the behaviour of binge-watching is a significant method of reading the media in the consumer society. Eyrek (2022, p. 83) has associated binge-watching, a phenomenon resulting from viewing habits in the new media age, with consumption, and has stated that watching on digital platforms creates a kind of "McDonaldsization" situation.

The distinguishing quality that differentiates digital platforms from traditional television is the difference in flow, which is fuelled by the understanding of being anytime and anywhere. Raymond Williams (2003, p. 79) asserts that television is characterised by a "flow" that is created successively and continuously. The theory of flow, as posited by Raymond Williams, is activated through television, thereby exerting a profound influence on the human mind. Television, in establishing its own reality, exerts a pervasive influence over the human mind through the phenomenon of flow. Williams's (2003) seminal work, which was based on the premise that films and commercials are often interrupted in private television in the US as opposed to British television, defined the presentation of multiple contents sequentially on television as flow. The streaming effect reinforces the idea that the viewer is prevented from changing the television channel and choosing a different type of program. Individuals, presumed to possess the capacity to disengage from a program and transition to another, are pacified by the streaming power of television and relinquish their autonomy to the streaming effect. In essence, Williams' streaming theory posits the notion that "viewers do not watch a program, they watch television" (Chandler & Munday, 2011, p. 426).

Conversely, the 1990s witnessed the emergence of the concept of flow in the context of digital media. The notion of streaming, which has been reintroduced through the utilisation of digital technologies since the 1990s, is delineated in two distinct ways. The first of these refers to the broadcasting of media over the internet in real time without any driver. The principal feature of the concept, which is also employed to describe on-demand service forms, is the provision of access to the media catalogue over internet protocols within a specified subscription fee (Gümüş, 2021, p. 152). While Raymond Williams' seminal work on the streaming theory was rooted in the domain of traditional television, the advent of on-demand digital platforms has served to further accentuate the significance of this concept. In contradistinction to the streaming effect of traditional television, the manner in which digital television offers on-demand content restores the concept of streaming to the agenda in diverse ways. The evidence suggests that digital platforms, such as Netflix, which offer on-demand broadcasting services, continue to exert significant influence over their audience. This is evidenced by the release of entire seasons of programming all at once, as well as the provision of personalised content recommendations. These factors serve to reinforce the conclusion that the streaming effect has not disappeared with digital platforms. The television streaming effect, which is experienced as a whole in traditional media with the successive scheduling of commercial generations and various program types, has updated the streaming effect on digital platforms that offer on-demand broadcasting services with features such as the broadcast of on-demand content and the ability to switch to a new episode immediately after an episode. Conversely, it can be posited that the streaming effect, which is producer-centric in traditional media, is user-centric on new media platforms.

Research

The present study is founded upon a qualitative research paradigm. In order to achieve the objectives of the study, a sample of 10 participants was selected purposively, with the proviso that they expressed a preference for digital platforms over traditional ones for the viewing of television series and films. The interviews were scheduled to last for approximately 30 minutes, utilising a semi-structured interview technique. The study was conducted with the approval of the Ethics Committee of Istanbul Gelisim University Ethics Committee, as per the decision dated 18/04/2025 and numbered 2025-06-105. The following questions were posed to the participants:

- What is your average daily digital screen time (including digital TV, smartphone, computer, tablet, etc.) in minutes?
- What types of content do you consume on digital platforms (e.g., TV series, movies, documentaries, short films)?
- Which devices do you primarily use to access digital content (e.g., smartphone, tablet, computer, smart TV)?
- What are your reasons for preferring digital platforms over traditional media for viewing TV series and movies?
- Do you typically watch content on digital platforms alone or with others? If so, why?
- While watching content on digital platforms, do you engage in other activities (such as sports, traveling, housework, or social media browsing), or do you focus solely on the screen?
- How have digital platforms influenced your viewing habits?
- When consuming TV series or movies on digital platforms, do you often use multiple screens (e.g., television, computer, phone) simultaneously?
- Do you binge-watch series or movies on digital platforms, similar to traditional television viewing? How does your ability to pause content affect your attention?
- How long does it typically take you to complete a series on digital platforms? Do you engage in binge-watching, and if so, what motivates this behavior?
- Do you believe that digital platforms encourage binge-watching? Why or why not?
- Do you perceive the content on digital platforms as more original, high-quality, and creative compared to traditional media? Please elaborate.
- If you are not enjoying a series on a digital platform, do you continue watching it, or do you stop immediately?
- Do you revisit TV series or movies that you have previously watched on a digital platform? If so, what motivates you to do so?

The data set was completed with the data obtained from semi-structured interviews based on the interview questions. The data set thus obtained was then subjected to content analysis, with the software program MAXQDA being utilised for this purpose. In the digital age, the utilisation of software programs serves to enhance the systematic nature of data analysis, thereby expediting the research analysis process. In the present study, MAXQDA was utilised for the analysis of the data. The analysis process with the MAXQDA program involved the initial coding of data, leading to the identification of categories and themes. The coding process in the study was carried out by another researcher one week after the initial coding, and it was found that there was a consensus between the coders. The findings were subsequently discussed in the conclusion section.

Analyze

The participants who consented to participate in the interviews conducted within the scope of the research were requested to sign a voluntary consent form, after which the interviews were conducted. During the interviews, participants were assigned codes beginning with the letter P and continuing sequentially up to 10. The identities of the participants were maintained in strict confidentiality in accordance with the established ethical guidelines. The resultant 30-page data set was then subjected to coding with the software program MAXQDA. The categories obtained through the coding process are presented in the following section, under the designated theme headings.

Table 1. Demographic characteristics of the participants

Participant No	Age	Gender	Education Level
P1	38	Female	Secondary school graduate
P2	22	Female	Undergraduate student
P3	18	Male	Undergraduate student
P4	45	Male	High school graduate
P5	25	Female	Associate degree graduate
P6	20	Female	Undergraduate student
P7	33	Male	Master's degree graduate
P8	38	Female	PhD graduate
P9	33	Female	PhD student
P10	29	Female	Master's degree graduate

continued on following page

Table 1. Continued

The participants exhibited a wide range of demographic characteristics, including different age groups, genders, and educational levels. The age range of the participants was from 18 to 45 years. The female participants constituted the majority, with a total of seven female and three male participants. With respect to educational attainment, the participants included secondary school graduates, high school graduates, associate degree graduates, bachelor's degree students, master's degree graduates and doctoral level education. A particularly noteworthy aspect is the significant proportion of participants engaged in or who have completed higher education, which is indicative of a well-educated and informed demographic. This distribution indicates that the study sample is characterised by individuals with a broad spectrum of educational attainment.

Table 2. Technological tools for following movie and television content

Participant No	Technological tools for following the content			
	Television set	Computer	Tablet	Mobile phone
P1	+	-	-	-
P2	+	+	-	+
P3	+	+	-	+
P4	+	-	-	+
P5	+	-	-	+
P6	-	+	-	+
P7	+	+	-	-
P8	-	+	-	-
P9	+	+	+	+
P10	-	+	-	-

The following table illustrates the technological devices preferred by participants for the consumption of films and television series. The data indicates that, while television remains a prevalent medium for content consumption, digital devices such as computers, tablets and smartphones are also utilised by a considerable proportion of the population. With respect to the consumption habits of television series and movies on digital platforms, it is observed that while some participants continue to utilise traditional television, there is an increasing tendency towards digital devices. Individual-oriented devices such as computers and phones are preferred especially due to their mobility and ease of personal access. However, the utilisation of tablets is comparatively constrained, a finding that can be interpreted as an indicator of the relationship between screen size and usage habits.

Table 3. Average daily screen time

Participant No.	Participants' daily screen time		
	2-4 hours	4-6 hours	7 hours or more
P1			
P2			
P3			
P4			
P5			
P6			
P7			
P8			
P9			
P10			

The table illustrates the mean daily screen time of the participants. The data indicates that the majority of participants spent between two and four hours using screens each day, with a smaller proportion spending seven hours or more. A further evaluation of the daily screen time of the participants in terms of age groups reveals that participants over the age of 30 (P1, P4, P7, P9) generally spend shorter periods of time in front of the screen. Conversely, participants between the ages of 18 and 29 (P2, P3, P5, P6, P10) exhibited a wider distribution of screen time. The presence of individuals with longer screen time among younger participants suggests that digital media is more widely consumed in this age group, potentially for educational, entertainment or social media interactions.

Reasons for Preferring Digital Platforms to Traditional Platforms

The present study set out to explore the reasons why participants expressed a preference for digital platforms over traditional platforms. Through a comprehensive review of the existing literature and an in-depth analysis of the data collected, it was possible to identify four categories that were deemed to be the primary factors in participants' preferences. These categories are as follows: independence from time and space, the existence of original stories and non-cliché content, ad-free viewability, and content diversity and personalised content options.

The initial category under the theme of preferring digital platforms to traditional channels is that of independence from time and space. Participant P1 articulated their perspective on the challenges they face in allocating time for media consumption during periods when children are typically active: "*They either take over the remote control or there is no environment in which I can focus my attention on what I am watching. Consequently, it is logical to view content after children's bedtime. This sentiment is further exemplified by the participant's sharing of a particular series that is viewed on Show TV, subsequently accessed on YouTube outside of its broadcast schedule, underscoring a preference for autonomy in media consumption. I am able to make my plans during the day according to myself.*" The most significant reason for this preference was the opportunity to act independently of time. In a similar vein, one of the participants, P4, stated that television programmes are broadcast at specific times, and that he is occasionally unable to watch them due to professional commitments. Conversely, digital platforms offer instantaneous access to content, a feature that is regarded as highly convenient. Participant P4 further elaborated on the practical benefits of mobile device usage, stating, "*It is more convenient to view a few items on the phone while commuting or during my return journey from work.*" The ability to view content irrespective of physical location was identified as a significant advantage. Participant P8 also highlighted the autonomy in scheduling that digital platforms offer, enumerating the reasons for her predilection for these platforms. "*The independence of time and space is the primary reason why I prefer digital platforms... However, I can exercise control over the content I consume. In other words, I can stop, close or fast forward at will*".

The second category under the theme of reasons for preferring digital platforms to traditional channels is the presence of original stories / non-cliché content. One of the participants, P6, explained her dislike of TV series and movies in traditional media with the sentence "*I don't support and watch any production made by mainstream media. It definitely does not appeal to me*". Similarly, P2 defined the reason for preferring digital platforms as "*not being able to find quality content in traditional media and the repetition of the same things*" and stated "*traditional content is repetitive and I don't think it appeals to young people anymore*". On the other hand, in their preference for digital platforms, the participants opened brackets to the existence of original stories and scenarios. Participant P1 said: "*I think there are more different stories and more different characters on digital. I think there is more quality work than in the past...it gives me what I want*", while participant P3 said "*...digital platforms generally offer more original productions in different genres. While some traditional TV series can be more commercial, digital platforms are open to more daring and experimental projects. Especially many of Netflix's original productions are of high quality and different*". Participant P8 said, "*I generally find the content on digital platforms to be more original, high quality and creative than traditional content. Digital platforms operate with less censorship and restrictions than traditional TV channels. This allows producers and writers to tell more original stories. On the other hand, the high budgets allocated to the big platforms naturally* *lead to the emergence of quality productions,*" attributing the non-cliché content libraries of digital channels to censorship and high budgets.

The third category under the theme of preferring digital platforms to traditional channels is that of ad-free viewability. Participant P4 articulated the following perspective: "*The act of changing channels or commercials on television can sometimes be a source of boredom. Digital platforms' provision of ad-free content fosters a more positive viewing experience.*" Participant P5 articulated their sentiments on the subject, stating, "*The presence of commercials on traditional television can be a source of significant frustration. When one is engrossed in a program, the commercial intermissions disrupt the flow of the event, leading to a decline in viewer engagement. In contrast, digital platforms offer ad-free content, which is perceived as more enjoyable.*" Participant P8 further elaborated on the benefits of ad-free content, underscoring its role in effective time management: "*It maintains the flow of the program and allows for time savings.*"

The fourth category under the theme of preferring digital platforms to traditional channels is content diversity/personalised content options. Participant P2 articulated that digital platforms "*enable me to watch a greater number of films, as they provide access to a wider array of content catering to my preferences*". Participant P9 expanded on the merits of personalised content diversity, stating, "*The personalised recommendations offered by these platforms have expanded my horizons, leading to the discovery of new content. Furthermore, they expressed a sense of autonomy in their media consumption, stating that they have complete control over the content they watch. I am able to pause, skip or turn off content at will*". Participant P10 further elaborated on this sentiment, stating, "*Traditional platforms often present content that has already been well-received and has been favorably reviewed. Consequently, their engagement with content from traditional platforms does not yield the same level of enjoyment.*" However, the ability to access a wider array of content on digital platforms, largely attributable to the customised nature of the algorithms, is a significant factor in determining preference. Participant P4 asserted that they possess the ability to locate a substantial amount of content within the genres that they prefer: "*Historically, individuals were compelled to consume whatever content was provided to them by television; however, in the contemporary era, they have the capacity to exercise agency over the content they consume, rather than being subject to the content provided to them by television*". Participant P3 concurred, stating that the proliferation of options in television series and films has become a key factor in their media consumption habits. They further elaborated on the significance of diversity in digital platforms, underscoring its role as a primary motivator for their media selection.

Distinctive Characteristics of Viewing Habits in the Age of Digital Platforms

The following categories are of particular note within the overarching theme of distinguishing qualities, which are becoming increasingly evident in viewing habits in the digital era: the cultural context of individual viewing habits; the practice of pausing during viewing; viewing habits across multiple screens (i.e. multi-screen viewing); the consumption of binge-viewing content (i.e. binge-viewing as a genre); selective viewing based on genre; and the consumption of new content.

The initial category that is evident under the theme of the distinctive qualities that are emerging in viewing habits in the age of digital platforms is that of individual viewing culture. The majority of participants indicated that they consume movies and television series on digital platforms in a solitary manner. A subsequent finding indicated a heightened propensity among younger participants (ages 18-25) to engage with digital platform content in a solitary manner. Participant P2 articulated their rationale for preferring solo viewing, stating, "*I watch alone because everyone usually opens and watches what they want from their own account. We all have different tastes. Naturally, each individual has their own account and watches content according to their preferences*".Participant P3 further elaborated on this sentiment, stating, "*I typically watch alone because I prefer to unwind while studying or to decompress during my leisure time.*" However, they did acknowledge that they occasionally engage in shared viewing experiences with friends or family. P6, who stated that she lives far away from her family due to her university education, said, "*I watch alone because I live alone now. Other than that, I watch with my friends or my brother, but we cannot watch digital platform productions together due to the generational and cultural difference between my parents and me*". Participant P10 concurred, stating that the optimal viewing experience for him is solitary, as it allows for autonomy in content selection, aligning with her personal preferences and inclinations. The most salient reason for the participants in this age group to realise the viewing experience as a solitary pursuit can be ascribed to the differentiation of expectations over the type of content and the generation gap. In contrast, the majority of participants in other age groups reported watching digital platforms in solitude, although they also indicated that they sometimes watched with their spouses, friends, or acquaintances, depending on the circumstances. Participant P7 articulated their tendency to engage in solitary viewing, attributing this behaviour to their tendency towards spontaneity and variability in their viewing habits: "*At times, an episode is watched and then paused; at other times, a season is watched over the course of several hours.*" However, the preference is to watch certain productions in the company of friends or family. As demonstrated by the research findings, there is an increasing prevalence of individual viewing habits. This shift is particularly evident among younger demographics, who have adopted this individual viewing culture more frequently. However, it should be noted that the individual viewing option is not the sole viewing choice available to participants.

The second category that merits attention under the theme of distinctive qualities emerging in viewing habits in the age of digital platforms is that of pause-watching. In the context of the research undertaken, participants were posed the following question: "Do you watch productions on digital platforms in a single sitting, akin to traditional television viewing? Do you pause-watch?" The responses obtained from this inquiry yielded notable insights. The vast majority of participants indicated that they engage in the practice of pausing while watching. Participant P9 articulated their experience with this phenomenon, stating. The option to pause and resume later enhances the frequency of pause watching, and digital platforms have played a pivotal role in fostering this behaviour. Participant P1 stated that they were obliged to pause the programme due to competing demands on their time, including childcare, domestic responsibilities, and household chores. Participant P7 stated that they typically discontinue watching due to competing commitments. "*If a film or television programme captures my attention, I will continue to watch it uninterruptedly; however, more often than not, I am distracted by other commitments.*" The findings emphasise the impact of digital platforms on the viewing experience and the importance of the flexibility they offer to viewers. Conversely, traditional television broadcasts mandate a passive viewing experience, contingent on a specific sequence of programming. In contrast, digital platforms empower viewers with autonomy, allowing them to consume content according to their own schedules. While the majority of participants indicated that they pause to watch content, they also emphasised that this is a necessity. Participant P2 stated, "*Unless my work is urgent, I prefer to finish the episode in one sitting and close it that way. When I have to pause and then continue, I may lose track of the subject or I may not feel inclined to watch it again.*" Participant P7 said, "*Stopping and watching sometimes makes it difficult to focus because I may not be in the same mood when I go back*". This observation highlights a potential challenge that could be experienced by some viewers, namely that this aspect might have a negative impact on their overall viewing experience. In conclusion, although the practice of pause viewing is regarded as a benefit offered by digital platforms, its impact varies depending on individual preferences and the context of viewing. While some adopt this practice due to the demands of daily life, others advocate for preserving the integrity of the uninterrupted viewing experience. Consequently, the flexibility and user-friendliness of digital platforms continue to exert a substantial influence on viewing habits.

The third category that merits attention under the theme of distinctive qualities emerging in viewing habits in the age of digital platforms is multi-screen viewing. The ubiquity of digital platforms has precipitated a substantial shift in audience habits. A salient feature of this transformation is the increased prevalence of concurrent multiscreen consumption, whereby individuals engage with content across multiple screens simultaneously. This phenomenon, termed multi-screen viewing, involves individuals engaging with multiple digital platforms concurrently, such as social media, messaging applications, and email, while also engaging with traditional media like movies and television series. Participant P5 articulated this phenomenon as follows: "*Especially when I share something on social media, I also browse the content I watch...So actually, following more than one screen at the same time has become a part of this age*". Participant P9 further elaborated on this phenomenon, stating, "*I predominantly engage with social media while watching content. However, the temporal and situational factors that influence this behaviour are multifaceted, and housework is cited as a potential competing activity.*" The motivation behind multiscreen use is largely driven by the desire to engage with social media. In the contemporary context, numerous viewers have adopted the practice of concurrently consuming content and engaging with other content. However, multi-screen use is not always limited to social media interaction. The propensity for multiscreen engagement is contingent on the quality of the content being viewed. Participant P8 stated, "In the event of viewing a significant film or television series, I do not allocate my attention to multiple screens concurrently. Interest in the phone is only piqued in cases of distraction or disinterest in the content, yet the viewing persists. The subject further elaborated on her approach to multiscreen tracking, stating that it is contingent upon the content's effect on him." P1 also expressed the impact of the content on multiscreen use, stating, "*For example, when I watched the first season of Squid Game, I watched it breathlessly and did not look at my phone. However, we just watched the second season, and I can say that I was on my phone a lot because I did not like it very much. I am unable to refrain from accessing my phone and social media while watching a programme.*" This practice exerts a multifaceted influence on the viewer's experience. Primarily, the utilisation of multiple screens has the potential to disrupt the viewing process by dividing the viewer's attention. This is particularly problematic during the viewing of films or television series, where viewers require undivided attention to follow the plot. However, some viewers attempt to maintain their focus by regulating the use of multiple screens. For instance, participant K2 articulated that she would only glance at incoming notifications while watching a movie, stating, "*I generally focus on the screen, but if I receive a notification on my phone, I will pause the movie to attend to it.*"As is evident from the participant statements, the practice of multiscreen viewing has become a prevalent aspect of the digital era. However, this phenomenon manifests itself in different ways depending on the type, duration and quality of the content viewed. While in-depth and remarkable content can sustain viewer interest for extended periods, superficial or repetitive content can prompt a transition to other screens. It can thus be concluded that digital platforms must develop more immersive and interactive formats if they are to retain viewer attention and determine effective content strategies.

The fourth category that merits attention under the theme of distinctive qualities emerging in viewing habits in the age of digital platforms is that of binge-watching. The unlimited access to content offered by digital platforms has radically transformed viewing habits. A salient manifestation of this transformation is the practice of binge-watching. Users frequently engage in binge-watching behaviour, particularly with regard to immersive series. One of the participants, K1, articulated this phenomenon as follows: "*We finished the new season of Squid Game in two days on a weekend; it went by in one breath. A similar phenomenon was observed with 'İlk ve Son'. I finished it very quickly, but I can also watch it slowly.*" This observation underscores the notion that the immersive nature of the content and the retention of viewer interest are pivotal factors in promoting binge-watching behaviour. P9, who stated that she does not binge watch due to the intensity of her daily work, nevertheless stated that she thinks that digital platforms cause binge watching behavior, stating that "*the wide range of content, personalized content recommendations, algorithmic interfaces and the opportunity to watch without ads. In addition, the lack of limitations such as space, time and means of viewing may also encourage binge viewing.*" One of the main reasons for binge-watching is the viewer's desire to constantly consume new content. Participant P1 drew attention to this point, saying: "*There is always a desire to watch something new. I've finished this one, let's watch the next one. I think everybody is like that. One of my colleagues will say, 'Have you seen this?' and then I go home and watch it. We watch a lot of TV series like that.*" She explains that the wide range of content available on digital platforms means that viewers are constantly consuming new productions. This situation creates a kind of content race between individuals and accelerates the viewing process.

Another important trigger for the binge-watching habit is the way in which the series lead the viewer into the next episode with intriguing scenes at the end of each episode. P2 explained: "*When I start a TV series, I usually don't stop until I've watched a few episodes, and if I'm hooked, I can keep watching and finish the season. I think the reason is that I always start the next episode because of the attention-grabbing, intriguing episode endings.*" This suggests that viewers are often unable to resist the urge to move on to the next episode and find themselves in long-term viewing processes.

In addition, the autoplay feature of digital platforms is another factor that encourages binge-watching. Participant P8, who believes that digital platforms encourage binge-watching, stated that "*offering personalised recommendations, not having time and space limits, being able to watch from different devices, i.e. offering multiple viewing features, and having content without advertising are also factors that pave the way for binge-watching*" and similarly, P5 explained how platforms support this process as follows: "*When an episode ends on digital platforms, the 'next episode' suggestion comes immediately, and that really appeals to me. In some series, especially if there are events that I am curious about, I can lose myself by saying 'let me watch another episode'. Sometimes I find myself watching content for hours because there is always new content and I want just a little bit more.*" These statements show how effective the strategies of digital platforms are in keeping the audience in the content and how users do not realise how time passes in this flow. However, some viewers use a controlled method of viewing against this fast consumption habit. P6 explains that she develops a conscious resistance against over-watching by saying: "*People want to consume and finish the ready-made thing, fast food concept is everywhere in our life now, but I try to watch one episode every day so as not to get bored.*" The same participant offers a different perspective on digital platforms, saying: "*I think it saves time, we don't have to watch commercials.*" It is clear from the research data that digital platforms have a structure that encourages excessive viewing and many viewers can consume content for hours, making time management difficult due to factors such as immersive content and autoplay. However, some users try to develop a controlled viewing habit to balance this rapid consumption. This suggests that individuals shape the speed of their content consumption according to their own preferences and daily routines, but the continuous streaming offered by digital platforms tends to extend viewing times.

The fifth category under the theme of distinctive qualities emerging in viewing habits in the age of digital platforms is genre-oriented selective viewing. The wide range of content offered by digital platforms allows viewers to determine their preferences more subjectively. Compared to the limited and mostly commercial content of traditional television, digital platforms offer viewers the opportunity to easily access the type of content they want. This situation brings the tendency of genre-oriented selective viewing to the fore in viewing habits. P1 stated that, thanks to digital platforms, she was no longer exposed to content in genres she did not want to watch: "*Also, I don't like to watch ridiculous and fake things like honour etc, but since TV was full of them, we watched them somehow. Since I like horror and romantic films and TV series very much, I usually watch those kinds of films.*" This statement shows that the restrictive structure of traditional television has been replaced by a personalised viewing experience. Digital platforms reinforce viewers' genre orientation by offering suggestions based on their interests.

Participant K2 stated that she had more viewing experience in the age of digital platforms as "*It allowed me to watch more movies because I could find more content in the genres I like*". The same participant summarized how the algorithms' presentation of content in line with user preferences affects the viewing experience as "*It draws the viewer in by offering movies similar to the type of movie they like*". This situation suggests that digital platforms encourage individuals to consume more content by increasing their interest in certain genres. Of particular note in the participants' statements are genre-based viewing definitions such as science fiction, drama, comedy and psychological thriller. Participant P3 described his own viewing preferences as "*I especially prefer science fiction, drama and sometimes comedy genres*", while participant P3 said "*Digital platforms often offer more original productions in different genres. While some traditional TV series can be more commercial, digital platforms are open to more daring and experimental projects. Especially Netflix original productions are of high quality and different.*" This suggests that digital platforms encourage individuals to consume more content by increasing their interest in certain genres. In the participants' statements, genre-oriented viewing definitions such as science fiction, drama, comedy and psychological thriller are particularly noteworthy. Participant P3 described his own viewing preferences as "*I especially prefer science fiction, drama and sometimes comedy genres*", while participant P3 said: "*Digital platforms often offer more original productions in different genres. While some traditional TV series can be more commercial, digital platforms are open to more daring and experimental projects. Especially Netflix original productions are of high quality and different.*" This statement suggests that digital platforms not only offer certain genres, but also enrich these genres with innovative and original content. As can be understood, digital platforms offer viewers a great deal of freedom in choosing content, popularising the habit of genre-oriented selective viewing. While the personalised recommendations offered by algorithms allow viewers to gravitate towards certain genres, the platforms' inclusion of original and innovative productions reinforces this tendency. In contrast to the limitations imposed by traditional television, digital platforms make it easier for viewers to access content that appeals to their interests and thus provide a more satisfying viewing experience.

The sixth category under the theme of distinctive qualities emerging in viewing habits in the age of digital platforms is content-driven viewing focused on new content. The large pool of content offered by digital platforms means that viewers are constantly discovering new content rather than watching it again. This makes the new content-oriented viewing tendency stand out in viewing habits. While participants tend to re-watch only productions with which they have a special connection, they generally find it more attractive to turn to new content. In this context, P3 stated that he did not want to waste time during the viewing process: "*If I don't like it, I stop immediately. I don't want to waste my time. If it didn't catch my attention at first, I'll move on to other alternatives.*" Similarly, participant P8 said: "*In general, I do not re-watch the content I watch. However, the content that I do re-watch is important and privileged for me, such as being included in my cult films that I find worth watching again.*" This statement shows that viewers quickly move away from productions that are of little interest to them. Similarly, participant P1 stated that it is more satisfying to discover new stories than to repeat a production that has already been seen: "*Watching it once is enough because I already understand everything and it makes more sense to watch new films and TV series than to re-watch what I have already watched. I want a new story that I don't know.*" In a similar vein, P10 asserted that "*the abundance of content on digital platforms is excessive. I have a greater interest in other content than in repeatedly viewing the same content.*" However, it should be noted that some participants also expressed a preference for revisiting certain productions. For instance, P2 articulated that revisiting familiar content offers a sense of reassurance, stating, "*I occasionally revisit my preferred television series or films because I am not always inclined to seek out new material. This practice is akin to a guarantee of satisfaction, as it is a known quantity that can be relied upon. It serves as a reliable source of entertainment, eliminating the need to explore new options, avoid disappointment, and engage in the time-consuming process of searching for a new source of entertainment.*" This phenomenon can be interpreted as indicative of a concern regarding the indecision and temporal expenditure associated with the discovery of new content.

However, it has been observed that the practice of rewatching is predominantly limited to older and more in-depth content. P4 stated that "*If there is a movie or TV series that I really like, I may like to watch it again after years.*" This inclination is attributed to the potential realization of hitherto unperceived nuances upon subsequent viewings. Nevertheless, it is important to note that the practice of rewatching is predominantly limited to older films and television series. With the emergence of new content, the focus shifts towards exploring these more recent releases. The motivation to rewatch is not typically associated with average works, as they do not offer sufficient content to justify the effort. This statement indicates that the motivation to rewatch is contingent on the quality and depth of the content. This phenomenon can be attributed to the abundance of content available on digital platforms, personalised recommendation systems, and continually updated catalogues. While viewers may rewatch only those productions that hold a special meaning or depth, they often find it more appealing to discover new and unknown stories. The ease with which content can be accessed, the rapid rate at which it can be consumed, and the plethora of alternative options provided by digital platforms have been identified as significant factors that contribute to a decline in re-watching behaviour, thereby encouraging viewers to constantly consume new content.

Future Research Directions

This study employs a qualitative lens to explore the evolution of viewing habits among digital platform users, unveiling significant insights. Nevertheless, there are still many research opportunities in this area. Firstly, it is recommended that future studies augment the sample size and diversify it to include different age groups, socioeconomic backgrounds and geographical regions. This would provide a more comprehensive picture of how digital viewing habits differ across social contexts.

Secondly, while the present research concentrated principally on audience preferences and behavioural changes, future studies could examine the psychological and emotional effects of new viewing practices such as binge-watching, pause-watching and multi-screen use. It is imperative that long-term studies are conducted in order to assess the effects of continuous use of digital platforms on attention span, content memory and emotional well-being.

Thirdly, the utilisation of algorithm-based recommendation systems by digital platforms should be subjected to rigorous examination in terms of its impact on user autonomy, content diversity and cultural consumption patterns. In this context, research could also encompass contemporary debates such as digital echo chambers, content over-personalisation and filter bubbles.

CONCLUSION AND DISCUSSION

The objective of this study is to explore and discuss the transformation of viewing experiences in the age of digital platforms. The study sought to answer the following research questions: what are the determinants of the preference of digital platforms over traditional media, and how have viewing habits been transformed, both positively and negatively, by digital viewing platforms? To this end, the qualitative research model was adopted, and semi-structured interviews were conducted with ten participants who stated a preference for digital platforms over traditional platforms. The data set obtained was analysed by content analysis.

The research revealed that the participants who expressed a preference for digital platforms over traditional platforms cited several key reasons for this preference. These reasons encompass the autonomy to choose when and where to engage with content, the presence of original narratives and non-clichéd content, the absence of advertisements, the capacity for content diversity and the availability of personalised content options. Participants further elaborated that these qualities, absent in traditional media, render digital platforms appealing and significantly influence their viewing experiences. Conversely, when probing the impact of digital platforms on viewing habits, it was observed that there has been an emergence of individual viewing cultures, pause viewing, multi-screen viewing, binge viewing, genre-oriented selective viewing and content-driven viewing focused on new content behaviours.

The paradigm of individual viewing culture underscores the notion of viewer autonomy in selecting content according to personal predilections. This approach aligns with the capitalist system's conceptualisation of the individual as a subjective entity. Individuals shape their viewing habits with a view to personal satisfaction and the articulation of their identities. A similar phenomenon is evidenced by genre-oriented viewing habits, which demonstrate that individuals realise themselves by turning to certain types of content. This phenomenon is significant in the context of individualisation processes and the fulfilment of postmodern desires. However, it is important to note that both individual viewing culture and genre-oriented viewing habits are predominantly manifested through new content. This emphasis on novel content can be seen as a reflection of viewers' pursuit of innovation and their desire to remain current in the rapidly evolving digital landscape. This behaviour is directly linked to consumption culture. Digital platforms enable viewers to engage with the constant stream of new content, thus fulfilling their role as consumers within a consumer society. Indeed, the existence of this content-oriented viewing behaviour is inextricably linked to the phenomenon of binge-watching. Digital platforms, which espouse the liberal discourse of "freedom", fully conform to the structure of postmodern capitalism.

In response to the structure of digital platforms organised around consumption, multi-screen viewing has been identified as a significant area of interest, given the observable transformation in participants' viewing behaviours. Participants have indicated that they perceive the content on digital platforms to be more authentic in comparison to that of traditional channels. However, they also indicated that they typically engage with this content across multiple screens, including phones and computers. Participants further elaborated that their utilisation of multiple screens is contingent upon the quality of the content, with their attention being redirected to other screens in the event of encountering superficial or repetitive content. In this context, despite users' perceptions that content on digital platforms is more authentic than traditional media, it is understood that these platforms are not yet at a level to fully concentrate attention on the content. This phenomenon, characterised by the viewers' tendency to multitask, has been interpreted as contributing to the perpetuation of popcorn culture.

REFERENCES

Adorno, T. W., & Horkheimer, M. (2007). *The Culture Industry* (Ülner, N., Tüzel, M., & Gen, E., Trans.). İletişim Yayınları. (Original work published 1944)

Alimoradi, Z., Jafari, E., Potenza, M. N., Lin, C. Y., Wu, C. Y., & Pakpour, A. H. (2022). Binge-watching and mental health problems: A systematic review and meta-analysis. *International Journal of Environmental Research and Public Health, 19*(15), 9707. DOI: 10.3390/ijerph19159707 PMID: 35955069

Altın, A. (2021). New trends in television broadcasting: Mobile broadcasting (Doctoral dissertation, Marmara University, Turkey).

Anghelcev, G., Sar, S., Martin, J. D., & Moultrie, J. L. (2021). Binge-watching serial video content: Exploring the subjective phenomenology of the binge-watching experience. *Mass Communication & Society*, *24*(1), 130–154. DOI: 10.1080/15205436.2020.1811346

Anozie, V. (2020). Effects of Emotion on Binge-watching. *Modern Psychological Studies*, *25*(1), 9.

Bilginer Kucur, A. (2022). Using The Second Screen In Digital Natives: Field Research. *Journal of History School*, *57*, 1358–1382.

Castells, M. (2008). *Ağ Toplumunun Yükselişi Enformasyon Çağı: Ekonomi, Toplum ve Kültür*. İstanbul Bilgi Üniversitesi Yayınları.

Çelik, F. (2023). Second screen. *Communication encyclopedia*. https://doi.org/DOI: 10.5281/zenodo.8252245

Chandler, D., & Munday, R. (2011). *Oxford A Dictionary of Media and Communication*. Oxford University Press. DOI: 10.1093/acref/9780199568758.001.0001

D'heer, E., Courtois, C., & Paulussen, S. (2012, July). Everyday life in (front of) the screen: The consumption of multiple screen technologies in the living room context. In *Proceedings of the 10th European conference on Interactive TV and video* (pp. 195-198). DOI: 10.1145/2325616.2325654

Erdoğan, İ., & Alemdar, K. (2010). *Öteki kuram: Kitle iletişiminde yaklaşımların tarihsel ve eleştirel bir değerlendirmesi* (3rd ed.). Erk Yayınları.

Erickson, S. E., Dal Cin, S., & Byl, H. (2019). An Experimental Examination of Binge Watching and Narrative Engagement. *Social Sciences (Basel, Switzerland)*, *8*(1), 19. DOI: 10.3390/socsci8010019

Eyrek, A. (2022). Time Front of the Screen: The McDonaldization of Television Viewing – Binge-watching. *Fenerbahce University Journal of Social Sciences (FBU-JOSS)*, 2(1), 83-96.

Flayelle, M., Maurage, P., Di Lorenzo, K. R., Vögele, C., Gainsbury, S. M., & Billieux, J. (2020). Binge-watching: What Do We Know So Far? A First Systematic Review of The Evidence. *Current Addiction Reports*, *7*(1), 44–60. DOI: 10.1007/s40429-020-00299-8

Gomez-Uribe, C. A., & Hunt, N. (2015). The Netflix Recommender System: Algorithms, Business Value, and Innovation. [TMIS]. *ACM Transactions on Management Information Systems*, *6*(4), 1–19. DOI: 10.1145/2843948

Gümüş, B. (2021). From Marathon Watching to Binge Watching: The Effect of Netflix on Watching Habits. *Turkish Review of Communication Studies*, (37), 147–169.

Hepkon, Z. (2011). Yeni iletişim teknolojileri tartışmalarının yeni olmayan boyutu: Teknolojik determinizm. In Hepkon, Z. (Ed.), *İletişim ve teknoloji olanaklar, uygulamalar, sınırlamalar* (pp. 121–141). Kırmızı Kedi Yayınevi.

Jenner, M. (2014). Is This TVIV? On Netflix, TVIII and Binge-watching. *New Media & Society*, •••, 1–17.

Lüders, M. (2022). Self-Determined or Controlled, Seeking Pleasure, or Meaning? Identifying What Makes Viewers Enjoy Watching Television on Streaming Services. *Poetics*, *92*, 101639. DOI: 10.1016/j.poetic.2021.101639

Matrix, S. (2014). The Netflix Effect: Teens, Binge Watching, and On-Demand Digital Media Trends. *Jeunesse: Young People, Texts. Cultures*, *6*(1), 119–138.

Mazıcı, E. T., & Can, E. N. (2021). Postmodern Consumption and Digital Media Reflections: An Assessment on Netflix. *Journal of Selcuk Communication*, *14*(2), 832–858.

Morley, D. (2003). *Television, Audiences and Cultural Studies*. Routledge. DOI: 10.4324/9780203398357

Neate, T., Jones, M., & Evans, M. (2017). Cross-device Media: A Review of Second Screening and Multi-Device Television. *Personal and Ubiquitous Computing*, *21*(2), 391–405. DOI: 10.1007/s00779-017-1016-2

Ort, A., Wirz, D. S., & Fahr, A. (2021). Is Binge-Watching Addictive? Effects of Motives for TV Series Use on the Relationship Between Excessive Media Consumption and Problematic Viewing Habits. *Addictive Behaviors Reports*, *13*, 100325. DOI: 10.1016/j.abrep.2020.100325 PMID: 33457488

Saeed, A. (2024). Investigating the Binge-Watching Behavior on Insomnia and Obesity Among Generation Z. *Pakistan Journal of Rehabilitation, 13*(1), 30–42. DOI: 10.36283/pjr.zu.13.1/005

Song, L., Zhang, Q., Hu, B., & Mou, J. (2022). To Resist or to Purchase: The Causal Mechanism of Binge-Watching and Program Purchase. *Journal of Retailing and Consumer Services, 68*, 103021. Advance online publication. DOI: 10.1016/j.jretconser.2022.103021

Starosta, J. A., & Izydorczyk, B. (2020). Understanding The Phenomenon of Binge-Watching—A Systematic Review. *International Journal of Environmental Research and Public Health, 17*(12), 4469. DOI: 10.3390/ijerph17124469 PMID: 32580289

Steiner, E., & Xu, K. (2018). Binge-watching Motivates Change. *Convergence (London), 135485651775036*. Advance online publication. DOI: 10.1177/1354856517750365

Steins-Loeber, S., Reiter, T., Averbeck, H., Harbarth, L., & Brand, M. (2020). Binge-watching Behaviour: The Role of İmpulsivity and Depressive Symptoms. *European Addiction Research, 26*(3), 141–150. DOI: 10.1159/000506307 PMID: 32074611

Tefertiller, A. C., & Maxwell, L. C. (2018). Depression, Emotional States, and The Experience of Binge-Watching Narrative Television. *Atlantic Journal of Communication, 26*(5), 278–290. DOI: 10.1080/15456870.2018.1517765

Thakur, A., Sharma, S., & Narula, A. (2025). K-Drama: A Study on Bedtime Procrastination and Binge Watching among University Students. *International Journal of Interdisciplinary Approaches in Psychology, 3*(1), 28–44.

Trouleau, W., Ashkan, A., Ding, W., & Eriksson, B. (2016). Just One More: Modeling Binge Watching Behavior. *Proceedings of the 22nd ACM SIGKDD International Conference on Knowledge Discovery and Data Mining - KDD '16*. DOI: 10.1145/2939672.2939792

Turner, G., & Tay, J. (2009). Introduction. In Turner, G., & Tay, J. (Eds.), *Television Studies After TV: Understanding Television in The Post-Broadcast Era* (pp. 1–7). Routledge. DOI: 10.4324/9780203878316

Ulusoy, E., Wirz, D. S., Eden, A., & Ellithorpe, M. E. (2025). Boundaries on A Binge: Explicating The Role of Intentionality in Binge-Watching Motivations And Problematic Outcomes. *Acta Psychologica, 252*, 104666. Advance online publication. DOI: 10.1016/j.actpsy.2024.104666 PMID: 39693967

Vaterlaus, J. M., Spruance, L. A., Frantz, K., & Kruger, J. S. (2019). College Student Television Binge Watching: Conceptualization, Gratifications, and Perceived Consequences. *The Social Science Journal, 56*(4), 470–479. DOI: 10.1016/j.soscij.2018.10.004

Williams, R. (1989). *Raymond Williams on Television: 1921-1988.* Routledge.

Williams, R. (2003). *Televizyon, Teknoloji ve Kültürel Biçim* (Türkbağ, A. U., Trans.). Dost Kitabevi.

Zengin, F. (2021). Artificial Intelligence and Personalized Viewing Culture: Hyper-Personalization of Art Works on Netflix. *TRT Akademi, 6*(13), 700–727. DOI: 10.37679/trta.959576

Additional Reading

Benavides, C., & Buzeta, C. (2025). 12 OTT Video Streaming: Redefining the Future of Television. De Gruyter Handbook of Media Technology and Innovation, 183.

Casetti, F., & Odin, R. (2025). From paleo-to neo-television: A semio-pragmatic approach. *Critical Studies in Television*, 17496020251321738.

Chayka, K. (2025). *Filterworld: How algorithms flattened culture*. Random House.

Hebben, K. C., & Piepiorka, C. (2025). Easy to snack—Hard to digest? Strategies of dis/array in streaming, social media, and television. *Media and Communication, 13*, 13. DOI: 10.17645/mac.9430

Johnson, C., Lobato, R., & Scarlata, A. (2025). Default Viewing: Reconceptualising Choice And Habit in Television Audience Research. *Media Culture & Society*, •••, 01634437241313040. DOI: 10.1177/01634437241313040

Perks, L. G. (2015). *Media Marathoning: Immersions in Morality*. Lexington Books.

Saritepeci, M., Balıkçı, H. C., & Ermiş, U. F. (2025). Factors associated with multi-screen addiction and academic resilience: A multigroup analysis by school level. *Quality & Quantity*, •••, 1–19. DOI: 10.1007/s11135-025-02076-z

Schopman, B., Brickly, D., Aroyo, L., van Aart, C., Buser, V., Siebes, R., . . . Raimond, Y. (2010). NoTube: making the Web part of personalised TV. In *WEBSCI* 2010.

Steiner, E. (2023). *Binge TV: The Rise and Impact of The Viewing Revolution.* McFarland.

Wayne, M. L., & Castro, D. (2025). Cultural Authenticity as Netflix Televisuality: Streaming Industry Discourse and Globally Commissioned Original Series. *Media and Communication*, *13*, 13. DOI: 10.17645/mac.9407

KEY TERMS AND DEFINITIONS

Individual Viewing Culture: The concept of individual viewing culture pertains to the tendency of viewers to consume media content in a solitary manner, often choosing what, when, and how to watch without the influence of others.

Binge-Watching: The term "binge-watching" is used to describe the practice of watching multiple episodes of a television series or an entire season in a single sitting.

Consumer Society: Consumer society is defined as a social system in which the acquisition and consumption of goods and services are central to the identity and lifestyle of individuals. In this context, the consumption of media assumes a significant role, with entertainment and information being commodified and marketed to satisfy the desires and needs of consumers.

Active Viewer: An 'active viewer' is defined as a media consumer who engages critically with the content they are consuming, often interpreting, analysing and discussing it. This dynamic stands in contrast to that of a passive viewer, who may merely observe without engaging deeply.

Multi-Screen: Multi-screen refers to the concurrent utilisation of multiple digital devices (e.g. a television, smartphone, tablet, or computer) for media consumption. This behaviour often involves engaging with different types of content across screens, such as watching a television programme while browsing social media or checking the internet.

Personalised Screen: The concept of personalised screens refers to the customisation of a viewer's media experience through tailored content and interfaces. The advent of technological advancements and sophisticated algorithms has enabled streaming platforms and applications to formulate content recommendations that are tailored to the individual preferences, viewing history and behavioural patterns of the viewer, thereby engendering a bespoke media consumption experience.

New Content-Driven Viewing: New content-driven viewing is defined as a contemporary viewing trend in which viewers consume media based on content-driven preferences rather than traditional streaming or channel loyalty. This approach is supported by the accessibility, diversity and personalisation offered by digital platforms.

Chapter 3
Television and Digital Platform Series in Turkey: A Structural and Content-Based Comparison

Damla Fatma Saylan
Ondokuz Mayıs University, Turkey

Ömer Çakın
https://orcid.org/0000-0001-7853-6460
Ondokuz Mayıs University, Turkey

ABSTRACT

In today's globalized world, the media industry has undergone a significant transformation due to digitalization and advancements in communication technologies. This study compares traditional Turkish television series with digital platform productions, analyzing structural aspects like duration, format, broadcasting, advertising, and financing. It explores how digital series blend cinematic and televisual elements to form hybrid narratives, and how these innovations reshape viewer experience. The research highlights the shift from passive to active audiences, emphasizing how viewer engagement now guides content creation. Ultimately, the study aims to uncover the impact of digital platforms on the series industry and their role in shaping future media trends in Turkey.

DOI: 10.4018/979-8-3373-1957-5.ch003

INTRODUCTION

Developments in technology have led to significant transformations in all sectors, including communication and media, and have paved the way for the emergence and evolution of the concept of "digitalization." The distinction between traditional media—which is characterized by a one-way structure and limited capabilities—and new media tools that have acquired a multilayered structure through advancements in internet technologies, emerges as a natural result of media digitalization (Timisi, 2003: 80). The television series industry has also been influenced by this widespread process of digitalization. In Turkey, the growing popularity of digital platforms and their venture into series production have initiated a new formation process, structurally and content-wise, that is distinct from traditional Turkish television series. From cinema to digital publishing, series have encountered various experiences (Günay and Yetkiner, 2022: 33).

The first digital platform initiative in Turkey began with the launch of BluTV in 2015, followed by Netflix's official entry into the Turkish market in 2016, which accelerated the process. Since 2015–2016, the increasing number of digital platforms has created a new and exciting space for viewers tired of traditional narrative structures, and for creative teams and production crews frustrated with censorship and restrictive broadcasting policies.

In television series produced for traditional channels, producers and creative teams are obliged to operate under certain conditions. Advertising revenues constitute the primary source of funding for television broadcasting, which results in prolonged episode durations and a strict censorship mechanism. These limitations prevent deviation from classical narrative structures and create challenges for viewers, creators, producers, and actors alike. In contrast, digital platforms develop their own unique structural and content features, offering viewers an alternative viewing experience and, through subscription systems, transforming them from passive consumers into active "users." Moreover, these platforms not only provide a freer creative space for writers and technical teams but also contribute to more humane working conditions for actors and set workers (Ayerdem, 2019: 53–71).

In light of these distinctions, it can be observed that, as in many other countries, two separate television industries have emerged in Turkey under the influence of digitalization. The emergence of these two distinct industries raises several fundamental questions:

What structural and content-related changes have occurred with this transformation?

Why do viewers prefer digital platforms?

What are the main differences between traditional television series and digital series in terms of content and structure?

How has the series and film industry developed a hybrid narrative structure through digitalization?

How has the transition of the viewer from a passive to an active role in the new media environment affected content producers?

To what extent have viewing experiences and consumption habits changed based on audience feedback and participation?

This study focuses on the structural and content-related differences between traditional media, represented by television broadcasting, and content produced for digital platforms. The primary aim is to identify the differences at both structural and content levels between traditional Turkish television series and those produced on digital platforms. Accordingly, the study first examines the historical development of the traditional television series sector in Turkey, then evaluates the emergence and proliferation of digital platforms through a literature review. Through a comparative analysis framework, the study aims to present findings that will offer predictions about the future of the series industry in Turkey.

A BRIEF HISTORICAL OVERVIEW OF THE DEVELOPMENT OF THE TURKISH TELEVISION DRAMA INDUSTRY

While the first television broadcast in the world took place on November 2, 1936, in a town in London, the arrival of television in Turkey took many years (Kar & Gündüz, 2024: 198). In Turkey, the first broadcast began in 1952 through efforts at Istanbul Technical University, followed by the trial broadcast of TRT Ankara Television on January 31, 1968. In 1971, with a protocol signed between TRT and ITU, the control of television broadcasting was completely handed over to TRT, thus initiating the development process of television broadcasting in Turkey. Consequently, TRT maintained a monopoly over television broadcasting in the country until the emergence of private channels in the 1990s (Özçağlayan, 2014: 42).

TRT's monopoly in series production and broadcasting came to an end with the rise of numerous private channels in the 1990s. To regulate and supervise these private broadcasters, the now-repealed Law No. 3984 came into force in 1994, under which the Radio and Television Supreme Council (RTÜK) was established. However, the law soon proved inadequate in light of the evolving dynamics of the sector, and following annulments of certain articles by the Constitutional Court, a revision became necessary. As a result, taking into account sectoral developments, the more comprehensive Law No. 6112 was prepared and enacted in 2011 (RTÜK, 2025).

Turkey's initial exposure to television series began in 1972 with TRT's broadcast of foreign productions. The first steps in domestic series production were taken with the broadcasting of Kaynanalar and Aşk-ı Memnu in 1974. Between 1974 and

1986, TRT continued producing various series. Until the 1990s, TRT was the sole producer of television dramas in Turkey. As a public broadcaster, TRT developed its programming by adhering to the cultural values of the Turkish family and social structure (İTO, 2022).

The introduction of the ratings system in Turkey during the same period led to a competitive environment based on advertising revenues. Private channels, which emerged during this time, began producing their own drama content. However, unlike TRT, these productions were largely commercialized and aimed at capturing a share of the advertising market. Nevertheless, in the early years, similar to TRT's approach, private channels also produced content that respected family and societal values. However, in the 2000s, with the increasing influence of popular culture, the thematic direction of Turkish television series shifted; the portrayal of traditional cultural values diminished while elements of Western culture became more prominent in narratives. This transformation is considered one of the effects of cultural imperialism (Ayerdem, 2019: 45–46).

For instance, the 2002 series Çocuklar Duymasın, aired on TGRT, portrayed the conflict between traditional/patriarchal order and the innovations brought about by modernization. It reflected this conflict through the troubled marriage of Haluk and Meltem a couple incorporating elements of Western culture—presented within the context of family representation and humor (Özsoy, 2006: 158–162). In this sense, the commercial and advertising-focused orientation of private broadcasters played a significant role in altering the content structure of Turkish series.

The time slot with the highest television viewership is referred to as "prime time" or "golden hours." While these hours vary by country, in Turkey, they generally span from 8:00 p.m. to 11:00 p.m. In pursuit of maximizing advertising revenues, Turkish television dramas are primarily broadcast during this time. Because this period overlaps with the leisure hours of the largest socioeconomic and demographic segments of the population, episodes are typically extended to a duration of 240–270 minutes, including a recap segment (Mutlu, 2008: 58–59). The extension of episode length, driven by advertising policies, complicates both the technical production and scriptwriting processes. The obligation for each television series to meet a specific airtime requirement directly affects the production process. This issue will be addressed in more detail in the section on structural differences.

Looking at the present day, in the 21st century—also referred to as the "Digital Age"—internet-based platforms have gained a central position, just as television did in its heyday, following its invention in 1923 and widespread use beginning in the 1960s. Much like television once drew audiences away from cinema halls, a similar transformation is currently occurring due to the influence of digital media platforms. For audiences weary of traditional broadcasting practices, creative teams constrained by censorship mechanisms, and television sector workers exhausted by long working hours, digital platforms now offer a compelling alternative.

THE EMERGENCE AND EXPANSION OF DIGITAL PLATFORMS IN TURKEY

The pioneer of digital broadcasting in Turkey was the Doğan Media Group, which had been operating since 1997. Under its leadership, BluTV was founded in 2015 by Aydın Doğan Yalçındağ, becoming the first digital streaming platform in Turkey. Operating under a paid subscription model, BluTV initially offered existing films and series; however, it later produced Masum (2017), Turkey's first digital platform series and BluTV's first original content. On January 19, 2021, Warner Bros-Discovery acquired a 35% stake in BluTV. Subsequently, on December 6, 2023, the company acquired full ownership of the platform. BluTV is expected to transition into the MAX platform as of April 15, 2025 (BBC, 2024).

PuhuTV, also established under the Doğan Media Group in 2016, adopted a model similar to YouTube by offering free, ad-supported content instead of a paid subscription system. PuhuTV made previously aired Turkish television series available to viewers free of charge and funded its operations through advertising. Its first original series was Fi (2018), followed by productions such as Şahsiyet (2018) and Dip (2018).

Netflix, which was founded in 1997 in the United States initially as a DVD rental service, later evolved into a global leader in digital streaming. It entered the Turkish market in January 2016 (Chen, 2020: 42). Netflix announced plans to invest in domestic productions, generating excitement among Turkish audiences seeking diverse content. Its first original Turkish production, Hakan: Muhafız (The Protector), premiered on December 5, 2018 (Ildır & Çelik Rappas, 2022: 255–271).

Following Netflix's entry, the number of digital platforms in Turkey increased, and this trend was joined by Gain, launched by Beyn Consultancy. Gain adopted a short-form video strategy with vertically oriented content designed for mobile viewing, typically producing short (10–15 minute) entertaining and educational videos (Türkiye, 2024). The platform's first original series was 10 Bin Adım (2020).

Exxen, a paid content platform, was launched on January 1, 2021, by Acun Ilıcalı under the Acun Medya umbrella. Its first original series, Şeref Bey (2021), was followed by numerous other Turkish productions, reflecting a strong domestic content focus.

In parallel with these developments, TRT launched its international digital streaming platform Tabii on May 2, 2023. Designed as a "Digital Home" for families, the platform aimed to meet the growing demand for family-oriented content (AA,

2023). While TRT continues to produce series on its traditional broadcast channel in line with its public service mission, the establishment of Tabii reflects an effort to keep pace with the digital age and evolving viewer habits.

Since their inception around 2015–2016, digital platforms in Turkey have increased significantly in both number and content production by 2018. Their rapid expansion can be attributed to the ease of access across various devices such as televisions, PCs, and tablets, as well as features unique to digital platforms—such as subscription models and personalized content experiences. These characteristics have clearly differentiated digital platforms from traditional television series. In the following sections of this study, these distinctions will be examined in terms of both structural and content-related dimensions.

DIFFERENCES IN THE PRODUCTION OF TURKISH TELEVISION SERIES AND DIGITAL PLATFORM SERIES

The emergence of digital streaming platforms, which operate under a structure distinctly different from traditional television broadcasting that has existed for decades, has significantly influenced the production processes of series in both structural and content-related aspects. This section of the study will focus on the impacts of these differences specifically within the context of Turkey.

Structural Differences

With the emergence of digital streaming platforms, which have developed with a different logic compared to traditional television broadcasting, the series production processes of both mediums have undergone significant changes. These differences manifest across several key factors, including duration, format, target audience, advertising revenue, distribution channels, and methods of measuring success.

Duration, Format, and Target Audience

The most significant difference between traditional television series and digital platform series lies in the duration of episodes, narrative structure, and target audience. Whether episodes are long or short affects the series throughout the production process, both structurally and content-wise. Traditional television series construct their narrative structure around the desires and tendencies of viewers, focusing on societal and cultural values. Digital platforms also prioritize audience expectations; however, unlike television, they do not target broad audiences defined by socio-economic and demographic factors, and they acquire funding through a different method than television. This results in a distinct narrative style that deviates from the uniform format of traditional television series.

Television determines its target audience using a ratings system, which classifies viewers into five categories: A/B, C1, C2, D/E. Groups A/B represent higher-income audiences, while C/D/E represent lower-income groups. The "Total" category represents the common subset of all these groups. Since the Total group represents the widest audience, production companies working for television create series that cater to this group. This commercial orientation leads to discomfort among viewers who are dissatisfied with content produced primarily for profit, driving them away from traditional television and towards digital platforms (Ayerdem, 2019: 58–59).

Şaban Özdemir, who examines generational media consumption habits in the age of social media, found that Generations Y and Z are more inclined to consume media content for entertainment purposes (Özdemir, 2021: 302–304). According to the We Are Social Digital Global 2024 report, the number of active social media and internet users worldwide is rapidly increasing. The average amount of time spent on the internet by users is determined to be 6 hours and 40 minutes per day. In countries with aging populations, this time has been observed to decrease, and older individuals use the internet less than younger generations. Additionally, the report indicates a decline in TV viewership. While there has been a slight increase in internet usage, a decrease of 8.2% in TV viewership was recorded compared to the previous year. This shows that the average internet user now watches 17 minutes less TV content per day compared to the same period last year (We Are Social Digital Global, 2024).

Usage on internet and social media platforms is continually increasing, particularly among younger generations. In this context, the internet-based nature of digital platforms, content promotions through social media via official production accounts and fan pages dedicated to the series, and the ease of access to content through smart TVs, tablets, PCs, and smartphones without spatial and temporal restrictions, indicate that their target audience predominantly consists of Generations Y and Z. In short, while digital platforms cater to a specific audience, television series are produced for a broader target audience. The fact that television follows a commercial-oriented strategy by offering advertising-prioritized programming, while digital platforms provide ad-free content and cater to a more specific target audience, shapes the duration and format of both types of series in distinct ways.

When looking at the history of TV series durations in Turkey, a major change can be observed between the past and present. During the period when TRT had a monopoly on Turkish television, the duration of the series it produced ranged from 25 to 30 minutes. At that time, viewers, who had no alternative options for watching TV series, would request the channel to extend the duration of the series in order to enjoy their experiences more. In response to these requests, the duration of the series was increased to 40–50 minutes. In the 1990s, with the breaking of TRT's monopoly and the widespread privatization of television channels, a competitive environment was created. Under the influence of this competition, the duration of series increased to 60 minutes. Starting from the 2010s, Turkish series were introduced to the global market, elevating the Turkish TV industry to an important position in terms of exports. As a result, the desire to increase advertising revenue on television led to an even further extension of the duration of series. In 2010, the Cinema Writers Association, troubled by the increasing lengths of TV series, held a protest under the slogan “Local Series Are Unnecessarily Long,” aiming to prevent the ever-growing duration of series, yet the episode durations did not decrease; on the contrary, they increased from 90 minutes to 120 minutes (Arık, 2023: 131).

When examining today's TV series, including the summary sections and commercial breaks, the total duration can reach up to 240 minutes. In other words, a television viewer must set aside 4 hours on the day and time of the broadcast (prime time) in order to watch the series until the end. In Turkey, TV series air one new episode per week. If a Turkish series, which begins airing in the fall, becomes successful, it concludes its season finale in the summer of the same year. This means that a viewer who follows a TV series will need up to nine months to watch an entire season of their favorite show.

On the other hand, digital platforms offer series with episode durations ranging from 10 to 60 minutes, depending on the genre. There are no summary sections like on TV. All episodes of a series are released under a single season heading at once. As a result, digital platform viewers are not required to spend long periods of time on a single episode, as they would with television series. Moreover, they have the opportunity to consume an entire season in one go. This aligns with the increasing emphasis on speed and interaction in the digital age, where viewers’ desire to consume content quickly contrasts with television series' commercial-driven approach, which extends episode durations.

In an interview with Sadullah Şentürk Köprü, a director of famous Turkish productions such as Kurtlar Vadisi Pusu (2007) and Behzat Ç. Bir Ankara Polisiyesi (2012), conducted by Ferit Çağıl and Funda Maskar Kara (2019), he pointed out the duration difference between TV series and digital platform series, explaining that it is due to the advertisement-oriented approach of national channels: “Furthermore, to broadcast more commercials, national channels have increased the minimum duration of their series to 135 minutes. These series sometimes reach 160–180 minutes. On digital platforms, however, episodes range between 45–60 minutes” (Çağıl and Maskar Kara, 2019: 16).

The increasing durations of TV series not only lead to a waste of time but also impact the aesthetic quality of the content. In 2023, during interviews conducted by Sezen Kayhan with 13 participants who had been part of the creative and technical teams of both TV and digital platform series, screenwriters expressed their dissatisfaction with the excessive lengths of TV series. They stated that due to the need to fill time, they could not go through a healthy writing process in terms of creativity and originality, and at times, they wrote just to fill space. They indicated that digital platforms offer an advantage in terms of duration. One of the participants, who had worked as a screenwriter for both television and digital platforms, explained this situation as follows:

"On television, we have to write and get the treatment and script approved within a week, and then adjust according to revisions. There have been weeks when I wrote nearly 500 pages. Of course, in this situation, you don't really care about the depth of the story or characters. You're just focused on finishing. In this sense, I can say that digital platforms allow for a bit of breathing room" (Kayhan, 2023: 107).

As a result, the fact that digital platform series and traditional television series produce content for different target audiences affects the duration and format of the series. The financing of television series through advertising revenues leads to longer durations. This, in turn, negatively impacts the content and aesthetics of the series. Most digital platforms, however, finance their content through subscription systems. Their target audience mainly consists of younger to middle-aged generations, who spend more time online and are more inclined to media content. Therefore, episode durations can be kept shorter compared to TV series, which allows them to present more quality content in terms of both storylines and cinematography.

Advertising and Financing Models

The desire of advertisers to promote their products and services to as wide an audience as possible can be effectively achieved through the visual and auditory nature of television. In this sense, television is also an advertising tool, and as an advertising medium, it has several functional characteristics such as reaching a broad audience, creating a competitive environment, influencing, and promoting. For this reason, television is an important mass communication medium in terms of its nature and position in the advertising sector (Kırlar, 1994: 58).

Television broadcasts typically feature advertising breaks lasting 10-15 minutes at regular intervals during the broadcast hours. The duration of these advertising breaks varies depending on the channel's broadcast policies, the type of content being aired, the time of the broadcast, the target audience, and RTÜK (Radio and Television Supreme Council) regulations (Zenith Media, 2025). According to Article 13 of the regulation amended by RTÜK on February 15, 2005, the amount of advertising time in a one-hour broadcast is limited to a maximum of 12 minutes (Çakır, 2013: 205).

In this context, several types of advertisements stand out in the television broadcasting field. These include spot advertisements, lower-third advertisements, promotional advertisements, product placements, scenario integration, and program sponsorships:

Spot Advertisements: Advertisements shown during the break, typically lasting 10, 20, or 30 seconds.

Lower-Third Advertisements: A type of moving advertisement that appears at the bottom of the screen for 8-10 seconds during the broadcast.

Promotional Advertisements: Detailed advertisements, typically lasting 60-90 seconds, presented by a host, actor, or a representative from the brand during the broadcast.

Product Placement: A type of advertising commonly used in TV series where a product or service is integrated into the broadcast content (Bolat, 2018: 15).

Scenario Integration: A form of product placement where the product or service is incorporated into the storyline without disrupting the flow of the plot.

Program Sponsorship: A type of advertisement that claims ownership of the broadcast content. This is done through phrases like "Presented by," "To be continued," "Continues," or "Brought to you by" at the beginning, during breaks, and at the end of the program (13Brave Media Agency, 2025).

Among these advertising types, the most frequently used in television series are product placement and sponsorship advertisements. Product placement is integrated into the storyline without disrupting the plot, distracting the audience, or breaking their focus. The product is typically promoted through the actors using it. In sponsorship advertisements, a different method is followed. To reduce production costs, products or services used in scenes are shown, but without explicitly mentioning the brand name or sponsor. These details are provided through phrases like "Presented by," "To be continued," or "Brought to you by" at the beginning, during breaks, and at the end of the show. While product placement may directly refer to the brand name, in sponsorships, even if the product is shown, information about the brand is only given during specific segments (Çakır and Kınıt, 2014: 24).

In line with its functions of reaching a wide audience, promoting, and influencing, television channels fund a large portion of their operations through advertising revenues. Within the competitive commercial television model, prime time defines the hours when the largest viewer group, characterized by socio-economic and demographic traits, is likely to be watching. Therefore, advertisements reach the audience most effectively during these hours, making prime time the most valuable time slot for television broadcasts. As a result, TV series are aired during prime time, and the most expensive and longest advertisements are shown during these hours (Mutlu, 2008: 58–59).

The advertisers' efforts to increase their brand visibility by reaching a wide audience combine with television's advertising revenue-based financing model to create a unique advertising understanding for television broadcasting. A noteworthy point here is that the most expensive and longest advertisements, which are aired during prime time on TV series, are not always a pleasant experience for the viewers. Television's advertising policies disrupt the viewers' experience of watching a series. In particular, the sudden insertion of ads during high-tension and suspenseful moments disrupts the viewers' attention and hinders their emotional connection with the characters.

In this context, the emergence of digital streaming platforms promising an "Ad-Free Content Experience" is significant. Viewers who are bothered by frequent and long commercial breaks in TV series find digital platforms advantageous for their viewing experience because of the ad-free nature of the content. One of the most important factors contributing to the preference for digital platforms is this feature of ad-free content. These platforms, unlike television, fund their operations through a "Paid Subscription System." Each platform sets its subscription fees according to its distribution network and the income level of its target audience. Posters, billboards, signs, and social media posts are used to promote TV series.

However, in recent years, with the increase in the number of digital streaming platforms and the intensity of content production, some platforms have introduced ad-supported subscription packages, developing a new revenue model (Tech Inside, 2025). As a result, two separate paid subscription options have emerged: "Ad-Supported" and "Ad-Free."

This hierarchical system, based on income levels, may appear similar to the advertising-focused approach of television at first glance, but in practice, it differs. While it is impossible for TV viewers to experience an ad-free viewing experience, digital platforms leave this choice to the viewers and offer partial control tools, such as the "Skip Ad" button. For instance, the subscription pricing for Disney Plus, one of the leading entertainment companies, is as follows: Disney+ Ad-Supported: Monthly 164.90 TL, Yearly 1,649.00 TL; Disney+ Ad-Free: Monthly 349.90 TL, Yearly 3,499.00 TL (Disney, 2025). While this system offers alternative options to the viewers, whether it is an advantage or disadvantage for the viewers depends on their income levels and is a matter of debate.

In conclusion, while the advertising-oriented structure of traditional television broadcasting and the attitudes of digital streaming platforms differ, they converge at the point of sharing the advertising pie. The emergence of private TV channels led to a competitive environment, which gave rise to an advertising-driven broadcasting model, causing the duration of TV series to increase. A similar situation is occurring today with digital platforms. The increase in the number of platforms and the variety of content production has created a competitive environment among digital platforms as well. Initially attracting attention with their promise of ad-free content, digital platforms, in the face of growing competition, have sought new financing models and have become more integrated with the advertising industry.

Viewing Area and Success Measurement Method

In line with internet-based technological developments, the broadcasting process of television has evolved, and the broadcasting model of digital streaming platforms has shaped itself within this process. With the transition from analog technology, transmitted via terrestrial, satellite, and cable, to digital, the addition of IP-based broadcasting has led to a new form of television broadcasting that has developed into a collaborative structure within itself (Kavi, 2019: 7).

Digital streaming platforms, on the other hand, broadcast series content through websites they have created for themselves on the internet. Devices such as phones, computers, tablets, and even smart TVs allow users to easily access the content of digital streaming platforms by connecting to the internet via television. Similarly, viewers can access TV channels' own websites through the internet, follow their series, and engage with them via social media accounts.

Another advantage of the internet environment is that viewers have the ability to pause, rewind, and continue watching from where they left off while watching series. Although the viewing areas differ in practice, it is evident that both industries benefit from the advancements in internet technology. However, the difference in viewing areas changes the way success measurement ratios for series are determined. While the success measurement of series on television is based on the rating system, digital streaming platforms determine these ratios through an algorithmic system that includes data on users' activities, personalizes the experience, and measures feedback. By using this algorithmic system, digital streaming platforms can predict in advance which content will be successful, thus avoiding the risk of reproducing the same content. In traditional television series, however, this method is carried out via the rating measurement system.

In Turkey, with the introduction of private channels, the rating measurement system began in 1989. The most widely known method for measurement is the Peoplemeter system. In television viewership measurements, concepts such as ratings, share, and total viewership rate (TVR) come to the forefront. With technological advancements in viewership measurements, these methods have been further diversified (Hatırnaz, 2006: 22–30).

In digital streaming platforms, however, the rating measurement system does not apply. Success measurement ratios are determined differently from television based on the types of content subscribed users watch, how much time they spend on these contents, and the feedback they

Contentual Differences

There are significant contentual differences between traditional television series and digital streaming platform series. Digitization has transformed the narrative structure, script content, and viewer experiences of series. It has fundamentally altered the working conditions of content creators and the interaction viewers have with the content. The constraints of traditional television series have been replaced by more dynamic and interactive content on digital platforms.

Script Content

The script content of television series produced under traditional broadcasting principles has created a conventional narrative framework. The emergence of digital streaming platforms as an alternative for series production has brought with it script content that can go beyond this traditional narrative structure. The main reasons for this change are directly related to the structural differences discussed in the previous section of the study. These factors, which influence the production process of series, shape the writers' scripts, the quality of the story that emerges, its cinematography, and the variety of genres.

The difference in episode durations influences the script content because time is crucial for screenwriters. The process of creating a script by developing the plot, theme, and characters varies from one screenwriter to another, so no definitive statements can be made. However, the shorter duration of series on digital platforms compared to television series changes the working conditions for screenwriters and allows them to save time. In a study where both creative and technical teams working for digital and television series were interviewed, screenwriters expressed that the shorter episode durations improved their working conditions (Kayhan, 2023: 107). In another study with screenwriters, one participant expressed the advantage of shorter durations as follows: "But in digital platforms, in terms of duration, I mean, we write 120 minutes, 130 minutes, 140 minutes for TV. Now on digital platforms, it's a maximum of 1 hour. And we work on something more limited, knowing the beginning and the end, like 10 episodes, 6 episodes, 8 episodes. That's an advantage" (Oduncu & Karaduman, 2021: 80). The difference in episode durations can be said to lead to a more unique writing process in terms of script content as it affects the working conditions of screenwriters.

The limited range of themes, genres, and topics addressed in Turkish television series is expanded on digital platforms, offering more variety. The lower level of censorship is also a contributing factor. While censorship on television—such as content being banned or fined—restricts the subject matter of television series, digital platforms impose fewer constraints, allowing screenwriters a greater degree of creative freedom. Series like Hakan Muhafız (2018), Atiye (2019), Şahmaran (2023), and Bir Başkadır (2020) stand out for their themes and genres that differ from those of traditional television series.

Since the early years of Turkish television series production, dramas have most often attracted viewers. The influence of Yeşilçam cinema, in particular, has played a significant role in shaping the content of Turkish series (Özsoy, 2024: 602). The dominance of the drama genre in Turkish television series supports this. The audience's initial interest in the drama genre led to an increase in the number of series produced in this genre. Looking at the Turkish series that aired in the 2024-2025 season, most of them are drama series, with plots revolving around specific themes. For example: Annem Ankara, Bir Gece Masalı, Deha, Karadut, Leyla, Siyah Kalp, Uzak Şehir, Sahipsizler, Kardelenler, Kral Kaybederse—and among the highest-rated recent shows, the majority are also dramas: Bahar (2024): 10.35 rating, Kızılcık Şerbeti (2022): 10.32 rating, Uzak Şehir (2024): 9.32 rating, İnci Taneleri (2024): 9.03 rating, Kızıl Goncalar (2023): 8.88 rating, Gönül Dağı (2020): 7.64 rating, Deha (2024): 6.98 rating (Box Office Türkiye, 2025).

On the other hand, digital platforms have offered new storytelling experiences to viewers by creating content in various genre categories. For example, Netflix's first original Turkish production, Hakan: Muhafız (2018), was a science fiction series, which was different in genre from the majority of Turkish TV shows. This series offered viewers not only a unique storyline but also a more striking cinematography with the use of visual effects. In a study analyzing viewer comments on Hakan: Muhafız, it was observed that local viewers, comparing it with traditional television series, found Netflix's content to be of higher quality (Başlar, 2021: 431). Moreover, elements such as profanity, slang, alcohol consumption, and sexuality—subject to intense censorship in TV series—can be shown more freely in digital platform series, affecting the content. For example, the Esas Oğlan (2024) series, broadcast on Gain, frequently depicts alcohol consumption, sexuality, and fantasy elements. It is much more difficult to portray such bold scenes on television compared to digital platforms, as they could result in severe penalties. For instance, the Çukur (2017) series received an administrative fine from RTÜK in 2018 due to alcohol use and explicit kissing and sex scenes (Diken, 2025). The airing of series on different platforms has led to a freedom of content in terms of genre and themes, which also affects the realism and depth of characters (Sirianni, 2019: 194-197). Looking at digital series, we can observe that the characters are often more complex and psychologically deep. An example of this is the 2018 series Şahsiyet.

This diversity in genre, character, and content in digital platform series has created a hybrid narrative structure within its own framework. The merging of classical, modern, and postmodern narratives due to technological developments has brought about a hybrid narrative form. This structure expresses a common form in terms of both style and content. The interaction between digital platforms and viewers—such as pausing, continuing from where they left off, and providing feedback—ensures diversity in this hybrid narrative (Altınkaya & Doğan, 2024: 11-14). In this regard, it can be said that digital platforms produce more enriched content compared to television series.

In traditional television series, episodes are broadcast weekly, and feedback from the audience and rating systems can influence the screenwriters' decisions on the next episode. In digital platforms, the uninterrupted release of an entire season allows screenwriters to avoid such influences. This difference in the release process, which affects the working conditions of screenwriters, also influences the script content. The main storyline, plot development, and character changes are shaped accordingly. In a study conducted by Öz and Pehlivan in 2024, in-depth interviews with 15 series screenwriters revealed that the ratings significantly affected the content of the scripts, whether the series would continue or not, and that screenwriters often wrote scripts based on ratings. The study also mentioned the effect of social ratings, where social media trending topics, user feedback, and seeing which scenes gained the most ratings influenced the direction of the story (Öz & Pehlivan, 2024: 310-311).

Censorship and Free Content Production: RTÜK

The advent of private TV channels in Turkey in the 1990s marked the breaking of the public monopoly on broadcasting. With the implementation of Law No. 3984 in 1994, which regulated private radio and television broadcasting, the Radio and Television Supreme Council (RTÜK) was established. However, due to technological advancements in broadcasting and the Constitutional Court's annulment of certain provisions, Law No. 3984 was later revised in line with the European Union's Audiovisual Media Services Directive. This led to the enactment of the Law No. 6112 on the Establishment and Broadcasting Services of Radio and Television on March 3, 2011. RTÜK is a public institution authorized to regulate and supervise the activities of radio and television broadcasts in Turkey. It issues licenses and broadcasting permits for organizations wishing to broadcast in Turkey. While RTÜK cannot intervene in program content before it is aired, it can apply sanctions after the broadcast if necessary, based on viewer complaints and reports. Broadcasting activities are monitored by RTÜK in three ways: direct monitoring by RTÜK experts, viewer/listener monitoring through complaints filed via the RTÜK Communication Center (Alo 178, RTÜK Mobile, 444 1 178, and e-Government channels), and self-regulation by broadcasters based on broadcasting ethics principles (RTÜK, About Us: 2025).

The supervision of television series by RTÜK significantly impacts the freedom of content production. When producing a TV series, it is not always clear whether the content will fall under the censorship mechanism; however, non-compliance with the provisions of Article 32 of Law No. 6112 is known to lead to sanctions by RTÜK. According to the 2023 annual report published by RTÜK, a total of 625 sanctions were imposed for violations of the provisions of Article 32 (RTÜK Activity Report, 2023). Therefore, it is difficult to talk about a completely free content production environment for producers and broadcasters of television series, as the broadcasting framework defined by these regulations imposes limitations on content creators. For example, in 2024, RTÜK imposed administrative fines and suspended programs for the series Arka Sokaklar (2006), Yabani (2023), Deha (2024), and Sahipsizler (2024) on the grounds of violating national and moral values, normalizing violence, and breaking the rules (AA, 2025).

In the early years of digital platforms, the fact that broadcasts were conducted over the internet excited both viewers and the industry, as it seemed to offer a space for content creation free from censorship mechanisms. On August 1, 2019, a regulation was published in the Official Gazette, granting RTÜK the authority to intervene in digital broadcasting platforms, including the issuance of broadcast rights and transmission licenses (Official Gazette, 2019). Prior to 2019, RTÜK could not intervene in digital platforms, which made the environment seem freer for content production compared to television. However, with the extension of RTÜK's regulatory powers to digital platforms, the content production environment has become more restrictive for both industries. One example of RTÜK's influence on digital content is seen in the case of Şimdiki Aklım Olsaydı, a series produced by Netflix and planned for release in 2021. Like all foreign productions in Turkey, Netflix submitted the script to the Ministry of Culture and Tourism for filming permission. While the series was denied permission, no explanation was provided. The screenwriter, Ece Yörenç, speculated that the reason for the denial was the inclusion of a gay character in the story. The team decided to remove the character from the script, after which filming permission was granted. However, following a meeting between Netflix officials and RTÜK in 2020, the series was ultimately canceled (Yücel, 2020). This example demonstrates how the censorship mechanism, particularly RTÜK's interference, significantly impacts the writing process, potentially hindering originality in script content.

In a 2020 interview with Ayşen Güven on self-censorship, screenwriter Ayşenur Sıkı discussed the intense effects of the censorship mechanism, stating that screenwriters automatically apply self-censorship due to external pressures. She said: "However, no matter which platform you're on, your pen is shaped according to its scale. This is undeniable. And without the producer or channel intervening, you do it automatically. Because now you're racing against time. There are things we change, thinking 'this may get flagged, let's not write it this way'" (Güven, 2020). In addition to RTÜK's censorship, the self-regulatory rules of channels, producers, digital platforms, and audience feedback also push screenwriters to apply self-censorship. Therefore, it can be said that both television and digital broadcasting industries face constraints that hinder the creation of truly free content. The effects of RTÜK's regulation, the rating concerns of channels, the specific rules of digital platforms, and audience feedback all influence the production of content, making it challenging to create in completely free conditions.

Conclusion: The regulatory influence of RTÜK, alongside the inherent pressures from television channels, digital platforms, and audience feedback, significantly shapes content production in Turkey. Although digital platforms once promised a more liberated environment for content creation, RTÜK's increasing influence over both television and digital platforms has imposed new limitations. This dynamic results in a complex environment where the creation of truly free content remains difficult in both sectors.

The Changing Role of Audiences and Its Impact on Content Production

The advent of digital platforms has transformed the role of viewers from passive consumers to active participants, significantly altering viewing habits and shifting the viewer's position. In traditional media, the audience simply consumed the content provided without the level of interaction seen today. However, with technological advancements and the rise of digital platforms and social media applications, the audience's position has changed, allowing them to shift from being passive consumers to active participants who can influence content production (Uluç, 2008: 116). Kristen Daly emphasizes that viewers have transitioned into an active role, interacting not only with content but also with other viewers, and has referred to this shift as "Cinema 3.0" (Daly, 2010: 81-90).

Viewers now engage in mutual interaction through social media platforms tied to TV series. For instance, platforms like X (formerly Twitter) and Instagram allow users to comment on posts related to episodes, scenes, characters, or other events, creating a space where viewers can interact not just with one another but also with content creators. This interaction between viewers and creators is a clear indication that audiences have, at least to some extent, an influence on the production of content. For example, trending on social media or commenting on a post can generate conversations, influence the narrative, and provide direct feedback to creators.

In an interview conducted by the Peak Mag YouTube channel with Ayça Üzüm, the screenwriter of Bahar (2024), she acknowledged the influence of viewer reactions on the storyline. She stated, "Viewer reactions do, of course, sometimes affect the script. More specifically, when you write a story and see it on screen or when a new character isn't well received, you understand that it's not resonating. At that point, you need to make a move. Sometimes, you're in tune with the audience's feelings and intervene, but we don't make changes because of social media pressure because that leads us to make mistakes" (Peak Mag, 2025).

In a study involving creative and technical teams, one of the screenwriters mentioned, "Writing a story with a fixed beginning and end is impossible on TV. The story starts, and if the ratings are good, it continues based on that. Sometimes, the story even changes based on social media reactions. However, on digital platforms, you can write a story with a clear beginning and end" (Kayhan, 2023: 11). Another study with screenwriters highlighted that social ratings, which include viewer comments and reactions, also influence the script (Öz & Pehlivan, 2024: 310-311).

The direct interaction between audiences and content creators, especially through social media, has indeed influenced the course of stories. This change suggests that viewers now have an impact on content production, a shift closely related to their evolving role in the new media landscape. On digital platforms, this influence extends beyond social media. Personalized user experiences and feedback algorithms allow platforms to measure viewer preferences and responses, adapting content accordingly. When a storyline fails to engage, the system can avoid similar content types in future productions, further reinforcing the audience's influence on content creation.

CONCLUSION

With the emergence of digital streaming platforms, particularly in the television industry, a new space for content distribution has been created, distinct from traditional broadcasting. These platforms offer innovative features that provide both content creators and viewers with new opportunities and experiences. The differences in the distribution channels have led to various similarities and differences in content production, which include factors such as target audiences, episode durations, content and genre diversity, censorship impact, the freedom to create, and the effects of changing viewer habits and roles.

According to the 2023 Household ICT Usage Survey by the Turkish Statistical Institute (TÜİK), 95.5% of households in Turkey have access to the internet at home (TÜİK, 2025). Dursun Güleryüz, General Manager of TİAK Anonim Şirketi, presented data to the parliament indicating that the average daily television viewing time per household in 2024 is six hours and seven minutes, with one hour and 37 minutes per person. This suggests that the interest in television still persists, despite the rise of digital platforms. Initially, there were concerns that digital platforms might replace television, but it is clear that television has not lost its functionality.

When we examine the structural differences between traditional and digital media, we see that TV series are often produced with long episodes based on a rating system aimed at reaching a wide audience. This can negatively affect the formal and aesthetic quality of content. In contrast, digital platform series tend to target more specific and homogeneous audiences, offering shorter episodes without the burden of advertising and providing viewers with the flexibility to access content without time or space constraints.

Television, with its ability to reach large audiences through visual and auditory means, has been a significant platform for advertising. Various types of commercials, especially during the prime-time slots, have contributed to high costs, interrupting the viewing experience and pushing audiences towards digital platforms. Initially, digital platforms gained attention with their promise of "ad-free content" and revenue from subscription models. However, the increase in the number of platforms has led to the introduction of ad-supported subscription packages, creating a new revenue model. While a system offering both ad-free and ad-supported options caters to user preferences, it also creates a media access divide based on income levels.

Technological developments in internet-based broadcasting have added new dimensions to television broadcasting, paving the way for the rise of digital streaming platforms. Traditional television, transitioning from analog to digital, has incorporated IP-based broadcasting, resulting in a multi-channel structure. On the other hand, digital platforms deliver content via the internet, accessible through smartphones, computers, tablets, and smart TVs, providing viewers with personalized control over their viewing experience, such as pausing or resuming content. Although both systems benefit from internet technologies, the methods of evaluating content success differ. While television series are evaluated using a Peoplemeter-based rating system, digital platforms rely on algorithms that measure viewer behavior, which reduces the risk involved in content production.

In television, where content is driven by ratings, screenwriters often shape the storyline based on viewer feedback and rating results. In contrast, digital platforms typically release episodes in bulk, making them less susceptible to such external influences. This approach positively impacts the narrative integrity, character development, and flow of the story. Digital series tend to portray characters in a more layered and realistic manner, enabling a deeper connection with the audience. Additionally, the development of hybrid narrative structures, combining classical, modern, and postmodern elements, has contributed to the emergence of new storytelling forms. In this context, digital platforms offer richer, more original, and diversified content compared to traditional television.

Since the emergence of private television channels in the 1990s, the public monopoly in broadcasting has come to an end in Turkey, and the Radio and Television Supreme Council (RTÜK) was established as a regulatory body in 1994. The sanctions imposed by RTÜK under the Law No. 6112 have created a censorship pressure on television content production. In 2019, digital platforms were also brought under RTÜK's supervision, limiting the freedom that these platforms initially offered. The cancellation of Netflix's Şimdiki Aklım Olsaydı series serves as an example of this digital censorship. Screenwriters not only face legal regulation but also self-censor due to pressure from producers, channels, and audiences. Therefore, content production on both television and digital platforms is subject to various forms of censorship.

With the widespread adoption of digital platforms and social media, viewers have transitioned from being passive consumers of traditional media to active participants in content production. Viewers can now directly interact with both other viewers and producers through social media, which can lead to changes in storylines and characters. Especially social media reactions and viewership statistics directly influence the process of shaping the storyline. On digital platforms, algorithms guide content production based on viewer preferences. This further emphasizes the audience's influence on content creation.

Although there is still strong interest in both industries, the competitive environment continues to intensify. The increase in the number of digital streaming platforms and the corresponding rise in content volume may lead to viewer and producer fatigue, and the risk of content becoming repetitive. Furthermore, the fact that TV content is shown on digital platforms after airing increases the volume of content on digital platforms, contributing to a “content clutter.” These and similar situations may prompt both viewers and content producers to seek new approaches in the future. In this context, with advancements in technology, it is expected that emerging techniques such as artificial intelligence, interactive series, and virtual reality will bring about new changes in the television and streaming industry, opening up new areas for research.

REFERENCES

Altınkaya, M. T., & Doğan, E. (2024). From Griffith to Netflix, From Classical Narrative to Hybrid Narrative Two Examples: The Birth of a Nation and Don't Look Up. *Kastamonu İletişim Araştırmaları Dergisi*, (13), 177–195. DOI: 10.56676/kiad.1535096

Altyazı, F. (2024, Şubat 20). Bakanlık ve RTÜK'ten sansür, Netflix'ten iptal kararı. https://fasikul.altyazi.net/pano/bakanlik-ve-rtukten-sansur-netflixten-iptal-karari/

Anadolu Ajansı (AA). (2024, Mart 8). RTÜK'ten kurallara uymayan dizi ve programlara yaptırım. https://www.aa.com.tr/tr/gundem/rtukten-kurallara-uymayan-dizi-ve-programlara-yaptirim/3406533

Arık, İ. (2023). Türk Televizyon Dizilerinin Dizi Süreleri Bağlamında Değerlendirilmesi. *Yeni Yüzyıl'da İletişim Çalışmaları*, *2*(6), 125–145.

Ayerdem, T. İ. (2019). *Türkiye'deki Dijital Medya Platformları ve İzler Kitle Profili (Yüksek Lisans Tezi)*. İstanbul Üniversitesi Sosyal Bilimler Enstitüsü.

Başlar, G. (2021). Yerel İçeriğin Küresel Dolaşımı Bağlamında Netflix: "Hakan Muhafız" İzleyici Yorumlarının Analizi. *Akdeniz Üniversitesi İletişim Fakültesi Dergisi*, (36), 415–435. DOI: 10.31123/akil.989340

Bolat, N. (2018). Ürün Yerleştirme Kavramsal Boyutlar ve Ürün Yerleştirme Ortemlarının İncelenmesi, Ürün Yerleştirme Uygulamaları İçinde, Konya: Literatürk Acadamia yayınları.

Box Office Türkiye. (2024, Mart 15). 2024 yılının en çok izlenen televizyon dizileri. https://boxofficeturkiye.com/haber/2024-yilinin-en-cok-izlenen-televizyon-dizileri--6544

Box Office Türkiye. (2024, Mayıs 1). Yeni sezonda başlayacak olan yerli televizyon dizileri (2024-2025). https://boxofficeturkiye.com/haber/yeni-sezonda-baslayacak-olan-yerli-televizyon-dizileri-2024-2025--6136

13. Brave. (n.d.). TV reklamları. https://www.13brave.com/tv-reklamlari/

Çağıl, F., & Masdar Kara, F. (2019). Dijital Dönüşüm Bağlamında Türkiye'de Dizi Sektörü ve Geleceği. *ARTS: Artuklu Sanat Ve Beşeri Bilimler Dergisi*, (1), 8–18. DOI: 10.46372/arts.570181

Çakır, V. (2013). Avrupa Birliğine Uyum Sürecinde Türkiye'de Televizyon Reklamlarına Yönelik Düzenlemeler. *Selçuk İletişim*, *5*(1), 198–209. DOI: 10.18094/si.57552

Çakır, V., & Kınıt, E. (2014). Televizyon Dizilerinde Ürün Yerleştirme ve Sponsorluğun Sonuçları. Selçuk Üniveristesi. *Küresel Medya Dergisi*, *5*(9), 19–47.

Chen, Y. N. (2020). *The development of the North American film industry in 2018. Cilt 1, Development of the Global Film industry*. Londra.

Daly, K. (2010). Cinema 3.0: The Interactive-Image. *Cinema Journal*, *50*(1), 81–98. DOI: 10.1353/cj.2010.a405349

Disney+.(n.d.).Disney + fiyatlandırma bilgileri. https://help.disneyplus.com/tr/article/disneyplus-price

Günay, M. A., & Yetkiner, B. (2022). Taşrada Sinema Deneyimi: Gaziantep Örneği. *Middle Black Sea Journal of Communication Studies*, *7*(1), 29–50. DOI: 10.56202/mbsjcs.1099581

Hatırnaz, B. (2006). *Televizyon izleme ölçümleri ve Program Planlamasındaki Rolü*. Marmara Üniversitesi Sosyal Bilimler Enstitüsü.

Hürriyet. (2023, Kasım 5). Televizyon hâlâ zirvede. https://www.hurriyet.com.tr/gundem/televizyon-hala-zirvede-42693721

Ildir, A., & Celik Rappas, I. A.Ildır. (2022). Netflix in Turkey: Localization and audience expectations from video on demand. *Convergence (London)*, *28*(1), 255–271. DOI: 10.1177/13548565211060301

İTO. 2022. Kültürel Değişim ve Endüstrileşme Sürecinde Türk Dizileri. İstanbul Ticaret Odası Sektörel Araştırmalar Yayınları 16.

Kar, A. T ve Gündüz, U. (2024). İTÜ -TV'den TRT'ye Türkiye'de Televizyon Tarihi ve Dijitalleşme. 10. Uluslararası Atatürk Kongresi Bildirileri, Cilt 1, Ankara.

Kavi, N. A. (2019). *Televizyonda Yayınlanan İnternet Dizileri Üzerine Bir İnceleme: Fi Dizisi Örneği*. İstanbul Üniversitesi Sosyal Bilimler Enstitüsü.

Kayhan, S. (2023). Televizyondan Dijital Yayın Platformlarına Türkiye'de Dizi Yapım Dinamiklerinin Değişkmi. Dijital Medya Çalışmaları, Özgür Yayınları, syf 97-120.

Kırlar, S. (1994). *Televizyon Reklamlarında Kadının İşlevi (Doktora Tezi)*. İstanbul Üniversitesi Sosyal Bilimler Enstitüsü.

Mutlu, E. (2008). *Televizyonu Anlamak*. Ayraç Yayınları.

Oduncu, P., & Karaduman, S. (2021). Türkiye'deki Senaristlerin Bakış Açısıyla Değişen Dizi Sektörü Üzerine Bir Araştırma. *Akdeniz Üniversitesi İletişim Fakültesi Dergisi*, (36), 72–89. DOI: 10.31123/akil.989010

Öz, S., & Muratoğlu Pehlivan, B. (2024). Yaratıcı Endüstriler Bağlamında Dizi Sektöründe Senaryo ve Senaristlerin Güncel Durumu ve Geleceği. *Kültür Ve İletişim, 27*(54), 287–324. DOI: 10.18691/kulturveiletisim.1491953

Özçağlayan, M. (2014). TÜRKİYE'DE TELEVİZYON YAYINCILIĞININ GELİŞİMİ. *Selçuk İletişim, 1*(2), 41–52.

Özsoy, A. (2006). Popüler Kültür Ürünü Olarak Durum Komedileri: Çocuklar Duymasın Örneğinde Aile Söylemi. Kültür Ve İletişim, 9 (2)(18), 143-173.

Özsoy, A. (2024). Dijitalleşme Sürecinde Türk Dizileri ve Yeni Nesil Türk Draması. *TRT Akademi, 9*(22), 601–607.

Radyo ve Televizyon Üst Kurulu (RTÜK). (2024). 2023 yılı faaliyet raporu. https://www.rtuk.gov.tr/Media/FM/2023_yili_faaliyet_raporu.pdf

Radyo ve Televizyon Üst Kurulu (RTÜK). (n.d.). Hakkımızda. https://www.rtuk.gov.tr/hakkimizda/1749

Resmî Gazete, T. C. (2019, Ağustos 1). Radyo, Televizyon Ve İsteğe Bağlı Yayınların İnternet Ortamından Sunumu Hakkında Yönetmelik. https://www.resmigazete.gov.tr/eskiler/2019/08/20190801-5.htm

Sirianni, J. M. (2019). Stranger Thnigs and the Pervasiveness of Nostalgic Television. In *Netflix nostalgia: Streaming the past on demand.* Lexington Books. DOI: 10.5040/9781978724631.ch-012

Susma24. (2023, Temmuz 25). Dizi senaristleri konuşuyor: "Yazmayın denmiyor ama yazarsak başımıza hoş şeyler gelmeyeceğini biliyoruz". https://susma24.com/dizi-senaristleri-konusuyor-yazmayin-denmiyor-ama-yazarsak-basimiza-hos-seyler-gelmeyecegini-biliyoruz/

TechInside. (2024, Nisan 10). Dijital platformlar abone sayısından çok gelire odaklandı. https://www.techinside.com/dijital-platformlar-abone-sayisindan-cok-gelire-odaklandi/

Timisi, N. (2003). *Yeni iletişim Teknolojileri ve Demokrasi.* Dost Kitabevi Yayınları.

Türkiye İstatistik Kurumu (TÜİK). (2023, Ağustos 25). Hanehalkı bilişim teknolojileri (BT) kullanım araştırması 2023. https://data.tuik.gov.tr/Bulten/Index?p=Hanehalki-Bilisim-Teknolojileri-(BT)-Kullanim-Arastirmasi-2023-49407

Uluç, G. (2008). *Küreselleşen medya: İktidar ve mücadele alanı.* Kırmızı Yayınları.

ADDITIONAL READING

Akbayır, Z. (2016), Bana Bir Hikâye Anlat: Marka İletişiminde Hikâyeleştirme ve İnternet, Karadeniz Teknik Üniversitesi İletişim Araştırmaları Dergisi,Cilt 3, Sayı 12, ss.67-84.

Akbulut, T. N., & Erdoğan, B. E. (2007). *Televizyon Reklam Film Yapımı Kavramlar, Uygulamalar, Sorunlar ve Telif Hakları*. Beta Yayınları.

Aktuğlu, I. K. (2006). Tüketicinin bilgilendirilmesi sürecinde reklam etiği. Küresel İletişim Dergisi, 2 (Güz), 1-20.

Aydın, İ. (2017). Pazarlama Perspektifinden Karşılaştırmalı Reklamlar, Muş Alparslan Üniversitesi Sosyal Bilimler Dergisi, C. 5, S. 3, ss. 899-921.

Ayna, A., & Postalcı, İ. E. (2020). Bilim Kurgu Filmlerinde 60'lardan Günümüze Beden Ve Mekân Algısına Dair Bir Okuma. *Yıldız Journal Of Art And Desıgn, Volume*, *7*(1), 1–29.

Baran, T., Baran, S. (2014). Televizyon Programları, Sembolik Tüketim ve Toplumsal Yansımaları, Karamanoğlu Mehmet Bey Üniversitesi Sosyal ve Ekonomik Araştırmalar Dergisi, Sayı 3, ss. 171-175.

Batı, U. (2010). Hedef Kitle Davranışını Etkileyen Bir Unsur Olarak Reklamlarda Müzik Kullanımı Konusundaki Yazının İncelenmesi, Uluslararası İnsan Bilimleri Dergisi, Cilt 7, Sayı 2, ss. 778-808.

Batı, U. (2010). *Reklamın Dili: Dilbilim – Strateji – Mesaj – Retorik– Göstergebilim*. Alfa Yay.

Batı, U. (2013). Reklamcılıkta Mizah İçerikli Mesajlar Ve Mesaj Türleri, Kocaeli Üniversitesi İletişim Fakültesi Araştırma Dergisi, Sayı 11, ss. 25-54.

Chang, C. (2009). Being hooked by editorial content: The implications for processing narrative advertising. *Journal of Advertising*, *38*(1), 21–34. DOI: 10.2753/JOA0091-3367380102

Coşkun, E., & Çepni Şener, B. (2023). Televizyon Ve Sosyal Medya Reklamlarında Müzik Kullanımına İlişkin Bir Değerlendirme. *Medya ve Kültürel Çalışmalar Dergisi*, *5*(2), 91–106. DOI: 10.55055/mekcad.1361626

Ebren, F., Güler, M. (2015). Etkileşim ve Televizyon Reklamları İlişkisi Üzerine Bir Araştırma, Türkbilim Dergisi, Sayı Temmuz. ss. 225 -240.

Ebuka, P., & Fountain, O. C. (2024). Guidelines for Making Product Demonstration Ads: A Focus on Custard, DOI: DOI: 10.13140/RG.2.2.16820.63361

Elden, M., & Bakır, U. (2010). *Reklam Çekicilikleri; Cinsellik, Mizah, Korku.* İletişim Yay.

Elden, M., & Kocabaş, F. (2015). *Reklamcılık Kavramlar, Kararlar, Kurumlar. İstanbul: İletişim Yayınları.Gürgen, H. (1990).* Reklamcılık ve Metin Yazarlığı, Anadolu Üniversitesi, Açık Öğretim Fakültesi Yayınları.

Hollensen, Svend ve Christian Schimmelpfennig (2015). "Developing a Glocalisation Strategy: Experiences from Henkel's Product Launches in the Middle East and Europe." Journal of Brand Strategy 4(3): 248-258.

Kotler, P., & Armstrong, G. (2004). *Principles of Marketing*. Prentice Hall Inc.

Lee, J., & Hong, I. B. (2016). Predicting Positive User Responses to Social Media Advertising: The Roles of Emotional Appeal, Informativeness, and Creativity. *International Journal of Information Management, 36*(3), 360–373. DOI: 10.1016/j.ijinfomgt.2016.01.001

Lou, C., & Koh, J. (2018). Social Media Advertising: An Unavoidable Trend. *Journal of Marketing Communications, 24*(2), 183–188.

Martín-García, M., & Alvarado-López, J. (2022). Digital marketing strategies and consumer behavior. *International Journal of Consumer Studies, 46*(1), 15–30.

Martínez-Costa, M. (2019). The impact of data-driven journalism on audience engagement. *Digital Journalism (Abingdon, England), 92*(4), 155–172.

McCracken, G. (1986). Culture and Consumption: A Theoretical Account of Structure and Movement of the Cultural Meaning of Consumer Goods. *The Journal of Consumer Research, 13*(1), 71–84. DOI: 10.1086/209048

Nwachukwu, S. L. S., Vitell, S. J.Jr, Gilbert, F. W., & Barnes, J. H. (1997). Ethics and Social Responsibility in Marketing. *Journal of Business Research, 39*(2), 107–118. DOI: 10.1016/S0148-2963(96)00146-4

O'Reilly, T. (2007). What is Web 2.0? *Communications of the ACM, 51*(1), 18–25.

Okmeydan, S. B. (2020). Kültür Eksenli Reklamcılıkta Diditalleşme, Reklamcılık ve Dijitalleşme içinde. (Ed. D. Öcal ve H. Polat.), Ankara: Nobel Yayınevi. ss. 277-320.

Okmeydan, S. B., & Saran, M. (2018). "Actors of International Public Relations". in International Public Relations Practices and Approaches. (Ed.) M. U. Tuncer. Berlin: Peter Lang. ss.29-52.

Okumuş, E. (2002). Küreselleşme ve medeniyetlerarası diyalog. *Marife Dini Araştırmalar Dergisi, 2*(2), 115–132.

Önlü, M. ve Saran, M. (2019). "Akademik Bir Disiplin Olarak Kültürlerarası İletişim ve Kuramsal Temelleri" içinde Kültürlerarası İletişim; İletişim Odaklı Güncel Yaklaşımlar. (Ed.) S. B. Okmeydan ve M. Saran. Konya: Eğitim Yayınevi. ss. 15-54.

Pahari, S., Bandyopadhyay, A., Kumar, V. M., & Pingle, S. (2024). A bibliometric analysis of digital advertising in social media. *Cogent Business & Management, 11*(1), 2–15. DOI: 10.1080/23311975.2024.2383794

Weinberger, M. G., Gulas, C. S., Weinberger, M. F. (2015). Looking in through outdoor: Asocio-cultural and historical perspective on the evolution of advertising humour. International Journal Of Advertising. 34 (3). ss. 447-472.

KEY TERMS AND DEFINITIONS

Digital Platform: Digital platforms are online exhibition spaces that provide internet-based visual and auditory content services. The content offered by these platforms is accessed via the internet. Unlike traditional broadcasting, they stand out with advantages such as personalized user experience, interactive content, accessibility from multiple devices, and saving time and space. Examples include Netflix, Disney+Plus, YouTube, Gain, and Exxen.

Television Series: These are serials created through a specific topic, character, or characters and are broadcast in episodes at regular intervals. They follow a traditional narrative structure and often include similar themes and genres.

Censorship: Censorship refers to the process of modifying or completely blocking all or part of any type of content either before or after it is presented to the public, due to being subject to control. It is implemented by state institutions, broadcasting organizations, content providers, etc.

Format: In content production, format refers to the standard structure shaped by unique characteristics such as the type of content, narrative style, duration, target audience, and language. Formats can be created originally or adapted from foreign versions into the local language.

Script: The script is the written form of visual and auditory storytelling produced in fields such as cinema, theater, television, and digital platforms. The subject, characters, and plot of a series are developed during the scriptwriting stage.

Content Production: This refers to the process of creating and presenting various types of visual and auditory content on digital or traditional media platforms.

Audience: Audiences are individuals or communities who follow, consume, interact with, or respond to broadcast content offered on traditional or digital platforms.

Chapter 4
Navigating the Digital Shift:
Ethical Considerations and Technological Advances in Broadcasting

Rashid Hashmi
https://orcid.org/0009-0006-3232-0705
Sharda University, India

ABSTRACT

The rapid transformation of digital broadcasting is reshaping content creation, audience engagement, and media ethics. With the integration of artificial intelligence, personalized broadcasting, and interactive streaming, the traditional broadcasting landscape has undergone significant changes. However, these advancements raise concerns about misinformation, algorithmic bias, and data privacy. This chapter examines the interplay between technological innovations and ethical considerations in digital broadcasting. It highlights the shift from linear television to on-demand, asynchronous viewing, the role of AI in content curation, and the emergence of deepfake technology. The discussion extends to the implications of algorithm-driven audience targeting, digital editing, and synthetic media. Moreover, the ethical and regulatory challenges associated with these innovations are analyzed, emphasizing the need for transparency, accountability, and audience protection. This chapter provides insights into maintaining responsible digital broadcasting practices in an AI-driven era.

DOI: 10.4018/979-8-3373-1957-5.ch004

1. INTRODUCTION

Broadcasting has long been at the forefront of both shaping the debate on public issues and the wider dissemination of information, as well as contributing to the formulation of cultural identity. In the early 20th century, broadcasting resonated with the golden radio era and with the advent of television after the war, broadcasting had a tremendous impact on that era's zeitgeist. Most of the early industry enjoyed centralised control of editorial decision making and one-directional communication – its programming schedules were linear or at least amenable to linear programming. The viewers and listeners were passive recipients of the scheduled broadcasts, tuned in based on the professional journalists and media executives' curated schedules. But in the turn of the millennium and with the diversification of the world that the internet brought, the broadcasting environment underwent an important change. This was not just about technological updates, it was about the paradigm of creation, exchange, and consumption of information being changed.

The features of the 21st century are digital broadcasting platforms, personalized content delivery systems, as well as real-time audience interaction models that undermine the traditional structure of media. More recently, artificial intelligence (AI) has accelerated this transformation, offering tools that can automate content production, recommend tailored content to individual users, and even simulate human presenters using virtual avatars. If one has to pick the moment when AI appeared in broadcasting, one will always be able to feel it in the almost all the key parts of the media value chain. From algorithms that recommend videos and news articles to large language models that draft scripts or generate voiceovers, AI is reshaping editorial decision-making and operational workflows. The increasingly heightened reliance on AI in media production and distribution opens up a wide range of ethical dilemmas, which starts with the systems not being transparent and replicating existing biases, and some other ones, as Trattner et al. wrote (2022).

One of the most revolutionary technologies has come in the form of large language models (LLMs), which have been able to generate coherent, human-sounding content, at times with little human involvement. As Bender et al. (2021) have noted, these technologies have major advantages, but also have quite serious downside. They are helpful for the efficiencies they create in content generation, but when they are trained on vast amounts of datasets, it run the risk of replicating problematic stereotypes, inaccuracies, or ultimately speculation. As with such technologies, absent robust regulation, they will sometimes inadvertently breed misinformation or sway public sentiment on significant issues.

The introduction of AI into broadcast news takes the questions beyond issues of accuracy, bias, or ownership to raise questions of responsibility. When an algorithm chooses a news feed, or who gets their voice in a debating format, the issue is 'who is responsible for the consequential effect' - is it the engineers, editors, platforms, or algorithms? Such argumentation justifies the call for the construction of ethical guidelines that inform the development and use of such AI technologies in media contexts. Floridi et al. (2018) contribute to the ethics of AI on a fundamentally solid basis on the grounds of the principles of transparency, fairness, and harm minimization. The deployment of these principles in broadcasting needs more than a technical fix; it needs attention to social responsibilities traditionally allocated to journalism and public communication.

In this context, of course, both the environmental and the societal costs of AI have to be taken into consideration. Crawford (2021) points out that taking the development and deployment of AI technologies forward requires large amounts of computational resources that push its use towards carbon emissions and energy consumption. Furthermore, while data for training these systems is often extracted through labour and infrastructure that is unevenly distributed across the globe, this constitutes a concern of exploitation and digital colonialism. Broadcasting organizations that adopt AI must therefore be mindful not only of the outputs their systems generate but also of the hidden costs that sustain these technologies.

The intended subject of this book chapter is to explore the ethical and technological implications of digital broadcasting with the help of AI. The paper investigates how media organizations are adept at manoeuvring this new terrain while maintaining the balance between the innovative and the responsible, and the tenets of such frameworks that might ensure that these transformations are consistent with the very core values of public communication. More specifically, it examines five main issues, including (1) the use of artificial intelligence in media processes, (2) ethical risks of the digital curation and the distribution of its content, (3) personalization of broadcasting utilizing algorithm filtration, (4) emergence of deepfake journalism and (5) environmental and social aspects related to AI deployment.

The role of artificial intelligence within media workflows encompasses attributes such as automated transcription, video editing, news writing, and visual effects, which increases and lowers the cost of producing that media. This raises an issue of labour ethics and the idea of quality of content. Although forms of automated processes may happen, they may also replace human workers, and AI's role within digital ethics is much more nuanced, as forms of automated decision-making can heighten echo chambers and filter bubbles, all of which can alter how people see the world around them. Personalization can be easy and mild, but it also heightens each experience we have with confirmation bias and reduces us to just one kind of information. This effect is seen most at a more serious level in politically and socially sensitive contexts.

The big concern is deep fake journalism. For the audience, it is often hard to verify what they are hearing in the audio and visuals, and whether they were authentic video and audio. This is extremely important for public trust in the media. In addition to technical safeguards, it will necessitate a rethinking of the protocols for verifying, handling, and awareness if we are to combat these risks, as Trattner et al. (2022) note.

2. BACKGROUND

The digital transformation of broadcasting is not merely a story of new tools—it reflects a broader shift in how societies consume, interpret, and respond to information. While technological advances have made access and interaction more accessible and more interactive, they have also generated new ethical, governance, and truth-related challenges. Among the considerations relevant for the current moment is the historical evolution of addressable broadcasting techniques through time, the rise of algorithmic systems and misinformation via synthetic media, and the ever-accelerating global response to these shifts.

2.1 From Linear TV to Streaming and On-Demand Platforms

Broadcasting began as a centralized model of communication. From the 1950s to the early 1990s, television programming was linear, scheduled by networks, watched (or, in the case of recording, recorded) in real time, and pretty alike for the audience. Positive regulatory bodies enforcing the content standards and delivering public interest objectives assured this structure. Until the late 1990s or early 2000s, however, cable, satellite, and internet-based broadcasting were the exception, not the rule. With this evolution, more channel diversity and time-shifted viewing options were being introduced, which paved the way for more personalized experiences.

The streaming service, companies like Netflix, YouTube, later Disney+, and Amazon Prime, drastically rewrote that broadcasting landscape. Other than the traditional TV, these platforms also provided on-demand content libraries, which meant viewers could choose to watch what they wanted to watch at that moment. This shift also disrupted existing revenue models based on advertising and syndication. Content became increasingly driven by data—platforms tracked viewer preferences, habits, and engagement metrics to inform production and recommendation strategies. With the advent of digital broadcasting, convenience and choice became easier, yet at the same time, the visibility and control of content were called into question. The result was that viewers gained agency over their media diets, but the platform algorithms started to have a decisive impact on what they chose to hear, see, consider unsafe, and possibly suppress. It represented the coming of age of algorithmic gatekeeping in modern media environments.

Table 1. Timeline of broadcasting technological milestones (1950–2025)

Year	Milestone
1950s	Emergence of national television broadcasting
1962	First live satellite TV broadcast (Telstar)
1980s	Widespread adoption of cable and satellite TV
1995	Introduction of digital TV broadcasting
2005	Launch of YouTube and the rise of user-generated media
2007	Netflix launches streaming service
2010s	Explosion of streaming platforms and smart TVs
2016	AI-driven content recommendation systems expand
2019	Real-time personalization in broadcast apps
2020–2025	Integration of generative AI and synthetic media

2.2 Rise of Algorithmic Content Curation

One of the most transformative changes in modern broadcasting is the use of algorithms to curate and prioritize content. Rather than editors or producers deciding what reaches the audience, machine-learning models now perform these tasks in real-time. These systems analyse vast amounts of user data—including watch history, location, click behaviour, and demographic information—to recommend content most likely to retain engagement.

While efficient, algorithmic curation is not without consequence. Diakopoulos (2019) states that automation in the newsroom can move editorial responsibility away from journalists onto technologists and destroy both traditional journalism values like impartiality and public interest. When recommendation algorithms prioritize sensational or polarizing content to maximize engagement, they risk distorting public understanding and weakening democratic discourse. Moreover, these systems are often opaque. Users rarely know why a particular piece of content is shown to them, and developers may be unaware of how algorithms evolve once deployed. The lack of transparency complicates accountability, especially when automated decisions affect news visibility or political narratives. According to Helberger et al. (2022), editorial norms should be reconsidered because of the growing role of AI in journalism. As algorithmic gatekeeping comes to figure more centrally within the broadcast sector, media organizations must question what values these systems entail. So, how do they balance personalization and pluralism? But what safeguards are needed to ensure responsible curation?

2.3 Deepfake Technologies and Misinformation Ecosystems

In addition to algorithmic curation, the emergence of deepfake technologies has added a new dimension of risk to digital broadcasting. Deepfakes—AI-generated audio or visual content that impersonates real individuals—can convincingly create speeches, events, or appearances. What was once the realm of science fiction is now within reach for anyone with a smartphone and simple software tools. These technologies have been used to some extent for satire and entertainment, and of course have been exploited most maliciously as a means for political manipulation, reputational damage, and misinformation. It is significant to broadcasting. Unlike traditional verification methods (fact-checking, source triangulation, etc.), these deepfake dissemination tools overwhelm any speed or scale that traditional verification processes can handle.

According to Nallasamy et al. (2024), misinformation is not just the definition of falsehoods; it is also the undermining of trust determined in the media ecosystems. Erosion due to deepfakes is caused by a blurring of the line between authentic and synthetic content. The closer that trust is to falling, the less that public institutions can communicate with citizens. The challenge for broadcasters is twofold: preventing the unintentional spread of deepfakes and restoring public confidence in verified content. This requires a combination of technical tools (e.g., deepfake detection software), human editorial judgment, and audience education. The goal is not just to stop false content but to reinforce the social contract between media institutions and the public.

2.4 Regulatory and Global Perspectives on AI and Media Ethics

These developments are being responded to by governments and some international organisations more or less unevenly. Deepfakes have already triggered legislation to curb the spread of deepfakes in some nations, algorithmic discrimination, or the misuse of data. Others are developing guidelines for how to develop ethical AI. At the same time, there is still no agreement on the way to regulate AI within the context of broadcasting. Fairness, accountability, transparency, and human oversight are, however, identified as several key principles mentioned in the commonality to most of the AI ethics frameworks by Khan et al. (2021). However, these principles are necessary, but difficult to principled in fast fast-moving, commercialized media environment. For example, algorithms need some mechanism or systems of audit, interpretation, and reverse if needed, their decisions, things that many platforms are not ready to provide or not ready to allow in the first place.

According to Diakopoulos (2024), automation in newsrooms is often revenue-driven, not edited, and a recourse to cost-cutting rather than editorial goals. In this sense, ethics can be simply set aside to gain efficiency or profitability. It simply embodies that which should be regulated, namely, setting standards and aligning incentives with responsible innovation in that space. An effort to harmonize AI ethics in the media has made some progress globally. Neither the European Union's Digital Services Act (DSA) nor its Artificial Intelligence Act is the only attempt to regulate content and technology platforms, but they are two of the most comprehensive. Such laws demand higher transparency in recommendation systems, prevention of harmful content, and risk assessments for critical AI systems. However, other regions fall behind, especially ones in the Global South with limited infrastructure and governance capacity. In this sense, then, it is important to highlight the role of media responsibility as done by Shiraliyeva (2025). With the technologization of broadcasting comes increased complexity of the technological mechanism. Yet, broadcasting is still socially important as a means of informing the public, creating a dialogue and guaranteeing democratic values. Being for ethics is not something you do later; they are in the design, in the strategy, in the operations.

Table 2. Key ethical concerns in digital broadcasting

Ethical Concern	Description
Algorithmic Bias	Skewed recommendations or suppression of marginalized voices
Lack of Transparency	Limited understanding of how content is curated or prioritized
Automation of Editorial Judgment	Shift of responsibility from journalists to algorithm designers
Misinformation and Deepfakes	Difficulty in verifying synthetic content and restoring trust
Data Privacy	Excessive or opaque collection of user data for personalization
Environmental Impact	High energy use and resource demands of AI infrastructures
Global Inequity	Uneven regulatory enforcement and digital colonialism risks

As digital broadcasting continues to expand, these concerns will only grow in importance. Ethical questions are no longer just about content—they are about systems, governance, and power. Who controls the media infrastructure? Who gets to be heard? And who is responsible when things go wrong? In response, some media organizations have begun to establish AI ethics boards or adopt transparency guidelines. However, these initiatives often remain voluntary and lack enforcement mechanisms. Lasting progress will depend on multilateral collaboration between broadcasters, technologists, regulators, and civil society.

3. FOCUS OF THE ARTICLE

This section critically analyses key dimensions along the intersection of artificial intelligence (AI), digital broadcasting, and ethics. Regarding content creation, curation, and distribution systems, as AI is being embedded, this brings both opportunities and complex ethical dilemmas. This section focuses on five interrelated domains: AI-driven personalization, deepfake journalism, ethical questions in automated content generation, algorithmic bias, and user privacy in media environments.

3.1 AI-Driven Personalization

Content has never been delivered to the viewers in such a personalized way as we see today with AI-driven personalization. Shanbhag et al. (2024) describe these systems as ones that analyse user behaviour like viewing history, click patterns, and preferences to provide 'content streams that are curated to individual interests'. Complex recommendation algorithms are used by Netflix and other such platforms to maintain the user's attention, and also increase user satisfaction and the time spent on the platforms. It brings the advantage of efficiency for users, spending less time searching, and more time consuming content according to their interests. This optimization, however, often costs. A phenomenon known as filter bubbles, where users are exposed to what the algorithms filter into their feeds, can separate individuals from different perspectives. As researched by Bakshy et al. (2015), algorithmic content exposure effects to greatly reduces ideological diversity. For instance, Bandy and Diakopoulos (2021) show that in the end, the platforms like Twitter select what to curate algorithmically, and they typically favour content that's popular over informative diversity. Noble (2018) also maintains that algorithmic design can reinforce social biases and inequalities when the algorithms are trained with corrupt or limited data. Concerns about these also suggest whether personalization in the media is truly serving public interest or creates ideological polarization and less healthy discussion. As users rely more and more on curated feeds, media literacy takes on added relevancy in equipping audiences for wondering and contextualizing content they consume. In addition, on the platform, the process of content delivery should also be balanced between being in terms of engagement and responsibility to ethics.

3.2 Benefits and Opportunities

AI-based recommendation engines make content more user-enhanced and engaging. It allows streaming platforms, the digital news portal, or social media services to elevate viewers' satisfaction and minimize the amount of information they are overloaded with (Shanbhag et al. 2024). In an age of massive digital content, this approach offers a great deal for users to find material tailored to their needs efficiently. Personalization of content is especially useful; nevertheless, issues of concern arise. One of the main issues is the creation of filter bubbles, where individuals are repeatedly exposed to the same points of view, thereby most likely deepening earlier cognitive biases (Bakshy et al., 2015). This occurrence threatens democratic debate and amplifies ideological polarization, as individuals become insulated from diverse opinions. Secondly, algorithmic curation processes are likely to amplify sensational or affective content, thereby distorting the public's perception of complex matters (Bandy & Diakopoulos, 2021). Moreover, content suggestions have the side effect of excluding minority voices or underrepresented opinions, thereby expanding representational gaps in the virtual world. Noble (2018) contends that algorithms tend to reflect the prejudices in the societies and developers who create them. Such systems, personalization can lead to exclusion and not inclusion, perpetuating systemic discrimination.

3.3 Deepfake Journalism and Misinformation

Central to news integrity are deep fake technologies, a form of AI that facilitates the generation of hyper-real digital fabrications. As video and audio content becomes easier to manipulate, it has become easier to bend journalism and the public's trust. According to Shoaib et al. (2023), deepfakes are a key means of spreading misinformation in the entire ecosystem, as during politically charged events. In 2020, a manipulated video of a world leader went viral, causing public confusion before it was debunked. In regions with weak digital regulation, deepfakes could be weaponised for defamation, extortion, and political manipulation, warns Nishal and Diakopoulos (2024), and weaponisation of deepfakes could be for political manipulation as much as it could for defamation and extortion. Morales (2025) stresses that the gap between satire, misinformation, and malicious verbiage has become so narrow that audiences can no longer differentiate real from fake. Verification of sources is now a challenge for journalists, who also need forensic tools and technical training to verify authenticity. Deepfakes spread, eroding legitimacy in news, creating an environment in whose inhospitable land "seeing is believing" no longer applies. The psychological effect of even a debunked deepfake can persist, influencing perceptions long after the truth is revealed. Moreover, bad actors exploit these technologies faster than regulations can adapt, creating a gap between capability and accountability. As a result, media outlets must adopt robust verification frameworks and collaborate with tech experts to build resilience against such threats. Synthetic media poses growing risks, and their joint countermeasures are incumbent upon both educational institutions, regulators, and platform providers, who need to find safeguards safeguarding democratic processes and public discourse. Journalistic institutions are hit hard by the credibility of deepfakes. Malicious actors can use this technology to fabricate statements by public figures, manipulate historical footage, or create fictional news reports. The potential to erode public trust in authentic media is immense (Shoaib et al., 2023). These concerns are heightened in conflict zones, elections, and crisis reporting, where misinformation can have real-world consequences.

Case Studies and Real-World Impact

During political campaigns and public health emergencies, Nishal and Diakopoulos (2024) document cases where synthetic media is used in attempts to spread misinformation. There was one instance where a deepfake video of a politician went around widely, only to be debunked, where the damage to reputation and public discourse had already taken place. As described by Morales (2025), such incidents remind us that most media organizations do not have appropriate detection mechanisms or editorial safeguards.

Table 3. Examples of deepfake incidents in news media (2019–2024)

Year	Description	Platform	Consequences
2019	Deepfake of a political figure inciting violence	Twitter	Sparked civil unrest
2021	Synthetic news clip on pandemic origins	YouTube	Led to public confusion
2023	Altered video of a journalist reporting the false event	Facebook	Undermined media credibility
2024	Fake interview using AI voice cloning	Telegram	Prompted legal inquiry

This growing threat emphasizes the urgent need for journalistic verification tools, editorial guidelines, and public literacy campaigns to mitigate the spread of synthetic disinformation.

3.4 Ethical Dilemmas in AI Content Creation

Even today, AI-generated content, the news articles or automated weather updates, has moulded the idea of present-day journalism. However, proliferation raises questions of responsibility and editorial integrity, as well as questions of authorship. The use of AI in content creation generates profound ethical questions in regards to authorship, accountability, and transparency. Robotic journalism, or automated journalism, is technological journalism that produces news content with minimal human involvement. This speeds up news production but makes the term of authorship difficult to define. Who should be the author, developers, editors, or the algorithm itself, is questioned by Montal and Reich (2017). When misinformation or bias is introduced through AI-generated content, this ambiguity becomes much more obvious. Linden (2017) reports that both the newsroom automation and stable employment paradoxically coexist, which would indicate that AI complements rather than replaces journalists. However, when algorithms are opaque, tracing decision-making is made difficult and erodes editorial accountability. To maintain public trust in AI systems used in journalism, Olanipekun (2025) argues that transparency has to be built into such systems. Equally as much, it places the ethical burden in deciding what editorial standards AI tools should adhere to — and in particular, what should be used on AI text-generating tools, particularly on such topics as health, politics, or social justice. Academic and regulatory domains are still growing in terms of the questions they pose about intent, correction mechanisms, and error liability. At the same time, emotional intelligence in algorithms is missing, so algorithms can be out of context and act in ways that cause harm when analysing subjects with high sensitivity. This means that media organizations must clarify their ethical guidelines, especially on the use of AI in producing content. While this means not just as a checkpoint but rather as a form of ethical stewardship to protect journalistic integrity even in the age of automated storytelling, there was no way out.

As algorithms take on the role of content producers, it becomes increasingly difficult to delineate authorship. Montal and Reich (2017) argue that when a story is generated by an algorithm, traditional notions of journalistic accountability are disrupted. Who is the author—the coder, the editor, or the system? Linden (2017) examines the paradox of growing automation in journalism coexisting with persistent employment. While newsrooms benefit from automation in low-stakes reporting, the lack of clear bylines in AI-generated content challenges transparency. This ambiguity can mislead audiences, especially when automated reports appear alongside human-authored journalism. Ethical journalism requires transparency in sourcing and accountability for errors. However, algorithmic content generation often lacks audit trails or explainability mechanisms. As Olanipekun (2025) notes, opacity in how AI systems generate and frame content can lead to misinformation or biased narratives, especially when training data is unbalanced or outdated. These dilemmas necessitate a reimagining of editorial workflows to incorporate AI while maintaining ethical standards. Media organizations must establish internal policies on disclosure, content review, and attribution of AI-generated work.

3.5 Algorithmic Bias and Diversity

Bias in algorithmic decision-making in broadcasting is a central concern in AI-based media, potentially distorting media narratives and silencing particular voices. The datasets used to train algorithms may themselves contain biases stemming from society. According to Bender et al. (2021), training large language models over massive internet corpora may indirectly transfer discriminatory considerations, such as racism, sexism, and other forms of oppression. In an allied observation, Noble (2018) says that when users enter seemingly innocuous queries, search engines have been found to disproportionately rank biased content, with racial and gender stereotypes. Bergstrom and Joseph (2019) coined the term 'information gerrymandering' to explain how skewed network structures may shape public opinion and preclude informed decision-making. These are particularly relevant in media systems, where algorithmic choices regarding the presentation of content and target audience can systematically disbar minority viewpoints. The penchant to amplify popular narratives at the expense of peripheral voices risks rendering public discourse univocal. Furthermore, biased artificial intelligence methods used in the production and curation of content may result in insufficient diversity concerning representation in newsrooms, coverage agendas, and storytelling. As a result, openness regarding training data and algorithmic processes is the most critical factor. While the efforts towards inclusive AI design, such as with diverse datasets and participatory modelling methods, are beginning to come into view, they are nevertheless far from generalized application. In addition, content moderation algorithms have to be reframed to forestall unjust censorship or disregard for minority concerns. Regulators and media watchdog groups must compel platforms and developers to undertake bias audits of their systems so that fair representation across various communities and contexts occurs in the arena of digital broadcasting.

3.6 Data Privacy and Surveillance

Privacy of data is at the core of AI-based media systems, particularly because personalization is predicated on the collection and processing of user information. Every time a user engages with digital content—clicks, likes, viewing time—the data feeds algorithmic engines so that future recommendations become better. Khazanchi and Saxena (2025) contend that the collection of personal information, if not regulated, can result in surveillance capitalism, where the user's activities are used to generate profits. Paik (2023) illustrates that media platforms always have obscure data policies, where users are unaware of how information about them is being gathered and utilized. Beyond that, Sun et al. (2022) establish that although many users enjoy convenience through means of personalized content, they are more and more fearful of loss of privacy and data misappropriation. Surveillance mechanisms built into media platforms even monitor emotional response and biometric indicators, leading to ethical issues regarding consent and manipulation. All of this has implications not only for personal autonomy but also for free speech, since users will silence what they perceive as monitored activity if they think that they are constantly being observed. Jurisdictional regulations such as the General

Data Protection Regulation (GDPR) have sought to address some of these issues, but enforcement across jurisdictions is still highly variable. On top of that, cross-border data flow makes accountability highly difficult, since media platforms are global but regulation is nation-bound. For broadcasting to remain ethically responsible, it must prioritize user consent, data minimization, and transparency in data usage. Ethical frameworks need to evolve alongside technology, ensuring that innovation in content personalization does not come at the expense of fundamental privacy rights.

Modern broadcasting platforms often employ sophisticated tracking tools to monitor user behaviour—what they watch, for how long, on which devices, and under what contexts. This data is then used to optimize content and advertising strategies. However, users are seldom fully informed about the extent and implications of such surveillance (Khazanchi & Saxena, 2025). Paik (2023) raises concerns about the commodification of personal data in journalism. The monetization of reader profiles can incentivize invasive data practices, compromising the ethical boundaries of editorial operations.

3.7 Public Awareness and Regulatory Concerns

Sun et al. (2022), based on a China-based public perception study, found that users express strong concern over AI's role in monitoring their media behaviours. Yet, few felt empowered to protect their data or influence how algorithms treated their information.

To address these concerns, broadcasters must implement transparent data policies, enhance user controls over privacy settings, and adhere to emerging data protection laws like GDPR and other jurisdiction-specific frameworks.

Table 4. Ethical risks vs technological benefits in AI-driven broadcasting

Domain	Technological Benefit	Ethical Risk
Personalization	Enhanced user experience	Filter bubbles, echo chambers
Content Automation	Efficiency, 24/7 updates	Lack of accountability
Deepfakes	Creative storytelling	Misinformation, deception
Data Analytics	Targeted advertising	Privacy violations
Recommendation Systems	Engagement boost	Ideological skewing

4. SOLUTIONS AND RECOMMENDATIONS

The evolution of digital broadcasting has brought remarkable opportunities, but it also calls for actionable, well-grounded responses to its ethical, technological, and regulatory challenges. The rapid integration of artificial intelligence in media systems cannot be met with static policies or outdated ethical paradigms. This section offers grounded strategies aimed at addressing these contemporary challenges through four interconnected pathways: policy and regulation, ethical AI design, newsroom practices, and public media literacy. Together, these provide a holistic vision for responsible innovation in broadcasting.

4.1 Policy and Regulation

Establishing a policy and regulation about digital broadcasting is an urgent and primary way to solve the ethical issues related to digital broadcasting. Media technologies are also transnational in scope, thus complicating the regulation of such technologies. This combination of enforcement imbalance and regulatory deficits in digital rights protection and algorithmic accountability leads to non-existent international standards. GDPR may be the highest standard for data protection in the world, but its enforcement outside of the EU lags. According to De-Lima-Santos et al. (2024), it is imperative to develop adaptive and enforceable ethics in different geopolitical contexts. While the application of artificial intelligence in journalism and broadcasting is being steered by the development of the digital ethics charters initiated by bodies such as UNESCO and the Council of Europe, these are not binding.

Formulating ethical frameworks is not the problem; it is, rather, challenging to equip regulatory (or any other) bodies with the needed resources, skills, and robust charter to monitor and oversee exactly the types of algorithmic systems (and the people within complex institutions that design and apply them). In his article, Ward (2021) recommends that national media councils and transnational oversight bodies reform their mandates, introducing algorithmic audits, transparency efforts, and a real-time system of monitoring. Without these initiatives, digital media companies often operate in murky legal waters using AI to increase engagement or tailor content to watch and survey. In exposing that the development of information and communication technology is ‘exceptional’ in its implications, Floridi et al (2018) argue that ethical regulation must also follow ‘exceptionally’, and that this is achieved through ‘collaboration between ethicists, engineers, lawyers, and media experts, all working together very closely to formulate policy’. Such a multi-stakeholder regulation is designed to ensure that the emerging technologies are compatible with democratic principles, protect the rights of citizens, and contribute to the welfare of society.

Policy-making must ensure that the views and values of the Global South are taken into account, where digital infrastructure is less pronounced but the influence of media technologies is nevertheless deeply felt. Transnational policies must heed the various economic, cultural, and legal environments of regions to prevent ethical imperialism and ensure equitable representation in global broadcasting norms. Harmonization of regulations, recognition of mutual standards, and cooperative enforcement actions could provide a common ethics platform, allowing governments and media institutions to tackle collectively misinformation, algorithmic bias, and privacy violations. Without this consistency, piecemeal approaches risk eroding public confidence and leading to wide gaps in ethics-based governance.

4.2 Ethical AI Design and Guidelines

The underlying philosophy of ethical digital broadcasting is the creation of artificial intelligence systems based on ethical principles, like fairness, accountability, and transparency. But these principles need to be incorporated right from the initial stages of the creation of algorithmic systems, and not as an afterthought. One of the key aspects of ethical AI design is intentional decision-making in the context of training data, algorithmic logic, model testing, and outcome evaluation. Pant et al. (2023) highlight that the process of ethical design goes beyond technical details; it has to be a collective effort by software engineers, sociologists, media studies scholars, and ethicists.

In broadcasting applications, fairness means that recommendation systems should not excessively favour some views or stifle minority opinions. Cao and Meng (2025) suggest a multi-layered fairness architecture of media algorithms where both input data and output options are audited periodically. These audits should check not only statistical balance but also socio-cultural effects, and spot patterns of marginalization or over-representation. For instance, if a news recommendation system systematically favours sensational over informative reporting, it distorts public debate and undermines civic participation. Systemic solutions need to go beyond code-tweaking—they need to re-evaluate the ethical presumptions underpinning algorithmic choices.

Meanwhile, accountability demands the identification of those with a responsibility for decisions that are made by AI systems. According to Trattner et al. (2022), black box algorithms weaken this accountability in particular, as black box algorithms' decision-making processes remain opaque not only to their creators but also to their users. If platforms need to implement mechanisms for the users to object to the algorithmic decisions, like a good decision or the reason as to why they should hide a piece of certain news, they have to become broadcasting platforms. These feedback systems empower users and introduce a layer of ethical responsiveness often missing from automated systems.

Academic discussions of transparency cannot end with them. Content created or curated by AI should be flagged using visual indicators or disclaimers to inform an audience. By establishing this design philosophy, trust is built, and the risk of misinformation or perceived algorithmic bias is mitigated. Additionally, open-source models and community oversight boards can bring in the participatory mechanisms of public stakeholders who have some roles in making the design of media algorithms ethical. With convergence between data science and broadcasting becoming more and more the norm, ethical design principles trump the optional; these principles have become essential for maintaining the media's democratic role in society.

4.3 Newsroom Practices

Newsroom integration of AI does not change that core journalistic integrity that has been a hallmark of trustworthy broadcasting. The rise of AI tools in the media sector is witnessing the use of automatic reporting, trend detection, and even headline generation by many of the media houses. But, as the reliance grows, so should the newsroom practices with which to exercise this growing reliance, in a way that champions an ethical use. Which is why the adoption of AI disclosure policies is one important step. The Associated Press (2023) says that if all the articles that get generated or even assisted pull AI involvement, this should be clearly stated to ensure transparency with audiences. It helped prevent the erosion of trust and make sure that the human editorial role stays visible and is worth very much.

Partially answering this problem, the Washington Post (2025) employs a hybrid editorial system that combines the use of AI systems to increase productivity while maintaining judgment. AI in this model provides a draft or summary; journalists are responsible for contextual accuracy, tone, and final publication. This collaborative model not only speeds up operations but also safeguards the ownership over publications. According to Murgia (2023), such workflows can redeploy AI as a no replacement for journalists, but rather as an editorial capacity augmenting tool. But this model is only going to be successful with exhaustive training. The journalists need to acquire the skills to understand how AI tools operate, their constraints, and the ethical issues associated with the use of AI tools.

In addition to making the newsroom process transparent and unidirectional, editorial oversight mechanisms must adapt to include algorithmic audits, where a newsroom editor periodically checks for alignment between how AI-generated outputs meet the values of the organization. In Cools and Diakopoulos (2024), newsrooms are encouraged to create AI ethics committees to attend to the social impact of AI-assisted journalism and notify on possible ethical deviations. These internal watchdogs exist to be the first line of defence for automated systems from bias, sensationalism, or misinformation. Equally important is diversity in newsroom leadership. Ethical decisions about AI deployment must include voices from underrepresented communities to prevent narrow or biased interpretations of newsworthiness. As AI systems increasingly influence story selection, framing, and prioritization, media organizations must ensure that their ethical frameworks are inclusive, participatory, and adaptable to evolving digital realities.

4.4 Media Literacy and Public Engagement

No ethical broadcasting ecosystem can succeed without informed and critical audiences. Media literacy, especially digital and algorithmic literacy, is essential to help individuals recognize AI-generated content, detect manipulation, and question automated recommendations. Nishal and Diakopoulos (2024) emphasize the importance of public education campaigns that demystify how media algorithms function and their potential impact on public opinion. Such initiatives are particularly crucial in societies where exposure to digital media outpaces formal education on media ethics. Morales (2025) suggests that digital literacy should not only cover how to consume media but also how to produce and verify it, encouraging civic participation and critical thinking. These educational efforts can be supplemented by community-based programs led by libraries, NGOs, and local media outlets.

User awareness can also be supported by interactive media field tools (e.g., browser plug-ins, mobile apps). These tools can explain why some content is recommended, why media may appear to have been altered, or suggest diversification of one's media sources. Shoaib et al. (2023) note that nudging users toward diverse viewpoints can counteract filter bubbles and foster pluralistic dialogue. However, these tools must be designed with user autonomy in mind—educational, not coercive.

It also encourages the public to participate in talks on media ethics and a culture of accountability. Public consultations, participatory research projects, and citizens' panels all offer means to give user voices into policy debates and platform governance. If audiences perceive in digital media an ethical direction and are invested in it, they will be more likely to engage in responsible innovation and less inclined to have manipulative content. Thus, media literacy is not just a defensive strategy—it is a proactive, empowering force in the digital transformation of broadcasting.

Table 5. Recommended AI ethics guidelines for media organizations

Guideline	Description
AI Disclosure	Indicate when content is generated or assisted by AI.
Fairness Audits	Regularly assess algorithms for demographic or ideological bias.
Transparency in Recommendations	Provide explanations for content curation and ranking algorithms.
Data Privacy Protections	Limit data collection and provide opt-out mechanisms for personalization.
Editorial Oversight	Maintain human review in AI-assisted content production.
Inclusive Design	Involve diverse voices in algorithmic development and content strategy.
Public Engagement	Educate users about algorithmic systems and gather feedback.
Ethical Review Boards	Establish internal committees to oversee AI ethics in newsroom practices.

5. FUTURE RESEARCH DIRECTIONS

As the media landscape continues to evolve under the influence of digital transformation and artificial intelligence, the academic community faces the responsibility of asking new questions and exploring emerging complexities. The intersection of ethics, technology, and journalism is not static, but a constantly shifting space shaped by cultural norms, technological innovation, political structures, and public behaviour. Despite growing attention to these areas, numerous gaps remain in current research—gaps that, if addressed thoughtfully, can contribute to more equitable, transparent, and resilient media systems. This section outlines several promising directions for future inquiry, each of which holds the potential to deepen understanding and improve practical responses to the challenges facing modern broadcasting.

One of the most pressing areas for scholarly development is the creation of ethical design frameworks specifically tailored to the field of journalism. While general frameworks for responsible AI already exist, such as those offered by IEEE, UNESCO, or the EU's High-Level Expert Group on AI, these are often too broad to account for the particular nuances and obligations of journalism. The need for domain-specific frameworks arises from journalism's foundational role in democracy, truth-telling, and public accountability. Ward (2021) emphasizes that ethical journalism requires a delicate balance between speed, accuracy, and fairness—considerations that are not fully addressed in generic AI ethics models. Future research should investigate how these frameworks can be operationalized in newsrooms, addressing issues such as the ethics of headline automation, the use of bots in political reporting, and algorithmic gatekeeping.

Another area that requires substantial scholarly attention is the cross-cultural interpretation of AI ethics in media environments. Much of the discourse around AI and ethics is dominated by Western philosophical traditions and regulatory perspectives. Broadcasting, though, is inherently global in reach and influence and requires metaphors of this potential global reach and influence, yet the ethical values on which media consumption and production based differ sharply from culture to culture. For example, 'privacy' may be understood and of value differently in Scandinavia than in Southeast Asia. Zhao and Phakdeephirot (2023) assert that no ethnic group is the same, and it is no surprise that a scientific religion like AI ethics cannot cater to all individual and ethnic differences. In the context of research in this area, there should be an exploration of how ethical standards could be adjusted to operate within a pluralistic environment, without violating basic rights, such as freedom of expression or protection from harm. Empirical grounding for more culturally inclusive ethical models can be provided by comparative ethnographic studies, interviews with regional media practitioners, and policy analyses.

In addition to cultural considerations, there is a growing need to explore the evolving dynamics of human-AI collaboration in content creation. As AI tools become more advanced, they are increasingly involved in the creative process, from drafting scripts to editing footage and even generating synthetic interviews. This collaboration challenges traditional notions of authorship, labor, and creativity within journalism. Farid (2023) points out that the blending of human judgment with machine-generated content complicates existing ethical boundaries, particularly when it comes to accountability and originality.

One of the most critical yet under-researched components in the use of AI in journalism is trust in the media. Trust is increasingly hinged on the drivers of trust, as algorithms increasingly shape what news people see, frame it, and whether they believe it. With regards to AI-mediated journalism, current literature has just started to examine user trust in algorithmic systems more generally, but there are no focused studies on this. While transparency and explainability are widely discussed as solutions, Manninen (2022) also points out that they don't automatically result in trust. Media audience's experience with previous media, readiness with politics, and digital literacy that they possess all influence the degree to which they would trust AI-generated / AI-curated news. As a result, in future research, public trust has to be measured and better understood using less simplistic approaches. Mixed-method studies that combine surveys, focus groups, and experimental design are suited because they create a multi-dimensional treatment of trust among diverse demographic and cultural groups. Additionally, it is also important to distinguish between trust in content and trust in platforms. For example, if a piece of information appears in the news with a piece attached to it, users may trust the information regardless of the platform, but not trust the platform. Looking at these layers of trust will help media organizations and policymakers identify technologically sound interventions that also speak to society.

Another interesting path is to devise better methods for assessing the societal reach of AI technologies applied in broadcasting. Much of the current assessment of the technical performance metric, for example, accuracy, speed, or engagement, but little is said regarding the long-term social impacts. Building on the body of work on algorithmic journalism, Bandy and Diakopoulos (2021) advocate for more robust frameworks of measurement as the impact of algorithmic journalism on political polarization, information diversity, and civic engagement. And the impacts are hard to quantify, but are key to AI's ethical viability for journalists. Research could build on existing computational models to create new indices or dashboards that measure exposure diversity, topic variety, or sentiment balance in news feeds. Additionally, studies could investigate the unintended consequences of algorithmic news filtering, such as the reinforcement of echo chambers or the marginalization of dissenting voices. Such metrics can guide editorial decisions and serve as benchmarks for ethical audits. Farid (2023) argues that environmentally responsible AI development must become part of ethical assessments, especially in industries like media, where public interest is paramount. Future studies should explore how media organizations can balance innovation with environmental stewardship, perhaps by incorporating sustainability metrics into their procurement and development decisions.

6. CONCLUSION

Great innovation and serious ethical dilemmas have marked the transformation of broadcasting in the digital age. The whole industry was then transformed from the traditional linear TV to streaming platforms where the content is then algorithmically geopolitically. Artificial intelligence is also integrated in journalistic workflows, and new delivery and audience engagement strategies are also created in this transformation. Nevertheless, these instruments are still gaining steam as forces favourable to changing people's views, and the media professionals, scholars, and policymakers cannot simply afford to neglect the ethical foundations of journalism and public communication. Now, as the benefits of technological development become more critical to be harnessed and the responsibility to maintain these principles is growing, this becomes more critical.

From the initial broadcast of information given, broadcasting has grown from a centralized, linear-based industry into a decentralized, on-demand, digital-based marketplace. This transformation has provided unprecedented accessibility and personalization, but has also brought about so many more questions about transparency, truth, and control. Algorithms determine today what audiences will see and how they will come to see it. The risk of ideological silos, filter bubbles, and less exposure to different points of view have been warned about by Bakshy et al. (2015) for this degree of algorithmic influence.

One of the primary difficulties in leveraging AI for personalization is its increasing prevalence. Personalization can enhance user experience and simplify interactions by tailoring content to individual preferences. However, it also exacerbates ideological division, as individuals tend to engage mainly with material that reinforces their existing beliefs. This poses a significant threat to democratic dialogue, particularly when considering how swiftly both truths and falsehoods can circulate compared to facts. Bandy and Diakopoulos (2021) highlight the risks associated with opaque algorithmic processes and the absence of responsibility in how news content is filtered and ranked.

Additionally, this complexity is heightened by the emergence of synthetic media technologies such as deepfakes. While the ability to create synthetic audio and video offers avenues for creativity and satire, its misuse in journalism has ushered in a new era of disinformation, where 'authenticity' can no longer be taken for granted. The media sector is apprehensive, given that the means to produce strikingly realistic yet entirely fictional content now exists. Shoaib et al. (2023) observe that deepfakes have been utilized to influence political discourse, fabricate false statements attributed to public figures, and instigate skepticism about verified news events. As these technologies evolve, verifying sources and sustaining credibility will become increasingly challenging for the media. Concerns extend beyond just the misuse of technology to include critical ethical questions: how can institutions respond effectively and mitigate the potential for such misuse?

In parallel, the incorporation of responsible artificial intelligence has become an imperative. In this regard, ethical approaches extend beyond mere avoidance of harm; they entail active encouragement of trust, inclusivity, and the common good in broadcasting by applying ethical AI principles. Floridi et al. (2018) established frameworks where transparency, justice, and beneficence are critical characteristics of AI systems. These values are particularly significant in journalism, a profession with immense influence on the shaping of public opinion, reinforcement of democratic processes, and promotion of human dignity. Instead of targeting typical, narrow-scope integrations, development needs to be conducted by varied teams with contextual knowledge, allowing for open dialogue on algorithmic decision-making, and ensuring an ongoing commitment to public accountability. Even though large language models, such as those used for improved classification and search capabilities that detect human beings of different skin tones, have immense power, they can also reproduce destructive biases if not well-designed and implemented, cautioned Bender et al. (2021). Ethical design cannot, therefore, be considered a fringe concern but a requirement for innovative and sustainable development of media.

The role of policies in guiding the adoption of artificial intelligence in broadcasting is of critical significance. Currently, institutions such as the European Union and UNESCO are publishing guidelines that aim to foster trustworthy AI, with a focus on the importance of such collaboration given the inherently global character of the media. Nevertheless, de-Lima-Santos et al. (2024) argue that ethical regulation must be flexible and enforceable to guard against the pursuit of innovation at the expense of the public interest. Media organizations without robust regulatory frameworks might prioritize competitive advantage at the expense of ethical standards, thus developing a situation where misinformation, bias, and manipulation are allowed to thrive without accountability. Hence, stakeholders in the formulation of regulatory strategies pertaining to technology and innovation must collaborate with technologists and journalists to establish systems that uphold journalistic integrity while driving innovation. This endeavor entails the uptake of interoperability standards, the assurance of auditability of algorithms, and the facilitation of inclusive contribution to the development of digital norms.

The worth of education, both in professional journalism and in society as a whole, is of utmost importance and cannot be overemphasized. As algorithmic recommendations and artificial media become part of the texture of everyday life, Nishal and Diakopoulos (2024) describe that media literacy must be reconceptualized for today's society. Audiences can no longer afford to take content at face value; they need to be ready to critically analyze its origins, intentions, and possible influences. Public engagement programs, educational curricula, and digital literacy training can be crucial means of equipping citizens to navigate the evolving media environment successfully. Education is more than a reaction to disinformation; it is a pledge to the strength of a democratic society. This chapter has explored the trajectory of digital transformation in broadcasting, including historical progress, algorithmic filtering of content, the development of deepfake technologies, regulatory responses, and the role of media literacy. The path forward is multifaceted and non-linear, but it is possible with prudent planning and foresight.

REFERENCES

Anderson, C. W. (2013). *Rebuilding the news: Metropolitan journalism in the digital age*. Temple University Press.

Bozdag, E. (2013). Bias in algorithmic filtering and personalization. *Ethics and Information Technology, 15*(3), 209–227. DOI: 10.1007/s10676-013-9321-6

Broussard, M. (2018). *Artificial unintelligence: How computers misunderstand the world*. MIT Press. DOI: 10.7551/mitpress/11022.001.0001

Clerwall, C. (2014). Enter the robot journalist: Users' perceptions of automated content. *Journalism Practice, 8*(5), 519–531. DOI: 10.1080/17512786.2014.883116

Diakopoulos, N., & Koliska, M. (2017). Algorithmic transparency in the news media. *Digital Journalism (Abingdon, England), 5*(7), 809–828. DOI: 10.1080/21670811.2016.1208053

Dörr, K. N. (2016). Mapping the field of algorithmic journalism. *Digital Journalism (Abingdon, England), 4*(6), 700–722. DOI: 10.1080/21670811.2015.1096748

Eubanks, V. (2018). *Automating inequality: How high-tech tools profile, police, and punish the poor*. St. Martin's Press.

Fink, K., & Anderson, C. W. (2015). Data journalism in the United States: Beyond the "usual suspects.". *Journalism Studies, 16*(4), 467–481. DOI: 10.1080/1461670X.2014.939852

Gillespie, T. (2014). The relevance of algorithms. In Gillespie, T., Boczkowski, P., & Foot, K. (Eds.), *Media technologies: Essays on communication, materiality, and society* (pp. 167–194). MIT Press. DOI: 10.7551/mitpress/9042.003.0013

Gillespie, T. (2018). *Custodians of the Internet: Platforms, content moderation, and the hidden decisions that shape social media*. Yale University Press.

Graefe, A. (2016). *Guide to automated journalism*. Columbia Journalism School. https://www.cjr.org/tow_center_reports/guide_to_automated_journalism.php

Hermida, A. (2010). Twittering the news: The emergence of ambient journalism. *Journalism Practice, 4*(3), 297–308. DOI: 10.1080/17512781003640703

Jarvis, J. (2014). *Geeks bearing gifts: Imagining new futures for news*. CUNY Journalism Press.

Lewis, S. C., & Westlund, O. (2015). Actors, actants, audiences, and activities in cross-media news work: A matrix and a research agenda. *Digital Journalism (Abingdon, England)*, *3*(1), 19–37. DOI: 10.1080/21670811.2014.927986

Lindgren, M. (2017). *Digital first journalism: Theory and practice*. Oxford University Press.

Marconi, F., & Siegman, A. (2017). *The future of augmented journalism: A guide for newsrooms in the age of smart machines.* Associated Press. https://insights.ap.org/uploads/images/the-future-of-augmented-journalism_ap-report.pdf

McChesney, R. W., & Nichols, J. (2010). *The death and life of American journalism: The media revolution that will begin the world again*. Nation Books.

Molyneux, L., & Holton, A. E. (2015). Branding (health) journalism: Perceptions, practices, and emerging norms. *Digital Journalism (Abingdon, England)*, *3*(2), 225–242. DOI: 10.1080/21670811.2014.906927

Morozov, E. (2013). *To save everything, click here: The folly of technological solutionism*. PublicAffairs.

Napoli, P. M. (2011). *Audience evolution: New technologies and the transformation of media audiences*. Columbia University Press.

Noble, S. U. (2018). *Algorithms of oppression: How search engines reinforce racism.* NYU Press. DOI: 10.18574/nyu/9781479833641.001.0001

O'Neil, C. (2016). *Weapons of math destruction: How big data increases inequality and threatens democracy*. Crown Publishing Group.

Pariser, E. (2011). *The filter bubble: What the Internet is hiding from you.* Penguin Press.

Pasquale, F. (2015). *The black box society: The secret algorithms that control money and information*. Harvard University Press. DOI: 10.4159/harvard.9780674736061

Pavlik, J. V. (2013). Innovation and the future of journalism. *Digital Journalism (Abingdon, England)*, *1*(2), 181–193. DOI: 10.1080/21670811.2012.756666

Powers, M. (2018). Understanding algorithms in journalism: A theory of sociotechnical interdependence. *Digital Journalism (Abingdon, England)*, *6*(3), 273–290. DOI: 10.1080/21670811.2017.1340770

Stray, J. (2012). Algorithmic accountability: A primer. *Tow Center for Digital Journalism.*https://www.cjr.org/tow_center_reports/algorithmic_accountability.php

Tandoc, E. C.Jr, & Maitra, J. (2018). News organizations' use of native videos on Facebook: Tweaking the journalistic field one algorithm change at a time. *New Media & Society*, *20*(5), 1679–1696. DOI: 10.1177/1461444817702398

Thorson, E., & Wells, C. (2015). Curated flows: A framework for mapping media exposure in the digital age. *Communication Theory*, *26*(3), 309–328. DOI: 10.1111/comt.12087

Thurman, N., Dörr, K. N., & Kunert, J. (2017). When reporters get hands-on with robo-writing: Professionals consider automated journalism's capabilities and consequences. *Digital Journalism (Abingdon, England)*, *5*(10), 1240–1259. DOI: 10.1080/21670811.2017.1289819

Tufekci, Z. (2015). Algorithmic harms beyond Facebook and Google: Emergent challenges of computational agency. *Colorado Technology Law Journal*, *13*, 203–218. https://ctlj.colorado.edu/?p=1306

van Dalen, A. (2012). The algorithms behind the headlines: How machine-written news redefines the core skills of human journalists. *Journalism Practice*, *6*(5–6), 648–658. DOI: 10.1080/17512786.2012.667268

Ward, S. J. A. (2010). *Global journalism ethics*. McGill-Queen's University Press. DOI: 10.1515/9780773585218

Ward, S. J. A. (2018). Disrupting journalism ethics: Radical change on the frontier of digital media. *Journalism Studies*, *19*(15), 2320–2337. DOI: 10.1080/1461670X.2017.1351238

Wardle, C., & Derakhshan, H. (2017). *Information disorder: Toward an interdisciplinary framework for research and policy making*. Council of Europe. https://rm.coe.int/information-disorder-report/1680764666

Weber, M., & Monge, P. (2017). Industries in turmoil: Journalism in the networked information economy. *Annals of the International Communication Association*, *41*(3–4), 204–210. DOI: 10.1080/23808985.2017.1402194

Westlund, O. (2013). Mobile news: A review and model of journalism in an age of mobile media. *Digital Journalism (Abingdon, England)*, *1*(1), 6–26. DOI: 10.1080/21670811.2012.740273

Zelizer, B. (2009). The changing faces of journalism: Tabloidization, technology, and truthiness. In Wahl-Jorgensen, K., & Hanitzsch, T. (Eds.), *The handbook of journalism studies* (pp. 335–349). Routledge.

Zelizer, B. (2019). Why journalism is about more than digital technology. *Digital Journalism (Abingdon, England)*, *7*(3), 343–350. DOI: 10.1080/21670811.2019.1571932

Zelizer, B., & Allan, S. (2010). *Journalism after September 11* (2nd ed.). Routledge.

Zelizer, B., & Tenenboim-Weinblatt, K. (2014). Journalism and memory. In Hanitzsch, T. P., & Wahl-Jorgensen, K. (Eds.), *The handbook of journalism studies* (pp. 195–211). Routledge.

Zelizer, B., & Wasserman, H. (2015). Journalism in times of crisis. *Journalism*, *16*(1), 1–7. DOI: 10.1177/1464884914568072

ADDITIONAL READING

Bandy, J., & Diakopoulos, N. (2021). Auditing News Algorithms: A Sociotechnical Framework for Analyzing Algorithmic News Curation. *Digital Journalism (Abingdon, England)*, *9*(3), 330–350.

Crawford, K. (2021). *Atlas of AI: Power, Politics, and the Planetary Costs of Artificial Intelligence*. Yale University Press.

de-Lima-Santos, M. F., Christofoletti, R., & de Andrade, L. A. (2024). Towards a Global Framework for Ethical AI in Journalism. *Journalism Studies*, *25*(2), 145–167.

Morales, L. (2025). *Synthetic Realities: Deepfakes, AI, and the Crisis of Authenticity in News*. MIT Press.

Trattner, C., Ferwerda, B., & Schedl, M. (2022). Ethical Challenges of AI in Recommender Systems for Media. *ACM Transactions on the Web*, *16*(4), 1–24.

KEY TERMS AND DEFINITIONS

Artificial Intelligence in Media: The term Artificial Intelligence in media is used to describe models and techniques of using machine learning and computation to automate or supplement people's work in journalism and broadcasting. It covers things like news making, content suggestion, audience awaiting, and visual editing. AI in media can include things like predictive analytics and personalisation engines or generators that create text, images, and video content that requires little to no human interaction.

Algorithmic Bias: Here we say algorithmic bias, based on undesired and usually discriminatory results that result from trained systems with unfair data, non-optimum model design, or an unequal distribution of digital resources. In media, algorithmic bias can show up in news curation, discrimination of minority content, or the reinforcement of polarizing content that already exists, which only stimulates current social inequalities.

Deepfake Journalism: The term deepfake journalism refers to the use of synthetic media technologies using deep learning algorithms to create manipulated audiovisual content that appears very realistic. But malicious deepfakes can fool the public by distorting facts, spreading misinformation or impersonating people in the situations of fake news scenario, and eroding public trust in credible reporting.

Digital Broadcasting Ethics: Digital broadcasting ethics are the moral principles and professional guidelines for content creation, distribution, and consumption in the new digital and AI-enabled media landscape. These ethics deal with concerns pertaining to the journalistic and broadcasting use of multiple digital technologies, such as truthfulness, accountability, inclusivity, transparency, and the social impacts of those digital technologies on society.

Personalized Content Delivery: Tailoring media outputs to individual users depending on their preferences, behaviours, and viewing history is called personalizing content delivery. However, there is a flip side to all of this, as this technique is not only improving engagement and satisfaction, but also undermining the values of echo chambers, the lack of content diversity, and the increased ideological polarization.

Chapter 5
The Evolution of Binge-Watching:
The New Watching Habit of the Digital Age

Serhat Erdem
https://orcid.org/0000-0002-3782-0147
Atatürk Üniversitesi, Turkey

ABSTRACT

The study examines the binge-watching habits popularized with the rise of digital media platforms and the effects of these habits on media consumption habits. Platforms such as Netflix, Amazon Prime Video and Hulu have encouraged binge-watching by making content instantly accessible, offering viewers a seamless viewing experience. Thanks to technological innovations, personalized content recommendations and advanced algorithms, these habits may deepen in the future. AI-powered systems can reinforce binge-watching behaviors by recommending content based on viewers' moods and viewing history.

INTRODUCTION

Binge-watching has become an important phenomenon transforming media consumption habits with the rise of digital media platforms. Platforms such as Netflix, Amazon Prime Video and Hulu make content instantly accessible and offer entire seasons at once, providing viewers with an uninterrupted viewing experience. This development has encouraged viewers to engage more intensely with content and has made media consumption continuous. Binge-watching has led to the emergence

DOI: 10.4018/979-8-3373-1957-5.ch005

of new viewing habits by offering viewers the freedom to watch content whenever they want, in contrast to traditional television viewing habits.

Technological innovations will further influence viewers' behavior and media consumption patterns. In particular, artificial intelligence and advanced algorithms will lead viewers to watch more content by providing personalized content recommendations based on viewer preferences. Such systems will reinforce binge-watching behaviors by offering content based on the viewer's viewing history and mood. In the future, the integration of technologies such as augmented reality (AR) and virtual reality (VR) into media consumption could make the way viewers interact with content more interactive and in-depth. This will enable viewers to watch content for longer and have more media experiences.

The social dimensions of binge-watching are also important. While digital platforms have made viewers' connection to content stronger, they have also changed the forms of social interaction. Instead of watching content alone, viewers have formed communities by sharing and discussing their content through social media and online forums. This interaction encourages viewers to think more about the content and exchange ideas with others. In the future, these communities will grow stronger and social experiences will be created around the content.

The future of the media industry will be shaped by the evolution of binge-watching habits. Digital platforms are increasing audience engagement and deepening viewers' interest in content by delivering content in a more personalized way. They are also transforming the way content is produced. Interactive content and projects that involve viewers in the story can make media consumption more participatory. Interactive projects such as Netflix's Bandersnatch are important examples of how this type of content will become more common in the future. In the future, media companies will continue to respond to audience demands with more creative content strategies.

Binge-watching has become a habit that has deepened and evolved with the technological innovations offered by digital media platforms. This phenomenon is reshaping the media industry and leading to major cultural and societal transformations, while changing the way audiences engage with content. Technological advances, personalized experiences and increased social interactions point to an era in which binge-watching will become more widespread and more effective in the future.

Binge-watching has become an important phenomenon in recent years, especially with the impact of digital media platforms. The habit of many viewers to binge-watch a season or series episode has created a radical change in media consumption habits. This habit has gone beyond being just an entertainment activity and has shown many effects at the social and individual level. Especially the effects of the digitalized world on social and cultural structures require a more in-depth examination of the binge-watching phenomenon. This research is based on a literature review to understand the change in media viewing habits in the digital age and the psychological and social reflections of this change.

SOCIAL AND PSYCHOLOGICAL REFLECTIONS OF BINGE-WATCHING

Binge-watching did not start as an entertainment practice, but has had significant social and psychological effects over time. The literature suggests that prolonged binge-watching habits have various effects on individual psychology and lead to changes in social relations. Binge-watching has also been studied as a phenomenon that affects brain chemistry; regular content viewing can stimulate the reward centers of the brain, triggering the viewer to watch more content. This demonstrates the direct effects of media on individual psychology (Kubey & Csikszentmihalyi, 2002).

The social effects of binge-watching are also noteworthy. The media's role in shaping the social structure restructures the social interactions of individuals. Through digital content, viewers have a more individualized experience compared to traditional media, while social norms are rapidly transforming. This change can also lead to increased social isolation (Kraut & Seay, 2006). Increasing social isolation and decreasing interpersonal relationships are considered as one of the negative consequences of the excessive use of digital technologies. (Kotan, 2024, p. 95).

The evolution of binge-watching is a critical phenomenon for understanding the effects of digitalized media environments on social structure and individual psychology. This habit has become more than just a form of media consumption; it has also affected individuals' lifestyles and social relations, changing cultural norms.

Definition and Historical Development of Binge-Watching

Binge-watching, while initially seen as a recreational activity, has become an important part of media consumption habits in the digital age. Binge-watching a series or movie season has become more common, especially with the popularization of internet-based digital platforms. This habit is defined by the viewer's preference for binge-watching several episodes of a TV series or movie, in order to experience the viewing experience in a more in-depth and intense way (Lobato, 2019). The evolution of binge-watching has followed a parallel process with the change in television viewing habits. Understanding how this phenomenon has gained an identity in digital media provides important data on how the media industry, social norms and individual psychology are shaped.

Impact of Digital Media Platforms

The most important impact of binge-watching is that the content offered by digital media platforms provides the viewer with an uninterrupted experience. Platforms such as Netflix, Amazon Prime Video and Hulu have created an environment where content accumulates and can be watched without interruption by offering "full season" broadcasts to viewers (Mikos, 2016). Unlike traditional television broadcasting, these platforms have made content available at the same time. In this way, viewers have the opportunity to watch the entire season or the entire series at the same time, rather than the series being broadcast one week at a time. This has fundamentally changed traditional viewing habits in terms of timing and content consumption. The content offered by digital platforms gives the viewer more control over when and how they watch.

Digital platforms have not only changed viewing habits but have also transformed the form of media production. Viewers, who used to follow a program flow determined by television channels, now have an experience that they shape according to their own viewing time and content preferences. This gives the viewer more autonomy and redefines television viewing habits (Creeber, 2015). With this process of change, in addition to the new approaches emerging for the audience with digitalization and digital transformation in message sharing, the time and space compression specific to traditional broadcasting is replaced by fluid time and virtual spaces. This fluidity enables communication, broadcasting and, more importantly, the socialization process to change meaning. In connection with these emerging needs, the importance of social media and its impact on television broadcasting is increasing with new tools, namely social media (Çakın & Bolat, 2018, p. 176).

Evolution in Television Viewing Habits

The historical evolution of binge-watching is based on fundamental changes in television viewing habits. Since the 1950s, television has become the most important source of home entertainment. However, television viewing habits were usually based on a weekly program schedule. In other words, viewers had to wait for the programs they preferred to watch on a specific day and time. At the societal level, this created a social ritual based on the hours that families watched together. This situation has led to television creating a viewing habit that directs the viewer and compresses them into a specific time frame.

However, since the late 1990s, with the impact of digital media, there has been a major shift in television viewing habits. Especially with the rise of DVDs and Blu-rays, viewers began to use various forms of media to complete a season of TV series. The real transformation, however, came with the rise of internet-based platforms.

Netflix's transformation from a DVD rental service to an online video streaming platform in 2007 accelerated the global spread of binge-watching (Creeber, 2015). Netflix's user-friendly interface and continuous streaming feature made it easy for viewers to watch several episodes or seasons in a single session. This feature made the television viewing experience more personalized and made viewers' viewing habits more independent. To summarize, with the emergence of online television broadcasting, the viewer has moved out of the fixed broadcast stream on televisions and has taken a more active position, giving the viewer the opportunity to watch, start, stop, re-watch, start and/or rewind the content they follow at any time. It is possible to state that this situation creates a free space for the viewer by eliminating time and space barriers (Demir & Akmeşe Demir, 2023). In addition, thanks to the second screen and Social TV applications, the opportunity to interact with other viewers has also improved and the television audience has entered into an active participation (Bayraktar, 2020).

Binge-Watching and Psychological Effects

Binge-watching, along with media consumption habits, also leads to significant changes on a psychological level. Many studies reveal that binge-watching can have specific effects on individuals' mental and emotional states. In particular, there are several factors that can have positive or negative effects on the mental health of the viewer. These include the type of content the viewer watches, the length of the content and the duration of viewing.

Studies on the psychological effects of binge-watching have found that when viewers watch content continuously, reward mechanisms in the brain are activated, which leads the viewer to watch more content (Kubey & Csikszentmihalyi, 2002). Long-term series viewing can increase the brain's production of dopamine, encouraging the viewer to constantly watch new content. This may lead to an addiction-like effect over time. On the other hand, some studies suggest that binge-watching has not only psychological but also emotional effects. In particular, the fact that viewers develop emotional bonds and increase their empathy for characters while watching TV series for a long time constitutes another important dimension of this phenomenon (Kraut & Seay, 2006).

Social Interactions and Social Structures

Binge-watching is not only an individual behavior, but also has an impact on social interactions. Continuous viewing of media content can change the ways in which viewers interact socially. While traditional television viewing habits create social bonds between family and friends, binge-watching can become a more isolated experience. This is because this habit is usually a solitary activity and the viewer has an experience in their own inner world rather than social bonds (Lobato, 2019). However, social interactions between viewers have been reshaped as digital platforms have enabled viewers to interact with shows on social media and forums.

Digital media has changed not only the way content is watched but also the way it is produced. With the digitalization of media, series can be produced in a shorter period of time and the demands of viewers can be responded to more quickly. This has led to the adoption of a more dynamic and audience-centered approach to content production (Mikos, 2016).

The evolution of binge-watching is directly related to the rise of digital media and this habit affects both social structure and individual psychology. Digital media platforms have drastically changed the way audiences access content and the speed at which they watch it. Television viewing habits have undergone a significant transformation with digitalization and this transformation has shaped viewers' behaviors, emotional and social interactions. Binge-watching has not only affected individuals' habits of watching content for entertainment purposes, but also the way media is produced and distributed.

THE RISE of DIGITAL MEDIA and THE EVOLUTION of BINGE-WATCHING

Mass media not only mixes art, politics, religion, philosophy and commerce harmoniously and often underhandedly, but also reduces these cultural spheres to a common condition, a commercial form (Yurdigül et al., 2015).

Digital media has developed rapidly over the last few decades and has radically changed media consumption habits. The widespread availability of the internet, the rise of digital platforms and the rapid delivery of content in digital environments have fundamentally changed people's relationship with media. As a result of this transformation, the viewing habit called binge-watching has emerged. Binge-watching is defined as binge-watching a season of a TV series or movie, and has been popularized by the viewing experience offered by digital media platforms. The emergence of this concept is directly related to audience demands in a digitized media environment, and over time this phenomenon has reshaped media viewing habits.

The Rise of Digital Media

Digital media underwent a major transformation process with the widespread use of the internet in the late 1990s. In the early 2000s, the internet began to offer an important alternative to traditional media forms such as television and radio. In this period, the distribution and accessibility of digital content became one of the biggest factors changing the habits of media consumers. With the widespread use of the Internet, television viewing habits have also been reshaped through digital platforms. YouTube, in particular, has emerged as a medium where video sharing has increased rapidly and the production and consumption of digital content has become more democratized (Lotz, 2014). However, the rapid development of the internet has also brought about a significant diversity in content production. Instead of traditional television channels, digital platforms have gained great interest with the different types of content and the viewing experience they offer to viewers regardless of time and space.

In 2007, Netflix's move to an online streaming model was one of the turning points in the rise of digital media. Netflix abandoned the DVD rental model and offered the opportunity to watch TV series and movies online without interruption. This move signaled the future of digital media platforms. By streaming content all at once, Netflix allowed viewers to consume content at their own pace, in contrast to traditional television viewing habits. In 2013, Netflix began producing original series, changing the power dynamics between content producers and digital platforms (Lobato, 2019). Netflix's strategy also paved the way for the emergence of the "binge-watching" phenomenon. People could now watch entire seasons in one go without having to wait weeks between episodes. Since the content offered by digital media platforms can be customized according to individual preferences, it has given the viewer more control.

Following Netflix, Amazon Prime Video, Hulu and many other digital platforms have offered content with a similar model, providing viewers with more and more options every day. This development has accelerated the digitalization of television viewing habits and enabled the rise of digital media platforms. While digital platforms encourage quick viewing of their content, they also offer personalized content recommendations by continuously monitoring and analyzing viewers' viewing preferences. This personalized experience enabled viewers to watch more content and encouraged binge-watching habits in the long run (Mikos, 2016).

Evolution of Binge-Watching

Binge-watching is a viewing habit that has become popular and rapidly expanding with digital media. However, this habit actually derives from an earlier form of viewing. In the mid-20th century, with the growing popularity of television series, viewers would wait for the weekends between episodes to catch up. However, this kind of viewing habit was often formed by the accumulation of weekly episode broadcasts. The "full season" and "binge-watching" options offered by digital platforms have allowed this kind of habit to evolve. While at first it was only common among a small audience, over time it has become a worldwide phenomenon.

When Netflix began streaming its original series in 2013, binge-watching really took off. In particular, shows such as House of Cards and Orange is the New Black released their entire seasons at the same time, giving viewers the opportunity to watch content in one go (Creeber, 2015). This strategy is one of the clearest examples of how digital platforms are changing content viewing habits. Younger viewers, in particular, have started to want to spend time binge-watching a series season in order to minimize the time between starting and finishing a series. By enabling uninterrupted viewing of content, digital media platforms have extended viewers' time in front of the television.

Another important step in the evolution of binge-watching was the development of content recommendation algorithms by digital platforms. Netflix has developed a system that recommends what to watch next based on viewers' viewing history. This prevented viewers from constantly searching for new content and encouraged them to watch the next episode, which was necessary to complete a season (Mikos, 2016). These recommendation algorithms play a major role in encouraging binge-watching habits.

The evolution of binge-watching is not only due to the ways in which content is delivered; the social and psychological effects of this habit must also be taken into account. Especially in the early 2010s, a number of studies were conducted on the health effects of this habit and its links to social relationships. Studies have shown that binge-watching has both positive and negative effects. Many studies have pointed out that binge-watching increases the release of dopamine by affecting brain chemistry, thereby creating an addiction-like effect (Kubey & Csikszentmihalyi, 2002). This has led to a tendency for viewers to watch more and more content.

On the other hand, binge-watching has also been observed to have effects on social relationships. It has been reported that individuals who binge-watch television often disengage from social ties and tend towards solitary viewing experiences. Binge-watching can increase feelings of loneliness and limit social interactions, especially among younger viewers (Kraut & Seay, 2006). However, digital platforms also encourage online social interactions among viewers. Viewers can form communities by interacting on social media platforms or various forums about the shows they watch.

BINGE-WATCHING and MEDIA CONSUMPTION HABITS

Binge-watching is a rapidly evolving and reshaping aspect of media consumption habits in the digital age. This phenomenon is directly related to the uninterrupted viewing experiences offered by television and digital media platforms. While binge-watching a season of a TV series or movie used to mean binge-watching only a few episodes, today this habit has started to have a deeper cultural, social and psychological impact. In order to understand how binge-watching has transformed social norms and individual viewing habits as well as changes in the media industry, it is necessary to consider this phenomenon in a broader context. Under this heading, the effects of binge-watching on media consumption habits, viewers' behavior, social dynamics and the transformation of media production will be examined.

Digitalization of Media Consumption Habits

Traditional media consumption habits were limited to the placement of television programs in specific time slots and weekly broadcast streams. In this period, when television series were considered as programs that viewers watched in a certain time period, viewers' viewing preferences were generally shaped by the broadcast stream. However, with the rise of digital platforms, these habits have undergone a major change. Digital platforms allow viewers to access content without time constraints, giving them the freedom to decide when and how to watch (Rubenking & Bracken, 2021). This new way of watching has created a significant shift in media consumption habits.

Digital platforms such as Netflix have changed the weekly episode format of traditional television by offering full seasons of content to viewers at the same time. This has reshaped the way viewers start and finish a series. With the launch of Netflix's original series in 2013, the phenomenon of binge-watching has spread to a wider audience (Jenner, 2017). These platforms made content fully accessible, allowing viewers to access content in a continuous way. This made it easier for viewers to continue watching for long periods of time, which naturally reinforced binge-watching habits.

The rise of binge-watching has led to significant changes not only in terms of content delivery, but also in viewer behavior. Digital platforms have enabled viewers to receive more recommendations based solely on the content they watch, by presenting content to the viewer in a personalized way. This is a factor that encourages viewers to spend more time on a TV series or movie and accelerates the viewing of content. This has also affected social media and online viewing habits, with viewers sharing and discussing TV series and movies on social networks (Niemeyer, 2014). This interaction has reshaped the social dimension of media consumption habits

The Effects of Binge-Watching on Audience Behavior

Binge-watching has influenced the way audiences approach content and the behaviors they exhibit while watching it. Binge-watching is more than just a habit of watching a TV show or a movie; it is also redefining the relationship viewers have with media and their viewing experiences. This transformation in the way they interact with media has led viewers to seek more in-depth content and make more emotional connections with the content they watch. In addition, binge-watching offers a more intense experience as the viewer watches a large amount of content in a short period of time. This can lead to both positive and negative psychological effects.

Many studies have shown that binge-watching can have psychological effects on viewers. The most notable of these effects is the strengthening of emotional attachment to media content as the frequency of viewing increases. Empathic bonds with series characters may increase the viewer's interest in the content they watch, which may trigger continuous viewing behavior (Mikos, 2016). On the other hand, the habit of binge-watching can negatively affect the viewer's physical and mental health. Watching television for long periods of time can encourage a sedentary lifestyle, which can lead to health problems such as obesity, especially among young viewers (Creeber, 2015). In addition, prolonged viewing can lead to reduced social interactions, increased feelings of loneliness and a sense of isolation that can be associated with psychological problems (Kraut & Seay, 2006).

Binge-Watching and Social Interactions

The social effects of binge-watching are also remarkable. The content offered by digital platforms has changed the forms of social interaction between viewers. In traditional forms of media, families or groups of friends would gather together to watch television, a habit that encouraged social interaction. With digital media, however, the viewing experience has become more individualized. Binge-watching is often a solitary activity, which has increased the tendency for viewers to watch content alone. This can lead to a more isolated experience (Rubenking & Bracken, 2021).

However, online communities offered by digital media platforms have increased social interaction among viewers. For example, discussing a TV series on social media platforms while watching it offers the opportunity to communicate with other viewers, suggest and discuss new content. This allows viewers to share and interact in a community with content that they previously watched alone. This social interaction has made media consumption habits more collective and creates a shared experience among viewers (Niemeyer, 2014).

Change in Media Production and Binge-Watching

Binge-watching has not only influenced audience behavior, but also transformed the processes of media production. Digital platforms follow a different production process than traditional television channels. While television series are usually broadcast in weekly episodes, digital platforms offer all episodes of a season at the same time. This requires content producers to construct shows and movies differently. By focusing on providing a holistic experience, digital platforms aim to ensure that the audience stays engaged with a season from start to finish (Jenner, 2017).

Binge-watching's impact on media production has particularly changed the form of storytelling. In traditional television series, the weekly episodes were often linked to the previous ones and the viewer waited in anticipation of what would happen next. Digital platforms, however, have changed this structure. Series now more independently present different sub-stories or characters in each episode, making it easier for viewers to consume content more quickly and seamlessly. It is also common to see the use of techniques such as cliffhangers in a season, which remain connected to the viewer, as this encourages binge-watching to continue.

CULTURAL DIMENSIONS OF BINGE-WATCHING

Binge-watching has become an important cultural phenomenon in recent years as part of digital media consumption. The rapid and uninterrupted viewing of television and digital media content has shaped not only viewers' relationship with media, but also cultural structures and social norms. The cultural dimensions of this phenomenon encompass many aspects of the media industry, from content production to audience behavior. The impact of binge-watching on global culture, its impact on viewers' daily lives, and the role of this habit in the cultural context require an in-depth analysis. While the content offered by digital media platforms enables the rapid spread of a global culture, how local cultures interact in the digital environment has also become an important area of research.

The Effects of Binge-Watching on Cultural Identity

Identity is a fundamental element that enables an individual to exist within the social system and to be positioned as a social being. In this context, identity, which is an important concept for individuals to gain a place in society and to define this system, makes it possible for the individual to be recognized and accepted in society (Akmeşe, 2020). Binge-watching has an important place as an activity that shapes individuals' cultural identities. Cultural identity refers to the ties that individuals establish with the society and culture they belong to, and media plays a major role in shaping this identity (Couldry & Hepp, 2017). Digital media, especially with the rise of streaming platforms, gives audiences the opportunity to construct their own cultural identity and present this identity to society through digital content. This leads to audiences using media content not only for entertainment purposes, but also as a means of self-expression and reinforcing their identities.

While digital media platforms make content globally accessible, they also allow local cultures to participate in global media. This enables specific cultural themes to be shared with international audiences through TV series and movies. Binge-watching makes it easier for viewers to connect with cultural themes by watching this content quickly and continuously. For example, TV series that feature the traditions, lifestyles or social issues of a particular culture allow viewers to learn more about that culture and internalize that knowledge. However, some content risks homogenization in the process of globalization of local cultures, which can lead to a reduction in cultural diversity (Tomlinson, 1999).

Digital Media and Cultural Hegemony

Another important cultural dimension of binge-watching is the hegemonic influence of the media industry. Digital platforms have great control over the production and distribution of content. These platforms offer content recommendations by monitoring user behavior, which in turn determines what kind of content viewers will be interested in. This mechanism can lead digital platforms to establish cultural hegemony. In particular, media giants such as Netflix and Amazon Prime create a global viewing experience by influencing viewers' cultural tastes. While this ensures universal viewing of content, it also paves the way for the imposition of certain cultural norms and values on a global audience (Artz, 2018).

Binge-watching is not only entertainment, but also a phenomenon that promotes the spread of cultural codes among viewers. On a global scale, certain cultural themes and lifestyles are disseminated through digital platforms. In particular, the fact that Hollywood productions reach a large audience around the world is one of the most obvious examples of this process of hegemony. However, while the spread of global content can create opportunities for local cultures and communities, it can also reduce the chances of local producers and content to compete in the global arena (Miller et al., 2005). This can make it difficult for media consumers to experience cultural diversity and create an environment of increasing monopolization in media content production.

Binge-Watching and Changing Social Norms

Binge-watching is a factor that transforms social norms and reshapes viewer behavior. While television viewing habits have historically been perceived as an activity that takes place over a certain period of time and when family or a group of friends gather together, with digital media, this habit has become more individualized. Binge-watching has led to a decrease in social interactions and an increase in viewers' habit of watching content alone. However, this individual experience can be offset by the opportunities for social interaction offered by digital platforms. In particular, social media and online forums encourage viewers to interact, share their thoughts and discuss their experiences with other viewers. This suggests that media consumption through digital platforms is changing social norms.

The social effects of binge-watching range from family relationships to work life. As people spend more and more time in front of the television, traditional family conversations and shared time together may diminish. In addition, the continuous viewing offered by digital platforms may lead viewers to take more time away from work and daily routines. This has led to debates in society on time management and work-life balance (Creeber, 2015). Furthermore, the negative effects of binge- watching on physical and mental health have also been discussed. Prolonged television viewing can lead to health problems such as obesity by encouraging a sedentary lifestyle.

Cultural Diversity and Binge-Watching

Digital platforms have the potential to increase cultural diversity on a global scale. Platforms such as Netflix offer content from different cultures to viewers around the world, creating a viewing experience that crosses cultural boundaries. Netflix's inclusion of content from different languages and cultures is an example of how cultural diversity can exist in the digital environment. At the same time, when global media producers broadcast content that deals with local cultures and issues, viewers can experience cultural differences. However, the global dissemination of this content may lead to the erosion or standardization of local cultures. In particular, the increase in cultural similarities with the globalization of media may lead to a decrease in cultural diversity.

Binge-watching encourages viewers to watch content from different cultures together, while at the same time creating challenges for the preservation of cultural heritage. Digital platforms can introduce local cultures to a global audience by rapidly delivering content from different cultures. However, the globalization of this content can be challenging for local producers and productions. The standardization of media content can limit the opportunities for local producers to promote unique cultural values and themes globally.

BINGE-WATCHING and MARKETING STRATEGIES in THE MEDIA INDUSTRY

Binge-watching has become a fundamental part of content consumption habits in the digital media landscape. This phenomenon refers to viewers binge-watching a season of a TV series or movie without interruption and has become even more widespread, especially with the "full season" streaming strategies offered by digital platforms. This behavior has greatly influenced the content production and marketing strategies of the media industry, changing the way they deliver media content in line with viewers' preferences. In particular, the content strategies of platforms such as Netflix, Amazon Prime and Hulu have been continuously developed to encourage the binge-watching habit and encourage the audience to watch more content. Under this heading, the place of the binge- watching phenomenon in the media industry and its impact on marketing strategies will be analyzed.

Binge-Watching and the Changing Dynamics of the Media Industry

Binge-watching has been an important factor in the evolution of the media industry. With the rise of digital platforms, traditional television viewing habits began to change. By offering viewers the entire season of a TV series or movie at the same time, these platforms have encouraged uninterrupted viewing of content based on a "full season". This viewing habit has also transformed the way television series and movie content are produced. While traditional television series encourage viewers to wait for the next episode with weekly broadcasts, digital platforms offer content in a way that allows viewers to watch content at their own pace and without interruption (Creeber, 2015). This has forced media producers to develop new content production methods. By making content constantly available, digital platforms encourage long-term viewing habits of viewers.

In 2013, Netflix started to release original series all at once, which led to the acceleration of the binge-watching habit (Jenner, 2017). This strategy has enabled viewers to engage more deeply with content and at the same time reshaped the way the media industry produces content. By enabling viewers to binge-watch content to complete a season, Netflix and similar platforms have increased the viewing time of content and gained more views. This strategy has increased viewers' loyalty to the platform, while at the same time providing content producers with a steady stream of viewers.

The Impact of Marketing Strategies on Binge-Watching

In order to understand how binge-watching has transformed marketing strategies in the media industry, it is necessary to look at how this phenomenon has impacted content consumption patterns. As binge-watching encourages viewers to watch content for longer periods of time and without interruption, the media industry has integrated this behavior into its marketing strategies to attract more viewers. These strategies have been implemented with the aim of making viewers more engaged with content by offering entire seasons at once, as opposed to releasing content on a regular basis (Rubenking & Bracken, 2021).

Digital platforms such as Netflix and Amazon Prime aim to keep viewers on their platforms for longer by adopting a “full season at once” strategy. This strategy aims to create a “seamless” viewing experience by offering viewers all content from a season at the same time. This type of marketing strategy encourages viewers to start watching the next episode as soon as they start a season. This allows viewers to watch more content before leaving the platform and increases their loyalty to the platform (Mikos, 2016). Netflix's algorithms aim to ensure continuous content viewing by providing content recommendations based on users' viewing history. This personalized recommendation system makes it easier for viewers to adapt not only to a series, but also to the habit of watching continuous content.

Binge-watching's impact on marketing strategies is not limited to the way content is presented. The phenomenon has also influenced campaigns and advertising strategies for the audience. Media companies promote content on social media and other digital platforms in order to increase viewers' interest in the content. Such marketing strategies make binge-watching more attractive and extend the time viewers spend on the platform.

Binge-Watching and Audience Engagement

Binge-watching has created an important strategic opportunity for the media industry to increase audience engagement. As digital platforms offer viewers the opportunity to binge-watch content, their loyalty to the platform increases. While this has enabled media companies to build long- term audiences, it has also transformed viewers' media consumption habits. Platforms such as Netflix, Amazon Prime and Hulu have adopted a strategy of continuous content delivery to ensure that viewers spend more time on the platform. This strategy has encouraged viewers to watch content without interruption, while at the same time making the media industry's marketing efforts more targeted.

Netflix's algorithms track users' viewing habits and provide them with personalized content recommendations. This is an important marketing tool that keeps viewers watching more content. By providing content recommendations based on the viewer's tastes, the algorithms encourage them to stay on the platform longer. In addition to increasing viewer engagement, this allows content producers to generate more revenue (Rubenking & Bracken, 2021). Moreover, as viewers will naturally want to watch the next season once they finish a season, continuous delivery of content becomes an effective strategy to increase the platform's viewership.

The Changing Face of Marketing and Advertising Strategies

Binge-watching's impact on the media industry has transformed advertising and marketing strategies. Traditional television viewing habits often required viewers to be exposed to advertisements. However, on digital platforms, content is often presented ad-free or with limited ad slots. This has changed advertisers' relationship with the media industry. Advertising strategies have become more creative and integrated as part of content production than established ad formats. For example, platforms such as Netflix combine their TV series and movies with sponsored content and branded collaborations to increase advertising revenues (Jenner, 2017).

The digital age, data mining, and efforts towards cable broadcasting have led to the replacement of mass marketing with personalized marketing (Yılmaz, 2017, p. 263). However, media companies are also making effective use of social media platforms to enable viewers to interact more while watching content. Social media has become an important tool for promoting content and engaging with audiences. Binge-watching habit encourages viewers to participate in discussions, comment on content and discover new content on social media after completing the content. This creates a dynamic that strengthens media companies' marketing strategies while increasing interest in their content (Mikos, 2016).

BINGE-WATCHING and CINEMA: NEW WATCHING EXPERIENCES

Binge-watching has become a rapidly growing cultural phenomenon with the proliferation of digital media platforms. Initially defined as the binge-watching of television series, this habit has become a broader concept over time and has spread to all visual media content, including cinema. Binge-watching's impact on cinema has radically altered audience experiences, especially with the transformation of digital content distribution methods. With the transition from movie theaters to digital platforms, binge-watching has played an important role in the evolution of viewing patterns, creating a new viewing experience that has reshaped the dynamics of cinema.

Cinema and Digital Platforms: New Viewing Experiences

Binge-watching has also transformed movie-going habits. The traditional cinema experience is based on audiences sharing a certain amount of time by watching a movie in front of a large screen. While movie theaters offer audiences the opportunity to have a shared experience as a group, digital platforms have made this experience more individualized and flexible. The collective viewing experience offered by movie theaters has transformed into individual viewing habits with digital media. People now have the opportunity to watch the movie they want at home, on their own devices, whenever they want.

While cinema is known for its long-form films and intense dramatic structures, the content offered on digital platforms is often shaped by shorter, faster-paced series with more episodes. This has created a significant change in the way cinema connects with the audience. The rapid development of content, especially in the series genre, has questioned the power of cinema to present long-lasting and in-depth stories. However, in order to adapt to the audience habits of digital platforms, the cinema industry has started to offer feature-length films on digital platforms. For example, Netflix has begun to question audiences' habits of watching movies in theaters, as it offers its original productions directly on the platform instead of screening them in movie theaters (Creeber, 2015).

Much of the content offered by digital platforms is structured in a way that encourages the viewer to watch selected content sequentially. This has increased viewers' tendency to watch continuous content and reshaped their feature film viewing habits. Cinema is no longer an event that can only be watched in theaters, but can now be watched on digital platforms. This transformation has led to content being offered in longer formats over time, and to the "transformation of feature films into series". Netflix's streaming of its original content and big-budget film projects on digital platforms has increased the impact of cinema in the digital environment (Jenner, 2017).

Digitalization of Cinema: Cultural and Artistic Change

The digitalization of cinema has changed not only viewing habits but also the way films are produced. The rise of digital technologies has radically changed the production process of motion pictures. Films can now be shot more quickly and visual effects are becoming more extensive and effective. In addition, digital platforms reach a wider audience by offering different types of content. This has led to an increased interest in cinema and a shift in film production towards more diverse themes (Rubenking & Bracken, 2021).

The effects of binge-watching on cinema have also changed the cultural dimension of cinema. Especially long-form series and miniseries have gained a large audience by adopting cinematic narrative techniques. The cinematic narrative forms of series content have become comparable to the movies watched in movie theaters. However, the content offered by digital platforms aims to create the same effects as movies watched in movie theaters. In these new forms of media, the audience is provided with an "uninterrupted" experience. This has reshaped audiences' approach to cinema and led to an increase in the cultural impact of digital platforms.

The Fusion of Cinema and Digital Media: Innovative Viewing Experiences

Binge-watching has merged with digital media as well as cinema to create new viewing experiences. While this experience has strengthened viewers' attachment to movies and TV series, it has also transformed the way the media industry produces and delivers content. Digital media offers viewers a viewer-centered experience that not only provides them with content, but also directs them to it. Binge-watching has made this experience more personalized by binge-watching content and increased viewers' engagement with it. Cinema has found its place in this new viewing experience and has been reshaped by the feature-length content offered by digital platforms (Lobato, 2017).

With the digitalization of cinema, filmmakers have started to produce more innovative and creative projects by taking advantage of the freedom offered by digital platforms. Platforms such as Netflix and Amazon Prime have produced big-budget projects by adopting a cinematic structure in content production and have enabled the integration of cinema into the digital environment. These projects have enabled the reinterpretation of cinematic language through digital platforms and the merger of cinema and digital media (Jenner, 2017).

Importance and Purpose of the Study

Binge-watching symbolizes a new dimension of media consumption in recent years. The "bingeable" content offered by digital media platforms encourages viewers to binge-watch content. The importance of this phenomenon is not only related to entertainment habits, but also to its effects on social structures, individual psychology and the media industry. With the growth of digital media platforms, the rapidly changing modes of production, distribution and viewing of media content have reshaped societies' viewing habits.

The aim of the study is to understand how the binge-watching habit has evolved in the digital age and to examine the social, cultural and psychological effects of this phenomenon in depth. Existing studies in the literature reveal that binge-watching is not only an entertainment habit, but also has significant psychological and social implications. In particular, the focus will be on how this phenomenon shapes individual psychology, social interactions and cultural norms.

Method

The research will adopt a qualitative approach based on a literature review to understand the evolution and effects of the binge-watching phenomenon. In contrast to quantitative analysis methods, a more in-depth literature analysis will be conducted to understand the social, individual and cultural dimensions of this phenomenon. The literature review will examine studies on the impact of digital media platforms on user habits and the psychological and social effects of binge-watching. This will bring together existing understandings of the topic to understand how the phenomenon has taken shape and under what factors it has evolved.

The main source of the research will be scientific articles, books and academic journals on media and digitalization. In particular, studies on media consumption and audience behaviors will address how digitalization transforms the social structure. The theories in the literature will illuminate the behavioral tendencies that individuals develop while watching TV series and the effects of media content on these tendencies.

Limitations

The limitations of the study are related to the fact that the research is based on a literature review only. The fact that the studies in the literature review are based on available time and geographical regions may limit the universal validity of the research. Furthermore, the effects of digital media platforms may differ in different cultural contexts; therefore, this research will be limited to the existing literature on digitized media consumption habits within a specific cultural framework. The study will only analyze academic texts without collecting individual user data or conducting quantitative analyses.

Population and Sample

The research is based on a large population of individuals who watch content on digital media. However, the research focuses on existing studies in the literature on the evolution of content viewing habits and their social impact. The sample of the research will be based on research and publications on digital media platforms based on the literature review. The sample will be limited to global media consumption studies and literature on audience behavior.

Netflix and Binge-Watching: An Analysis on Audience Behavior and Content Viewing Habits

As the pioneer of digital media platforms, Netflix has played an important role in the development of content consumption habits and binge-watching habits. The platform has provided viewers with an uninterrupted viewing experience by offering all seasons of content at once, thus encouraging the binge-watching phenomenon. This research aims to analyze the content viewing habits and behaviors of individuals who actively use Netflix. This analysis is an attempt to understand the impact of the platform on viewers and how it transforms their content viewing habits.

Netflix and Digital Content Consumption

Netflix introduced an innovation that shook traditional television viewing habits by switching to online video streaming in 2007 (Creeber, 2015). Unlike traditional television broadcasts, which require users to watch in a specific time frame, the content offered by Netflix is completely under the viewer's control. Users can watch the content they want, when they want, and watch entire seasons in one go. This allows viewers to engage with content more quickly and watch a TV series or movie from start to finish quickly. In 2013, when Netflix started streaming all seasons of its original series at once, the foundations of the binge-watching habit were laid (Jenner, 2017).

Netflix's strategy encouraged viewers to binge-watch an entire season of a TV series and developed an alternative model to the traditional weekly episode release. By offering an uninterrupted viewing experience, Netflix's content has led viewers to watch more content and stay on the platform longer. This has created a significant transformation in the evolution of viewer behavior. Binge- watching habits have not only become an entertainment habit, but have also affected media consumption patterns, audience relations and the functioning of the media industry.

Audience Behavior and Binge-Watching Habits

The impact of binge-watching on audience behavior has led to more intense and continuous media consumption. Netflix users are becoming more attached to the shows they watch and binge- watching these shows deepens their interest in the content. Binge-watching often leads to a viewer's prolonged engagement with a piece of content, which in turn leads to a stronger emotional connection with a character or story (Mikos, 2016). To strengthen these bonds, Netflix strategically designs its content and presents it in a way that makes it easy for the viewer to move on to the next episode. This behavioral feature offers the viewer a kind of "consumption" experience; the viewer experiences a sense of satisfaction by consuming content quickly.

The psychological effects of binge-watching can lead to an addiction-like behavior as well as the development of emotional attachments to the content. Jansz and Tanis (2007), in their study examining the psychological effects of online media consumption, stated that people who watch content for a long time, the satisfaction they get from the content affects their brain chemistry and triggers the desire to watch more content. Netflix's content recommendation algorithms reinforce this cycle by constantly recommending new content based on viewers' viewing history. These recommendations enable viewers to spend more time on the platform and consume content quickly.

Demographic Characteristics and Binge-Watching

Individuals who actively use Netflix may have various demographic characteristics, such as different age groups, genders and social statuses. This demographic diversity plays an important role in understanding how binge-watching habits vary across different groups. Various studies show that factors such as age group and gender have an impact on individuals' binge-watching habits. For example, young adults have been found to watch more TV series and have a higher commitment to digital platforms (Creeber, 2015). It has also been observed that women generally spend more time with longer-form content such as dramas and romantic comedies, while men are more interested in action and science fiction genres (Rubenking & Bracken, 2021).

Social factors such as income and education level can also affect audience habits. Individuals with higher income levels tend to subscribe to more digital platforms and generally watch more content. In addition, individuals with higher levels of education are more likely to be more critical of media content and watch different types of content (Jenner, 2017). These factors provide important data to understand the effects of Netflix and similar digital platforms on the audience.

Netflix and Binge-Watching: Social and Cultural Dimensions

Netflix has become not only an entertainment platform but also a medium through which cultural and social norms are shaped. Binge-watching, as a form of behavior that affects social norms, can also change individuals' social interactions. Content viewing habits on digital platforms have changed when and how people interact with each other. For example, families who used to watch an episode of a TV series together, now prefer to watch it on their own devices. At the same time, however, the opportunities for social interaction offered by Netflix can offset this transformation. Netflix offers a variety of opportunities for its users to comment on the content they watch and share it on social media. This allows viewers to interact with each other on content.

Binge-watching has also changed viewers' perception of time. Binge-watching has transformed television viewing habits, which viewers have come to see as "part of the day". While this has changed viewers' expectations of media consumption, it has also allowed the media industry to reshape its content production and distribution strategies (Lobato, 2017).

Research shows that Netflix's effects on viewers are not limited to media consumption, but also shape their social and psychological behavior.

Amazon Prime Video and Binge-Watching: An Analysis of Audience Behavior and Content Viewing Habits

With the rise of digital media platforms, Amazon Prime Video has become one of the most important services transforming media consumption habits. This platform has further popularized binge-watching habits by offering viewers the opportunity to watch content without interruption. Users of Amazon Prime Video can access the content on the platform at their own pace, making the media consumption of viewers more independent.

The Rise of Amazon Prime Video and Content Consumption

As one of the major players in digital media streaming services, Amazon Prime Video, along with other platforms such as Netflix, represents a turning point in changing digital content consumption habits. At first, Amazon's video streaming service started as part of a shopping service, but it quickly evolved into an independent media platform and built a large audience. The content offered by Amazon Prime Video encourages binge-watching habits, especially with the ability to watch entire seasons at once. With every episode available, viewers can quickly watch TV series and movies from start to finish (Mikos, 2016). This freedom gives viewers the opportunity to consume content quickly, which increases user loyalty to the platform.

Prime Video uses content recommendation algorithms to provide continuous content recommendations based on viewers' preferences. These recommendations influence viewers' choices of TV shows and movies and encourage them to spend more time on the platform. This recommendation system, based on the content users watch, works as a strategy that reinforces binge- watching behaviors. Amazon's content strategy constantly offers new and engaging content to make viewers' content consumption faster and more intense (Creeber, 2015). These strategies create a dynamic that drives viewers to watch the full content and increases viewer engagement.

Amazon Prime Video and Binge-Watching Habits

Binge-watching refers to the habit of binge-watching a season of a TV series or movie, which has been particularly encouraged by the "full season" streaming offered by digital platforms. Amazon Prime Video is an important platform that makes this experience more attractive to users. Viewers' deep engagement with a piece of content is an important factor in the content offered by Amazon Prime Video. Binge-watching allows viewers to develop emotional attachments to content and build a stronger relationship with characters. This increases viewers' interest in a series or movie and leads them to spend more time on the platform (Jenner, 2017).

Binge-watching habits often lead to viewers becoming more intensely engaged with content, leading to longer viewing times and 'consumption' of media content. Amazon Prime Video offers entire seasons of its content in one place, allowing viewers to quickly watch a TV series or movie and at the same time find motivation to complete a season. Following Netflix, Amazon Prime Video has implemented a similar model, encouraging viewers to watch entire seasons in one session. This type of content delivery is a factor that reinforces binge-watching habits (Mikos, 2016).

Demographics and Amazon Prime Video Users

Amazon Prime Video is a platform that appeals to a wide demographic audience, and users come from different age groups, genders, education levels and social statuses. This diversity plays an important role in understanding how binge-watching habits vary across different groups and what factors shape viewer behavior. Various studies have found that age group and gender have an impact on binge-watching habits. Young adults, especially those between the ages of 18-34, spend more time on digital platforms and there is a marked increase in content consumption. Amazon Prime Video is very popular among young viewers, who have often developed binge-watching habits of digital content.

Gender is also an important factor. Research has shown that female viewers tend to watch more drama, romantic comedy and thriller content, while male viewers are more interested in action, science fiction and sports content (Rubenking & Bracken, 2021). These demographic characteristics are another important factor shaping the viewing habits of Amazon Prime Video users. Audience behavior can be further analyzed based on such demographic data, which helps to understand the time viewers spend on the platform and their interest in content types.

Factors such as income and education level can also have an impact on content consumption. Individuals with higher incomes tend to invest more in digital platforms and generally watch more content. At the same time, individuals with higher levels of education may prefer a wider variety of content. The wide variety of content offered by Amazon Prime Video allows viewers to discover different types of content and thus increase their viewing time (Creeber, 2015).

Amazon Prime Video and Cultural Influences

Binge-watching habits not only influence viewers' behavior, but also transform cultural dimensions. The content offered by Amazon Prime Video is a tool that allows viewers to explore content in different cultural contexts. In particular, viewers in different geographical regions can switch between content from their local culture and global popular culture. By offering a combination of multinational content and local productions, Amazon Prime Video allows viewers to experience cultural contexts in a broader perspective (Lobato, 2017).

The dissemination of cultural diversity through digital media enables individuals to become more familiar with different cultures. Many of Amazon Prime Video's original productions offer content that reflects local cultures. This content allows local viewers to share their own cultures with audiences around the world, while at the same time offering new cultural experiences to a global audience (Rubenking & Bracken, 2021).

Amazon Prime Video has an important place among digital media platforms and has transformed viewers' content viewing habits. Binge-watching habits have been supported by the platform's ability to watch all seasons at once, allowing viewers to build stronger connections to content. Analyses of audience behavior, demographic factors and social characteristics help us better understand the impact of the platform on its audience. From content production to audience engagement, Amazon Prime Video is transforming the digital media ecosystem and having a major impact on the future of the media industry.

Hulu and Binge-Watching: An Analysis of Audience Behavior and Content Viewing Habits

Hulu is an important content streaming service in the rapidly evolving world of digital media platforms, especially in the US. The platform plays an important role in changing viewer behavior and the development of binge-watching habits, as content can be watched without time constraints. The uninterrupted viewing experience offered by Hulu has deepened viewers' engagement with content, while at the same time reshaping the media consumption habits of the platform's audience.

Hulu and Digital Content Consumption

Since Hulu started offering digital content streaming services in 2007, it has had a significant impact on content consumption habits. While Hulu has enabled the digital streaming of content from television networks, it has also built a large audience with its original TV series and movie content. The content offered by Hulu allows viewers to watch content without interruption. In particular, the fact that the content is available all at once allows viewers to quickly complete a series or movie season (Mikos, 2016). This is an important factor that encourages binge-watching habits.

Hulu's "all season in one" streaming allows users to binge-watch content that they can watch whenever they want. This flexibility has made viewers' content consumption habits independent. With its content recommendation systems, Hulu recommends content based on viewers' previous viewings. This increases viewers' engagement with the content and makes them watch more content. In addition, Hulu offers the option to watch ad-supported content, which leads viewers to use the platform more frequently (Creeber, 2015).

Binge-Watching Habits and Audience Behavior

Binge-watching refers to the habit of watching an entire season of a TV show or movie in one session. By offering this experience to viewers, Hulu helps viewers build a stronger connection with content. Binge-watching allows viewers to spend more time with a piece of content, while at the same time strengthening their emotional connection to it. This habit leads viewers to binge-watch content and to seek out new content (Rubenking & Bracken, 2021). The fact that the content offered by Hulu can be watched in one session has led viewers to develop habits of continuous content viewing.

The psychological effects of binge-watching on viewers are not limited to the rapid consumption of content. Prolonged content viewing can affect a viewer's mood, which can help people avoid emotional experiences such as loneliness. Some studies on the psychological effects of online media consumption have found that people who watch intense content derive emotional satisfaction from it, which affects brain chemistry and triggers a desire to watch more. Hulu reinforces this addiction-like effect with its constant stream of content and recommendation systems.

Binge-watching has also been a habit that has changed social interactions. While digital platforms allow viewers to watch content on their own, their social interactions have taken a different form. Hulu encourages viewers to share content on social media and interact with other viewers. However, the social interactions of individuals who watch content alone may be limited. On the other hand, content discussions on platforms such as Hulu allow viewers to interact more with content and share it with other viewers (Jenner, 2017).

Demographics and Hulu Users

Hulu users represent a broad audience with different age groups, genders, education levels and geographical regions. Demographics are important factors influencing viewers' content consumption habits. Research shows that young viewers (especially between the ages of 18-34) are more interested in digital platforms and consume digital content intensively (Creeber, 2015). Hulu has been a popular platform among young viewers, who often share and discuss content through social media.

Gender plays a significant role in viewers' content preferences. It has been observed that female viewers are generally interested in genres such as dramas, romantic comedies and psychological thrillers. Male viewers, on the other hand, prefer action, science fiction and sports content. These demographic differences are an important factor in shaping Hulu's content delivery strategies (Rubenking & Bracken, 2021). In addition, income and education levels can have an impact on viewers' engagement with the platform. Individuals with higher incomes tend to subscribe to more digital platforms and watch more content.

Hulu and Cultural Influences

Hulu is a platform that appeals to a large global audience. This allows viewers to interact with different cultural contexts and media content. Hulu bridges local content with global audiences and promotes cultural diversity. In particular, content from different geographies allows viewers to both explore their local culture and interact with global popular culture (Mikos, 2016). The diversity of content offered by Hulu helps the platform to create cultural interaction between viewers from different cultures.

Hulu is a platform that transforms viewer behavior and media consumption habits by offering instant and uninterrupted viewing of content. Binge-watching has become a habit that strengthens viewers' engagement with content and increases their viewing time. Hulu supports this habit, enabling viewers to engage more deeply with content. Demographic factors play an important role in shaping viewers' content viewing habits. Hulu's content strategies and recommendation systems encourage viewers to watch content continuously and increase viewer engagement. Hulu's content delivery has reshaped viewer behavior and radically changed media consumption habits.

BINGE-WATCHING IN THE FUTURE: TECHNOLOGICAL INNOVATIONS AND NEW CONSUMPTION HABITS

Binge-watching has gained momentum with the emergence of digital media platforms and has radically changed the way audiences approach media content. This phenomenon has transformed not only viewing habits but also a wide range of media production processes and audience interaction. It is expected that binge-watching will further deepen and evolve in the future. It is a fact that artificial intelligence contributes to the reshaping of life by providing creative solutions to the problems encountered in all areas of daily life (Gervais, 2019, cited in Özkemahlı & Er, 2024, p.132).Factors such as technological innovations, the development of new media platforms, artificial intelligence and personalized content recommendations will further shape audience behavior and give rise to new consumption habits

Until now, one of the main triggers of binge-watching has been the delivery of content at the pace of the viewer. Digital platforms have made content immediately available, allowing the viewer to watch it whenever they want. However, the future of this process will be shaped by the introduction of more sophisticated technologies and algorithms. One of the most important innovations offered by technology will be personalized content recommendations and more interactive viewing experiences. Platforms such as Netflix, Amazon Prime and Hulu already make content recommendations by observing users' viewing habits. In the future, thanks to artificial intelligence and advanced algorithms, these recommendations will become much more unique and tailored to the viewer's mood, time and content. In particular, there may come a time when AI-supported systems will be able to read the viewer's emotional reactions and recommend the most appropriate content. This kind of personalization could further influence viewer behavior and reinforce binge-watching habits.

Future technological innovations will change not only the way media content is viewed, but also the way it is produced. Interactive TV series and movies can make content consumption more participatory by providing experiences where viewers can intervene in the story and change the fate of characters. This kind of content production can lead to viewers engaging with content for longer periods of time. Netflix's interactive movies, such as Bandersnatch, are an early example of this kind of experience. The ability of viewers to make choices about content and shape their own stories represents a major shift in media consumption habits. This kind of media will enable viewers to build a stronger connection with content and may increase their propensity to watch content continuously. However, the impact of augmented reality (AR) and virtual reality (VR) technologies on media consumption will also be significant in the future. AR and VR technologies can offer viewers the opportunity to experience content in a more interactive and realistic way, encouraging longer and more in-depth content consumption.

Binge-watching has not only become an entertainment habit, but has also changed forms of social interaction. From watching content on their own, viewers have formed online communities through digital platforms and started discussions about the content. These communities may become even stronger in the future. Social media platforms and digital media will enable viewers to instantly comment on a TV series or movie, share their opinions and interact about the content. Especially when content is shared on social media and goes viral, it will socialize the audience's media experience. In the future, media content will provide tools that enable viewers to share and create social experiences through the content they watch. This will create more interaction among the audience and allow individual viewing experiences to be socialized.

The future of binge-watching is not only about the viewing habits of the audience, but also about the forms of monetization of content. Digital platforms generate revenue through advertising and subscriptions. In the future, increased viewership of content will increase the revenues of media companies, which will allow platforms to further personalize their content strategies. Furthermore, increased competition between platforms may encourage more innovative and user-centered forms of content delivery. In particular, the use of micropayment systems could allow viewers to pay only for content they are interested in. Such a system could encourage binge-watching habits, enabling viewers to consume more content.

In addition to technological innovations, cultural change and social norms are also expected to play an important role in the evolution of binge-watching habits. Digital media has transcended traditional social norms, leading viewers to consume content not only for entertainment, but also for personal escape, emotional release or social interaction. In the future, society's view of digital media and binge-watching may reach a point where this habit will become even more accepted and widespread.

Binge-watching is no longer just a recreational activity, but an experience that fulfills the emotional and social needs of viewers. This shift will lead media producers to consider not only entertainment but also emotional fulfillment and social interaction when designing their content.

Binge-watching will become even more prevalent in the future and will be shaped by technological innovations that will profoundly affect audience behavior. Personalized content recommendations, interactive experiences, integration of AR and VR technologies, and increased social media interactions will change media consumption habits by enabling audiences to watch content for longer periods of time. Technological innovations and cultural change will lead to a deepening of binge- watching and the emergence of new consumption habits. By responding to viewers' expectations, digital platforms will reshape the future of the media industry and make viewers' content consumption experiences more personalized, interactive and integrated.

CONCLUSION

Binge-watching has become a phenomenon that has spread rapidly with the rise of digital media platforms and radically changed media consumption habits. Platforms such as Netflix, Amazon Prime Video and Hulu have become important tools that encourage binge-watching, as they offer viewers instant and uninterrupted access to content. Technological innovations, personalized content recommendations and interactive viewing experiences will lead to further expansion and evolution of binge-watching habits in the future. In particular, AI-powered content recommendation systems will take into account viewers' viewing history and preferences, encouraging them to watch more content. In the future, systems that analyze viewers' moods and behaviors to provide them with more specific content may reinforce binge-watching as a habit. Integrating these technologies will extend viewers' time on the platform and increase their engagement with content.

Binge-watching's impact on the media industry has changed not only the way content is presented, but also the processes of content production. Digital platforms offer entire seasons of content at once, encouraging viewers to consume content quickly. This represents a major departure from traditional television broadcasting and transforms how media producers create and deliver their content. Moreover, the rise of interactive content and new forms of media will enable viewers to have a more participatory experience and deepen their engagement with the media. However, this type of content enables audiences to consume content not only for entertainment purposes but also for their psychological and emotional needs, changing the social dimension of media consumption.

Binge-watching's impact on audience behavior has led to more intense engagement, more content viewing, and changing patterns of social interaction. Content discussions on digital platforms further strengthen viewers' attachment to content and reshape social interactions. In particular, content sharing and comments on social media allow viewers to discuss TV series and movies in more depth and interact with each other. This situation takes individual viewing experiences to a social dimension and creates a collective experience around media content.

The combination of technological innovations and social interactions will lead to a greater prevalence of binge-watching in the future, reshaping viewers' relationships with media content. Advanced algorithms and personalized content recommendations will extend the time viewers spend on the platform, making media consumption habits more intense and continuous. In the future, the integration of new technologies such as augmented reality and virtual reality will offer viewers a more interactive and in-depth media experience, leading to a more participatory binge-watching experience. This will further consolidate the impact of digital platforms by increasing viewers' engagement with media content.

Binge-watching, together with the innovative content streaming systems offered by digital media platforms and technological developments, has radically changed the media consumption habits of audiences. This change has become an important dynamic shaping the future of the media industry. While digital platforms enable audiences to interact with content more deeply, they are also transforming content production processes. Future technological innovations will make binge- watching an even more integrated and interactive experience, making viewers' behavior more personalized and intense. These developments will pave the way for structural changes in the digital media and entertainment industry and completely redefine the audience's relationship with media.

REFERENCES

Akmeşe, E. (2020). An analysis on the existential crisis of the individual in the context of the dialectics of othering: Majority 2010. *Middle Black Sea Journal of Communication Studies*, *5*(1), 57–64.

Artz, L. (2018). *Global Media Practices and Cultural Hegemony: Growing*. Harvesting, and Marketing the Consuming Audience., DOI: 10.1163/9789004364417_003

Bayraktar, R. (2020). İyileştirme Kuramı Bağlamında Geleneksel TV'den IPTV'ye Dönüşen İzleyici Tercihleri: Literatür Üzerine Teorik Bir İnceleme. *Atatürk İletişim Dergisi*, (19), 79–93. DOI: 10.32952/atauniiletisim.702436

Couldry, N., & Hepp, A. (2017). *The Mediated Construction of Reality*. Polity Books. Creeber, G. (2015). *The Television Genre Book,* Bloomsbury Publishing, UK.

Jansz, J., & Tanis, M. (2007). Appeal of playing online first person shooter games. *Cyberpsychology & Behavior, 10*(1), 133–136. DOI: 10.1089/cpb.2006.9981 PMID: 17305460

Jansz, J., & Tanis, M. (2007). The Social and Psychological Impact of Online Gaming. *Journal of Media Psychology, 12*(3), 201–212.

Jenner, M. (2017). *Netflix and the Reinvention of Television*. In *Reinventing Television* (pp. 35-49). Cambridge University Press.

Kotan, S. (2024). *Digital Apocalypse Narrative in Cinema Specific to the Movie "Leave the World Behind". Innovative Research in Communication Sciences 1* (Durur, E. K., Yılmaz, A., & Cinisli, Z., Eds.). Gazi Bookstore.

Kraut, R.E., & Seay, A.F. (2006). Project massive: the social and psychological impact of online gaming.

Kubey, R., & Csikszentmihalyi, M. (2002). Television Addiction is No Mere Metaphor. *Scientific American, 286*(5), 74–81. DOI: 10.1038/scientificamerican0202-74 PMID: 11828703

Lobato, R. (2019). *Netflix Nations: The Geography of Digital Distribution*. New York University Press. DOI: 10.18574/nyu/9781479895120.001.0001

Lotz, A. (2016). The Paradigmatic Evolution of U.S. Television and the Emergence of Internet- Distributed Television. Revista ICONO14. Revista científica de Comunicación y Tecnologías emergentes. 14. 122. .DOI: 10.7195/ri14.v14i2.993

Mikos, L. (2016). Digital Media Platforms and the Use of TV Content: Binge Watching and Video-on- Demand in Germany. *Media and Communication*, *4*(3), 154–161. DOI: 10.17645/mac.v4i3.542

Miller, T.. (2005). *Television Studies: Theories and Approaches*. British Film Institute.

Niemeyer, K. (2014). Introduction: Media and Nostalgia. In Niemeyer, K. (Ed.), *Media and Nostalgia*. DOI: 10.1057/9781137375889_1

Özkemahlı, K. K., & Er, M. H. (2024). *Yapay Zekâ Destekli Fotoğrafik Yaklaşım: Portre ve Mekân Temelinde Mustafa Kemal Atatürk Fotoğraflarının Yeniden Üretilmesi*. Disiplinlerarası Sanat Pratikleri II, Detay Yayıncılık.

Rubenking, B., & Bracken, C. C. (2021). Binge watching and serial viewing: Comparing new media viewing habits in 2015 and 2020. *Addictive Behaviors Reports*, *14*, 100356. DOI: 10.1016/j.abrep.2021.100356 PMID: 34124334

Tomlinson, J. (1999). *Globalization and Culture*. University of Chicago Press.

Yılmaz, R. (2017). Structural Transformation of Advertising Narrative in Turkey in the Digital Age.

Yurdigül, Y., et al. (2015). Frankfurt Okulu'nda Birey ve Toplum: İnsanın Şeyleşmesi ve Kültürün Metalaşması Üzerine Eleştirel Okumalar, *Atatürk Üniversitesi Sosyal Bilimler Enstitüsü Dergisi 2015 19 (2)*, s. 97-110

ADDITIONAL READING

Ferchaud, A. (2021). *Binge and bingeability: The antecedents and consequences of binge-watching behavior*. Routledge.

Flayelle, M., Maurage, P., Di Lorenzo, K. R., Vögele, C., & Billieux, J. (2020). Binge-watching: What do we know so far? A first systematic review of the evidence. *Current Addiction Reports*, *7*(1), 44–60. DOI: 10.1007/s40429-020-00299-8

Gabbiadini, A., Baldissarri, C., Valtorta, R. R., Durante, F., & Mari, S. (2021). Loneliness, escapism, and identification with media characters: An exploration of the psychological factors underlying binge-watching tendency. *Frontiers in Psychology*, *12*, 785970. DOI: 10.3389/fpsyg.2021.785970 PMID: 35069369

Hamilton, J. (2016). Television Beyond the Screen: The Impact of Digital Platforms on Viewing Habits. *International Journal of Medical Students*, *12*(3), 209–224.

Harris, M. A., & Stevens, E. L. (2018). Exploring the Phenomenon of Binge-Watching: A Social and Psychological Perspective. *Media Psychology*, *20*(1), 35–56.

Mendelsohn, D. (2019). *The Binge Watcher's Guide to the New Television*. Penguin Books.

Nieborg, D. B., & Poell, T. (2018). The Platformization of Cultural Production: The Intermediary Role of Digital Platforms in the Cultural Industries. *Media Culture & Society*, *40*(4), 1–21.

O'Leary, K. (2018). The Changing Nature of Television and the Rise of Binge-Watching. *Journal of Digital Media & Policy*, *9*(2), 151–167.

Starosta, J. A., & Izydorczyk, B. (2020). Understanding the phenomenon of binge-watching—A systematic review. *International Journal of Environmental Research and Public Health*, *17*(12), 4469. DOI: 10.3390/ijerph17124469 PMID: 32580289

Walton-Pattison, E., Dombrowski, S. U., & Presseau, J. (2018). "Just one more episode": Frequency and theoretical correlates of television binge watching. *Journal of Health Psychology*, *23*(1), 17–24. DOI: 10.1177/1359105316643379 PMID: 27106091

KEY TERMS AND DEFINITIONS

Binge-Watching: Binge-watching refers to the habit of watching an entire season of a show or a movie in one sitting. Digital media platforms encourage this behavior by offering entire seasons at once. Viewers form stronger connections to the storylines by watching content in one go. This habit has become widespread with the continuous content flow provided by streaming services. Binge-watching makes media consumption more intense and continuous.

Digital Media Consumption: Digital media consumption refers to consuming content through digital platforms. The widespread use of the internet and mobile devices has rapidly increased this consumption. Users can now access content anytime and anywhere. This shift has accelerated the transition from traditional media formats to digital media. Digital media has made access to content more flexible for users.

Streaming Platforms: Streaming platforms are services that provide digital content delivery over the internet. Platforms like Netflix, Hulu, and Amazon Prime Video allow viewers to watch content instantly. These platforms do not require physical media and offer immediate access to content. With these platforms, watching digital content has become easier and faster. Streaming services have fundamentally changed television and movie-watching habits.

Viewer Engagement: Viewer engagement refers to how viewers interact with the content they consume. Viewers comment on, share, and discuss content on social media, which increases interaction. This engagement leads to more views and strengthens viewer loyalty. Viewer engagement is enhanced by features provided by digital platforms to foster greater participation. It makes the viewing experience more social and dynamic.

Personalized Content: Personalized content refers to recommendations tailored to viewers based on their past viewing preferences and behaviors. Digital platforms use algorithms to suggest content suited to the viewer's tastes. These recommendations are shaped by the types of shows and movies the viewer has previously watched. Personalized content suggestions encourage viewers to stay longer on the platform and watch more content. This method makes the viewing experience more personalized and relevant.

Interactive Media: Interactive media is a form of media that allows viewers to actively engage with the content. Viewers can make choices, intervene in the storyline, or influence events within the content. Unlike traditional passive viewing experiences, interactive media is more participatory. Interactive media appears in various formats like video games and interactive series. Viewers have a deeper experience with this type of content.

Media Industry Trends: Media industry trends refer to new patterns in media production and consumption. Digital platforms have transformed every process from content creation to distribution. The increasing popularity of streaming services has caused traditional television broadcasts to fall behind. New media formats are changing the way media companies present content. These trends shape the evolution of viewer behavior and the future of the media industry.

Chapter 6
TRT's International Digital Platform "Tabii" and Transmission of Turkish Culture Through TV Series

Ayşegül Akaydın Aydın
https://orcid.org/0000-0001-5772-4008
İstanbul Aydin University, Turkey

ABSTRACT

This study examines the role of the TRT-established digital platform Tabii in the representation and promotion of Turkish culture in response to the growing cultural hegemony imposed by international streaming services, particularly Netflix. Drawing upon theoretical frameworks such as Antonio Gramsci's concept of cultural hegemony and Adorno and Horkheimer's culture industry, the article investigates how digital platforms have become central to the transmission of cultural narratives. The study focuses on TRT's international digital platform "Tabii" and this platform's historical dramas available exclusively on the platform and utilizes Roland Barthes' semiotic approach to analyze cultural representations embedded in these narratives. The selected sample includes five series—Mahsusa Trablusgarb, Kızıl Elma, Akif, Rumi, and Hay Sultan—which span various epochs of Turkish history and foreground themes central to Turkish identity.

DOI: 10.4018/979-8-3373-1957-5.ch006

INTRODUCTION

Culture, which is a multidimensional notion, has made a name for itself with different characteristics throughout human history. Therefore, as a result of this multidimensionality, it is used in disciplines such as sociology, anthropology and also communication. Especially in order to make sense of the transformation of societies, it is necessary to observe which social dynamics affect culture.

Cicero (106-43 BC) used the concept of culture as "kultura animi", which he defined as human reasoning, criticism and self-discipline. In the historical process, culture was translated into English as "cultura" in the early 15th century, meaning farming and growth. With the 16th century, culture began to be used in the sense of human development and self-education (Oğuz, 2011, p.125).

According to sociologist Anthony Giddens, culture adresses to people's way of life, daily routines and beliefs. In addition, Giddens states that culture is a system of meanings and symbols shared among individuals belonging to a particular community (Giddens, 2000, p.25). With this definition, Giddens emphasizes that culture changes between societies and individuals within the changing events of history. Culture transforms in line with different social, economic, political or technological dynamics. In this respect, it is possible to say that communicative processes have a strong influence during cultural transformation. Communication is a structure that uses language, writing and discourses in both interpersonal and mass contexts. This communication establishes the link between cultural forms and society (İrvan, 2002, pp-7-9).

Professor Ünsal Oskay explains the relationship between society and culture in the following words:

"Communication is a reflection of human socialization, which is a species characteristic. Unlike all other species that adapt to their natural environment directly, human beings adapt to the storms, cold, lakes and seas in their natural environment through the culture they have created through socialization (Oskay, 2000, p.310)."

Communication, culture and society exist as an interactive structure. On the other hand, communication, which started as interpersonal, has changed societies culturally with the technological development of communication tools. Marshall McLuhan, one of the most important proponents of technological determinism in the field of communication, classifies this change as oral culture, written culture, typographic culture and electronic culture. According to McLuhan, each cultural period begins with the emergence of different means of communication on the stage of history. Oral culture emerged before writing, written culture with the invention of writing, typographic culture with the invention of printing, and electronic culture with telegraph, radio and television (McLuhan, 2007, pp. 50-55).

Today, digital culture is referred to as the dominant culture with the combination and spread of internet and computer technologies. Especially in the mid-19th century, growing institutions based on mass production, the global dissemination of information accelerated the process of transition to the information society and at the end of this process, digital culture began to spread (Gere, 2019, p. 41).

The reach of culture to different dimensions through mass media has accelerated especially thanks to television, which stands out with its visual and auditory features. Television has attracted global attention, influenced people with its credibility and both entertained and informed individuals with different content. Therefore, television has also created its own culture, in a sense cultural hegemony. The cities formed with the industrial revolution made consumption compulsory and at the same time created new social class relations. In these new class relations, a group of people who settle in the city to work come to the fore and these individuals need to consume quickly while producing. The most important tool of popular culture that emerged for this purpose has been television. The producers of popular culture convey their products as a way of life to the audience through television in an entertaining way. In this way, fast consumption is encouraged and at the same time individuals dependent on television emerge (Cereci, 2016, pp. 55-56).

As the power of television over people became clear, it started to be used for the dissemination of the dominant culture. There are now culture wars managed through media and communication. Based on Italian literary critic Umberto Eco's (2012, p.223) sentence "War does not create culture", it can be said that the war on the front line does not create culture, but a new culture is created through the media and affects societies.

In this section, the cultural imperialism created by digital platforms is mentioned and TRT's digital platform named "Tabii", which was established in response to this, is analyzed. Based on the argument that historical drama series promote Turkish history and create a structure against cultural hegemony, the cultural elements in such series are analyzed. Mahsusa Tripoli, Red Apple, Akif, Rumi, Hay Sultan are the series selected as a sample. The first episodes of these series were analyzed semiotically. The theme of family is especially prominent in these historical series that aim to fulfill the founding purpose of the "Tabi" platform. In addition to the family theme, homeland, national anthem and religion were also identified as the carrier elements of culture.

CULTURE: CONCEPTUAL AND THEORETICAL PERSPECTIVES

Culture, an interdisciplinary concept with different definitions, changes dynamically with internal and external factors. Apart from Kroeber and Kluckhohn, many cultural theorists state that culture is learned, acquired and transmitted unchanged over generations (Brinkmann, 2017, p.31). According to Kroeber and Kluckhohn (1952), American cultural anthropologists, culture is defined as a whole that includes beliefs, artistic products and all other habits acquired by people who are members of society (Kroeber & Kluckhohn, 1952, pp. 81-82).

According to anthropologist Clifford Geertz, culture is a system that analyzes and directs human behavior. Geertz defines culture as "the network of symbols that give meaning to people's lives" and argues that analyzing this network is the main task of anthropology (Geertz, 1973). According to him, culture is not only the sum of behaviors, but also the totality of the symbolic meanings behind these behaviors. Geertz's approach is shaped by "thick description", a method based on interpreting culture. The "thick description" method requires focusing not only on what cultural practices are, but also on what they mean. This perspective sees culture as a dynamic and interpretable process rather than a static construct. Inspired by the philosopher Gilbert Ryle, he mentions that a blink of an eye can have a physical meaning as well as a symbolic one. Geertz also says that context is important for understanding action (Scheneider, 1987, p. 810). Sosyal psikolog Geert Hofstede'ye göre ise kültür, toplumsal grupların birbirlerinden ayırt edici özelliklerinin tümüdür. On the other hand, Hofstede mentions that culture has various layers. These layers are named as values, heroes, rituals and symbols. Values are the building blocks of culture. The symbol layer of culture in a society is stated as clothing, monuments, flags, logos. Heroes are well-known and successful people who are respected in a society. Finally, the rituals layer is defined as the behaviors and rules that individuals in a society must follow. (Öztürk, Altundağ, 2023, pp.68-69).

In addition to anthropology, culture has been and is being discussed and analyzed in a sociological context. From a sociological perspective, culture is not considered independent of the society in which it exists. According to Max Weber, culture is the process of making sense of the environment in which humans live. According to him, culture is a reality woven with meanings (Weber, 1949, p. 86).

Karl Marx, who brings a different perspective to culture, sees human beings as a part of nature and sees human labor as a process that continuously transforms itself and its environment. Therefore, Marx defines culture as the accumulation of human beings apart from nature. On the other hand, Marx emphasizes that culture is a structure outside the economy, but that the economy has an impact on social consciousness. Thus, he states that the dominant subjects in society, in other words, the ruling class, are effective in the development of culture (Kulak, 2017, pp. 36-

37). On the other hand, Marx divides society into two basic components. These components are: infrastructure (base) and superstructure (superstructure). While infrastructure represents the economic structure, superstructure includes socialization mechanisms such as language, religion, education, law, ideology, mass media and the military. What should be emphasized here is that Marx sees the economic basis as the determinant of social, political and cultural structure. In other words, the superstructural institutions of a society are shaped by its economic infrastructure (El Aidi & Yechouti, 2017, p.2).

As the effects of mass communication on societies are analyzed, the importance of cultural studies in this field has begun to be understood. Critical theory, or in other words, the Frankfurt School tradition, which stands out as a Marxist tradition, has come to the fore with the study of the culture industry. Frankfurt School thinkers Theodor Adorno and Max Horkheimer, in their book "Dialectics of Enlightenment", emphasize that culture in modern societies standardizes people and makes them consumption-oriented. Adorno states that cinema and television are part of the culture industry and that the universe they create distracts people from their daily troubles. However, he says that this state of distancing and rest prevents people from thinking, that is, it transforms them into unquestioning beings (Adorno, 2009, pp. 56-60). According to them, culture is one of the tools that direct and control people within the capitalist system. Cultural products (movies, music, television, fashion) are like goods produced for consumption rather than being authentic. Individuals only consume this culture, they are not producers. This hinders social criticism and ensures the reproduction of the existing order. Frankfurt School thinkers, who favor Marxist thought, view culture from an ideological perspective.

While Karl Marx evaluates culture within the economic framework, the critical tradition examines culture mainly in the context of mass communication. The Italian philosopher Antonio Gramsci, who also examines culture in Marxist thought and emphasizes the concept of hegemony, brings a different point of view to this field by mentioning that the sovereign government manages society through culture. Gramsci is an important thinker who pioneered a Marxist political theory with Marx's theoretical and conceptual perspective and organized the working class struggle in the 1920s. Gramsci, one of the 20th century's leading Marxist theorists, introduced the concept of hegemony (Tazefidan & Porsuk, 2023, p. 1531).

Gramsci does not give a precise definition of culture in his works. The closest characterization to culture in his works is the concept of "Hegemony". Gramsci defines hegemony as the social direction given by the dominant group in society to the rest of the population due to its position and function, or the spontaneous consent given to the ruling class by the majority of the population. The Italian thinker asks the following question around the concept of hegemony:

"Which components of a dominant culture obtain the consent of the ruled?" (Jackson Lears, 1985, p.568).

Gramsci answers this question as the values, perceptions, beliefs, emotions and prejudices created by the ruling classes, the decision-makers who control production. In sum, cultural hegemony is the determination of what is seen as 'normal' or 'acceptable' in society by allowing dominant groups to impose their worldview as the universal standard. In this way, these groups can perpetuate stereotypes, reinforce power imbalances and prevent the advancement of more diverse or egalitarian cultural expressions. According to DEI, in the context of cultural hegemony, some groups are marginalized while the power of the ruling class is reinforced through mass media. In a culturally hegemonic environment, underrepresented groups find it difficult to make their voices heard or gain visibility (DEI dictionary, oxfordreview.com). Cultural hegemony uses mass communication to spread. In this way, it increases its sphere of influence by reaching more people. Another school that argues that the dominant ideology is reproduced through mass communication and puts culture at the center of its thoughts is British Cultural Studies.

The tradition of British Cultural Studies emerged particularly from the ideas of Richard Hoggart and Raymond Williams in the late 1950s, rooted in the belief that mass communication media provided a means for the dominant discourse to be reproduced in society in a renewed and powerful way. Raymond Williams defined culture as a way of life. Initially focusing on literary studies, the British Cultural Studies School engaged with the works of Louis Althusser and Karl Marx. Later, under the leadership of Stuart Hall, Marxist thought continued to exert influence within the school until the late 1960s. The school's perspectives evolved around Antonio Gramsci's concept of cultural hegemony, concentrating particularly on the ideological discourses present within media texts (Erdoğan & Alemdar, 2002, pp. 386-387). Consequently, television programs, news broadcasts, films, advertisements—in short, every product emerging from mass communication media—were regarded as media texts. Gramsci argued that every media text disseminates the dominant ideology to society and that these media channels serve to reproduce the prevailing ideology. Building upon this idea, Hall proposed that media texts undergo different processes of reception by audiences or readers. In analyzing this process, Hall introduced the concept of reception theory. According to reception theory, texts encoded by the sender and decoded by the receiver convey the ideologies of the senders but can also be interpreted differently by audiences. Hall identified three types of readings that audiences (receivers) may perform: dominant-hegemonic reading, negotiated reading, and oppositional reading, particularly in the decoding of meanings embedded in cultural texts, notably within television discourse (Martin, 2007, pp. 1-3).

Among the modes of television reading identified by Hall, the hegemonic reading aligns closely with Gramsci's definition of cultural hegemony. Television disseminates the ideology of the culturally dominant power through images, metaphors, sounds, and slogans. Viewers of television texts—such as television programs, series, and news broadcasts—which are imbued with these elements, are culturally and ideologically influenced. In the 21st century, this cultural hegemony is being reproduced through the content offered by digital platforms, which strongly attract audience interest. This phenomenon mirrors the concept of the culture industry described by Adorno and Horkheimer years ago after observing the influence of Hollywood cinema in America. Only the instruments have been transformed by digitalization; the commodification of culture, however, has remained unchanged. On the other hand, as Byung-Chul Han points out, Homo digitalis (2024, p. 21) refers to the digital human, a solitary individual who communicates via networks. This suggests that the digital human seeks to alleviate their loneliness by consuming content on digital platforms. However, this new loneliness, which is a consequence of the digital world, is seen as an opportunity by global platforms such as Netflix. According to Rabon Lobato, Netflix is a global distributor as well as a content producer. It thus invests in local production ecosystems to gain cultural legitimacy and audience loyalty. According to Lobato, by commissioning original series in languages such as Spanish, Korean and Turkish, Netflix is positioning itself not only as a foreign distributor but also as a cultural stakeholder in local media industries (Lobato, 2019, pp.107-112). Anamik Saha emphasizes the 'Myth of Cultural Democracy' discourse on digital platforms and culture. Saha argues that the claims that digital platforms, especially Netflix, are "open to everyone" and "include everyone's stories" are in fact liberal discourses that cover up hegemonic structures. In this way, cultural hegemony operates not only through coercion but also through the production of consent (Saha, 2018, pp. 29-31). From this perspective, the field offers a new analysis by blending Adorno and Horkheimer's cultural view with digital platforms. In this way, digital platforms, which produce global content and at the same time quickly distribute this content globally, have a say in shaping the perceptions of individuals. In short, cultural hegemony is reproduced through digital platforms.

AN OUTLINE OF TRT'S HISTORICAL DEVELOPMENT

Broadcasting in Turkey evolved through three distinct phases until the early 1990s: the radio era (1926–1936), the state monopoly period (1936–1964), and the TRT (Turkish Radio and Television Corporation) era (1964–early 1990s). The emergence of radio as a significant mass communication tool and the state's assumption of broadcasting responsibility played an influential role in Turkey's modernization process. However, a new era in Turkish broadcasting commenced with the establishment of TRT in May 1964, following the enactment of the broadcasting law in 1963 (Kejanlıoğlu, 2001, pp. 87–90). Meanwhile, indicators of cultural and political transformation became noticeable during this new period. TRT, a public broadcasting institution, made its first broadcast in 1968. Moreover, TRT contributed to the nation-building process by offering a variety of programs, including those focused on education, arts, news, and public discussions. American sociologist and media theorist Todd Gitlin emphasizes that the cultural massification facilitated by media plays a significant role in the formation of nations (Gitlin, as cited in Mutlu, 2001, p. 27).

The process of cultural massification described by Gitlin began in Turkey with the establishment of TRT. For instance, TRT 1 broadcast programs themed around Turkish folk music and Anatolian culture. Educational programs were designed to encourage individuals to learn foreign languages. TRT 2 offered programs featuring discussions on arts and literature, as well as broadcasts of classical music. In 1989, TRT-GAP was launched to support the Southeastern Anatolia Project (GAP), providing agricultural information to viewers. TRT-GAP, which shared joint broadcasts with TRT 3, also marked Turkey's first instance of rotational broadcasting. By the 1990s, TRT began to air foreign television series such as Bonanza, The Fugitive, and The Young and the Restless, which attracted considerable viewer interest.

In addition, TRT became one of the founding members of the European Broadcasting Union (EBU) in 1972 and signed the Asia-Pacific Broadcasting Union (ABU) agreement in 2004. Currently, TRT operates 14 television channels and 19 radio stations. It also broadcasts television channels in multiple languages, including Turkish, English, Arabic, Azerbaijani, and Kurdish (TRT, 2024). As Turkey's national public broadcaster, TRT continues to hold an important position today. However, it faces challenges in attracting audiences amidst the dominance of digital broadcasting platforms within Turkey. In an effort to adapt to this new environment, to compete with global platforms such as Netflix, Disney+, and Amazon, and to resist the cultural hegemony these platforms aim to disseminate globally through their content, TRT launched its first international digital platform, Tabii.

The Tabii platform launched on May 7, 2023. This platform is significant as it represents TRT, Turkey's public broadcaster, becoming the first international digital video platform of the organization. The promotional meeting for the platform took place on May 2, 2023, at the Beykoz Kundura Factory in Istanbul. During this meeting, TRT Director-General Zahid Sobacı emphasized that TRT is a "memory" and highlighted the cultural importance of the Tabii platform. Some details from Sobacı's speech are as follows:

"We will be the primary platform to meet the global demand for family-oriented content. In addition to our films and series, we will become the new digital home for the families who trust us, offering brand-new animated content for our children, whom we regard as entrusted minds and hearts. Within this vision, I would like to state that our international digital platform is a pure, natural, and new source, created in response to those who seek to wash all of humanity in the same water. Our platform will make significant contributions to the promotion of our beautiful homeland, from tourism to economy, and from sharing our cultural wealth. Initially, the TRT international digital platform will feature content in Turkish, English, Spanish, Urdu, and Arabic. With 30 new productions and 184 episodes, it will be the platform with the richest original content at its launch stage. Along with our successful projects, the platform will also feature popular TRT productions, and it will be made available to our viewers in Turkey starting May 7." (AA, 2023).

In his speech, Sobacı emphasizes the theme of family, which is a fundamental aspect of Turkish culture. He also highlights the role of Turkish TV series in promoting tourism, thanks to their compelling storylines.

In Sobacı's interview in 2024, the concepts of representation and content diversity are brought to the forefront.

"As Turkey, we cannot remain within the boundaries drawn by others. We cannot allow anyone to impose content on us or shape the narrative of our country. Therefore, Tabii is extremely important for the true representation of our country in the digital world. In addition, there is a need for diversity and perspective, which is an issue in the international arena where space is narrowing and production has become increasingly difficult. Every concept produced cannot simply be thrown into the universal values set and forced upon everyone." (Platinonline, 2024).

One year after the platform's establishment, Anadolu Agency reported the following details about the platform:

"According to a statement from TRT, the domestic and national digital platform, Tabii, with the slogan 'Stories that unite us,' has offered a wide range of content from action to romantic comedy, crime dramas to youth series. The platform has reached over 4 million subscribers and 164 million views, hosting more than 32 original productions, 616 series and films, and over 20,000 hours of content. Tabii's social media accounts have also surpassed 30 million followers." (AA, 2024).

In addition to these original Turkish TV series, The Tabii platform also broadcasts UEFA Champions League, UEFA Europa League, Conference League, and Super Cup matches. In this way, the platform is expanding its subscriber base by also attracting sports viewers.

Considering that television is an excellent storyteller, TRT executives have positioned Tabii in the digital broadcasting market under the slogan *"Stories that unite us."* The platform, which especially features historical drama productions, highlights religious and political figures from Turkish history.

Within the "Series" section, original Turkish-language productions are featured. Among these, the series Gassal, which began airing in December 2024, stands out. Notably, the promotional phrase associated with the series, "When I die, who will wash me?", garnered significant attention even before the series Gassal release on the platform. Additionally, historical drama series within this section are particularly prominent, as they aim to highlight important figures from various periods of Turkish history and to preserve traditional cultural elements.

Within the "Series" section, there are several subcategories, including: "Exclusive to Tabii," "International Productions," "Adaptations from Books," "Following the Action," "Historical Stage," "Family Entertainment," "Corner of Laughter," and "Dramatic Touches."

Similarly, the "Films" section features its own subcategories: "Science Fiction," "Adrenaline Rush," "Guaranteed Laughter," "Life Stories," "Emotional Journeys," "Family Cinema," "Festival Enthusiasts," and "Nostalgic Films." Turkish productions dominate the content across these categories. In both the series and film sections, particularly within the "Adaptations from Books" and "Nostalgic Films" subcategories, viewers can access classic Turkish television productions.

In the "Children's" section, the platform prioritizes animated productions aimed at young audiences. To support children's learning through entertainment, subcategories such as "Eco-friendly Little Ones," "Learning Adventures," and "Curious Explorers" have been created.

The "Documentaries" section is organized into subcategories as well, including: "Animal Kingdom," "Dusty Pages of History," "The Power of Knowledge," "Undiscovered Paths," "Art for Everyone," "Extraordinary Lives," "Nature's Stage," "Gastronomic Discoveries," "Cultural Window," "On Humanity," and "Concerts at Home." Notably, the "Dusty Pages of History" subcategory features productions that document various periods of Turkish history through archival materials.

The structure of TRT's international platform, its founding slogan, and the nature of its content indicate that it was established with the aim of preserving and promoting Turkish culture. Tabii adopts a content strategy that positions itself against global platforms such as Netflix, Disney+, and Amazon Prime, which dominate both the Turkish and international digital broadcasting markets. A significant portion of Netflix's content, for example, promotes American culture. In the words of Adorno and Horkheimer, individuals consume media—and thus popular culture—rapidly and superficially. Today, this pattern of mass consumption is further encouraged by digital platforms. Popular series adapted from books, Korean productions, and reality shows have transferred the "magical screen" experience of traditional television into the digital realm. Furthermore, thanks to the flexibility of digital media, this magical screen has become even more appealing, allowing individuals to access the content they desire anytime and anywhere.

AIM, SAMPLE AND METHODOLOGY

In this section, the cultural themes present in the historical series broadcast on the Tabii platform are analyzed. Five series were selected through a random sampling method from among the twenty-five series listed under the "Historical Stage" category. These selected series are listed below.

- Mahsusa Trablusgarb (Mahsusa Tripoli)
- Kızıl Elma: Bir Fetih Öyküsü (Red Apple: A Story of Conquest)
- Akif
- Rumi
- Hay Sultan

With the rapid advancement of digitalization, the ever-evolving media landscape has given rise to a new form of cultural industry: global digital platforms. These platforms offer audiences a content consumption experience characterized by similar narratives across different cultures. However, during this experience, viewers are also exposed to elements such as youth cultures, everyday life practices, languages, and religions from various cultural backgrounds. This study examines "Tabii," the international digital streaming platform launched by TRT, as a counter-hegemonic response to the cultural dominance established by global digital platforms. The platform aims to promote Turkish culture, history, and language through original productions. Using a random sampling method, a selection of historical drama series has been chosen for analysis. The reason for focusing on this specific genre lies in the notable success of Turkish television dramas—initially broadcast on traditional television channels—on a global scale, particularly in the Middle East. For instance, the series *Gümüş* (*Noor*), which aired between 2005 and 2007, gained significant popularity in Tunisia. Subsequently, the success of historical dramas such as *Muhteşem Yüzyıl* (*The Magnificent Century*) has contributed to Turkish tourism. Today, the popularity of Turkish dramas extends beyond the Middle East, reaching audiences in Latin America and Eastern Europe as well (PolitikaAkademisi, 2020). Due to this global success, the genre of historical drama within the series category has been selected as the focal point of this study.

The selected television series have been analyzed using Roland Barthes' semiological method. Barthes, a prominent French theorist, critic, and semiotician, is renowned for his work on media, mythology, and language. He critically examined signs embedded in everyday life, questioning their structural properties and cultural functions (Culler, 2000, p. 43). Moreover, Barthes asserted that narratives containing signs have existed since the beginning of human history and that all peoples, societies, and cultures possess their own forms of narrative (Barthes, 2009, p. 103). According to Barthes, signs give rise to a meta-language—an analytical discourse that enables the examination of how representations are structured and encoded (Aydınalp, 2021, p. 207). In his transition from linguistic theory to semiotic analysis, Barthes employed key concepts such as meaning and connotation. He also emphasized that cultural elements themselves function as signs. Within this framework, his triadic model of sign, signifier, and signified was applied. The selected series were analyzed through the lens of core cultural components such as language, religion, and tradition, followed by an interpretation of how these elements collectively construct the concept of family.

ANALYSIS AND FINDINGS

Mahsusa Trablusgarb (Mahsusa Tripoli)

The "Tabii" series *Mahsusa Trablusgarb* portrays the events of the Italo-Turkish War (1911–1912), focusing on a group of volunteer Ottoman soldiers who, under the leadership of Enver Pasha and Mustafa Kemal, travel to Tripoli to defend the region against Italian occupation. The series consists of two seasons and a total of eighteen episodes.

The first episode, titled *"Yola Çıkış" (Departure)*, depicts the preparations made by Enver Pasha, Mustafa Kemal, and other volunteer soldiers before their journey to Tripoli. The main characters are Enver Pasha and Mustafa Kemal. Enver Pasha is portrayed as a composed and diplomatically skilled military officer, while Mustafa Kemal is represented as a patriotic, optimistic, and family-oriented young soldier.

Set across various cities and locations, the episode begins with an artillery defense launched by Turkish troops near the port of Tripoli against the Italian navy. Subsequently, the narrative shifts to a heated debate in the Ottoman Parliament in Istanbul (Meclis-i Mebusan), where members argue over Italy's occupation of Tripoli. Following this, the storyline introduces Talat Pasha, who collaborates with Enver Pasha to devise a plan for the Tripoli campaign. This plan involves recruiting other patriotic soldiers, including Mustafa Kemal.

Throughout the episode, numerous cultural signs and symbols are identified. These semiotic elements, which reflect language, national identity, military values, and traditions, are documented and categorized in the following table.

Many cultural indicators are identified in the series. These indicators are given in the table below.

Table 1. Analysis table of the series Mahsusa Tripoli

Sign	Signifier	Signified
Object	Turkish flag	Homeland, defense of the nation
Human & Object	Italian soldiers making a pilgrimage gesture upon approaching the shore	Religious representation, fear of the Italian soldiers
Human & Object	Quarreling deputies in the Ottoman Parliament and the gavel sound	Disagreement over Tripoli, diplomatic turmoil
Object	Red Apple	A covert action (a Turkish soldier executing an enemy soldier in a symbolic way)
Object	Amulet	Divine protection sought by soldiers
Object	White handkerchief	Purity, prayer, affection, and protection of Mustafa Kemal's mother as he departs for Tripoli
Object	Ring	Ottoman Empire and power
Object	Prayer beads	Remembering God and Patience
Human & Object	Turkish soldiers lying dead with the flag	Patriotism, willingness to die for the homeland
Object	Italian Flag	Occupying force, especially shown as Italian soldiers salute near the bodies of Turkish troops
Human	Mustafa Kemal kissing his mother's hand	A cultural gesture of respect
Object	British flag and barbed wire	Invasion of land and imprisonment of Turkish people

An analysis of the signs used in the series reveals the prominent themes of nationalism, religion, and patriotism. Given that the narrative is set during a historical period of war, conflict naturally emerges as a central element. This conflict, primarily between Italian and Turkish forces, is introduced to the audience in the first episode through the motif of territorial struggle.

Several dialogues in the first episode are particularly noteworthy for their ideological implications. For instance, a Turkish soldier refers to the Italians by saying, *"The Italians dream of establishing a new Roman Empire,"* which alludes to the expansionist policies pursued by Italy during that era.

Another significant example occurs during a conversation between Mustafa Kemal and Fethi Bey at the Pink Mansion in Istanbul. Here, Mustafa Kemal quotes from Namık Kemal's famous poem *Vatan* (*The Homeland*), stating:

> *"What did Namık Kemal say in The Homeland? 'The glory of our ancestors is known throughout the world. Do not assume that nature changes; this blood is still the same blood.'"*

This reference to Namık Kemal, one of the leading figures in Turkish nationalism, serves not only to evoke patriotic sentiment but also to introduce a significant piece of Turkish poetic heritage to the audience.

Kızıl Elma: Bir Fetih Öyküsü (Red Apple: A Story of Conquest)

The series tells the story of the reign of Murad II and the childhood years of Mehmed II. Starting with the birth of Mehmed II, the series also deals with the power struggles within the palace. In the first episode of the series titled "Şehzade Dangerously", the events begin with the birth of Mehmed II.

Mehmed II is a curious, knowledgeable for his age, headstrong and active child. His father, Murad II, is a strong and loyal ruler. The rulers around Murad II talk about Sheikh Hacı Bayram Hazret. Upon this, the sultan orders the sheikh to be brought to the palace. At the same time, a Serbian princess is brought to the palace to be married to Murad II. However, the princess does not want to marry the sultan. For this reason, she escapes from the janissaries where they are camped. Meanwhile, Mehmed II is in the river to fish. Drifting with the effect of the current, Mehmed II swallowed water. The princess finds him immobilized on the river. Thus the prince is saved. In addition to the plot consisting of many side stories, there are also cultural indicators.

Table 2. Signifiers the series Kızıl Elma: Bir Fetih Öyküsü (Red Apple: A Story of Conquest)

Sign	Signifier	Signified
Object	Holy Book (The Quran)	Islam
Object	Rain and thunder	Power and abundance
Object	Mosaic of the Virgin Mary and Jesus Christ	Christianity
Human & Object	Christian cleric making the sign of the cross	Christianity
Object	Lightning striking the statue of the Eastern Roman Emperor	The Conquest of Istanbul

continued on following page

Table 2. Continued

Sign	Signifier	Signified
Human & Object	Mehmed II, miniature cannon, and gunpowder	The Conquest of Istanbul
Object	Ruler	Wisdom, rationality, discipline
Object	White dove	Peace
Object	Roses	Faith in God
Object	Scorpion	Evil

In the first scene of the series, Murad II's recitation of the Koran and the birth of Mehmed II at that time tells us that a very blessed person was born. When naming his son, Murad II says: "*We will call him Mehmed according to the Oghuz tradition.*" Here it is stated that the lineage of Turks goes back to the Oghuz. It speaks of an empire that is loyal to its ancestors and strives to follow in their footsteps.

In the series, Mehmed II is characterized as a mischievous child. However, there is a reference to the Conquest of Istanbul in every scene. When Akşemseddin is brought to the palace in Edirne, the scorpion stings the janissary who wants to kill him and Akşemseddin treats him, representing benevolence and kindness. Akşemseddin, who would later become the teacher of Mehmed II, was also a poet and physician.

Akif

The series *Akif*, which portrays the life of the poet Mehmet Akif Ersoy—the author of the Turkish National Anthem—also introduces the audience to lesser-known aspects of the poet within a historical context.

The first episode, titled "Perseverance," opens with a war scene in which a young soldier is shot while fleeing during an assault by troops at the front. In later scenes, it is revealed that this soldier is Akif's son, Mümtaz. Although Akif and his family initially welcome Mümtaz's return from military service with joy and pride, they soon discover that he was actually shot while deserting the battlefield. Furthermore, it emerges that Mümtaz has joined an anti-military group and has been distributing a poem published by this group to military recruits. As Akif investigates the authorship of the poem distributed by his son, he confronts the poet Tevfik Fikret. In the series, Tevfik Fikret questions religion, military service, and war; his poems have become a guide for young men who wish to avoid combat. Additionally, the Protestant Society is depicted as assisting these young men in fleeing to New Zealand in order to avoid military service.

The indicators in the series are listed in the table below.

Table 3. Signifiers of the series Akif

Sign	Signifier	Signified
Object	Soup	Military food
Object	Turkish soldier at the front	Nationalism
Object	Turkish flag	Patriotism, Nationalism
Object	Dining Table	Unity and solidarity, family
Object	Stuffed cabbage	Emphasis on national values through local culinary elements; represents Turkish cuisine
Object	Turkish Coffee	National values
Human & Object	Mümtaz kissing his mother's hand	Respect and affection for elders
Object	Akide candy (Kind of Turkish candy)	National values

The first episode of the series *Akif* predominantly conveys messages centered around military service. For instance, Mümtaz's mother expresses that her son has attained the honorable status of a war veteran upon seeing him, which reinforces this thematic emphasis. Moreover, through the depiction of traditional Turkish dishes, the episode also seeks to evoke feelings of family, trust, and sincerity in the audience.

Rumi

The series, which focuses on the life of the Persian poet and pioneer of Sufi thought, Mevlana Jalal al-Din Rumi, begins with his migration to the capital of the Anatolian Seljuk State, Konya, as a result of the Mongol invasion. The narrative opens in the year 1242, depicting Rumi's spiritual foresight of the impending Mongol threat and his efforts to warn the Seljuk ruler. During a dhikr (remembrance ritual) in the madrasa, Rumi senses the approach of the Mongols toward Konya. At the same time, the Mongol forces advance toward the Seljuk fortress located in Erzurum. In response, Ömer Atabek, a trusted Seljuk soldier, dispatches two men to reinforce the fortress. However, before reaching their destination, the soldiers witness the approaching Mongols and turn back to alert Konya.

The first episode is titled *"Find that path or be lost in it,"* which symbolizes Rumi's spiritual quest for truth and his readiness to endure the challenges along the way. The series, which spans three seasons, stands out with its extensive cast and elaborate production.

The following table presents the key semiotic elements featured in the series.

Table 4. Signifiers of the series Rumi

Sign	Signifier	Signified
Object	Bow	War, warrior spirit
Human & Object	Rumi in a red robe	Emphasis, drawing attention, significance
Object	Moth circling a flame	Divine messenger
Object	Sandstorm	Mongol invasion
Object	Door	Divine symbol – transition from the material world to the realm of meaning
Human & Object	Tattoo on a Mongol warrior	Cultural signifier – status, bravery
Object	Eagle	Power
Object	Floor dining setup (traditional meal)	Family unity and togetherness
Object	Ring	Sovereign authority and power
Object	Skull	Barbarism, invasion

The analysis of the series reveals the presence of several religious symbols, most notably the motif of the door, which in Sufi belief symbolizes the stages of an individual's inner journey, the act of spiritual surrender, and ultimately the pursuit of divine truth. This notion is further reinforced through Rumi's dialogues with his own likeness, wherein he is repeatedly reminded of his obligation to seek the truth. Accordingly, the central conflict of the series is constructed around the human quest for spiritual truth. In addition to this metaphysical dimension, the historical conflict between the Seljuks and the Mongols introduces a dynamic and dramatic layer to the narrative. For instance, the Mongol ruler smearing the blood of a slain soldier onto his forehead, the recurring imagery of sandstorms, and the placement of a skull on a spike beside the Mongol flag all serve to reinforce the portrayal of the Mongols as invaders and warriors. Furthermore, the theme of family is emphasized through scenes depicting Rumi's extended family gathering around a traditional floor dining arrangement. This visual not only conveys familial unity, but also highlights the significance of collective identity and tradition.

Hay Sultan

The narrative of the series centers on a pivotal episode from the life of the prominent Islamic scholar and mystic, Abd al-Qadir al-Gilani. In the first episode, titled *"The Road to Baghdad,"* a Seljuk emir dispatches a royal messenger to deliver an important message to the caliph in Baghdad. However, the messenger is ambushed in the desert, only to be rescued by al-Gilani. The two then continue their journey to Baghdad together. Upon their arrival, the city is depicted as suffering from severe drought and widespread illness. In stark contrast, the caliph's palace is shown as a place of opulence and abundance. Throughout the episode, al-Gilani's patience, tolerance, and moral integrity are highlighted, and the socio-economic disparity between wealth and poverty is conveyed through various symbolic and narrative elements.

The following table presents the key semiotic elements featured in the series.

Table 5. Signifiers of the series Hay Sultan

Sign	Signifier	Signified
Object	Water	Peace, Abundance
Object	Staff	Wisdom
Object	Tortoise	Wisdom, patience
Human&Object	Dancing concubines	Wealth, extravagance
Object	Murky water	Disease

The series suggests that Abd al-Qadir al-Gilani is emerging from a period of seclusion and is preparing to return to Baghdad. This is implicitly conveyed through his reflective statement: *"The waters of the Tigris are murky; it must need a moment to breathe,"* showing his contemplative withdrawal from public life. Drawing upon the visual and narrative symbols throughout the episode, it can be argued that the themes of patience and wisdom are prominently emphasized. In addition, the recurrent use of water as a symbolic element is particularly noteworthy. While clean water is associated with abundance and peace, the depiction of impoverished neighborhoods in Baghdad where residents only have access to muddy water highlights socio-economic deprivation. Al-Gilani's actions—gathering the marginalized residents, offering them food at his lodge, and bringing together individuals from various sectarian backgrounds—convey strong messages of hospitality, unity, and tolerance.

FUTURE RESEARCH DIRECTIONS

Since it has been understood that visual arts have a significant impact on human perception, cinema, television, painting, and graphic design have become powerful tools of propaganda. In this context, the American lifestyle—portrayed as happy, successful, and filled with wealth—marketed by Hollywood cinema has attracted the attention of global audiences for decades. This portrayal has led many individuals to desire such a life. People wished to be part of the glamorous life they saw on screen.

For instance, individuals, much like Truman Burbank, found themselves living in an artificial reality. Digital platforms, dominated by American cultural hegemony, have attempted to impose this culture particularly through television series.

Following this study, culture-based research will focus on digital platforms and the various series produced by them. The primary reason for this focus is the necessity of closely observing individuals' preferences and viewing habits to understand a nation's consumer culture, traditions, and everyday cultural practices. As in the past, culture will continue to transform. Within this transformation, communication tools will play a central role in shaping cultural dynamics. With digitalization, new tools will emerge, and digital platforms will potentially be replaced by interactive content or different forms of social media. At this point, one of the most critical aspects to consider in future research is that cultural elements (such as language and traditions) will inevitably be disseminated through these forms of content.

CONCLUSION

Throughout history, civilizations have influenced one another through various means such as warfare, trade, and intermarriage. As a result of these interactions, cultures have come to recognize each other, often adopting rituals, customs, and practices from one another. However, with the advent of modernity, cultural interaction began to occur increasingly through communication tools rather than solely physical or political contact.

Although the precise temporal boundaries of modernity remain ambiguous, it is generally acknowledged that the process began to take shape between the 15th and 18th centuries. By the 19th century, driven significantly by the Industrial Revolution and the rise of mass communication technologies, cultural transformation became more visible and pervasive. From this period onward, the influence of newspapers, radio, and later television on cultural dynamics became more pronounced.

In this context, the notion of the "culture industry" proposed by Adorno and Horkheimer becomes particularly relevant. Their framework critiques how individuals are influenced by the content they consume—especially via television—and how this consumption leads to the internalization of certain values and a turn toward material consumption. Indeed, one of the most effective ways to comprehend a society's cultural codes, everyday practices, and consumer behavior is to observe the media content its people engage with and favor.

In the case of Turkey, Netflix began operating in 2016, offering globally produced content to Turkish audiences. It is plausible to argue that such platforms contribute to the global culture industry and foster a form of cultural hegemony. The recurring similarities in narratives, casting choices, and visual settings across different series indicate an ongoing process of standardization in content production. In response to this homogenization and with the aim of representing and promoting Turkish culture on a global scale, the national broadcaster TRT launched its own streaming service, "Tabii." A significant portion of the series available on this platform consistently incorporates the theme of family, which serves as a central narrative element. Moreover, in an effort to promote Turkish culture to a global audience, the platform also broadcasts series that depict the life stories of various historical figures. In this sense, the platform implicitly conveys that the foundations of Turkish culture lie in its deep-rooted history and strong familial ties.

Based on a semiotic analysis in the tradition of Roland Barthes, it can be argued that the platform strategically utilizes its historical series to enhance the translatability and recognition of Turkish culture on a global scale. The primary cultural themes employed for this purpose include family, religion, military service, and nationalism. The key signifiers representing these themes are communal dining scenes symbolizing family unity, the act of reciting prayers as a religious marker, and the recurring presence of the Turkish flag as a nationalist symbol. Furthermore, the narratives suggest that tolerance and patience are among the most prominent characteristics attributed to the Turkish people.

When comparing the historical drama series on this platform to conventional television series broadcast in Turkey, it becomes evident that the aforementioned themes are more deliberately emphasized and systematically integrated into the storytelling. This approach highlights a conscious effort to construct and disseminate a curated image of Turkish identity through culturally resonant narratives. The prominent position of Turkish television series within the traditional broadcast market has been further solidified through their presence on this digital platform.

In summary, the digital streaming platform Tabii positions itself as a cultural counterbalance to the hegemonic influence of foreign media platforms. Through its curated selection of content, Tabii aims to promote and disseminate Turkish culture to both domestic and international audiences. By foregrounding culturally significant themes—such as family, history, religion, and national identity—the platform seeks not only to preserve cultural heritage but also to present an alternative narrative to global viewers, one rooted in Turkish values and traditions.

Furthermore, Tabii explicitly aligns its cultural objectives with broader economic and strategic goals. One of its central ambitions is to foster cultural tourism by sparking international interest in Turkey's historical sites, lifestyles, and local traditions depicted in its series. In parallel, the platform aspires to catalyze the development of a new Turkish drama industry that is economically sustainable and globally competitive. By investing in original productions and cultivating local talent, *Tabii* contributes to the cultural economy while simultaneously asserting Turkey's soft power in the international media landscape.

REFERENCES

Adorno, T. (2009). *Kültür Endüstrisi-Kültür Yönetimi. (Culture Industry-Culture Management).* İthaki.

Anadolu Ajansı. (2023). TRT'nin Uluslararası Dijital Platformu "Tabii" Tanıtıldı. *(TRT's International Digital Platform 'Tabii' has been introduced.*https://www.aa.com.tr/tr/kultur/trtnin-uluslararasi-dijital-platformu-tabii-tanitildi/2887338#

Anadolu Ajansı. (2024). Tabii ilk yılında 164 milyon izlemeye ulaştı. *(Tabii reached 164 million views in its first year).*https://www.aa.com.tr/tr/gundem/tabii-ilk-yilinda-164-milyon-izlenmeye-ulasti/3228964

Aydınalp, E. B. (2021). Roland Barthes'ta Metin ve Eleştiri Dinamiği. (Dynamics of Critic and Text in Roland Barthes). *Edebi Eleştiri Dergisi.Journal of Literary Criticism, 5*(1), 203–214.

Barthes, R. (2009). *Göstergebilimsel Serüven. (Adventure of Semiotic).* Yapı Kredi Publishing.

Brinkmann, K. (2017). Culture: Defining an Old Concept in a New Way. *Journal of Culture. Social Development, 35*, 31–34.

Cereci, S. (2016). *Televizyon Sosyolojisi (Television Sociology).* İstanbul: Phoenix.

Culler, J. (2000). *Literary Theory-A Very Short Introduction.* Oxford University Press.

Eco, U. (2012). *Yengeç Adımlarıyla-Sıcak Savaşlar ve Medyatik Popülizm (Turning Back the Clock: Hot Wars and Media Populism).* Doğan Books.

El Aidi, A., & Yechouti, Y. (2017). Antonio Gramsci's Theory of Cultural Hegemony in Edward Said's Orientalism. *Galaxy: International Multidisciplinary Research Journal., 6*(5), 2–10.

Erdoğan, İ., & Korkmaz, A. (2002). *Öteki Kuram. (Other Theory).* Pozitif Publishing.

Geertz, C. (1973). *The Interpretation of Cultures.* Basic Books.

Gere, C. (2019). *Dijital Kültür (Digital Culture).* Salon Publishing.

Giddens, A. (2000). *Sosyoloji (Sociology)* (Çev. H. Özel & C. Güzel). Ankara: Ayraç Publishing.

Han, B-C. (2024). *Sürünün İçinde-Dijital Dünyaya Bakışlar. (In the Swarm: Digital Prospects).* (Z. Sarıkartal.Trans.). İstanbul: İnka. DEI dictionary, *Cultural Hegemony,* oxfordreview.com.

İrvan, S. (2002). *Medya Kültür Siyaset. (Media, Culture, Politic).* Alp Publishing.

Jackson Lears, T. J. (1985). The Concept of Cultural Hegemony: Problems and Possibilities. *The American Historical Review*, *90*(3), 567–593. DOI: 10.1086/ahr/90.3.567

Kejanlıoğlu, B. (2001). Turk:ish Broadcasting Policy in a Historical Context: Continuties and Discontinuties in the 1990s. [Culture and Communication]. *Kültür ve İletişim.*, *4*(2), 85–104.

Kejanlıoğlu, B., Çelenk, S., & Adaklı, G. (2001). *Medya Politikaları. (Media Politics).* İmge Publishing.

Kroeber, A. L., & Kluckhohn, C. (1952). *Culture: A critical review of concepts and definitions*. Harvard University Press.

Kulak, Ö. (2017). *Theodor Adorno: Kültür Endüstrisinin Kıskacında Kültür. (Theodor Adorno: Culture in the Grip of the Culture Industry).* İthaki.

Lobato, R. (2019). *Netflix Nations: The Geography of Digital Distribution*. NYU Press. DOI: 10.18574/nyu/9781479895120.001.0001

Martin, J. (2007). *Audiences and Reception Theory*. Sociology Made Simple.

McLuhan, M. (2019). *Gutenberg galaksisi (Gutenberg Galaxy)* (Korkmaz, Z., Trans.). Yapı Kredi Publishing.

Oğuz, E. S. (2011). Toplum Bilimlerinde Kültür Kavramı. *(The Concept of Culture in Social Sciences).Journal of Faculty of Letters*, *28*(2), 123–139.

Oskay, Ü. (2000). *XIX. Yüzyıldan Günümüze Kitle İletişiminin Kültürel İşlevleri (Cultural Functions of Mass Communication from XIX. Century to Present).* Der Publishing.

Öztürk, C., & Altundağ, P. (2023). Kültürel Boyutlar Teorisi Bağlamında Türkiye-Güney Kore Organizasyon Kültürü İncelemesi. (Analysis of Turkiye-South Korea Company Culture in The Context of Hofstede's Theory of Cultural Dimensions. *Journal of Oriental Languages*, *8*(2), 65–95.

Platinonline. (2024). Bir Türkiye Markası: Tabii. *(A Turkish Brand: Tabii).*https://www.platinonline.com/yasam/bir-turkiye-markasi-tabii-1089150

Politika Akademisi. (2020). Türk Dizileri ve Türkiye'ye Katkıları *(Turkish TV Series and Their Contribution to Turkey*). https://politikaakademisi.org/2020/09/09/turk-dizileri-ve-turkiyeye-katkilari/

Saha, A. (2018). *Race and Cultural Industries*. Polity Press.

Schneider, M. (1987). Culture-as-Text in the Work of Clifford Geertz. *Theory and Society, 16*(6), 809–839. DOI: 10.1007/BF00138070

Tazefidan, K., & Porsuk, S. (2023). Çağdaş Sosyal Teoride Antonio Gramsci. (Antonio Gramsci in Contemporary Social Theory). *Afyon Kocatepe University Journal of Social Sciences., 25*(4), 1526–1539. DOI: 10.32709/akusosbil.1116215

Weber, M. (1949). *The methodology of the social sciences.* Free Press.

ADDITIONAL READING

Baumann, Z. (2000). *Liquid Modernity.* Polity Press.

Eco, U. (2024). *Televizyona Dair. (About Television).* Can Publishing.

Hall, S. (2017). *Temsil-Kültürel Temsiller ve Anlamdırma Uygulamaları.(Representation-Cultural Representations and Signification Practices).* Pinhan.

Hofstede, G., Hofstede, G. J., & Minkov, M. (2010). *Cultures and organizations: Software of the mind* (3rd ed.). McGraw-Hill.

Innis, H. A. (2007). *Empire and communications* (Watters, M. W., Ed.). Rowman & Littlefield.

McLuhan, M., & Powers, B. R. (2020). *Global Köy. (The Global Village).* Scala.

Morley, D. (1992). *Television, audiences and cultural studies.* Routledge.

Weber, M. (2011). *Protestan Ahlakı ve Kapitalizm Ruhu. (The Protestant Ethic and the Spirit of Capitalism).* Bilgesu Publishing.

Williams, R. (1983). *Keywords: A Vocabulary of Culture and Society.* Oxford University Press.

Williams, R. (2003). *Televizyon, Teknoloji ve Kültürel Biçim. (Television, Technology and Cultural Form).* Dost Publishing.

Williams, R. (2013). *Kültür ve Materyalizm. (Culture and Materialism).* Sel Publishing.

KEY TERMS AND DEFINITIONS

Digital Media: The development of mass media with internet technology and its ubiquitous accessibility.

Cultural Transmission: The transmission of elements of culture across generations. This transmission takes place through different forms of communication. However, cultural transmission has accelerated with digital media.

TRT (Turkish Radio and Television Corporation): Turkey's first and only public broadcaster.

Netflix: Founded in 1997 as a DVD rental company in the United States and launched in Turkey in 2016, the global streaming platform...

Disney+: US-based global video streaming platform.

Cultural Belonging: Individuals feel themselves as part of a society.

Cultural Codes: It is a set of symbols and indicators that constitute a culture.

Chapter 7
From Radio Magazines to Social Media:
Audience Seek Out Their Radio Stations

Ufuk İnal
https://orcid.org/0000-0001-8638-0662
Ondokuz Mayıs University, Turkey

ABSTRACT

This study examines the evolution of radio audience interaction from the early days of letter writing and radio magazines to contemporary engagement through social media platforms such as Instagram, Facebook, and X. Using the netnography method, it analyzes audience behavior toward Turkey's most listened-to radio stations and prominent presenters. The findings reveal a shift in audience loyalty from radio institutions to individual broadcasters, driven by the immediacy and accessibility of social media. While traditional communication emphasized respectful, delayed feedback, today's interaction is fast, direct, and often informal. Social media has enhanced the visibility of broadcasters, increased feedback opportunities, and provided new revenue sources, ultimately reshaping the relationship between listeners, radio, and content creators.

INTRODUCTION

Dostoyevsky defines man as an ungrateful two-legged creature. According to him, man has developed science and technology in order to pave the way for himself and has an innate tendency to create. For this reason, he describes man as an insatiable and ungrateful being who is not satisfied with what exists. From this

DOI: 10.4018/979-8-3373-1957-5.ch007

perspective, it can be seen that the fundamental driving force behind technology-supported change from yesterday to today has always been the need to know and communicate. Humanity's appetite for knowledge has resulted in the discovery of various mass communication tools, from the telegraph to the telephone, from the phone to the radio, to television, and the internet. However, no device has yet been sufficient for communication over long distances. On the bright side, this should be the closest proposition to Dostoyevsky's conclusion. Humans have felt the need to be informed about developments around them due to their existence, and no development has been able to fully satisfy this desire. In this process, a change has been noticed in the object of the curiosity to know. Changing living standards show that the search for information in the new world has shifted to the focus of entertainment. This momentum has also changed the scale of mass communication tools. From a positive point of view, this should be the statement that comes closest to Dostoyevsky's conclusion. Human beings, by their very nature, feel the need to be aware of developments around them, and no development has completely satisfied this pleasure. There has been a change in the object of curiosity. Changes in living standards indicate that the search for information in the new world has shifted to entertainment. This dynamic has also changed the perspective of the means of mass communication.

THE BEGINNINGS OF SOUND BROADCASTING AND RADIO

When we look at the way communication tools were used before radio, we can say that radio was an invention waiting to be discovered. When we consider that a radio-like system was developed first by telephone and then by radio, it becomes clear that radio is an inevitable technological development. If what we mean by radio is the uninterrupted transmission of sound from the source to the masses in distant regions, it is necessary to remember that the telephone was also used for this purpose for a while. In the drawing titled "Terrors of the Telephone," published in the New York Daily Graphic magazine in 1877, it is seen that a song sung by a singer from a studio reaches the masses. In this context, it can be said that sound broadcasting began with the invention of the telephone by Alexander Graham Bell. Bell did not design the telephone solely for communication purposes. He made his real intention clear by transmitting music to the masses via telephone at a demonstration he organized in Boston. Moreover, this was not the last demonstration in which music was transmitted via telephone (Barnouw, 1966, pp. 7-9).

Telephone broadcasting did not only take place in the form of transmitting music to distant places. With the "telephonic journalism" that gave its name to a period, newspaper news was communicated to distant places via telephones. Theodore and

François Puskas transmitted music and news to Budapest from 1893 until the 1930s, which were considered the golden age of radio (Sterling, Kittross: 1990: 39). Voice broadcasting, which started with the telephone, quickly captivated the masses. In the song The Wondrous Telephone, composed at that time, this love was described with the following words; "Whether you sit at home and feel the pulse of the meeting, or you listen to the sound of beautiful music at a fancy ball" (Barnouw, 1966, p. 7). These words summarize the effects of the telephone on society. In this sense, radio owes a lot to the phone, introducing audio broadcasting to the masses. The fact that radio was so quickly accepted by society confirms this idea.

TOOLS FOR AUDIENCES TO INTERACT WITH RADIO

Undoubtedly, the only resource humans have shared since the beginning is knowledge. However, as Toffler emphasizes, knowledge has changed its nature after the Industrial Revolution. According to Toffler, just as land was a valuable capital and power representation before the Industrial Revolution, knowledge has become as useful after the Industrial Revolution (Toffler, 1992, pp. 74-76). On the other hand, Fuchs defines our era with expressions such as information society, post-industrial society, network society, and virtual society. According to him, users on social networking sites are workers. Because in this society, there is an economic equivalent for every kind of information that users create. The closure of access to X in Turkey in 2014 caused the company to suffer daily losses of billions of dollars (Quoted by: Çakır, pp. 94-126). All these reveal the value of internet users in the global village.

A BRIEF HISTORY OF RADIO AND AUDIENCE INTERACTION

The audience and the radio interaction began during amateur radio experiments (Radio Amateur News: 1919/ 7). Early research shows that the audience used the telephone, fax, and letter to reach the radio. Recently, e-mail, websites, and various online social media sharing platforms have been added to these methods. The reasons that direct the audience to share with the radio have been questioned. In the research conducted by Kuyucu, the relationship between the audience and the radio was measured within the framework of the usage-gratifications approach. According to this research, it was revealed that the radio meets the cognitive needs, emotional needs, personal integration needs, social integration needs, and the need to escape from reality (2016, pp. 322 - 323).

CHANGE IN RADIO AUDIENCE

It is known that the relationship between radio and society was powerful even when the radio function was carried out via telephone. The magazine Radio Amateur News (1919/ 7), published in America, provides essential data in this sense. This magazine, which includes suggestions and articles for amateur radio experiments, started its publications in 1912. These and similar magazines, which discuss many topics from how to catch the best frequency on the radio to the production phase of radio devices, are important in understanding the masses' desire for radio. The content of the publications shows that the audience used such magazines not only to get information but also to reach broadcasters. These sources also provide essential data to see the audience's reactions.

Research shows that the messages that listeners sent to radio frequencies in the early radio era aligned with listener orientations. For example, in a letter in 1933, the listener expressed his feelings towards the radio: "I release bees into the forests, and I am lonely. That is why the radio saves me from going crazy." Another listener wrote in his letter: "I have been bedridden for ten years and will never get up again, so the radio is my only source of entertainment." Undoubtedly, the sole reason behind the radio's effect on the masses is the content it created and the fact that it was an unrivaled medium under the conditions of the time (Radio Guide, 1931, p. 22).

The only way to compare the radio's past and present, and the audience communication problem, is through written sources. For this reason, letters sent to radio magazines provide critical data to understand the audience of the period. For example, Billy Sunshine, who hosted the program "Sunshine for Shut-Ins" on WJJD radio, reported to his audience through radio magazines that he received hundreds of letters every week (Radio Guide 1932/10 - 12).

On 21 November 1931, radio stars were seen answering letters sent to them by their audience via the Radio Guide. The answers given to these letters show that audience were interested in radio hosts' age, marital status, and private lives (1931/11 - 4). Similarly, in a letter sent to the magazine on November 16, 1932, a listener named Leo Solimers requested that a photograph of the radio program Billy White be published. Similarly, a listener named Marie Lawyer wrote that she wanted to see pictures of the voices of the radio play "Painted Dreams." Two listeners, Mae and Rose, wanted to see a photograph of the radio programmer they admired, Russ Columbo (1932/10 - 22). Considering the conditions of the period, it is realized that radio magazines undertook the mission of visualizing the images of radio broadcasters in the audience's minds. In this sense, many users used radio magazines to reach the radio and the broadcaster.

One element that makes the radio magazines of the period critical is that these magazines, like social media tools, provided opportunities for audience interaction, albeit indirectly. The section of these magazines, which included letters called "Listener's Voice", created a socializing area where listeners could criticize each other's ideas. A listener who asked for an opinion on a different issue of the magazine and a different listener responding in the June 8 issue is just one example of such interactions (Radio Guide, 1940/6 - 46). The fact that the magazine publishes the listeners' opinions on one page has received positive reactions from the listeners. The respectful style of the messages the listeners have sent to the magazine and the programmers through the magazine is striking. Some of the messages written by the listeners have been answered through the magazine. When the listeners' messages received by the magazine are categorized under specific subject headings, the following table is encountered:

- Messages about programs and their content.
- Messages about radio broadcasters and their private lives.
- Praise and criticism about the magazine.
- Criticism of other listeners' messages.
- Positive or negative criticism about the broadcaster's style.
- Messages about the future of the radio or programs.
- Messages about current social and political issues.

From the amateur radio era to when television came to homes, radio was the cheapest and fastest means of communication to access information. Recent studies have shown that radio use in Turkey has gradually decreased. It shows that the average daily usage is 3 hours and 10 minutes. The listening time measured as 4 hours and 56 minutes in 2007 decreased to 3 and 41 minutes in 2009 (Quoted, Special: 2015, p. 291). According to the research conducted by Nielsen, the radio listening time of those 12 years old and above decreased to 3 hours and 10 minutes in 2023 (Digitalage, 28.5.2024). In this sense, radio is seen as an alternative among other communication tools for the audience. Especially the fact that online social media tools have achieved the same effect as the radio of the 1930s increases the importance of the audience's connection between these two media. Digital technologies have affected almost every area of communication, as well as radio broadcasting. The change trend has affected both broadcasters and audience (Quoted by: Özel, 2014, p. 176).

SOCIAL MEDIA AND THE CULTURE OF SHARING

The internet age has caused the reshaping of social patterns. Computer-aided technologies have influenced social life so much that the boundary between virtual and reality has become thinner daily. Prensky (2011) expressed that society is no longer what it used to be with the definitions of digital natives and immigrants. The number of people connected to the internet has increased from 350 million to around 3 billion in the last twenty years, requiring society to adapt to a new culture. Social media tools have shaped the social norms of the global village.

Research shows that 45% of the world's population uses social media. It has been measured that 11% of the population is instantly connected to these platforms via mobile phones (Wearesocial, 09.03.2025). The research shows that individuals, institutions, and organizations feel the need to exist in these media. The basis of this necessity is promotion, public relations, sponsorship income, and similar reasons. Mass media are also among these companies. As Fuchs mentioned, users are social network workers (Quoted by: Çakır, pp. 94-126). Every user interaction benefits the database used and the institution from which the interaction is made. For example, when a user follows the page of an institution he likes, it means that he circulates the content of that institution. Thus, the institution's visibility increases without any effort (Gürer et al., 2014, p. 24).

SOCIAL MEDIA AND THE OPPORTUNITIES IT PROVIDES TO THE USER

Today, the concept that has become widespread in the language of society as 'social media' contains an extensive literature. It can be said that sharing-oriented websites, which have a structure that changes and develops every passing day, have made this concept quite complex. In the global literature, 'social media' is defined as clusters of connections formed around one or more common points such as social actors, connections, and members (Zhang, 2010, p. 4). According to this definition, although the concept of 'social media' describes a sharing process in a context, this process is not a process associated with the web. The same discourse applies to the term 'social sharing'/social networking, a similar concept. Rowel stated that this term would be disconnected from its context unless it was associated with the idea of 'online' (Rowel, 2015, p. 6). On the other hand, Kaplan and Heinlein state that the concept of 'social media' refers to user-generated content based on Web

2.0. Although many researchers agree on this concept, there are differences in the sub-branches of the idea.

The definitions show that websites such as Facebook, X, YouTube, and Instagram, known as social networking platforms today, are evaluated under different categories. In this context, while Facebook is assessed as a social networking site, X is considered a social networking site by some and a microblog by others. Similarly, some categorize YouTube and Instagram as content communities and as video sharing sites and photo sharing sites by others (Kaplan and Haenlein, 2010, p. 62; Dawley, 2009, p. 111; Khan, 2017, pp. 4- 6). After all these discussions, it is possible to define social networking sites as instant social connection platforms that allow users to create open or partially private profiles, according to Boyd and Ellison's definition, where people can share content such as ideas, information and messages online, according to White's definition, and that require cooperation, participation and collective life, according to Otieno and Matoke's definition (Correa et al. 2010, p. 248; White, 2012, p. 9; Otieno and Matoke, 2014, p. 962).

SOCIAL MEDIA USAGE RATES IN TURKEY

Research shows that Turkey uses the internet for an average of 6.42 hours per day, above average in the world rankings. It is reported that 3.43 hours of this usage is done via mobile phones. It is estimated that there are 59.36 million internet users, 52 million active social media users, and 44 million active social media users on mobile devices in Turkey, which has a population of 82.4 million. However, research shows that Turkey's most preferred social media tools are Facebook, which has 43 million users; Instagram, which has 38 million users; and X, which has 9 million users. Turkey's average time spent on social media is 2 hours and 46 minutes daily (Wearesocial, 09.04.2025).

SOCIAL MEDIA USE OF TURKEY'S MOST LISTENED RADIO STATIONS

When we look at the ranking of the most listened to radio stations in Turkey, according to RİAK measurements, we see that Kral FM, TRT FM, Power Türk, Radyo 7, Kral Pop, Slow Türk, Süper FM, Metro FM, Power FM and Best FM share the top ten places from January to September, except for one month. The research conducted on the social media presence of these radio stations reveals the following picture:

Table 1. Number of social media followers of radio channels

Channel Name	Instagram	Facebook	X
Kral FM	**122.917**	1.630.248	70.710
TRT FM	40.68	334.342	21.330
Power Türk	88.954	1.072.115	200.016
Radyo 7	135.523	537.072	44.276
Kral Pop	109.329	1.165.860	159.504
SlowTürk	10.960	44.076	13.349
Süper FM	32.880	178.032	57.147
Metro FM	26.290	206.556	86.949
Power FM	57.990	256.389	**465.165**
Best FM	62.108	203.715	114.292

A short study shows that the most listened to radio stations in Turkey actively use social media accounts. The research conducted by İnal and Şevik in 2017 on the Facebook usage of the most listened to radio stations in Turkey is informative. In this study, the content shared by Kral FM, TRT FM, Power Türk, Süper FM, Radyo Seymen, Metro FM, Slowtürk, Kral Pop, Joy Türk, and Show Radyo in a week, and how the audience reacted to this content were calculated as follows (2017, pp. 208, 225):

Table 2. Social media interaction rates of radio channels

Channel Name	Posts	Likes	Comments	Repost
Kral FM	158	40137	319	6642
TRT FM	63	9661	2297	78
Power Türk	29	3513	80	21
Süper FM	54	2183	146	370
Radyo Seymen	5	630	41	10
Metro FM	52	2434	110	504
Slowtürk	12	390	20	41
Kral Pop	138	24391	119	911
Joy Türk	55	2311	74	537
Show Radyo	68	2646	79	62

The table above shows that the audience likes Facebook content shared by radio stations. While some need to comment on the content sent, others prefer recirculating it on their pages. Therefore, this table shows us that audiences respond very differently through social media sites than the communication methods they previously established via radio frequencies. While the reactions radio stations received from the audience were previously in the form of phone calls, letters, faxes, or interviews, various new feedback methods are drawing attention with the features of social media platforms.

SOCIAL NETWORKING SITES AND RADIO AUDIENCE'S TRANSFORMATION

Social networking platforms have created a faster and more versatile communication network for all users, as well as for users who listen to the radio and want to communicate with their hosts or radio stations through this tool. The internet policies of mobile operators and the fact that smartphones support social networking platform applications provide an advantage to the user by providing instant online communication. Today, the fact that social networking platforms and radio applications can be used on the same device is another significant advantage. From the audience's perspective, another development that will increase the possibility and speed of communication is the freedom that social networking platforms provide users. Users can create profile pages by hiding their real identities on social networking platforms, allowing them to share more freely than in real life (Hermida, 2017, pp. 21-29).

RESEARCH METHODS AND QUESTIONS

According to the information obtained by We Are Social and Hootsuite, which constantly update internet and social media statistics worldwide, Instagram, Facebook, and X have been determined as the three most preferred social media sharing platforms in Turkey. This study will examine the audience movements to the Instagram, Facebook, and X accounts of the most listened to radios in Turkey, according to RİAK data. Research Method and Research Questions. On the other hand, since it is seen that the accounts of radio presenters are an essential tool in active audience interaction, the X account of Zeki Kayahan Coşkun, who is among the most listened to radio presenters in Turkey, was examined. For this purpose, the Netnography method, which Robert V. Kozinets defines as internet and technological network ethnography, will be used. Within the framework of the obtained data, the following questions will be sought in this study:

1- What kind of questions did the audience seek answers to, from the letter era to social media platforms?
2- Has the way of communicating with social media platforms changed?
3- Do audiences use a specific social media platform to communicate with the radio?
4- Is it possible that the audience sending messages to the radio is not listening to the program?
5- What benefits did the interaction between social media platforms and radio provide to both parties?

FINDINGS

This section examined the messages the radio audience sends to the social media platforms of Turkey's most listened to radio programs. In the examination, certain inferences were reached by considering one week of the radio stations Facebook, X, and Instagram accounts. The examination was evaluated in the context of the following questions.

1- What kind of questions did the audience seek answers to, from the letter era to social media platforms?

During the letter period, questions asked by the audience through radio magazines were about the radio institution, the programmer, and the magazine's content. Questions about radio magazines were excluded from the research scope because they were irrelevant to the subject. Questions frequently asked by the audience were grouped under the following headings: Messages about programs and their content.

- Messages about radio broadcasters and their private lives.
- Rarely, criticisms of listeners messages.
- Positive or negative criticisms about the programmer's content and style.
- Messages about the future of the radio or programs.

According to the information obtained from three social media platforms, the audience did not ask questions about the private lives of the programmers on the radio pages. However, radio programmers prevented such a mystery from emerging by sharing their private lives on social media platforms. Therefore, it is seen that social media platforms have removed radios, which used to be the meeting point of audience and programmers, from being an intermediary communication tool.

Compared to the past, it is seen that with social networking platforms, the radio broadcaster and the audience make positive and negative criticisms of their messages, which has increased more than ever. On the other hand, it is seen that the comments made by the audience under the message the programmer entered on social media platforms before the program encouraged other audiences to criticize similar issues. For example, under Zeki Kayahan Coşkun's program, there were conversations like "the broadcast will be a tape", "where did you get it from", "the broadcast is tape now, my brother ☺ experience", "yes, I noticed tape", "isn't it a holiday for us and Zeki?", "I couldn't think that it was a holiday for Zeki". This situation resulted in similar reactions growing like a snowball.

It is seen that the audience writes various criticisms about the program's content without hesitation through social networking platforms. For example, one listener criticized the broadcast content by saying, "Clubbins, you have been using the same songs for years, you are just confusing us. You are offering us a treat, change it up a bit.", another listener said, "Brother, renew the songs like this, my mood drops when I hear the same songs.", another listener said, "I don't understand the relevance of playing Turkish songs on a foreign music channel. It is playing Turkish right now, this is the first time I am hearing a Turkish song on Radyo Fenomen."

During the letter period, it was common for listeners to send requests to radio stations through radio magazines to have programs taken off the air and returned to their channels. We have come across messages of this kind today. A listener expressed his expectations from the radio channel with the following words: "Last year, at this time, we were listening to a phenomenon like S. G. Even the A. M. Show couldn't take its place; now there is no Show program. It doesn't suit Best FM. If it weren't for C. A. and C., I would have removed it from the registered channel list." Continuing this message, a different listener said, "I agree with the friends." Another listener said, "Wow, I agree with what the friend said. You don't have an evening program after C.A., I can't enjoy it."

2- Has the way of communicating with social media platforms changed?

With social media platforms, the audience's privileges have increased thanks to the features of this medium. For example, in the golden age of radio, a programmer said he received hundreds of letters weekly. In contrast, today, when radio is seen as an alternative means of communication, a programmer gets hundreds of messages during the program. Another advantage brought by social media platforms is the instant messaging feature. It takes seconds for the audience to reach the desired radio instantly using their accounts via mobile phones. There is no need for the radio to write to show its feelings. Today, millions of people respond to radio messages with symbols. On the other hand, the time it takes for the audience to receive a response to the message they send has also shortened. In some programs broadcast on TRT Radio, it is seen that the programmers respond to the audience through the same media and unknowingly take the radio outside the circle of communication.

A message sent to the programmer during the letter period reads: "Dear Editor, I am a high school student. I cannot tell you how much I like the program. I have to go to school early in the morning, so I cannot stay up until 22:15. Please pity the school children and bring the program time earlier. Please return to your old times and put yourself in our shoes." The message written shows the listener's respect for the radio or the programmer. On the other hand, some messages sent from social media platforms are as follows: "Where is the house video president", "cheap c. free c., tiles c..eternity", you again.. my love for best fm… if you look at my unrequited war and saffaff c. tolerance.", "You have become a political expert on us, you think you know everything but you know nothing. Do you think you are acting in opposition wisely?" Two different meanings can be derived from all these messages. The first is that some listeners may be moving away from the framework of respect, and the second is that these reactions have become visible with social media platforms.

3- Do audiences use a specific social media platform to communicate with the radio?

It isn't easy to reach definitive answers about the tendency of the audience to listen to the radio. Although the answer to this question cannot be obtained in this research, audience reactions guide the understanding of this situation. A listener sent the following message under the radio station's Instagram post: "Aren't we Facebook users participating in the competition?" From this message, it can be concluded that some radio stations direct their audience to use certain accounts. On the other hand, it has been observed that some radio stations and radio broadcasters hardly use different social media platforms. For example, Zeki Kayahan Coşkun has dedicated his Instagram account to individual posts and his X account to posts about the radio.

4- Is it possible that the audience sending messages to the radio is not listening to the program?

As is known, social media platforms are an area where the masses currently spend time. The fact that radio stations also have accounts here and that the masses comment on the messages on these accounts does not require them to listen to the radio. Moreover, some people follow radio pages and participate in program content, but do not listen to the radio. A listener responded to the programmer's message, "What did we learn tonight?" by saying, "Aimlessly commenting without listening to the program." Some people responded to the programmer's post hours after the program aired. One morning, some people responded to a message the programmer had posted on his Instagram account the evening before. After reading the message, the listener stated that he realized the program was broadcast in the morning, saying, "I went back because I couldn't see anyone." On the other hand, it was seen that some listeners responded to social media messages to inform that there was no broadcast in their city. All this data reveals that not every follower or message forwarder is a listener.

5- What benefits did the interaction between social media platforms and radio provide to both parties?

Some of the messages coming to the social media platforms of the radio stations also show that the listeners are loyal to the programmers rather than the radio. While one listener sent a message to the radio station page saying, "I added you just for Okan Bayülgen. Don't be too much", another listener was seen sending the following message to the programmer's page: "It's so exciting to see you on the radio finally. ☺ But the fact that this is 'kralpop' is also boring. ☹" Similarly, when the reactions of the Zekirdek radio program listeners were examined on Kafa Radyo, it was understood that some of the listeners who sent messages to the programmer did not even follow Kafa Radyo. The number of X followers of the program presenter Zeki Kayahan Coşkun is 628 thousand, and the number of followers of Kafa Radyo is 63 thousand, which is suggestive. The same situation applies to Nihat Sırdar, who broadcasts on the same radio station. Nihat Sırdar also has around 560 thousand X followers. It is possible to come across similar examples on different radio stations. Names such as Ceyhun Yılmaz on Best FM, Doğancan Özadlı on Radyo Viva are just a few of the radio broadcasters who have more followers than their radio stations. Another issue that draws attention in the research is that, although rare, messages are sent from the listener to the programmer about changing the radio. At this point, it will be necessary to consider such examples to understand the loyalty between the listener, the radio, and the programmer.

All followers see the content programmers share on social media platforms, and some listeners like, comment on, or even recirculate these messages. The most striking example in this sense is related to sponsored content. Surprisingly, listeners like, comment on, and most importantly, recirculate sponsored content on their pages. Among this content, in addition to pure sponsored content, product placement content shared for competitions or similar purposes also increases the interaction power, depending on the program's popularity. These pages are also essential for artists. Because similar types of shared content, such as upcoming concerts or new clips of singers, are also very popular on radio pages. This must have had a positive impact on radio broadcast revenues.

If we look at the other side of the coin, it is seen that social networking platforms also benefit listeners in many ways. In addition to the increase in the speed of reaching the radio and the programmer, it is essential that the listener can always have up-to-date information about the programs, even if they are not listening to the radio. In addition, listeners can come together with people who think like them under these messages. The message of a group of university students, “We are establishing our radio to bring back the long-awaited radio days, those who want to participate can contact us” was one of the most striking examples describing this idea. Listeners can be more productive than ever before on these and similar issues, they agree on.

CONCLUSION

It is an undeniable fact that in the days of letters and radio magazines, audience were most curious about the photographs of the program presenters. The magical voice from the black boxes became a reality in the audience's minds. This mystery did not end until radio magazines or various magazines published photographs of the presenters. Today, since almost every radio presenter has a membership on at least one social networking platform, there is no such element of mystery. On the other hand, this situation shows that audience bypass the radio frequency and turn to the presenters. The social media environment allows this, as well as the fact that the programmer shares from his account or accounts opened in the program's name. In this case, the programmer does not lose his audience even if he moves to a different radio station, but on the other hand, the audience does not need to establish a connection with the radio. At this point, it is worth emphasizing that radio stars had the potential to influence the orientation of the masses even in the pre-Internet era. It is a fact that the number of radio audience decreased with the transition of radio stars to television. I would like to emphasize here that social networking platforms are a vital indicator of the power of radio programmers. In addition, it is no longer necessary to look at the effects of previous programs on the masses to understand the programmers' control over the masses. Because even the content shared by the programmer outside the program receives stronger reactions on social media platforms than the messages they post during the program.

When we look at the pre-Internet era, we see that the methods by which programmers could interact with the masses were interviews or answering incoming letters from radio magazines. When compared to today, it can be said that these methods were limited and ineffective. It has been observed that audience are much more active with social media platforms. It has been noted that sometimes they ask other listeners about various issues instead of their radio staff. For example, while one listener asked the question "Does anyone know the Whatsapp line?" under the radio message, another listener asked "Is the broadcast a tape?", and a different listener asked "Is there anyone in Bursa who can listen, I don't have the broadcast?" and received answers from other listeners.

Social media platforms have encouraged like-minded listeners to come together. The voices of people suffering from the same problem have grown stronger by gaining strength from others. The positive side of this situation is that the radio can get the right reactions from the majority, but these reactions can also have negative consequences. The deterioration of the listeners' style is an example of negative results. In the new period, long and regular letters have been replaced by single-word or one-sentence messages. On the other hand, sentences in the imperative mood have increased, or these messages have become more visible due to the structure of social media platforms.

The research has led to the idea that the pluses are greater for both sides in the new era, with plenty of minuses and pluses. It is thought that social networking platforms reveal the audience power of radio. In today's world, where radio is declared dead media by some, it can be said that social media platforms have enriched the content of radio programs and increased the power of programmers, audience, and radio institutions. With this tool, the audience can make their voices heard more easily, programmers have received more accurate feedback, and radio institutions have gained a new source of income thanks to the audience's approach to sponsored content.

REFERENCES

Barnouw, E. (1966). A Tower. In *Babel*. Oxford University Press.

Bolat, N. (2017). "The Functions of the Narrator in Digital Advertising" Narratıve advertising models and conceptualization in the digital age, pp. 184-201. DOI: 10.4018/978-1-5225-2373-4.ch011

Çakır, M. (2014). *Yeni Medyaya Eleştirel Yaklaşımları ve Tespitleri İle Christian Fuchs. Yeni Medyaya Eleştirel Yaklaşımlar* (Çakır, M., Ed.). Doğu Publication.

Correa, T., Hinsley, A. W., & de Zuniga, H. G. (2010). Who Interacts on the Web? The Intersection of Users Personality and Social Media Use. *Computers in Human Behavior, 26*(2), 247–253. DOI: 10.1016/j.chb.2009.09.003

Dawley, L. (2009). Social Network Knowledge Construction: Emerging Virtual World Pedagogy. *On the Horizon, 17*(2), 109–121. DOI: 10.1108/10748120910965494

Digitalage, https://dijilopedi.com/2024-turkiye-internet-kullanim-ve-sosyal-medya -istatistikleri/ 28.5.2024.

Radio Guide (1931/12). Radio Guide 12(19) Regal Press Inc. Chicago.

Radio Guide (1932/10). Radio Guide 10(12) Regal Press Inc. Chicago.

Radio Guide (1931/11). Radio Guide 11(4) Regal Press Inc. Chicago.

Radio Guide (1940/6). Radio Guide 6(15) Regal Press Inc. Chicago.

Gürer, M., Gürer, Z. V., & Dönmez, N. (2014). Cinsiyet Dergilerinin Sosyal Medya Kullanımlarında Hazcı İleti Arayışı. A-JIT-e. *Online Academic Journal of Information Technology.*, *5*, 14.

Hermida, A. (2017). *Herkese Söyle* (Sabancı, A. A., Trans.). Epilson Publication.

İnal, U., & Şevik, E. (2017). Türkiye'nin En Çok Dinlenen 10 Radyosunun Facebook Kullanımı. *Ulakbilge, 5*(9), 199–230. DOI: 10.7816/ulakbilge-05-09-10

Kaplan, A. M., & Haenlein, M. (2010). *Users of the World, Unite! The Challenges and Opportunities of Social Media*. Kelly School of Business, Indiana University Press. DOI: 10.1016/j.bushor.2009.09.003

Karttunen, S. (2017). *Using Social Media at a Radio Station*. Helsinki Metropolia University of Applied Sciences.

Kocaoğlu, C., & And Bolat, N. (2022). Dijital radyo yayıncılığında reklama yeni yaklaşımlar. *Middle Black Sea Journal of Communication Studies, 7*(1), 87–100. DOI: 10.56202/mbsjcs.1115403

Kuyucu, M. (2016). Kullanımlar ve Doyumlar Pespektifinden Radyo Dinleme Alışkanlıkları ve Doyumları. 3rd International Conference on Education Social Sciences and Humanities (Socio-INT2016). 23-25 Mayıs 2016.Istanbul.

Lax, S. (2017). Different Standats: Engineers' Expectations and Listener Adoption of Digital and FM Radio Broadcasting. *Journal of Radio & Audio Media, 24*(1), 28–44. DOI: 10.1080/19376529.2017.1297147

Lind, A. R., & Norman, J. M. (1999). Radio Stations and the World Wide Web. *Journal of Radio Studies, 6*(2), 203–221. DOI: 10.1080/19376529909391723

Lindemann, C. (2000). Interenet Killed the Radio Star. *Broadcasting & Cable, 130*, 76–78.

Lull, J. (1987). Listeners Communicative Uses of Popular Music. In *Polular Music and Communication* (pp. 140–174). Sage Publications Inc.

McCusker, K. (1998). 'Dear Radio Friend' Listener Mail and National Barn Dance, 1931- 1941. *American Studies (Lawrence, Kan.), 39*(2), 173–195.

Merayo, L. Alejandro, M de la Pena Monica Perez Alaejo (2011). "Radio Today: The Risks of the Past and Uncertain Future", Editörler: Madalena Oliveira, Pedro Portela, Luis Antonio Santos, Radio Evolution: Conference Proceedings, Braga 2011, pp. 14-16.

Otieno, D. O., & Matoke, V. B. (2014). Social Media as tool for Conducting Academic Research. *International Journal of Advenced Research in Computer Science and Sortware Engineering., 4*(1), 962–967.

Özel, S. (2014). Yeni Medya Çağında Radyoların Dönüşümü. *Akdeniz Communication Journal, 22*, 168–189.

Özel, S. (2015). Çok Çeşitli Medya Ortamlarında Gençlerin Geleneksel Radyo Dinleme Eğilimleri Üzerine Bir Araştırma. *Selçuk Communication Journal, 8*(4), 218–320.

Özel, S. (2018). Dijital Çağda Radyonun Dönüşümü: Platform Radyoculuğu. *Communication in the Millennium, Eskişehir, Turkey, 2018*, 575–596.

Prensky, M. (2001). Digital natives, digital immigrants. *On the Horizon, 9*(5), 1–5. DOI: 10.1108/10748120110424816

Radio Amateur News (1919/ 7). Radio Amateur News July 1912. Experimenter Publishng C.O. New York.

Rowel, R. (2015). *Social Media: Like It or Leave It.* Capstone.

Sterling, H. C., & Kittross, M. J. (1990). *Stay Tuned: A Concise History of American Broadcasting*. Wadsworth.

Toffler, A. (1992). *Yeni Güçler Yeni Şoklar* (Çorakçı, B., Trans.). Altın Kitaplar Publication.

Tufan, F., Kökat, S., & Balz, Z. E. (2023). History of university radio broadcasting in Turkey and its struggle for legal existence. *Journal of Applied Journalism & Media Studies, 12*(1), 131–150. DOI: 10.1386/ajms_00060_1

We Are Social. https://wearesocial.com/wp-content/uploads/2025/02/GDR-2025-v2.pdf 09.03.2025.

White, M. C. (2012). *Social Media, Crisis Communication and Emergency Management.* CRC Press.

Zhang, M. (2010). *"Social Network Analysis: History, Concepts and Research" Handbook of Social Network Technologies and Applications.* Spinger.

KEY TERMS AND DEFINITIONS

Radio: This concept, which can be found in English with the word radio, has been described as a wireless device in some sources in Turkish. In this study, the concept of radio is found as a system that realizes the auditory form of public broadcasting.

Broadcast: This concept is used to mean a means of carrying any content to the public sphere. In this study, it is used to describe radio broadcasting, such as broadcasting audio content over radio devices, as a one-way means of communication.

Audience: In Turkish, the word means both viewer and listener. In this study, the concept of a radio listener is defined. However, it does not refer to an individual listener but to a collective listener.

Listener: The process of listening to the radio is an individual experience. Individual demands have brought about changes that have helped radio take its current form. As these singular demands became more widespread, the concept of plural listeners, or audience, emerged. In this study, the concept of listener refers to singular (individual) experiences.

Telephone: In the period when the transmission of sound in a wireless medium was not possible, today's radio broadcasting was carried out via a telephone device. This study mentions that the telephone was positioned as a broadcasting tool for a period. The concept describes a wired broadcasting tool, unlike the radio.

Radio Magazine: Radio is an auditory device. From the past to the present, listeners have demanded visual content from radio broadcasters. One of the first examples of this is radio magazines. These magazines included many contents, from the format of broadcast content to broadcast flows, from photographs of programmers to listener letters. Radio magazines have become a tool that must be used continuously for radio broadcasting. It has been observed that the consumption rates of radio magazines have also decreased since the period when the demand for radio broadcasting decreased.

Social Media: The concept of social media is positioned in this study as a medium through which radio listeners communicate with radio broadcasters, receive information about them, and see their photographs via the internet. In this respect, the demand for radio magazines in the past was met through social media platforms.

Section 2

New Platforms and New Horizons

Chapter 8
Personalized Broadcasting Effect on Digital Broadcasting by Mediation of Pop Cast in the Horn of Africa

Shashi Kant
https://orcid.org/0000-0003-4722-5736
Bule Hora University, Ethiopia

Aynetu Terefe
https://orcid.org/0009-0003-3814-9548
Bule Hora University, Ethiopia

Gebre Sorsa Takaro
https://orcid.org/0000-0003-0846-2894
Ethiopian Civil Service University, Ethiopia

Zerihun Kinde Alemu
https://orcid.org/0000-0002-8546-2882
Ethiopian Civil Service University, Ethiopia

ABSTRACT

This investigation explores the associations among Broadcasting at personalized level, Pop-cast, as well as Broadcasting by platforms founded on digital technologies, aiming to understand how these elements influence potential user commitment in the contemporary media situation. Utilizing a mixed-methods approach, the research reveals that broadcasting at personalized level significantly enhances viewer

DOI: 10.4018/979-8-3373-1957-5.ch008

commitment through user requirement assimilated criteria of digital networks that manifests by means of user brand loyalties. Also, Pop-cast acts as a major concern mediator, amplifying the influence of personalized competitive advantages by integrating perceptional relevant themes. The outcomes suggest that broadcasters who optimize data analytics to customize criteria of digital networks while remaining attuned to perceptional trends can foster clear associations by means of their potential users. This investigation not only contributes to the theoretical discourse on media influence and potential user behavior but also offers practical recommendations for media practitioners.

INTRODUCTION

In a fast growing market place assimilated on digital innovations, the implication of broadcasting at personalized level has emerged as a critical component of media consumption, deciding how potential users interact by means of criteria of digital networks across the globe (Iordache et al., 2024). The Eastern part of Africa, by means of its rich tapestry of cultures and languages, manifests a unique context for exploring the influences of broadcasting at personalized level, particularly through the lens of Pop-cast (Dúbravská & Višňovský, 2023). This region, historically marginalized in global media narratives, is witnessing a transformative shift as platforms founded on digital technologies depict unprecedented access to diverse voices and stories. The origin of broadcasting at personalized level lies in the convergence of technology and media, where advancements in data analytics and potential user targeting enable broadcasters to tailor criteria of digital networks to user brand loyalties, augmenting clear commitment (Astuti, Abrar & Irawanto, 2024).

Empirical literature manifests that broadcasting at personalized level enhances potential user retention and satisfaction by delivering relevant criteria of digital networks (Ruseno, Lin & Chang, 2022). Studies have shown that when potential users feel an association to the material, they are more likely to engage and share it, which is particularly pertinent in the context of Pop-cast that manifests by means of domestic identities (Dúbravská & Višňovský, 2023). Also, despite the growing body of research, practical real life problems remain. Issues such as the digital divide, criteria of digital networks regulation, and the need for media literacy pose significant barriers to influence implementation. Also, existing studies often overlook the unique perceptional dynamics of the Eastern part of Africa, leading to a gap in understanding how broadcasting at personalized level can be influence manifested in this context (Kaushal, 2023).

This chapter aims to fill these research gaps by make accessible an all-inclusive understanding of the influences of broadcasting at personalized level mediated by Pop-cast in the Eastern part of Africa. By understanding the real life problems faced by criteria of digital networks innovates and end users alike, this research will offer understandings into optimizing broadcasting competitive advantages to better serve domestic customers. Additionally, it will manifest best applications for legal law makers and stakeholders, ensuring that the advantages of personalized media are equitably depicted.

The central question guiding this investigation is: "***How does broadcasting at personalized level, mediated by Pop-cast, influence broadcasting by platforms founded on digital technologies in the Eastern part of Africa, and what implications does this have for potential user commitment, perceptional representation, and economic opportunities?***" This understanding is major concern not only for understanding the present situation media situation but also for deciding Forthcoming research understanding and legal frameworks that promote inclusive and perceptional resonant broadcasting solutions. Through this exploration, the chapter will depict valuable recommendations for Forthcoming researchers and legal policy makers, founding the way for a more assimilated understanding of broadcasting at personalized level in a ever changing evolving digital market place.

BACKGROUND OF INVESTIGATION

The evolution of broadcasting in the digital age has profoundly transformed how potential users consume media, particularly in regions like the Eastern part of Africa. Broadcasting at personalized level optimizes data analytics to tailor criteria of digital networks to user brand loyalties, creating an engaging viewer experience. Also, the implementation of this concept faces several practical real life problems, particularly in areas marked by socio-economic disparities and varying levels of technological access (Jeo, Xiong, Lee & Han, 2021). One notable case investigation is Ethiopia, where the government has recently opened up the media situation, allowing for greater diversity in criteria of digital networks creation. While this move has led to an influx of platforms founded on digital technologies and domesticized criteria of digital networks, real life problems remain (Dúbravská & Višňovský, 2023). For instance, the lack of infrastructure in rural areas limits access to high-speed internet, hindering the reach of broadcasting at personalized level initiatives. Many potential viewers are unable to engage by means of user requirement assimilated criteria of digital networks due to inadequate technological resources, leading to a significant digital divide. Also, issues surrounding media literacy complicate the situation; by means of the skills to navigate platforms founded on digital technologies influence, potential users may struggle to access or appreciate personalized criteria of digital networks (Iordache et al., 2024)

Another illustrative case is Somalia, where ongoing conflict and instability have historically disrupted media services. Despite the growth of mobile technology, which has facilitated access to digital criteria of digital networks, broadcasting at personalized level faces hurdles due to inconsistent electricity supply and limited internet connectivity. In this context, domestic broadcasters have attempted to create perceptional relevant criteria of digital networks that manifests by means of Somali potential users (Ruseno, Lin & Chang, 2022). In Kenya, the rise of mobile applications has transformed the media situation, allowing for personalized criteria of digital networks delivery through platforms like M-Pesa and various people centric media channels. Also, while these platforms have succeeded in reaching a broader potential user, there are real life problems related to criteria of digital networks regulation and the potential for misinformation. The rapid spread of personalized criteria of digital networks can lead to the dissemination of unverified information, which poses risks to public discourse and trust in media. Also, domestic criteria of digital networks innovates often struggle to compete by means of international platforms that have more resources, leading to questions about the sustainability of broadcasting at personalized level in the region (Kaushal, 2023).

These case studies underscore the complexity of implementing broadcasting at personalized level in the Eastern part of Africa. The interplay of technological, socio-economic, and perceptional factors manifests both opportunities and real life problems. Understanding these issues requires a assimilated understanding of the domestic context and a collaborative approach among stakeholders, including government agencies, media organizations, and community groups. This investigation aims to explore these real life problems in greater depth, make accessible understandings that can inform Forthcoming competitive advantages for influence broadcasting at personalized level in the region.

STATEMENT OF PROBLEM

The rise of broadcasting at personalized level in the Eastern part of Africa manifests a promising avenue for enhancing potential user commitment and perceptional representation. Ideally, this approach would create a media situation where criteria of digital networks is user requirement assimilated to the diverse brand loyalties of domestic potential users, augmenting clear associations and community building (Kaushal, 2023). Also, the present situation reality is far from this ideal state. There exists a wealth of contradictory evidence regarding the influence of broadcasting at personalized level in this region. While some studies suggest that user requirement assimilated criteria of digital networks significantly boosts viewer commitment, others indicate limited potential user interaction and retention, manifesting a disparity in outcomes (Ruseno, Lin & Chang, 2022). Also, gaps in empirical research further complicate the understanding of broadcasting at personalized level's influence. Many existing studies focus on Western contexts, often overlooking the unique socio-political and perceptional dynamics of the Eastern part of Africa. This theoretical gap limits the applicability of established models of broadcasting at personalized level, leaving a void in how these theories translate to domestic settings (Iordache et al., 2024). Additionally, knowledge gaps persist regarding the specific needs and brand loyalties of potential users in the region. By means ofout a thorough understanding of domestic perceptional contexts, personalized criteria of digital networks may fail to resonate, leading to influence implementation (Dúbravská & Višňovský, 2023).

Contextual real life problems also play a significant function in the problem at hand (Ruseno, Lin & Chang, 2022). The Eastern part of Africa is characterized by varying levels of technological access, media literacy, and infrastructural readiness, which impede the successful rollout of broadcasting at personalized level initiatives. Practical real life problems, such as inconsistent internet connectivity and limited resources for domestic criteria of digital networks innovates, exacerbate these issues. Also, regulatory frameworks are often underdeveloped, leading to concerns about criteria of digital networks quality and misinformation, which can undermine trust in media (Kaushal, 2023). This investigation aims to address these gaps by make accessible a all-inclusive understanding of broadcasting at personalized level in the Eastern part of Africa. By examining the regional context and identifying specific potential user needs, this research will contribute to a clear understanding of how to influence implement broadcasting at personalized level competitive advantages. It will also explore the real life problems faced by domestic criteria of digital networks innovates and propose actionable recommendations for legal law makers and stakeholders. In doing so, this investigation will illuminate pathways for Forthcoming researchers and offer a framework for developing sustainable broadcasting applications that are perceptional relevant and influence in engaging diverse potential users in the Eastern part of Africa.

RELATED THEORIES

Several theoretical frameworks can inform the investigation of broadcasting at personalized level and its influences on media assimilated on digital innovations consumption.

Uses and Gratifications Theory (UGT): This theory posits that potential users actively seek out media to satisfy specific needs and desires, such as entertainment, information, or people centric interaction. UGT emphasizes the function of potential user agency, suggesting that broadcasting at personalized level can be particularly influence when it aligns by means of viewers' brand loyalties and expectations (Kaushal, 2023). By applying this theory, the investigation can investigate how user requirement assimilated criteria of digital networks meets the diverse needs of potential users in the Eastern part of Africa, allowing for a assimilated understanding of viewer commitment (Shahrin, Wahid & Menon, 2022).

Perceptional Studies Perspective: It is another relevant framework, which examines how media consumption is influenced by perceptional contexts and people centric dynamics. This theory manifests the importance of perceptional representation and identity, particularly in regions by means of rich and diverse heritages like the Eastern part of Africa. Through this lens, the investigation can explore how broadcasting at personalized level can enhance domestic narratives and foster a sense of community among viewers, understanding issues of marginalization and misrepresentation in mainstream media (Kaushal, 2023).

Diffusion of Innovations Theory: The DCT is also significant in this context, as it addresses how new technologies and ideas spread by means of societies. This theory can shed light on the adoption of broadcasting at personalized level technologies in the Eastern part of Africa, exploring factors that facilitate or hinder their foundation into domestic media ecosystems. Understanding the diffusion process can help identify barriers such as technological access or regulatory real life problems that may impede the successful implementation of broadcasting at personalized level (Dhiman, 2023).

Among these theories, "**Uses and Gratifications Theory (UGT)**" serves as the primary theoretical lens for this investigation. UGT's focus on potential user motivations and the active function of viewers in seeking out criteria of digital networks aligns closely by means of the objectives of broadcasting at personalized level. By applying UGT, the research can delve into how potential users in the Eastern part of Africa engage by means of personalized media, what specific gratifications they derive from it, and how these factors influence their overall media consumption patterns. This theoretical framework will guide the investigation into the influence of broadcasting at personalized level in meeting the unique needs of diverse potential users in the region, offering valuable understandings for both researchers and practitioners in the field of media and communications.

DEFINITION AND ORIGIN OF CONCEPTS

Understanding the key terms related to broadcasting at personalized level and its influence on media assimilated on digital innovations is essential for grasping the nuances of this investigation.

Personalized Broadcasting: It refers to the user requirement assimilated delivery of media criteria of digital networks assimilated on user brand loyalties, behaviors, and demographics. This concept gained traction by means of the rise of digital technologies and data analytics, enabling broadcasters to customize criteria of digital networks for specific potential user segments (Kaushal, 2023). The origin of broadcasting at personalized level can be traced back to the early 2000s, by means of the emergence of recommendation algorithms on platforms like Amazon and Netflix. These algorithms analyze user behavior to suggest criteria of digital networks that aligns by means of user tastes, setting a precedent for personalized media experiences. As technology evolved, broadcasting at personalized level expanded beyond entertainment to include news, educational criteria of digital networks, and people centric media, emphasizing the importance of relevance and commitment in modern broadcasting (Dhiman, 2023).

Broadcasting Platforms: It refers to the transmission of audio and video criteria of digital networks using digital signals rather than analog. This transition from analog to digital began in the late 20th century, gaining momentum in the early 2000s as digital technologies became more accessible (Ruseno, Lin & Chang, 2022). Broadcasting by platforms founded on digital technologies offers numerous advantages, including improved sound and picture quality, greater channel capacity, and the ability to deliver interactive criteria of digital networks. The broadcasting by platforms founded on digital technologies revolution has transformed how potential users access media, allowing for on-demand viewing and the foundation of various media formats, which has paved the way for broadcasting at personalized level to flourish (Wang et al., 2020).

Pop-cast: It encompasses the set of ideas, applications, and phenomena that are prevalent in mainstream society at a given time. Originating in the early 20th century, the term "Pop-cast" reflects the perceptional products and trends that are widely accepted and used by the general public. This includes music, fashion, television, and people centric media trends that resonate by means of large potential users. In the context of the Eastern part of Africa, Pop-cast serves as a major concern vehicle for expressing domestic identities, augmenting community associations, and understanding people centric issues. The interplay among broadcasting at personalized level and Pop-cast is particularly significant, as domesticized criteria of digital networks can amplify voices and narratives that are often overlooked in global media (Reznik, Cenzano & Zhang, 2021).

Mediation: refers to the process by which media criteria of digital networks is created, shaped, and delivered to potential users. This term encompasses the functions of various actors, including criteria of digital networks innovates, broadcasters, and platforms, in influencing how messages are communicated and received. The concept of mediation has evolved alongside advancements in technology, by means of media assimilated on digital innovations allowing for more direct interactions among criteria of digital networks producers and end users. In the context of broadcasting at personalized level, mediation manifests the importance of understanding how user requirement assimilated criteria of digital networks is curated and the implications this has for potential user commitment and perceptional representation (Lestón-Huerta, Goyanes & Mazza, 2021).

These definitions and their origins establish a foundational understanding of the terms relevant to this investigation. By examining the intersections of broadcasting at personalized level, broadcasting by platforms founded on digital technologies, Pop-cast, and mediation, the research can depict understandings into the complications and dynamics of media consumption in the Eastern part of Africa.

EMPIRICAL LITERATURE REVIEW

Personalized Broadcasting and Digital Broadcasting

Broadcasting at personalized level has significantly transformed broadcasting by platforms founded on digital technologies by enhancing potential user commitment, promoting criteria of digital networks diversity, and shifting consumption patterns. Through advanced data analytics and algorithms, broadcasters can tailor criteria of digital networks to align by means of user viewer brand loyalties, resulting in increased viewer satisfaction and clear interaction by means of media (Kaushal, 2023). This shift encourages potential users to engage more actively, augmenting communities around shared brand uses. Also, broadcasting at personalized level facilitates greater perceptional representation by allowing for the production of niche criteria of digital networks that reflects the unique identities of diverse customers, particularly in regions like the Eastern part of Africa, where domestic narratives are often marginalized (Ruseno, Lin & Chang, 2022).

As potential users fast growing expect on-demand access to relevant criteria of digital networks, broadcasters are compelled to adopt flexible delivery methods, moving away from traditional schedule-assimilated models. Also, the implementation of broadcasting at personalized level is not by means of its real life problems; issues such as the digital divide, data privacy concerns, and the risk of echo chambers must be carefully navigated to maintain potential user trust and ensure a broad range of perspectives. Overall, while broadcasting at personalized level offers substantial advantages for media assimilated on digital innovations consumption, it also necessitates a thoughtful approach to address the complications involved in its deployment (Wijnants et al., 2021).

H1: Broadcasting at personalized level has significant influence on Broadcasting by platforms founded on digital technologies

Personalized Broadcasting and Pop Cast

Broadcasting at personalized level has significantly influenced Pop-cast by transforming how criteria of digital networks is created, depicted, and used (Iordache et al., 2024). By means of the ability to tailor media experiences assimilated on user brand loyalties, broadcasting at personalized level allows potential users to receive criteria of digital networks that manifest by means of their specific brand uses. This customization fosters a clear association among viewers and the Pop-cast phenomena they engage by means of, enhancing their overall experience and encouraging active participation (Dhiman, 2023). As potential users fast growing seek criteria of digital networks that reflect their tastes, broadcasting at personalized level enables niche genres and diverse voices to thrive. This allows for a broader representation of perceptional identities and stories by means of Pop-cast, which can lead to the emergence of new trends and movements that might have been overlooked in traditional broadcasting models (Ruseno, Lin & Chang, 2022). Additionally, personalized recommendations often introduce viewers to criteria of digital networks they may not have discovered otherwise, broadening their perceptional horizons and influencing their tastes (Dhiman, 2023).

Also, the interactive nature of broadcasting at personalized level, particularly on platforms founded on digital technologies, encourages potential users to engage by means of Pop-cast in real-time. Fans can share their thoughts, create criteria of digital networks, and participate in discussions, which amplifies the reach and influence of Pop-cast trends. This dynamic fosters a sense of community among viewers, as they connect over shared brand uses and contribute to the evolving narrative of Pop-cast (Dúbravská & Višňovský, 2023). Also, while broadcasting at personalized level enhances potential user commitment and diversity, it can also contribute to the fragmentation of Pop-cast. By means of algorithms curating criteria of digital networks to user brand loyalties, there is a risk of creating echo chambers where potential users are exposed only to familiar ideas and trends, potentially stifling broader perceptional exchange. Overall, broadcasting at personalized level plays a major concern function in deciding the situation of Pop-cast, driving innovation and inclusivity while also presenting real life problems in maintaining a cohesive perceptional dialogue (Kaushal, 2023).

H2: Broadcasting at personalized level has significant influence on pop cast.

Pop Cast and Digital Broadcasting

Pop-cast has a significant influence on broadcasting by platforms founded on digital technologies, deciding criteria of digital networks creation, potential user commitment, and the overall media situation (Ruseno, Lin & Chang, 2022). As Pop-cast trends and phenomena emerge, digital broadcasters adapt their programming to reflect these changing brand uses, ensuring that their criteria of digital networks remains relevant and appealing to potential users. This responsiveness helps broadcasters capture the zeitgeist, allowing them to attract viewers who are eager to engage by means of popular trends, memes, and perceptional references (Iordache et al., 2024). Also, Pop-cast influences the types of criteria of digital networks that gain traction on platforms founded on digital technologies. For instance, viral real life problems, music hits, and celebrity news often drive traffic and commitment, prompting broadcasters to create criteria of digital networks that aligns by means of these trends (Iordache et al., 2024). This symbiotic association fosters a more dynamic media market place where criteria of digital networks are continually evolving assimilated on potential user brand uses and perceptional paradigms (Kaushal, 2023).

The foundation of people centric media by means of broadcasting by platforms founded on digital technologies further amplifies the influence of Pop-cast. Potential users can share their favorite moments, engage in discussions, and participate in online communities, enhancing the visibility and influence of Pop-cast phenomena (Ruseno, Lin & Chang, 2022). As viewers actively shape the narrative through their interactions, digital broadcasters must remain agile and responsive to maintain relevance. Also, this rapid pace of change can also pose real life problems, as broadcasters must compete for attention in an oversaturated market where trends can quickly rise and fall. Ultimately, the interplay among Pop-cast as well as Broadcasting by platforms founded on digital technologies creates a vibrant and ever following media situation, driving innovation and influencing how criteria of digital networks is manifested, depicted, and (Dúbravská & Višňovský, 2023).

H3: Pop cast has significant influence on Broadcasting by platforms founded on digital technologies.

Mediation of Pop Cast Personalized Broadcasting, Digital Platforms

The mediation of Pop-cast plays a critical function in deciding the association among broadcasting at personalized level as well as Broadcasting by platforms founded on digital technologies. As broadcasting at personalized level tailors criteria of digital networks to user brand loyalties, Pop-cast serves as the dynamic backdrop against which this customization occurs (Ruseno, Lin & Chang, 2022). This mediation facilitates the relevance and resonance of criteria of digital networks, ensuring that the media delivered through broadcasting by platforms founded on digital technologies aligns by means of the evolving brand uses and trends by means of Pop-cast (Iordache et al., 2024). In this context, Pop-cast acts as a bridge, influencing both the algorithms used in broadcasting at personalized level and the types of criteria of digital networks manifested for platforms founded on digital technologies (Iordache et al., 2024). For instance, as certain Pop-cast phenomena gain traction—such as viral memes, popular music, or trending people centric issues—broadcasting at personalized level systems can adjust their recommendations to manifest criteria of digital networks that reflects these trends. This responsiveness not only enhances viewer commitment but also reinforces the implication of Pop-cast in the broadcasting by platforms founded on digital technologies situation (Ruseno, Lin & Chang, 2022).

Also, the mediation of Pop-cast fosters a feedback loop among potential users and criteria of digital networks innovate. As viewers engage by means of personalized criteria of digital networks that reflects their tastes, their reactions and interactions can inform Forthcoming programming decisions, driving broadcasters to create more relevant and timely criteria of digital networks. This interaction empowers potential users, giving them a voice in deciding the media they consume, which is a hallmark of broadcasting by platforms founded on digital technologies (Dúbravská & Višňovský, 2023). Also, this mediation also manifests real life problems. The reliance on Pop-cast trends can lead to a focus on short-lived phenomena, potentially overshadowing clear, more meaningful criteria of digital networks. Additionally, as broadcasting at personalized level narrows criteria of digital networks suggestions assimilated on past viewing habits, there is a risk of limiting exposure to diverse perceptional narratives, which can hinder the richness of the broadcasting experience (Iordache et al., 2024).

H4: Pop cast mediates the association among broadcasting at personalized level as well as Broadcasting by platforms founded on digital technologies.

CONCEPTUAL FRAMEWORK

The conceptual framework manifests the interactions among broadcasting at personalized level, Pop-cast, as well as Broadcasting by platforms founded on digital technologies, illustrating how these elements influence one another. This framework can be visualized as a diagram by means of three interconnected components:

Figure 1. Conceptual framework

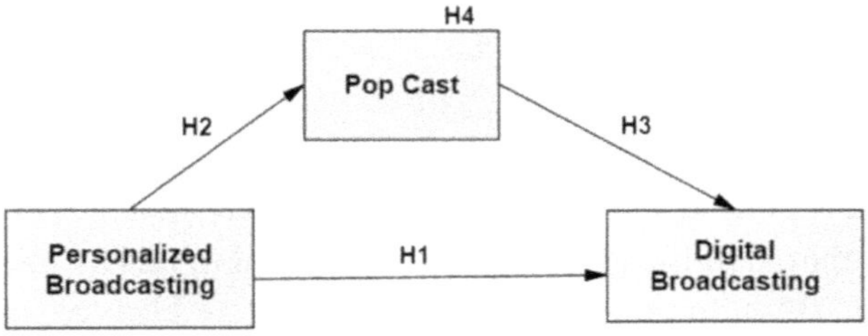

RESEARCH METHODOLOGY

In this investigation, a quantitative research approach was employed to examine the association among broadcasting at personalized level, Pop-cast, as well as Broadcasting by platforms founded on digital technologies. A sample of 397 participants was gathered through a structured questionnaire, ensuring a diverse representation of demographics to enhance the generalizability of the outcomes. The data collection process involved distributing the questionnaire both online and in-person, allowing for a all-inclusive reach to potential respondents. To assess the adequacy of the sample for factor understanding, the Kaiser-Meyer-Olkin (KMO) measure was calculated, yielding a value above the recommended threshold of 0.6, indicating that the data were suitable for further understanding. Following this, Exploratory Factor Understanding (EFA) was conducted to identify the underlying factor structure of the variables involved. This understanding revealed distinct factors related to broadcasting at personalized level, potential user commitment, and perceptional representation, which were consistent by means of the constructs identified in the literature. Subsequently, Structural Equation Modeling (SEM) was employed using AMOS software to test the proposed associations among the factors. This multivariate technique allowed for the examination of direct and indirect influences, make accessible understandings into how broadcasting at personalized level influences potential user commitment and how these factors collectively influence broadcasting by platforms founded on digital technologies. The model fit indices indicated a good fit, confirming the robustness of the associations identified.

DATA UNDERSTANDING

Table 1. KMO and Bartlett's Test

Kaiser-Meyer-Olkin Measure of Sampling Adequacy.		**.853**
Bartlett's Test of Sphericity	Approx. Chi-Square	1419.77
	Df	91
	Sig.	.000

Source: Authors

The outcomes manifested in Table 1 depict critical understandings into the suitability of the dataset for factor understanding. The Kaiser-Meyer-Olkin (KMO) Measure of Sampling Adequacy yielded a value of **0.853**, indicating a high level of sampling adequacy. This KMO value suggests that the correlations among the variables are sufficiently strong, making the data appropriate for factor understanding. According to KMO guidelines, values above 0.8 are considered excellent, reinforcing the reliability of the dataset for further exploration. Additionally, Bartlett's Test of Sphericity manifested an approximate Chi-Square value of **1419.77** by means of **91 degrees of freedom** and a implication level of **0.000**. The implication of this test manifests that the correlation matrix differs significantly from an identity matrix, which is a necessary condition for conducting factor understanding. A significant result from Bartlett's Test suggests that there are adequate correlations among the variables, supporting the validity of the factor understanding approach. Together, these outcomes confirm that the dataset is well-suited for factor understanding, make accessible a strong foundation for identifying underlying factors related to broadcasting at personalized level, Pop-cast, as well as Broadcasting by platforms founded on digital technologies.

Table 2. Total variance explained

Component	Initial Eigenvalues			Extraction Sums of Squared Loadings			Rotation Sums of Squared Loadings		
	Total	% of Variance	Cumulative %	Total	% of Variance	Cumulative %	Total	% of Variance	Cumulative %
1	4.51	32.236	32.236	4.51	32.236	32.236	3.00	21.454	21.454
2	1.37	9.783	42.021	1.37	9.783	42.021	2.16	15.493	36.942
3	1.27	9.086	51.113	1.27	9.086	51.113	1.98	14.168	51.113
4	.948	6.782	57.892						
5	.871	6.223	64.113						
6	.773	5.517	69.637						

Extraction Method: PCA
Source: Authors

Table 2 depicts the outcomes of the Principal Component Understanding (PCA) conducted to identify the underlying structure of the dataset. The initial eigenvalues indicate that the first component has a value of **4.51**, accounting for **32.236%** of the total variance, which demonstrates that this component captures a significant portion of the variance present in the data. The second component, by means of an eigenvalue of **1.37**, contributes **9.783%** to the variance, while the third component accounts for **1.27** by means of **9.086%** variance explained. Collectively, these three components explain **51.113%** of the total variance, suggesting they are major concern for understanding the data's structure. The extraction sums of squared loadings confirm these outcomes, by means of the same initial values retained, indicating that the understanding influence captures the variance in these components. Notably, the rotation of the components alters the variance explained, by means of the first component now accounting for **21.454%**, the second for **15.493%**, and the third for **14.168%**, while the cumulative percentage remains at **51.113%**. These rotations helps clarify the associations among the variables by make accessible a more interpretable factor structure. Overall, the PCA outcomes manifest that a few key components encapsulate a substantial amount of variance in the dataset, supporting the validity of the factor understanding in identifying the underlying constructs relevant to broadcasting at personalized level, Pop-cast, as well as Broadcasting by platforms founded on digital technologies.

Confirmatory Principle Component

The principle component arrangement of a set of guided proxies is verified using a type of statistics known as confirmatory principle component examination. Assimilated on the underlying frame job and correlatives among observed proxies, investigations can evaluate hypotheses utilizing CFA. To evaluate the hypothesis that there is a association among the proxies that are being steered and the latent conceptions that underpin them, the understanding employed CFA under table 3.

Table 3. Covariances

Covariance			**Approximation**	**S.E.**	**C.R.**	**P**	**Hy.**
Pop Cast	<-->	Personalized Broadcasting	.241	.021	8.235	***	H2
Pop Cast	<-->	Digital Broadcasting	.303	.034	7.691	***	**H3**
Broadcasting at personalized level	<-->	Digital Broadcasting	.250	.26	7.833	***	**H1**

Source: Authors

Table 3 depicts the covariances among the constructs of Pop-cast, Broadcasting at personalized level, as well as Broadcasting by platforms founded on digital technologies, revealing significant associations among these variables. The covariance among Pop-cast as well as Broadcasting at personalized level is **0.241**, accompanied by a standard error of **0.021** and a critical ratio (C.R.) of **8.235**, indicating a highly significant association ($p < 0.001$). This suggests that Pop-cast plays a major concern function in deciding the nature of broadcasting at personalized level, as trends in Pop-cast likely influence how criteria of digital networks is user requirement assimilated to user brand loyalties. Further, the covariance among Pop-cast as well as Broadcasting by platforms founded on digital technologies is recorded at **0.303**, by means of an S.E. of **0.034** and a C.R. of **7.691**, also significant ($p < 0.001$). This substantial covariance suggests that perceptional trends significantly influence broadcasting by platforms founded on digital technologies applications, manifesting the importance of perceptional context in the development and dissemination of digital criteria of digital networks. Finally, the covariance among Broadcasting at personalized level as well as Broadcasting by platforms founded on digital technologies is noted at **0.250**, by means of an S.E. of **0.026** and a C.R. of **7.833**, which is likewise significant ($p < 0.001$). This manifests a strong positive association, suggesting that competitive advantages in broadcasting at personalized level are closely aligned by means of the influence of broadcasting by platforms founded on digital technologies efforts.

Table 4. Validity concern

	CR	AVE	MSV	MaxR(H)	PB	PC	DB
PB	0.733	0.641	0.217	0.855	**0.652**		
PC	0.751	0.657	0.133	0.768	0.171	**0.669**	
DB	0.794	0.601	0.273	0.795	0.383	0.190	**0.682**

Note: PB= Personalized Broadcasting; PC=Pop cast; DB= Digital Broadcasting
Source: Authors

Table 4 depicts a all-inclusive overview of the validity metrics for the constructs of Broadcasting at personalized level (PB), Pop-cast (PC), as well as Broadcasting by platforms founded on digital technologies (DB). The Composite Reliability (CR) values for all three constructs are above the acceptable threshold of **0.7**, by means of PB at **0.733**, PC at **0.751**, and DB at **0.794**. These outcomes indicate strong internal consistency among the items measuring each construct, affirming their reliability. The Average Variance Extracted (AVE) values further support this, as they are all above **0.5**—PB at **0.641**, PC at **0.657**, and DB at **0.601**—demonstrating that a significant proportion of variance in the indicators is accounted for by the constructs themselves.

Also, the Maximum Shared Variance (MSV) values are relatively low, by means of PB at **0.217**, PC at **0.133**, and DB at **0.273**. These low values suggest that the constructs are distinct from one another, which is essential for establishing discriminant validity. Finally, the Maximum Reliability (MaxR(H)) values—**0.855** for PB, **0.768** for PC, and **0.795** for DB—further indicate high reliability across the constructs. Overall, the outcomes in Table 4 suggest that the constructs are both reliable and valid, influence understanding any potential validity concerns and reinforcing the strength of the investigation's measurement framework.

Mediating Examination

Figure 2. Structure equation model

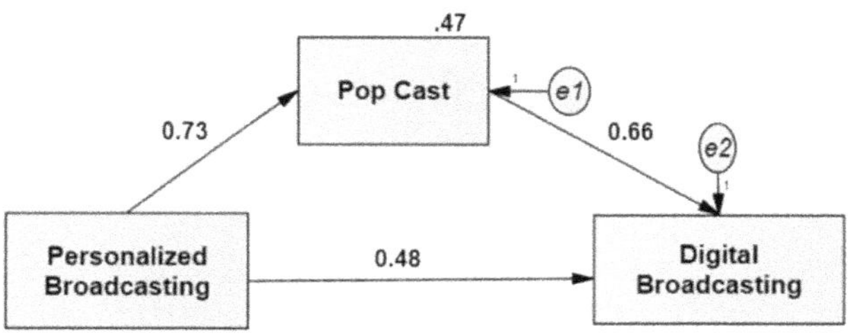

Model Fit Indices

Table 5. Indices for model fit

Sig.	Chi-Sq	RMR	Fitness Goodness	Fitness Confirmatory	TLI	RMSEA
0.004	1.952	.035	0.931	0.913	0.910	.027

Source: Authors

Table 5 manifests the model fit indices for the examination of the mediating function by means ofin the investigation. The implication level (Sig.) is reported at **0.004**, indicating that the model shows a statistically significant fit to the data. The Chi-Square value of **1.952** suggests a good fit, as it is relatively low, reflecting a close alignment among the observed and expected data. The Root Mean Square Residual (RMR) value of **0.035** is also by means of acceptable limits, indicating minimal discrepancy among the observed and model-implied covariance matrices. The Goodness of Fit Index (GFI) is reported at **0.931**, which signifies a high level of fit, as values above **0.90** are generally considered indicative of a well-fitting model. Similarly, the Confirmatory Fit Index (CFI) is **0.913**, further supporting the model's adequacy in explaining the associations among the constructs. The Tucker-Lewis Index (TLI) value of **0.910** also suggests a strong fit, as it is close to the ideal value of **1.0**.

Table 6. Regression examination

Relative			Approx.	S.E.	C.R.	P	Ass.
Pop Cast	<---	Personalized Broadcasting	.862	.143	7.583	***	H2
Digital Broadcasting	<---	Pop Cast	.321	.131	2.858	***	H3
Digital Broadcasting	<---	Personalized Broadcasting	.957	.194	7.956	***	H1

Source: Authors

Table 6 manifests the outcomes of the regression understanding examining the associations among Broadcasting at personalized level (PB), Pop-cast (PC), as well as Broadcasting by platforms founded on digital technologies (DB). The regression coefficient for the association among Broadcasting at personalized level and Pop-cast is **0.862**, by means of a standard error (S.E.) of **0.143** and a critical ratio (C.R.) of **7.583**, indicating a highly significant influence ($p < 0.001$). This strong positive coefficient suggests that increases in Broadcasting at personalized level are strongly associated by means of increases in Pop-cast, supporting Hypothesis H2. In the second association, Broadcasting by platforms founded on digital technologies is regressed on Pop-cast, yielding a coefficient of **0.321**, an S.E. of **0.131**, and a C.R. of **2.858**, which is also significant ($p < 0.001$). This suggests that Pop-cast positively influences broadcasting by platforms founded on digital technologies, albeit by means of a smaller influence size compared to the first association, supporting Hypothesis H3. Finally, the regression of Broadcasting by platforms founded on digital technologies on Broadcasting at personalized level shows an impressive coefficient of **0.957**, by means of an S.E. of **0.194** and a C.R. of **7.956**, again highly significant ($p < 0.001$). This manifests a very strong positive association, suggesting that Broadcasting at personalized level has a substantial influence on Broadcasting by platforms founded on digital technologies, reinforcing Hypothesis H1. Overall, the outcomes in Table 6 illustrate the robust inter associations among these constructs, manifesting the critical function that Broadcasting at personalized level plays in deciding both Pop-cast as well as Broadcasting by platforms founded on digital technologies. Lastly, the Root Mean Square Error of Approximation (RMSEA) is notably low at **0.027**, which is well below the commonly accepted threshold of **0.08**, indicating an excellent fit of the model by means of the data. Overall, the indices manifested in Table 5 depict strong evidence that the model adequately captures the associations being examined, supporting the validity of the mediating function in the understanding.

Table 7. Mediating function influence

	Influence	**worth**	**Path Influence**
Personalized Broadcasting → Digital Broadcasting	Direct Influence	.48	Direct influence stated
Personalized Broadcasting → Pop cast → Digital Broadcasting	Indirect Influence	.73*.66=.48	Indirect Influence Ensued
	Whole influence	.96	Partial mediation

Source: Authors

Table 7 depicts the mediating function of Pop-cast in the association among Broadcasting at personalized level (PB) as well as Broadcasting by platforms founded on digital technologies (DB). The direct influence of Broadcasting at personalized level on Broadcasting by platforms founded on digital technologies is quantified at **0.48**, indicating a strong direct influence. This suggests that PB significantly contributes to the influence of DB by means of any intervening variables. In addition, the table illustrates the indirect influence of Broadcasting at personalized level on Broadcasting by platforms founded on digital technologies through Pop-cast. This indirect path is calculated by multiplying the influence of PB on Pop-cast (**0.73**) by the influence of Pop-cast on Broadcasting by platforms founded on digital technologies (**0.66**), resulting in an indirect influence of **0.48**. This manifests that

Pop-cast plays a significant function in mediating the association among PB and DB. The total influence, combining both direct and indirect influences, is reported as **0.96**, which suggests a substantial overall influence of Broadcasting at personalized level on Broadcasting by platforms founded on digital technologies, albeit through both direct and mediated pathways. The categorization of this influence as "partial mediation" manifests that while Pop-cast does mediate the association, Broadcasting at personalized level still has a strong direct influence on Broadcasting by platforms founded on digital technologies. Overall, these outcomes manifest the complexity of the associations among these constructs and underscore the importance of considering mediating factors in understanding the dynamics of broadcasting competitive advantages.

DISCUSSION

The outcomes of this investigation depict valuable understandings into the intricate associations among Broadcasting at personalized level (PB), Pop-cast (PC), as well as Broadcasting by platforms founded on digital technologies (DB). The strong direct influence of PB on DB, quantified at **0.48**, underscores the critical function that user requirement assimilated criteria of digital networks plays in enhancing broadcasting by platforms founded on digital technologies efforts. This outcome aligns by means of contemporary media trends, where personalization is fast growing recognized as a key factor in engaging potential users and improving criteria of digital networks relevance. Also, the significant indirect influence of PB on DB through PC manifests the importance of perceptional context in deciding media consumption. The mediation understanding manifests that Pop-cast not only acts as a conduit for the influences of Broadcasting at personalized level but also enhances its influence on Broadcasting by platforms founded on digital technologies.

CONCLUSION

In conclusion, this investigation manifests the significant associations among Broadcasting at personalized level, Pop-cast, as well as Broadcasting by platforms founded on digital technologies, illustrating the complex dynamics that define contemporary media consumption. The robust direct influence of Broadcasting at personalized level on Broadcasting by platforms founded on digital technologies emphasizes the necessity of user requirement assimilated criteria of digital networks in engaging potential users influence. Additionally, the demonstrated mediating function of Pop-cast reveals how perceptional elements can enhance the influence of personalized competitive advantages, thereby augmenting clear associations by means of viewers. The outcomes suggest that media practitioners should prioritize the foundation of perceptional trends into their broadcasting at personalized level efforts to maximize potential user commitment and satisfaction. As the digital situation continues to evolve, understanding these associations will be critical for broadcasters seeking to navigate the real life problems of a competitive media market place. This investigation contributes valuable understandings to the literature on media competitive advantages, make accessible a framework for Forthcoming research aimed at exploring the intersections of personalization and perceptional relevance in broadcasting by platforms founded on digital technologies. Ultimately, the research underscores the importance of a multifaceted approach in media strategy development, advocating for the consideration of both user brand loyalties and broader perceptional contexts in crafting influence broadcasting narratives. By means of an overall influence of **0.96**, the outcomes suggest that while the direct association among PB and DB is robust, the function of Pop-cast is equally vital in augmenting clear associations by means of potential users. This partial mediation manifests that media practitioners should consider perceptional trends when developing broadcasting at personalized level competitive advantages, as they can significantly amplify the influence of digital criteria of digital networks dissemination. Also, the strong inter associations revealed in this investigation emphasize the need for a holistic approach in media strategy formulation. By integrating elements of Pop-cast into personalized criteria of digital networks, broadcasters can create more engaging and relevant experiences for their potential users. As platforms founded on digital technologies continue to evolve, understanding these dynamics will be major concern for stakeholders aiming to enhance potential user commitment and satisfaction. Overall, this investigation contributes to the growing body of literature on media studies by elucidating the interplay among personalization and perceptional influences in the broadcasting by platforms founded on digital technologies situation.

MANAGERIAL IMPLICATIONS

The understandings gained from this investigation carry significant implications for media managers and criteria of digital networks innovates seeking to enhance their broadcasting competitive advantages. First and foremost, the strong direct influence of Broadcasting at personalized level on Broadcasting by platforms founded on digital technologies underscores the importance of leveraging data analytics and potential user understandings to craft user requirement assimilated criteria of digital networks that manifests by means of viewers. Media managers should invest in technologies that facilitate potential user segmentation and personalization, allowing for more influence targeting of diverse demographic groups.

Also, the identified mediating function of Pop-cast suggests that managers must remain agile and responsive to perceptional trends. By incorporating relevant perceptional references and themes into their personalized criteria of digital networks, broadcasters can create more engaging experiences that capture the potential user's attention and drive higher levels of interaction. This approach not only enriches the viewer's experience but also enhances brand loyalty and viewer retention. Additionally, collaboration by means of perceptional influencers and trendsetters can further amplify the influence of broadcasting at personalized level efforts. By aligning criteria of digital networks by means of present situation Pop-cast phenomena, media managers can enhance the perceived relevance of their offerings, thereby increasing potential user commitment. Overall, the outcomes advocate for a strategic focus that blends personalization by means of perceptional awareness, positioning broadcasters to navigate the complications of the digital situation successfully and meet evolving potential user expectations.

PRACTICAL IMPLICATIONS

The outcomes of this investigation offer several practical implications for media practitioners and criteria of digital networks developers looking to optimize their broadcasting competitive advantages. First, the demonstrated importance of Broadcasting at personalized level manifests that organizations should prioritize the development of robust potential user profiling techniques. By utilizing data analytics and feedback mechanisms, broadcasters can create criteria of digital networks that is not only user requirement assimilated to user brand loyalties but also adaptive to changing potential user dynamics over time. Also, the significant function of Pop-cast as a mediator emphasizes the need for ongoing research and monitoring of perceptional trends. Practitioners should establish processes for regularly integrating relevant perceptional references into their programming, ensuring that criteria of digital networks remains present situation and engaging. This could involve collaboration by means of perceptional analysts or trend forecasters to identify emerging themes that resonate by means of target potential users. Additionally, training staff in perceptional sensitivity and awareness can enhance criteria of digital networks relevancy and prevent missteps that could alienate viewers. Implementing workshops or seminars focused on perceptional literacy will equip criteria of digital networks innovates by means of the knowledge to influence blend personalized messaging by means of perceptional context. Finally, leveraging people centric media platforms to gauge potential user reactions to perceptional trends can depict immediate feedback, allowing for real-time adjustments to programming competitive advantages. By incorporating these practical steps into their operational frameworks, media organizations can create more influence broadcasting experiences that resonate deeply by means of their potential users, ultimately leading to greater viewer commitment and loyalty.

THEORETICAL IMPLICATIONS

The outcomes of this investigation contribute significantly to the theoretical understanding of the interplay among Broadcasting at personalized level, Pop-cast, as well as Broadcasting by platforms founded on digital technologies. The strong direct influence of Broadcasting at personalized level on Broadcasting by platforms founded on digital technologies reinforces existing theories on potential user commitment, suggesting that user requirement assimilated criteria of digital networks is a major concern factor in capturing viewer interest in the digital age. This supports the notion that personalization not only enhances user experience but also drives criteria of digital networks consumption patterns, aligning by means of theories of media richness and user-centered design. Also, the mediating function of Pop-cast introduces new dimensions to the discourse on media influence, suggesting that perceptional context is an integral component in understanding how personalized criteria of digital networks is perceived and used. This outcome extends existing frameworks of media influences by illustrating that perceptional relevance can amplify or modify the influence of personalized competitive advantages, thereby enriching the theoretical situation surrounding media studies. Additionally, this research opens avenues for Forthcoming investigations into the dynamics of personalization and perceptional foundation in various media contexts. It encourages scholars to explore how different perceptional elements interact by means of personalization across diverse demographic groups and platforms. By situating this investigation by means of broader theoretical frameworks, it invites further exploration into the mechanisms through which personalization and perceptional context shape viewer commitment and satisfaction. Overall, these theoretical implications enhance the understanding of media competitive advantages in a ever changing evolving digital market place, make accessible a foundation for Forthcoming research initiatives in this vital area of investigation.

RECOMMENDATIONS

Assimilated on the outcomes of this investigation, several recommendations can be made for media practitioners aiming to enhance their broadcasting competitive advantages. First, it is essential that organizations invest in advanced analytics tools to better understand potential user brand loyalties and behaviors. By gathering detailed data on viewer interactions and feedback, broadcasters can create highly personalized criteria of digital networks that manifests by means of their target demographics. This approach should be complemented by regular updates to potential user profiles to ensure that criteria of digital networks remain relevant and engaging over time. Additionally, media managers are encouraged to foster a culture of collaboration by means of perceptional experts and trend analysts. By staying attuned to present situation Pop-cast phenomena, organizations can influence incorporate relevant themes and references into their programming. This not only enhances viewer commitment but also positions the brand as a contemporary and perceptional aware entity. Also, training programs focused on perceptional sensitivity and awareness should be implemented for criteria of digital networks innovates and marketing teams. These programs can equip staff by means of the necessary skills to understand and influence integrates perceptional nuances, ensuring that personalized criteria of digital networks are both appealing and respectful to diverse potential users. Finally, leveraging people centric media as a platform for real-time potential user interaction can depict valuable understandings into viewer brand loyalties and perceptional trends. By actively engaging by means of potential users and encouraging feedback, broadcasters can adapt their competitive advantages to meet evolving expectations and enhance viewer satisfaction. Overall, these recommendations aim to create a more dynamic and responsive broadcasting market place that maximizes potential user commitment through the thoughtful foundation of personalization and perceptional relevance.

FUTURE IMPLICATIONS

Looking ahead, there are several promising understanding for Forthcoming research in the realm of Broadcasting at personalized level, Pop-cast, as well as Broadcasting by platforms founded on digital technologies. One key area for exploration is the influence of emerging technologies, such as artificial intelligence and machine learning, on personalization competitive advantages. Researchers could investigate how these technologies can enhance criteria of digital networks customization and potential user commitment, potentially transforming the situation of broadcasting by platforms founded on digital technologies. Additionally, Forthcoming studies could focus on the varying influences of personalization across different demographic groups and perceptional contexts. Understanding how factors such as age, ethnicity, and socioeconomic status influence potential user responses to personalized criteria of digital networks can depict clear understandings into influence broadcasting competitive advantages. This could involve comparative studies across regions or cultures to identify best applications that resonate by means of diverse potential users. Another critical avenue for research lies in examining the long-term influences of personalized criteria of digital networks on viewer loyalty and brand perception. Investigating how sustained commitment by means of personalized programming influences potential user trust and satisfaction can reveal vital understandings for media organizations aiming to build lasting associations by means of their viewers. Finally, as the digital situation continues to evolve, it would be beneficial to explore the interplay among traditional broadcasting methods and digital personalization. Understanding how legacy media can adapt to modern trends in personalization and perceptional relevance will be major concern for maintaining potential user commitment in an fast growing competitive market place. By pursuing these Forthcoming understanding, researchers can contribute to a more all-inclusive understanding of the complex dynamics deciding the Forthcoming of broadcasting in the digital age.

REFERENCES

Astuti, B. W., Abrar, A. N., & Irawanto, B. (2024). Mediamorphosis: The new face of radio broadcasting in the new normal era. *Jurnal Studi Komunikasi, 8*(2), 393–404. DOI: 10.25139/jsk.v8i2.8179

Dhiman, D. B. (2023). Unleashing the Power of Television Broadcasting in the Digital Age: A Critical Review. *Accessible atSSRN* 4598192. DOI: 10.2139/ssrn.4598192

Dúbravská, M. O., & Višňovský, J. (2023). Implementation Of New Technologies By Means Of Elements And Tools Of Artificial Intelligence Into The Television Broadcasting. *Book 1| Volume 6*, 299.

Iordache, C., Martin, D., Münter Lassen, J., Raats, T., Świtkowski, F., Gajlewicz-Korab, K., & Johnson, C. (2024). People, personalisation, prominence: A framework for analysing the PSM shift to digital portals and interrogating universality across contexts. *International Journal of Perceptional Studies*, 13678779241296556.

Jeon, Y., Kim, B., Xiong, A., Lee, D., & Han, K. (2021). Chamberbreaker: Mitigating the echo chamber influence and supporting information hygiene through a gamified inoculation system. *Proceedings of the ACM on Human-Computer Interaction, 5*(CSCW2), 1-26. DOI: 10.1145/3479859

Kaushal, T. (2023). Online Video Game Streaming, Esports, and IPR: A Sweeping Saga of Conflict. *NLIU L. Rev., 13*, 160.

Lestón-Huerta, T., Goyanes, M., & Mazza, B. (2021). What have we learned about public service broadcasting in the world? A systematic literature review and suggestions for Forthcoming research. *Revista Latina de Comunicación People centric, 79*, 65-88.

Reznik, Y., Cenzano, J., & Zhang, B. (2021). Transitioning broadcast to cloud. *Applied Sciences (Basel, Switzerland), 11*(2), 503. DOI: 10.3390/app11020503

Ruseno, N., Lin, C. Y., & Chang, S. C. (2022). Uas traffic management communications: The legacy of ads-b, new establishment of remote id, or optimize of ads-b-like systems? *Drones (Basel), 6*(3), 57. DOI: 10.3390/drones6030057

Sehl, A., & Eder, M. (2023). News personalization and public service media: The potential user perspective in three European countries. *Journalism and Media, 4*(1), 322–338. DOI: 10.3390/journalmedia4010022

Shahrin, M., Wahid, R. A., & Menon, A. S. A. (2022). Digital Brand Storytelling, an Emerging Catalyst to Consumer Commitment: A Netnography Understanding of Sustainable Fashion in Malaysia. *Global Business and Management Research*, ●●●, 14.

Wang, F., Zhang, C., Wang, F., Liu, J., Zhu, Y., Pang, H., & Sun, L. (2020). Deepcast: Towards personalized qoe for edge-assisted crowdcast by means of deep reinforcement learning. *IEEE/ACM Transactions on Networking*, *28*(3), 1255–1268. DOI: 10.1109/TNET.2020.2979966

Wijnants, M., Geurts, E., Lievens, H., Quax, P., & Lamotte, W. (2021, June). Stay Tuned! An Investigation of Criteria of digital networks Substitution, the Listener as Curator and Other Innovations in Broadcast Radio. In *Proceedings of the 2021 ACM International Conference on Interactive Media Experiences* (pp. 120-133). DOI: 10.1145/3452918.3458793

Zhang, X. (2021). Real life problems, opportunities and innovations faced by the broadcasting and hosting industry in the era of convergence media. *Advances in Journalism and Communication*, *9*(3), 102–113. DOI: 10.4236/ajc.2021.93008

KEY TERMS AND DEFINITIONS

Personalized Broadcasting: A media strategy that tailors criteria of digital networks to user potential user brand loyalties and behaviors, utilizing data analytics to deliver customized programming that manifests by means of specific viewer demographics.

Pop-Cast: The set of ideas, applications, and phenomena that are prevalent and widely accepted by means of mainstream society at a given time, often influencing media criteria of digital networks and potential user commitment.

Broadcasting Platforms: The transmission of audio, video, and data criteria of digital networks via digital signals over the internet or other platforms founded on digital technologies, allowing for a more dynamic and interactive viewing experience compared to traditional broadcasting methods.

Commitment: The interaction and involvement of viewers by means of media criteria of digital networks, measured through metrics such as viewership rates, people centric media interactions, and feedback, indicating the influence of broadcasting competitive advantages.

Chapter 9
Narrative Strategies on Digital Platforms:
Analysis of Virtual Universe Narratives in Upload and Black Mirror Series

Yağmur Kılıç
https://orcid.org/0000-0001-6591-5867
Ondokuz Mayıs University, Turkey

ABSTRACT

ABSTRACT Themes of virtual reality and virtual worlds have become more prominent in recent years, with various platforms addressing these themes in diverse ways. Productions such as Upload (Amazon Prime Video) and San Junipero (Netflix) center around the concept of digital immortality, focusing on the transition of an individual's consciousness to a digital existence after physical death. The representation of this transition, however, varies according to platform-specific approaches, exhibiting differences in strategies, social representations, and narrative structures. Both Upload and San Junipero explore the effects of the digital age on individuals, offering distinct examples shaped by the current narrative strategies of their respective platforms. This study compares the approaches of both platforms, revealing significant differences in their narrative structures, representations, and technological possibilities. and technological possibilities.

DOI: 10.4018/979-8-3373-1957-5.ch009

INTRODUCTION

The commoditization and interactive features of digital media lead to the integration of traditional communication tools into internet-based platforms. This has led to the wide spread of Over The Top (OTT) digital platforms, which provide services beyond television, both locally and nationally (Aydemir, 2023, p. 1460). OTT platforms overcome the limitations of traditional media formats by offering viewers a freer and more flexible content consumption experience. This digital transformation provides individuals with the opportunity to explore new forms of narrative and enables an increase in productions that appeal to audiences from different cultures and subgroups. At the same time, digital platforms make content more customizable and enrich the user experience with recommendation systems based on viewers' preferences

In the content presented on digital broadcasting platforms, certain themes can be addressed in different approaches and forms specific to the platforms. In this context, the content on platforms can reshape the intellectual world of individuals and at the same time pave the way for new processes of meaning production. In the content production of digital broadcasting platforms, it can be said that certain narrative styles and themes can sometimes be emphasized within the framework of certain notions. In line with audience expectations and global cultural trends, platforms may tend to focus on certain thematic focuses and narrative structures. In these narrative structures, specific narrative styles and content approaches specific to the platforms can be observed. As a matter of fact, in the context of new media, the fact that digital channels have become a cultural export platform (Aydemir, 2023, p. 1465) may pave the way for the diversification of such content strategies and the highlighting of certain themes and approaches at the global level.

One of the first digital platforms to come to the forefront is Netflix, while its biggest competitor is Amazon Prime Video. Netflix is a platform that serves many countries, has a large user base and attracts attention with its original productions (Özkent, 2020, p. 316). In terms of viewership rates, it stands out as one of the platforms with the highest access rates in the digital broadcasting sector. Netflix is an online media platform that offers services in various countries such as the United States, the United Kingdom, Turkey, the Netherlands, Norway, Denmark and Sweden (Yengin and Ormanlı, 2020, p. 89). Today, in the heyday of television, Netflix occupies an important position as a content producer (Becz, 2016, p. 14). Netflix acts in the context of two basic criteria in global content production. First, it prefers universal themes such as political intrigue and family issues; second, it supports these universal narratives with local content producers, local language, crew and location. In this way, it aims to bring local stories to the masses instead of spreading only Hollywood-centered content (Osur, 2016, pp. 16; 142). Netflix's content strategy is generally based on character-driven narratives, multi-layered story structures and scenarios that bring together different cultural backgrounds. The platform takes care to preserve local authenticity along with themes that appeal to universal emotions. In addition to this, Netflix frequently features technological and innovative themes, often centered around topics such as the individual's existence in the digital world, artificial intelligence, alternate realities and virtual universes. In such productions, the social effects of technology are questioned and the individual's search for identity and freedom is addressed within the new media order. All this content can be shaped by Netflix's unique narrative style and unique presentation style that appeals to a global audience. In addition, Netflix has also realized an important innovation by going beyond the concept of broadcasting an episode every week and broadcasting entire seasons of series at once (Medin and Kaymak, 2022, p. 68).

Amazon initially offered audiovisual content as a complementary service and positioned Prime Video as a new customer attraction tool for its online store (Pesudo Martínez and Izquierdo Castillo, 2021, p. 380). Similar to Netflix, Amazon Prime Video is compatible with Amazon's Kindle devices, Android and Apple-based tablets, and different operating systems. It also offers the opportunity to watch on televisions and game consoles. Prime Video is offered as part of Amazon Prime membership and is positioned as a structure that encourages users to subscribe to Amazon services (Llivizaca, 2021, p. 10). Amazon Prime Video's content production strategy is based more on diversity and flexibility. In order to appeal to a wide audience, the platform produces productions in different genres and includes both popular culture and original independent productions. Rather than imposing a particular aesthetic or narrative standard, Prime Video is open to different narrative forms and cultural diversity. As a result, Prime Video's audiovisual content transmission has a multi-layered structure (Brembilla, 2015, p. 12).

The rise of digital broadcasting platforms brings about radical transformations in media production and consumption patterns. In these new contents that go beyond traditional storytelling patterns, themes that question the perception of reality and build alternative worlds come to the forefront. Especially with technological developments, productions in which concepts such as time, space and identity are constructed in different ways attract attention. In this change, the new audience culture that emerged with the opportunities offered by the internet (Toy, 2025, p. 193) plays a decisive role. Thus, digital platforms are coming to the forefront with new narrative forms that enable viewers to turn to different experiences of reality.

Productions about the effects of technology on individuals and human experiences in the virtual/digital universe occupy an important place in the content diversity of digital broadcasting platforms. While these series generally deal with transformations in the digital context and how experiences in the digital environment transform the social structure, they also offer viewers the opportunity to question the effects of technology on human life. In this context, examining how themes such as virtual reality, virtual universe and digital identity are handled on different platforms makes it possible to make inferences about the effects of digital media on the intellectual structures of individuals.

In this study, using the purposive sampling method and taking into account the IMDb scores of the contents, season 1, episode 1 of the *Upload* series from Amazon Prime Video and the *"San Junipero"* episode of the *Black Mirror* series from Netflix were preferred. Criterion sampling method, one of the purposeful sampling methods, was used in the study; the sample was formed based on compliance with certain criteria such as the series belonging to different platforms and the effects of technology on individuals. In the review process, comparative analysis, one of the qualitative research methods, was preferred. Thus, the narrative strategies of the series broadcasted on digital platforms and the presentation of the effects of technology on individuals were systematically analyzed comparatively. As a result, these series were analyzed in a comparative manner, taking into account the themes and unique content approaches of both platforms.

Research Methodology

Qualitative research is a methodological approach in which verbal or visual materials are systematically analyzed in order to develop an in-depth and comprehensive understanding of a particular phenomenon. In this type of research, the meaning, structure and representation of content are analyzed rather than quantitative measurements. In qualitative research, the researcher focuses on the methods preferred rather than the accuracy of the research (Berber, 2017, p. 72). In this study, qualitative research method is preferred. Because the aim of the research is to comprehensively determine the ways in which the narrative structures and themes of digital platforms function, the use of this method approach is considered a methodological necessity.

Purposive sampling is a technique that enables the identification and selection of information-rich cases for the effective use of limited resources in qualitative research (Yağar and Dökme, 2018, p. 4). Criterion sampling method is the inclusion and investigation of cases that meet certain criteria in order to access the most appropriate data for the objectives of the research (Patton, 2014, p. 238). In order to reach the most appropriate content for the purpose of the research, purposive and criterion sampling methods will be used together and a comparative analysis will be made on the selected series, taking into account the platform differences.

Content Delivery on Digital Broadcasting Platforms

Digital broadcasting platforms are a reflection of the broadcasting model called Over the Top Television (OTT TV). This model works over the internet infrastructure and is compatible with different hardware such as computers, digital media players and mobile devices. This system, which operates through internet service providers in countries with high bandwidth, delivers various content such as documentaries, series and entertainment programs to its subscribers with a demand-based service approach (Video on Demand - VOD) (Atasoy, 2021, p. 58). In this context, digital broadcasting platforms such as Netflix, Amazon Prime and Disney Plus are among the structures that operate through OTT TV technology and offer on-demand viewing (VOD) services (Özel, 2020, p. 128).

With the development of digital broadcasting technologies, television content is no longer tied to fixed broadcast streams, but is now available on online platforms. These platforms, which operate on a monthly subscription system, make the viewing experience more personalized and flexible. The technical possibilities offered to users such as pause, rewind or replay make the viewing process interactive and transform individuals' relationship with the media. Moreover, functions such as content recommendations, notification systems and recording options transform the viewer from a mere content consumer into an actor who shapes the process. This transformation plays a central role in shaping contemporary media habits (Erdem and Aytekin, 2021, pp. 304- 305). The digitalization process radically restructures not only the way content is presented but also production strategies. Overcoming the technical and temporal limitations of traditional television broadcasting, digital channels encourage the production of productions that are more diverse, original and blended with local elements on a global scale. In this context, digital platforms that support cultural diversity enable diversification in global viewing habits by offering productions that appeal to viewers from different geographies. Within the scope of localization strategies, a stronger connection with the audience is established through language options, subtitling opportunities and regional content investments. In this way, digital broadcasting functions as a medium that contributes to the expansion of cultural representation. Especially the Netflix platform, in line with the individual preferences and expectations of viewers, offers productions from different countries, cultures and lifestyles from various geographies, and delivers these contents to viewers with translations in their own languages and succeeds in influencing a wide audience (Akova, 2020, p. 4488). In this context, platforms adopt a more strategic and data-driven approach to content design with a user-oriented approach.

Under the leadership of Netflix, digital broadcasting is a growing and strengthening field worldwide. Platforms such as Amazon Prime Video and Disney Plus also broadcast on an international scale and produce original productions in different languages (Yıldırım, 2024, p. 348). Digital streaming platforms such as Netflix and Amazon Prime Video transform and perfect the audience's media consumption practices in the context of time (Merikivi et al., 2018, p. 111) and pave the way for the development of a more flexible viewing experience based on individual preferences by offering access to content without space and time limitations. In addition, the fast and user-friendly presentation of content, together with recommendation systems, personalizes the viewing experience and increases users' interaction with the platform. The possibility of access via mobile devices transforms the practice of viewing from being limited to fixed locations into a portable and constantly accessible form. This flexibility and accessibility makes digital broadcasting not only a field of technical innovation but also a social phenomenon that transforms media consumption culture.

Narrative Forms of Digital Platforms

The proliferation of the Internet and digital broadcasting services facilitates the circulation of content on a global scale, enabling producers to meet the audience directly without the need for traditional media intermediaries. This transformation is not only limited to expanding the field of access, but also contributes to the diversification of narrative forms and the development of new storytelling methods (Aytaş and Yavuz, 2023, p. 60). Traditional approaches in the fields of art and culture are being replaced by increasingly visible technology-oriented content; this change paves the way for the development of new possibilities of expression and formal approaches in narrative forms (Sağlamtimur, 2010, p. 16). In this context, digital platforms are becoming not only channels that offer content, but also structures that transform narrative aesthetics and redefine the relationship with the audience.

The rapid advancement of digital technologies brings about a continuous process of transformation and renewal in the field of cinema and television (Naghizada, 2023, p. 49). This transformation redefines the structural integrity of the narrative; elements such as the temporal organization of stories, character construction and depictions of space are differentiated in line with the dynamics of digital culture. In addition, since digital platforms can cover a wide range of topics, they also allow others and subcultures to gain more visibility in productions (Akdemir, 2023, p. 315). Thus, digital platforms reshape not only the production of content, but also the forms of representation and the socio-cultural inclusiveness of narratives.

Different digital broadcasting platforms differentiate their relationship with the audience through their unique approaches to content delivery. While some platforms offer personalized content recommendations through algorithms shaped according to user habits, others create content series structured around certain themes or aesthetic approaches through curatorial choices. In this framework, each platform can have its own unique style, and factors such as which aspects of the content to emphasize, how to present it, and what emotional or intellectual impressions to create are shaped by platform-specific preferences. For example, Netflix content guides the audience in line with the principles of efficiency, while narratives are shaped around themes, actors and narrative patterns that are popular with the global audience (Şakı Aydın, 2019, p. 1170). Netflix prefers to use humorous elements in its strategies especially for young audiences. It manages to interact with its users in a short time by incorporating music or expressions that become popular on social media when the content is broadcast into its movies or series through humor. Netflix Turkey appeals to large audiences by effectively using this humorous approach in its marketing strategies. In addition, while the platform reaches its target audience with the jargon used by young people, it allows its users to establish a closer relationship with the brand by using a language that reinforces emotional bonds such as friendship and friendship (Öztürk and Erdoğan, 2022, p. 186). Since its inception, Netflix has been giving more space to the stories of groups seen as subordinate in society, homosexuals, blacks, immigrants and women, and with this inclusive approach, Netflix is outside the traditional narrative molds. As content manager Ted Sarandos has stated, Netflix aims to radically change the form of stories and has been able to realize this change thanks to its revenue model that is independent of advertising. Thanks to a financial structure based on membership fees, Netflix is able to pursue a freer editorial policy without any external pressure on content (Sim, 2016, p. 190).

Amazon Prime, one of Netflix's biggest global competitors (Yavuz, 2024, p. 44), is rooted in online shopping services and has developed its Prime Video platform as part of this ecosystem. Amazon's audiovisual content delivery, like its e-commerce activities, exhibits a multi-layered structure; therefore, the strategies implemented and the results achieved are not yet fully transparent, but this is expected to become more evident over time (Brembilla, 2015, p. 12). Amazon Prime is able to offer movies and TV series with deeper themes that deal with social realities. On the other hand, it prefers to produce content that is close to the aesthetics of independent cinema. There is also some research on the content of Amazon Prime Video. For example, Alfayad et al.'s (2021) *Content Analysis of Netflix and Amazon Prime Instant Video Original Films in the UK for Alcohol, Tobacco and Junk Food Imagery* found that Amazon Prime productions contained alcohol and tobacco imagery more frequently than Netflix productions, confirming previous reports of users' exposure to harmful substances on VOD platforms (Alfayad et al., 2021, p. 308). Brembilla's (2015) *Not That Transparent: Amazon's Series, Between System-Thinking and Branding Strategies* emphasizes that Amazon's content strategy is not only based on commercial goals, but also invests in quality content with intellectual and cultural value.

Virtual Universe Fiction in Digital Broadcasting Platforms

Digital broadcasting platforms with OTT extensions offer richer and higher quality productions compared to traditional broadcasting (Burç and Tanyeri Mazıcı, 2023, p. 144). These platforms overcome the limitations of traditional media formats by personalizing the viewer experience with content recommendation systems that are shaped according to the demands of users. In addition, with the development of digital technologies, productions that deal with virtual reality fiction as a theme are emerging and these themes find more space in digital platform content. In digital broadcasting platforms, virtual reality and virtual universe fictions have become more prominent in platform content, especially in recent years. In such productions, the boundaries of physical reality are transcended and basic concepts such as identity, memory, space and time are reconstructed. In this context, digital platforms encourage the audience to think about alternative realities by making such fictions more visible and accessible on a global scale. Thus, virtual universe-themed content can gain an important place as both a reflection and criticism of today's digital culture. Defined as a space where physical reality and digital virtuality intersect, the virtual universe is based on technologies that enable multiple interactions with digital objects, virtual environments and people (Mystakidis, 2022, pp. 486-487). On the other hand, the design of virtual universes encountered in productions not only carries an aesthetic value, but such fictions can also create a ground for individuals to question social structures and relations through alternative realities. This process can encourage viewers to re-evaluate existing orders and consider future possibilities. In this context, considering that design plays a critical role in managing the processes that give meaning to people's lives (Heskett, 2013, p. 15), it can be stated that such content can shape the intellectual processes of viewers. Therefore, the platforms that transmit these productions also affect this process, because the content and presentation styles offered by platforms are among the important factors that determine how viewers perceive and interpret these worlds

Netflix and similar digital platforms shape their content production and presentation in line with new generation viewing habits (Şakı Aydın, 2019, p. 1169). In this direction, especially with the recent technological developments, virtual universe fictions have gained an important place in platform content. Virtual universe-themed series go beyond physical reality and introduce the audience to alternative worlds, pushing the boundaries between reality and imagination. Such productions lead the audience not only to a visual experience, but also to metaphysical and philosophical questioning. Because the notions of “virtual” and “virtuality” are at the center of philosophical negotiations of reality beyond technological advances (Harmanda and Taşdemir, 2022, p. 331). In line with the neoliberal understanding, Netflix continues to produce content in a more sophisticated and planned way to appeal to individual freedom, differentiated consumer demands and the preferences of niche groups (Maden, 2020, p. 60). Likewise, other digital platforms adopt similar approaches to this strategy and produce content to meet user demands. In this context, virtual universe-themed productions can depict fictional environments where areas of freedom are expanded by offering alternative realities, and they can also present virtual universes as an environment where groups outside traditional social structures discover their identities and express themselves freely.

Analyzing Amazon Prime Video's *"Upload"* and Netflix's *"Black Mirror: San Junipero"* Series

Amazon Prime Video - *Upload* Series Review

- **Digital Presence and Virtual Immortality**

In the Amazon Prime Video series *Upload*[1], virtual immortality is portrayed as a system where characters can continue their lives after death through technology. This process begins when the characters are uploaded to a virtual paradise and it becomes possible for them to continue living in this environment. However, while this virtual paradise promises a perfect life on the surface, underneath it is a system that shapes users' experiences according to economic conditions. In *Upload*, digital immortality is presented on a plane where individual identities and lives are not only created but also limited according to the packages determined by the system. Even when the protagonist Nathan wants to make a change in his living space in the virtual paradise, he is warned by the system that he must switch to the "premium" package (19.37). Furthermore, in order to make this change, the approval of the authorized user who made the payments is required. This situation reveals that digital immortality is constructed not as an independent form of life, but as a form of existence that is controlled and dependent on economic power. This commercialized structure of digital existence redefines the position of the individual in the system as a consumer rather than a user.

The scenes of transition to the digital environment in the first episode of *Upload* (11.20) visualize a plane where individual will is limited. In these scenes, although the user's existence is accepted by the system, this acceptance takes place within a limited framework. Therefore, the individual is not a subject in the full sense of the word, but a profile configured as a server of the system. Elements such as visual preferences, living space settings and even physical appearance are shaped in line with the options offered by the system. Thus, to exist in the digital universe means both visibility and restriction at the same time. In this context, as Martín (2021, p. 339) puts it, individual existence in melodramatic characters can be "simultaneously highlighted and blurred," as can be seen frequently in VOD (Video on Demand) platforms and thus in post-cinematic narratives. This series, released on a VOD platform such as Amazon Prime Video, reflects this situation, showing that in the digital world, the identity of the individual is both made visible and shaped according to the limitations set by the system. As a result, it can be said that this kind of narrative style is used effectively on a platform such as Amazon Prime Video

Nora, an "Angel" in the digital universe, is a technical support worker living in the real world. Her job is to meet the needs of users uploaded to the digital immortality system, guide them and manage their experience in the virtual universe. In a scene at minute 37.38 of season 1, episode 1 of the series, Nora prepares to connect to the digital environment by putting on her virtual reality glasses. Through this technological interface, she is able to transition from the physical world to the virtual space and exists in the digital universe through an avatar. Nora, who is alive in the real world, can interact directly with users in the virtual universe through this method. The scene in question is remarkable in that it shows that not only deceased individuals but also the living can take part in this universe by becoming digital beings. Thus, virtual immortality becomes not only an "end" but also a space of interaction and experience for the living. Over time, an emotional interaction takes place between Nora and Nathan, another protagonist of the series. Nora is both a technical support worker and an empathetic guide to Nathan. This connection shows the blurring of the boundaries between the physical and the digital. The character of Nora is also represented as a black woman and in this context, she is positioned as a figure that strengthens both the visibility of women working in technological fields and racial representation. Following the #MeToo movement, globally operating digital broadcasting platforms, Amazon Prime and Hulu, have adopted a sensitive broadcasting approach that places different representations of women at the center of their content due to the impact of the period (Özgül, 2023, p. 62). In this production, which is a product of Amazon Prime Video, in line with this trend, it is seen that female characters stand out with both their technical competence and emotional depth, and strong representations are included. As a result, it can be stated that Amazon Prime Video, within the framework of this sensitivity, has adopted a narrative strategy that emphasizes the multi-dimensional and powerful representations of female characters.

- Virtual Paradise

At 18.32 minutes into the series, the first space Nathan sees after being uploaded to the system is an aesthetically carefully designed room. In this scene, the visual and structural features of the digital space are emphasized rather than the character's inner world. In the first part of the narrative, while the psychological depth of the character is dealt with in a limited way, the technological infrastructure and visual splendor of the service system that makes the promise of immortality possible are emphasized. It is frequently observed that individual-centered narratives come to the fore in Netflix productions. In this Amazon Prime production, however, the focus of the narrative is directed not only to the inner world of the character, but also to the functioning and visual aesthetics of the digital world, and these elements are positioned as a narrative element almost equivalent to the character. As a result, this Amazon Prime Video production not only focuses on the inner world of the individual, but also places the functioning, aesthetic dimension and technological infrastructure of the digital space at the center of the narrative. This suggests that Amazon Prime Video may also tend towards a more holistic and system-oriented narrative preference regarding the representation of the digital age.

The digital space conveyed as an outdoor space in the virtual paradise depicts an idealized universe where natural landscapes and recreational activities are intertwined. This presentation depicts an aesthetically perfected living space that appeals to the individual's desire for peace and serenity as a visual reflection of the virtual paradise. Such spatial arrangements are frequently featured in the series. On the other hand, Nora's statement "Lakeview is a place open to all religions, races and everyone" (18.55) in the first scenes shows that this digital paradise is not only a place that offers individual fulfillment, but is also constructed as an inclusive space where different identities and beliefs can coexist. Thus, this environment is not only a place where individuals rebuild their digital identities, but also a virtual universe that accepts and accommodates social diversity.

The scene at 21.41 minutes in which two men, one black and one gay, spend time together in the digital universe shows that the idealized living space in the film is constructed with the principles of inclusivity and diversity. This representation reflects the imagination of a digital utopia where both ethnic and sexual identities can exist freely. The representation of homosexual identity, which is frequently encountered in Netflix productions, gains visibility through a short scene, although it is not very prominent in the *Upload* series of Amazon Prime Video. As a result, it is seen that the narrative includes the intense use of visuals about the perfected form of the digital universe and the representation of homosexual identity. Within the digital platform logic of Amazon Prime Video, the perception of a digital utopia is constructed through the use of all the representations and visuals in the narrative to evoke aesthetic pleasure in the audience (Martín, 2021, p. 343). In this context, Amazon Pime Video presents idealized virtual living spaces in this virtual paradise-themed narrative, often accompanied by nature landscapes, while at the same time including identities representing social diversity.

- Digital Life

The construction of digital life in the series is read as a process shaped from both technological and commercialized perspectives. This process is shaped by the presentation of the virtual world not only through technical infrastructure and visual design elements, but also through user interaction. The virtual paradise presented in the series not only provides individuals with a sensory enriched experience, but also encourages them to certain orientations, paving the way for consumption practices to take place in the digital environment. In the scene presented at 23.07 minutes, when the character tries to buy a product from the minibar in his digital room, the fact that the object becomes available only when purchased reveals an important detail about the functioning of the virtual world. This structure, in which the boundaries of the digital paradise are determined by the economic power of the users, is a recurring theme in the series. *Upload*, which is produced by Amazon Prime Video, thus presents the idea of digital immortality, and although it conveys the many possibilities of this universe on the surface, it clearly reveals that it works with a commercialized order in the background. In this context, Prime Video constructs the narrative of technological utopia through a structure intertwined with consumer culture. On the other hand, the fact that the products in the van are presented with known brands shows that the scene can be read not only on a narrative level, but also within the framework of a product placement strategy. This strategy is frequently used in the rest of the series. While this narrative form emphasizes that even in the digital universe, the individual is primarily positioned as a consumer; with this presentation, the platform itself becomes a part of this order. Therefore, while the platform invites the audience to realize this situation, it simultaneously exhibits a practice that is included in this framework. In this context, Amazon Prime Video can be considered as an example among digital platforms that constructs its narrative world not only on the basis of content, but also through intertextual forms of consumption and visual placement strategies.

In a scene set in a virtual paradise, the lead character Nathan Brown's video communication with his girlfriend in the form of a reflection with a hand gesture at 26.52 minutes is both an opportunity provided by technology and a reconstruction of a form of communication that already exists in the physical world in a digital environment (In the series, it is a form of communication frequently used by those living in the real world). Here, the term "reflection" reveals a form of interaction in which the digital and physical worlds merge. This interaction can offer the viewer an intellectual journey about how technology is intertwined with the physical world and how digital environments are integrated into human experiences. On the other hand, at minute 24.15, Nathan's ability to change the climatic conditions outside from a switch inside the house makes visible the possibilities offered by the digital world. This shows the capacity of individuals to directly shape their environment through the digital systems provided by technology. With this narrative emphasizing the fusion of the digital and physical worlds, *Upload* offers a perspective on how technology can transform individuals' lives. This shows that Amazon Prime Video has the capacity to reflect the multi-layered aspects of technological transformation through its production *Upload*.

Although the series features a virtual universe narrative, it frequently includes food products with high fat, sugar and salt content (HFSS) (such as in minutes 23.10 and 30.10). In a study conducted by Alfayad et al. (2022), it was stated that the density of HFSS products in original content on Netflix and Amazon Prime Video platforms was similar, but the content on Amazon Prime included more such products (Alfayad et al., 2022, p. 306). The more intense coverage of HFSS products in the content on the Amazon Prime platform may increase the likelihood of normalization and acceptance of such food products by the audience. In this universe, which is fictionalized as a virtual paradise, the transfer of elements of the physical world - especially habitual objects such as unhealthy food - to the digital space may also suggest that this universe is a simulation that reflects the habits of the current world rather than an ideal future.

- The Limits of Individual Freedom

Nora is a system agent that monitors and manages all the daily needs of users in the digital paradise, supervising data flow and providing service access. She also has the role of continuously monitoring users' interactions and behaviors. On the other hand, Nathan's girlfriend, as an authorized user in the virtual paradise, determines the services Nathan receives. This situation shows that Nathan's digital life is shaped under the control of neither his girlfriend nor Nora and that his freedom in the digital environment is limited. In conclusion, there is surveillance in the series and this surveillance shapes the experiences of users in their virtual lives. The evolution of technology into surveillance mechanisms is a theme that is frequently addressed in the context of digital culture, especially in Netflix productions. In this respect, Amazon Prime Video can offer a similar trajectory to *Upload* both on a structural level and in terms of the narrative strategies it presents to the audience; it can simultaneously open the idea of digital freedom and the practice of surveillance to discussion.

Netflix- Black Mirror- San Junipero Episode Review

- Digital Presence and Virtual Immortality

In the episode of *Black Mirror* titled *San Junipero*[2], the theme of digital immortality is explored through the uploading of individuals' consciousness into a virtual reality environment. This fiction makes it possible for the individual to live a life beyond his/her physical body, allowing the mental existence to continue in a technological system. In the episode *San Junipero*, a digital "paradise" is depicted where elderly or dying individuals can upload their consciousness on a weekly basis and continue their existence indefinitely after their death. In *San* Junipero, the individual is presented as a conscious subject, not just as "data". In other words, the characters not only exist within the system, but also continue to live emotional experiences such as love, loss, regret and freedom. Thus, digital existence is constructed not as a mere extension but as a new form of life. This makes the episode meaningful not only on a technological but also on a philosophical level. In conclusion, while the Netflix production *San Junipero* presents digital immortality as a kind of salvation, it also proceeds through how the individual makes sense of and relates to this new way of life. Unlike *Upload*, which has a scenario that deals with commercialized and class distinctions, *San* Junipero constructs digital immortality around the themes of emotional freedom, personal confrontation and existential choice

Under the guise of a quiet seaside town, *San Junipero* offers a nostalgic space where youth and unlimited fun are digitally reproduced. Users can exist here at any physical age and appearance they wish, thus eliminating age, illness or physical limitations. Yorkie, one of the main characters, has the opportunity to experience the fun and freedom that she has never experienced in her life for the first time in this simulation. In a club he has never been to before, he drinks drinks he has never drunk, and moves freely to music he has never listened to. The bars and clubs in *San Junipero* are not only places of entertainment, but also scenes where Yorkie can experience his youth and come into direct contact with life for the first time. This environment offers him the freedom not only to move, but also to feel, experience and exist. This is where Yorkie meets Kelly, another leading character, and their moments together allow Yorkie to embark on a new journey of freedom and self-expression in the digital world (04.09). The digital universe of *San Junipero* functions not only as a space where entertainment and youth are relived, but also as a stage where individuals can realize their desires that they cannot experience in life and freely express their repressed identities. In this context, Yorkie's story shows that identity and existence can be reconstructed in a technological universe. This narrative is presented in a postmodern framework where technology is not only a tool but also a new door to the inner world of the individual. As in this episode, Netflix pioneers narratives that question how the digital age transforms the human experience by giving a wide space to scenarios shaped around technology. In this context, Netflix is encountered as a platform that shapes the cultural structure (Yaman, 2023, p. 71). Because through such content, Netflix creates a narrative space that shapes the cultural dynamics of the digital age by influencing the intellectual world of viewers.

In the series, access to the digital system is possible both for the living and for individuals at the end of their lives. For limited periods of time - usually a few hours a week - the living experience transferring their consciousness into this digital environment. During this process, their minds temporarily reside in *San* Junipero while their bodies continue to exist in the physical world. However, after death, the person's consciousness can be completely transferred to this digital environment and continue to exist permanently in *San Junipero*. Thus, this system functions as a digital living space that can be both "experienced" before death and "inhabited" after death. The idea of transhumanism (Kanburoğlu, 2022, p. 4), which has recently appeared in Netflix content, centers on the desire to overcome the physical limitations of human beings. In this context, the platform not only reproduces traditional narrative forms, but also creates original fictional universes that examine the effects of technological developments on individual existence. Productions such as *San Junipero*, for example, explore the concept of transhumanism in a digital medium, questioning the idea that human consciousness can exist independently of the physical world. Such productions demonstrate that technology can reshape fundamental existential elements beyond biological life, such as identity, freedom and relationships. In this way, Netflix not only offers entertaining and thought-provoking content, but also creates alternative realities that address the effects of digital life and technological transformation on the individual.

In the following frames, Kelly and Yorkie are euthanized in the real world and relocated to the digital world in order to make the permanent transition to *San Junipero*. At the end of the series, at minute 59.20, the small devices containing Kelly and Yorkie's consciousnesses are connected to a large machine containing devices containing the consciousnesses of hundreds of other individuals. This process allows them to completely separate from the physical world and exist only in the digital universe. Once they begin to live in the digital environment, both their individual identities and their existence become fully integrated into the digital universe of *San* Junipero. This narrative structure reveals that Netflix is not only about content that serves popular culture, but also offers in-depth structures that question the effects of technological developments on the individual's self, memory and perception of death. As a result, it can be said that digital platforms such as Netflix offer individuals multiple and extraordinary content (Kılıç and Akbayır, 2023, p. 270).

- Virtual Paradise

Behind the colorful, nostalgic and peaceful atmosphere of *San Junipero* lies a darker side of the system. Presented at 25.23 minutes, this dark club in a digital paradise, characterized by noisy music, chaotic relationships and occasional scenes of violence, is like a refuge for repressed emotions. This space is called "the swamp" among users. The existence of such a place in this digital universe, which is ostensibly a paradise, shows that the consciousnesses present here are not only happy, but also carry dark and complex emotions. This reveals that the system does not offer a one-way peaceful environment, but has a multi-layered structure that can take on different meanings according to individual experiences. Yorkie goes to this place to find Kelly and tries to understand her escapes, fears and reservations. Compared to television channels, digital platforms have the flexibility to cover more unusual topics (Akdemir, 2023, p. 315). This narrative freedom makes it possible to construct *San* Junipero not only as a peaceful paradise, but also as a multi-layered universe that allows for the expression of repressed desires, emotional conflicts and individual traumas. This can be seen as a reflection of Netflix's approach to producing content that allows space for different emotional depths.

In *San* Junipero's digital universe, individuals have a choice not only of space but also of time. Going to different years such as 1980 (27.36), 1996 (28.16), 2002 (29.06) allows users to shape their existence according to the cultural texture, music, fashion and social atmosphere of certain periods in the past. However, Yorkie's main purpose in traveling to different years is to find Kelly. Kelly is not only a desire for Yorkie, but also a figure that shapes her new life and identity. Finding Kelly means an opportunity for her to rebuild her lost self in the real world. In this context, the multi-layered structure of the narrative built around time and identity points to a narrative style that differs from traditional linear story structures. In the converging media universe, new approaches to storytelling have emerged. Classical narrative forms are being replaced by multidimensional and intertwined structures (Pavlik and Bridges, 2013, p. 5); just like the structure of *San Junipero*, which is woven around time and identity, it places the viewer at the center of plural experiences, not a fixed presentation. By enabling the proliferation of such content presentations and narratives, Netflix contributes to the exploration of multidimensional forms of storytelling that transcend traditional boundaries.

- Digital Life

Although *San Junipero*'s digital universe is built with advanced technology, there are almost no technological elements in the environment that users experience. Although this virtual paradise is based on a digital infrastructure, it expresses itself not through technology but through nostalgia. Equipped with neon-lit streets, vintage cars, analog jukeboxes, and CRT televisions, this world deliberately avoids appearing technological, despite the fact that it contains a highly sophisticated technology such as consciousness transference. This preference shows that it places the emotional transformation and relational bonds of the characters, not technology, at the center of the narrative. Based on a book or a play that is the subject of the production, Netflix involves the audience through the character (Yengin and Ormanlı, 2020, p. 89); therefore, it adopts a character-driven narrative style. *In San Junipero*, Netflix prefers to direct the audience to emotional and human-oriented stories by presenting technology as an invisible infrastructure; here, technology does not get in the way of emotional experiences, on the contrary, it deepens them and draws the audience into the inner journeys of the characters. In this context, Netflix demonstrates its potential to develop original and multi-layered scenarios by transforming conventional narrative structures with the example of *San Junipero* .

In *San Junipero*, alcohol is encountered as an essential part of social interaction and entertainment. Bars, dance floors and drink services are elements that reconstruct the youthful atmosphere that users have experienced in the past. Alcohol consumption takes place in this digital universe as a means for individuals to express themselves comfortably, to establish intimacy and to revitalize familiar social roles. Thus, this virtual paradise, which is constructed as a technological utopia, offers an idealized but familiar life experience by hosting the habits and pleasures of the traditional world. Previous research has also shown that alcohol and tobacco content is remarkably frequent in programs offered through VOD services (Alfayad et al., 2022, p. 308). In this context, Netflix, as a VOD service, includes the alcohol and tobacco elements seen in the *San Junipero* example and presents these elements as a natural part of the narrative in the context of character construction and social interaction.

The detached nature of *San Junipero* from physical reality is revealed in the scene (31.16) in which Kelly punches the mirror in the bar's sink. This act is seen as a sudden expression of his repressed anger and inner conflict. However, neither the mirror is broken nor Kelly's hand is damaged after the blow, thus depicting an artificial order in the digital universe where physical pain and material effects are ignored. This scene represents a breaking moment in which Kelly pushes the boundaries of digital existence and her body, accustomed to real-world pain, is unrequited here. Through this narrative, Netflix reflects the depth of emotional and psychological experiences within a digital artificiality.

Towards the end of the series, the characters' choices regarding the digital world bring about emotional conflicts. Kelly proposes marriage to Yorkie so that she can permanently transition *to San Junipero*; Yorkie accepts this proposal. Only the approval of family members is legally required for Yorkie, who is in a vegetative state in real life, to transition to digital life. This process will be completed by euthanizing Yorkie in the real world. After their marriage, Kelly approves Yorkie's transition to *San* Junipero. However, Yorkie asks Kelly to continue in the digital paradise permanently. Kelly refuses this offer and an argument breaks out due to emotional conflicts between them. Kelly then gets into a car accident (54.33) and is unharmed. In this context, the reality in *San Junipero* goes beyond physical pain and harm, where no physical harm occurs, but emotional and psychological conflicts persist even in the digital environment. This suggests that digital existence shapes not only bodily experiences but also individual internal states. In this context, Netflix's unique storytelling style of keeping its audience on their toes by having characters in constant action (Özkent and Can, 2021, p. 690) is also evident in these scenes of *San* Junipero, and the production supports the platform's unique narrative style in this respect.

- The Limits of Individual Freedom

In *San Junipero*, the freedom in the digital paradise allows individuals to construct their identities in the way they want. Kelly describes *San Junipero* as a "party city" (11.16) and emphasizes that everything is free in this digital universe. Here, people can dress according to the period fashions of the past, dance, drink alcohol and express their existence freely. With this kind of content, Netflix glorifies individual freedom and desires by offering the viewer an uncontrolled and free space. By putting this freedom and choice at its center, *San Junipero* depicts a universe where identities and desires are reshaped in the digital environment. This also reflects Netflix's aim to offer its viewers experiences through more diverse lifestyles and identities

Kelly and Yorkie's intimacy in *San Junipero* takes shape as an expression of individual freedom and emotional choices in a universe free from the confines of the physical world and social norms. Presented at minute 18.01, Kelly and Yorkie's first intimacy is the moment when their emotional connection begins. *San Junipero*, as a digital paradise where homosexual relationships can be lived freely, offers a space free from social limitations. The fact that Yorkie is black symbolizes the existence of an environment where everyone can freely express their identity and relationships. Netflix aims to increase the sense of representation by offering rich and diverse content. This approach shows that the platform is not only inclusive, but also follows a marketing strategy that prioritizes diverse communities (Altın and Demirci, 2024, p. 727). In this context, the *San Junipero* episode not only presents a love story, but also reveals the possibility of an alternative social structure where different identities gain visibility within the digital universe. Thus, Netflix aims to establish a deeper connection with its global audience by expanding its spheres of representation. Netflix's original productions, although relatively low-budget, present narratives that deal with universal themes; in these narratives, disadvantaged groups, especially LGBTQ+ people and ethnic minorities, are often included and positive discrimination is practiced. Although such content includes social and political criticisms through characters, these criticisms are often shaped within the boundaries of the existing system and presented in a structure that does not contradict the dominant narratives (Yaman, 2023, p. 71). In this framework, *San Junipero*, while increasing the visibility of alternative identities, also reproduces this representation within the boundaries of the system.

At the end of the series, Kelly and Yorkie are reunited and dance together at *San Junipero*'s entertainment center (59.30). Yorkie, previously unable to fully experience her freedom in the digital world, is finally free; freed from the limitations of her body, she is now able to dance and express herself. This moment represents a turning point in which freedom in the digital world is rediscovered, both physically and emotionally. *San Junipero* offers a space where individuals can freely live the life they desire, free from physical pain, limitations or the pressures of society. This dance is a symbol of both Kelly and Yorkie finding their identities and desires in this digital world, of their liberation. However, this final scene of the series is presented in a disconnected way from the previous scene. Because in the previous scene, Kelly states that she refuses to stay in *San Junipero*. This narrative style is an example of the postmodern narrative style, a feature frequently encountered in Netflix's original content. While appealing to different cultures and offering content to various countries, Netflix uses the possibilities of postmodern narratives to present narratives that are more fragmented and spread over different time periods. An important feature of postmodern narrative is that it includes interrupted, fragmented narrative forms instead of a holistic narrative (Özkent, 2020, p. 316).

CONCLUSION

This study comparatively analyzes two different VOD (Video-on-Demand) platform productions, *Upload* (Amazon Prime Video) and *San Junipero* (Netflix), which center on the theme of digital immortality. While both productions focus on the individual's transition to a digital existence through consciousness transference after physical death, they exhibit certain differences in terms of the ways of representing this transition, platform strategies, social representations and narrative structures. *Upload* on Amazon Prime Video and Netflix's *San* Junipero stand out as examples that question the effects of the digital age on the individual; at the same time, they stand out as structures shaped by contemporary narrative strategies.

As in the order of analysis, if we first talk about the Amazon Prime Video series *Upload*, individual existence can be made visible and blurred at the same time through melodramatic character structures, as is common in VOD platforms and therefore in post-cinematic narratives. Amazon Prine Video, while integrating this narrative strategy used in *Upload* with the idea of a digital paradise, reinforces the visibility of the individual not only through technological possibilities but also through consumption-oriented arrangements integrated into this technological system. In this context, digital immortality, which can be achieved through the transmission of consciousness, is reconstructed not only as a technical possibility but also through profit-oriented models and service levels, and individual identity can exist within the boundaries defined by the system. On the other hand, the presentation of Nora, another protagonist at the center of the narrative, as a black female character, equipped with technical skills, with emotional depth and in a subject position, coincides with the sensitive representation policies that digital platforms have recently adopted. In addition, in the *Upload* series, the presentation of the digital universe in a perfected form and the representation of homosexual identity coincide with the literature that all representations and visuals in the narrative are used to arouse aesthetic pleasure in the audience in line with the digital platform logic of Amazon Prime Video. This shows that the platform offers a kind of "ideal" digital life design in terms of both visual aesthetics and representation. These narrative choices reveal that Amazon Prime Video is shaped in line with the current representational politics of VOD platforms. Furthermore, this production, in which product placement strategies are used extensively, reveals that platforms are positioned not only as storytellers but also as structures that reproduce consumption patterns. In this context, Amazon Prime Video can be considered as an example of a digital platform that constructs its narrative world not only on the basis of content, but also through intertextual forms of consumption and visual placement strategies. Previous research has shown that HFSS (high in fat, sugar and salt) products are frequently visible in the content on the Amazon Prime Video platform. In the *Upload* series, despite the depiction of a digital paradise, such food and beverages are prominently featured. This situation reveals that even idealized digital living spaces are not constructed independently from the norms of today's consumer culture. As a reflection of the platform's content production approach, the placement of such products shows that Amazon Prime Video shapes the digital world not only narratively, but also in a cultural context as a structure that reflects consumption habits.

Netflix pioneers narratives that question the human experience of the digital age through scenarios shaped on the axis of technology; in this respect, it is positioned not only as a platform that offers content, but also as an actor that transforms the cultural structure. In recent years, as the idea of transhumanism has become a central theme in Netflix productions, the desire to transcend the physical limitations of human beings and the reshaping of individual existence has become a central theme in these productions. This allows the platform to not only reproduce traditional narrative forms, but also to create original fictional universes that question the effects of technological developments on the individual. Productions such as *San Junipero* reflect a transhumanist approach by exploring the idea that human consciousness can exist in a digital environment, independent of the physical body. In this context, Netflix abandons classical narrative patterns and adopts multi-layered and intertwined story structures, thus contributing to the development of narrative forms that go beyond traditional boundaries. In addition, Netflix generally adopts a character-driven narrative style, and this narrative style is evident in the San Junipero episode. The narrative, which progresses through the characters' inner conflicts, emotional transformations and their connection to the past, encourages the audience to focus on individual experiences. This approach shows that even in a transhumanist universe, human emotions, the search for identity and personal choices are prioritized. On the other hand, alcohol and tobacco use, which are frequently encountered in productions offered through VOD services, are also prominently featured in *San Junipero*; in this context, Netflix presents these elements as a natural part of the narrative within the framework of character construction and social interaction. Netflix's unique storytelling style of keeping the audience on their toes by having the characters constantly in action is also evident in these scenes of San Junipero; the production supports the platform's unique narrative style in this aspect. Despite their relatively low budgets, Netflix productions often focus on universal themes and make space for the representation of disadvantaged groups, especially LGBTQ+ individuals and ethnic minorities. *San Junipero* continues this approach and supports the platform's inclusive narrative policies by presenting the virtual paradise as a space of freedom and acceptance for these individuals. In addition to all these, this example, where a fragmented narrative structure is preferred, reveals that Netflix is moving away from traditional holistic narrative patterns and towards a flexible and multi-layered story structure that appeals to contemporary audience habits.

REFERENCES

Akdemir Dilek, B. (2023). "Uysallar" Dizisinde Punk Alt Kültürün Sinematografik Araçlarla Yeniden İnşası. *Sizefilozofi*, *8*(16), 298–318. DOI: 10.31122/sinefilozofi.1199053

Akova, S. (2020). Kültürlerarası İletişim Bağlamında Ötekileştirme Olgusunun Dijital Taşıyıcılığına Dair Netflix Dijital Televizyonu Üzerinden Bir Bakış: 13 Commandments (13 Emir) Dizisi Üzerinden Göstergebilimsel Analizi. *Opus International Journal Of Society Researches*, *15*(26), 4479–4516. DOI: 10.26466/opus.680136

Alfayad, K., Murray, R. L., Britton, J., & Barker, A. B. (2022). Content Analysis Of Netflix And Amazon Prime Instant Video Original Films İn The Uk For Alcohol, Tobacco And Junk Food İmagery. *Journal of Public Health (Oxford, England)*, *44*(2), 302–309. DOI: 10.1093/pubmed/fdab022 PMID: 33675356

Amazon Prime Video. (2020). *Upload – Season 1, Episode 1: "Welcome To Upload*". Retrieved from: Watch Upload - Season 1 | Prime Video (Retrieved on April 29, 2025).

Atasoy, A. A. D. (2021). *Dijital Platformlarda Kullanılan Yapay Zeka Teknolojilerinin Kullanıcı Motivasyonları Üzerinden İncelenmesi: Netflix Örneği* [Unpublished Doctoral Dissertation]. İstanbul Universty, İstanbul.

Aydemir, M. (2023). Dijital Platformlarda İçerik Mülkiyeti Stratejileri: "Sadece" Modeli Üzerine Bir İnceleme. *Nevşehir Hacı Bektaş Veli* Universty *Sbe Journal,* 13(3), 1457-1478. Https://Doi.Org/10.30783/Nevsosbilen.1271624

Becz, P. (2016). *Netflix Goes To Cinema: The New Chapter Of Quality TV Conquers The Big Screen* (Master's Thesis, University Of Copenhagen). Retrieved From Http://Bit.Ly/3llmm87

Berber, A. (2017). Yönetimde Kavramsal Çerçeve Belirleme Ve Nitel Araştırma Yöntemleri. *İstanbul Üniversitesi İşletme Fakültesi Dergisi,* 46, 71-73.

Brembilla, P. (2015, July 7–9). *Not That Transparent: Amazon's Series, Between System-Thinking And Branding Strategies* [Paper Presentation]. *Media Change International Conference*, University Di Urbino Carlo Bo, Dıscum, Urbino, Italy.

Burç, M., & Tanyeri Mazıcı, E. (2023). Kültür Endüstrisi Aracı Olarak Dijital Yayıncılık: Dijital Tv Platformları Üzerine Durum Çalışması. *İletişim Ve Toplum Araştırmaları Dergisi*, 3(1), 133-166. Https://Doi.Org/10.5281/Zenodo.7785622

Erdem, N., & Aytekin, B. A. (2021). Covid-19 Pandemisinde İzleyici Deneyimi: Netflix Ekseninde Dijital Platformlara Bakış. *Akdeniz University İletişim Fakültesi Der*gisi (36), 302-325. Https://Doi.Org/10.31123/Akil.988565

Harmanda, A., & Taşdemir, B. (2022). 360 Derece Film Mizanseni Nedir? Tasarım Ve Yapım Sürecine Dair Temel Açıklamalar. *Akdeniz Sanat,* 16(30), 325-344. Https://Doi.Org/10.48069/Akdenizsanat.1117313

Heskett, J. (2013). *Tasarım.* (E. Uzun, Trans.) Ankara: Dost Kitapevi. (Original Work Published, 2002)

Kanburoğlu, S. (2022). *Netfli x Yapimlarinda Transhümani zm Ve Gelecek Tasarimi* (Master's Thesis, Izmir Katip Celebi University (Turkey)).

Kılıç, S., & Akbayır, A. (2023). Postmodern Bireyin Temsili: The Witcher Dizi Örneği. *Kastamonu İletişim Araştırmaları Dergisi* (11), 262-289. Https://Doi.Org/10.56676/Kiad.1262904

Llivizaca Criollo, R. M. (2021). *Análisis comparativo de las plataformas de streaming: Netflix y Amazon Prime Video en el Ecuador* (Bachelor's Thesis, Universidad Técnica de Babahoyo).

Maden, A. (2020). *Postmodern Bağlamda Netflix'te Lgbtq+ Söylemler.* (Unpublished Master's Thesis). İstanbul İbn Haldun University, İstanbul.

Medin, B., & Kaymak, A. (2022). *Sinema Ve Dijital Platformlar* (1st ed.). Doruk Yayımcılık.

Merikivi, J., Salovaara, A., Mäntymäki, M., & Zhang, L. (2018). On The Way To Understanding Binge Watching Behavior: The Over-Estimated Role Of İnvolvement. *Electronic Markets, 28*(1), 111–122. Https://Doi.Org/10.1007/S12525-017-0271-4. DOI: 10.1007/s12525-017-0271-4

Mystakidis, S. (2022). "Metaverse". *Encyclopedia,* 2, 486–497. Https://Doi.Org/10.3390/encyclopedia2010031

Naghizada, S. (2023). *Türk Dizilerinde Algı Yönetimi Ve Ürün Yerleştirmesinin Incelenmesi: Netflix Platformu Erşan Kuneri Dizisi Örneği* (Doctoral Dissertation, Maltepe University (Turkey)).

Netflix. (2016). *Black Mirror – Season 3, Episode 4: "San Junipero".* Retrieved from: Https://Www.Netflix.Com/Tr/Title/70264888?S=A&Trkid=13747225&Trg=Cp&Vlang=Tr&Clip=81996955 ((Retrieved on April 29, 2025)).

Osur, L. (2016). *Netflix And The Development Of The İnternet Television Network.* (Phd Thesis. Abd: Syracuse University).

Özel, S. (2020). Talebe Bağlı Video Servisleri Çağında Netflix Etkisi. *İnsan ve İnsan*, 7 (26), 115-138.

Özgül, İ. (2023). *Toplumsal Cinsiyet Bağlamında Dijital Platformlardaki Annelik Kavramı: Big Litlle Lies ve Litlle Fires Everywhere Örnekleri*. (Published Master's Thesis). Akdeniz University, Institute of Social Sciences, Antalya.

Özkent, Y. (2020). Postmodernizmi Netflıx'ten Seyretmek: Metinlerarasılıktan Nostaljiye Stranger Thıngs. *Moment Dergi*, 7(2), 314-333. Https://Doi.Org/10.17572/Mj2020.2.314333

Özkent, Y., & Can, A. (2021). "Nitelikli Televizyon": Netflix Platformunda "Nitelikli Drama"Nın Yeniden İnşası. *Selçuk İletişim*, 14(2), 674-698. Https://Doi.Org/10.18094/Josc.871771

Öztürk, N. B. & Erdoğan, Y. (2022). Netflix'te Dijital Pazarlama Stratejileri İle Gündem Belirleme: Pera Palas'ta Gece Yarısı Örneği. *Akademik Hassasiyetler Dergisi*, Cilt 9, Sayı: 20, Syf, 161-195

Patton, M. Q. (2014). *Nitel Araştırma Ve Değerlendirme Yöntemleri* (Bütün, M., & Beşir Demir, S., Eds. & Trans.). Pegem.

Pavlik, J. V., & Bridges, F. (2013). The Emergence Of Augmented Reality (Ar) As A Storytelling Medium İn Journalism. *Journalism & Communication Monographs*, *15*(4), 4–59. DOI: 10.1177/1522637912470819

Pesudo Martínez, J., & Izquierdo Castillo, J. (2021). Los Gigantes Tecnológicos Conquistan El Audiovisual. El Caso De Amazon Prime Video. *Área Abierta, 21*(3).

Sağlamtimur, Ö. Z. (2010). Dijital Sanat. *Anadolu University Sosyal Bilimler Dergisi*, Cilt 10, Sayı: 3, Syf, 213-238

Şakı Aydın, O. (2019). Yeni İzleme Biçimleri ve Netflix İçerikleri: Ritzer'in McDonaldlaşma Tezi Ekseninde Bir Değerlendirme. *Journal of International Social Research*, *12*(63), 1167–1172. DOI: 10.17719/jisr.2019.3305

Sebastián-Martín, M. (2021). Refabricating Individualism And Commodifying Anti-Capitalism: Melodramatic Sf And Vod Spectatorship. *Science Fiction Studies, 48*(Part 2 (144)), 332-353.

Sim, G. (2016). Individual disruptors and economic gamechangers: Netflix, new media, and neoliberalism. In McDonald, K., & Smith-Rowsey, D. (Eds.), *The Netflix effect: Technology and entertainment in the 21st century* (pp. 185–202). Bloomsbury Academic.

Yağar, F., & Dökme, S. (2018). Niteliksel Araştırmaların Planlanması: Araştırma Soruları, Örneklem Seçimi, Geçerlik Ve Güvenirlik. *Gazi Sağlık Bilimleri Dergisi, 3*(3), 1–9.

Yaman, E. (2023). *Netflix'te Oryantalizm: Orta Doğu Konulu Dizilerde Emperyal İzler*. (Unpublished Master's Thesis). Akdeniz University, Antalya.

Yavuz, G. (2024). *Sayısal Yayın Platformlarında Belgesel Sinemanın Dönüşen Anlatı Yapısı: Netflix Örneği.* (Master's Thesis). Selçuk University, Konya.

Yengin, D., & Ormanlı, O. (2020). İnteraktif Kurgu Örneği Olarak Bandersnatch Filminin Analizi. *Turkish Online Journal Of Design Art And Communication, 10*(2), 83–96. DOI: 10.7456/11002100/002

Yenigün Altın, Ş., & Demirci, K. (2024). Kültürel Hegemonya Tartışmaları Çerçevesinde Netflix Türkiye Yerli Dizileri İncelemesi Ve İzleyici Deneyimi. *Trt Akademi*, 9(22), 724-751. Https://Doi.Org/10.37679/Trta.1519715

Yıldırım, N. (2024). Yerli Dijital Platformlarda Alternatif Türler: Sahte Belgesel '500t' Dizisi Örneği. *İnönü Üniversitesi İletişim Fakültesi Elektronik Dergisi* (İnif E-Dergi), 9(2), 347-368. Https://Doi.Org/10.47107/İnifedergi.1515792

ADDITIONAL READING

Braun, J. (2013). Going Over The Top: Online Television Distribution As Sociotechnical System. *Communication, Culture & Critique*, *6*(3), 432–458. DOI: 10.1111/cccr.12015

Büyükçelikok, T. Ö., & Dilmen, N. E. (2024). Dijital Yayın Platformları Teknik Özelliklerinin Kullanılabilirliğinin Kullanıcı Deneyimine Etkisi: Netflix Örneği. *İletişim Çalışmaları Dergisi*, 10(3), 359-372.

Ceylan, G. E. (2024). *Dijital Platformlarda Pagan Sembolleri: Netflix'in Hakan: Muhafiz Ve Atiye Dizileri* (Master's Thesis, Istanbul Sabahattin Zaim University (Turkey)).

Sadana, M., & Sharma, D. (2021). How Over-The-Top (Ott) Platforms Engage Young Consumers Over Traditional Pay Television Service? An Analysis Of Changing Consumer Preferences And Gamification. *Young Consumers*, *22*(3), 348–367. DOI: 10.1108/YC-10-2020-1231

Sarı, Ü., & Sancaklı, P. (2020). Küyerelleşmenin Dijital Platformların İçerik Tanıtımına Etkisi: Netflix Örneği. *Erciyes İletişim Dergisi*, *7*(1), 243–260. DOI: 10.17680/erciyesiletisim.647463

Sarı, Ü., & Türker, H. (2021). Dijital Platform Kullanıcılarının İzleme Alışkanlıklarına Yönelik Bir Araştırma: Netflix Örneği. *Anadolu Üniversitesi Sosyal Bilimler Dergisi*, 21(1), 59-80. Https://Doi.Org/10.18037/Ausbd.902558

Shih, W. C., Kaufman, S. P., & Ve Spinola, D. (2009). *Netflix*. Harvard Business School.

Tiwary, I. (2020). Amazon Prime Video: A Platform Ecosphere. In A. Athique & V. Parthasarathi (Eds.), *Platform Capitalism İn India* (*Global Transformations İn Media And Communication Research – A Palgrave And IAMCR Series*). Palgrave Macmillan. Https://Doi.Org/10.1007/978-3-030-44563-8_5

Ünlü, T. T., & Akyol, O. (2025). Türkiye'de Dijital Platformlarda Yayınlanan İnteraktif Yapımların İncelenmesi. *Communicata*, (29), 48–59. DOI: 10.32952/communicata.1619972

Van Vliet, H. (2002). Where Television And Internet Meet. *New Experiences For Rich Media, 9*(11), 2020.

KEY TERMS AND DEFINITIONS

Digitalization: Digitalization refers to the process of converting physical or analog data into digital formats and the subsequent processing, storing, and transmitting of this digital data, driven by technological advancements. Digitalization transforms the daily lives of individuals, the way companies operate, communication methods, and how information is accessed within societies.

Netflix: Netflix is an online digital media streaming platform. In 2007, it transformed from a physical DVD rental service to an online video streaming service as part of the digitalization process. Users can watch content such as TV series, movies, and documentaries over the internet.

Amazon Prime Video: Amazon Prime Video is an online digital media streaming platform offered by Amazon. Users can watch TV shows, movies, documentaries, and other content via Amazon's Prime membership. With this platform, Amazon has created a major shift in digital content distribution and has become a significant player among subscription-based media platforms.

Virtual Universe: A virtual universe is a digital reflection of the real world, created as an environment or universe where users can interact. This universe is typically built with 3D graphics and offers virtual worlds where users can navigate and engage. Virtual universes have evolved particularly in relation to gaming, social media, and virtual reality (VR) technologies.

Platform Strategies: Platform strategies are the structural choices through which digital platforms create, direct, and engage audiences via content production and distribution. These strategies are not only economic but can also involve ideological and cultural preferences.

Platform Presentation: Refers to how a digital content (such as a movie, TV series, documentary, etc.) is presented to the audience, including the platform, format, timing, and strategy used. It also involves the presentation preferences shaped by the target audience, representation policies, and content emphasis, which are crucial parts of platform presentation. This strategy plays a critical role in enhancing content visibility, fostering engagement, and shaping the user experience.

Platform Broadcasting Platforms: Digital broadcasting platforms are online services that provide content via the internet, allowing users to watch or listen to digital media (such as movies, TV series, music, documentaries, etc.). These platforms typically operate on a subscription-based model, enabling users to access content at any time and on any device they choose.

ENDNOTES

1 Upload - Season 1, Episode 1 (2020). *Amazon Prime Video.* Access address: Watch Upload - Season 1 | Prime Video

2 Black Mirror - San Junipero - Season 3, Episode 4 (2016). Netflix. Retrieved from: https://www.netflix.com/tr/title/70264888?trackId=14170286

Chapter 10
Netflix's Effort to Enhance User Experience With Gaming Strategy:
Netflix Gaming Strategy

Mert Gürer
https://orcid.org/0000-0002-2940-2009
Kocaeli University, Turkey

Gözde İslamoğlu
https://orcid.org/0000-0002-0910-5744
Kocaeli University, Turkey

Emel Ateşçi
https://orcid.org/0000-0002-4170-7745
Kocaeli University, Turkey

ABSTRACT

Digital gaming has evolved from traditional physical games to interactive experiences, becoming a dynamic part of the entertainment industry. Games now serve as tools for social interaction, education, and cultural expression, with mobile and multiplayer games fostering global communities. Netflix's gaming initiatives influence the storyline, transforming passive viewing into active participation. These games are analyzed for features like playability, user ratings, language diversity, and social interaction potential. Netflix's approach aligns with broader trends in digital platforms, which use AI, big data, and augmented reality to personalize user experiences. Gaming strategy exemplifies this transformation, blending entertainment with interactivity to redefine user engagement. Within the scope of the study, analyses will be carried out on the types of digital games offered by Netflix and

DOI: 10.4018/979-8-3373-1957-5.ch010

quantitative data on usage practices. This study highlights the platform's efforts to adapt to evolving digital trends and sets the stage for further research into user behavior and preferences.

INTRODUCTION

Digital gaming culture has become one of the most dynamic and rapidly growing areas of the entertainment industry. With technological developments, games have gone beyond being just a means of entertainment and are now accepted as a part of social interaction, education and even art. Especially online multiplayer games increase intercultural interaction by creating a global community. Mobile games, on the other hand, reach out to users of all ages, further popularising the gaming culture. Digital games have become not only a hobby but also a lifestyle and a form of cultural expression.

Digital games have a very important share in today's entertainment industry. In this sense, it attracts the attention of other fields. Role-playing as a type of digital games, taking on a character while playing; popular film and series content is seen as a suitable adaptation area for the digital game field. The ability of players to direct their favourite TV series or film characters on a digital platform brings along the continuation of their viewing experience on a virtual platform. In this sense, digital games bring benefits to films and series in terms of enabling them to continue their own universes.

The future of digital platforms is undergoing a transformation, especially with the addition of technologies such as artificial intelligence, big data analytics and augmented reality. One of the most important innovations offered by these platforms is personalised user experience. Artificial intelligence-based algorithms analyse user preferences, making the practice of viewing more targeted and individualised. User loyalty is increased with recommendation systems based on user habits. In the future, this personalisation offers viewers fully individualised content or virtual environments.

Netflix aims to enhance its dominance in the digital entertainment sector by venturing into the mobile gaming industry, striving to create a multifaceted user experience. The platform offers its members not only films and series but also an interactive gaming experience through games spanning 14 different categories. This strategy seeks to increase user engagement on the platform while strengthening brand loyalty by appealing to diverse age groups and interests. Notably, games in popular categories such as action, adventure, and strategy support this goal with high download numbers and positive user ratings.

Netflix's gaming portfolio is designed to synergize with its original content. Game adaptations of series like *Stranger Things* and *Squid Game* allow users to interact with the universes they love. This approach fosters continuity across content while deepening users' emotional connection. Additionally, games based on Netflix originals such as *Too Hot to Handle* and *Money Heist*are part of the platform's strategy to deliver a multi-dimensional experience. Such games enable users to transition from passive viewers to active participants.

Another factor enriching the user experience is the inclusion of diverse features such as age restrictions and multiplayer options. Adult-oriented games like *GTA: San Andreas* and educational games for children like *CoComelon: Play with JJ* reflect Netflix's goal of reaching a broad audience. Multiplayer modes encourage social interaction, fostering competition and collaboration among users. This diversity demonstrates Netflix's ability to cater to varied user needs. The offline play feature ensures users can engage with the platform even without an internet connection. These features underscore Netflix's commitment to user satisfaction and technological flexibility.

The first part deals with the transformation of television broadcasting under the influence of technological developments, digitalisation and changing consumer behaviour. mpaperxnes Initially based on terrestrial and satellite broadcasting, television has evolved through cable TV and later web-based streaming, enabling on-demand content consumption and breaking fixed schedules. Platforms such as Netflix have revolutionised the industry by moving from DVD rental to global streaming, encouraging binge-watching cultures and interactive audience engagement. Digitalisation transforms passive viewers into active producers, algorithms personalise content and social media enhance collective viewing experiences. The rise of IPTV and streaming platforms has replaced linear broadcasting with non-linear, fragmented content, appealing to different preferences and marginalised voices. Netflix's expansion into gaming and original productions demonstrates how digital platforms are becoming multi-faceted entertainment ecosystems, prioritising user engagement and loyalty through innovative, cross-platform strategies.

The second part of study deals with the digital streaming platforms are evolving beyond one-dimensional content by embracing interactive and multi-optional experiences, particularly through game development. Platforms like Netflix are entering the gaming industry, transforming passive viewers into active participants and offering new ways to engage with content, such as games based on popular TV series or films. This strategy not only enhances user experience by blending entertainment with interactive gameplay but also expands the platform's economic and cultural impact, diversifying revenue models and fostering global subscriber growth. By integrating games into their ecosystems, these platforms create synergies between media content and gaming, appealing to wider audiences and reinforcing their position in the competitive digital landscape.

In the data collection and analysis part of this study examines Netflix's mobile gaming platform, aiming to categorize its games and analyze how they enhance user experience while contributing to a multifaceted entertainment ecosystem. Using qualitative data analysis, the study evaluates games based on criteria like age restrictions, player count, offline playability, ratings, and downloads, focusing on Turkish users. It highlights Netflix's strategy of integrating original content with games to maintain brand coherence and appeal to diverse age groups, reflecting the media industry's shift toward multi-dimensional entertainment. The research is limited to a specific timeframe and generalizes certain details, such as rating differences across platforms, leaving room for future in-depth analyses.

The Transformation of Television Broadcasting

The widespread adoption and personalization of computers have catalyzed a transformation in broadcasting. Television, once reliant on terrestrial broadcasts, has evolved alongside technological advancements. The launch of satellites by the Soviet Union and later the United States marked the shift to satellite broadcasting. Cable TV improved image quality, and today, web-based streaming has replaced traditional methods.

Television has always been a dynamic mass communication tool. Since the mid-1990s, digitization has revolutionized its technology, distribution, economics, media policies, and usage patterns (Mikos, 2016: 154). Digitization has also fostered collaboration between television broadcasting and computer technology.

The ability of content creators to distribute their work directly to audiences via web pages has redefined the concept of viewership. Audiences are no longer passive consumers but active producers, sharing their own content. This shift has driven television networks to adopt internet-based broadcasting models.

Television viewers demand on-demand access to content, breaking free from fixed broadcast schedules (Tryon, 2013). Netflix's "binge-watching" culture exemplifies this change. Users now consume content continuously, abandoning the traditional weekly episode format and reshaping the television industry's content production strategies. The advent of IPTV, facilitated by the internet, has eased the transition from traditional television to internet-based viewing. Alongside live broadcasts, viewers can access content tailored to their preferences.

The rise of digital platforms has been shaped by advancements in internet technology and shifts in consumer behavior. In the early 2000s, platforms like Netflix began as DVD rental services and evolved into global streaming giants (Jenkins, 2006). This transformation has upended content distribution models, empowering users to transition from passive viewers to interactive participants. The new form of television broadcasting has transformed the consumption of popular culture, politics, information and entertainment, as well as shaping how viewers access and experience content (Dhiman, 2023). This convergence of television broadcasting with the Internet has transformed viewing into an experience and the viewer into a user.

Streaming platforms such as Netflix appeal to niche audience profiles when producing content. Unlike traditional audience categories, Netflix defines niche audience groups as "taste communities". Instead of creating separate content for each audience group, they produce content at the intersection of these communities based on audience data (Lotz, 2018). Therefore, it is seen that there is a differentiation in the sociodemographic understanding of the audience of platform broadcasting television and traditional television. This differentiation is important when it comes to content production, as it provides essential data for broadcasting. When digital streaming platforms first emerged, they wanted to be known for the kind of productions that would make a splash. They adopted investing in original content as a strategy for branding and initially invested in dramas (Doyle, 2016).

Unlike traditional broadcasting, in Internet-based television broadcasting, new content is important for the brand value of the platform. However, licensed older content is also included in the libraries of streaming platforms. These productions, which have their own unique value, are also beneficial in terms of the economic and cultural value they carry (Gilbert, 2019). In addition to new and original productions, television content that viewers are already familiar with is also included in building the content library. Productions that were popular with viewers at the time they were broadcasted are added to the platform's stream, creating a familiar and nostalgic connection.

Digital streaming platforms essentially have control over the content they offer to their viewers. Although the viewer thinks that he/she chooses from the available content at a desired time, the platform actually directs this choice (Tefertiller, 2018). Platforms open an interactive door that allows the audience to access and watch the content they want from a non-linear broadcast library. However, at this point, it does not leave the viewer completely alone with himself/herself, but guides him/her by using the viewing data it obtains. The fact that it offers content to each viewer in accordance with his or her own viewing experience is a concrete manifestation of this functioning.

Binge watching, a new form of viewing that comes with transforming television broadcasting and digital streaming platforms, offers the viewer a viewing experience that is not interrupted by commercials. The viewer can binge watch as many episodes as they wish in a planned period of time. At this point, the viewer approaches the content not as a part of the television stream, but as a complete text (Jenner, 2014). When it comes to the television viewing experience instead of traditional television viewing, there are differences in terms of the interactive consumption of content as well as its perception. The content watched has a unity in itself, telling its own story like a single book selected from a library. If the viewer does not want the flow of the story to be disrupted, they can allocate a separate period of time in which they concentrate on the content, engaging in a higher level of interactivity than in the traditional way. This transforms viewing into a new kind of experience.

Digital platforms have personalized content consumption while turning it into a tool for social sharing (Boyd, 2014). Younger generations, in particular, discuss shows on social media, creating a collective experience. This shift symbolizes the move from family-centric viewing practices to individualized, mobile-focused models.

Streaming platforms have fundamentally altered traditional broadcasting. Audiences now access a wide array of international and genre-diverse productions via internet-based applications. Linear content consumption has given way to non-linear streaming. Williams (1970s) conceptualized broadcasting as a natural flow, but in the digital era, this flow has become a cultural practice (Kompare, 2002: 3). Media no longer merely functions as a flow; it is now designed to flow. Viewers can select content at will, watch multiple episodes, and extend their time on the platform. The fragmented nature of digital content and its representation of marginalized concepts, identities, and cultures have forged a seamless bond between streaming platforms and audiences.

In the 21st century, digital platforms have radically transformed media consumption habits, reshaping traditional entertainment models. Netflix, a pioneer in this shift, began as a content distribution platform but has since evolved into a comprehensive digital entertainment ecosystem through original productions, interactive content, and strategic entries into the gaming sector (Lotz, 2017; Johnson, 2021). This expansion aims not only to increase market share but also to enhance user loyalty by delivering a multi-dimensional experience.

Digital platforms have transcended the one-way nature of traditional television by offering personalized content through user-centric algorithms (Lotz, 2017). Netflix's recommendation system curates content based on viewer preferences, boosting user engagement. Features like multi-device support and offline viewing further enhance flexibility.

Netflix's foray into gaming reflects the creative approaches of digital platforms in content delivery. Beyond traditional film and series consumption, the platform offers free mobile games to subscribers, aiming to extend user interaction and unify diverse entertainment formats under one umbrella (Jenkins, 2006).

Netflix seeks to enrich the user experience by entering the gaming sector and offering interactive content (Johnson, 2021). This move underscores how digital platforms have evolved from mere viewing tools into multifaceted entertainment ecosystems. Academic research predicts that such cross-platform strategies will play a critical role in fostering user loyalty and expanding market share.

Digital Streaming Platforms and Game Development

Digital broadcasting platforms are no longer channels that offer one-dimensional content. They have started to take steps towards preparing interactive and multi-optional content for their users. It is noteworthy that some platforms prefer to directly participate in the gaming industry while doing so. This may also make a difference in terms of transforming the position of the audience. Digital platforms that are orientated towards game development do not only see their viewers as users who consume content, but also lead them to have different experiences by taking an active role. Thus, the individual who practices playing games with the opportunities offered by digital platforms encounters an alternative reality within the daily life flow. Games go beyond being a leisure time activity and lead people to a space where they can position and express themselves in different ways and discover new experiences.

It is possible to look at the game as a phenomenon that can imitate, complement or transform the order of everyday life. In this context, the game development strategy of the digital broadcasting platform reshapes not only the forms of production, distribution and consumption of media content but also the audience. Huizinga (2010) underlines that the game creates order and even is the order itself. According to him, the game creates a field of activity with its unique tendencies, rules and structure. In this respect, it contributes to entering a privileged space that is separated from the chaos in everyday life. The game also has an attraction to itself.

Connolly et al. (2012) state that games have different types and functions. Games that include entertainment are gradually increasing the interest they attract by offering interesting activities. The most important factors in this increase are the new consoles, platforms and technologies used in game presentation. The fact that games are accessible and numerous suggests that they can be frequently preferred for different purposes. In addition to entertainment, games can offer people different experiences and alternative ways for a specific purpose. It also seems possible to comment that a wide variety of games may enable a wide range of users to be addressed.

Playing games is also a way for people to realise themselves. Life is reshaped here and new possibilities are developed. Gaming is an activity that distracts from life for a while and gives the feeling of being in an alternative place, of being in an easier, lighter and better life (Fink, 2015). This experience is also valid for digital games. They can reach people quickly and participate in everyday life.

Kerr and Cawley (2012) highlight that digital games are developed by cultural workers as primary information products and services for end consumers. Since the mid-1990s, gaming consoles have brought these games into homes, driving their success. The gaming industry has diversified to include casual games, with consoles becoming internet-compatible. This has led to the geographic expansion of production networks owned by developers, publishers, and distributors.

Today, the gaming industry has become a serious global power with 3.4 billion players worldwide. According to the Türkiye Gaming Industry Report 2024, the gaming industry has reached a serious size of $187.7 on a global scale. The largest share of this income belongs to mobile games. Mobile games constitute 49% of the total income, equivalent to approximately $92.6 billion (Aydemir, 2024).

As the gaming industry develops and diversifies, different sectors are integrating games into their own strategies. Here, gamification theory draws attention. Gamification is the use of game-specific design elements in non-game contexts to increase users' motivation and encourage certain behaviors. It offers a reward and reputation system. This includes points, badges, levels and leaderboards (Deterding et al., 2011). In this context, design elements that can stimulate people's motivation are at the center of gamification. It is aimed to make participation continuous by providing a sense of progress towards a goal. Gamification theory is gaining importance in many sectors. This theory has begun to be applied in areas such as education, marketing, health and media, especially with the spread of digital technologies.

When evaluated in terms of new generation publishing, gamification can be a strategic tool to increase users' interest and accelerate content circulation. Passive audiences in traditional media have begun to take part in an interactive and participatory environment with the rise of digital platforms. These transformations allow the use of gamification techniques, especially in the production, consumption and circulation of digital media content.

Nowadays, the gaming industry also attracts the attention of TV series broadcasting platforms. With the involvement of digital platforms in this sector, the relationship between broadcasting, gaming and audience experience has gained a new dimension. A comparable platform to Netflix's gaming application is Amazon's cloud gaming service, Luna. Launched in the United States in 2022, Amazon Luna is currently not available in Turkey. While Amazon Prime Video provides downloadable games in Turkey through Prime Gaming, it does not offer a unified platform for both video streaming and gaming. In contrast, Netflix uniquely delivers both services in Turkey, enhancing user engagement and mobile usage by gamifying its original series. Consequently, for a viewer who is a fan of Stranger Things and prefers mobile devices, Netflix's gaming application may be considered particularly appealing.

Offering mobile game access in addition to viewer subscription enables to attract existing users and a wider audience interested in games. Thus, cross-promotions and synergy opportunities can be created between Netflix's local content consisting of TV shows and films and games. In this framework, it becomes possible for viewers to experience popular programmes and games while benefiting from the content library, and to make connections and transitions between them (Bozduganova, 2023).

Users who have transformed from viewers to gamers encounter different content depending on the type of game. The type of game also affects the purposes for which it is produced. Connolly et al. (2012) state that digital commercial games are developed with priorities such as entertainment, having a good time and resting. However, when it comes to serious games that will provide game-based learning, learning behavior change is aimed. Grand Theft Auto, which is in Netflix's game pool, is an example of digital commercial games.

Netflix's gaming strategy is an important example to understand the current dynamic structure and prevalence of digital platforms. The effort to enrich the user experience reveals the platform's vision of becoming an interactive entertainment ecosystem rather than just a streaming service. Academic studies confirm that this strategy is supported by elements such as content diversity, ease of access and personalisation (Başer & Akıncı, 2020). This strategy reinforces the platform's "entertainment ecosystem" vision, encouraging users to spend more time within its ecosystem. The relationship established with the game industry leads the audience to a magical world as in films and TV series. The interactive games offered by Netflix offer users not only the role of being a content consumer but also the opportunity to be involved in that content.

Netflix's gaming strategy also reflects its endeavour to expand the economic and cultural impact of digital platforms. As the gaming industry has become a multi-billion dollar market globally, Netflix aims to diversify its revenue model and grow its global subscriber base by investing in this area. An analysis in Think with Google suggested that cloud gaming platforms could transform traditional games marketing with a Netflix-style subscription model (Think with Google, 2021). Furthermore, the potential to develop games based on local content offers cultural richness in line with the platform's "glocalisation" strategy. This demonstrates Netflix's willingness to position the user experience not only as entertainment but also as a means of cultural interaction.

Purpose of the Study

This study aims to categorize the games offered on Netflix's mobile gaming platform, analyze thematic how they enrich the user experience, and examine digital platforms' efforts to create a multifaceted entertainment ecosystem. Games are evaluated based on criteria such as age restrictions, player count, offline playability, ratings, and download numbers to reveal the platform's strategic diversity and user appeal. Additionally, the study highlights Netflix's integration of original content with games to maintain brand coherence and its contribution to gaming culture while targeting diverse age groups. By exploring the transition from traditional content delivery to multi-dimensional entertainment experiences, this study captures the transformation within the media industry.

Methodology

Qualitative data analysis, which is used in the classification and interpretation of written or visual material in the study, enables to create meaning with its implicit and explicit dimensions. Details are reached by elaborating and interpreting the general categories created based on the data (Mezmir, 2020: 15). Qualitative data collection provides the opportunity to reach the answers to why and how as well as what is related to the research topic, and in some cases, they can illuminate why and how the results were obtained for various findings, including unexpected effects (Holtrop, Rabin & Glasgow, 2018: 2). In qualitative data analysis, coding is fluid and constantly reorganisable. Data are treated as potential indicators of concepts; indicators are compared with each other to determine which concepts they best fit (Bryman, 2012: 568). Based on the views of other researchers, Creswell lists the basic elements of qualitative data analysis as coding the data, combining the codes into broader categories or themes, and making comparisons in data graphs, tables and charts (2013: 180).

The games offered by Netflix to Turkish users were tabulated under 14 categories, each analyzed in detail. Tables included game names, age restrictions, player count, offline playability, ratings, and download numbers, enabling comparative evaluation. Analyses considered factors such as popularity, user feedback, and alignment with the platform's content strategy.

Scope and Limitations

The study focuses on mobile games offered by Netflix to Turkish users. However, it is limited to games accessible during a specific timeframe and treats details like rating differences between iOS and Android platforms from a general perspective. In-depth mechanical analyses of game content were not conducted; the focus remained on user experience and platform strategy. These limitations present opportunities for future research.

Findings

Within the scope of this study, firstly, the games offered by the Netflix platform to its members were tabulated within the framework of the categories created by the platform itself. The tables include game name, age limit, number of players, offline play feature, scoring system according to the downloaded platform and number of downloads. There are 14 categories in the games; action, adventure, arcade, card, educational, music, party, puzzle, racing, RPG, simulation, sports, strategy and board game. The ranking of the games in the tables was carried out by taking into account the scores they received from the most downloaded game to the least downloaded game. The games are compatible with Android and iOS. However, score, comment information and details may differ. In addition, the Netflix game controller application in 32 languages, including Turkish, can also be downloaded on iOS. Thus, the phone or mobile device can be used as a game controller.

An active Netflix membership is required to play the games. Regardless of the age limit, all games can be accessed from the adult profiles in the membership. Only Squid Game: Breaker by Breaker is available to users without a membership for a limited time. In the adventure category, OXENFREE II: Lost Signals in the adventure category can also be purchased for various game consoles without a subscription. Netflix's mobile games offered to users in Türkiye are as follows:

Table 1. Games in the action category (Data as of April 20, 2025)

Game Name	Age limit	Number of Players	Play Offline	Play Store Score	App Store Score	Number of downloads
GTA: San Andreas	17+	Single Player	Yes	3,3	3,7	10 Mn+
Squid Game: Kıran Kırana	12+	Multiplayer	No	4,3	4,5	5 Mn+
Snake.io – Yılan Oyunu	9+	Single Player Multiplayer	Yes	4,8	4,8	1 Mn+
Into the Dead 2: Unleashed	17+	Single Player	Yes	4,7	4,8	1 Mn+
TMNT: Shredder's Revenge	9+	Single Player Multiplayer	Yes	4,7	4,8	1 Mn+
Sonic Mania Plus	9+	Single Player	Yes	4,7	4,7	1 Mn+
Death's Door	12+	Single Player	Yes	3,6	3,9	500 B+
Rainbow Six: SMOL	12+	Single Player	Yes	3,2	3,6	500 B+
Poinpy	9+	Single Player	Yes	4,3	4,2	100 B+
Rival Pirates	9+	Multiplayer	No	3,9	2,3	100 B+

continued on following page

Table 1. Continued

Game Name	Age limit	Number of Players	Play Offline	Play Store Score	App Store Score	Number of downloads
Relic Hunters: Rebels	12+	Single Player	Yes	3,0	4,2	100 B+
Dust&Neon	12+	Single Player	Yes	3,0	3,8	100 B+
Steel Paws	12+	Single Player	No	3,8	3,0	50 B+
Tomb Raider Reloaded NETFLIX	12+	Single Player	No	3,2	4,6	100 B+
Hades	12+	Single Player	Yes	-	4,8	-

There are 15 games in the action category. Among these games, Hades is only supported by iOS. 11 of the games are only single player and 2 of them are multi-player. 2 games can be played as single player or multiplayer. Multiplayer only games do not have offline use. One of these games is Squid Game: Breaker by Breaker is a game adaptation of Netflix original content. Ninja Turtles (TMNT), Sonic and Tomb Raider game characters appear in both TV series and films and games.

This table lists the games in the action category according to age limit, number of players, offline play, ratings and number of downloads. The game with the highest number of downloads is "GTA: San Andreas" (10 Mn+), while the highest rated games are "Snake.io - Snake Game" and "Into the Dead 2: Unleashed" (4.8). Over 10 million downloads is one of the highest in all categories. While most games offer single-player modes, some also include multiplayer options.

Netflix's selection of games in the action category appeals to a wide age range. Adult games such as "GTA: San Andreas" and games suitable for younger audiences such as "Snake.io" are offered together. Games that offer multi-player options strengthen user loyalty by increasing social interaction. High download numbers and app store scores show that these games are liked by users. Netflix increases the attractiveness of its platform by appealing to different tastes with this diversity.

Games in the action category often offer high adrenaline and fast-paced experiences. Among the games in this table, classics such as "GTA: San Andreas" and modern titles such as "Into the Dead 2: Unleashed" stand out. The games range in age from 9+ to 17+, indicating that the target audience appeals to a wide range of people. In terms of player numbers, single player mode is prevalent, but multiplayer titles such as "Squid Game: Squid Game", but there are also multiplayer options such as "Squid Game. Offline play is available in many games, which means that users can experience the game without an internet connection. Ratings generally range from 3.0 to 4.8, indicating that the games have received generally positive user feedback. The number of downloads ranges from 100,000 to 10 million, indicating the popularity of the games.

Table 2. Games in the adventure category (Data as of April 20, 2025)

Game Name	Age limit	Number of Players	Play Offline	Play Store Score	App Store Score	Number of downloads
Scriptic: Crime Stories	17+	Single Player	Yes	4,7	4,1	1 Mn+
Dead Cells: Netflix Edition	12+	Single Player	Yes	4,6	3,7	1 Mn+
Stranger Things: 1984	12+	Single Player	Yes	4,1	2,6	1 Mn+
Stranger Things 3: The Game	12+	Single Player Multiplayer	Yes	4,0	4,1	1 Mn+
LEGO Legacy: Heroes Unboxed	9+	Single Player	No	3,7	4,5	1 Mn+
Twelve Minutes	17+	Single Player	Yes	3,7	4,3	1 Mn+
Before Your Eyes	12+	Single Player	Yes	4,3	4,8	500 B+
Valiant Hearts: Coming Home	12+	Single Player	Yes	4,1	4,4	500 B+
Raji: Kadim Bir Destan	12+	Single Player	Yes	3,9	4,1	500 B+
OXENFREE: Netflix Edition	12+	Single Player	Yes	3,5	4,4	500 B+
Laya's Horizon	4+	Single Player	Yes	3,5	4,2	500 B+
Carmen Sandiego	4+	Single Player Multiplayer	Yes	4,7	5,0	100 B+
Lucky Luna	9+	Single Player	Yes	4,7	4,6	100 B+
Dragon Up	4+	Single Player	No	4,3	4,3	100 B+
This is a True Story	12+	Single Player	Yes	4,2	4,5	100 B+
OXENFREE II: Lost Signals	12+	Single Player	Yes	4,1	4,8	100 B+
Highwater	12+	Single Player	Yes	3,8	4,8	100 B+
Kentucky Route Zero	12+	Single Player	Yes	3,2	3,7	100 B+

There are 18 games in this category. While 2 of these games have the option to play multiplayer with single player, 2 of them do not offer the option to play offline. The games have been downloaded over 100 thousand, 500 thousand and 1 million. Stranger Things and Carmen Sandiego are the game versions of the content broadcast on the Netflix platform.

Adventure games include "Scriptic: Crime Stories" and "Dead Cells: Netflix Edition" and "Dead Cells: Netflix Edition" stand out. "Carmen Sandiego" has the highest App Store score (5.0), while games like "LEGO Legacy: Heroes Unboxed" cannot be played offline. Downloads across the category ranged from 1 Mn+ to 100 B+. Adventure games are designed in line with Netflix's story-driven content strategy. Games like "Scriptic: Crime Stories" draws users in with interactive stories. Games linked to Netflix's original series (e.g. the "Stranger Things" series) enrich the user experience while ensuring brand integrity. High ratings and download numbers prove the success of this category.

Adventure games provide users with story-driven and exploration-based experiences. This category includes popular titles such as Dead Cells: Netflix Edition and the Stranger Things series. Age limits range from 4+ to 17+, suggesting a variety that appeals to both children and adults. Most games have a single-player mode, but multiplayer options are also available, such as 'Stranger Things 3: The Game'. Offline play is supported in many games. Ratings generally range between 3.5 and 4.8, indicating that the games are well received by users.

Table 3. Games in the arcade category (Data as of April 20, 2025)

Game Name	Age limit	Number of Players	Play Offline	Play Store Score	App Store Score	Number of downloads
Bloons TD 6	9+	Single Player Multiplayer	Yes	4,6	4,9	5 Mn+
Sonic Prime Dash	9+	Single Player	Yes	4,7	4,7	1 Mn+
Bowling Ballers	4+	Single Player	Yes	4,6	4,8	1 Mn+
Pinball Masters	9+	Single Player	No	4,5	4,7	1 Mn+
Teeter Up Remastered	4+	Single Player	Yes	3,3	4,6	1 Mn+
World of Goo Remastered	4+	Single Player	Yes	2,3	3,7	1 Mn+
Shooting Hoops	4+	Single Player	Yes	3,1	4,7	500 B+
Skies of Chaos	9+	Single Player Multiplayer	Yes	3,4	5,0	100 B+

All 8 games in the Arcade category are only related to video games. They have no connection with the content of Netflix series, films and programmes. The games are generally single player. Only two games offer both single player and multiplayer options. Unlike the others, Pinball Masters cannot be played offline. The most downloaded game in the category has been downloaded more than 5 million times and offers single and multiplayer options.

Among arcade games, "Bloons TD 6" stands out with both a high score (4.9) and a high number of downloads (5 Mn+). "Sonic Prime Dash" and "Bowling Ballers" also received high scores. While most games offer a single-player mode, "Skies of Chaos" offers a multiplayer option. Arcade games appeal to a wide audience with their simple and fun structure. Strategy-based games like "Bloons TD 6" and fast-paced options like "Sonic Prime Dash" fulfil users' need for short-term entertainment. High scores in this category reflect the quality of the games and user satisfaction.

Arcade games are characterised by simple mechanics and fast gameplay. The age limits in this category range from 4+ to 9+, indicating that they appeal to a younger audience. Most games have a single-player mode, but there are also multiplayer options such as "Skies of Chaos". Scores generally range between 2.3 and 4.8. The number of downloads varies between 100,000 and 5 million.

Table 4. Games in the card category (Data as of April 20, 2025)

Game Name	Age limit	Number of Players	Play Offline	Play Store Score	App Store Score	Number of downloads
Exploding Kittens	9+	Single Player Multiplayer	Yes	3,4	2,5	1 Mn+
Hearts	4+	Single Player	Yes	4,3	4,9	100 B+
Card Blast	4+	Single Player	Yes	3,7	No	100 B+
Arcanium: Rise of Akhan	9+	Single Player	Yes	3,6	3,0	100 B+

There are 4 games in the card category. All of these games can be played offline. The most downloaded game in the category is Exploding Kittens, the game version of the Netflix animated series with the same name. This game has offline, single player and multiplayer options.

Among card games, Exploding Kittens has the highest number of downloads (1 Mn+). "Hearts" has the highest App Store score (4.9), while games like "Arcanium: Rise of Akhan" have lower scores. Games in the category generally offer a single-player mode. Card games are characterised by their structure that encourages social interaction. While most games have a single-player mode, games that offer a multi-player option, such as "Exploding Kittens", increase competition among users. Games in this category offer a different experience by combining strategy and luck.

Card games combine the elements of strategy and luck. The most popular games in this category are "Exploding Kittens" and "Hearts". Age limits range from 4+ to 9+. The scores vary between 2.5 and 4.9. The number of downloads of the games is between 100 thousand and 1 million.

Table 5. Games in the educational category (Data as of April 20, 2025)

Game Name	Age limit	Number of Players	Play Offline	Play Store Score	App Store Score	Number of downloads
CoComelon: Play with JJ	4+	Single Player	Yes	4,2	No	500 B+

The only game in the educational category was adapted from a cartoon film whose content is also broadcast on Netflix. In this game, which includes songs, shapes, numbers and letters are taught. Only "CoComelon: Play with JJ" is included. The game offers educational content with 500 B+ downloads and a Play Store score of 4.2. It can be played offline.

Netflix offers content for children with educational games. Games like "CoComelon: Play with JJ" aims to teach while entertaining. The limited number of games in this category shows that Netflix has the potential to develop more content in this area. Educational games combine learning and entertainment. In this category, "CoComelon: Play with JJ" is a game especially for children. The age limit is set at 4+. The game has a single-player mode.

Table 6. Games in the music category (Data as of April 20, 2025)

Game Name	Age limit	Number of Players	Play Offline	Play Store Score	App Store Score	Number of downloads
Hello Kitty Mutluluk Geçidi	4+	Single Player	No	3,7	3,3	1 Mn+

Hello Kitty, which has a single-player mode in the music category, progresses by moving according to the rhythms of the songs given to the players. This game, which has over 1 million downloads, can only be played online in single-player mode. Only "Hello Kitty Happiness Parade" is included in the music category. The game has 1 Mn+ downloads and a Play Store score of 3.7. It cannot be played offline.

Music-themed games have a limited place in Netflix's content portfolio. Games such as "Hello Kitty Happiness Parade" appeal to a younger audience. Expanding this category may offer more options to the platform's music-loving users. Music games offer rhythm and music-themed experiences. This category includes a colourful option such as "Hello Kitty Happy Parade".

Table 7. Games in the party category (Data as of April 20, 2025)

Game Name	Age limit	Number of Players	Play Offline	Play Store Score	App Store Score	Number of downloads
Nailed It! Baking Bash	4+	Single Player Multiplayer	Yes	2,1	5,0	1 Mn+
Heads Up!	4+	Multiplayer	Yes	2,7	3,0	100 B+

Nailed It! Baking Bash, one of the two games in the party category, is the game version of the Nailed It programme on Netflix in which bakers compete. In this game, which offers a multiplayer option, users can compete with their friends. Heads Up!, on the other hand, is based on guessing cards consisting of Netflix content with clues and can only be played with multiple players. However, the number of downloads is very low compared to the other game and remains at 100 thousand.

"Nailed It! Baking Bash" has the highest App Store score (5.0), while "Heads Up!" offers a multiplayer mode. The number of downloads varies between 1 Mn+ and 100 B+. Party games are designed to increase social interaction. Fun and competitive games such as "Nailed It! Baking Bash" provide an enjoyable time among friends and family. Netflix allows users to have fun together with games in this category. Party games aim to increase social interaction. This category includes fun options such as "Nailed It! Baking Bash" and "Heads Up!". The age limit is 4+ and multiplayer mode is supported. Scores range from 2.1 to 5.0.

Table 8. Games in the puzzle category (Data as of April 20, 2025)

Game Name	Age limit	Number of Players	Play Offline	Play Store Score	App Store Score	Number of downloads
Storyteller	12+	Single Player	Yes	3,6	4,4	10 Mn+
Cut the Rope Daily	4+	Single Player	Yes	4,4	4,7	1 Mn+
Monument Valley 1	4+	Single Player	Yes	4,8	4,9	1 Mn+
Monument Valley 2	4+	Single Player	Yes	4,9	4,9	500 B+
Monument Valley 3	4+	Single Player	Partially	4,8	4,9	500 B+
Word Trails	4+	Single Player	Yes	4,8	4,9	500 B+
Krispee Street	4+	Single Player	Yes	4,6	4,8	500 B+
Knittens	4+	Single Player	No	4,4	5,0	500 B+
The Rise of the Golden Idol	12+	Single Player	Yes	4,7	4,9	100 B+
Mayın Tarlası	4+	Single Player Multiplayer	Yes	4,6	4,9	100 B+

continued on following page

Table 8. Continued

Game Name	Age limit	Number of Players	Play Offline	Play Store Score	App Store Score	Number of downloads
Puzzle Gods	9+	Single Player	Yes	4,5	4,5	100 B+
TED Tumblewords	4+	Single Player Multiplayer	Yes	4,4	4,8	100 B+
Yabani Şeyler: Hayvan Macerası	4+	Single Player	Yes	4,4	4,6	100 B+
Diner Out	12+	Single Player Multiplayer	No	4,3	4,4	100 B+
Braid, Anniversary Edition	12+	Single Player	Yes	4,1	4,2	100 B+
The Case of the Golden Idol	12+	Single Player	Yes	4,0	5,0	100 B+
Ghost Detective	12+	Single Player	No	3,9	4,5	100 B+
Arranger	9+	Single Player	No	4,7	5,0	50 B+
Sanal Ülke: Çocuk Cosmo	12+	Single Player	No	4,7	4,8	50 B+

There are 19 games in the Puzzle category. With more than 10 million downloads, Storyteller is based on creating stories by placing fairy tale characters on the page. While 16 of the games offer only single player option, 3 of them can be played with multiple players. 14 of the games can be played offline. The second-ranked Cut the Rope Daily is a game about Om Nom, a cute green monster available on Netflix, and consists of daily tasks. In the middle of the category, Krispee Street, with more than 500,000 downloads, is a game version of a popular web comic. The game is about finding hidden objects and characters. At the bottom with 50,000 downloads, Virtual Land: Cosmo for Kids is based on the Netflix science fiction film The Electric State.

The "Monument Valley" series (1, 2, 3) stands out with high scores (4.8-4.9) and downloads. "Storyteller" has 10 Mn+ downloads. Games in the category generally offer a single-player mode. Puzzle games aim to develop intelligence and strategy skills. Highly rated games such as the "Monument Valley" series are highly appreciated by users. Netflix appeals to different age groups with the diversity in this category.

Puzzle games are aimed at developing intelligence and strategy skills. This category includes popular choices such as the 'Monument Valley' series and 'Cut the Rope Daily'. Age limits range from 4+ to 12+. Most games have a single-player mode. Scores range from 3.6 to 4.9. Downloads are between 50,000 and 10 million.

Table 9. Games in the racing category (Data as of April 20, 2025)

Game Name	Age limit	Number of Players	Play Offline	Play Store Score	App Store Score	Number of downloads
Asphalt Xtreme	12+	Single Player Multiplayer	No	4,2	4,8	1 Mn+

There is 1 game in the Racing category. The game, which can be played both single-player and multiplayer, does not have an offline play option. There is only "Asphalt Xtreme" in this category. The game has 1 Mn+ downloads and an App Store rating of 4.8. It offers multiplayer mode.

Racing games offer adrenaline-filled experiences. Games like "Asphalt Xtreme" stand out for their competitive nature. The limited number of games in this category shows Netflix's potential to produce more content in this area. Racing games offer speed and competition-themed experiences. Ages 12+ and multiplayer supported. Rated 4.2 and over 1 million downloads.

Table 10. Games in the RPG category (Data as of April 20, 2025)

Game Name	Age limit	Number of Players	Play Offline	Play Store Score	App Store Score	Number of downloads
Transformers – Savaşçılar	12+	Single Player Multiplayer	No	4,2	4,2	1 Mn+
Gölge ve Kemik	12+	Single Player	Yes	4,7	4,8	100 B+
Moonlighter	9+	Single Player	Yes	3,6	3,5	100 B+
Dungeon Boss: Respawned	9+	Single Player Multiplayer	No	3,4	4,5	100 B+

There are 4 games in the role-playing category. 2 of these can be played offline with a single player. The other two games have both single player and multiplayer options. Shadow and Bone was inspired by the book series and the fantasy series developed for Netflix. Transformers is also one of the movies available on Netflix.

"Shadow and Bone" has the highest ratings (4.7-4.8), while "Transformers - - Warriors" has 1 Mn+ downloads. Most games offer a single-player mode. RPG games are characterized by deep storylines and character development. Games like "Shadow and Bone" synergize with Netflix's original content. Games in this category offer ideal options for strategy and adventure lovers.

RPG games offer deep storylines and character development. This category includes options like "Shadow and Bone" and "Moonlighter". Ages range from 9+ to 12+. Most games have a single-player mode. Scores range from 3.4 to 4.8. Downloads are between 100,000 and 1 million.

Table 11. Games in the simulation category (Data as of April 20, 2025)

Game Name	Age limit	Number of Players	Play Offline	Play Store Score	App Store Score	Number of downloads
SüngerBob: Mutfakta	4+	Single Player	Yes	4,7	4,8	5 Mn+
Farming Simulator 23	4+	Single Player	Yes	4,5	4,3	5 Mn+
Too Hot to Handle 2	17+	Single Player	No	4,8	4,7	1 Mn+
Too Hot to Handle: Aşk Bir Oyundur	17+	Single Player	No	4,7	4,8	1 Mn+
Too Hot to Handle 3	17+	Single Player	No	4,7	4,8	1 Mn+
Netflix Stories	17+	Single Player	No	4,2	4,1	1 Mn+
Money Heist: Ultimate Choice	12+	Single Player	No	3,8	4,4	1 Mn+
FashionVerse	12+	Single Player Multiplayer	No	4,5	4,5	500 B+
Spiritfarer	12+	Single Player	Yes	4,0	4,4	500 B+
Kediler ve Çorba	4+	Single Player	Yes	3,9	3,8	500 B+
Game Dev Tycoon	4+	Single Player Multiplayer	Yes	3,9	3,7	500 B+
Townsmen - A Kingdom Rebuilt	9+	Single Player	Yes	3,6	4,3	500 B+
Secrets By Episode	17+	Single Player	No	4,6	4,7	100 B+
Kırsaldaki Dostlar	9+	Single Player Multiplayer	No	4,4	4,7	100 B+
Cozy Grove: Hayalet Kamp	9+	Multiplayer	No	4,4	4,7	100 B+
Vineyard Valley	12+	Single Player Multiplayer	Yes	4,3	4,5	100 B+
Ültimatom: Seçimler	17+	Single Player	No	4,1	4,2	100 B+
Flutter Butterflies	4+	Single Player	No	3,9	5,0	100 B+
Black Mirror: Thronglets	12+	Single Player	No	3,8	4,6	100 B+
Immortality	17+	Single Player	Yes	2,6	2,3	100 B+
RollerCoaster Tycoon	12+	Single Player	No	1,4	1,5	100 B+

The simulation category consists of 21 games. While there is only 1 game with multiplayer option, 4 games have both single and multiplayer options. 8 games offer players the opportunity to play offline. In this category, Money Heist and Too Hot to Handle are based on Netflix original content. Netflix Stories is an interactive fiction game based on Netflix's popular romantic movies and TV series. SpongeBob and Black Mirror are also streamed on the platform.

"SpongeBob: In the Kitchen" and "Farming Simulator 23" stand out with 5 Mn+ downloads. The "Too Hot to Handle" series received high ratings. The category is dominated by games that cannot be played offline. Simulation games bring real-life experiences to the digital realm. Fun games like "SpongeBob: In the Kitchen", entertaining games like "SpongeBob: In the Kitchen", which stimulate users' creativity. Netflix appeals to different interests with the diversity in this category.

Simulation games mimic real-life experiences. In this category, "SpongeBob: In the Kitchen" and "Farming Simulator 23" are popular choices. Age limits range from 4+ to 17+. Most games have a single-player mode. Scores range from 1.4 to 4.8. Downloads are between 100,000 and 5 million.

Table 12. Games in the sports category (Data as of April 20, 2025)

Game Name	Age limit	Number of Players	Play Offline	Play Store Score	App Store Score	Number of downloads
Football Manager Mobile 2024	4+	Single Player	Yes	4,2	4,5	5 Mn+
Wonderputt Forever	12+	Single Player	Yes	4,1	4,2	500 B+

2 games in the sports category (soccer and golf) are single player. However, they can be played offline. "Football Manager Mobile 2024" is the most popular game with 5 Mn+ downloads and an App Store score of 4.5. "Wonderputt Forever" has a lower number of downloads.

Sports games stand out for their competitive nature. Games like "Football Manager Mobile 2024" appeal to strategy and sports fans. The limited content in this category could be one of Netflix's potential areas of expansion. Sports games offer experiences themed around competition and physical activity. This category includes a game like "Football Manager Mobile 2024". The age limit is 4+ and the game has a single-player mode. The play store score of the game is lower than the other app and is 4.2.

Table 13. Games in the strategy category (Data as of April 20, 2025)

Game Name	Age limit	Number of Players	Play Offline	Play Store Score	App Store Score	Number of downloads
Ludo King	12+	Single Player Multiplayer	Yes	4,1	2,2	1 Mn+
Terra Nil	4+	Single Player	Yes	3,6	4,5	1 Mn+
Narcos: Cartel Wars Unlimited	12+	Single Player Multiplayer	No	4,9	4,8	500 B+
Into the Breach	9+	Single Player	Yes	4,8	4,8	500 B+
Reigns: Three Kingdoms	12+	Single Player Multiplayer	No	1,7	2,2	500 B+

In the strategy category consisting of 5 games, 2 games are single player, while 3 games offer single and multiplayer options. 2 games do not have the option to play offline. Only the Narcos game in the category is due to Netflix original content.

"Narcos: Cartel Wars Unlimited" has the highest score (4.9), while "Ludo King" has 1 Mn+ downloads. Games such as "Into the Breach" received high scores. Strategy games emphasize intelligence and planning skills. Games like "Terra Nil" offer entertainment while raising environmental awareness. Netflix aims to improve users' strategic thinking skills with games in this category.

Strategy games aim to develop tactical and planning skills. In this category, options like "Terra Nil" and "Narcos: Cartel Wars Unlimited" and "Narcos: Cartel Wars Unlimited". Age limits range from 4+ to 12+. Most games have a single-player mode. Scores range from 1.7 to 4.9. Downloads are between 500,000 and 1 million.

Table 14. Games in the board game category (Data as of April 20, 2025)

Game Name	Age limit	Number of Players	Play Offline	Play Store Score	App Store Score	Number of downloads
Solitaire	4+	Single Player	Yes	4,7	4,8	1 Mn+
Mahjong Solitaire	4+	Single Player	Yes	4,8	4,8	500 B+
The Queen's Gambit Chess	9+	Single Player Multiplayer	Yes	3,9	4,6	100 B+

There are 3 games in the board game category. The Queen's Gambit Chess is created from Netflix original content and can be played both single and multiplayer. All 3 games in this category offer the option to play offline. Classic games like "Solitaire" and "Mahjong Solitaire" stand out in this category with high ratings (4.7-4.8) and downloads. "The Queen's Gambit Chess" offers a multiplayer mode.

Board games digitize the traditional gaming experience by bringing it to digital platforms. Games like "Solitaire" and "Mahjong Solitaire" help users relax. Netflix appeals to users of all ages with games in this category. Age limits range from 4+ to 9+. Most games have a single-player mode. Scores range between 3.9 and 4.8. The number of downloads is between 100 thousand and 1 million.

CONCLUSION

Digital platforms are constantly expanding and diversifying their content portfolios to meet user demands. Platforms such as Netflix not only offer films and TV series, but also documentaries, animations and reality shows. This diversity aims to grow the global audience by appealing to different demographic and cultural groups. Netflix offers interactive content (Black Mirror: Bandersnatch) and experimental formats to enrich the user experience. Such content allows the viewer to intervene in the story, encouraging a shift from passive consumption to active participation. It also aims to increase user engagement through gamification techniques.

Netflix aims to diversify the user experience by stepping into the gaming industry as well as content production. The platform appeals to a wide range of ages and interests with games in 14 different categories. In addition to popular genres such as action, adventure and strategy, it meets the different needs of users with thematic categories such as educational and party games. This diversity shows that Netflix is on its way to becoming an integrated entertainment ecosystem, not just a streaming platform.

The diversity in Netflix's game categories clearly reflects the platform's goal of enriching the user experience. The games offered in popular categories such as action, adventure and strategy appeal to a wide audience by appealing to different age groups and tastes. For example, the combination of adult games such as "GTA: San Andreas" with options suitable for younger audiences such as "Snake.io" shows the inclusiveness of Netflix's content strategy. This diversity contributes to users spending more time on the platform and increasing their loyalty.

One of the most striking aspects of the platform's gaming strategy is the synergy between original content and games. "Squid Game: Squid Game: Breaker vs. Breaker", the "Stranger Things" series and game adaptations of Netflix productions such as "Narcos" attract users' attention while maintaining brand integrity. These adaptations strengthen users' loyalty to the platform by encouraging not only content consumption but also interactive experiences. Moreover, the fact that some games are accessible without requiring a subscription is used as an effective marketing tool to attract potential subscribers to the platform. This strategy creates synergies between content while strengthening brand loyalty, and the fact that some games, such as “OXENFREE II”, can be purchased without a subscription also reflects Netflix’s efforts to diversify its revenue models.

The technical features of Netflix games are also geared towards optimising the user experience. The offline play feature of most games allows users to continue interacting with the platform even without an internet connection. In addition, offering single-player and multiplayer mode options enriches the gaming experience by increasing social interaction. Multiplayer options, especially in the party and board game categories, strengthen the social aspect of the platform by allowing users to have fun with their friends. Factors such as offline playability, multiplayer modes and language support facilitate user access. Games designed especially for mobile devices enable users to access entertainment anytime and anywhere. However, the limited number of content in some categories (for example, racing and educational games) indicates that Netflix needs to invest more in these areas.

Netflix’s gaming strategy also aims to offer personalised experiences by leveraging user data. In particular, the popularity of games such as ‘GTA: San Andreas’, ‘Bloons TD 6’ and ‘Monument Valley’ is evidence that Netflix has chosen the right content.

User feedback and download numbers prove the success of Netflix games. The fact that games such as ‘Bloons TD 6’ and ‘Monument Valley’ stand out with high scores and millions of downloads shows that these contents are adopted by users. Moreover, games in niche categories such as educational and simulation games reflect the platform’s endeavour to appeal to different interests. However, the limited number of content in some categories shows that Netflix needs to feed these areas with new content.

As a result, Netflix’s gaming strategy seems to aim to further connect its users to the platform and gain a competitive advantage, and games are positioned as an integral part of Netflix’s vision of digital entertainment, not just as an additional service. A variety of categories appealing to different age groups, tastes and gaming styles enable users to spend more time on the platform. This situation reveals that in the transforming television broadcasting, the flow does not only consist of television content; the viewer, who becomes a user, is constantly in the system with content such as interactive games. The alignment between original content and games increases brand equity, while technical specifications and user feedback support the success of the strategy. In order for Netflix to fully realise its potential in this field, it is important for the future to make new investments, especially in categories where the number of content is limited, and to carry out new studies on user experience in order to adopt innovative approaches that will further increase user interaction. The analysis of Netflix’s game strategy in this study will not only reveal the way platforms gain competitive advantage, but will also serve as a reference for future studies on understanding changes in user behaviour and future media consumption trends.

REFERENCES

Aydemir, O. (2024). Türkiye Gaming Industry Report 2024. Accessed May 17 2025. https://www.gaminginturkey.com/files/pdf/turkiye-oyun-sektoru-raporu-2024.pdf

Başer, E., & Akıncı, S. (2020). Kullanıcı deneyimi ve kişiselleştirme bağlamında bir dijital platform incelemesi [An analysis of a digital platform in the context of user experience and personalization]. *Selçuk İletişim Dergisi*, *13*(2), 866–897.

Boyd, D. (2014). *It's complicated: The social lives of networked teens*. Yale University Press.

Bozduganova, T. (2023). *Netflix's expansion into the video game industry: Strategic issue management and brand extension strategies* [Master's thesis, Erasmus University Rotterdam].

Broadbent, B., & Guerrieria, P. (2021). *Oyun endüstrisini değiştiren 6 trend*. Think with Google. [https://www.thinkwithgoogle.com/intl/tr-tr/icgoruler/tuketici-trendleri/oyun-dunyasi-pazarlama-trendleri/]

Bryman, A. (2012). *Social research methods* (4th ed.). Oxford University Press.

Connolly, T. M., Boyle, E. A., MacArthur, E., Hainey, T., & Boyle, J. M. (2012). A systematic literature review of empirical evidence on computer games and serious games. *Computers & Education*, *59*(2), 661–686. DOI: 10.1016/j.compedu.2012.03.004

Creswell, J. W. (2013). Qualitative inquiry & research design: Choosing among five approaches. *Sage (Atlanta, Ga.).*

Deterding, S., Dixon, D., Khaled, R., & Nacke, L. (2011). From game design elements to Gamefulness: defining gamification. In *Proceedings of the 15th International Academic MindTrek Conference: Envisioning Future Media Environments*. 9-15. DOI: 10.1145/2181037.2181040

Dhiman, D. B. (2023). *Unleashing the power of television broadcasting in the digital age: A critical review. SSRN.* https://papers.ssrn.com/sol3/papers.cfm?abstract_id=4598192 DOI: 10.2139/ssrn.4598192

Doyle, G. (2016). Digitization and changing windowing strategies in the television industry: Negotiating new windows on the world. *Television & New Media*, *17*(7), 629–645. DOI: 10.1177/1527476416641194

Fink, E. (2015). *Bir dünya sembolü olarak oyun* (N. Aça, Trans.). Dost Kitabevi Yayınları. (Original work published earlier).

Gilbert, A. (2019). Push, pull, rerun: Television reruns and streaming media. *Television & New Media*, *20*(7), 686–701. DOI: 10.1177/1527476419842418

Holtrop, J. S., Rabin, B. A., & Glasgow, R. E. (2018). Qualitative approaches to use of the RE-AIM framework: Rationale and methods. *BMC Health Services Research*, *18*(1), 177. DOI: 10.1186/s12913-018-2938-8 PMID: 29534729

Huizinga, J. (2010). *Homo ludens: Oyunun toplumsal işlevi üzerine bir deneme* (3rd ed.). (Yayınları, A., Trans.). M. A. Kılıçbay. (Original work published 1938)

Jenkins, H. (2006). *Convergence culture: Where old and new media collide*. NYU Press.

Jenner, M. (2014). Is this TVIV? On Netflix, TVIII and binge-watching. *New Media & Society*, *18*(2), 257–273. DOI: 10.1177/1461444814541523

Johnson, D. (2021). *Media franchising*. Routledge.

Kerr, A., & Cawley, A. (2012). The spatialisation of the digital games industry: Lessons from Ireland. *International Journal of Cultural Policy*, *18*(4), 398–418. DOI: 10.1080/10286632.2011.598515

Kompare, D. (2002). *Flow to files: Conceiving 21st century media*. Paper presented at the Media in Transition 2 Conference, Cambridge, MA. https://cmsw.mit.edu/mit2/Abstracts/DerekKompare.pdf

Lotz, A. (2017). *Portals: A treatise on internet-distributed television*. Michigan Publishing. DOI: 10.3998/mpub.9699689

Lotz, A. D. (2018). Evolution or revolution? Television in transformation. *Critical Studies in Television*, *13*(4), 491–494. DOI: 10.1177/1749602018796757

Mezmir, E. A. (2020). Qualitative data analysis: An overview of data reduction, data display, and interpretation. *Research on Humanities and Social Sciences*, *10*(21), 15–27.

Mikos, L. (2016). Digital media platforms and the use of TV content: Binge watching and video-on-demand in Germany. *Media and Communication*, *4*(3), 154–161. DOI: 10.17645/mac.v4i3.542

Tefertiller, A. (2018). Media substitution in cable cord-cutting: The adoption of web-streaming television. *Journal of Broadcasting & Electronic Media*, *62*(3), 390–407. DOI: 10.1080/08838151.2018.1451868

Tryon, C. (2013). *On-demand culture: Digital delivery and the future of movies*. Rutgers University Press.

ADDITIONAL READINGS

Brereton, J., Jones, B., Reeve, C., Zborowski, J., & Bramwell-Dicks, A. (2025). Play your way into production: Game-based skills development for the film and TV industry. *Popular Communication*, 1–22. Advance online publication. DOI: 10.1080/15405702.2025.2486773

Dovey, J., & Kennedy, H. W. (2006). *Game cultures – computer games as new media*. Open University Pres.

Juul, J. (2010). *A casual revolution: Reinventing video games and their players*. The MIT Press.

Katerynych, P., Goian, V., & Goian, O. (2023). Exploring The Evolution of Storytelling in the Streaming Era: A Study Of Narrative Trends in Netflix Original Content. Communication Today, Vol. 14, No. 2. https://communicationtoday.sk/wp-content/uploads/03.-KATERYNYCH-et-al.---CT-2-2023.pdf

McErlean, K. (2018). *Interactive Narratives and Transmedia Storytelling*. Routledge. DOI: 10.4324/9781315637570

Murray, J. (2004). From game-story to cyberdrama. N. Wardrip-Fruin, P. Harigan (Eds.). First person: new media as story, performance and game (pp. 2-11). MIT Press.

Ortega, V. R. (2024). Audiovisual streaming, networked memory & Netflix: The spectator-interface. *Creative Industries Journal, 17*(3), 535–550. DOI: 10.1080/17510694.2022.2150814

Petruska, K. (2014). The digital television transition, consumer power and the limits of cultural citizenship. *Creative Industries Journal, 7*(1), 19–32. DOI: 10.1080/17510694.2014.892266

Waldfogel, J. (2017). How digitisation has created a golden age of music, movies, books, and television. *The Journal of Economic Perspectives, 31*(3), 195–214. DOI: 10.1257/jep.31.3.195

Wang, A., Whyke, T. W., & Dean, L. (2023). The interplay between digital platforms and user-generated content in reinterpreting and recreating mythological narratives with traditional Chinese cultural elements: The animated series Yao-Chinese Folktales. *Creative Industries Journal*, 1–22. Advance online publication. DOI: 10.1080/17510694.2023.2252423

KEY TERMS AND DEFINITIONS

Mobile Gaming: It refers to digitally based games that players can play by using their mobile devices such as mobile phones, tablets, etc. or by downloading them to these devices.

Simulation: It is a category that can be used to characterise games created by copying real-life events, situations and characters.

Interactive: It is the mutual communication in an interactive way.

Digital Platform: It enables publications to be transferred to electronic media through the use of communication technologies, especially the internet. Access is realised through smart devices.

Arcade: It is used to characterise video games played by throwing coins into machines in arcades. Digital games inspired by this genre can be downloaded from applications.

Active Participant: Transforming television broadcasting encourages the viewer to be constantly present in its fragmented flow. The viewer, who consumes the content of his/her choice within the digital flow, also chooses at which point to stop watching the content. All the choices of the viewer mean that he/she interacts with the digital streaming platform. In this context, the viewer is now an active participant.

Digital Streaming: In Internet-based television broadcasting, content is organised and filed separately from each other. This situation creates a digital flow different from the traditional flow understanding. There is content consumption in the form of streaming the selected content and/or continuing the flow from there by switching to another content.

Chapter 11
AI-Powered Digital Video Broadcasting:
Nvidia Broadcasting

Volkan Cetin
https://orcid.org/0000-0003-1159-162X
Istanbul Bilgi University, Turkey

ABSTRACT

In this study, a comparative analysis method was used to compare traditional video broadcasting processes with AI-powered digital video broadcasting processes. The analysis focused on content production, editing, distribution, and audience interaction aspects. A literature review was conducted to identify areas where artificial intelligence is applied in digital video broadcasting. Then, using the case study method, differences between traditional and AI-powered systems were analyzed in terms of efficiency, production time, cost, quality, and viewer experience.

INTRODUCTION

Digital video broadcasting has been experiencing unprecedented growth and transformation in recent years. The transition from traditional television broadcasting to internet-based platforms has fundamentally changed the dynamics of content production and consumption. The rise of platforms such as Twitch, YouTube, Facebook Live, and Instagram has enabled not only professional broadcasters but also individual content creators to reach global audiences. According to NVIDIA's reports, the number of broadcasters on the Twitch platform alone increased by 89% in 2020, while the number of viewers increased by 56% (NVIDIA, 2020). This

DOI: 10.4018/979-8-3373-1957-5.ch011

growth accelerated during the COVID-19 pandemic and has established a permanent trend as digital content consumption has become an indispensable part of daily life.

Today, the digital video broadcasting ecosystem encompasses various formats such as livestreaming, video conferences, educational content, e-sports events, virtual events, and social media content. This diversity brings with it different technical requirements and quality expectations. High-resolution video, clean audio quality, low latency, and uninterrupted broadcast stream have become essential requirements for successful digital broadcasting. However, traditionally, expensive equipment, specialized studio environments, and technical expertise are required to produce high-quality broadcasts. This situation creates a significant barrier, especially for small-scale broadcasters and individual content creators with limited resources. In this context, artificial intelligence technologies have begun to play a critical role in the democratization of broadcasting.

TRADITIONAL VIDEO BROADCASTING PROCESSES

Traditional video broadcasting processes form a complex ecosystem involving detailed planning, meticulous production, and effective distribution of content intended for broadcasting. These processes typically follow specific stages, allowing for the construction of an organized and systematic structure. The first phase is the development of content strategy, during which target audience, content type, and distribution channels are carefully determined. Content strategy encompasses not only academic or educational film projects but also various entertainment broadcasts. The importance of this phase stems from determining the necessary parameters for creating the most appropriate content for the target audience. These processes are enriched by bringing together various disciplines to ensure effective dissemination of video content.

The broadcast production process typically begins with writing a script, which is a crucial step. The script plays a defining role in determining story structure, character depth, and dialogue flow. After the script is completed, the production team selection takes place, during which it is of significant importance to bring together professionals with various areas of expertise such as directors, cinematographers, and production designers. During the shooting phase, images are captured using different technical equipment and technologies. Additionally, elements such as sound recording, lighting arrangements, and set design are among the critical factors directly affecting video quality. Following the completion of all these related processes, the post-production phase begins; here, applications such as acceleration, editing processes, sound design, and special effects are carried out, meticulously producing the final product. Each stage is vital for the success of the project and therefore must be conducted with care.

Finally, the distribution of produced content constitutes a critical phase of the process. This phase aims to provide access to a broad target audience through traditional television channels, cable companies, and digital platforms, thus ensuring the content reaches more people. Content can be presented in a structure that aims to reach more viewers by being supported through channels such as social media and digital advertising in accordance with effective marketing strategies. Thus, traditional video broadcasting can be defined as a highly dynamic process covering all these stages with both artistic and commercial aspects. Although this process has evolved over time, it is still widely used today and maintains its importance. In this context, contemporary elements such as artificial intelligence and digital technology are being integrated into traditional processes, allowing for the development of more effective and innovative approaches. Thus, innovations in content distribution advance both creative and commercial processes even further.

AI-POWERED VIDEO BROADCASTING PROCESSES

Artificial intelligence is significantly reshaping video broadcasting processes, offering revolutionary opportunities in content production and distribution. This transformation is not limited to technological advancements but is a reflection of new dynamics and approaches in content production. One of the most critical stages of these processes is content creation. Rapid developments in artificial intelligence are fundamentally changing creative processes such as automatic video editing, content recommendations, and even script development. For example, software supported by machine learning algorithms can deeply analyze existing videos to determine which scenes most affect and interest viewers; thus, content creators gain the ability to produce more attractive, engaging, and target-focused videos that align with viewer trends. This contributes to both improving content quality and strengthening viewer loyalty. Especially considering viewer feedback and interactions helps the content creation process progress more easily. (Türten, 2024)

Another important process is the effective distribution and marketing of video content. Artificial intelligence plays a vital role in viewer analytics and data-driven content recommendations. Advanced algorithms that analyze user behaviors make a significant contribution to determining the most suitable content for the target audience, while through this process, broadcasters gain the opportunity to develop more efficient and target-focused marketing strategies. Additionally, AI-based automatic content distribution systems are effectively used to optimize videos across various platforms and ensure they reach viewers with the right timing. These applications significantly increase broadcasters' potential to reach wide audiences while offering the opportunity to meet more viewers by increasing the accessibility of content. Thus, video content becomes more functional and effective for both creative users and viewers (Chetouani, 2024).

In conclusion, artificial intelligence stands out as a revolutionary tool and method in content creation and distribution in the video broadcasting process. The adoption of these modern technologies not only provides broadcasters with a competitive advantage but also offers the opportunity to establish deeper and more meaningful interactions with viewers. Artificial intelligence not only automates business processes but also produces innovative solutions for renewing content strategies and meeting evolving viewer expectations. This dynamic structure effectively supports the flexibility and innovation necessary for sustainable growth in the media industry. This process supports establishing a stronger bond with the audience while enhancing user experience in addition to increasing content efficiency. As a result, artificial intelligence provides a more effective and directive content flow by bringing together creative thinking and technology in video broadcasting.

AI SUPPORT IN DIGITAL VIDEO BROADCASTING

Artificial intelligence technologies are increasingly being used in all stages of digital video broadcasting. These applications affect the entire broadcasting value chain, from content production to distribution, from audience analysis to monetization. Artificial intelligence automates and improves video content creation and editing processes. Operations such as automatic video editing, visual effect creation, sound editing, and subtitle addition can be performed by artificial intelligence algorithms. For example, Adobe's Sensei AI platform uses artificial intelligence technologies to automate and accelerate video editing processes. Artificial intelligence algorithms improve low-quality audio and video to enable the production of professional-quality content. Processes such as noise reduction, image sharpening, color correction, and resolution enhancement can be accomplished with artificial intelligence. NVIDIA Broadcast is one of the prominent applications in this field. Artificial intelligence systems can automatically analyze video content to create metadata about the content. This allows content to be categorized, tagged, and optimized for search engines. For instance, Google's Video AI API can automatically recognize objects, activities, and speech in video content. Machine learning algorithms can analyze user behaviors to offer personalized content recommendations. Platforms such as Netflix, YouTube, and Amazon Prime Video use advanced recommendation systems to suggest content based on users' viewing habits. Artificial intelligence can dynamically optimize broadcast quality according to network conditions and device characteristics. Adaptive bit rate technologies optimize bandwidth usage and provide an uninterrupted viewing experience using artificial intelligence algorithms. AI-powered translation and subtitle systems enable content to be presented in different languages and according to different accessibility needs. Automatic speech recognition and translation technologies can create real-time subtitles even for live broadcasts. Artificial intelligence can analyze viewer behaviors to provide valuable insights. These insights can be used for developing content strategy, determining target audiences, and optimizing advertisements.

These developments have accelerated the adoption of artificial intelligence technologies in the broadcasting industry. According to Deloitte's 2024 Media and Entertainment Sector Report, 78% of media companies are investing in artificial intelligence technologies and integrating these technologies into their business processes. The same report shows that AI-Powered content production and distribution can achieve operational cost savings of 25-30%.

AI-POWERED DIGITAL VIDEO BROADCASTING TECHNOLOGIES

Audio Processing and Enhancement Technologies

Audio quality is one of the most important factors affecting the viewer's experience in digital video broadcasting. AI-Powered audio processing and enhancement technologies enable broadcasters without access to professional studio equipment to produce high-quality sound. Artificial intelligence algorithms can detect and filter background noise perceived by the microphone. These noises include keyboard sounds, fan sounds, room noises, street sounds, and sounds of household appliances. NVIDIA Broadcast's noise reduction feature uses deep learning models to filter such noise in real-time while preserving speech. In tests conducted, NVIDIA Broadcast's noise reduction feature was found to be more effective than other noise-canceling solutions such as Discord and G HUB (Technopat, 2021). Artificial intelligence models can detect and eliminate room echoes that occur during sound recording. This provides a significant advantage especially for broadcasters recording in acoustically non-optimized environments. NVIDIA Broadcast's room echo removal feature uses artificial intelligence to filter sound echoes and reverb. Artificial intelligence algorithms can analyze audio signals to optimize frequency balance and improve sound quality. This enables the production of professional-quality sound even with low-quality microphones. NVIDIA's Studio Voice feature, introduced in 2025, significantly improves sound quality with AI-powered microphone effects and brings the sound closer to studio quality (Techolay, 2025). Artificial intelligence models can separate mixed audio signals into their components. For example, speech, music, and background sounds can be separated and each processed individually. This allows broadcasters to better control their audio mix. AI-Powered sound synthesis technologies can produce speech from text and automate dubbing processes. Amazon's Prime Video platform began testing an AI-Powered dubbing feature in 2025. This technology aims to collaborate with professional localization experts, where artificial intelligence creates the initial dubbing version, after which these recordings are edited by humans and quality control is ensured (Webrazzi, 2025).

Image Processing and Enhancement Technologies

Image quality is another important factor affecting viewer experience in digital video broadcasting. AI-powered image processing and enhancement technologies enable broadcasters to produce high-quality images without professional camera equipment and studio environments. Artificial intelligence algorithms can distinguish a person from the background in webcam images, offering the ability to change or blur the background. This allows for professional-looking broadcasts without requiring a green screen. NVIDIA Broadcast's virtual background feature uses deep learning models to distinguish the person from the background and can replace the background with a desired image. With updates made in 2025, the foreground/background separation has been further improved (Techolay, 2025). Artificial intelligence models can analyze camera images to track a person's face and movements and automatically reframe the image. This ensures that the image stays in focus even if the broadcaster moves. NVIDIA Broadcast's auto frame feature uses artificial intelligence to zoom in on the image to track head movements. Thus, even if you move left or right, the focus point does not shift from the user (NVIDIA, 2020). Artificial intelligence algorithms can enhance low-quality camera images to produce clearer and more professional-looking video. This includes processes such as improving image quality in low light conditions, reducing noise, and color correction. NVIDIA Broadcast's video noise reduction feature reduces camera noise that typically occurs in low light conditions. Artificial intelligence models can analyze a person's gaze direction to simulate eye contact. This allows the broadcaster to appear as if making eye contact with viewers even when not looking directly at the camera. NVIDIA Broadcast's eye contact feature simulates a lens effect by darkening the corners of the frame for a cosmetic effect. With updates made in 2025, gaze stability has been improved for a more natural look (Techolay, 2025). This beta feature introduced by NVIDIA in 2025 reduces shadows by relighting the face and offers a more professional appearance. This technology, which creates the effect of two main light setups, offers an ideal solution especially for chat-style live streams and video conferences (Techolay, 2025). AI-powered vignette effect darkens the corners of the screen to simulate a lens effect and gives the image a cosmetically professional appearance. NVIDIA Broadcast can apply this effect in real-time.

Content Production and Editing Technologies

AI-powered content production and editing technologies enable broadcasters to create content more efficiently and creatively. AI-powered speech recognition technologies can automatically convert speech in video content to text to create subtitles. This increases the accessibility of content and facilitates reaching audiences in different languages. YouTube introduced automatic subtitle creation in 2009 and has continuously improved it since then.

Artificial intelligence models can create video content from text input. This is particularly useful technology for educational content, explanatory videos, and product introductions. Platforms like Synthesys offer artificial intelligence video technology with lip synchronization to create videos from text. Media creators and companies need no more cameras or film crews to create videos. Artificial intelligence algorithms can analyze long video content to detect important moments and automatically create summaries. This allows viewers to quickly grasp the main points of the content. Platforms like Pictory offer automatic summarization of long videos. AI-powered translation systems enable video content to be presented in different languages. This facilitates reaching a global audience. Platforms like DeepBrain AI facilitate global content creation by offering voiceovers in more than 80 languages and with more than 100 realistic AI voices. Artificial intelligence technologies can create realistic avatars, allowing content creators to produce video content without appearing on camera. DeepBrain AI allows users to create custom avatars using a smartphone or webcam. This significantly reduces the time and cost associated with traditional video production (Unite.AI, 2025).

AI-Powered Broadcast Optimization

AI-powered broadcast optimization technologies are used to improve broadcast quality and viewer experience. Artificial intelligence algorithms can dynamically optimize broadcast quality according to network conditions and device characteristics. This allows for high-quality broadcasting even under limited bandwidth conditions. NVIDIA's NVENC (NVIDIA Encoder) technology reduces CPU workload to increase frame rates in games and offers the best video quality on the market (NVIDIA, 2020). Artificial intelligence models can use various optimization techniques to reduce broadcast latency. This is especially important for live broadcasts and interactive content. NVIDIA's RTX GPUs offer video encoding and decoding processes optimized for low latency. AI-powered adaptive broadcasting technologies can automatically adjust broadcast quality according to the viewer's internet connection and device characteristics. This provides an uninterrupted viewing experience. Platforms such as Netflix, Amazon Prime Video, and YouTube optimize the viewer experience using adaptive bit rate technologies. Artificial intelligence algorithms optimize the performance of content delivery networks, ensuring content reaches viewers faster and more efficiently. This is especially important for platforms broadcasting on a global scale. Artificial intelligence models optimize the use of system resources (CPU, GPU, RAM) during broadcasting, allowing the broadcaster to perform different activities simultaneously, such as playing games or running other applications. NVIDIA Broadcast enables the selection of the most suitable effect for the system with the GPU usage indicator added in 2025 (Techolay, 2025).

AI OPPORTUNITIES FOR BROADCASTERS

Production Efficiency and Cost Advantages

Artificial intelligence technologies significantly improve broadcasters' production processes and reduce costs. AI-powered automation tools accelerate time-consuming tasks such as video editing, audio processing, and applying effects. For example, automatic subtitle creation can be up to 90% faster compared to manual subtitle addition. This allows broadcasters to produce more content or focus more on the quality of existing content. AI-powered software reduces the need for expensive hardware equipment. For instance, applications like NVIDIA Broadcast can eliminate the need for green screens, professional microphones, and studio lighting. This is a significant advantage, especially for small-scale broadcasters and individual content creators with limited budgets. By automating technical tasks, AI allows broadcasters to dedicate more time to creative processes. For example, automatic video editing tools enable editors to focus on creative storytelling rather than routine cutting and merging operations. AI technologies enable broadcasters to easily scale their production capacity, offering flexibility to quickly respond to increasing demand or expanding target audiences. For instance, multiple language support and automatic translation features facilitate rapid content delivery in different languages, making global growth easier. AI optimization algorithms can reduce energy consumption in broadcasting processes, providing both cost savings and contributing to sustainability goals.

Improving Content Quality

AI technologies help broadcasters significantly improve content quality. AI-powered audio and image processing technologies enable professional quality content production even with amateur equipment. NVIDIA Broadcast's noise reduction, virtual background, and automatic frame adjustment features make it possible to broadcast at studio quality even in a home environment. AI algorithms ensure consistency in content quality, improving viewer experience and strengthening brand image. For example, automatic color correction and audio normalization features ensure that content recorded under different conditions can be presented with consistent quality. AI-powered effects and filter tools make it easier to add creative and visually rich elements to content. NVIDIA Broadcast's Virtual Key Light and vignette effect features give content a professional appearance. AI technologies can improve content quality in real-time, even during live broadcasts. This provides a significant advantage, especially in situations where unexpected technical issues or environmental changes occur. AI algorithms analyze viewer feedback and interaction data to continuously improve content quality, allowing to produce content that better responds to viewer expectations.

Accessibility and Inclusivity

AI technologies help broadcasters make their content more accessible and inclusive. AI-powered speech recognition and image processing technologies enable accessibility features such as automatic subtitle creation and sign language translation, making content more accessible to deaf or hard-of-hearing viewers. AI-powered translation and dubbing technologies enable content to be presented in different languages. Amazon Prime Video's AI-powered dubbing feature facilitates reaching a global audience by making content accessible in different languages (Webrazzi, 2025). AI algorithms can automatically analyze visual content to create audio descriptions, helping visually impaired viewers better understand the content.

AI technologies make it easier to adapt content to the needs of different viewer groups. For example, age-appropriate versions for children or versions adapted to different cultural contexts can be created. AI-powered compression and optimization technologies ensure quality content delivery even in low bandwidth conditions, making it easier to reach viewers in regions with limited internet access.

Personalized Content Delivery

AI technologies allow broadcasters to offer personalized content to their viewers. AI algorithms can analyze viewer behaviors to provide personalized content recommendations, improving viewer experience and increasing time spent on the platform. Platforms like Netflix, YouTube, and Amazon Prime Video use advanced recommendation systems to suggest content based on users' viewing habits. AI technologies can dynamically adapt content according to viewer preferences and behaviors. For example, different content segments or alternative endings can be presented based on the viewer's interests. AI algorithms can segment viewers according to demographic characteristics, interests, and behavioral patterns, enabling the development of customized content strategies for each segment. AI technologies can personalize content according to the viewer's real-time interactions, providing significant advantages especially for interactive live broadcasts and game streams. Advanced AI algorithms can analyze the viewer's emotional state and present appropriate content, increasing viewer loyalty and satisfaction.

New Revenue Models and Business Opportunities

AI technologies offer new revenue models and business opportunities for broadcasters. AI algorithms can analyze viewer data to make more targeted and effective ad placements, increasing advertising revenue and improving viewer experience. AI-powered content analysis and metadata creation facilitate the licensing and distribution of content across different platforms and in different formats, allowing broadcasters to generate more revenue from their content. AI algorithms can be used to optimize subscription models. By analyzing viewer behaviors, pricing strategies, content packages, and special offers can be developed. AI-powered virtual reality (VR) and augmented reality (AR) technologies provide opportunities to offer new types of digital events and experiences, allowing broadcasters to diversify their revenue sources. Broadcasters with AI-powered content production tools can use these technologies to provide services to other content creators and brands, creating a new revenue stream.

Democratization Effect on Small and Medium-Sized Broadcasters

AI technologies create a democratization effect in the broadcasting industry, enabling small and medium-sized broadcasters to compete with large media organizations. AI-powered tools lower the barriers to enter the broadcasting industry by reducing the need for expensive equipment and large technical teams. Applications like NVIDIA Broadcast enable the production of professional quality content with minimal hardware requirements. User-friendly AI-powered tools automate tasks that require technical expertise, making it possible for broadcasters with limited technical knowledge to produce quality content. AI technologies offer scalable solutions for small-scale broadcasters in their growth process, providing flexibility to quickly respond to increasing demand or expanding target audiences. AI-powered analysis tools facilitate the identification of niche viewer segments and the production of specialized content for these segments, allowing small broadcasters to gain a competitive advantage by specializing in specific areas.

AI-powered translation and localization tools make it possible even for small broadcasters to reach global audiences, significantly expanding potential viewership and revenue opportunities. The democratization effect of AI technologies in the broadcasting industry increases content diversity and creates a more competitive ecosystem, benefiting both broadcasters and viewers.

NVIDIA BROADCAST AND ALTERNATIVES

NVIDIA Broadcast is an innovative and pioneering application powered by NVIDIA's extraordinary graphics processing capabilities that has fundamentally transformed how content creators approach broadcasting and video communication in the modern digital environment. Designed with advanced artificial intelligence capabilities, this application significantly enhances broadcast quality by effectively using real-time processing techniques to improve audio and video elements. The application includes various features such as the highly popular virtual background generation, which allows users to easily replace their physical backgrounds with different digital representations without requiring a green screen. This remarkable innovation is particularly beneficial for content creators who want to maintain a clean and professional appearance, making it possible to minimize distractions during important live broadcasting events, webinars, or intensive gaming sessions. Thus, content creators can interact with their audiences with greater focus and clarity

In addition to offering a wide range of visual enhancements, NVIDIA Broadcast significantly improves audio quality with advanced AI-powered noise reduction technology. By intelligently distinguishing between background noise and the speaker's voice, this innovative application successfully filters out unwanted sounds such as distracting keyboard clicks, constant traffic noise, or other disturbing sounds that could hinder the communication experience. This advanced feature is extremely important for broadcasters aiming to deliver clear, crisp, and engaging narration. The powerful combination of sophisticated noise cancellation and effective echo reduction not only enriches the audio environment but also ensures that the speaker remains the center of attention throughout the broadcast. By using this technology, content creators can maintain their professionalism while offering their viewers a seamless listening experience, resulting in more effective presentations that impress their audiences (Starowicz & Zieliński, 2024).

Furthermore, NVIDIA Broadcast seamlessly integrates with various popular broadcasting platforms and basic video conferencing tools. This allows content creators to apply these advanced enhancements effortlessly and efficiently. Due to its user-friendly interface, even individuals without extensive technical knowledge or background can easily manage settings to customize their broadcasting environments according to their specific preferences and needs. As the demand for high-quality digital content continues to increase at a rapid pace globally, NVIDIA Broadcast positions itself as an indispensable tool for broadcasters, educators, and various professionals. The application caters to the special requirements of different users. By harnessing the power of artificial intelligence technology, this application not only effectively simplifies the production process but also offers new opportunities for content creators to establish more effective and meaningful connections with their audiences. This ensures that content presented through NVIDIA Broadcast stands out remarkably in the competitive and constantly evolving digital video landscape, regardless of which platform is used (Kumar et al., 2024).

What is Nvidia Broadcast?

NVIDIA Broadcast is an AI-powered video broadcasting application that provides content creators and game broadcasters with advanced working capabilities in various areas. This platform is not only an advanced software solution but also enhances audio and video quality and is equipped with features such as background noise reduction by leveraging the capabilities of NVIDIA's graphics processing units (GPUs). These features enable live broadcasts and video recordings to gain a more professional appearance and clarity. While NVIDIA Broadcast allows users to showcase their creativity in their studios, it also deepens and strengthens viewer engagement. Thus, content creators have the opportunity to establish a more effective connection with their viewers and create compelling content. This technology raises industry standards by offering impressive and quality broadcasting experiences (Akmanlar, 2024).

NVIDIA Broadcast offers impressive features such as virtual backgrounds, audio removal, and automatic framing. The virtual background function allows users to broadcast with various and colorful visuals that reflect their personal style and brand without needing a physical background. This not only provides a more engaging experience for viewers but also gives content creators the opportunity to showcase their creativity. The audio removal feature effectively filters out unwanted background noise, providing viewers with a clearer and more fluid listening experience, which is a significant advantage especially in music or audio content broadcasts. Thus, viewers can focus solely on the content while background noise is minimized. The automatic framing function ensures that the frame continuously adjusts as users move while maintaining the focus point on the screen, allowing viewers to always see the main subject clearly. The combination of these features creates a more professional impression throughout the broadcast, making content creators' broadcasts more effective and attention-grabbing. These features provide significant convenience for individuals with creative content in expressing themselves.

Broadcasters can strengthen their position in digital video broadcasting thanks to this innovative solution offered by NVIDIA Broadcast. This application not only improves broadcast quality but also offers the opportunity to reach a wide audience by creating impressive and attention-grabbing content. The additional features provided by the application make content more attractive while leaving a lasting impact on viewers. As a result, NVIDIA Broadcast has become a critical tool in AI-powered digital video broadcasting, providing content creators with significant advantages both technically and aesthetically. This allows broadcasters to achieve a more professional image and gain a competitive edge.

Features Of Nvidia Broadcast

NVIDIA Broadcast is a software solution that offers innovative opportunities to content creators and significantly improves the user experience in the field of video broadcasting. This impressive software has notably enhanced audio and video processing capabilities by leveraging artificial intelligence technologies. It provides users with the ability to achieve professional quality in their videos through various processes such as effectively eliminating ambient noise, creating virtual backgrounds, and facial recognition. For example, while filtering out unwanted background sounds, it creates a positive effect on viewers by offering an opportunity to focus. Thanks to these features, broadcasters can enhance the viewer experience in a versatile way by increasing the quality of their broadcast streams. NVIDIA Broadcast provides great convenience to users at every stage of content production, paving the way for them to create more impressive and professional content (Akmanlar, 2024) (KAYAALP et al.).

Another striking and remarkable feature of NVIDIA Broadcast is its virtual background creation capacity. Users can make significant changes in their environments in real-time without having a physical background. This represents a major advantage especially for broadcasters producing various types of content, as it offers the opportunity to increase viewer interest and make the content more attractive by creating different themes. Additionally, the most advanced face and body tracking technologies are used for precise background segmentation. This ensures that as users move, the background adapts dynamically accordingly, enriching the user experience. All these features allow content creators to produce more creative, engaging, and impressive broadcasts. NVIDIA Broadcast greatly simplifies this process with its technological infrastructure.

NVIDIA Broadcast features remarkable multi-platform compatibility. Its integration with prominent platforms such as YouTube, Twitch, and Zoom allows users to conduct their broadcasts seamlessly across different channels and formats. Beyond these features, NVIDIA's AI-powered technology offers content creators not only quality audio and video but also the opportunity to enhance interaction and engagement. Thus, broadcasters can establish a stronger and more lasting connection with their viewers through professional and dynamic communication. Such innovative tools play an important role in shaping the future of digital broadcasting and have the potential to fundamentally transform content creation processes. As a result, broadcasters will gain significant advantages in producing more interactive and impressive content thanks to these advanced technologies. (Karaca, 2024)

Nvidia Broadcast and Video Quality

NVIDIA Broadcast is an extremely powerful application specifically developed to leverage the extraordinary capabilities of NVIDIA's advanced graphics cards. This software plays a transformative and pioneering role for broadcasters, content creators, and remote working professionals in various fields by significantly enhancing video quality. Using the latest artificial intelligence algorithms, this software elevates both visual and audio experiences, allowing users to create high-quality content without the extensive technical knowledge or expensive equipment investment typically required to achieve professional results. Users can greatly benefit from innovative features such as background removal or replacement, noise cancellation, and virtual green screens, which significantly increase the overall production value of live broadcasts and recorded videos, thus allowing content creators to focus more on their content and viewer interaction rather than technical setups and limitations. The application enables users to optimize their images dynamically and efficiently; for example, the automatic framing feature ensures that the presenter always remains centered and well-positioned, ultimately providing a refined and professional appearance that enhances the viewing experience. (Azzarelli et al., 2025)

NVIDIA Broadcast goes beyond ensuring visual broadcast quality by also offering seamless integration with popular broadcasting platforms and commonly used video conferencing tools. This level of compatibility allows content creators to both increase their production and maximize workflow efficiency while maintaining high and consistent production standards. As the extraordinary growth in digital content consumption continues, the integration of powerful tools like NVIDIA Broadcast is becoming an indispensable component for content creators aiming to distinguish themselves in an increasingly competitive environment, beyond being a simple enhancement tool. By simplifying the complexities and challenges of video production while enhancing overall quality, this software makes a significant contribution to the evolution of digital broadcasting. It offers capabilities that will constitute a valuable and indispensable asset for modern broadcasters or content creators seeking to establish themselves in the digital space. (Kumar et al., 2024)

Advantages and Disadvantages of Nvidia Broadcast

Advantages of NVIDIA Broadcast:

- High-quality and accurate artificial intelligence models
- Low latency and high performance thanks to Tensor cores
- Comprehensive feature set (audio and video processing)
- User-friendly interface and easy installation
- Free to use (for RTX GPU owners)
- Regular updates and new features

Disadvantages of NVIDIA Broadcast:

- Works only with NVIDIA RTX GPUs
- Compatibility issues with some older or specialized cameras
- Beta features require high GPU power
- Limited customization options (compared to other professional software)
- No support outside Windows operating system

Similar Applications and Their Features

XSplit VCam is an application offering virtual background and background blurring features. Similar to NVIDIA Broadcast, XSplit VCam provides the ability to change backgrounds without requiring a green screen. However, XSplit VCam's artificial intelligence models are not as advanced as NVIDIA Broadcast and show lower performance in edge detection.

Krisp is an application that offers AI-powered noise reduction. Like NVIDIA Broadcast, Krisp filters microphone and speaker noise. Krisp's advantage is that it doesn't require an NVIDIA RTX GPU and offers wider hardware compatibility. However, Krisp's noise reduction performance is not as effective as NVIDIA Broadcast and requires a monthly subscription.

Adobe's video editing software offers AI-powered audio and video processing features. The Adobe Sensei AI platform provides features such as automatic color correction, audio enhancement, and content-aware scaling. However, this software focuses on post-production rather than real-time processing and is more complex and expensive compared to NVIDIA Broadcast.

OBS Studio can be extended with various AI-powered plugins. These plugins offer features such as noise reduction, virtual backgrounds, and automatic subtitle creation. However, the installation and configuration of these plugins are more complex, and their performance is not as high as NVIDIA Broadcast.

Market Position and Competitive Analysis

NVIDIA Broadcast holds a strong position in the market for AI-powered broadcasting tools. The application's free availability (for RTX GPU owners) and high performance provide a competitive advantage. However, its limitation to only work with NVIDIA RTX GPUs restricts its potential user base. The market is becoming increasingly competitive. Hardware-independent solutions like Krisp appeal to a wider user base. Large software companies like Adobe are integrating AI-powered features into their products. Additionally, open-source platforms like OBS Studio are being extended with AI-powered plugins. In the future, the market for AI-powered broadcasting tools is expected to grow and diversify further. For NVIDIA Broadcast to maintain its position in the market, it needs to offer wider hardware compatibility, add more customization options, and continuously improve its artificial intelligence models.

The Advantages of AI-Powered Broadcasting

AI-Powered broadcasting presents transformative opportunities in the media industry with significant advantages. Firstly, there is a need to place greater emphasis on accelerating the content production process. Compared to traditional methods, AI systems offer notable time-saving benefits through data analysis and content creation stages. For instance, AI algorithms learn from vast data sets, enabling effective analysis of viewer preferences and providing highly accurate predictions about when and how certain content should be presented. Such in-depth analysis enhances broadcasters' ability to quickly respond to audience demands while also contributing significantly to the development of more targeted and impactful content strategies. In this context, broadcasters strengthen their interactions with viewers while increasing their chances of standing out in modern broadcasting.

Additionally, AI-powered broadcasting offers substantial benefits in personalizing content. Today's digital environment sees viewers demanding increasingly personalized and individually tailored content that aligns with their interests. AI analyzes users' viewing habits, preferences, and interactions in detail, enabling it to provide content recommendations customized for each individual, meeting their specific needs. This approach effectively increases user loyalty and higher watch rates. On the other hand, AI's ability to automatically generate text and visually edit content reduces production costs by a significant margin. It also allows broadcasters to allocate more resources elsewhere, providing a critical opportunity for small and medium-sized broadcasters with limited budgets to enhance quality in content creation. Therefore, the advantages offered by AI bring revolutionary changes to the broadcasting industry, making it more efficient (Çakmak, 2024).

In conclusion, the benefits of AI-powered broadcasting are not limited to innovations in data analysis, personalization, and cost efficiency. AI also enhances the traceability of content, contributing to broadcasters' profitability and market share growth. This dynamic plays a decisive role in shaping competition within the media sector and enables broadcasters to achieve sustainable growth in future digital ecosystems. Broadcasting strategies that integrate AI represent not just a technology-driven transformation but also one that enriches user experiences. Furthermore, data analyses conducted through AI applications facilitate deeper understanding of user behavior, which is then used to more effectively reach target audiences. Personalization processes, facilitated by content recommendation systems, provide users with not only topics matching their interests but also uniquely designed content, enhancing user satisfaction. This improves the quality and impact of the broadcaster's content while strengthening brand loyalty. AI stands out as a tool capable of creating revolutionary potential in the creation, distribution, and consumption of media content.

Automation and Time Efficiency

Automation plays a crucial role in enhancing efficiency in digital video production by streamlining content creation and editing processes compared to traditional methods. AI-powered solutions automate repetitive tasks, increasing productivity while reducing human errors. For example, advanced machine learning algorithms can quickly and accurately perform complex operations during video editing, such as color corrections, audio matching, and automatic cuts. This allows broadcasters to focus more on their content, allocate more time to creative processes, and improve efficiency by ensuring a better-quality output. As a result, teams save time while achieving effective results, creating new opportunities for innovation in digital video broadcasting.

Timesaving is one of the most significant advantages provided by automation and has a substantial impact across many sectors. Autonomous systems not only minimize working hours but also enable the creation of more content, enhancing efficiency in the process. For example, tools that automatically generate video subtitles overcome language barriers, enhance accessibility, and simplify reaching a broader audience. Such automations are crucial in encouraging global sharing of content. Additionally, automated community management systems manage viewer feedback, comments, and interactions more effectively, strengthening broadcasters' connections with their audiences and contributing to increased viewer engagement. Comprehensive automation solutions play a major role in enhancing content strategies and viewer interaction; thus, broadcasters investing in automation gain a competitive edge. The use of these systems facilitates the production of higher quality content with less time spent.

The necessity for broadcasters to optimize their workflows and use resources more efficiently has made automation a crucial requirement. This situation becomes an important factor in determining competitive advantages within the sector. This process not only enhances efficiency but also allows broadcasters to develop more flexible and intelligent solutions for their operations. The increase in efficiency aids broadcasters in gaining more flexibility and control over their budget management by saving time and reducing costs. These systems accelerate content production in the digital environment, improving quality and playing a critical role in capturing user interest. In this context, broadcasters not only speed up content production but also have more opportunities to focus on marketing and promotional strategies. Ultimately, automation and timesaving become indispensable necessities in digital video broadcasting, significantly accelerating transformation within the sector. This change not only increases competition in broadcasting but also contributes to further improving content production processes with innovative approaches.

Personalized Content

Personalized content is an essential component of digital broadcasting, consisting of specially crafted content that takes into account individual preferences, interests, and viewing habits. The creation of such content is made possible today by the rapid and continuous evolution of artificial intelligence and machine learning technologies. A deep analysis of user data provides broadcasters with extremely important and valuable opportunities to produce the most suitable content for viewers' expectations. Personalized content strategies play a critical role in capturing viewer attention, enhancing the user experience with supporting elements that engage users more deeply. Therefore, digital content creators gain a significant advantage by effectively using personalized content strategies to better understand their audience and deliver more appropriate content to them (Kırık & Özkoçak, 2023).

Digital broadcasting platforms employ complex algorithms to analyze user behavior, thereby automating their content production processes. These algorithms examine a user's past viewing habits, favored genres, and interactions with specific content to create a personalized stream of information for them. For instance, if a viewer consistently selects fantasy movies, new content and recommendations in that genre will be prioritized for them. This user-centric approach not only enhances viewer loyalty but also reinforces the platform's recommendation system efficiency, encouraging users to return frequently. However, providing personalized content must consider ethical concerns and data privacy issues. Safeguarding user data is crucial for ensuring these platforms remain reliable and user-satisfying. Ultimately, users feeling secure is essential for the sustainability of such platforms, emphasizing the importance of trust in their continued success.

Another significant advantage of personalized content is its ability to segment target audiences more precisely and detail-oriented, allowing for the development of tailored campaigns aimed at different viewer groups. These targeted and unique approaches significantly increase broadcasters' potential to boost advertising revenue while also laying the groundwork for a more meaningful, deeper, and impactful connection between the content and the audience. Therefore, such strategies play a major role in driving innovative and creative transformations in both content production and distribution. Personalized content not only enhances user experience but also serves as a strategic and effective tool for broadcasters to maintain their presence dynamically and competitively in the market. This development process ultimately aims to better understand viewers' needs and expectations, enabling the creation of matching content that increases user satisfaction and supports the sustainable growth of businesses.

COMPARISON OF TRADITIONAL AND AI-POWERED BROADCASTING

In traditional broadcasting, broadcasters focus on dynamically reaching specific target audiences within certain time and medium constraints. They use conventional media tools to create and distribute content within a business model framework. Key components include selecting the right content that aligns with audience interests, crafting compelling stories, ensuring quality through editorial processes, and effectively distributing the content. Feedback mechanisms in traditional broadcasting are essential for understanding audience preferences but may not be as quick or detailed.

Broadcasters often rely on long-term analyses to gauge what works, which can take years to surface. AI-supported broadcasting, on the other hand, leverages artificial intelligence (AI) for data analysis, trend prediction, and tailored content distribution. This modern approach enhances efficiency and customization by streamlining editorial processes and reducing manual intervention. AI allows broadcasters to adapt quickly to changing market conditions and audience demands, making their operations faster and more accurate. (Akşit, 2024).

On the other hand, AI-supported broadcasting provides a faster and more comprehensive content production process, especially with the integration of data analytics and machine learning technologies. AI algorithms enable real-time analysis of viewer behavior, preferences, and immediate reactions, which facilitates the dynamic adjustment of content strategies. Regularly updated data allows broadcasters to more effectively segment their target audiences and also helps in increasing viewer interaction by personalizing content. In addition, advanced algorithms allow for more detailed data analysis, which also lays the groundwork for creating content that enhances the user experience. Moreover, innovative technologies like automatic content generation and natural language processing speed up the production process, reduce costs, and decrease the need for human intervention in creation (Doğanay, 2024) .In conclusion, AI-supported broadcasting enhances content quality and assists broadcasters in developing more effective strategies. This comprehensive approach to content production ensures that broadcasters can adapt quickly to audience needs, optimize resources, and ultimately deliver higher-quality content efficiently

In contrast to traditional approaches, AI-supported broadcasting offers significant advantages in content creation and distribution. The integration of artificial intelligence allows for real-time feedback during analysis and dissemination, enabling dynamic adjustments that enhance content quality and relevance. However, conventional methods often fall short in providing such adaptability.

Traditionally, the broadcasting model has favored fixed frameworks and predictable outcomes, maintaining a cautious approach to change. On the other hand, AI-driven approaches are more open to evolution, readily adapting to shifts in media environments and fostering innovation. Despite these contrasting models, there is an opportunity to combine both methods effectively. This fusion allows broadcasters to benefit from the reliability and proven effectiveness of traditional techniques while embracing the flexibility and efficiency that AI technologies offer. As a result, content creation becomes richer, more accessible, and interactive, enhancing viewer engagement through diverse offerings. Such integration not only deepens the interaction between audiences and media but also paves the way for transformative changes within the industry. Ultimately, this approach offers new opportunities for content creators and broadcasters to thrive in an ever-evolving landscape.

COST ANALYSIS IN DIGITAL VIDEO BROADCASTING

Cost analysis plays a crucial role in the digital video broadcasting ecosystem. It provides critical data for financial sustainability and profitability for broadcasters by evaluating strategic aspects across operations. Broadcasters utilize AI-supported tools to optimize costs from content production to distribution, marketing strategies, and performance analysis. They meticulously assess these opportunities to enhance efficiency. AI algorithms analyze viewer behavior deeply, identifying popular content types and aiding in cost reduction strategies. This foundation allows for innovative financial management within broadcasting processes. Ultimately, this approach strengthens broadcasters' market positions and enhances viewer experience by tailoring content to preferences, increasing satisfaction.

The cost elements of digital video content are generally divided into main categories such as content production, editing, distribution, and marketing. Conducting a detailed cost analysis for each stage is of great importance. For example, equipment used in content production, software, production times, and staff employed directly affect costs. Control and planning activities during this process also come to the fore. In addition, platform fees, technical infrastructure investments, and distribution methods used at the distribution stage play significant roles. AI applications are crucial in improving efficiency in each of these stages and reducing total costs. For example, automatic editing software reduces studio hours, while machine learning-supported marketing analyses identify which platforms target audiences spend more time on, enabling more efficient and effective use of marketing budgets. This increases the accessibility of content and has a positive impact on investment returns. In summary, understanding and optimizing each cost element is essential for effective digital video broadcasting, especially with AI applications driving efficiency and reducing overall costs (Çiltaş & İlhan, 2023).

In conclusion, cost analysis in digital video broadcasting is not only a mechanism for controlling costs but has also become a strategic decision-making tool with a significant role. In this context, its importance has increased. Today's dynamic market conditions allow broadcasters to achieve competitive advantages by taking into account the high efficiency offered by AI and opportunities for data analysis while conducting these analyses. Thus, cost analysis is not only limited to evaluating the current situation but also serves as a solid foundation for determining future investments and strategies. This makes it possible for broadcasters to take more strategic and efficient steps toward achieving sustainable growth in digital media. The information obtained during the cost analysis process plays a critical role in adaptation and innovation in competitive market conditions. Therefore, cost analysis is not just a financial tool; it is an essential element for the long-term success of the business. The detailed breakdown of costs involved in digital video content—such as production, editing, distribution, and marketing—is crucial for ensuring optimal resource allocation and profitability. By leveraging AI applications to enhance efficiency across these stages, broadcasters can significantly reduce overall costs while improving the effectiveness of their strategies. This approach not only maximizes investment returns but also ensures that digital media content remains accessible and impactful in a competitive market landscape. In summary, cost analysis empowers broadcasters to make informed decisions, optimize resources, and maintain a competitive edge in the ever-evolving digital media industry. It is an indispensable tool for achieving sustainable growth and long-term success.

SPEED AND EFFICIENCY

In today's fast-paced digital landscape, AI-supported digital video broadcasting offers revolutionary opportunities for speed and efficiency. This approach empowers content creators and broadcasters with tools that streamline processes and enhance productivity. Traditionally, the publication process involves several labor-intensive stages such as planning, shooting, editing, and broadcasting, each requiring significant time, manpower, and financial resources. However, integrating AI systems into these stages introduces a transformative shift in efficiency and speed. For instance, automatic video editing software enables users to complete lengthy editing processes in mere minutes, drastically reducing production times. Similarly, content recommendation algorithms swiftly deliver tailored content that aligns with viewer preferences, enhancing engagement and interaction. These advancements not only allow creators to establish stronger connections with their audiences but also enable broadcasters to reach broader demographics effectively. As a result, AI-supported digital video broadcasting is redefining the content creation process, opening new horizons for growth and innovation in the industry. In summary, AI-driven solutions in digital video broadcasting are revolutionizing traditional methods by optimizing resources and enhancing efficiency, ultimately paving the way for more dynamic and impactful content creation.

Additionally, AI-based analytical tools meticulously track viewer behavior, providing broadcasters with critical and valuable information for shaping content strategies. This comprehensive data encompasses which contents are more watched, optimal broadcasting time slots for the audience, and demographic details of viewers. Consequently, broadcasters can effectively utilize this information to optimize their content and broadcast schedules, laying a solid foundation for developing more effective and efficient marketing strategies. This leads to increased production efficiency, significantly reducing production costs, benefiting not only independent content creators but also large-scale media companies with positive results. In this context, analysis systems equipped with AI solutions have become an indispensable tool for achieving success in the increasingly competitive media environment. These tools enable broadcasters to make informed decisions based on precise data, ensuring that their efforts are well-targeted and resource efficient. By leveraging these advanced tools, content producers can enhance their market presence and ensure long-term growth, making AI a cornerstone of modern digital video broadcasting strategies. The integration of AI-driven solutions not only streamline operations but also fosters innovation, allowing broadcasters to adapt quickly to evolving market demands. This approach ensures that resources are optimally allocated, leading to cost-effective production processes and enhanced content quality. As such, AI-supported analytics empower broadcasters to navigate the dynamic media landscape with precision and confidence, ensuring sustained success in an ever-changing industry (Kaba, 2024).

As a result, AI-supported digital video broadcasting transforms content production into faster and more efficient processes. In comparison to traditional methods, this technology enables content creation to be completed much more quickly. Additionally, utilizing advanced analysis systems that enhance viewer interaction allows broadcasters to establish deeper and more effective communication with their audience. Furthermore, the opportunities for cost reduction contribute to making broadcasters economically more sustainable. Considering the continuous evolution of technology, the integration and further development of such systems herald a new era filled with unexpected opportunities in digital video broadcasting.

USER EXPERIENCE (UX) IN DIGITAL VIDEO BROADCASTING

In the context of digital video broadcasting, user experience (UX) is a critical factor aimed at optimizing viewer interaction and satisfaction. For broadcasters, enhancing UX not only increases the number of viewers but also lays the foundation for building a loyal audience. This involves strategic planning across various elements from content distribution to platform design. The text emphasizes that viewer interactions with the interface (UI), as well as their processes of discovering and accessing content, are key factors in shaping user experience. These interactions directly influence how much value users perceive from the platform, thus affecting their loyalty. A well-designed UI/UX makes the content flow more intuitive and provides personalized recommendations tailored to user needs, leading to a more meaningful and satisfying experience for viewers. In summary, enhancing UX involves creating interfaces that intuitively guide users to desired content through tailored recommendations, thereby increasing viewer satisfaction and loyalty in digital video broadcasting (Ekmekci, 2024).

Digital video broadcasting heavily relies on user experience (UX), which is critical for optimizing viewer interaction and satisfaction. UX improvement not only increases viewer numbers but also builds a loyal audience. It involves strategic planning across elements like content distribution, platform design, interface interactions, and content discovery processes. Advanced technologies such as data analytics and AI continuously enhance UX by analyzing viewer behaviors to offer content recommendations and improve interface designs. AI personalizes suggestions based on user interests, boosting satisfaction. Enhanced UX leads viewers to spend more time on the platform, increasing content consumption. Comprehensive understanding of UX enables broadcasters to refine their strategies and content diversity, allowing them to effectively reach target audiences. This better understanding of viewers' needs results in higher quality, engaging content, giving broadcasters a competitive edge.

In the realm of digital video broadcasting, user experience (UX) is a critical factor for optimizing viewer interaction and satisfaction. Enhancing UX not only increases viewer numbers but also helps build a loyal audience. This involves strategic planning across various elements from content distribution to platform design. The integration of data analytics and AI technology plays a significant role in continuously improving UX. By analyzing user feedback, broadcasters can refine their strategies and content diversity, enabling them to reach target audiences more effectively. Successful UX management is essential for future success in digital video broadcasting, allowing broadcasters to strengthen their market positions through innovative approaches. In conclusion, the strategic management of user experience ensures that digital platforms evolve dynamically, enhancing viewer satisfaction and engagement. This approach not only boosts current user satisfaction but also attracts new users, making it a cornerstone for successful digital content distribution.

CONTENT PRODUCTION PROCESSES

Digital video broadcasting is revolutionized by AI-driven strategies that focus on enhancing user experience (UX). These strategies optimize the production process, personalize content recommendations based on viewer data, and reduce costs through automation. By leveraging advanced analytics, broadcasters can better understand their audience's preferences, enabling them to create more engaging and specific content. Additionally, continuous improvements in UX ensure a dynamic platform evolution, keeping up with fast-changing trends. This approach not only boosts efficiency but also enhances viewer satisfaction by providing tailored experiences, giving broadcasters a competitive edge in the evolving digital landscape (Özdemir & Günay, 2023).

AI plays a crucial role in optimizing the content creation process for digital video broadcasting. From scripting to filming, AI tools support creative processes by helping users save time and minimize human error. For example, AI-supported scriptwriting applications can offer suggestions based on existing content, fostering more creative frameworks and encouraging idea development. During the filming stage, AI systems can optimize camera positioning, determining the most effective angles for shooting. This not only enhances production quality but also significantly improves the efficiency of the production process. As a result, content creators gain a competitive edge by achieving their goals with a more efficient workflow (Pamuklu et al.).

In conclusion, the distribution process of content has been optimized through the capabilities provided by AI-supported algorithms. Analytical data from the distribution phase can be effectively utilized to determine which platforms and time slots are most effective. As a result, content is delivered to the target audience in the most suitable and impactful manner, increasing view rates. AI supports strategic decision-making throughout the entire lifecycle of content, helping broadcasters maintain their competitive advantages. These innovations in content production processes, combined with the dynamic nature of digital video broadcasting, shape future paradigms for content creation and offer more innovative solutions. In this ever-changing environment, correctly managing and distributing content is critical to the success of brands.

THE CHALLENGES OF AI-POWERED VIDEO BROADCASTING

AI-supported broadcasting represents a revolutionary change in the media sector, offering numerous benefits while also presenting various challenges. The primary challenge lies in the high level of automation provided by AI during content creation and distribution processes, which can impact human creativity. While broadcasters benefit from algorithms generating content that can engage users and increase viewer loyalty, they face significant issues due to the lack of human touch and authenticity in production. Particularly, the quality and reliability of content generated by AI have become controversial topics regarding trustworthy media principles. The risk of spreading incorrect information increases due to these systems' reliance on algorithms, potentially damaging the broadcaster's reputation. Therefore, media organizations must adopt a cautious and informed approach during content creation and distribution in this AI-supported era (Yıldırım & Can, 2024).

In addition, AI's impressive data analysis capabilities play a crucial role in aligning content with target audiences, from posters to interactive content. However, advanced data collection and user analysis methods raise concerns about privacy and security. Broadcasters must ensure they fulfill their responsibilities regarding user privacy while also fighting against the negative effects of algorithm-generated content. Thus, there is an urgent need for both effective and ethical content strategies.

In conclusion, AI-supported broadcasting requires broadcasters to strategically plan by leveraging technological opportunities and continuously developing innovative solutions. Overcoming challenges in AI-driven content strategies is critical for enhancing viewer engagement and achieving sustainable success in the sector. By implementing diverse strategies and innovative approaches, broadcasters can strengthen their position in a competitive environment.

TECHNOLOGICAL DEPENDENCY AND ITS EFFECTS

Technological dependency refers to an excessive and compulsive reliance on digital devices, social media platforms, and online environments. Key components of this dependency include distractibility, difficulties in time management, and withdrawal from social interactions. Users may feel a constant need to stay online, which can negatively impact on their daily lives, productivity, and the quality of their relationships. This dependency is particularly significant for younger generations, influenced by the design of social media platforms and systems governed by user feedback and algorithms. Such factors contribute to an increased reliance on technology, affecting individuals' social lives and overall health. Considering these challenges, developing methods and strategies to overcome technological dependency becomes crucial for enhancing the quality of life for those affected (Akarcan, 2024).

This dependency has a significant impact on individuals' psychological and physical health, leading to severe and long-lasting consequences. Scientific research reveals that excessive screen time disrupts sleep patterns significantly, contributing to mental health issues such as depression, anxiety, and attention deficit disorder. Furthermore, digital dependency not only affects individual well-being but also profoundly impacts social dynamics. The decrease in face-to-face communication, the weakening of social skills, and the erosion of a sense of community are critical outcomes that demand serious attention. Additionally, in professional and academic settings, technological dependency can lead to difficulties in maintaining focus and reduced productivity, negatively impacting individuals' careers and academic achievements. In essence, excessive reliance on digital technologies has far-reaching consequences, affecting not only personal health but also social interactions and professional success. Addressing this issue requires a comprehensive approach that considers both individual well-being and the broader implications for society (Akpınar, 2024).

Technological dependency has significant impacts on both individual mental health and broader societal dynamics. The excessive use of digital devices and social media leads to issues such as distraction, poor time management, and withdrawal from social interactions. It can also contribute to mental health problems like depression, anxiety, and attention deficits, while also disrupting sleep patterns.

The text highlights the role of AI-supported systems in mitigating these negative effects by providing tools to analyze user behavior and create solutions for healthier screen time management. Broadcasters have an ethical responsibility to encourage healthy technology use. Implementation challenges include balancing user privacy and engagement without making restrictions too intrusive. Redesigning social media platforms to encourage healthier usage while maintaining user engagement is a significant challenge. Additionally, considering age-specific strategies and educational programs could help younger generations manage their digital consumption better. Mental health aspects are crucial, emphasizing the need for balance between technology use and offline activities that promote well-being. Overall, thoughtful implementation of AI tools can create a healthier digital environment, but challenges around privacy, effectiveness, and ethical considerations must be addressed to ensure successful outcomes.

PRIVACY AND SECURITY ISSUES

In digital media broadcasting, the increased user interaction comes with privacy and security concerns. Broadcasters cannot avoid collecting audience data while using it for purposes such as content recommendations and targeted advertising. However, this raises ethical responsibilities regarding how data is collected, processed, and secured. Ensuring user trust and maintaining confidentiality requires transparency in data collection methods and processing. This not only benefits broadcasters by building credibility but also protects users' rights, making it a critical aspect of digital media management.

To address privacy concerns effectively, it is essential for broadcasters to clearly define their data security protocols and comprehensive privacy policies for users. Specifically, there should be clear communication regarding which data is collected, why it is collected, and the steps involved in its processing. Additionally, various technologies, encryption methods, and access control mechanisms used to ensure data security must be taken into consideration. In this way, user data will be effectively protected, enhancing the credibility of broadcasters and increasing users' trust in the platform.

To effectively address data privacy and security concerns, broadcasters should develop central strategies that go beyond mere regulatory compliance. They must adopt an inclusive approach that builds sustainable and reliable relationships with users, aligning with international standards like GDPR to enhance user willingness to share personal data. Proactively addressing privacy and security in digital video broadcasting is crucial for creating a sustainable and profitable business model. Simply complying with current regulations isn't enough; broadcasters must also respect user preferences and establish trust relationships, ensuring a secure and trusted environment for all stakeholders.

CONCLUSION

This research examines the current state of artificial intelligence (AI)-supported digital video broadcasting technologies, the opportunities they offer for broadcasters, and particularly the role of the NVIDIA Broadcast application in this field. According to this: AI technologies are being increasingly used at every stage of digital video broadcasting. Advances in AI subfields such as deep learning, computer vision, natural language processing, and speech recognition are transforming broadcasting processes. AI-supported broadcasting tools lower entry barriers for content creation, enabling more individuals and small-scale broadcasters to enter the market. This increases content diversity and fosters a more competitive ecosystem. AI technologies significantly improve the efficiency of broadcasters' production processes while reducing costs. Automatically handling time-consuming tasks like video editing, audio processing, and effect application shortens production times and optimizes human resources. AI-supported audio and video processing technologies enable the creation of professional-quality content even with amateur equipment. Features like noise reduction, virtual backgrounds, and automatic framing make it possible to conduct studio-quality broadcasts from a home environment. AI technologies help broadcasters make their content more accessible and inclusive. Automatic captioning, multilingual support, and audio descriptions facilitate access for diverse audiences. NVIDIA Broadcast stands out among AI-supported broadcasting tools. The application's AI models, powered by Tensor Cores, provide high-quality and real-time audio and video processing. In addition to core features like noise reduction, virtual backgrounds, and automatic framing, new features such as Virtual Key Light and Studio Voice expand the application's capabilities. The development of AI-supported digital video broadcasting brings challenges related to data privacy, copyright, and deepfake risks, among others. It is essential to address these challenges and develop proper regulatory frameworks. Trends like real-time 3D modeling, AI-supported content creation, personalized viewer experiences, and AR/VR integration are shaping the future of AI-supported digital video broadcasting. These trends will create new opportunities and challenges in the broadcasting industry.

To fully benefit from the opportunities provided by AI-supported digital video broadcasting, the following strategic recommendations are made for broadcasters. Broadcasters should develop their basic knowledge and understanding of AI technologies. This will facilitate the effective use of current tools and adapt to future developments. Broadcasters should align their investments in AI-powered tools with their business goals and content strategies. Starting with free or low-cost tools like NVIDIA Broadcast, they can transition to more advanced solutions as needed. Broadcasters must redesign their processes to integrate AI technologies into their existing workflows. This includes identifying tasks that can be automated and redirecting human resources toward creative and strategic roles. While AI tools improve technical quality, the uniqueness, creativity, and value of content still depend on the human factor. Broadcasters should focus not only on technical improvements but also on content quality and storytelling. Develop a comprehensive data strategy: Broadcasters should collect, analyze, and gain insights from viewer data. This will enable personalized content delivery, targeted marketing, and content optimization. By integrating AI-powered accessibility features (such as automatic captions and multilingual support), broadcasters can reach a broader audience. Broadcasters must act in accordance with ethical principles and legal regulations when using AI technologies. Responsibilities include data privacy, copyright, and content accuracy. Broadcasters should remain open to new tools and techniques as AI technologies evolve rapidly. Continuous learning and adaptation will provide a competitive advantage.

This study comprehensively examines the current state and future of AI-supported digital video broadcasting. The findings highlight the potential of AI technologies to transform the broadcasting industry and the role of applications like NVIDIA Broadcast in this transformation. The recommendations for broadcasters, technology developers, and researchers aim to contribute to the responsible and effective development and use of these technologies.

Although AI's support in video production primarily focuses on technical improvements and facilitating the process, its benefits in content creation are evident. After this study, it is essential to investigate how AI can be integrated into character creation, story development, and visual effects within the film industry

All these developments have enabled the digital broadcasting sector to overcome its challenges and enhance its ability to respond to the constantly evolving expectations of viewers. At the same time, this process involves ethical considerations, ensuring content security, and improving the viewer experience, which are critical elements. The assurance of viewer trust has become a vital component for broadcasters' long-term sustainable success, as it directly relates to the improvement of content quality. In addition to leveraging the potential offered by AI, there is a need to focus on enhancing the quality of media content within a framework of social responsibility and encouraging sensitivity in societal contexts. Media organizations should consider not only technological advancements but also the responsibilities they bring when building a healthy relationship with their audience. In this context, the transformative potential of AI applications in digital video broadcasting contributes significantly to shaping the future media ecosystem. This dynamic environment will continue to demand constant change and innovation. It is no longer sufficient to merely adapt to these changes; developing strategies that address viewers' expectations becomes one of the fundamental responsibilities of media professionals.

REFERENCES

Akarcan, M. (2024). Dijital Medya Bağımlılığının Getirdiği Sorunlar ve Çözüm Önerileri. (Problems Caused by Digital Media Addiction and Solution Suggestions). *Black Sea Journal of Public and Social Science*, *7*(1), 47–54. DOI: 10.52704/bssocialscience.1383503

Akmanlar, S. (2024). Fotoğrafta Yapay Zeka: Tanıtım Fotoğrafına Etkileri ve Geleceği. Yayımlanmamış doktora/yüksek lisans tezi. Marmara Üniversitesi GSE Fotoğraf Anasanat Dalı. https://tez.yok.gov.tr/UlusalTezMerkezi/TezGoster?key=KMB79M3N7zK1UR2WYeRgQm1bDnq6yQ0ZO0wthhZIFWBu9IAQ-F33i6dp4xksqWUD. 41-45

Akşit, Z. A. (2024). Ütopya Kavramı ve Görsel Sanatlar: Klasik Dönemden Postmodern Döneme Bir Kesişim Alanı.(The Concept of Utopia and Visual Arts: An Intersection Arena from the Classical to the Postmodern Eras). [Tykhe Journal of Art and Design]. *Tykhe Sanat ve Tasarım Dergisi.*, *9*(17), 377–399.

Azzarelli, A., Anantrasirichai, N., & Bull, D. R. (2025). Intelligent Cinematography: A review of AI research for cinematographic production. *Artificial Intelligence Review*, *58*(108), 108. DOI: 10.1007/s10462-024-11089-3

Çakmak, A. Ç. (2024). Yapay Zekâ ile Marka İnşası. (Branding Building with Artificial Intelligence). *Kahramanmaraş Sütçü İmam University Journal of Social Science.*, *21*(2), 624–635.

Chetouani, N. (2024). *Yapay zeka uygulamalarının habercilik pratiklerine etkileri. (Effects Of Artificial Intelligence Applications on Journalism Practices).* (MA Thesis). Selçuk University. Social Science Institute. Konya.

Çiltaş, E., & İlhan, V. (2023). Dijital Medyada İçerik Üretim Süreçlerine Yönelik Bir Bakış. (An Overview of Content Production Processes in Digital Media). [Türkiye Media Academy Journal]. *Türkiye Medya Akademisi Dergisi.*, *3*(6), 429–464.

Deloitte. (2024). *Medya ve Eğlence Sektörü Raporu 2024. (Media and Entertainment Report).*

Doğanay, A. (2024). Veri gazeteciliği, algoritmik habercilik ve yapay zekanın, gazetecilik üzerindeki dönüştürücü etkisi. Yayımlanmamış yüksek lisans tezi. Marmara Üniversitesi Sosyal Bilimler Enstitüsü Gazetecilik Ana Bilim Dalı Medya Ekonomisi ve İşletmeciliği Bilim Dalı. https://tez.yok.gov.tr/UlusalTezMerkezi/TezGoster?key=weFMBHaUra8rsS5wi2bmHDBDAOXrF1RJSx6u8PqI9O19RWkTbSNg545JKCYZ0G23. 87

Kaba, K. (2024). Yapay zekâ haberciliği ve dijital etik (Artificial intelligence journalism and digital ethics). (MA Thesis). *Sakarya Üniversitesi, Sosyal Bilimler Enstitüsü. (Sakarya University Social Sciences Institute).*

Karaca, S. (2024). Dijital oyun tasarımında illüstrasyon. (Illustration in Digital Game Design). (MA Thesis). Selçuk Üniversitesi. Sosyal Bilimler Enstitüsü. *(Selçuk University Social Sciences Institute).*

Kırık, A. M., & Özkoçak, V. (2023). Medya ve İletişim Bağlaminda Yapay Zekâ Tarihi ve Teknolojisi: Chatgpt ve Deepfake ile Gelen Dijital Dönüşüm. (The History and Technology of Artificial Intelligence in The Context of Media and Communication: Digital Transformatıon with Chatgpt And Deepfake). [Karadeniz International Science Journal]. *Karadeniz Uluslararası Bilimsel Dergi*, (58), 73–99. DOI: 10.17498/kdeniz.1308471

Korkut, C. (2022). Değişen Televizyon Yayıncılık Teknolojileri. https://www .egitimyayinevi.com/doc/457. 111

Kumar, T., Sharma, P., Tanwar, J., Alsghier, H., Bhushan, S., Alhumyani, H., & Alutaibi, A. I. (2024). Cloud-based video streaming services: Trends, challenges, and opportunities. *CAAI Transactions on Intelligence Technology*, *9*(2), 265–285. DOI: 10.1049/cit2.12299

NVIDIA. (2020). *NVIDIA Broadcast Uygulama Kurulum Kılavuzu. (NVIDIA Broadcast Manuel).* https://www.nvidia.com/tr-tr/geforce/guides/broadcast-app-setup-guide

NVIDIA. (2020). *Huzurlarınızda NVIDIA Broadcast Uygulaması. (NVIDIA Broadcast Application).* https://www.nvidia.com/tr-tr/geforce/news/nvidia-broadcast-app

Özdemir, A., & Günay, M. (2023). GRAFİK TASARIMIN GELECEĞİ (YAPAY ZEKA). TURAN: Stratejik Arastirmalar Merkezi. https://avesis.gelisim.edu.tr/publication/showdocument/897f855a-5b44-420d-aedf-3c812df52f78. 120

Pamuklu, A. G., Özkartal, M., & Pamuklu, E. (2024). Dede Korkut Karakterleri Görsel Temsillerinin Yapay Zekâ ile Yeniden Üretimi. (Reproduction of Visual Representations of Dede Korkut Characters with Artificial Intelligence). *(The Journal of International Language, Literature, Culture, History, Art and Education Research).* 18. 276-293.

Starowicz, A., & Zieliński, M. (2024). Sustainable acoustics: The impact of AI on acoustics design and noise management. *Technical Sciences.*, *202*. Advance online publication. DOI: 10.31648/ts.10297

Technopat. (2021). *NVIDIA Broadcast kullanımı ve inceleme. (NVIDIA Broadcast Usage and Analyse)*

Techolay. (2025). *Yeni NVIDIA Broadcast Özellikleri. (New NVIDIA Broadcast).*

Türten, B. (2024). Sinemada dağıtım ve gösterim ağında yapay zekâ uygulamaları. (Artificial intelligence applications in cinematic distribution and screening network). *Journal of Humanities and Tourism Research, 14*(13), 376–402.

Unite.AI. (2025). *İyi 10 Yapay Zeka Video Oluşturucu. (10 Best Artificial Intelligence Video Creators).*

Webrazzi. (2025). *Prime Video, yapay zeka destekli dublaj özelliğini test ediyor. (Prime Video is testing an AI-powered dubbing feature).* Webrazzi.

Yıldırım, E., & Can, A. (2024). Yapay Zekanın Reklamcılık Alanında Kullanımı Yapay Zeka Kullanarak Yazılmış Reklam Film Analizi.(The Use of Artificial Intelligence in the Field of Advertising Advertising Film Analysis Written Using Artificial Intelligence*).* [Pamukkale University Communication Science Journal]. *Pamukkale Üniversitesi İletişim Bilimleri Dergisi., 3*(2), 268–287.

ADDITIONAL READING

Bourtsoulatze, E., Chadha, A., Fadeev, I., Giotsas, V., & Andreopoulos, Y. (2019). Deep Video Precoding. https://dl.acm.org/doi/abs/10.1109/TCSVT.2019.2960084

Camilo Zemanate Zúñiga, J., Andrés Muñoz Hidalgo, J., & Luis Arciniegas, J. (2014). Detection of advertising spaces from audiovisual scenes to product placement. https://core.ac.uk/download/229159541.pdf

Costalago Serrano, R. (2019). Aplicaciones de la inteligencia artificial en la industria publicitaria. https://uvadoc.uva.es/handle/10324/36896

Htut Soe, T. (2021). AI video editing tools. What editors want and how far is AI from delivering? https://www.hsu-hh.de/imb/wp-content/uploads/sites/677/2021/08/AI-video-editing-tools-What-editors-want-and-how-far-is-AI-from-delivering.pdf

Kose, U., & Sert, S. (2017). Improving content marketing processes with the approaches by artificial intelligence. https://arxiv.org/pdf/1704.02114

Kraus, L. (2019). Artificial intelligence in the value chain of book publishing.https://run.unl.pt/handle/10362/69198

Midoglu, C. A., Hicks, S., Thambawita, V., Kupka, T., & Halvorsen, P. (2022). MMSys'22 Grand Challenge on AI-based Video Production for Soccer. https://www.researchgate.net/publication/358306833_MMSys'22_Grand_Challenge_on_AI-based_Video_Production_for_Soccer

Nir, O., Vidra, I., Neeman, A., Kinarti, B., & Shamir, A. (2024). VCR: Video representation for Contextual Retrieval. https://arxiv.org/pdf/2402.07466

Yıldız, M., & Fulya Yıldırım, B. (2018). The Effects O Artificial Intelligence And Robotic Systems On Librarianship. https://www.researchgate.net/publication/324428346_Yapay_Zeka_ve_Robotik_Sistemlerin_Kutuphanecilik_Meslegine_Olan_Etkileri_The_Effects_of_Artificial_Intelligence_and_Robotic_Systems_on_Librarianship

Zhang, H., Li, Y., Ai, Q., Luo, Y., Wen, Y., Jin, Y., & Binh Duong Ta, N. (2020). Hysia: Serving DNN-Based Video-to-Retail Applications in Cloud. https://dr.ntu.edu.sg/handle/10356/152998

KEY TERMS AND DEFINITIONS

Digital Video: Digital video is an electronic form of moving images that is represented by a digital data stream.

Broadcasting: Broadcasting refers to the process of disseminating information or media to a broad audience simultaneously. This method ensures that multiple recipients receive the same content at the same time, enabling widespread access to information, entertainment, or educational materials.

Artificial Intelligence: Artificial intelligence (AI) refers to the simulation of human intelligence in machines that are programmed to think like humans and mimic their cognitive functions. These cognitive functions include learning, problem-solving, decision-making, perception, and language understanding.

Nvidia Broadcasting: NVIDIA Broadcasting" refers to a comprehensive set of tools and features developed by NVIDIA designed to enable high-quality video streaming, particularly tailored for gaming.

Image Processing: Image processing is a broad field that involves manipulating and analyzing digital images to enhance their quality, extract information, or prepare them for specific applications. It encompasses both fundamental techniques and advanced methods, often incorporating artificial intelligence and machine learning.

Noise Cancelling: Noise canceling is a technology designed to reduce unwanted sounds (noise) in audio.

Digital Streaming: Digital streaming is the process of delivering digital content, such as videos, music, or live events, over the internet in real-time. Unlike downloading, where you have to wait for the entire file to download before accessing it, streaming allows you to start watching or listening immediately as the data arrives.

Streaming Optimisation: Streaming optimization refers to a comprehensive approach aimed at enhancing the delivery of digital content over the internet by improving efficiency, quality, and user experience.

Chapter 12
The Modern Dilemma Exploring the Boundaries of Smartphone Overuse and Dependency

Fahrettin Kayan
https://orcid.org/0000-0002-8099-7271
Akdeniz University, Turkey

ABSTRACT

The rapid advancement of digital technology has significantly reshaped human interaction, communication and information consumption. Smartphones in particular have become indispensable tools in both personal and professional contexts. However, along with their benefits, excessive smartphone use has also brought about various social, psychological and physiological challenges. This chapter explores smartphone overuse and addiction, analysing its prevalence, causes and consequences, as well as consumer behaviour and potential intervention strategies. Drawing on interdisciplinary research, this study examines smartphone addiction from psychological, social and neurological perspectives, with a particular focus on its effects on marketing, social interaction and digital wellbeing. The findings provide a comprehensive understanding of smartphone addiction and contribute to the ongoing discourse on responsible digital consumption.

DOI: 10.4018/979-8-3373-1957-5.ch012

INTRODUCTION

In recent years, the accelerated proliferation of digital technologies has profoundly impacted the routines of individuals on a daily basis. One such technology is the smartphone, which has become an integral component of both our personal and social lives. The convenience afforded by smartphones is manifold. Instant access to information, communication, and entertainment is made possible by the various features these devices offer. However, with the pervasive use of these devices, the potential dangers of excessive and unmonitored usage have also emerged. The phenomenon of smartphone addiction has emerged as a significant concern in contemporary societies. This form of addiction, which pertains to the excessive and uncontrolled use of smartphones, has the potential to negatively impact the social, psychological, and physical well-being of individuals (Moqbel et al., 2023). This phenomenon has reached alarming proportions, particularly among adolescents and young adults.

A number of studies (Luo & Hu, 2022; Matar Boumosleh & Jaalouk, 2017) have demonstrated a correlation between smartphone addiction and the onset of various psychosocial issues, including feelings of loneliness, depression, social anxiety, and sleep disturbances. The objective of this study is to examine the prevalence, causes, and effects of smartphone addiction on individuals and to examine the methods of measuring and evaluating this addiction. In the context of this study, an extensive review of existing literature on smartphone addiction was conducted, and the current approaches to this subject were evaluated. Furthermore, the relationship between smartphone addiction and social and demographic factors, its effects on individuals' mental health, and potential solutions to reduce this addiction were discussed. In this context, in light of the existing literature on smartphone addiction, important questions are raised regarding how societies should deal with this new type of addiction and the measures that can be taken. In the following sections of the study, the causes and effects of smartphone addiction and strategies to reduce addiction will be discussed comprehensively.

SMARTPHONE USE AND ADICTION

The Concept and Definition of Smartphone Addiction

The term "smartphone addiction" is used to describe a specific type of behavioral addiction, typically characterized by excessive and uncontrolled use of smartphones. Such addiction can have deleterious effects on the social, psychological, and physical health of individuals. Smartphone addiction is frequently compared to other behavioral addictions, such as pathological gambling and internet addiction.

It is associated with the criteria for addiction as defined in the DSM-5 (Loleska & Pop-Jordanova, 2021).

The phenomenon of smartphone addiction is characterised by a loss of control, the emergence of negative consequences in the event of continued use, and the experience of withdrawal symptoms (Mehrnaz et al., 2018). Furthermore, addiction manifests itself in symptoms such as an inability to rationally evaluate one's needs for the device in question and feelings of unease when one is unable to access the device (Körmendi et al., 2016). Moreover, individuals with smartphone addiction frequently utilize applications that facilitate social interaction, such as social media and instant messaging. This evidence suggests that the need for social connection is a significant factor in the increased use of smartphones (Mahapatra, 2019).

In defining the concept of addiction, the distinction between overuse and addiction is emphasized. Although numerous studies categorize smartphone addiction as a behavioral addiction, some researchers contend that this designation may be overly simplistic and propose alternative terms, such as problematic smartphone use" (Panova & Carbonell, 2018). These terms describe the adverse effects experienced by users, including the frequency of use and a lack of control, but do not always reach the threshold of addiction. In contrast to addiction, problematic use can result in a reduced level of negative consequences and typically necessitates less rigorous treatment (Nikolić, 2021).

The neurological effects of smartphone addiction have been the subject of investigation, with studies indicating that addiction can result in structural and functional changes in the brain. For example, studies have demonstrated a reduction in gray matter volume in the brains of individuals with smartphone addiction, accompanied by alterations in their cerebral activities (Horvath et al., 2020). Neuroimaging studies have revealed significant structural alterations, particularly in the anterior insula and anterior cingulate cortex regions, which have been linked to the severity of addiction (Schmitgen et al., 2020).

Smartphone addiction is frequently linked to psychosocial issues such as loneliness, depression, and social anxiety. Research indicates that individuals with elevated levels of social anxiety are more susceptible to developing smartphone addiction and are more engaged with digital platforms such as social media (Darcin et al., 2016). In contrast to fulfilling the need for social connection, such usage may result in users experiencing feelings of loneliness and isolation (Yu & Sussman, 2020). In particular, younger individuals are vulnerable to adverse psychological consequences associated with smartphone addiction and excessive social media usage (Daysal & Yılmazel, 2020).

A variety of scales have been developed for the purpose of defining and evaluating smartphone addiction. These scales are utilized to ascertain the extent of addiction among individuals and to determine whether such individuals require treatment. For example, the Problematic Smartphone Use Scale (PSUS) is a frequently utilized scale for assessing individuals' smartphone usage habits (Aljomaa et al., 2016). This scale employs a multidimensional approach to measuring addiction, encompassing factors such as frequency of use, social effects, and physical symptoms. Additionally, as with other forms of addiction, genetic, environmental, and psychological factors may contribute to the development of smartphone addiction (Choi et al., 2015).

Prevalence of Smartphone Addiction

The phenomenon of smartphone addiction is increasingly recognized as a significant public health concern on a global scale. While the prevalence of smartphone addiction varies across different age groups and demographic segments, it has emerged as a pervasive phenomenon, particularly among younger individuals. The research on the prevalence of smartphone addiction offers a more comprehensive understanding of the impact of this addiction and provides insights into the development of effective treatment approaches.

A review of the literature reveals that research on the global prevalence of smartphone addiction indicates that this phenomenon is relatively common among children and youth. For example, a meta-analysis study conducted among children and adolescents revealed that the average prevalence of problematic smartphone use in this age group was 23.3% (Sohn et al., 2019). In the same study, problematic smartphone use was found to be associated with various mental health problems, including depression, anxiety, and poor sleep quality.

The university student population represents one of the most extensively researched groups in the context of smartphone addiction. In studies conducted among this group, the prevalence of addiction was found to be relatively high. For example, a study conducted among university students in Saudi Arabia revealed that 48% of the participants exhibited signs of smartphone addiction (Aljomaa et al., 2016). Furthermore, the study revealed that the prevalence of addiction increased with an increase in both daily smartphone usage time and time spent on social media. In a separate study conducted among university students in Egypt, the prevalence of addiction was reported to be 59% (Okasha et al., 2021). This study revealed a strong association between smartphone addiction and psychiatric disorders, including depression, anxiety, and sleep disturbances.

The phenomenon of smartphone addiction is influenced by a multitude of social and demographic factors. This addiction is more prevalent among younger age groups and is observed at higher rates in men and single individuals (Kheradmand & Amirlatifi, 2022). Furthermore, individuals who spend a greater amount of time on social media and online gaming platforms are at an elevated risk of developing a smartphone addiction (Cha & Seo, 2018).

A study conducted in China revealed that addiction is prevalent among young adults and high school students, with a decline in addiction rates observed with increasing age. Nevertheless, the risk of addiction was found to increase in tandem with the duration of access to social networking sites and smartphone use (Haug et al., 2015). The detrimental effects of smartphone addiction extend beyond mere psychological consequences; they also manifest in physical health. A study conducted in Brazil revealed that neck and back pain is prevalent among individuals with smartphone addiction and that this is associated with prolonged mobile phone usage (Apv et al., 2020). Furthermore, individuals with high addiction levels exhibited elevated rates of insomnia and stress. In studies on mental health, it has been demonstrated that addiction is associated with adverse outcomes, including depression, anxiety, and a diminished quality of life. For example, a study on the relationship between depression and smartphone addiction revealed that individuals with smartphone addiction exhibited higher levels of depression (Alhassan et al., 2018).

Diagnosis and Measurement Methods of Smartphone Addiction

The prevalence of smartphone addiction is increasing, particularly among adolescents and young adults. A number of scales have been developed for the purpose of diagnosing and accurately measuring this addiction. One such instrument is the Problematic Smartphone Use Scale (PSUS), which is a widely utilized tool for assessing smartphone addiction across diverse cultural contexts. This scale was developed for the purpose of assessing whether or not individuals' phone usage habits have acquired a pathological dimension, and it examines different aspects of addiction in great detail.

The PDQ is a specialized scale for assessing smartphone addiction, grounded in psychometric standards and validated for reliability. It builds on prior internet addiction tools, focusing on digital addiction symptoms. The scale includes various subscales that cover addiction factors, validated through single- or multi-factor analyses (Kwon et al., 2013). Its reliability is confirmed by a high Cronbach's alpha of 0.93 (Lopez-Fernandez, 2017), and its construct validity has been supported by exploratory and confirmatory factor analyses. Additionally, multilingual adaptations, such as translations into Spanish and French, have confirmed its validity across cultures (Nikolić, 2021). Studies have linked the PDQ to smartphone addiction symptoms and usage duration, showing that it reliably predicts addiction without significant impact from personal factors like age or gender (Lee & Kim, 2021). The scale evaluates key addiction dimensions: tolerance, loss of control, daily activity disruption, withdrawal symptoms, excessive use, and time disturbance. Each factor includes specific questions to capture addiction symptoms, enabling a comprehensive analysis of addiction's effects (Lin et al., 2016).

The "tolerance" factor in the scale describes the phenomenon of increasing need for individuals to use the device. This factor assesses whether users exhibit a proclivity to utilize the device with increasing frequency over time. The "loss of control" factor gauges the extent to which users experience difficulty in putting the phone down or limiting the duration of use. Furthermore, the assessment of "withdrawal symptoms" encompasses the psychological distress experienced by users when separated from the device, thereby encompassing the psychological dimension of addiction (Panova & Carbonell, 2018). The PDQ has been demonstrated to possess both validity and reliability in a multitude of studies. For example, in a study conducted in Taiwan, the Chinese version of the scale was utilized, and it was determined to accurately measure addiction symptoms among children (Huang et al., 2020). In this study, it was demonstrated that the scale exhibited validity in accordance with the criteria set forth in the DSM-5 for diagnosing addiction, and that it could accurately describe the symptoms of addiction. Moreover, it is regarded as one of the most efficacious instruments for discerning the social and psychological ramifications of addiction. The scale has been identified as a powerful tool for determining the effects of addiction level on social life, and thus constitutes a useful measurement tool that can be employed in the context of addiction treatment (Kwon et al., 2013). The psychometric properties of the scale provide an accurate assessment of addiction symptoms and are employed to ascertain the prevalence of addiction.

EFFECTS OF SMARTPHONE ADDICTION ON THE INDIVIDUAL

Effects on Psychological Health

Anxiety and depression are frequently associated with smartphone addiction. In particular, smartphone addiction has been linked to a notable elevation in anxiety levels, particularly among younger individuals. It has been observed that the use of smartphones increases stress levels by distracting individuals during the day and interfering with their daily tasks (Elhai et al., 2017). This relationship between anxiety and smartphone addiction can also be explained by the fact that individuals experience distress when they are separated from their smartphones, which in turn increases their stress levels. In particular, individuals with social media addiction may experience heightened anxiety when they are unable to access their social media platforms (Hawi & Rupert, 2017).

Depression and anxiety are frequently observed to co-occur in individuals with smartphone addiction. Ge et al. (2023) posited that these two conditions may exert a common effect, whereby depression may indirectly elevate anxiety levels. In particular, executive dysfunction serves as a mediating factor in the relationship between depression and anxiety. This impairment may elevate stress levels by impairing an individual's capacity to plan and execute daily activities, potentially leading them to utilize smartphone usage as a means of avoidance.

The available evidence indicates that the quality of sleep experienced by individuals with smartphone addiction is inferior. For example, a study conducted in India revealed that 66% of young people exhibit high levels of smartphone addiction and 53% suffer from sleep disorders (Youssouf et al., 2019). This study revealed a positive correlation between sleep disorders and smartphone addiction. Another study has demonstrated that smartphone addiction can directly impact sleep quality, with lower sleep quality observed in young people with high addiction levels (Nikolić & Šipetić-Grujičić, 2023).

The use of smartphones has been linked to a notable reduction in both the duration and time required for individuals to fall asleep. In a study conducted by Zhang & Wu (2020) in China, approximately one-third of university students with smartphone addiction exhibited poor sleep quality. The study indicates that addiction results in a reduction in sleep duration and an increase in the time required to fall asleep. As the level of addiction increases, individuals tend to utilize their smartphones until late at night, which disrupts sleep patterns by prolonging the time required to fall asleep (Mehrnaz et al., 2018). A further study conducted in Korea demonstrated that smartphone addiction was associated with increased daytime sleepiness among young people (Chung et al., 2018). The findings of this study indicate that individuals with smartphone addiction experience a decline in sleep quality and an increase in daytime fatigue. Furthermore, a reduction in sleep duration may impair the productivity of these individuals in their daily tasks and negatively impact their overall quality of life. Another prevalent behavior among individuals with smartphone addiction is the postponement of sleep onset. Such behavior may have a detrimental impact on sleep quality and lead to sleep deprivation. Zhang & Wu (2020) investigated the positive correlation between smartphone addiction and the postponement of bedtime, demonstrating that this behavior results in a decline in sleep quality. Those with a smartphone addiction may continue to use the device before bedtime, which can result in a reduction in the amount of sleep obtained.

Furthermore, the relationship between smartphone addiction and sleep disorders is associated with psychological disorders such as depression and anxiety. In a study conducted by Demirci et al. (2015) on university students in Turkey, it was reported that smartphone addiction was associated with decreased sleep quality, increased anxiety, and elevated depression levels. As an indirect consequence of smartphone addiction, sleep disorders have a deleterious impact on individuals' mental health and increase the risk of developing mental disorders (Sohn et al., 2021 Such awareness-raising programs, particularly among younger individuals, can mitigate the symptoms of addiction and encourage the adoption of healthier sleep habits. It is of great importance to increase awareness about today's technology in order to protect sleep health.

Effects on Social Interactions

The phenomenon of smartphone addiction has been demonstrated to have a deleterious impact on the quality of social interactions. In particular, the enjoyment and satisfaction derived from social interactions are diminished during phone use, which subsequently results in a reduction in overall social satisfaction. A study conducted in Italy revealed that the use of smartphones disrupts face-to-face interactions and reduces the happiness obtained from social relationships. The study indicated that individuals exhibited a diminished level of satisfaction and enjoyment during social interactions when their phones were in use (Rotondi et al., 2017). Such behavior may result in individuals distancing themselves from close social relationships and narrowing the scope of their face-to-face social networks. This phenomenon has been observed with greater frequency, particularly among younger individuals. A reduction in social connectedness has been observed to result in a corresponding weakening of social support networks, leading individuals to seek out smartphones as a source of solace (Ihm, 2018).

The reduction in social interactions caused by this addiction may intensify feelings of loneliness among individuals with smartphone addiction, while simultaneously reinforcing the use of social avoidance strategies. As a consequence of smartphone addiction, individuals tend to dedicate a greater proportion of their time to digital platforms, thereby reducing their engagement in face-to-face interactions. This situation results in the weakening of the ties between individuals with phone addiction and their social environment, leading to a reduction in the level of social support they require (Bian & Leung, 2015). It causes individuals to prefer digital communication over face-to-face communication, which in turn results in a decrease in the number of face-to-face interactions. A review of the literature reveals that studies conducted on young people and university students indicate that this addiction causes individuals to prefer digital communication over face-to-face communication. This situation results in a reduction in face-to-face meetings, which in turn alters the natural tendencies of individuals in social communication (Verduyn et al., 2020).

A growing body of research indicates that the use of smartphones during social interactions impairs communication quality by causing distraction. The reduction in face-to-face interactions results in a loss of social satisfaction and leads to the formation of less reliable social relationships (Dwyer et al., 2017). Furthermore, smartphone addiction may also have a detrimental impact on face-to-face interactions within the family unit. In particular, within family units, the frequency of face-to-face communication is observed to decline, with digital communication via smartphones becoming the predominant mode of interaction. As the level of addiction increases, research indicates a corresponding decrease in face-to-face interactions between family members, which in turn weakens family ties (Alwi et al., 2022). A study conducted in Baghdad revealed that individuals with smartphone addiction in the family experience social interaction anxiety, which reduces face-to-face interactions. The findings of this study indicate that family members tend to gravitate towards digital communication channels over in-person interactions, which can have a detrimental impact on familial communication (Krishna et al., 2019). Such behavior increases the perception of social isolation and loneliness, which in turn leads to a decreased preference for face-to-face interactions. This situation results in individuals disengaging from their social environments and instead engaging with the digital world. It has been observed that social isolation exacerbates the psychological distress experienced by individuals with smartphone addiction, prompting these individuals to disengage from face-to-face social interactions (Dissing et al., 2019).

Digitalization can intensify loneliness by reshaping social interactions. A meta-analysis shows that appropriate digital technology use can reduce loneliness by 30% and strengthen social support, while misuse or overuse can increase loneliness (Shah et al., 2020). Excessive digital use, especially among young people, is linked to social isolation, with over 60% spending substantial time on social media, which heightens loneliness and reduces face-to-face interactions (Dedov & Komissarova, 2020). Older adults with low digital literacy also experience increased loneliness, as adaptation to digital tools influences feelings of isolation (Joo et al., 2023). Digital technology impacts loneliness differently depending on its use; for example, using the internet for social connections reduces loneliness, while using it to avoid social interactions increases it (Nowland et al., 2018). Active engagement on digital platforms can help older adults build social support networks and reduce loneliness (Wilson, 2017), while passive usage may lead to isolation. Furthermore, extended social media use is linked to greater loneliness and psychological issues such as depression. Misuse of digital technologies contributes to loneliness and social isolation.

DEMOGRAPHIC DIFFERENCES IN SMARTPHONE USAGE

Age and Gender-Based Usage Differences

Young people utilize smartphones with greater frequency, particularly for entertainment and social media interaction. A study that analyzed data from over 30,000 participants revealed that young people use smartphones for an average of 166.78 minutes per day, with usage declining with age (Andone et al., 2016). Among younger individuals, this usage is primarily oriented towards entertainment-oriented content, such as social media applications and online video platforms. In contrast, older individuals utilize their mobile devices for shorter periods and primarily for the purposes of obtaining information or engaging in basic communication. Gender significantly impacts smartphone usage habits. Research indicates that women utilize smartphones for longer periods of time and tend to employ communication-oriented applications, such as social media and messaging, more frequently than men. In contrast, men tend to demonstrate a greater inclination towards content categories such as information, news, and games (Ok, 2020). Men in different age groups tend to gravitate towards content outside of social media, whereas women are more inclined to utilize social connection and sharing applications. Young women assume a more active role in social media and online interaction than men. A study conducted in Finland with young people aged 16-20 indicates that women tend to utilize a greater number of social media applications and spend more time on these platforms (Wilska, 2003). This can be attributed to their utilization of social media, particularly as a conduit for enhancing social connections and personal expression. A greater proportion of younger women than older women use smartphones. However, these individuals also utilize smartphones to maintain social connections. In this context, older women tend to prefer smartphones, particularly for communicating with their families, and they typically spend less time on social media (Baron & Campbell, 2012). As they age, older women tend to gravitate towards more traditional forms of communication, leading to a decline in their usage of social media platforms. Among male users, it is observed that the use of smartphones for digital games and information is a prominent phenomenon. A study conducted among university students in Nigeria indicates that men frequently utilize their mobile devices for gaming and information-seeking activities (David & Hart, 2021). It is evident that men are more inclined to seek out information and entertainment-related content, whereas women are more drawn to social communication-oriented content.

Usage Habits According to Education and Income Level

Smartphone usage patterns vary significantly by education and income level, influencing how often and for what purposes devices are used. Higher education levels correlate with more frequent smartphone use for information retrieval, business tasks, and active social media engagement, as educated individuals tend to access more information via smartphones (Rashid et al., 2020). Conversely, those with less education primarily use smartphones for basic communication, like calls and messaging, with limited access to information (Puspitasari & Ishii, 2016). Income also shapes smartphone habits: higher-income individuals prefer advanced smartphones and use them for diverse activities like social media, online shopping, and entertainment, often investing in high-speed internet and data-intensive apps (Jamalova &

Constantinovits, 2020). Lower-income users typically focus on essential functions with low-cost devices and data-saving apps, rarely engaging in data-heavy activities (Saraswathi, 2017). These disparities reflect a digital divide, as higher-income and educated individuals have greater access to mobile technology and digital content, enhancing their social participation, while those with lower income and education levels face limitations (Zhao et al., 2018).

Socioeconomic Inequalities and the Digital Divide

The digital divide highlights disparities in access to information and communication technologies, with higher-income and more educated individuals enjoying greater access to the internet and smartphones than those of lower socioeconomic status. A study of over 40,000 households in India found that low-income, less-educated individuals face significant challenges in device ownership and usage (Tewathia et al., 2020). Beyond device access, there are differences in usage: higher-income groups often use the internet for education and professional growth, while lower-income groups use it more for entertainment (Rallet & Rochelandet, 2007). This gap restricts social and economic opportunities for disadvantaged groups. For example, university students with lower education levels in Europe showed low digital literacy (Sianou-Kyrgiou & Tsiplakides, 2012). In Brazil, higher-income individuals have greater digital access, amplifying educational and career opportunities (Nishijima et al., 2017). The digital divide contributes to social exclusion, limiting lower-income individuals' access to e-government and online education, reducing the benefits of digitalization (Robinson et al., 2020).

MAIN FOCUS OF THE CHAPTER

The Role of Smartphones in Marketing Strategies

Mobile devices present a multitude of possibilities for marketing communications. For example, mobile devices facilitate innovative strategies such as location-based marketing, which provides consumers with immediate local offers and tailors shopping experiences. The use of geolocation, algorithmic targeting, and augmented reality allows marketers to monitor consumer behavior with greater precision, enabling informed decision-making (Carah, 2020). Personalized mobile marketing strategies have emerged as a crucial tool for capturing consumer attention. In light of the considerable time consumers devote to mobile devices, the provision of personalized content represents an effective strategy for enhancing marketing effectiveness. The extant research on mobile marketing indicates that personalized notifications and offers are associated with increased consumer satisfaction and greater customer loyalty. In particular, personalization in mobile applications facilitates more profound engagement with the brand (Tong et al., 2020). Social media represents one of the most pervasive platforms for digital marketing through smartphones. While social media advertising enables brands to reach large audiences, it also benefits from the tendency of mobile users to be engaged with social media. The use of social media applications on mobile devices enables brands to implement targeted advertising campaigns and communicate directly with their users in an effective manner (Persaud & Azhar, 2012).

The integration of mobile marketing strategies and social media platforms amplifies the influence of brands in shaping consumer behavior. The use of smartphones provides an optimal setting for the facilitation of increased advertising interactions. The extant literature on the subject indicates that mobile advertisements have a positive effect on brand awareness and purchase intention. Consumers are better able to make informed and expedient decisions based on the rapid dissemination of information afforded by mobile advertisements (Martins et al., 2019). The technical capabilities of smartphones represent a significant determinant of the future trajectory of digital marketing. The incorporation of technologies such as NFC and QR codes into smartphones has the potential to further enhance brand engagement with consumers. In addition to serving as a conduit for marketing initiatives, smartphones have emerged as a catalyst for consumer behavior and a conduit for enhanced experiences. In addition to serving as a communication tool for marketers, smartphones also function as an experience platform that influences customer loyalty and purchase behavior (Amirkhanpour et al., 2014).

Consumer Behavior and Mobile Marketing

Attitudes toward mobile advertisements are influenced by multiple factors. Research shows that consumers react negatively to ads they do not approve of but respond favorably to personalized and useful ads, while irrelevant ads are perceived as annoying (Tsang et al., 2004). Location-based strategies in mobile ads, which analyze consumer behavior by time and location, can increase engagement by 19% among potential buyers (Zubcsek et al., 2017). SMS ads offer direct consumer engagement but elicit mixed reactions; positive attitudes arise when SMS content is informative and entertaining, while annoyance leads to negative responses (Shadkam, 2017). Consumer responses vary based on the entertainment and informativeness of ads, with engaging ads improving recall and purchase intent (Aramendia-Muneta & Olarte-Pascual, 2019). Additionally, trust and privacy concerns are crucial; consumers favor ads they perceive as trustworthy and privacy-protective, making trust a key factor in ad acceptance, especially for brands (Davis et al., 2011).

Mobile devices have features that increase users' tendency for impulse purchases. Social media integration in mobile apps makes discovering and quickly buying products easier. A study among Xiaomi users shows that social influence accounts for up to 30% of impulse buys, highlighting the impact of immediate purchasing on mobile devices (Arif & Saputra, 2022). Factors like entertainment and user satisfaction also drive instant purchases; engaging user experiences and interactive interfaces capture attention, making unplanned shopping more likely. One study found that entertainment boosts instant purchases on mobile platforms by 50% (Sari & Laksmidewi, 2021). Social media significantly influences consumer behavior, with 60% of users making immediate purchases when shown personalized ads. Algorithms that display content based on user interests can trigger buying impulses, and users respond well to personalized ads, leading to unplanned buys. The bond consumers form with brands on social media further drives impulse buying (Zafar et al., 2020).

Smartphones, constantly carried by consumers, play a key role in triggering impulse buying. Smartphone addiction is linked to anxiety experienced during device separation, making users more prone to impulsive decisions when holding their devices. This connection between addiction and anxiety strengthens consumers' attachment to smartphones, raising the likelihood of unplanned purchases. Gui et al. (2023) found that individuals with smartphone addiction feel heightened anxiety without access to their devices, spurring impulsive buying. Increased anxiety leads to more smartphone use, especially on social media and e-commerce platforms, making impulsive behavior a crucial factor in marketers' targeting strategies.

Sales promotions and discounts are major factors driving impulse purchases, with 45% of consumers making unplanned buys due to promotional campaigns, especially on e-commerce platforms. On smartphones, fast and attractive offers support quick decision-making, enhancing both brand loyalty and impulse buying behavior (Al Mutanafisa & Retnaningsih, 2021). Discounts and appealing promotions increase consumers' inclination toward quick purchases, bypassing long-term planning. Mobile commerce combines these strategies with convenient access, encouraging immediate purchasing. Mobile marketing taps into consumer psychology and social influences, key drivers of impulse buying, influenced by personal traits, social circles, and the ease of mobile shopping. Social media interactions, for example, often exert social pressure that impacts consumers' buying decisions, shaping mobile commerce strategies.

Mobile shopping platforms simplify product discovery and purchasing. Key factors such as system quality, information quality, and service quality directly impact customer satisfaction. System quality, for instance, contributes 35% to user satisfaction in mobile shopping apps (Chen, 2013). Design features also influence loyalty and purchase intent; optimized, easy-to-use applications boost customer loyalty (Nigam & Amirtharaj, 2018). High-quality user experiences encourage repeat purchases, as seen with Shopee users who spend more time on platforms they enjoy (Berlian & Balqiah, 2019). A study shows that 45% of users keep shopping apps on their phones, increasing their impulse purchase tendency (Kim et al., 2017). Short-form video platforms like TikTok enhance the mobile shopping experience by quickly showcasing products, with content quality positively impacting loyalty (Yang & Lee, 2022). Improved user experiences make e-commerce apps more attractive, as seen in an Indonesian study where enhanced UX increased app attractiveness by 30% (Muslim et al., 2019).

RESEARCH METHOD

This study examines the extant literature on smartphone addiction and digital marketing. The literature review was conducted primarily using scientific articles, reports, and meta-analyses that investigated the phenomenon of smartphone addiction, digital marketing strategies, and their effects on mobile marketing. The studies were selected from academic databases, including Google Scholar, PubMed, and ResearchGate. The sources examined consisted of articles published within the last 10 years and containing the most recent findings on the subject. In this context, the terms "smartphone addiction," "digital marketing," "mobile marketing," and "advertisement" were employed as keywords. To ensure the accuracy of the information obtained from the literature, the validity and reliability of the sources were also taken into consideration.

Data Collection Tools

In the study, the following demographic information was collected from individuals: gender, age, educational status, and income. The data were collected using the Mobile Phone Problematic Use Scale. A total of 674 individuals participated in the research study, which employed a 5-point Likert-type scale to collect data. The scale comprised a total of 20 items, each of which was presented on a 5-point Likert scale. The scale total score, as well as the sub-dimensions of addiction, social relations, and results, were subjected to analysis. The scale was developed for the purpose of measuring the excessive use of mobile phones, the impact of mobile phone use on social relationships, the level of addiction, and the adverse effects of long-term use (Augner & Hacker, 2012). In 2012, the scale was adapted from German to Turkish as part of an adaptation study. With regard to the scoring of the scale, each item in the addiction and social relations section is assigned a value between 0 and 4 points (0 = strongly disagree, 4 = strongly agree), while each item in the results section is scored on a Likert scale ranging from 0 (never) to 4 (very often) points. The total score is obtained by summing the scores assigned to each response. The total score for the entire scale ranges from 0 to 80. A high score on the results section of the scale indicates that the individual is engaging in problematic mobile phone use (Tekin et al., 2014).

Data Analysis

The statistical analysis of the data collected from the scientific study, which included the "Mobile Phone Problematic Use Scale" and demographic information, was examined. In the study, in which data were collected from 674 individuals, descriptive statistics, scale mean, standard deviation values, scale total score, and sub-dimensions of addiction, social relations, and results were compared. Furthermore, correlation analysis was employed to investigate the interrelationships between the sub-dimensions. The initial stage of any scientific study in the social sciences is to observe and make notes on any changes that occur. In the process of transforming data into information, research questions are formulated, hypotheses are established, and models are developed. The planned models are of great importance for the prediction and research to be conducted in a qualified manner. In order for a statistical analysis to be performed in a systematic manner, it is essential that the data in question adhere to a normal distribution. Once this equilibrium has been attained, statistical analyses may then be initiated (Kaya, 2015). In the scientific research, normality tests were conducted, and the data were found to be normally distributed. Prior to commencing the Cronbach's Alpha measurement tool and scale statistical calculations, a normality analysis was conducted to ascertain the reliability of the scale. Ultimately, the study employed multiple regression analysis. Regression analysis is a statistical tool employed in research to examine the relationship between two or more variables. In examining the relationship between two variables, regression analysis is the preferred method. When there are multiple variables, multiple regression analysis is the preferred approach. Multiple linear regression analysis represents the relationship between independent variables and dependent variables through the use of numerical symbols, thereby facilitating a mathematical representation (Çakıcı et al., 2015).

RESULTS

The individuals included in the study were asked a series of questions, comprising 22 items within the scope of the scale. These questions were designed to determine the participants' gender, age, educational status, and income variables. Table 1 display the descriptive statistics, including the demographic information and analysis of test statistics, employed in the research.

The results of the statistical analysis test for the Mobile Phone Problematic Use Scale are presented below. Prior to commencing the statistical analysis, a normality test was conducted on the research data. A normality test is a decision-making method that must be conducted at the outset of the analysis. This is done in order to ascertain which test will be performed, in accordance with the distribution of the data. Parametric tests are employed when the data exhibit a normal distribution, whereas non-parametric tests are utilized when the data do not display a normal distribution. Normality tests are classified into two categories: the Kolmogorov-Smirnov test and the Shapiro-Wilk test (Buskirk et al., 2013). In the event that the number of samples included in the research is 30 or less, the Shapiro-Wilk test is employed; conversely, if the number of samples is 30 or more, the Kolmogorov-Smirnov test is utilized. In this study, the Kolmogorov-Smirnov test was utilized, as the individuals included in the research constituted 674 people, 30 and over.

Table 1. Demographic information descriptive test statistics

Gender	**N**	%
Male	284	42,1
Woman	390	57,9
Total	674	100
Age	**N**	%
13-24	452	67,1
25-36	136	20.9
37-48	48	7,5
49-60	22	3,3
60 and above	8	1,1
Education Status	**N**	%
Primary education	16	2,4
Secondary Education	70	35,9
Licence	392	58,2
Master's Degree	17	2,4

continued on following page

Table 1. Continued

Gender	**N**	**%**
PhD	6	1
Income Status	**N**	**%**
0-17.002	369	54,7
17.003-35.000	159	23,7
35.001-52.000	63	16,3
52.000 and above	25	3,2

When the demographic information of the individuals participating in the study was analysed, it was seen that the ratio of women and men was close to each other. In the age range, it was seen that the majority of the individuals participating in the study were in the 13-24 age group at a rate of 67%. When the descriptive statistics of the educational status were analysed, it was seen that the majority of the participants were at the undergraduate level. In the case of income included in the study as an economic indicator, it was seen that 54% of the density was 0-17.002. According to the density of the age group of the research, it is considered normal that the income is in the range of 0-17.002. In the research, age, educational status and income status appear as a more heterogeneous group than gender. In general, the research population was spread in the 13-24 age range, 0-17.002 education level and undergraduate level.

The normality analysis performed with the Kolmogorov-Smirnov test statistically calculated that the data had a normal distribution ($p>.05$). Results are given in Table 2. The fact that the kurtosis and skewness coefficient values are between (-2, +2) indicates that the distribution is normal (Hair, Black, Babin, Anderson, & Tatham, 2013). As another criterion, the fact that the Z value obtained by dividing the kurtosis and skewness coefficient value of the scores in question by its standard error is between (-1.96,+1.96) is also seen as evidence that the distribution is normal (Howitt & Cramer, 1997). Finally, Kolmogorov-Smirnov (K-S) and Shapiro Wilks (S-W) tests, which determine whether the score distribution in question shows normal distribution characteristics by testing a statistical hypothesis, were used. If the statistical value calculated for these tests was not significant ($p>0.05$), it was assumed that the distribution was normally distributed (Bryman & Cramer, 2001).

Table 2. Normality test for problematic use of mobile phone scale

	Test statistic	s.d	Sig(p.)
Commitment	0.8694	415	0.638
Social Dependency	0.9924	415	0.923
Results	0.7753	415	0.542
Total	1.256	415	0.772

In the Cronbach's Alpha (α) test, in which the reliability test of the scale sub-dimensions and scale total scores were performed, it is seen that the dependency (0.79), social relationship (0.81), results (.78) and finally the scale total scores (0.80), respectively. Results are given in Table 3. With these results, it can be statistically stated that the validity and reliability of the scale is at a sufficient level. When the Cronbach's alpha coefficient test statistics of the original scale and the adapted scale were examined, it was seen that it was calculated between 0.76 and 0.83. Test statistics show that these results are in parallel with the original and adapted scale.

In the analysis of the scale sub-dimensions and total scores for the gender variable of the research, no significant difference was calculated between male and female individuals ($p>.05$). Results are given in Table 4.

Table 3. Internal consistency-Cronbach's alpha test statistics of problematic use of mobile phone scale

Scale	Number of Articles	Cronbach's Alpha(α)
Addiction	7	.79
Social Relationship	7	.81
Results	6	.78
Total	20	.80

In the original scale of the research, a significant difference was found between male and female individuals, but it should be taken into consideration that the gender variable was not homogeneously distributed in the original study and that it was predominantly female, because no significant difference was found in the gender variable in the study in which the research was adapted to Turkish.

Table 4. Examination of total scale score and sub-dimensions according to gender - independent sample t-test

Gender	Centre.	S.S	p.
Male	32.77	10.93	0.554
Woman	31.91	10.02	

In the research, it is seen that the descriptive aggregation is seen as 13-24 years old, which is also reflected in the statistical results. Results are given in Table 5. In particular, it was observed that the age range in which the frequency of mobile phone use is the most common constitutes the majority in the group. In the analysis where the difference between the averages was calculated, a significant difference was calculated according to age ($p<.05$). The age variable, which is an important indicator in many studies, has also taken its place as an important variable in this study, and it was calculated that there was a statistically significant difference between the ages of 13-24, where there is a density.

Table 5. Examination of the total scale score and subscales according to age-one way anova test

Age	Centre.	S.S.	p.
13-24	27.62	8.73	0.047*
25-36	31.01	12.32	
37-48	34.53	11.23	
49-60	28.66	12.02	
60 and above	33.45	9.07	

In the study, educational status, one of the main dimensions of education indicators, was analysed and one-way ANOVA test was conducted to measure significant differences between groups. Results are given in Table 6. When the test statistics were analysed, no significant difference was found according to educational status (p.>05). When the original and adaptation results of the research were analysed, it was calculated that there were no significant differences in the educational status variable. The high literacy rate in our country indicates the importance of educational indicators. It is thought that the concentration of the study at the undergraduate level affected the result of the research.

Table 6. Investigation of total scale score and sub-dimensions according to educational status - one way anova test

Education Status	Centre.	S.S.	p.
Primary education	33.45	9.17	0.166
Secondary Education	34.22	11.91	
Licence	32.09	10.78	
Master's Degree	33.67	11.57	
PhD	34.55	10.76	

In the scientific study in which the intervals determined in today's world where the economic process is fluctuating and constantly changing, no significant differences were found according to income status (p.>05). Results are given in Table 7. It is noteworthy that no significant differences were found in today's world where economic variables are important indicators.

Table 7. Investigation of scale total score and sub-dimensions according to income status - one way anova test

Income Status	Centre.	S.S.	p.
0-17.002	29.22	11.29	0.207
17.003-35.000	30.51	12.54	
35.001-52.000	30.63	11.77	
52.000 and above	29.34	11.76	

In the correlation test in which the relationship test of total scores and sub-dimensions was performed in the research, the results that provide importance in terms of research quality are shown in the Table 8. In the Table, especially the correlation between addiction and social relationship draws attention. In dependency and social relationship, especially strong social relationship is observed to increase dependency, while it is statistically calculated that the total results are highly correlated with the sub-dimensions. Correlation analysis gives us the direction and strength of the relationship between variables. In this analysis, the relationship between total scores, addiction, social relationship and outcomes was calculated. It was statistically calculated that all variables were positive and highly correlated.

Table 8. Correlation analysis test results between scale sub-dimensions and variables

Correlation	Total	Addiction	Social Relationship	Results
Total	1	,782	,816	,732
Addiction	,782	1	,832	,677
Social Relationship	,816	,832	1	,881
Results	,732	,677	,881	1

The literature review shows that smartphone addiction has various effects on psychological, social and physical health. While this addiction causes psychological disorders such as anxiety and depression in individuals, it also causes problems such as sleep disorders and decreased social interactions. Smartphone addiction, which is especially common among young people, increases the risk of anxiety and depression. Social media addiction causes individuals to compare themselves with others, creating a negative self-perception and reinforcing the risk of depression. Research shows that the risk of anxiety and depression is significantly higher in individuals with smartphone addiction.

Smartphone addiction also negatively affects individuals' sleep patterns. Long-term phone use prolongs the time to fall asleep, shortens sleep duration and increases daytime fatigue. Disruption of sleep patterns in young people puts additional pressure on mental health by increasing stress and fatigue levels. In addition to physical health, this addiction also negatively affects social relationships. Smartphone addiction reduces face-to-face communication and the increase in the time spent with digital communication strengthens the feeling of loneliness. Individuals' social support mechanisms weaken and the tendency to move away from face-to-face interactions and turn more towards digital environments increases. Especially among young people, digital platforms are preferred instead of face-to-face communication, which negatively affects the quality of social relations.

A strong link between digital marketing and smartphone addiction has also been observed. Personalised content and location-based notifications via mobile devices attract users' attention and increase mobile shopping behaviours. While social media platforms cause users to become more sensitive to digital marketing content, this situation reinforces smartphone addiction. Mobile marketing strategies target individuals with smartphone addiction, enabling them to spend more time with advertisements and other marketing content. Thus, smartphone addiction stands out as a factor that shapes digital marketing strategies and causes users to stay longer in digital environments.

CONCLUSION AND EVALUATION

This study reveals that smartphone addiction significantly harms individuals' psychological, social, and physical well-being. Excessive smartphone use is linked to mental health issues such as anxiety and depression, and negatively affects quality of life by disrupting sleep patterns. Young people are particularly affected, with social media addiction heightening loneliness and weakening offline relationships and social support networks. Moreover, smartphone addiction amplifies digital marketing effectiveness, as mobile marketing targets those with high addiction levels, maintaining engagement with personalized content. While beneficial for marketers, this cycle reinforces smartphone dependency, impacting public health. Therefore, it is essential to develop policies and educational programs that raise awareness about digital addiction, encouraging a balanced and conscious use of digital tools to minimize negative effects and promote responsible digital engagement.

In the scientific research, the "Problematic Use of Mobile Phone" scale was employed, and the original version, which was written in German and presented to the scientific community by Augner and Hacker, as well as the version that was adapted to Turkish by Tekin, Güneş, and Çolak in 2014, were also included in the research literature. This section presents a comparison of the test statistics derived from both scales, along with an analysis of the observed differences. The use of mobile phones, which represent one of the most significant mass communication tools of the digital age, continues to proliferate. This widespread use has been linked to a range of problematic outcomes. While technological advancements offer numerous advantages and facilitate efficient time management, they also give rise to a range of challenges. The problematic use of mobile phones is included in the study's fundamental principles and objectives, and the dimensions affected by it are examined. Although the telephone has facilitated communication from the moment it entered our lives, its subsequent development has enabled the formation of different dimensions of communication. The mobile phone has become an integral part of our lives, not only as a means of communication but also as a platform for a multitude of applications. One such application is the game, which represents one of the fundamental concepts of human interaction. The game is an entertainment tool that facilitates social interaction. In the contemporary era, mobile phones and other personal and portable digital devices have become ubiquitous in daily life, particularly among younger demographics (Gong & Li, 2008; Sultan et al., 2009). The integration of the mobile phone into this entertainment medium has facilitated a shift in the nature of social interaction. Prior to the advent of the digital age, the majority of games necessitated the physical presence of participants. The advent of the digital age has facilitated the transition of the game from a physical to a digital format, thereby enabling individuals to engage in gameplay without the need for physical proximity.

Upon examination of the test statistics from the research, the variables that should be included in scientific research and that emphasize qualifications were studied. The research examined the impact of gender, age, income, and education status on the observed differences and relationships between groups. Firstly, the normality of the data was assessed using the Kolmogorov-Smirnov test, as the sample size exceeded 30. The test statistics indicated that the data exhibited a normal distribution. Conversely, the validity analysis revealed that the scale exhibited a statistically high level of validity when compared with the results of the original and adapted scales. In our country, where the literacy rate is high, it has been observed that the educational status is concentrated at the undergraduate level. Conversely, in our country, where economic fluctuations are a common occurrence, the agglomeration level is observed to be at its lowest point. It is important to note, however, that the age group range of 13-24, which exhibits agglomerations in the research, encompasses 0-17.002 economic indicators. This phenomenon can be attributed to the fact that individuals are not engaged in any form of employment during the period in which they are engaged in reading activities. The study has demonstrated the necessity of incorporating the employment status (i.e., working or not working in any job) into the research design. The distinction between the groups is also likely to yield informative results in the study. The study revealed no significant differences in problematic mobile phone use based on gender, educational status, or income status, with the exception of age. With regard to the age variable, it is effective to aggregate on a specific group. The scientific study indicates that the problematic use of mobile phones by individuals is influenced by a multitude of factors. Nevertheless, the elevated mean scores indicate that the problematic use of mobile phones among the general population, as represented by the research sample, is currently prevalent at numerous points. The incorporation of a vernacular into scientific inquiry, one that is utilized extensively within society, has led to the estimation that individuals across a spectrum of demographics, including age, socioeconomic status, educational attainment, and gender, exhibit elevated rates of problematic behaviors. The correlation test results indicated a relationship between addiction, social relationships, and results.

Furthermore, the network of social relations has undergone a transformation as a consequence of the increased usage of mobile phones. Marketing communication can be defined as the sharing of a product's total offering with consumers in a manner that assists them in achieving their objectives while simultaneously advancing the organization's own goals (Odabaşı & Oyman, 2007). In the contemporary era, where marketing has assumed diverse forms and technology occupies a central role, it is crucial to consider the intended use of any given technology, as well as its potential benefits to humanity, society, and the future.

In this scientific study, which identified high levels of problematic mobile phone use, it was revealed that social relationships and addiction should be examined in greater depth. Marketing plays an essential role in facilitating healthy communication within society. It has been observed that marketing should be employed in a responsible manner for the benefit of society and the future in today's world, where technology is used in a problematic manner. The advent of mobile technology has facilitated convenient communication, information access, emailing, and document exchange, even when one is not connected to a fixed device, including while on the move. Since the mid-twentieth century, developments in the field of electronics have had a profound impact on social structures. Technological products, including the radio, camera, television, and microcomputer, have constituted a significant portion of this transformation. Of these technological products, the computer has had the most significant impact, particularly in the business sector. In the late 20th century, with the advent of new telecommunication and information technology, the entertainment sector became increasingly integrated with mobile communication and mobile marketing. In the contemporary era, mobile phones are capable of transmitting a multitude of messages to users, including health-related information, results of sporting competitions, news, stock market values, and weather conditions. In addition to these functions, mobile phones are also capable of facilitating communication (Walker et al., 2003).

The relationship between problematic mobile phone use and demographic variables has been examined in scientific research, and the results of this research may be further elaborated in future studies, particularly if scales that determine more psychometric qualities are added to the scale of problematic mobile phone use. Furthermore, an individual's preparedness for communication, perspective, and frequency of use may also provide additional insight into the development of problematic mobile phone situations. In the contemporary era, where marketing has become increasingly mobile and mobile marketing is a rapidly growing phenomenon, it is imperative to examine the nexus between social relations and addiction, particularly in the context of mobile marketing. Shopping is an area in which individuals may become addicted, fulfilling their basic and social needs in the process. In addition to the dimensions of addiction and social relationships, which are frequently cited in studies examining the purpose of mobile phone use, namely, shopping for marketing purposes, it would be beneficial for future scientific research to examine the relationship between mobile phone use and mental health. In a study, the relationship between university students' problematic use of mobile phones and leisure time satisfaction was examined, and a significant negative relationship was identified between the two variables (Akyürek, 2018). In another study on problematic mobile phone use, the relationship between university students' identity development and burnout levels was examined (Pamuk, 2016). Given the importance of this topic, it was necessary to gather demographic information and scales indicating the psychological and psychometric characteristics of individuals.

Solutions and Recommendations

To mitigate the adverse effects of smartphone addiction, a comprehensive approach that integrates public policy, educational initiatives, and technological interventions is essential. Public health campaigns can raise awareness of the risks associated with excessive smartphone use, particularly among young individuals, and underscore the importance of managing screen time. Educational programs in schools can enhance digital literacy and promote balanced smartphone usage by informing students about the potential dangers of social media and smartphone addiction. Furthermore, mobile app developers and digital platforms should assume responsibility by incorporating features that encourage healthy usage, such as reminders to take breaks or limit screen time. Lastly, promoting face-to-face social activities and mindfulness practices can assist individuals in strengthening their offline relationships, thereby reducing the appeal of constant digital interaction.

Future Research Directions

Future research should explore the psychological and social mechanisms by which smartphone addiction impacts mental health, particularly in relation to anxiety, depression, and loneliness. Additionally, studies could investigate how demographic factors - including age, gender, socioeconomic status, and education level - affect susceptibility to smartphone addiction and the effectiveness of digital marketing strategies. Given the growing importance of mobile marketing, it is essential to examine the relationship between smartphone addiction and consumer behavior, with a focus on the ethical implications of targeting vulnerable populations. Furthermore, longitudinal studies could provide valuable insights into the long-term effects of smartphone addiction on personal relationships, academic performance, and overall quality of life, thereby informing policies and interventions aimed at reducing digital dependency and enhancing well-being.

REFERENCES

Abbas, N., Ahmed, T., Shah, S. H. U., Omar, M., & Park, H. (2019). An overview of cyber-physical systems' architecture, applications, and security. *Sensors (Basel)*, *19*(14), 3071. PMID: 31336796

Akyürek, G., Kars, S., & Bumin, G. (2018). Investigation of the relationship between problematic use of mobile phones and leisure satisfaction in university students. *Journal of Occupational Therapy and Rehabilitation*, *6*(3), 191–196.

Akyürek, G., Kars, S., & Bumin, G. (2019). The relationship between mobile phone use and identity development in university students. *Journal of Occupational Therapy and Rehabilitation*, *7*(2), 85–90.

Al-Mansoori, R. S., Al-Thani, D., & Ali, R. (2022). The ethical responsibility of tech companies in addressing digital addiction: A comprehensive review. *Journal of Ethics and Information Technology*, *24*(3), 215–231.

Alrobai, A., Algashami, A., Dogan, H., Corner, T., Phalp, K., & Ali, R. (2019). COPE.er: A community-based platform for digital addiction awareness and support. *Journal of Digital Society and Wellbeing*, *5*(2), 119–134.

Aramendia-Muneta, M. E., & Olarte-Pascual, C. (2019). Understanding consumer attitudes towards advertising: An updated vision. *Marketing Intelligence & Planning*, *37*(6), 700–716.

Arif, D., & Saputra, A. (2022). An investigation of impulsive buying behaviour among smartphone users in Indonesia. *International Journal of Consumer Studies*, *46*(3), 321–330.

Athanasiou, N., Sanford, J., Khan, K. S., & Miotto, K. (2018). Mobile technology addiction: Prevention and treatment with digital literacy programmes. *Journal of Addiction & Prevention*, *9*(4), 42–54.

Attaran, M. (2021). 5G wireless networks and their impact on the IoT and AI-based mobile applications. *Journal of Telecommunications Policy*, *45*(5), 102076.

Augner, C., & Hacker, G. W. (2012). Associations between problematic mobile phone use and psychological parameters in young adults. *International Journal of Public Health*, *5*(2), 437–441. DOI: 10.1007/s00038-011-0234-z PMID: 21290162

Berlian, P., & Balqiah, T. (2019). The impact of customer satisfaction on mobile shopping application loyalty. *Indonesian Journal of Business Management*, *12*(2), 156–165.

Bian, M., & Leung, L. (2015). Linking loneliness, smartphone addiction symptoms, and patterns of smartphone use to social capital. *Social Science Computer Review, 33*(1), 61–79. DOI: 10.1177/0894439314528779

Bryman, A., & Cramer, D. (2001). *Quantitative data analysis: a guide for social scientists*. Routledge.

Buskirk, T. D., Willoughby, L. M., & Tomazic, T. J. (2013). Nonparametric statistical techniques. In Little, T. D. (Ed.), *Statistical analysis* (pp. 106–142). The Oxford handbook of quantitative methods. Oxford University Press.

Çakıcı, M., Oğuzhan, A., & Özdil, T. (2015). *Statistics*. Ekin Basım.

Carah, N. (2020). Targeted advertising and data ethics in digital media. *Media International Australia, 175*(1), 86–99.

Cham, S., Algashami, A., Aldhayan, M., McAlaney, J., Phalp, K., & Almourad, M. B. (2019). Examining the effects of self-control and online experiences on smartphone addiction in the UK. *British Journal of Psychology, 110*(4), 691–714.

Chen, L. Y. (2013). Antecedents of customer satisfaction and purchase intention with mobile shopping system use. *International Journal of Services and Operations Management, 15*(3), 259–274. DOI: 10.1504/IJSOM.2013.054442

Davis, R., Sajtos, L., & Chaudhri, A. (2011). Consumer trust in mobile service advertising. *International Journal of Mobile Communications, 9*(2), 197–210.

Dedov, H., & Komissarova, O. A. (2020). Psychological dependence on mobile gadgets among youth. *Journal of Russian Psychology, 15*(2), 67–79.

Dissing, A., Jørgensen, T., Gerds, T., Rod, N. H., & Lund, R. (2019). The role of smartphone use on mental well-being: A study among young adults in Denmark. *Scandinavian Journal of Public Health, 47*(5), 570–576.

Dwyer, R., Kushlev, K., & Dunn, E. W. (2017). Smartphone use undermines enjoyment of face-to-face social interactions. *Journal of Experimental Social Psychology, 78*(9), 233–239.

Ekeke, J. T. (2016). Cyberpsychology and online behaviour: A look into digital addiction and interventions. *Cyberpsychology, Behavior, and Social Networking, 19*(8), 468–472.

García, C.L., Sánchez Gómez, M.C., & Muñoz-Repiso, A.G. (2022). *Digital literacy and healthy habits: An intervention programme to prevent digital addiction.* Computers in Human Behaviour, 137, Article Number 107475.

Gong, W., & Li, Z. G. (2008). Mobile youth in China: A cultural perspective and marketing implications. *International Journal of Electronic Business*, *6*(3), 261–281. DOI: 10.1504/IJEB.2008.019107

Griffin, C. (2021). The ethics of persuasive technology and its impact on digital addiction. *Ethics and Information Technology*, *23*(3), 417–430.

Gui, D. Y., Dai, Y., Zheng, Z., & Liu, S. (2023). Smartphone addiction and anxiety among college students: A study on mental health consequences. *Journal of Behavioral Addictions*, *12*(2), 231–242.

Hair, J. F., Black, W. C., Babin, B. J., Anderson, R. E., & Tatham, R. L. (2013). *Multivariate data analysis*.

Howitt, D., & Cramer, D. (1997). *A guide to computing statistics with SPSS for Windows*. Prentice Hall.

Ihm, J. (2018). Different degrees of digital inequality: The role of age and social network proximity in smartphone use among older adults. *New Media & Society*, *20*(5), 1775–1794.

Jamalova, M., & Constantinovits, M. (2020). Exploring the mobile phone usage patterns of consumers with different income levels. *International Journal of Mobile Marketing*, *15*(3), 210–225.

Jones, P., & Comfort, D. (2020). Corporate social responsibility and digital addiction: Examining the responsibility of technology firms. *Journal of Public Affairs*, *20*(1), 1965.

Joo, S., Lee, Y., & Kim, H. (2023). Digital literacy and smartphone usage among older adults: Socioeconomic factors and implications. *Technology in Society*, *73*, 102131.

Kadena, E., Qose, S., & Zoltán, R. (2023). 5G technology and national security concerns: The case of European countries. *Journal of European Studies*, *15*(4), 389–403.

Kaya, A. (2015). Model, data and human risks in information systems. *Selçuk University Akşehir Vocational School of Social Sciences Journal*, *2*(6), 1–15.

Khan, R., Kumar, P., Jayakody, D., & Liyanage, M. (2020). A survey on security challenges in 5G networks. *IEEE Communications Surveys and Tutorials*, *22*(3), 1965–1990.

Kim, M., Kim, J., Choi, J., & Trivedi, M. (2017). Mobile shopping through applications: Understanding application possession and mobile purchase. *Journal of Interactive Marketing*, *39*(C), 55–68. DOI: 10.1016/j.intmar.2017.02.001

Krishna, N., Doshi, D., Kulkarni, S., Reddy, M., Srilatha, A., & Satyanarayana, D. (2019). Understanding mobile phone addiction and its impact on family interactions. *Family Medicine & Primary Care Review*, *8*(4), 1051–1055.

Luo, X., & Hu, C. (2022). Loneliness and sleep disturbance among first-year college students: The sequential mediating effect of attachment anxiety and mobile social media dependence. *Psychology in the Schools*, *59*(9), 1776–1789. DOI: 10.1002/pits.22721

Martins, J., Costa, C., Oliveira, T., Gonçalves, R., & Branco, F. (2019). How smartphone advertising influences consumers' purchase intention. *Journal of Business Research*, *94*(1), 327–336. DOI: 10.1016/j.jbusres.2017.12.047

Matar Boumosleh, J., & Jaalouk, D. (2017). Depression, anxiety, and smartphone addiction in university students-A cross sectional study. *PLoS One*, *12*(8), 0182239. DOI: 10.1371/journal.pone.0182239 PMID: 28777828

Mockel, P., & Makala, B. (2019). Using AI in mobile health apps: Opportunities and challenges. *Journal of Healthcare Informatics Research*, *8*(3), 225–239.

Moqbel, M., Nevo, S., & Nah, F. F. H. (2023). Unveiling the dark side in smartphone addiction: Mediation of strain and moderation of hedonic use on well-being. *Internet Research*, *33*(1), 12–38. DOI: 10.1108/INTR-01-2021-0003

Morra, L., Mohanty, S., & Lamberti, F. (2020). AI-based recommendation systems for e-commerce: The impact on consumer behaviour. *Journal of Electronic Commerce Research*, *21*(2), 115–129.

Morton, K., Dennison, L., Bradbury, K., Band, R., May, C., Raftery, J., Little, P., McManus, R., & Yardley, L. (2018). Promoting digital detox among university students through awareness campaigns. *Digital Health Journal*, *4*(1), 1–15.

Muench, C., Feulner, L., Muench, R., & Carolus, A. (2020). Time to log off: The impact of digital detox programmes on digital addiction symptoms. *Journal of Behavioral Addictions*, *9*(3), 644–655.

Muslim, E., Moch, B. N., Wilgert, Y., Utami, F.F., & Indriyani, D. (2019). User interface redesign of e-commerce platform mobile application (Kudo) through user experience evaluation to increase user attraction. *IOP Conference Series: Materials Science and Engineering,* 508, Artcile Number 012030.

Navarro-Ortiz, J., Romero-Díaz, P., Sendra, S., Ameigeiras, P., Ramos-Muñoz, J., & López-Soler, J. M. (2020). A comprehensive survey on 5G communications. *IEEE Access : Practical Innovations, Open Solutions*, *22*(2), 905–929.

Nigam, P., & Amirtharaj, P. (2018). Role of mobile applications quality and smartphones attributes in online shopping. *Jaipuria International Journal of Management Research*, *7*(2), 45–57.

Nowland, R., Necka, E. A., & Cacioppo, J. T. (2018). Loneliness and social internet use: Pathways to reconnection in a digital world? *Perspectives on Psychological Science*, *13*(1), 70–87. DOI: 10.1177/1745691617713052 PMID: 28937910

Odabaşı, Y., & Oyman, M. (2007). *Marketing communication management*. MediaCat.

Pamuk, M., Kutlu, M., & Kuloğlu, A. (2016, November). *Problematic use of mobile phone and student burnout in university students* [Paper presentation]. *International Academic Research Congress*, Antalya, Turkey.

Prodanova, J., & Chopdar, P. K. (2023). Mobile shopping personalisation and its impact on consumer engagement. *Journal of Retailing and Consumer Services*, *67*(1), 102916.

Rotondi, V., Stanca, L., & Tomasuolo, M. (2017). Connecting alone: Smartphone use, quality of social interactions, and well-being. *Journal of Economic Psychology*, *63*(1), 17–26. DOI: 10.1016/j.joep.2017.09.001

Salehan, M., & Negahban, A. (2013). Social media addiction among users: A study of Facebook and its effects on lifestyle. *Journal of Information Systems*, *27*(3), 129–141.

Sari, K., & Laksmidewi, D. (2021). Impulsive buying behaviour in mobile commerce: The influence of hedonic motivation and purchase intentions. *Asia Pacific Journal of Marketing and Logistics*, *33*(4), 1243–1261.

Satterfield, D., & Abel, T. D. (2020). The evolving role of AI in voice assistants: A study of consumer satisfaction with Siri, Google Assistant, and Alexa. *The Journal of Consumer Research*, *47*(3), 571–587.

Sultan, F., & Rohm, A. J. (2005). The coming era of 'brand in the hand' marketing. *MIT Sloan Management Review*, *47*(1), 83–90.

Tekin, C., Güneş, G., & Colak, C. (2014). Adaptation of problematic mobile phone use scale to Turkish: a validity and reliability study: a validity and reliability study]. *Medicine Science*, *3*(3), 1361–1381. DOI: 10.5455/medscience.2014.03.8138

Walker, O., Boyd, H., & Mullis, J. (2003). *Marketing strategy a decision focused approach*. McGraw-Hill-Irvin Publication.

ADDITIONAL READING

Demirci, K., Akgönül, M., & Akpinar, A. (2015). Relationship of smartphone use severity with sleep quality, depression, and anxiety in university students. *Journal of Behavioral Addictions, 4*(2), 85–92. DOI: 10.1556/2006.4.2015.010 PMID: 26132913

Dwyer, R. J., Kushlev, K., & Dunn, E. W. (2017). Smartphone use undermines enjoyment of face-to-face social interactions. *Journal of Experimental Social Psychology, 78*, 233–239. DOI: 10.1016/j.jesp.2017.10.007

Elhai, J. D., Levine, J. C., Dvorak, R. D., & Hall, B. J. (2017). Non-social features of smartphone use are most related to depression, anxiety and problematic smartphone use. *Computers in Human Behavior, 69*, 75–82. DOI: 10.1016/j.chb.2016.12.023

Gong, W., & Li, Z. G. (2008). Mobile youth in China: A cultural perspective and marketing implications. *International Journal of Electronic Business, 6*(3), 261–281. DOI: 10.1504/IJEB.2008.019107

Griffin, C. (2021). The ethics of persuasive technology and its impact on digital addiction. *Ethics and Information Technology, 23*(3), 417–430.

Horvath, J. (2020). Structural brain alterations and their association with smartphone addiction. *Psychiatry Research: Neuroimaging, 303*, 111134.

Kwon, M., Kim, D. J., Cho, H., & Yang, S. (2013). The smartphone addiction scale: Development and validation of a short version for adolescents. *PLoS One, 8*(12), e83558. DOI: 10.1371/journal.pone.0083558 PMID: 24391787

Lin, Y. H., Chiang, C.-L., Lin, P.-H., Chang, L.-R., Ko, C.-H., Lee, Y.-H., & Lin, S.-H. (2016). Proposed diagnostic criteria for smartphone addiction. *PLoS One, 11*(11), e0163010. DOI: 10.1371/journal.pone.0163010 PMID: 27846211

Martins, J., Costa, C., Oliveira, T., Gonçalves, R., & Branco, F. (2019). How smartphone advertising influences consumers' purchase intention. *Journal of Business Research, 94*, 327–336. DOI: 10.1016/j.jbusres.2017.12.047

Panova, T., & Carbonell, X. (2018). Is smartphone addiction really an addiction? *Journal of Behavioral Addictions, 7*(2), 252–259. DOI: 10.1556/2006.7.2018.49 PMID: 29895183

Persaud, A., & Azhar, I. (2012). Innovative mobile marketing via smartphones: Are consumers ready? *Marketing Intelligence & Planning, 30*(4), 418–443. DOI: 10.1108/02634501211231883

Sohn, S. Y. (2019). Prevalence of problematic smartphone usage: A systematic review and meta-analysis. *PLoS One*, *14*(3), e0213734.

Tong, S., Luo, X., & Xu, B. (2020). Personalized mobile marketing strategies: An integrative framework and future research directions. *Journal of the Academy of Marketing Science*, *48*(1), 48–69. DOI: 10.1007/s11747-019-00693-3

KEY TERMS AND DEFINITIONS

Smartphone Addiction: This term refers to the compulsive and excessive use of smartphones that has the potential to interfere with an individual's daily life, thereby causing emotional, social, and cognitive disruptions.

Digital Marketing: Digital marketing is defined as the practice of promoting products or services through online channels, such as mobile applications and social media platforms. This marketing strategy is distinguished by its emphasis on personalized consumer engagement, leveraging technology to target specific audiences and customize marketing messages to them.

Marketing Communication: This term refers to the adaptation and dissemination of communication strategies across various channels, including mobile and digital platforms, in order to promote brands, products, and services.

Mobile Marketing: Marketing practices that target consumers via smartphones and tablets, using tactics such as personalized notifications, app-based offers, and geolocation strategies.

Impulse Buying: Impulse buying is defined as the act of making a spontaneous and unplanned purchase. This phenomenon is heavily influenced by mobile advertisements and app-based marketing.

Social Isolation: The phenomenon of social isolation is characterized by the weakening of real-life social bonds and an increase in feelings of loneliness due to excessive reliance on smartphone communication.

Youth Vulnerability: The elevated probability of developing smartphone addiction among adolescents and young adults is attributable to neurodevelopmental and behavioral factors.

Chapter 13
Reproduction of Television Serires on Social Media

Abdulkadir Cabuk
https://orcid.org/0000-0003-1249-4506
Üsküdar Üniversitesi, Turkey

Esennur Sirer
Independent Researcher, Turkey

ABSTRACT

This study examines the reproduction of television series on social media, focusing on how audiences participate in the transformation of narrative elements, character developments, and thematic interpretations. By drawing upon theoretical frameworks such as Jenkins' participatory culture, Toffler's concept of the "prosumer," and Terranova's insights into free labor in digital economies, the research seeks to elucidate the socio-cultural and economic dimensions of this phenomenon. It explores how users, through activities such as meme creation, fan fiction writing engages in practices that blur the lines between production and consumption, thereby contributing to the life cycle and cultural significance of television series beyond their original broadcasts. Understanding the mechanisms behind this digital reproduction is crucial, not only for comprehending contemporary media consumption patterns but also for recognizing the broader shifts in cultural production in the digital age.

DOI: 10.4018/979-8-3373-1957-5.ch013

INTRODUCTION

With the spread of television, the first attempts at series began to appear in the 1940s. In the 1950s, television series began to become increasingly popular in the United States. *I Love Lucy* (1951) was one of the most famous series of this period and was a major production that shaped the format of television series (Boddy, 1990). In the 1960s, television series began to diversify more. During this period, cult series such as *The Twilight Zone* and *Star Trek* appeared (Anderson, 2008).

The 1970s saw series such as *All in the Family* and *MASH** and the introduction of television productions that dealt with more social and political themes (Anderson, 2008). The late 1980s and early 1990s are considered the golden age of television series. Popular series such as *Friends*, *The X-Files*, *The Simpsons*, and *Seinfeld* have cemented the cultural influence of television (Gray, 2006). In the 1990s, a large number of quality series began to be broadcast, and series began to reach large audiences (McCabe & Akass, 2007). From the early 2000s, premium channels (such as HBO, Showtime) began to make a name for themselves with quality series. With series such as *The Sopranos*, *The Wire*, and *Breaking Bad*, television series have become cinema-quality productions (McCabe & Akass, 2007). In the same period, web series and digital platforms began to rise. Platforms such as Netflix and Hulu have had great success with their own original series (Tryon, 2013). By the 2010s, digital platforms such as Netflix, Amazon Prime, and Disney+ have made television series more accessible. These platforms have produced TV shows and movies that appeal to a global audience. In addition, online viewing habits have become a factor shaping the future of traditional television (Tryon, 2013).

Television and TV series have undergone a great evolution over time. Television, which started with black-and-white and limited broadcasting options at first, has experienced a great transformation with color broadcasts, cable and satellite systems, digitalization and broadcasting over the internet. The series, on the other hand, started with simple stories at first, but over time they were enriched with more complex, in-depth characters and turned into a global media phenomenon. Today, streaming services have ushered in a new era in the evolution of series. The history of television and TV series sheds light on cultural and social changes in parallel with technological developments.

HISTORY OF TELEVISION

The foundations of television were laid with the first experiments that began to be made in the 1920s. The first television signal was sent by Philo Farnsworth in 1927, and this was a critical step for the future of television. At the same time, other scientists, such as John Logie Baird, were working on the mechanical systems of television. In the 1930s, television began to become more tangible. In 1936, the BBC began making regular television broadcasts in London (Aziz, 1981). In the same years, television broadcasts were started in the USA. However, the fact that television reaches large masses of people, 2. It was not possible until after World War II. From the mid-1950s, televisions were developed to broadcast in color and began to become popular rapidly. The U.S. began its first color television broadcast in 1954. In the 1960s, television began to become the main source of entertainment in the home. In the 1970s, cable television and satellite systems began to become widespread. In this way, television viewers were faced with more channel and content options. The 1980s, in particular, were marked by the diversification of the television industry. Since the early 2000s, digital television and streaming platforms (Netflix, YouTube, etc.) have changed the traditional structure of television. Smart televisions, internet connections, and digital broadcasting have transformed television viewing habits.

In Türkiye, the history of television begins with the first broadcast made with Istanbul Technical University in 1952 under the leadership of Professor Mustafa Santur. This publication, which started in 1952, continued with intermittent interruptions until 1971 (Öngören, 1972, p. 274-27; akt. Emir, 2019). However, the channel-based broadcast started on January 31, 1968, at TRT Ankara Television's Mithatpaşa Studio with the opening speech of Mahmut Tali Öngören (trt.net, 2022). In 1968, the first year of its establishment, TRT broadcast three days a week (Tuesday-Thursday-Friday). With the agreement made between TRT and ITU in 1971, television broadcasting in Türkiye was left to TRT (Yengin, 1994).

When Turkish television is evaluated in terms of content, it is possible to say that fictional content, especially television series, is the most preferred genre by both channels and viewers. In television series, where the television audience finds something from itself, they can also find problems close to their own problems and solutions close to it. Türkoğlu (2010) states that the representation needs of people who have difficulty in expressing themselves in society are met through series such as Perihan Abla, Super Baba and Second Spring, which are broadcast in Prime Time. In such series, various segments of society such as urban, peasant, rich and poor are represented. Again, the venues are chosen in accordance with this representation. Thus, it is ensured that the audience always finds something from themselves. The effect of the characters in the series on the audience and the intertwining of the story told with real life can be explained by the fact that this format is very suitable for the structural features of television, making it easier for the audience to connect. Gerbner (1998) states that the style of television content is realism and makes viewers feel as if they are a part of television. With the characters and events in the television series, the individual has information about the world he is in by encountering changing human relations, problems and definitions.

As of 2022, it is possible to say that television is a powerful mass communication tool in Türkiye and maintains its popularity. Turkish television, which is one of the televisions with the highest number of channels in the world, is a mass communication tool that the Turkish society follows with interest. According to TİAK Television Viewing Measurement Yearbook (2020), the average television viewing time in the world is 2 hours and 54 minutes, while it is 4 hours and 43 minutes in Türkiye. At the same time, television viewing times are increasing every year both in the world and in Türkiye.

Television was initially broadcast with an analog system. However, since analog broadcasts offered limited bandwidth, they led to limitations in terms of quality and a large number of channels. Since the late 1990s, the first steps of the transition to digital publishing have been taken around the world. Digital broadcasting is a system in which digital signals are used instead of analog signals. Digital television offers higher resolution picture and sound quality, providing viewers with a clearer experience (Federal Communications Commission [FCC], 2009). In addition, digital signals allow for more channels and higher quality content. The 2000s were a time when digital television broadcasts began to spread rapidly. Countries have started the process of transitioning from analog broadcasting to digital broadcasting. In 2009, Europe completely ended analogue broadcasting and switched to digital broadcasting (European Commission, 2010). Likewise, the U.S. introduced digital television broadcasts in 2009 and gradually phased out analog broadcasting (FCC, 2009).

One of the great innovations that digital television provided was that it offered images in higher resolution. This became possible with the advent of HD television (Lotz, 2014). From the mid-2000s, HD televisions were introduced, and these televisions offered much sharper, clearer, and more detailed images than the older CRT televisions. HD broadcasting has given us the opportunity to offer more channels and content (Uricchio, 2009). In the early 2010s, 4K televisions began to become popular. 4K offers four times the resolution of HD resolution, providing viewers with much clearer and more vivid images. 8K resolution, on the other hand, is a technology that is expected to become more widespread in the future, as the highest resolution level for now.

IPTV is a system that allows television broadcasts to reach the audience as data packets over the internet. This technology has gone beyond traditional television broadcasting, making it possible to offer viewers interactive features and content based on personal preferences (Cisco Systems, 2017).

One of the most important developments in the digitalization process is the rise of streaming services that provide the ability to watch series, movies and television programs over the internet. From the late 2000s, platforms such as Netflix, Hulu,

Amazon Prime Video, and Disney+ gained immense popularity. These services have changed traditional television viewing habits and offered viewers the opportunity to watch on-demand content. One of the most important developments in the digitalization process is the rise of streaming services that provide the ability to watch series, movies and television programs over the internet. From the late 2000s, platforms such as Netflix, Hulu, Amazon Prime Video, and Disney+ gained immense popularity. These services have changed traditional television viewing habits and offered viewers the opportunity to watch on-demand content.

The popularization of OTT (Over-The-Top) TVs has also caused some changes in viewing practices. With the advent of digital platforms, the concept of overwatching, which is a monitoring practice, has begun to be addressed. Compared to the old TV, this new TV is fast, smart and dynamic. The viewer is able to download content and pay for all these features (Jenner, 2015). OTT TVs have gained popularity because they offer many features that traditional television does not have and are accessible despite subscription fees. The fact that the number of Netflix subscribers is 231 million is another indicator of this popularity (statista.com, 2023). With OTT TVs, a new viewing practice has emerged. A new monitoring practice, 'binge watching', is also subject to some criticism. Gold, Frost-Pineda and Jacobs say that in the psychology and medical literature, bing watching is thought of as an addiction and that the reason why the viewer puts himself into this viewing practice is 'the desire to escape from reality'. Psychologists see this behavior as 'doing too much in a short time' and define excessive eating and drinking behaviors with concepts such as 'binge eating' and 'binge drinking'. (Schewidel, A, & Moe, W, 2014). This viewing practice, which comes with OTT TVs, is criticized as a kind of 'addiction'.

TRADITIONAL TELEVISION AND VIEWER EXPERIENCE

Since the middle of the 20th century, television has been one of the most important tools of social memory and cultural production. Television programs, which reach the audience at certain times depending on the broadcast flow, met with the audience over the weekly broadcast rhythm and certain time periods when they were set up in series format. This traditional publishing structure was based on the control of content by a central authority and a one-way communication model. While the viewers were passive consumers in front of the screen, the series producers presented the content unilaterally. As television became more prevalent, patterns of indoor social interaction began to shift accordingly. Families who used to gather around the radio turned to this new media tool with the spread of television, and a significant part of the time spent at home was devoted to watching television. Especially in the second half of the 20th century, television has become one of the main tools that meet the need for news and entertainment, and television programs have created a common viewing ritual for family members (McQuail, 2010).

Traditional television has evolved various types of content over time. News bulletins, entertainment programs, series, documentaries and sports broadcasts have become among the main formats of television. In particular, news bulletins have been an important communication tool with the power to form public opinion. Important events of the 20th century, such as the moon landing, the fall of the Berlin Wall, and the Gulf War, were followed live on television screens by millions of people (Williams, 1974). Thus, television has become a platform where social events and crises are widely watched, beyond being just a means of entertainment.

One of the most important features of traditional television is that it is based on program streaming. Viewers had to go to the screen at the specified time to watch a certain program. This has been instrumental in shaping daily routines (Lotz, 2014). Especially the evening hours, which are called prime-time, have come to the fore as the time period when television watching habits are the most intense. However, one disadvantage of this structure is that viewers have limited freedom in their choice of content. Since traditional television broadcasts the programs it offers to viewers according to a predetermined stream, individuals were limited in choosing content according to their own preferences (McQuail, 2010).

The television viewer experience has changed in line with technological developments. The invention of the remote control has influenced viewer behavior by facilitating the process of changing channels. In addition, video recorders have made the experience offered by television more flexible by allowing viewers to record programs and watch them whenever they want (Ellis, 2000). However, traditional television has survived as a model that requires viewers to adapt to the flow of programs.

Television advertising is another important factor that affects the viewer experience. Advertisements have occupied an important place as the main source of income for television channels. In the traditional television model, advertisements placed between programs interrupted the viewer experience but also influenced consumer behavior (Lotz, 2014). Thanks to advertisements, brands have had the opportunity to reach large audiences and television has become of great importance as a marketing tool. This situation has also caused television programs to be shaped in line with the expectations of advertisers.

The impact of traditional television on the viewer experience has also led to a change in viewing habits in a societal context. Although television is seen as a tool that brings family members together, it has also spread individual viewing habits over time (Briggs & Burke, 2010). Especially with the development of multi-channel systems and the placement of televisions in more than one room in homes, individual television viewing practices have increased. As a result, television has become a part of both common and individual consumption. However, the traditional television viewer experience has undergone a significant transformation with the development of digital technologies. Since the beginning of the 21st century, the spread of the internet has changed viewer preferences and created an alternative to the traditional model of television (Lotz, 2014). Video streaming platforms, on-demand content services, and media accessible on mobile devices have made the experience offered by traditional television more personalized. This has affected television viewership and sparked debate about the future of traditional broadcasting.

As a result, traditional television has played a decisive role in mass communication for many years and has shaped the viewer experience. While the program streaming-based model has made television a ritual, technological innovations have changed viewing habits. Although the impact of traditional television on the audience has decreased with digitalization, television still exists as an important media tool. Given these changes, the future of television will be reshaped depending on audience expectations and technological developments.

DEFINITION AND HISTORY OF SOCIAL MEDIA

Social media is online spaces where people can share, comment, like, and react to each other's posts of various types of media such as text, photos, videos, audio, etc. Social media is a powerful tool that enables not only personal interactions but also for businesses, brands, and organizations to communicate with their target audience.

The foundations of the concept of social media date back to the 1960s when the internet was first developed. The development of the ARPANET and newsgroups such as Usenet in the 1980s made it easier for people to share and discuss information (Rheingold, 1993). In the mid-1990s, the first social platforms such as GeoCities and TheGlobe.com emerged, where people began to create their own web pages and interact with communities (Boyd & Ellison, 2007).

With the 2000s, social media platforms have become more advanced and started to appeal to a large audience. Important platforms such as LinkedIn in 2003, Facebook in 2004, YouTube in 2005 and Twitter in 2006 emerged (Kaplan & Haenlein, 2010). These platforms have radically changed the role of the internet in mass communication, enabling users to become active content producers.

Facebook was founded in 2004 by Mark Zuckerberg and his friends at Harvard University. Facebook, which initially catered only to university students, soon gained popularity all over the world and became one of the social media giants (Kirkpatrick, 2010). Over time, Facebook has transformed the world of social media by introducing a range of features, such as the ability for users to add friends, share photos and content, create groups, and interact with the business community.

Founded in 2005, YouTube has become the pioneer of video-sharing platforms. Users could upload, watch, comment, and share videos with others here. YouTube has quickly become the world's largest video-sharing platform and has been a part of the digital media revolution (Burgess & Green, 2018).

Twitter was founded in 2006 and allowed users to share short messages with 140 characters (currently 280 characters). This platform has become a medium where news spreads quickly and the public can share their thoughts instantly (Murthy, 2018).

Instagram was founded in 2010 as a platform for sharing photos and short videos. It attracted a lot of attention with its photo editing and instant sharing features. It was acquired by Facebook in 2012 and grew rapidly (Leaver, Highfield, & Abidin, 2020).

With the widespread use of smartphones, social media platforms have started to focus on mobile compatibility. Platforms such as Instagram in 2010, Snapchat in 2011, and TikTok in 2016 have popularized new forms of content, such as short video formats and story sharing (Zulli & Zulli, 2020). Furthermore, artificial intelligence and algorithms play an important role in personalizing the social media feed (Gillespie, 2018).

Social media is a phenomenon that is discussed with both positive and negative effects. It has positive aspects such as facilitating access to information and bringing different communities together (Shirky, 2011). However, problems such as the spread of fake news, privacy issues, and digital addiction have also come with it.

The future of social media will become more diversified with artificial intelligence-supported algorithms, virtual reality and blockchain-based platforms. A period in which user experiences are more personalized and data privacy becomes more important awaits us (Van Dijck, 2013).

In conclusion, the evolution of social media from early internet communities to today's algorithm-driven, mobile-compatible platforms reflects not only technological progress but also profound changes in how people communicate, interact, and construct digital identities. As social media continues to develop, its impact on society will remain a dynamic and critical field of study.

CULTURAL IMPACT OF MEDIA

In the traditional media era, series productions were carried out by large production companies and state-sponsored broadcasters. This structure also reflected a certain status quo in economic and cultural terms. The series were effective in reinforcing the values, norms and ideologies that were in the collective memory of the society. In addition, the collective viewing experience that occurred during the series broadcasts created a common language between family members and the social environment. People shared the excitement and emotional charge of the series, creating shared experiences that were symbolic of social cohesion. However, the limitations of the traditional broadcasting model, especially the lack of audience interaction and instant feedback, have revealed the necessity of digital transformation over time. The need for viewers to share their instant comments and criticisms of the content has been one of the factors that have increased the importance of social media in the reproduction process of television series.

The cultural impact of the media contributes to the formation of cultural identities by reaching large audiences, especially through television, radio, newspapers and digital platforms. For example, television series and movies help viewers internalize societal norms and values (Hall, 1997). Cultural narratives are disseminated through media content, and this brings about a process of cultural change on a national and global scale (Silverstone, 1999).

The media also has an important role in the creation of cultural identity. While national television channels and local media outlets produce content to reinforce a particular cultural identity, global media platforms increase the interaction between different cultures (Morley & Robins, 1995). In this context, the media has a contradictory effect on both cultural homogenization and the preservation of cultural diversity.

Advertising and popular culture products are also important components of the cultural impact of the media. Especially with globalization, the media has established a western-centered cultural hegemony and has a dominant influence on local cultural elements (Tomlinson, 1999). For example, Hollywood movies and American TV series have had an impact on local values by determining the cultural consumption habits of individuals in different countries (Baudrillard, 1981).

The rise of digital media and the internet has changed cultural interactions and individual forms of expression. Social media platforms provide a more democratic structure compared to traditional media tools by providing the opportunity for individuals to create and share their own cultural identities (Jenkins, 2006). However, the management of these platforms by global companies has also led to the formation of a great control mechanism over digital culture (Manovich, 2001).

The cultural influence of the media is also evident in areas such as language use, fashion, music and art. Especially young people adopt different cultural currents by being influenced by media content, and these trends accelerate the transformation process of local cultures (Storey, 2018). For example, the globalization of hip-hop music has created a common cultural bond between young people in different countries (Mitchell, 2001).

As a result, the media is one of the most important forces shaping cultural dynamics. It functions as a tool that determines the identities, values, and lifestyles of individuals on both a local and global scale. The cultural impact of the media is in a constant process of change and transformation, and it is becoming more evident with technological developments and digitalization. In this process, individuals' development of critical media literacy stands out as an important factor in understanding the cultural effects of media content.

AUDIENCE ENGAGEMENT ON SOCIAL MEDIA

Social media has redefined the relationship between television series and the audience. Viewers can instantly participate in discussions on social media during or after the broadcast of series episodes, and share their comments on the characters and plot. This situation has also attracted the attention of series producers and media institutions, and plans have started to be made to take social media interaction into account in content strategies.

Especially on platforms such as Twitter, "live tweet" events play an important role in seeing the instant reactions of the audience communities and creating discussions about the series in line with these reactions (Highfield & Leaver, 2016). Viewers can instantly share their feelings, expectations, and criticisms about the series with the tweets they send during the episodes; this creates a basis for a collective discussion (Deller, 2011). Facebook groups, Reddit, and other forum platforms have become the sites where more in-depth analysis, theories, and fan theories are produced (Booth, 2010).

Various social media tools and platforms used in the digital reproduction of series are at the center of this process. The unique characteristics and user base of each platform allow sequences to be reproduced in different forms:

- **Twitter (X):** The short and instant sharing format allows reactions to spread quickly during the episode. Thanks to hashtags and the tagging system, communities of viewers are centered around specific topics.
- **Facebook:** Group and page structures are the sites for more in-depth discussions, fan theories, and alternative narratives. The ability of users to write long articles makes it possible to deepen sequence analysis and interpretations.
- **Instagram:** This visually-heavy platform stands out in the sharing of cutaways, illustrations and short video clips from the series. The Story feature provides an ideal environment for series instant announcements and visual feedback.
- **YouTube:** Unlike traditional media intermediaries, YouTube provides an environment where users can create their own content and interact with other users. Unlike traditional television broadcasting, creating content on YouTube does not require large production teams or technical infrastructure (Jenkins, 2006). Individual broadcasters, bloggers, companies, and academic

institutions use YouTube for various purposes, such as entertainment, education, news, and marketing (Van Dijck, 2013). Users create new content by remaking existing videos or editing them from a different perspective. For example, it is common to rearrange movie scenes to give them a new meaning or create parodies of popular videos (Lobato, 2016). Another common form of reproduction on YouTube is reaction videos. A user watches an existing video, comments, reacts, and presents it as new content (Burgess & Green, 2018). The academic or critical examination, analysis, and presentation of existing content to offer new information also fall within the scope of reproduction. News channels and independent journalists revisiting current events with their own commentary and presenting news videos from different perspectives are also considered part of this category.

- **TikTok:** With its short, fast-paced video format, it allows for humorous reinterpretation of sequence scenes, lines, and character traits.
- **Twitch:** Twitch is primarily known for video game streaming, but it has become an increasingly important platform for co-viewing TV series, hosting reaction sessions, and live fan discussions. Users are both viewers and performers, engaging with audiences through real-time chat interactions. This live engagement dynamic represents a heightened form of prosumerism, where the boundary between performer and spectator collapses (Taylor, 2018).

Each of these platforms can be considered as areas where different narrative techniques are used in the reproduction of the series narrative and audience participation emerges in various ways. Thanks to digital tools, viewers can make creative interventions on the content of the series, both individually and collectively, thus creating new cultural products beyond the original narrative.

Digital Audience Behavior and Participatory Culture

Digital audience behavior refers to the ways in which viewers interact with media content, which emerged with the rise of the internet and digital media platforms. Unlike traditional media consumption behaviors, these behaviors are shaped by viewers transitioning from being passive recipients to active participants.

The foundations of participatory culture are extensively discussed in Henry Jenkins' work Convergence Culture. Jenkins explains that participatory culture refers to the involvement of users in content creation and interpretation processes, and this involvement creates new dynamics in media production. Digital media allows for content to be produced not only by media companies and professional content creators but also by individuals. As a result, media content becomes a process of production and reproduction (Jenkins, 2006). With the influence of participatory culture, viewers no longer just passively consume content but also reinterpret and modify it, creating their own perspectives and cultural meanings.

Another significant factor in the emergence of participatory culture is the accessibility of media technologies. The widespread reach of digital technologies has made content production more common. Now, every individual, with a smartphone and an internet connection, can produce content and reach a global audience. This has particularly allowed communities, which previously lacked the means to produce content in the media field, to amplify their voices. Communities leveraging the power of participatory culture have contributed to societal and cultural change processes through social media and have raised issues that traditional media outlets often ignored (Benkler, 2006).

One of the most distinctive features of digital viewers is their flexibility in content consumption. Instead of watching programs aired at specific times on traditional media channels, digital platform users can access content whenever they want (Anderson, 2006). This shift has emphasized individual preferences and increased the importance of algorithms and personalized recommendation systems. For example, video streaming platforms analyze users' viewing habits to offer personalized content recommendations (Van Dijck, 2013).

Moreover, multi-screen viewing habits also play a significant role in digital audience behavior. Today, many people browse social media on their smartphones or tablets while watching television (Carr, 2010). This multi-screen usage has forced brands and content creators to develop new marketing strategies. The advertising sector, taking this trend into account, has developed content strategies aiming to reach their target audiences more effectively and directly (McQuail, 2010).

The attention spans of digital viewers also show significant differences when compared to traditional media. In the fast-flowing information age, viewers are more inclined toward short and concise content rather than long-duration media (Hargittai & Hinnant, 2008). Social media platforms have responded to this need with short videos and story formats. Especially platforms like TikTok, Instagram Reels, and YouTube Shorts have gained popularity due to their ability to provide maximum information or entertainment in a short time (Lobato, 2019).

Interaction and participation are also key factors that shape digital audience behavior. While viewers were passive consumers in traditional media, they have transformed into active participants in the digital world (Livingstone, 2004). Users not only consume content but also play more active roles in the media world by commenting, sharing, and creating content. Social media platforms offer various tools for users to voice their opinions and engage directly with brands (Baym, 2010). This creates both an opportunity and a challenge for brands and media organizations.

Digital viewers also place great importance on the quality and reliability of content. Particularly in information-based content, platforms that present false or misleading information can quickly lose trust (Sundar, 2008). Therefore, digital media providers must carefully assess their content for accuracy. Additionally, content's aesthetic and technical professionalism is a significant factor in capturing viewers' interest (Couldry, 2012).

Demographic characteristics and cultural differences of digital viewers are also important aspects that content creators must consider. Digital content, accessible globally, must address various age groups, geographical regions, and cultural backgrounds (Jenkins, 2009). Therefore, understanding the audience and providing content tailored to their expectations is considered a cornerstone of a successful digital strategy.

Digital audience behavior is characterized by a constantly changing dynamic, and understanding this change is crucial for content creators, marketers, and media organizations. With technological advancements, viewers' expectations and habits will continue to evolve, and the digital media world will have to adapt (Napoli, 2011). In the digital environment, content is shaped according to users' usage patterns. The development of algorithms and AI-driven recommendation systems has changed media consumption by offering personalized content to viewers (Napoli, 2011). Platforms like YouTube, Netflix, and Spotify analyze users' viewing habits to provide recommendations. This shapes viewer behavior and increases media consumption based on individual preferences. However, the "filter bubble" and "echo chamber" effects created by algorithms have drawn attention; this phenomenon can result in viewers being exposed only to content that supports their own beliefs (Pariser, 2011).

Furthermore, personalized content consumption may highlight specific content while pushing other content into the background. This may prevent viewers from seeing different perspectives and influence their information-gathering processes. For example, Netflix's recommendation algorithm tends to favor genres users have previously watched, making it harder for them to discover new genres (Sunstein, 2017). Personalization enhances the viewer experience while also becoming an important guiding force in shaping individual preferences.

EXPANSION OF THE DIGITAL ECOSYSTEM AND NEW BUSINESS MODELS

Digitalization has become one of the most defining dynamics of the 21st century, fundamentally transforming both economic structures and social organizations. At the heart of this transformation lies the expansion of the digital ecosystem. The digital ecosystem is a networked structure composed of interconnected actors supported by technological infrastructures. This structure includes individuals, companies, public institutions, and technological platforms. Through digitalization, data-driven decision-making mechanisms, AI-supported processes, and automation systems have transformed—if not entirely replaced traditional business models (Brynjolfsson & McAfee, 2014).

The expanding digital ecosystem has particularly gained attention with the emergence of the platform economy. Platforms such as Amazon, Uber, and Airbnb have not only offered technological services but have also transformed their intermediary positions into strategic business models, playing a significant role in global markets. These platforms process user data to optimize both demand-side and supply-side operations, thereby removing traditional sectoral boundaries (Parker, Van Alstyne & Choudary, 2016).

New business models are shaped within the digital ecosystem through structures such as network effects, multi-sided marketplaces, and subscription-based services. Especially subscription-based models have become one of the essential elements of sustainability in the digital economy, offering advantages like customer loyalty and consistent revenue streams. Companies such as Netflix and Spotify have successfully applied this model, creating significant transformations in traditional media industries (Rochet & Tirole, 2003).

Moreover, blockchain technology and decentralized finance (DeFi) applications are redefining the digital ecosystem. These technologies minimize the role of intermediaries, transform trust-based business practices, and enable users to participate more actively in the economy (Tapscott & Tapscott, 2016). At the same time, AI-powered solutions are laying the foundation for new business models in areas such as personalized customer experiences, demand forecasting, and process automation.

In this context, the expansion of the digital ecosystem has not only transformed the economic structure but has also reshaped business practices, consumer behavior, and competitive strategies. This transformation presents both opportunities and risks. Issues such as data protection, digital inequality, and algorithmic transparency are critically important for the sustainability of new business models. Therefore, alongside economic aspects, the growth of the digital ecosystem must also be evaluated through ethical and societal lenses.

Global Perspective and Intercultural Interaction

The process of reproduction in social media is an important factor that increases cultural interaction. In particular, the fact that individuals reinterpret the content of different cultures and make local cultural elements accessible at the global level changes the nature of intercultural communication (Lévy, 1999).

For example, on platforms such as TikTok and Instagram, users from different cultures enrich the production process by participating in a certain trend or challenge with their own cultural codes. This contributes to the expansion of intercultural dialogue in the new media environment by increasing cultural hybridization and global interaction (Castells, 2011).

The cross-border nature of social media brings the reproduction of television series to a global dimension. Viewers from different cultures create a common discussion area over the same series; This contributes to the development of intercultural interaction and understanding. In particular, the fact that the series universes are shaped around universal themes makes it possible for viewers from different geographies to share and interpret the same narrative. In this context, the multi-language options, subtitling and dubbing technologies offered by digital platforms in the future will further deepen cultural interaction.

Although the concept of reproduction begins with Karl Marx's economic analysis (Marx, 1867), it gains a cultural dimension with Walter Benjamin's work titled *The Work of Art in the Age of Technological Reproducibility* (Benjamin, 1936). According to Benjamin, works of art lose their "aura" when they are technically reproduced. Through means such as television, cinema, and digital media, a visual or sound recording can be reproduced over and over again and becomes an object of mass consumption. In this case, the difference between the original and the copy is eroded and the way reality is perceived changes (Benjamin, 1936).

Baudrillard, on the other hand, argues that reproduction through media is related to the concept of hyperreality (Baudrillard, 1981). The images that appear in the media represent a reality that is not authentic and tend to trap the consumer in a world of simulation. For example, ideological narratives in the news media or the concern to appear "flawless" on social media platforms play an important role in the process of reproducing reality.

In this context, both Benjamin's conceptualization of the "loss of aura" and Baudrillard's critique of "hyperreality" compel us to fundamentally reconsider our relationship with representations of reality in contemporary media environments. The images reproduced through media are not merely aesthetic copies but powerful instruments that shape individuals' perceptions on ideological and cultural levels. Therefore, the phenomenon of reproduction in the digital age is no longer a purely technical matter; it has evolved into a complex social experience where the boundaries between reality, authenticity, and representation become increasingly blurred.

The Transformation of Media and Reproduction

With the evolution of mass media, the concept of reproduction has undergone a profound transformation. In earlier stages, traditional forms of media such as print publications, television broadcasts, and radio programs served as the primary channels for distributing information and fostering social consciousness (McQuail, 2010). These mediums operated within a centralized structure where content creation was limited to professionals, institutions, or organizations with access to resources and infrastructure.

However, the emergence of digital media and the rapid proliferation of social networking platforms have radically shifted this paradigm (Jenkins, 2006). Today, virtually anyone with internet access can become a content creator, regardless of professional background or institutional affiliation. This democratization of media production has enabled individuals to generate, modify, and share visual, textual, and auditory content on an unprecedented scale (Bruns, 2008). The boundaries between producer and consumer have blurred, giving rise to what scholars often refer to as "*prosumer*" culture—a hybrid role where users simultaneously consume and produce content (Toffler, 1980). As a result, the reproduction of media is no longer confined by technological or institutional limitations, but instead operates within a dynamic, participatory, and constantly evolving digital landscape.

One of the most obvious examples of this is social media phenomena and "influencers". These individuals reproduce their own images, ideas and lifestyles over and over again, turning them into an object of consumption. At the same time, the mainstream media adopts these new dynamics and carries the content of traditional media to the digital environment. Influencers engage with their followers by creating content on social media platforms. Their business models generally include brand collaborations, establishing their own brands, generating revenue through live streaming, and offering consultancy services. Brands have also shifted away from traditional advertising strategies and started reaching their target audiences in a more natural and sincere way through influencers (Brown & Hayes, 2008). As influencers become key business partners in the digital age, their influence is expected to grow further with the continued expansion of this marketing field.

In the context of Pierre Bourdieu's concept of cultural capital, social media platforms are seen as spaces where individuals internalize and reproduce certain social values and norms (Bourdieu, 1986). Social media users reinforce existing social and economic structures while producing their own content (Couldry & Mejias, 2019).

Social media platforms transform users content production processes as an economic value, and this value is capitalized by large technology companies (Zuboff, 2019). This transformation has enabled individuals to become active content producers rather than just content consumers. Thus, media is no longer shaped by central authorities but by a wide range of users.

Example of Series Like Prens, Gibi and Leyla ile Mecnun

The series *Gibi* has garnered significant attention on digital platforms as a production that breaks conventional comedic molds through its absurdist sense of humor. The narration of mundane events surrounding the main character, Yılmaz, in an absurd tone opens up both intellectual and emotional spaces for the audience. The series has activated the humorous production potential of social media users; its scenes, character dialogues, and gestures have quickly become subjects of edits, memes, and user-generated videos.

The series *Prens*, on the other hand, presents a narrative that approaches contemporary times with an ironic and at times grotesque style. The modern equivalents of its characters are blended with historical parodies, granting the series a multilayered structure. *Prens* has particularly captured the attention of historical content creators on platforms such as Twitter/X, TikTok, and Instagram. It has been reproduced in various contexts, creating a wide sphere of interaction and reinterpretation.

Another significant example is *Leyla ile Mecnun*, which has maintained a strong presence in the digital sphere despite its original airing over a decade ago. With its absurdist narrative, philosophical undertones, and emotionally resonant characters, the series has generated a lasting fan culture that actively engages in reproducing its content on social media platforms. Users frequently share edited scenes, nostalgic montages, and meme-based reinterpretations, particularly on Twitter and Instagram. The show's iconic lines and character-based humor continue to inspire fan videos, aesthetic edits, and intertextual references, enabling the series to remain culturally relevant through continuous digital rearticulation. Much like *Gibi* and *Prens*, *Leyla ile Mecnun* exemplifies how a television series can evolve into a participatory cultural object through the practices of online communities.

These series have been extensively edited by social media users. These edits vary widely—from scene cuts, dialogue montages, video collages with altered background music, and "POV" (point of view) style content, to aestheticized visuals and short videos infused with diverse cultural references.

Notably on TikTok, short videos labeled as "Yılmaz's POV" or scenes from *Prens* accompanied by foreign music have enabled these contents to transcend their original context, integrating into a more universal sense of humor. These creative acts have transformed the series from being merely watchable content into tools through which users express their own digital identities.

While re-editing scenes, users embed their own sense of humor, political positions, or nostalgic emotions, thus constructing multilayered narratives. This not only leads to the reinterpretation of the content but also reinforces the individual's agency over media.

Users often form emotional bonds with characters from these series, adapt them into their everyday lives, and express this adaptation through edits shared across social media platforms.

In this process, the prosumer increases their own social capital while simultaneously contributing to the popularity of the series. This creates a reciprocal feedback mechanism wherein the boundaries between the original content producers (the series creators) and content reproducers (the users) become increasingly blurred. When considered within this context, the reproduction practices surrounding *Gibi*, *Prens* and *Leyla ile Mecnun* represent clear examples of free labor. Users who create video edits are not merely engaging in creative activity; they are also enhancing the visibility of these series, keeping them relevant, feeding platform algorithms, and driving traffic to these platforms. Thus, these practices are not only aesthetic but also bear economic and political value. According to Terranova, the "free" nature of such labor does not imply it is without value; on the contrary, it is a form of labor whose compensation is rendered invisible and is open to systemic exploitation.

From Terranova's perspective, these user-generated productions clearly constitute a labor process. Individuals mobilize not only their technical skills but also their emotions, aesthetic instincts, sense of humor, and cultural capital in this process (*Terranova, 2000*). Yet the output of this labor ultimately transcends personal satisfaction and is integrated into the platform economy. These contents feed into the algorithmic circulation of TikTok or Instagram. Edits and memes make the series go viral, increasing viewership and thus generating economic profit for digital platforms. Even though users may not directly gain monetary income from this content, the value they produce returns to the capitalist system as "added value."

Therefore, this production process fits precisely the definition of invisible but systematically exploited digital labor, as articulated by Terranova. Despite appearing creative and liberating, this labor form has become central to the capitalist cycle of production.

CONCLUSION

Reproduction through the media plays a critical role in the reconstruction of societal norms and ideological structures. Especially in the political and economic context, media outlets shape public opinion by highlighting certain discourses. For example, the fact that news channels present events from a specific point of view can transform the way the viewer perceives reality.

In addition, the process of reproduction through the media has become quite evident in the dissemination of popular culture. Recurring themes and stereotyped images in movies, TV series, music, and advertisements transform consumer habits and aesthetic perceptions.

Beyond traditional media, the rise of digital media platforms and the increasing role of social media productions have significantly transformed the media reproduction process within the framework of political economy. In the context of social media, content production is no longer solely under the control of large media corporations; rather, it has become decentralized and democratized. However, this decentralization does not eliminate economic and ideological dynamics. Instead, it reshapes them by incorporating user-generated content into capitalist frameworks of attention, engagement, and commodification.

The concept of the "*prosumer*" an individual who simultaneously consumes and produces content has become central in understanding this new media environment. Through platforms like YouTube, Instagram, TikTok, and Twitter, users create, remix, and disseminate content, often without direct financial compensation, contributing to the perpetuation of digital capitalism. As David Hesmondhalgh (2013) emphasizes, cultural production, including digital media production, is deeply entangled with capitalist market dynamics and political forces. While the digital era promotes new forms of participation, it simultaneously conceals the persistent structures of corporate control and economic exploitation. Although the rise of user-generated content is often celebrated as a form of democratization, it frequently results in free labor that disproportionately benefits platform owners rather than the users themselves.

Reproduction through the media has thus become an integral component of both social structures and individual perceptions in today's world. With the benefits of the digital era, consumers have also turned into producers and started to reconstruct reality in a multidimensional way. This phenomenon not only creates new opportunities for participation and expression but also brings new risks, such as increased surveillance, data commodification, and the reinforcement of dominant ideological structures under the guise of participatory culture. As a result, the dynamics of the media age are now determined by the complex interplay between technological empowerment and economic exploitation.

REFERENCES

Anderson, C. (2006). *The long tail: Why the future of business is selling less of more*. Hyperion.

Anderson, C. (2008). Television networks and the industry's development. In Wasko, J. (Ed.), *A companion to television* (pp. 47–70). Blackwell Publishing.

Assmann, J., & Assmann, A. (1997). *Cultural memory and early civilization: Writing, remembrance, and political imagination*. Cambridge University Press.

Baudrillard, J. (1981). *Simulacra and simulation* (Glaser, S. F., Trans.). University of Michigan Press. (Original work published 1981)

Baym, N. K. (2010). *Personal connections in the digital age*. Polity Press.

Benkler, Y. (2006). *The wealth of networks: How social production transforms markets and freedom*. Yale University Press.

Berners-Lee, T. (1990). *Information management: A proposal*. CERN.

Berners-Lee, T. (2006). The semantic web. *Scientific American*.

Booth, P. (2010). *Digital fandom: New media studies*. Peter Lang Publishing. DOI: 10.3726/978-1-4539-1654-4

Bourdieu, P. (1986). *The forms of capital*. Greenwood Press.

Boyd, D. M., & Ellison, N. B. (2007). Social network sites: Definition, history, and scholarship. *Journal of Computer-Mediated Communication, 13*(1), 210–230. DOI: 10.1111/j.1083-6101.2007.00393.x

Briggs, A., & Burke, P. (2010). *A social history of the media: From Gutenberg to the internet* (3rd ed.). Polity Press.

Brown, D., & Hayes, N. (2008). *Influencer marketing: Who really influences your customers?* Elsevier. DOI: 10.4324/9780080557700

Bruns, A. (2008). *Blogs, Wikipedia, Second Life, and beyond: From production to produsage*. Peter Lang.

Brynjolfsson, E., & McAfee, A. (2014). *The second machine age: Work, progress, and prosperity in a time of brilliant technologies*. W. W. Norton & Company.

Burgess, J., & Green, J. (2018). *YouTube: Online video and participatory culture* (2nd ed.). Polity Press.

Carr, N. (2010). *The shallows: What the internet is doing to our brains*. W. W. Norton & Company.

Castells, M. (2011). *The rise of the network society* (2nd ed.). John Wiley & Sons.

Cisco Systems. (2017). *Cisco visual networking index: Forecast and methodology, 2016–2021*. Cisco Public.

Couldry, N. (2012). *Media, society, world: Social theory and digital media practice*. Polity Press.

Couldry, N., & Mejias, U. A. (2019). *The costs of connection: How data is colonizing human life and appropriating it for capitalism*. Stanford University Press.

Deller, R. A. (2011). Twittering on: Audience research and participation using Twitter. *Participations*, *8*(1), 216–245.

Deuze, M. (2007). *Media life*. Polity Press.

Ellis, J. (2000). *Seeing things: Television in the age of uncertainty*. I.B. Tauris. DOI: 10.5040/9780755604784

European Commission. (2010). *Digital broadcasting: Transition from analogue to digital TV*. Publications Office of the European Union.

Federal Communications Commission (FCC). (2009). *The digital television transition: What you need to know about DTV*.

Fuchs, C. (2014). *Social media: A critical introduction*. SAGE Publications. DOI: 10.4135/9781446270066

Gillespie, T. (2018). *Custodians of the internet: Platforms, content moderation, and the hidden decisions that shape social media*. Yale University Press.

Gray, J. (2006). *Watching with The Simpsons: Television, parody, and intertextuality*. Routledge.

Halbwachs, M. (1992). *On collective memory*. University of Chicago Press. DOI: 10.7208/chicago/9780226774497.001.0001

Hall, S. (1997). *Representation: Cultural representations and signifying practices*. Sage Publications.

Hargittai, E., & Hinnant, A. (2008). Digital inequality: Differences in young adults' use of the internet. *Communication Research*, *35*(5), 602–621. DOI: 10.1177/0093650208321782

Hesmondhalgh, D. (2013). *The cultural industries* (3rd ed.). Sage Publications.

Highfield, T., & Leaver, T. (2016). Instagrammatics and digital methods: Studying visual social media, from selfies and GIFs to memes and emoji. *Communication Research and Practice*, *2*(1), 47–62. DOI: 10.1080/22041451.2016.1155332

Jenkins, H. (2006). *Convergence culture: Where old and new media collide*. New York University Press.

Jenkins, H., Ford, S., & Green, J. (2013). *Spreadable media: Creating value and meaning in a networked culture*. New York University Press.

Kaplan, A. M., & Haenlein, M. (2010). Users of the world, unite! The challenges and opportunities of social media. *Business Horizons*, *53*(1), 59–68. DOI: 10.1016/j.bushor.2009.09.003

Kirkpatrick, D. (2010). *The Facebook effect: The inside story of the company that is connecting the world*. Simon & Schuster.

Leaver, T., Highfield, T., & Abidin, C. (2020). *Instagram: Visual social media cultures*. Polity Press.

Livingstone, S. (2004). The challenge of changing audiences: Or what is the audience researcher to do in the age of the internet? *European Journal of Communication*, *19*(1), 75–86. DOI: 10.1177/0267323104040695

Lobato, R. (2016). The cultural logic of YouTube. *International Journal of Communication*, *10*, 363–380.

Lobato, R. (2019). *Netflix nations: The geography of digital distribution*. New York University Press. DOI: 10.18574/nyu/9781479895120.001.0001

Lotz, A. D. (2014). *The television will be revolutionized* (2nd ed.). New York University Press.

Manovich, L. (2001). *The language of new media*. MIT Press.

Marx, K. (1867). *Capital: Critique of political economy* (Fowkes, B., Trans.). Penguin Books.

McCabe, J., & Akass, K. (Eds.). (2007). *Quality TV: Contemporary American television and beyond*. I.B. Tauris. DOI: 10.5040/9780755696376

McQuail, D. (2010). *McQuail's mass communication theory* (6th ed.). Sage Publications.

Mitchell, T. (2001). *Global noise: Rap and hip-hop outside the USA*. Wesleyan University Press.

Morley, D., & Robins, K. (1995). *Spaces of identity: Global media, electronic landscapes and cultural boundaries*. Routledge.

Murthy, D. (2018). *Twitter: Social communication in the Twitter age* (2nd ed.). Polity Press.

Napoli, P. M. (2011). *Audience evolution: New technologies and the transformation of media audiences*. Columbia University Press.

O'Reilly, T. (2005). *What is Web 2.0? Design patterns and business models for the next generation of software*. O'Reilly Media.

Parker, G. G., Van Alstyne, M. W., & Choudary, S. P. (2016). *Platform revolution: How networked markets are transforming the economy and how to make them work for you*. W. W. Norton & Company.

Rheingold, H. (1993). *The virtual community: Homesteading on the electronic frontier*. Addison-Wesley.

Rochet, J. C., & Tirole, J. (2003). Platform competition in two-sided markets. *Journal of the European Economic Association, 1*(4), 990–1029. DOI: 10.1162/154247603322493212

Schroeder, R. (2016). Big data and the emergence of Web 4.0. *Journal of Information Technology, 31*(2), 155–161.

Shirky, C. (2011). *Cognitive surplus: How technology makes consumers into collaborators*. Penguin Books.

Silverstone, R. (1999). *Why study the media?* Sage Publications. DOI: 10.4135/9781446219461

Storey, J. (2018). *Cultural theory and popular culture: An introduction* (8th ed.). Routledge. DOI: 10.4324/9781315226866

Sundar, S. S. (2008). The MAIN model: A heuristic approach to understanding technology effects on credibility. In *Digital media, youth, and credibility* (pp. 73–100).

Tapscott, D., & Tapscott, A. (2016). *Blockchain revolution: How the technology behind Bitcoin is changing money, business, and the world*. Penguin.

Terranova, T. (2000). Free labor: Producing culture for the digital economy. *Social Text, 18*(2), 33–58. DOI: 10.1215/01642472-18-2_63-33

Tomlinson, J. (1999). *Globalization and culture*. University of Chicago Press.

Tryon, C. (2013). *On-demand culture: Digital delivery and the future of movies.* Rutgers University Press.

Turan, Y. (2018). Media consumption in the digital age: The reproduction of television series on social media. *Journal of Communication Research, 10*(2), 45–67.

Uricchio, W. (2009). Contextualizing the broadcast era: Nation, commerce, and constraint. In Holt, J., & Perren, A. (Eds.), *Media industries: History, theory, and method* (pp. 164–175). Wiley-Blackwell. DOI: 10.1177/0002716209339145

Van Dijck, J. (2013). *The culture of connectivity: A critical history of social media.* Oxford University Press. DOI: 10.1093/acprof:oso/9780199970773.001.0001

Williams, R. (1974). *Television: Technology and cultural form.* Routledge.

Zuboff, S. (2019). *The age of surveillance capitalism: The fight for a human future at the new frontier of power.* PublicAffairs.

Zulli, D., & Zulli, D. J. (2020). Extending the internet meme: Conceptualizing technological mimesis and imitation publics on TikTok. *New Media & Society, 22*(3), 1–18.

ADDITIONAL READING

Alvin Toffler. (1980). *The Third Wave.* William Morrow and Company, Inc.

Booth, P. (2010). *Digital fandom: New media studies.* Peter Lang Publishing. DOI: 10.3726/978-1-4539-1654-4

Bruns, A. (2008). *Blogs, Wikipedia, Second Life, and beyond: From production to produsage.* Peter Lang.

Christian Fuchs. (2014). *Social Media: A Critical Introduction.* SAGE Publications Ltd.

Henry Jenkins. (2006). *Convergence Culture Where Old and New Media Collide.* New York University Press.

Jenkins, H., Ford, S., & Green, J. (2013). *Spreadable Media: Creating Value and Meaning in a Networked Culture.* New York University Press.

José van Dijck. (2013). *The Culture of Connectivity a Critical History of Social Media.* Oxford University Press.

Matt Hills. (2002). *Fan Cultures*. Routledge.

Shifman, L. (2013). *Memes in digital culture*. MIT Press. DOI: 10.7551/mitpress/9429.001.0001

Tiziana Terranova. (2000). *Free Labor: Producing Culture for the Digital Economy*. Duke University Press.

KEY TERMS AND DEFINITIONS

Participatory Culture: A media environment where users actively contribute to the production, distribution, and interpretation of content, challenging traditional producer-consumer boundaries.

Prosumer: A hybrid role combining producer and consumer, where individuals simultaneously consume and produce media content, especially in digital and networked contexts.

Digital Reproduction: The process by which media content is copied, modified, and redistributed through digital technologies, facilitating rapid circulation and transformation in online environments.

Social Media Platforms: Digital infrastructures that enable users to create, share, and interact with content and one another, forming participatory and algorithmically curated communication spaces.

Audience Engagement: The active involvement of media audiences through interaction, feedback, and content co-creation, often measured by participation levels across platforms.

Media Convergence: The merging of traditional and new media forms, technologies, and industries, resulting in a hybrid media landscape characterized by cross-platform content flows.

Fan Practices: Creative and affective activities performed by fans—such as fan fiction, memes, and remixes—that extend, reinterpret, or critique original media texts.

Television Series Recontextualization: The reinterpretation and transformation of television narratives by audiences across platforms, often involving memes, edits, or commentary that shift meaning in new cultural or social contexts.

Section 3
Transformation of Reality and Space

Chapter 14
Artificial Intelligence-Themed Films in the Digital Publishing Ecosystem:
A Comparative Analysis of Platform Strategies

Tuğçe Karaca Özdemir
https://orcid.org/0009-0009-2733-1284
Ondokuz Mayıs University, Turkey

ABSTRACT

As digital publishing platforms undergo a significant transformation in content production, AI-themed films have become central to this shift. These platforms present such content through varying strategies—some focus on popular and accessible productions, while others prioritize philosophical and niche themes. This study examines how AI-themed films are represented on digital publishing platforms and how these narratives shape the broader media ecosystem. Through a comparative analysis of Netflix's JUNG_E and Apple TV+'s Swan Song, the study finds that while JUNG_E offers a critique of class exploitation and gender through an action-driven and dystopian narrative, Swan Song explores themes of individual consciousness through ethical and existential questions. In both films, the representation of the body and the boundaries between humans and artificial intelligence are addressed through cultural and ideological codes. Moreover, the content strategies of the platforms significantly influence the form and presentation of the films.

DOI: 10.4018/979-8-3373-1957-5.ch014

INTRODUCTION

The idea of projecting moving images onto the screen was realized with the technical advances that accelerated in the second half of the 19th century. In this process, Eadweard Muybridge's photographic works documenting the movement of horses constitute an important turning point. Muybridge took 24 shots of galloping horses and scientifically proved that the horses' feet were off the ground (Abisel, 2010, pp. 24-25). The birth of cinema was made possible by inventions such as the kinetoscope developed by Thomas Alva Edison and William K. L. Dickson in 1888 (Abisel, 2010, p. 14). While the kinetoscope offered an individual viewing experience, another step was taken with the development of the cinematograph for mass screening by the Lumière brothers in 1895. With its lightweight structure and the ability to record sixteen frames per second, the cinematograph was instrumental in the transformation of cinema into an industrial art form (Abisel, 2010, p. 31).

Lev Manovich defines the digitalization process in cinema as the reinvention of cinema. According to him, with the effect of digitalization, cinema is in a sense returning to the experimental structure of its early years (Lev Manovich, 2014, p. 172). Although the concept of "home cinema" was used to refer to individual movie-viewing practices during the era of the pelic screen, this practice did not have a significant impact on the communal viewing culture of cinema. However, with digitalization, this situation has undergone a radical change. The proliferation of videocassettes, optical disc technologies such as DVD and Blu-ray, the emergence of online movie viewing platforms and the development of interactive narrative forms have encouraged individual viewing practices at home and created a structural transformation in cinema consumption habits. In this context, McLuhan's following statement should be underlined: "We shape the tools and then the tools shape us" (Murphy, 2011, p. 17 as cited in Öztürk, 2013, p. 5). Similarly, Castells (2005, pp. 3-26) states that advances in information technologies have paved the way for the construction of a "network society" across the world. From this perspective, it can be said that individuals today are adapting to rapidly changing technologies and in this process, an interaction is taking place that transforms social structures as well as individuals.

Especially during the COVID-19 pandemic, the retreat of cinema audiences to homes has accelerated the trend towards video streaming platforms such as Netflix, Amazon Prime Video, Apple TV+ and Disney+ as an alternative to movie theaters. This great wave of orientation created an intense competitive environment in the film industry in a short time, and digital platforms enriched their catalogs with original and diverse content in order to gain new subscribers in this competition. Thus, a multi-layered transformation process has begun in the film industry, ranging from content production to viewing practices.

Both the integration of advanced technologies such as artificial intelligence (AI) into content production processes and the thematic level of content are reshaping the content strategies of digital platforms. This transformation affects production styles, narrative structures and thematic diversity. In this context, the fact that artificial intelligence-oriented narratives appear more frequently and in various forms on digital platforms shows the interaction of media with technological evolution.

Although artificial intelligence-themed narratives have a long history in the history of cinema, with the proliferation of digital platforms, they have become more diversified and have started to be reproduced in different narrative forms and for different audience segments. This situation provides important clues about the content production and presentation strategies of platforms. For example, while some platforms offer popular and accessible content that appeals to a wider audience, others focus on producing specialized productions with deeper, philosophical or niche themes. Therefore, it can be argued that AI-themed films are both a content genre and strategic tools that represent digital platforms' relationship with audiences. How this content overlaps with the content strategies of platforms is important for understanding the future of digital publishing.

Although there are studies in the literature on audience relationship and user experience in the context of digital broadcasting (Yıldırım, 2021; Erdem & Aytekin, 2021; Şahin, 2024); content production and women's identity (Yünkül, 2024; Demirci, 2024); digital broadcasting and platform strategies (Toptaş & Yazıcı, 2022; Aydemir, 2023); technical features and user experience (Büyükçelikok & Dilmen, 2024); marketing strategies and globalization (Yıldırım, 2024); technology and usability (Coşkun, 2023), studies on the representation of artificial intelligence-themed content in this context are limited. In particular, addressing thematic analyses in relation to platform policies can fill an important gap in terms of both media studies and digital culture.

This study aims to fill this gap and addresses the problem of "How are AI-themed movies represented on digital publishing platforms and how do these themes shape the digital publishing ecosystem?". In this context, the aim of the study is to compare the strategies of digital publishing platforms for AI-themed content, to examine how these contents are presented to the target audiences of the platforms and to understand the effects of the transformation in the digital publishing ecosystem. Within the scope of the study, two films were selected as a sample from Netflix and Apple TV+ platforms by using purposive sampling method, taking into account criteria such as different content production strategies, the way they appeal to audience groups, content diversity and access level. The films were selected based on factors such as the theme of artificial intelligence and the fact that they are exclusive productions of these platforms. In this context, Netflix original production *JUNG_E (Sang-hoYeon- 2023)* and Apple TV+ original production

Swan Song (BenjaminCleary- 2021) were selected as samples. The selected films are analyzed by comparative film analysis method.

Digital Publishing Ecosystem Transformation

Digitalization can be defined as a transformation that involves the process of converting information into digital format and the storage of data in digital media and its use on various platforms. Digitization is defined as a mechanism that converts analog processes into digital format and enables data to be stored and processed effectively in computer environments (Karakaş et al., 2009, p. 39). It is seen that the role of Web 2.0 technology in the rapid development of the Internet today is extremely decisive. This technology should not be considered as a change that only consists of updating existing web pages. Web 2.0 offers a new medium and perspective that shapes the dynamics of the digital age, where users can actively participate in content production. Thanks to the developing network infrastructure, the data volume of Web 2.0 technology is constantly increasing and the types of content are becoming more diverse. This significantly increases user interaction and brings about the continuous updating of digital applications and the expansion of related platforms (Musser & O'Reilly, 2006, p. 10). With this transformation, it becomes more evident how digital systems make a difference in the processes of media production and consumption.

Although digital systems are sometimes seen as equivalent to traditional media forms such as television and cinema, they are actually structurally quite different. The functioning of these systems is basically made possible by the possibilities offered by Web 2.0 technologies and the internet access of a computer. In this context, digitalization allows individuals to actively participate in the processes of producing, shaping and distributing data as well as accessing data. In addition, digital environments offer the user the flexibility to watch, listen and consume visual and audio content through different digital devices (Alioğlu, 2011, p. 26). Therefore, digitalization refers to both a development that transforms the technical infrastructure and a multi-layered transformation process that restructures the processes of content production, distribution and consumption in the media industries.

The concept of Web TV was used between 2004 and 2008 to describe the first examples of content broadcasting over the internet. Attempts in this period were often limited to short and unprofessional content and failed due to launching before the target audience was established and poor content quality. The term was also used between 1996 and 2013 as a trade name for a service that utilized televisions for internet access. The first predictions about web TV date back to 1995, when internet access was not yet widespread (Lotz, 2017, pp. 6-7).

Television broadcasting over the Internet is called IPTV and this model is based on the Internet infrastructure. Modern society has transformed into a network society, where individuals have the opportunity to access the Internet at any time and place. The distinctive feature of the network society is that it enables two-way interaction, which allows users to instantly change and personalize the broadcasts they watch. In IPTV broadcasting, viewers can interactively direct the broadcast content through feedback. This structure transforms the traditional television viewer into an active participant and enables content consumption based on personal preferences (Yaman, 2017, pp. 251-252).

Another important concept related to television broadcasting over the Internet is the term “OTT” (Over-the-Top), which has evolved in the television industry. This concept, which first emerged in 2005, did not become widespread until 2010. Conceptually, OTT is used to describe content streams that are transmitted over networks controlled by cable and telecommunications companies, but are not directly connected to these infrastructures. This structure, which differs from traditional broadcasting models, has transformed the content consumption habits of viewers; cable subscriptions have been replaced by on-demand content services provided through digital platforms. In this context, platforms such as Netflix, Apple TV+, Amazon Prime Video and Disney+ reach a large audience on a global scale and become decisive actors in the field of digital broadcasting by developing content strategies based on user behavior (Lotz, 2017, pp. 7-9).

The platform-based broadcasting model goes beyond the traditional media economy and aims to offer data-driven personalized experiences. In this way, viewers' preferences, past viewing habits and tendencies directly shape the content production and presentation strategies of platforms (Flew & Smith, 2021, as cited in Holat & Polan, 2024, p. 265). According to Rogers (1986, pp. 5-7), the most prominent feature of new media is “demassification”. Thanks to this feature, customized content can be offered in accordance with the individual characteristics and preferences of users. On digital broadcasting platforms, viewers are transformed from traditional passive users into active users who can select content according to their interests. These platforms develop personalized content recommendations by analyzing users' past viewing and search behavior, online interactions and preferences. Thus, the user is treated as a unique profile and is guided with the appropriate content within the platform (Sun et al., 2020; Srinivasan et al., 2002, cited in Holat & Polan, 2024, p. 265). Therefore, digital broadcasting can be considered as a technological innovation and a structural transformation that reshapes cultural production.

In conclusion, while the digital publishing ecosystem is transforming the way content is produced and distributed, it is also radically transforming the way audiences relate to the media. While elements such as artificial intelligence, algorithms, user experience and content diversity play a critical role in this ecosystem, it can be said that how these elements are used determines the content policies and representation practices of platforms.

Platform-Based Content Strategies: Netflix and Apple TV+

Digital broadcasting platforms' strategies for content curation are basically shaped around two main approaches: audience-oriented and content acquisition-based. The audience strategy aims to select content that meets the needs and preferences of specific audience segments. This strategy ensures that content targeted at niche audience groups, especially those underrepresented by traditional television broadcasting, is highlighted. On the other hand, the content acquisition strategy aims to diversify the platform's archive by purchasing content from different producers or global markets. These two strategies enable digital platforms to both build user loyalty and appeal to a wide audience (Lotz, 2017, p. 24).

Netflix started its operations in 1998 by offering DVD rental and sales services, and provided a continuous cash flow by switching to a subscription model in 1999. In 2007, it switched to a streaming service and digitized its content offering. In 2010, it discontinued DVD delivery by offering an internet-only plan. However, it continued to contract with distribution centers until 2010, and the company's international expansion only began in 2010 with Canada. Although the potential of Netflix's online model is limitless, its operations are still limited to national borders due to challenges related to property rights (Ladeira, 2013, pp. 152-153).

According to Oskay, since the information sources of the internet and social media are "personalized and customized, the individual creates his own television channel" (Oskay, 2007, p. 15). Netflix also differentiates its content strategy from the traditional mass broadcasting approach and adopts an approach defined as "conglomerate niche". In line with this strategy, instead of offering the same content to all subscribers, the platform develops or licenses customized content that appeals to different tastes and audience segments. This non-linear approach aims to direct users only to content that may be of interest to them, thereby personalizing the individual viewing experience. Netflix's algorithm-based recommendation systems and curation policy based on user data aim to provide each subscriber with a different "Netflix" experience while reducing negative impressions and feedback. This structure, which is independent of limitations such as time and broadcast capacity, not only creates mass scale, but also builds a content ecosystem that can respond to multifaceted user expectations (Lotz, 2017, pp. 26-28).

Content differentiation in the context of the portal is achieved by recommending specific productions to specific audiences based on data collected on users' viewing habits and preferences. This personalization strategy is evident in the homepage layouts and recommendation systems of platforms such as Netflix, where different TV series and movies are highlighted for each user based on their past viewing behavior, thus offering a unique viewing experience to each subscriber (Lotz, 2017, p. 74).

Netflix, as Hooper and his colleagues put it, enables “people to consume content anywhere, anytime and on any device” (Hooper et al., 2010, as cited in Aydemir, 2023, p. 1463). The company is seen as an actor with an accurate positioning in the market and a clear target audience; it also carefully carries out processes to focus on “personal experience that finds the most enjoyable titles from around the world for each person” (Wang, 2022, cited in Aydemir, 2023, p. 1463). In this direction, Netflix differentiates itself from the traditional television and movie sectors by offering its subscribers the ease of access to the content they want, whenever they want, and continues this strategy with determination.

Before entering the content distribution sector, Apple had already established a significant market presence through its own hardware products, such as the iPod. In 2007, the company introduced Apple TV as a service that enables the purchase of content through television devices. By connecting directly to the iTunes Store, Apple TV creates a different dynamic in the content purchase process. This strategy aims to integrate both devices and content into the Apple ecosystem. By partnering with content providers, Apple connects users to its own hardware and software systems, thereby positioning devices as a tool to drive content consumption. This approach therefore allows Apple to integrate hardware and content more strongly than its competitors (Ladeira, 2013, pp. 154-155).

In contrast to Netflix's algorithm-driven and audience segmentation-based content strategy, Apple TV+ adopts a more curatorial approach to its content strategy, aiming to reach specific audience segments with original and prestigious series of high cinematic quality, rather than producing popular productions that appeal to large audiences. Although productions such as “Foundation”, “For All Mankind” and “Silo” have been praised by critics, the platform has struggled to build a large audience. This situation reveals that Apple TV+ should prioritize the production of quality content, while targeting a more niche audience and shaping its brand identity accordingly (Motamayor, 2024).

According to Başer and Akıncı (2021, pp. 8701-872), Netflix has many innovative features to improve the user experience. Customizable interface design, multilingual subtitle and dubbing options, country-specific content and original productions that appeal to the user are among these features. The platform also draws attention with profiles suitable for different age groups, high-resolution audio and video quality, adaptive connection options that adapt to internet speed, and ease of use such as binge-watching. Affordable subscription options, ad-free content delivery and access from various devices also reinforce Netflix's user-centered approach.

Apple TV+ focuses on high picture and sound quality to maximize the user experience. The platform offers Dolby Atmos technology with 4K HDR video support and promises its viewers a movie theater quality viewing experience. It also provides a seamless and focus-enhancing viewing environment thanks to its ad-free content policy (PCMag, 2024). Apple TV+ offers multi-device support, enabling accessibility on many different platforms such as iPhone, iPad, Mac, Apple TV, smart TVs, game consoles and streaming devices. In this way, users can access content from any device (Apple, 2024a). In addition, thanks to the accessibility features developed by Apple with the tvOS 18 update, the viewing experience has been made more inclusive. Improvements to the subtitling system, voice highlighting technology that enables clearer understanding of dialogues, and the InSight feature that provides real-time information about content such as actors, characters or music during viewing are noteworthy (Apple, 2024b).

Through partnerships with companies such as Samsung and Apple, Netflix integrates directly into television sets and offers viewers a high quality viewing experience similar to traditional television with HD broadcast quality. In addition, customer-focused innovations such as reduced commercial breaks and flexible subscription models enable the company to develop next-generation strategies. These strategies position Netflix in new and unexplored market areas where competition is not intense, within the framework of Netflix's *Blue Ocean Strategy*. As defined by Kim and Mauborgne (2014, as cited in Aydemir, 2023, p. 1466), *the Blue Ocean Strategy* aims to create uncontested market space, render competition irrelevant, create new demand, disrupt the value-cost balance, and pursue differentiation and low cost together. Netflix's transition from a DVD rental model to an online content streaming service is a successful example of this strategy. *The Only on Netflix* policy, developed as another step of the strategy, aims to produce original content only available on the Netflix platform. This approach both increases user loyalty and strengthens dependency on the platform. As a result, Netflix strengthens its leading position in the global media industry by using both strategies together (Aydemir, 2023, p. 1466).

The content and user experience strategies of Netflix and Apple TV+ show how digital broadcasting is being reshaped by both technological developments and changing cultural expectations.

Media Representation of Artificial Intelligence Themed Content

Stuart Hall (2017), who has made significant contributions to the concept of representation, defines representation as a fundamental process by which meaning is produced and shared among members of a culture. This process involves the use of linguistic, auditory and visual signs that symbolize or depict things. According to Hall, representation means saying something meaningful about a phenomenon or object or describing it in a meaningful way. He argues that representation not only reflects reality but also constructs meaning. In this respect, representation is handled by Hall with three different approaches: reflective, intentional and constructivist. Hall especially emphasizes the constructivist approach, emphasizing that meaning is produced through language in social and cultural contexts rather than an objective reality (Hall, 2017, p. 23). In this context, considering that representation is not only the reflection of objects but also the process of social construction of meanings, how narratives on artificial intelligence are presented in media tools is also shaped by these representations.

Artificial intelligence-themed narratives have diversified and deepened in many media genres, especially cinema and digital publishing, in parallel with technological developments and social transformations. Especially in science fiction cinema, the representation of artificial intelligence characters has ceased to be merely a technical innovation over time; it has become central to philosophical and sociological questions such as ethics, identity, consciousness and humanity (Karaca Özdemir, 2025, pp. 168-173). The evolution from robots to artificial intelligence in cinema is seen as an important process that comprehensively reflects these developments. In the 1900s, the theme of artificial intelligence in cinema gained popularity with science fiction films, and the increasing presence of artificial intelligence characters in cinema, especially in the second half of the 20th century, led to the further spread of this genre (Acar, 2007, p. 64). In the early period, artificial intelligence was generally imagined in the form of robots or computers, and over time, these figures were integrated into cinema with different narratives.

From the early periods of cinema until the 1960s, the presence of artificial intelligence as a character in cinema has generally been shaped through oppositions and syntheses. Fritz Lang's *Metropolis* (1927) is one of the earliest examples of an artificial intelligence character, and although it is not a full-fledged artificial intelligence because the robot's decisions are directed, it can be defined as a cybernetic being (cyborg). In the 1960s and 1970s, the threats posed by artificial intelligence become more complex, and films such *as Colossus: The Forbin Project* (1970) emphasized that technology posed a potential danger to humanity and could lead to catastrophe if left unchecked.

Stanley Kubrick's *2001: A Space Odyssey* (1968) emphasizes the dangerous potential of artificial intelligence by highlighting HAL-9000's transformation from friend to foe, exhibiting human-like negative emotions and scientific accuracy (Nisanoğlu, 2021, p. 80). In the 1970s, while artificial intelligence characters undertake important tasks by establishing emotional bonds with humans in films such as *Star Wars*, Ridley Scott's *Alien* (1979) brings up the ethical questions of artificial intelligence characters and draws attention to Ash's secret plans. In the 1980s, films such as *Blade Runner* (1982) and *Terminator* (1984) depict artificial intelligence characters as a threat to humanity, while productions such as *Short Circuit* (1986) and *Spaceballs* (1987) use robots as comedic elements, and *Tron* (1982), the pioneer of the cyberpunk movement, highlights the dystopian and hostile aspects of technology. In the 1990s, the development of technology, the widespread use of the Internet and virtual reality themes were prominent in films such as *Terminator 2: Judgment Day* (1991), *The Matrix* (1999), as well as Steven Spielberg's *A.I. Artificial Intelligence* (2001), which questions humanity and artificial intelligence with its emotionally connected artificial intelligence characters and impressive visual effects.

Between 2000 and 2024, it is observed that the themes of artificial intelligence in science fiction cinema were covered in depth, more realistic and scientifically based films increased with the advances in computer technologies and artificial intelligence research, and in this period, with the depiction of artificial intelligence characters as individuals with human emotions, productions questioning the emotional ties between them and humans increased, but the cinema again progressed within oppositions such as enemy-savior and threat-opportunity. In the 2000s, it is observed that the representations of artificial intelligence in popular culture developed further and became more human-like, and narratives modeling artificial intelligence on the human body became widespread with the contributions of biotechnology and prosthetic technologies, especially with the influence of cyberpunk culture. In this period, science fiction cinema treats artificial intelligence as a phenomenon that can be encountered in daily life rather than a distant future, and offers a critical perspective to the audience through scientific research and philosophical discussions (Kavas, 2022, p. 38).

In recent years, films such as *Minority Report* (2002), about an artificial intelligence system that predicts crimes; *I, Robot* (2004), which emphasizes robots' relationships with humans and their threats; *Eagle Eye* (2008), about individuals under the control of secret artificial intelligence; *Transcendence* (2014), which deals with the transfer of mental processes to an artificial system; *Ex Machina* (2014), about artificial intelligence with emotional consciousness; *Chappie* (2015), which examines its integration into society; and *Blade Runner 2049* (2017) stand out.

Method

This study was conducted within the framework of a qualitative research approach, using a comparative film analysis method. The main purpose of the study is to examine how artificial intelligence-themed content is represented on digital publishing platforms and to evaluate the effects of these themes on the digital publishing ecosystem. Qualitative research is defined as a method that adopts an interdisciplinary holistic approach that examines the research problem from an interpretive perspective. The phenomena and events analyzed are analyzed in their own contexts and interpreted through the meanings that people attribute to these phenomena and events (Altunışık et al., 2010, p. 302).

Purposive sampling method was adopted in sample selection; two films were selected among the original productions of different digital platforms that deal with the theme of artificial intelligence. Netflix original production *JUNG_E* (2023) and Apple TV+ original production *Swan Song* (2021) are the examples selected in this context. The films were evaluated in terms of both content and distribution strategies. Purposive sampling is a sampling method in which the researcher consciously selects people or objects that can provide the most appropriate data for a specific purpose. The decisive factor in this method is compliance with the objectives of the research (Aziz, 2014, p. 55).

In the analysis process, five main criteria were identified: artificial intelligence themes, content presentation style, target audience strategy, aesthetic and narrative style, and broadcast ecosystem and distribution practices. In line with these criteria, Netflix's *JUNG_E* and Apple TV+'s *Swan Song* were analyzed comparatively. Thus, how artificial intelligence-themed content is structured both on the aesthetic and narrative level and how it is positioned in the context of digital publishing strategies is revealed with a holistic approach.

Netflix Movie *JUNG_E* movie Synopsis

Director: Sang-ho Yeon
Screenplay: Sang-ho Yeon
Producer Byun Seung-Min
Production Company: Climax Studio, WOW Point
Year of Production: 2023
Country: South Korea
Duration 98 minutes
Language: Korean
Genre: Science fiction, action, drama
Streaming Platform: Netflix
Main Cast: Kim Hyun-joo (Jung_E), Kang Soo-youn (Yun Seo-hyun), Ryu Kyung-soo (Kim Sang-Hoon)

Plot Summary: The movie takes place in the world of 2135, which has become uninhabitable due to climate change. Humanity is trying to establish a new life by building shelters in space. However, some of these shelters declare independence as the Adrian Republic and go to war with the remaining settlements. This conflict drags humanity into a war that lasts for many years. Captain Yun Jung-yi, a legendary mercenary of the Allied Forces, joins the wars to pay for the treatment of his daughter

Seo-hyun. However, he fails in his last mission and falls into a coma. Kronoid, an artificial intelligence development organization, clones Jung-yi's brain and turns him into a combat AI called *JUNG_E*. At the helm of this project is her daughter Seo-hyun, now grown up and a scientist. In 2194, the war is coming to an end and companies are turning to other markets instead of war robots. The project is about to be canceled. But Seo-hyun takes action to protect her mother's honor and to stand against the unethical aspects of the system. Jung_E escapes from the facility with one of his prototypes. The film is centered on Jung_E's regaining her free will and the struggle of a subject for existence against an inhumane technological system.[1]

Apple TV+ Movie *Swan Song* Movie Synopsis

Director: Benjamin Cleary
Screenplay: Benjamin Cleary
Producers: Jonathan Cavendish, Julie B. May, Ben A. Williams
Production Company: Apple TV+
Year of Production: 2021
Duration 112
Language: English
Genre: Drama, Science Fiction
Streaming Platform: Apple TV+
Lead Actors: Mahershala Ali, Naomie Harris, Awkwafina
Plot Synopsis: The film centers on Cameron Turner (Mahershala Ali), a terminally ill man who is faced with the choice of creating his own clone in order to spare his family pain. As Cameron begins to consider this ethically and emotionally complex solution, she struggles to make the right decision for her future and that of her family.[2]

COMPARATIVE OF ARTIFICIAL INTELLIGENCE THEMED FILMS

In the context of the comparative analysis of the films *JUNG_E* (Netflix, 2023) and *Swan Song* (Apple TV+, 2021) regarding the representation of artificial intelligence-themed content on digital broadcasting platforms, the table below systematically compares how the artificial intelligence themes of both films are processed, the forms of presentation through which the content is conveyed to the audience, their strategic positioning towards target audiences, the way digital platforms approach these contents and the way artificial intelligence depictions are characterized.

In this framework, under the heading of artificial intelligence themes, how the films address technological, ethical and emotional dimensions; under the heading of content presentation style, storytelling methods, visual style and in-platform presentation strategies were evaluated. The target audience strategy section reveals the age and interest groups for which each platform tailors its content, while the platform approach section focuses on Netflix and Apple TV+'s original content production and distribution policies. Finally, the depiction of artificial intelligence analyzes how artificial intelligence characters are portrayed in both films in terms of human characteristics, moral dilemmas and search for identity.

Table 1. Comparison of artificial intelligence themed films

Criteria	JUNG_E (Netflix, 2023)	Swan Song (Apple TV+, 2021)
Artificial Intelligence Themes	- Transfer of consciousness into an artificial body - The use of artificial intelligence in warfare technologies - Memory and personal rights - Exploitation of technology	- Consciousness transference and human replication - The question of identity and authenticity - Artificial intelligence mimicking human emotions - Problems of individual existence in the face of death
Content Presentation Format	- Focused on action and science fiction - Dystopian atmosphere - Fast-paced narration - Visual effects intensive - Dramatic Korean narrative language	- Emotional science fiction - Minimalist and slow-paced narration - Character-driven - Aesthetic and artistic shots - Dialog-heavy structure
Target Audience Strategy	- Young and adult science fiction audience - Action and technology enthusiasts - Netflix's global strategy for the Asian market	- Mature audience looking for emotional depth - Those interested in character development and ethical questioning - Artistic audience profile as part of Apple TV+'s "prestige content" strategy
Aesthetics and Narrative Style	- Korean futuristic aesthetics - Action-centered, character depth is secondary - Yeon Sang-ho's comic book-like, visual action style	- Minimalist but high-quality cinematography - Mahershala Ali's powerful performance in dual roles, emotional intensity - Benjamin Cleary's approach focused on slow tempo, intellectual structure and inner questioning
Publishing Ecosystem and Distribution Practices	- Global simultaneous launch; wide visibility with Netflix algorithm - Reaching a global audience with multiple dubbing and subtitling options - Visibility advantage in trend lists thanks to algorithmic distribution	- Limited access for Apple TV+ users only - More limited reach, but high quality of localization and authentic language use - Simple but attention-grabbing recommendation system due to low content

Artificial Intelligence

Although *JUNG_E* and *Swan Song* deal with the concept of artificial intelligence from different perspectives, they both focus on the blurring of boundaries between humanity and technology

Commonly, in both films, artificial intelligence is treated as a technical tool but also as an emotional and ethical issue. The idea of transferring human consciousness to artificial systems is a fundamental building block in both narratives. In this context, the reproduction of individual identity, memories and emotions through artificial intelligence opens up the effects of technology on human nature for discussion. On the other hand, the differences seem to emerge more in the emphasis points of the narratives.

While *JUNG_E* deals with the cloning of the human mind to produce warrior AI soldiers in a post-war future, it also criticizes the militarization of technology and the instrumentalization of human values. Artificial intelligence is considered here more in the context of a collective technology policy.

Through the theme of artificial intelligence, director Yeon Sang-ho presents a vision of the future that questions not only technological developments but also the social and ethical implications of these developments. Indeed, in the film, the idea of transferring the posthumous consciousness of individuals into synthetic bodies addresses the discourse of digital immortality together with a class hierarchy. While wealthy individuals can continue to live in synthetic bodies with all human rights, the middle class has access to this opportunity with more limited rights in exchange for data sharing. For the lower classes, the only option is to sell their mind data for commercial or scientific purposes. This structure shows how artificial intelligence is intertwined with the capitalist system and the risk of commodification of individual consciousness.

Swan Song, on the other hand, is based on an individual story; it focuses on a terminally ill man who creates a copy of himself in order not to cause pain to his family. In this film, artificial intelligence is dealt with in a more personal, emotional and existential dimension. The AI copy carries the love, fears and memories of the original individual, further complicating the issue of identity.

In *Swan* Song, the theme of artificial intelligence takes shape around immortality, raising a more personal ethical question: Does the reproduction of a person's identity and emotional bonds after their death create a true experience of immortality? The power of artificial intelligence to reconstruct individual identity and emotional connection creates a multi-layered ethical problem. Does replicating a person's exact "self" amount to violating their existential rights? Or, perhaps, is this kind of technological rebirth an option that is acceptable enough to ensure the continuation of the human being as a permanent presence beyond life? These questions test the ethical boundaries between humanity and technology and raise the question of how far artificial intelligence should interfere with human identity. In discussing the profound and sometimes dangerous effects of technology on human experience, both *JUNG_E* and *Swan Song* can be said to raise important questions about the extent to which these ethical issues are acceptable to humanity.

In conclusion, while both films relate artificial intelligence to human existential concerns, *JUNG_E* deals with social and military themes on a more macro level, while *Swan Song* prefers an individual and emotional perspective on a micro level. This shows that both productions create unique thematic depths in their approach to artificial intelligence.

Content Presentation Format

In the movie JUNG_E, artificial intelligence is predominantly constructed in a military context. In this narrative set in the future, the idea of artificial intelligence directing war robots and transferring human consciousness to digital media comes to the fore. In this context, artificial intelligence is presented as a functional technology that will replace humans on the battlefield and is handled with a very pragmatic approach. However, this use of artificial intelligence in the film raises various ethical and moral questions at the individual and social level. Especially in the context of war technology, the potential effects of artificial intelligence on human will and basic human values are opened to discussion; the boundaries between technology and the human body are rethought. As a matter of fact, Karabağ's (2021, p. 305) doctoral dissertation on science fiction series on Netflix has similar themes. Karabağ states that in these series, artificial intelligences are constructed as alternatives to humans in roles such as servants, sex robots, fighters, doctors, spouses/lovers or friends. When evaluated in this context, it can be said that the representations of artificial intelligence in Netflix's series are similarly reflected in the platform's movie content.

In the movie Swan Song, artificial intelligence goes beyond military or strategic contexts and is dealt with in a more personal and emotional framework. The movie is about an individual who is terminally ill and creates an artificial copy of himself that contains all his memories, personality and consciousness in order to protect his family from suffering. In this context, artificial intelligence is presented as a means of personal salvation for the individual to survive after death. The power of technology to reconstruct an individual's emotional ties and identity raises many questions both existentially and ethically. Especially the reproduction of a deceased individual through artificial intelligence turns into an experience that pushes the boundaries of being "human". As Reese (2020, p. 212) emphasizes, the purpose for which and how artificial intelligence is designed is of great importance in terms of its consequences. According to Reese, equipping artificial general intelligence with high cognitive capacities developed through sloppy programming may bring risks that may have serious consequences. In this respect, Swan Song centers on the question of whether artificial intelligence is a tool that serves the continuity of human life or a structure that threatens individual identity.

Both films examine the effects of technology on the human body and consciousness in the relationship between artificial intelligence and humanity. Thematically, both *JUNG_E* and *Swan Song* focus on how artificial intelligence can penetrate human identity, personality and emotional structure. Moreover, in both films, artificial intelligence is presented as an entity that has the power to somehow control or influence human life.

According to Köse (2013, pp. 76-77), beyond being a biological entity, the body is a structure that is shaped within cultural, social and political practices and whose meaning is constantly reproduced. This approach overlaps with Judith Butler's view that "the body is constructed in line with naturalized gender norms". According to Butler, the body is not a fixed essence; it is constructed along with gender through performatively repetitive actions and discourses (Butler, 2008, p. 34). Therefore, while the body is a visible entity, it is positioned as the carrier of power relations and cultural codes.

In this framework, in the film *JUNG_E*, the attempt to transform the artificial intelligence character Jung_E into a sex robot by removing her warrior identity shows how the female body is reshaped and instrumentalized by capitalist and patriarchal systems. The female body is constructed as both an instrument of war and an object of desire, and the continuity of the masculine gaze is ensured through the technological body.

In *Swan Song*, on the other hand, the AI body is completely desexualized and placed at the center of an ethical and emotional problematic. The replica body that replaces Cameron is positioned as a way to maintain family ties, while the physical representation of the AI serves an idealized human continuity. The distinction between these two examples is not only thematic but also related to the narrative strategies of the platforms. While Netflix's tendency to produce more striking, corporeal and provocative representations is evident in films such as *JUNG_E*, Apple TV+ presents a content approach that prioritizes more emotional, ethical and philosophical depth through *Swan Song*.

The differences in the way the films present content are mostly found in the way artificial intelligence is treated. *While JUNG_E* focuses on action and warfare, artificial intelligence is treated more as a military force. Artificial intelligence, as a war technology, replaces humans and aims to control human life. *Swan Song* discusses the effects of artificial intelligence through a more emotional and personal narrative. In this movie, artificial intelligence aims to recreate human emotional experiences such as death and loss, and in this context, it is seen that a more individual, moral and emotional approach is taken. Furthermore, whereas in *JUNG_E* AI is an entity in a constant process of rebirth and remembrance, in *Swan* Song AI is shown as a means of personal "rebirth".

In conclusion, both films deal with the effects of artificial intelligence on the human experience in different ways, focusing on war and its effects on the social level on the one hand, and on death and the search for individual identity on the other. It can be said that these themes enrich the AI-themed content of both films in different ways.

Target Audience

The films *JUNG_E* (2023) and *Swan Song* (2021) seem to deal with the theme of artificial intelligence in quite different fictional contexts and audience expectations. Both films are positioned to appeal to unique target audiences in line with the content strategies of different digital streaming platforms (Netflix and Apple TV+).

According to Siapera (2014, p. 156), unlike the passive recipients of the traditional mass communication model, online audiences are more active, participatory and dynamic. This new generation of digital viewers is positioned not only as consumers of content but also as producers, interpreters and part of social interaction. Digital streaming platforms such as Netflix shape their content strategies to respond to the demands of this audience profile. In this context, the movie *JUNG_E*, with its dystopian structure blending action and science fiction elements, targets especially the young adult and science fiction action audience. The film deals with themes such as artificial intelligence, war technologies, robotic transformation and the digitization of human consciousness; the narrative, supported by fast-paced editing, intense visual effects and dramatic scenes, appeals to a wide global audience. This production, which is in line with Netflix's strategy of multilingualism, cultural diversity and speed-oriented content production, can be considered as an example that reflects the platform's global accessibility and attractiveness goals.

In contrast, in line with Apple TV's strategy of presenting "inspiring and original stories with emotional depth, filled with compelling characters from all walks of life" (Apple, 2019), *Swan* Song opts for a simpler, emotional and philosophical narrative. In line with the platform's policy of producing more selective and "prestigious" content, the film stands out for its character-driven structure, emotional intensity and ethical debates. The theme of artificial intelligence, on the other hand, is explored here through deeper issues such as death, the self, the continuity of personal identity and human relationships; in this respect, it appeals to an adult audience looking for a more intellectual and emotional viewing experience. Apple's Racial Equality and Justice Initiative (REJI) projects (Apple, 2021), launched to combat systemic racism and promote racial equality across the country, demonstrate the importance the company attaches to diversity in representation in content production. Apple's corporate strategy is supported by the fact that the character of artificial intelligence in *Swan Song* is played by Mahershala Ali, a black actor, and his wife is played by Naomie Harris, also a black woman.

As a result, while both films thematically center on artificial intelligence, they format their content according to the audience profile they target; *JUNG_E* adopts a more popular and action-based strategy, while *Swan Song* appeals to a more elitist and introverted audience.

Aesthetics and Narrative

The basic elements of cinematic narrative are camera movements, editing techniques, acting, character design, color, light, costume and space (Yaylalı, 2019, p. 217). These elements come together to create an interactive structure that ensures the aesthetic and narrative integrity of the film.

The aesthetic narrative style of JUNG_E is based on dark and cold visual elements reflecting a dystopian future. It can be said that the color palette and the use of light play an important role in the aesthetic structure of the film (Kırık, 2013, p. 71). In JUNG_E, the intense use of cold gray tones and neon lights highlights the dystopian themes in the film. Gray tones symbolize the dark and gloomy effects of technology, neon lights emphasize the dominance of digital environments and artificial intelligence. Sterile and industrial space designs express a world where human consciousness is subjected to technology. The advanced visual effects in the film support the themes of artificial intelligence and war. On the other hand, the narrative structure is shaped around individual identity, class inequality and ethical issues.

Annie Beauchamp and Shannon Gottlieb, the set designers of *Swan Song*, emphasize in an interview with director Benjamin Cleary *(*Beauchamp & Gotlieb, 2021*) that he* prefers a warmer and more nature-friendly aesthetic in futuristic science fiction, moving away from the traditional cold and metallic visuals. In line with this approach, wood textures and organic materials are emphasized even in technical spaces such as laboratories. These choices can be said to symbolize the relationship between man and nature, but they also add an emotional layer to the narrative. Mahershala Ali's performance in a double role increases the dramatic intensity of the narrative. Cleary's slow-paced and character-centered narrative style offers the opportunity to question a technological theme on a human and ethical level. The film draws attention with its minimalist aesthetic and takes the viewer on a visual and intellectual journey.

Both films offer different aesthetic approaches to the subject of artificial intelligence by shaping the basic elements of cinematic narrative in line with their own thematic priorities. both films reveal different dimensions of the technology-human relationship through aesthetic and narrative choices, offering the audience a multi-layered viewing process both visually and intellectually.

Publishing Ecosystem and Distribution Practices

As part of Netflix's global content strategy, *JUNG_E* has the opportunity to reach a wide audience with the advantage of a global simultaneous launch. Thanks to Netflix's algorithmic content recommendation system, its visibility is increased with recommendations tailored to user profiles in different regions of the platform; and thanks to multiple dubbing and subtitling options, the content overcomes linguistic barriers and provides ease of global access (Urrutia, 2025). This allows JUNG_E to not only remain a South Korean sci-fi movie, but also to create international engagement through digital publishing.

On the other hand, *Swan Song* is only available on Apple TV+, giving it a more limited audience reach. The fact that the platform offers less content in general leads to a simpler but more targeted algorithmic recommendation system, which makes it easier for *Swan* Song to stand out among the remarkable productions. Furthermore, Apple TV+'s high localization quality and emphasis on the use of authentic languages (Apple, 2025) can be considered as a factor that supports the emotional narrative power of the film. However, its global reach remains narrower than that of JUNG_E due to its limited subscription base.

In this context, both films exhibit different distribution practices according to the strategic orientations of their respective broadcast platforms: *JUNG_E* has a distribution model that prioritizes broad audience reach, while *Swan Song* is characterized by a more niche, selective and narrative-driven distribution strategy.

CONCLUSION

The digitalization process has radically transformed the structural characteristics and usage practices of mass media, paving the way for the rise of digital broadcasting platforms. Thanks to their user-oriented interface designs and personalized content presentations, network-based channels reach large audiences and provide an alternative to traditional television broadcasting. Digital platforms such as Netflix and Apple TV+ use artificial intelligence algorithms to shape their content recommendation systems according to audience habits and integrate artificial intelligence into their content strategies at both the technological infrastructure and thematic narrative level. In this context, AI-themed films are considered both as narrative forms and as strategic elements that determine the direction of the digital publishing ecosystem.

The films *JUNG_E* (2023) and *Swan Song* (2021) analyzed in this study bear the traces of the content production and presentation strategies adopted by different platforms in line with the audience profiles they target. The findings show that artificial intelligence-themed content has an increasing importance in digital broadcasting and that these themes are at the center of platform strategies. In this framework, the ways of representation of artificial intelligence-themed productions constitute a remarkable area in terms of the cultural and technological evolution of digital broadcasting.

JUNG_E and *Swan Song* open up a multilayered view of the human-technology relationship by addressing representations of artificial intelligence as technological developments and their ethical, social and existential dimensions. Both productions center on the reproducibility of human consciousness through digital systems and address this theme through different narrative strategies, aesthetic choices and platform politics. While JUNG_E evaluates the use of artificial intelligence within militaristic and capitalist systems in the context of class inequality and exploitation, it also establishes a critical ground in relation to patriarchal structures through the instrumentalization of the female body. *Swan Song*, on the other hand, presents a more philosophical narrative that questions the meaning of being human by positioning artificial intelligence as an ethical, emotional and existential issue in a moment of individual death-identity rupture.

In both films, the representation of the body is dealt with not only in a physical context but also as a structure woven with cultural, social and ideological codes, and questioning areas regarding ethical boundaries are formed through the claim of artificial intelligence replicas to be "human". On the aesthetic level, JUNG_E presents an action-oriented structure with dark and mechanical visuals that support the dystopian atmosphere, while *Swan* Song creates a more visceral aesthetic experience with spaces in harmony with nature, warm tones and minimalist narrative. These differences deepen the emotional and intellectual connection with the audience, while reinforcing thematic stances on a platform basis.

Moreover, the digital platforms on which both films are released play a decisive role in the shaping of these productions. Thanks to Netflix's global reach, algorithmic recommendation system and multilingual options, JUNG_E reaches a wide audience, bringing a local production into a global sphere of interaction. Apple TV+, on the other hand, with its more selective, prestige-oriented and character-deep content strategy, brings *Swan* Song to a niche audience and highlights it in terms of narrative integrity and emotional intensity. Thus, both films represent different faces of digital broadcasting and platform-specific production dynamics, demonstrating both the formal and thematic diversity of artificial intelligence-themed content.

In conclusion, the films JUNG_E and *Swan Song* blend artificial intelligence narratives with the cultural, ethical and aesthetic codes of the digital age, creating spaces for critical thinking about the place of technology in human life. In addition to being contemporary examples of the science fiction genre, these films can be considered as intellectual structures that show how technological imaginaries are intertwined with social norms, value systems and platform strategies in the digital publishing ecosystem.

REFERENCES

Abisel, N. (2010). *Popüler sinema ve türler*. İletişim Publishing.

Acar, E. (2007). *Ölümlülük, Ölümsüzlük Ve Yapay Zeka*. Altkitap Publishing.

Alioğlu, N. (2011). *Yeni Medya Sanat ve Estetiği*. Papatya Publishing.

Altunışık, R., Coşkun, R., Bayraktaroğlu, S., & Yıldırım, E. (2010). *Sosyal Bilimlerde Araştırma Yöntemleri: SPSS Uygulamalı* (6th ed.). Sakarya Publishing.

Apple. (2019, March 25). Apple Unveils Apple TV+, The New Home For The World's Most Creative Storytellers. Apple Newsroom. https://www.apple.com/tr/newsroom/2019/03/apple-unveils-apple-tv-plus-the-new-home-for-the-worlds-most-creative-storytellers/ Retrieved April 28, 2025

Apple. (2021, January 13). Apple Launches Major New Racial Equity And Justice Initiative Projects To Challenge Systemic Racism, Advance Racial Equity Nationwide. Apple Newsroom. https://www.apple.com/newsroom/2021/01/apple-launches-major-new-racial-equity-and-justice-initiative-projects-to-challenge-systemic-racism-advance-racial-equity-nationwide/ Retrieved April 29, 2025

Apple. (2024a). Where To Watch Apple TV+. https://support.apple.com/en-us/HT210740 Retrieved April 22, 2025

Apple. (2024b). About Tvos 18 And İts Accessibility Features. https://support.apple.com/en-us/HT211331 Retrieved April 22, 2025

Apple. (2025, 5 Mart). Apple TV+ Hakkında. Apple Support. https://support.apple.com/tr-tr/119599 Retrieved April 30, 2025

Aydemir, M. (2023). Dijital Platformlarda İçerik Mülkiyeti Stratejileri: "Sadece" Modeli Üzerine Bir İnceleme. *Nevşehir Hacı Bektaş Veli Üniversitesi Sosyal Bilimler Enstitüsü Dergisi*, *13*(3), 1457–1478. DOI: 10.30783/nevsosbilen.1271624

Aziz, A. (2014). *Sosyal Bilimlerde Araştırma Yöntemleri Ve Teknikleri* (9th ed.). Nobel Akademik Yayıncılık Eğitim Danışmanlık Ticaret Ltd. Şti., https://www.nobelyayin.com

Başer, E., & Akıncı, S. (2020). Kullanıcı Deneyimi Ve Kişiselleştirme Bağlamında Bir Dijital Platform İncelemesi. *Selçuk İletişim Dergisi*, *13*(2), 866–897.

Beauchamp, A., & Gotlieb, S. (2021, December 30). Interview: Annie Beauchamp and Shannon Gotlieb on the futuristic set design of Swan Song. Awards Radar. https://awardsradar.com/2021/12/30/interview-annie-beauchamp-and-shannon-gotlieb-on-the-futuristic-set-design-of-swan-swong/ Retrieved April 29, 2025

Butler, J. (2008). *Cinsiyet Belası: Feminizm ve Kimliğin Altüst Edilmesi* (Ertür, B., Trans.). Metis Publishing.

Büyükçelikok, T. Ö., & Dilmen, N. E. (2024). Dijital Yayın Platformları Teknik Özelliklerinin Kullanılabilirliğinin Kullanıcı Deneyimine Etkisi: Netflix Örneği. İletişim Çalışmaları Dergisi, 10(3), 359–372. https://doi.org/DOI: 10.17932/IAU.ICD.2015.006/icd_v010i3005

Castells, M. (2005). *Enformasyon Çağı: Ekonomi, Toplum Ve Kültür Birinci Cilt: Ağ Toplumunun Yükselişi* (Kılıç, E., Trans.). Istanbul Bilgi University Press.

Cleary, B. (Director). (2021). Swan Song [Film]. Apple TV+. https://tv.apple.com/us/movie/swan-song/umc.cmc.2u5ulzjcxh7e50uhichjjlsv6. Retrieved April 30, 2025.

Coşkun, M. Ç. (2023). Instrument Development To Evaluate The Usability Of OTT Platforms (Master's thesis). Istanbul Technical University, Istanbul.

Demirci, H. (2024). Dijital Platformlarda Müslüman Kadın Kimliği: Élite Dizisi Örneği (Master's thesis). Erciyes University, Kayseri.

Erdem, N., & Aytekin, B. A. (2021). Covid-19 Pandemisinde İzleyici Deneyimi: Netflix Ekseninde Dijital Platformlara Bakış. *Akdeniz Üniversitesi İletişim Fakültesi Dergisi, 36*(36), 302–325. DOI: 10.31123/akil.988565

Hall, S. (2017). *Temsil: Kültürel Temsiller Ve Anlamlandırma Uygulamaları* (Dündar, İ., Trans.). Pinhan Publishing. (Original work published 1997)

Holat, O., & Polan, Ş. (2024). Dijital Yayın Platformu "Netflix" Üzerine Hazırlanan Lisansüstü Tezlerin Bibliyometrik Analizi. [KİAD]. *Kastamonu İletişim Araştırmaları Dergisi*, (13), 263–287. DOI: 10.56676/kiad.1450854

Karabağ, M. (2021). Dijital Televizyon Platformlarında Yayınlanan Bilim Kurgu Dizilerinde Yapay Zeka Olgusu: Netflix Örneği (Doctoral dissertation). Istanbul University, Institute of Social Sciences.

Karaca Özdemir, T. (2025). Bilim Kurgu Sinemasında Yapay Zeka Karakterlerinin İnşası (Master's thesis). Ondokuz Mayıs University, Samsun.

Karakaş, S., Rukancı, F., & Anameriç, H. (2009). Belge Yönetimi Ve Arşiv Terimleri Sözlüğü. T.C. Cumhurbaşkanlığı Devlet Arşivleri Başkanlığı. https://www.devletarsivleri.gov.tr/varliklar/dosyalar/eskisiteden/yayinlar/genel-mudurluk-yayinlar/belge_yonetimi_ve_arsiv_terimleri_sozlugu.pdf

Kavas, B. (2022). 2000 Sonrası Bilimkurgu Sinemasında Robotların Cinsiyetlendirilmesi (Master's thesis), Ankara University, Institute of Social Sciences, Department of Radio, Television, and Cinema.

Kırık, A. M. (2013). Sinemada Renk Öğesinin Kullanımı: Renk Ve Anlatım İlişkisi. 21. Yüzyılda Eğitim ve Toplum Eğitim Bilimleri ve Sosyal Araştırmalar Dergisi, 2(6), 71–83. https://dergipark.org.tr/tr/download/article-file/59561

Köse, H. (2013). Tüketim Toplumunda Bir "Sosyal Beden" Kurgusu Olarak Kadın. *Selçuk İletişim Dergisi*, *6*(4), 76–89.

Ladeira, J. M. (2013). Negócios De Audiovisual Na İnternet: Uma Comparação Entre Netflix, Hulu E İtunes-Appletv, 2005-2010. Revista Contracampo, 26(1), 145-162. https://www.uff.br/contracampo

Lotz, A. D. (2017). *Portals: A Treatise On İnternet Distributed Television.* Michigan Publishing., DOI: 10.3998/mpub.9699689

Manovich, L. (2014). HTML'den Borges'e yeni medya. In Çakır, M. (Ed.), *Yeni medyaya eleştirel yaklaşımlar* (pp. 157–182). Doğu Publishing.

Motamayor, R. (2024, July 24). Apple TV+ Has Great Shows — So Why İs No One Watching Them? SlashFilm. https://www.slashfilm.com/1628281/apple-tv-great-shows-no-one-watching-them/ Retrieved April 21, 2025

Murphy, S. (2011). *How Television Invented New Media, New Brunswick*, New Jersey ve Londra: Rutgers University.

Musser, J. ve O'Reilly, T. (2006). Web 2.0 Principles and Best Practices. (1. Baskı). USA: O'Reilly Media.

Nisanoğlu, K. (2021). Artıfıcıal Intellıgence And Humankınd Relatıons In Scıence Fıctıon Cınema. (Master's thesis). Bahçeşehir University.

Oskay, Ü. (2007). *İletişimin ABC'si*. İnklap Publishing.

Öztürk, G. (2013). *Dijital Reklamcılık ve Gençlik*. Beta Publishing.

PCMag. (2024). Apple TV Plus Review. https://www.pcmag.com/reviews/apple-tv-plus Retrieved April 22, 2025)

Reese, B. (2020). *Yapay Zekâ Çağı – Dördüncü Çağ: Akıllı Robotlar, Bilinçli Bilgisayarlar Ve İnsanlığın Geleceği* (Doğan, M., Trans.). Say Publishing.

Rogers, E. (1986). *Communication Technology: The New Media İn Society*. Free Publishing.

Şahin, R. N. (2024). Dijital Platformlar Kullanıcı Motivasyonu: Netflix Örneği (Master's thesis). Hacı Bayram Veli University, Ankara.

Siapera, E. (2014). From Couch Potatoes To Cybernauts: The Expanding Notion Of The Audience On TV Channels' Websites. *New Media & Society*, *16*(6), 155–172.

Urrutia, K. (2025, January 18). Netflix Marketing Strategy: Disrupting The Entertainment İndustry With İnnovation And Personalization. Voy Media. https://voymedia.com/netflix-marketing-strategy/ Retrieved April 30, 2025

Yaylalı, H. (2019). Sinemasal Anlatının Örneklerle Analizi: "Film Çalışmaları". *Etkileşim Üsküdar Üniversitesi İletişim Fakültesi Akademik Dergisi*, *2*(3), 214–217. DOI: 10.32739/etkilesim.2019.3.55

Yeon, S. H. (Director). (2023). JUNG_E [Film]. Netflix. https://www.netflix.com/title/81465109. Retrieved April 30, 2025

ADDITIONAL READING

Alan, E. (2025). *Yapay zeka çağında dijitalleşme ve CRM*. Optimist Publishing.

Çağıl, F. (2025). Dijital sinema kavramı çerçevesinde sinemada kameranın geleceği. *Yeni Medya Elektronik Dergisi*, *9*(1), 31–49.

Hall, F. (2014). *Dijital yayıncılık (H. Vardar* (Üstün, M., & Küçük, C., Eds. & Trans.). Profil Publishing.

Karşanbaş, L. (2022). Dijital platformlar ve belgesel sinema. *Maltepe Üniversitesi İletişim Fakültesi Dergisi*, *9*(1), 152–156.

Manovich, L. (2001). *The Language of New Media*. MIT Press.

Şenlik, A. C. (2025). *Teknoloji kabulü ve teknolojik yatkınlığın tüketicilerin dijital yayın platformlarını kullanım niyeti ve sıklığı üzerine etkileri Master's thesis, Hacettepe University*. Hacettepe University Institute of Social Sciences.

Temel, M., & Koçak, Ö. F. (Eds.). (2021). *Dijital çağda iletişim kültür ve medya 1: Dijitalleşme ve iletişim*. Çizgi Publishing.

Torun, A. (2021). Sinemada veya Netflix'te – dijital izleme ortamları ve yeni alışkanlıklar – bir sosyal ortam olarak sinema ve film izleme pratiklerindeki dijital dönüşüm. *SineFilozofi*, *6*(11), 370–387. DOI: 10.31122/sinefilozofi.871301

Tryon, C. (2013). *On-demand culture: Digital delivery and the future of movies.* Rutgers University Press.

Büyükçelikok, T. Ö. (2024). Dijital yayın platformu özelliklerinin kullanıcı deneyimine etkisi: Netflix örneği Doctoral dissertation, Marmara University. Marmara University Institute of Social Sciences.

KEY TERMS AND DEFINITIONS

Artificial Intelligence (AI): Artificial intelligence can be defined as computer systems, software or intelligent machines that can think, learn, make decisions and automate tasks like humans. Today, artificial intelligence is used effectively in many fields from health to education, from banking to industry, from defense systems to autonomous vehicles, and penetrates every aspect of life.

Digital Publishing: is the digital publishing of content such as news, videos, music and books over the internet. In other words, it is a new form of traditional publishing shaped by the development of technology and the internet.

Digital Platforms: are online spaces where users can interact with content such as watching, listening and sharing content via the internet. Today, platforms such as Netflix and YouTube are effectively used in this direction.

Media Ecosystem: Media ecosystem refers to the communication space where the content of different media tools such as television, radio, internet and social media interact with each other; where information and news are produced, shared and consumed.

Content Personalization: Platforms can be defined as determining the interests of users according to their previous preferences and presenting them with content tailored to their personal interests and tastes.

Platform Politics: the rules and strategies that digital platforms set for content production, which audience to address and how to shape the user experience.

Sci-Fi Cinema: Sci-fi cinema refers to a genre of films about utopian or dystopian worlds, different planets and colonies, space travel, the future, technology, artificial intelligence, multiple universes and alternative realities, shaped by scenarios based on imagination.

ENDNOTES

1 "JUNG_E" access address: Netflix (2023). Jung_E. https://www.netflix.com/tr/title/81465109?s=i&trkid=258593161&vlang=tr

2 "Swan Song" Access Address: Apple TV+. (2021). *Swan Song*.https://tv.apple.com/us/movie/swan-song/umc.cmc.2u5ulzjcxh7e50uhichjjlsv6

Chapter 15

Experiencing Social Reality Through "Found Story" in 360-Degree VR Narratives

Ummuhan Molo
https://orcid.org/0000-0002-3651-4818
Faculty of Communication, Istanbul Yeni Yüzyıl University, Turkey

Kubra Nisanoglu
https://orcid.org/0000-0002-3271-5401
Faculty of Communication, Istanbul Yeni Yüzyıl University, Turkey

ABSTRACT

Cinema, with its use of virtual technologies that immerse the audience in the narrative and present reality in new ways, reinvokes Siegfried Kracauer's concept of the 'found story'. Kracauer states that everyday reality can be captured through cinema and defines this as the 'found story'. This study aims to explore that concept within the framework of VR film technology. The research focuses on National Geographic's 360-degree VR series Plastic on the Ganges, which addresses social reality. The series depicts how plastic waste pollutes oceans and drinking water, affecting both human health and ecosystems. Its impact comes not only from what it tells but also from how it allows the audience to experience the story in an immersive way. The audience becomes part of the scene, among real individuals whose health is at risk. Thus, the 'found story' does not express the spectacle of a reality, but its experience.

DOI: 10.4018/979-8-3373-1957-5.ch015

INTRODUCTION

The development and diversification of narrative forms and technologies in cinema today often trigger the need to theoretically return to the past and reconsider them from a contemporary perspective. Unlike most other disciplines, in social science studies, especially in cinema studies, it is not possible to find a theoretical approach that is either agreed upon or rejected and isolated by clear boundaries. Academic studies in the field often reconsult to existing theories as a starting point, and re-reading the present day through dissertations put forward in the past is also the key to a unifying and holistic understanding. In this context, the concept of the "found story" discussed in this study and articulated by Siegfried Kracauer provides a critical framework for understanding how narratives emerge not through deliberate authorial construction but through the organic, often chaotic unfolding of reality. Initially formulated in the context of historiography and traditional media, the idea of the found story has gained renewed importance in the aesthetics of new media environments, particularly in the immersive formats of 360-degree virtual reality (VR) storytelling, offering the possibility of a refreshing rereading. Unlike classical narrative structures that impose coherence and causality on fragmented life events, VR narratives (especially those based in documentary or social realist traditions) offer the potential to preserve the disjointedness, randomness, and immediacy of lived experience. The spatial and experiential possibilities of 360-degree VR create an embodied mode of spectatorship that blurs the boundary between observer and participant by placing viewers within the narrative's environment. At the same time, this immersive positioning invites users to navigate the storyworld in a way that reflects Kracauer's vision of the found story encountering: not as a predetermined and constructed plot, but as a dynamic, emergent reality.

This study analyzes case studies in which social problems are portrayed through immersive VR environments, examining narrative techniques that eschew overt dramatization in favor of presenting the complexity and unpredictability of real life. It also explores how the technological possibilities of VR contribute to new modes of presence, perception, and emotional interaction, in line with Kracauer's call for a more authentic representation of physical reality. The analysis section of the chapter examines how the *Plastic on the Ganges* series mobilizes the aesthetics of the found story to facilitate an experiential transmission of social realities. By analyzing the series' narrative structure, visual strategies, and spatial organization, it investigates how the immersive possibilities of 360-degree VR technologies allow viewers to experience environmental degradation not through didactic display, but through an emotional and sensory engagement with the experienced textures of everyday life. In doing so, the chapter argues that VR narratives such as *Plastic on the Ganges* offer a renewed model of social storytelling that resists the closure and teleology of traditional narratives and instead embraces the open-ended, fragmented, and embodied nature of contemporary social experience. The absence of a singular, central plot invites users to make sense of their embodied experiences in the virtual space and aligns closely with Kracauer's vision of encountering historical and social reality as contingent and emergent.

While Kracauer's insights are rooted in early 20th-century media and historiographic theory, they have a renewed importance within the evolving aesthetics of new media, particularly in immersive 360-degree virtual reality (VR) environments. Here, narrative does not simply emerge; it is encountered through a dynamic interplay of immersion, presence, and agency. *Plastic on the Ganges*, a 360-degree VR documentary series focusing on plastic pollution along the Ganges River, exemplifies how found-story aesthetics are operationalized in contemporary media practices. Through a high degree of immersion and presence, viewers are positioned not as passive spectators but as embodied participants navigating a multisensory landscape. The effect of 360-degree navigation allows users to define their focal points and paths of attention, emphasizing a participatory mode of meaning-making that mirrors the serendipitous emergence of Kracauer's found story. Moreover, *Plastic on the Ganges* operates within the broader logic of remix culture and algorithmic aesthetics, where fragments of reality (individual testimonies, environmental sounds, urban textures) are captured, reassembled, and spatially arranged without the imposition of coherence by a single authorial voice. The algorithmic construction of VR environments, which continually recalibrate perspective based on viewer interaction, further emphasizes the dissolution of fixed narratives in favor of experiential fluidity. In this context, embodiment becomes a critical dimension: the VR user's bodily orientation, movement, and perceptual choices are not peripheral but central to the narrative experience. Unlike traditional film, where framing and montage dictate meaning, in VR, the viewer's embodied exploration co-constructs the emergent story. Thus, the story found in Plastic on the Ganges is not merely shown; it is totally experienced.

Finally, this chapter explores in depth how the intersection of these concepts (immersion, presence, activity, embodiment, remix culture, and algorithmic aesthetics) redefines the transmission of social realities in 360-degree VR narratives through Kracauer's understanding of reality and the concept of the "found story." Through a focused analysis of *Plastic on the Ganges*, the study aims to show that VR does not merely represent social worlds; it restructures the conditions of their experiences, offering new forms of social participation that align with, yet transform, Kracauer's core vision of authentic, unfiltered storytelling. At the same time, through this research, the chapter aims to reposition Kracauer's found story not as a static theoretical artifact, but as a dynamic and evolving principle that continues to inform the aesthetics of emerging media forms.

New Media Aesthetics and Narrative Forms

Understanding the evolving scope of new media aesthetics, its conceptual foundations, and the critical theoretical studies it has been subject to is important in order to gain a holistic perspective on the concept as a whole. Concepts such as digitization and digital representation emphasize a transformation toward independent and digitally manipulable data. These now make possible features such as modularity and automation that were largely absent from their earlier analog predecessors. The structural variability of digital objects, together with their capacity for constant change, transformation, and adaptation, stands in sharp contrast to the formal fixity of traditional media. In addition, the technological facilitation of transcoding across platforms and formats amplifies new dimensions of cultural exchange and interpretation, and the variability of aesthetic understanding in new media is substantiated through such phenomena. These new possibilities brought to new media productions can be examined under several different concepts on the axis of formal structure and audience. The starting point of these comprehensive concepts is immersion. The concept of immersion within new media theory is complex and multifaceted, and which is evolving alongside relevant technological advancements.

These new possibilities provided by new media content can be examined under several different concepts on the axis of form and audience. The beginning of these rather comprehensive concepts is *immersion*. The concept of immersion in new media theory is complex and multifaceted, and develops in direct proportion to the relevant technological developments. It's not simply about 'being there', but rather a confluence of factors that contribute to a sense of deep engagement with a mediated experience. By that, the relevant technologies create a sense of presence and engagement. In this respect, the state of being there mentioned here is similar to the concept of 'dasein' (being there/being in the world) mentioned by Heidegger; it is not just about being there and observing, but also about sensory interactions established with that environment and objects. What makes the act of being there meaningful is the provision of experiences that allow for active interaction from passive spectatorship, and this is exactly what new media aesthetics promises. Immersion is not a monolithic concept. It varies depending on the medium, the user, and the context.

Often intertwined with immersion, *presence* refers to a psychological sense of 'being there' in a mediated environment (Slater and Wilbur, 1997). This is particularly relevant in VR technologies, where users can feel physically present in a virtual space. To summarize, presence is the state in which a person feels mentally and perceptually present in a virtual environment, despite being physically somewhere else. For Mel Slater, presence is not just about 'being immersed'; it is about experiencing the virtual elements in one's environment as if they were real. "Given the same immersive system, different people may experience different levels of presence, and also different immersive systems may give rise to the same level of presence in different people" (Slater, 2003, p.2). Immersion can be achieved in two main ways in this medium: One through narrative immersion, and the other through technological one. The narrative immersion concept focuses on how storytelling techniques can draw users into a narrative world. This involves creating compelling characters, believable environments, and engaging plotlines. Thus, narrative theory, particularly in relation to digital storytelling, explores how new media can create immersive narratives through non-linear structures and interactive elements. On the other hand, technological immersion refers to the technical capabilities of a medium to create a sense of immersion. These include high-resolution visuals, surround sound technology, and haptic feedback, which can contribute to the viewer's technological immersion stage. It is also closely linked to developments in VR, AR, and other immersive technologies that are constantly pushing the boundaries of what is possible in these environments. Then, another important concept that is quite intertwined with immersion is *interactivity*. The concept of interactivity in new media theory is a dynamic and evolving one, playing a major role in fundamentally changing our understanding of the relationship between media and its audience. It helps to move the understanding of media from traditional, passive reception to active participation and interaction. In its technological structure, interactivity refers to a two-way or multi-way exchange between users and the media, which ensures a constant variability of options throughout the process. It also refers to user affect, that is, the sense of control and influence in the user experience, as a fundamental component of interactivity. This process also contains the ability to influence the content, form, or flow of the media experience. Because of this agency and reciprocity, it also provides feedback to user actions by creating a sense of responsiveness. Whether this feedback can be immediate or delayed, at the same time, it can take various forms such as visual, auditory, or haptic. By all these stages, interactivity options encourage user participation, blurring the lines between creator and consumer, in this case, the audience. Now they are able to contribute content, modify the existing one, and collaborate with others through the influence of their personal choices and social backgrounds.

New media serve as a tool that embodies its own distinct aesthetic values and narrative forms. What distinguishes it from other media and artistic disciplines is its unified structure, which amalgamates elements from cinema, television, photography, journalism, the internet, and various interactive environments. This unified structure does not have a sharply defined or easily identifiable boundary, resembling Nicholas Mirzoeff's concept of visual culture;

I describe the resulting hybridity of visual forms with each other and non-visual media as intervisuality. Intervisuality comprises the intertextuality of visual media, the interdependence of visual and non-visual media, the interface of viewer, technology, and the viewed, and the new infrastructures being created to support these changes (Mirzoeff, 2001, p.124).

The possibility of interaction with the visual given to the recipient is an important and effective factor in the construction of this aesthetic understanding and new media narrative. According to Mieke Bal, visual images also have a 'narrative aspect', and it is important to examine how the narrative and its potential to interpret that narrative are communicated to the recipient, because this potential of visual culture contains dynamics of power and representation (Bal, 2003). In this representation process, technologies that can enable interactivity evolves directly proportional to *remix culture*. The concept of remix culture is a cornerstone of new media theory, describing a society where creative Works are not just consumed but also actively transformed, repurposed, and shared. It's a shift from a 'read-only' culture to a 'read-write' culture, enabled by digital technologies. This form of participation resembles Barthes' *writerly text* concept, in which the meaning is not stable and limited; the reader (in that case participant/audience) needs to actively rewrite the text, where the reader is transformed into a content creator with the writer. Remix culture thrives on the ability to sample, copy, and manipulate existing media content, which can involve anything from music and video to images and text. Those digital platforms facilitate collaborative creation and sharing, allowing users to build upon each other's work. Thus, it often emphasized open Access to information and creative works by challenging traditional notions of copyright and intellectual property. To clarify, remix is not just about copying; just as it is described in writerly text concept, it's about transforming existing content, adding new layers of meaning, and reinterpreting it in new contexts. It also challenges the media consumer by inviting them to the production phases. Henry Jenkins, who has presented one of the most important studies on this subject in the field, also touches on the importance of participatory culture. According to Jenkins, consumers are not only passive but also active participants, playing a significant role in creating, sharing, and interacting with content and other users. In this context, participatory culture shortens the barriers in artistic expression and individual interaction, and contributes to the idea that users' contributions matter and that they remain socially connected. According to Jenkins, none of us has a comprehensive knowledge of what this media convergence, collective intelligence, and participatory culture are, and these changes produce anxiety, ambiguity, and panic because we have difficulty imagining a consumption process outside the influence of institutional and conventional controlling media power (Jenkins, 2006).

Algorithmic aesthetics is a concept that belongs to a constantly evolving field within new media theory, and whose outputs are fascinated by the masses, especially considering the age of artificial intelligence we are currently experiencing. This concept generally deals with how algorithms shape and affect our perception and design processes in the field of fine arts. It helps to understand how computational processes create aesthetic experiences and how these experiences differ from traditional artistic expressions. In this rapidly growing and developing computational design sector, materials to be examined aesthetically can be produced with different methods. The content designed automatically by algorithms has a unique and unpredictable structure. This includes a variety of products from generative art to music, from video games to coding. At the same time, with its features of visualizing given data and spontaneously producing works of art, it pushes us to question the nature of concepts such as creativity and originality. It is important to analyze the mathematical structure behind the cultural products produced by computers, especially digital images, sounds, and data processing systems, from a cultural perspective, because the computer now functions as a cultural machine; knowledge and cultural memory are also digitalized accordingly (Kittler, 1996). Algorithmic aesthetics as a concept also raises questions about the role of the artist in computational production phases, whether the artist is a programmer, algorithms themselves, or the user? It's also pointing us to reconsider the role of the consumer, by eliminating the solid and basic structure of traditional media consuming processes, by changing the designated position.

Considering all these developments, change does not only occur at an instrumental or consumption level; the consumed content itself is at the very center of this evolution process. Traditional narrative forms differ among traditional art types, but they have their consistencies and rules, and styling and aesthetic norms are already based on these recurring patterns. However, throughout the history of art, some artists thought that these rules were the walls that chained the free spirit of art and artists by restricting their development area, and rejected the traditional narrative form sought by the pre-structuralist perspective. Just like the break that came with the impressionist approach, when painters such as Monet, Renoir, and Pisarro began to depict nature, light, and instant impressions in the mid-19th century, defying the strict rules of academic painting. Over the centuries, similar approaches were seen in cinema, following painting, literature, and music.

The emergence of experimental narrative structure in cinema is largely the result of an objection to the classical narrative norms represented by mainstream cinema, and includes the re-questioning of the aesthetic and ideological structure of classical narrative. This structure has been observed in productions since the first half of the 20th century, influenced particularly by modernist and avant-garde art movements. It has been seen as an alternative cinema language that adopts the formal elements of the narrative and can be established in a way different from the generally accepted patterns. The basic characteristics of classical narrative, such as causality, continuity in time and space, character-centered and linear editing that directs the audience's perception, have been questioned. Rather than treating cinema as a narrative tool, it positions it as an area of audiovisual experience. Non-linear narratives, user-centered narratives, narratives that include gamification, etc., can be given as examples of these, and examples where actors turn to the camera to enter into a dialogue with the audience to remove the audience from a passive position are also among the experimental narrative techniques. With the development of camera and editing technologies, individual production has risen, and independent filmmaking processes have become easier compared to the past, thus expanding the areas of creative expression and increasing diversity. On new media platforms, experimental narrative diversity has developed in direct proportion to the technological possibilities offered. Different examples can be mentioned, such as internet-based projects, digital artworks (or NFTs), interactive documentaries and series, and social media narratives. The 2018 production "Bandersnatch: Black Mirror", which was added to the platform as a part of the Black Mirror series produced by Netflix, has been one of the frequently mentioned and examined examples in that regard, and is an interactive film with narrative features based on multiple endings and plotline choices, where the viewer can intervene in the decisions of the character. Similarly, the animated film "Puss in Book: Trapped in an Epic Tale (2017)", another Netflix production, is produced in an interactive structure. Again, developments have occurred in the field of theater; following the 2011 interactive theater performance "Sleep No More", the play "The Invisible Hours", which was staged in 2017, also offered the audience a physical experience through virtual reality technologies.

It has become a narrative form that stands in stark contrast to the classical narrative structure, with the story shifting to a different perspective, the absence of a linear and definitive narrative form, and the active participation of the audience in the storytelling process, transforming the consumption process from spectatorship to experience. To summarize, experimental narrative structure has some distinctive qualifications that brought new horizons to new media narrative style and aesthetics. Fragmented plots support the idea of non-linearity, rather than viewing, visual and auditory exploration is emphasized. Thus, subjectivity and abstraction are supported through narrative processes. Unlike the extensive idea of conventions, experimental narrative style focuses on the medium itself by encouraging the user's exploration of consciousness. By that understanding, experimental filmmakers/content creators aim to eliminate the limits of classical narrative styles that affect reception processes, by using the opportunities provided by new media technologies.

Narrative Structure Created by VR Technologies

Traditional narrative forms are undergoing transformation in direct proportion to technological developments, and virtual reality (VR) is seen as one of the most striking examples of this transformation process. With these technologies, narrative processes are restructured by placing users in the position of subjects who not only watch the story but also experience it. In addition to the new media concepts mentioned in the previous section, VR technology also has various possibilities contributed by itself. These are examined in order through concepts such as immersion, presence, agency, spatial storytelling, and embodiment.

- **Audience Experience**

Immersion means that the viewer temporarily breaks his/her connection with the physical world and participates in the virtual world holistically. In VR narratives, immersion allows not only watching the story but also experiencing the filmic time and space directly. With various VR tools, the viewer is involved in the narrative universe not only mentally but also emotionally and sensually. This situation, with the help of intermediary apparatus, significantly increases the credibility of the narrative and its striking effect on the viewer. Because with the help of developments such as walking platforms and consoles, the viewer is no longer limited to looking at a rectangular screen from a chair, but can travel every inch of the filmic universe with the help of relevant technology.

Figure 1. Omni One Walking Platform, Virtuix.com.

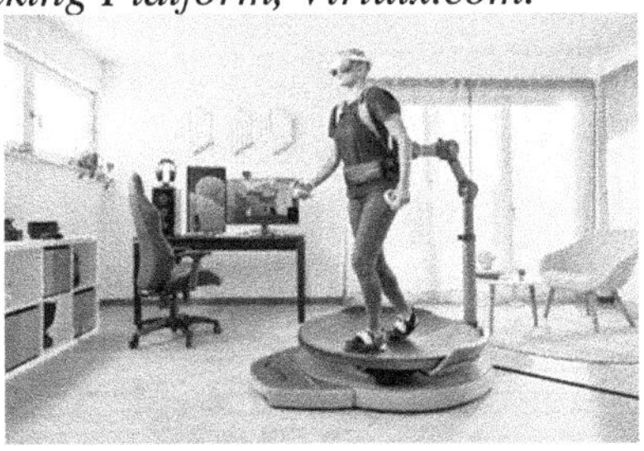

Presence is closely related to the viewer's feeling of being truly present in the virtual environment, and a high level of presence allows for a strong bond to be established between the user and the virtual narrative universe. Especially in dramatic or experiential narratives, the viewer's sensory perception of being there triggers an emotional and empathic approach to the narrative. This situation enables the possibility to not only to watch the narrative but also to experience it simultaneously. Wherever the viewer turns with the headset, the perspective and the universe of events are there, enabling the perception of a narrative universe that is instantly variable and fluid; this indirectly gives the viewer the feeling that they are in control of the relevant spatial plane. At this point, the feeling of being one with the place prepares the base for being immersed with the narrative. New media objects, which Lev Manovich describes as ‘images that escape the cinema screen’, exist in VR technologies as materials that surround the user and place him/her directly into the narrative. For this reason, new media objects are rarely experienced as fixed representations; they are always open to user interaction, adjustment, and participation (Manovich, 2001).

Embodiment is the situation where the viewer has a body in the virtual environment, and this body reacts in synchronization with the user's movements. VR technology creates a multidirectional universe, and “affords embodied listening through the headphones and head-tracking provided by the technology to create the illusion of perceiving sound in 3D space, for example, spatial audio” (De Villiers Bosman et al., 2025, p.49). This feature deepens the identification with the character and offers the possibility of some physical matching. In the VR environment, the user not only understands the character; he/she experiences it directly by taking on its body, and the control of the physical and mental experiences that the character should have in the plot is now, in a sense, the responsibility of the viewer. This situation creates a strong empathy effect, especially in social, ethical, or traumatic narratives. When considered spatially, this matching situation makes the viewer open to some illusions about physical presence. For Slater, considering three illusions to be key distinguishing features that are unique to VR: the illusion of being located at another location (place illusion), the illusion that depicted events are really happening (plausibility illusion), and the illusion of virtual body ownership (ownership illusion) (Slater, et al, 2022). With VR technology, the user’s avatar or bodily representation becomes a part of the narrative, while a fiction emerges in which the body is reproduced through software manipulation. This provides the narrative with not only empathy but also a sense of concrete presence. Thus, the interface (in this case, the digital body) participates in the basic structure of the narrative as a digital cultural form.

- **Interactive and Multilayered Structure**

Digital media, intertwined with the state of embodiment, transforms the user into a ‘navigator’ and ‘operator’, and in VR narratives, this situation finds its response in the concept of agency; the user is no longer just the receiver of the narrative, but also a perpetrator who determines its course. VR narratives are designed as data sets that are shaped by the user's choices, rather than a fixed plot. This conceptual distinction puts the user in the position of being the author of the VR narrative because the narrative becomes a structure that takes shape as the user moves and makes choices. Nevertheless, the narrative is transformed from a linear structure into multiple scenarios that branch out. The user not only follows the story; they also become an active subject who determines the course of the narrative, and this makes it possible to personalize and reproduce the narrative.

In VR environments, the narrative is not only constructed through the plot; it is also constructed through space. Space becomes a component of the narrative and is now an element that offers the user the opportunity to explore and make sense of the story. A multi-layered story texture is woven through objects, sounds, light effects, or gaps, which corresponds to a holistic understanding of space. This structure represents a transition from the 'time-flow-dependent' narrative format in classical narrative to a narrative model that is shaped through the user's experience and is not strictly linear. These digital environments, which are seen as navigation spaces, are combined with the concept of spatial storytelling in VR applications. This concept corresponds to the story being embedded in space; the user physically walking around the space and discovering the story, which allows the narrative to take on a non-linear, discovery-based structure. VR narratives function as a 'navigable space of information', as Manovich puts it: every object, sound, or light source is a part of the narrative and waiting to be revealed by the user (Manovich, 2013). In VR, the narrative is constructed through the user's body movements, interactions, and trajectory, making it not only interactive but also multi-layered and multi-faceted. To understand cinematic understanding of space, we must think that it includes two different kinds of spaces, the ones inside the frame and the ones outside the frame. Based on this, off-screen space is divided into six segments, four of them are defined by the four dimensions of the frame; the fifth segment is the space behind the camera, and the sixth one is encompassing the space existing behind the set or some object in it (Burch, 1981). With the use of diegetic sound and the addition of dialogues, a holistic time-space structure that can be perceived as '360 degrees' is constructed. While in cinema, this is realized by imagining off-screen spaces and with limited frames, in 360-degree VR productions, the audience has the chance to experience this situation as a participant, and by choice.

As a result, VR narratives offer unique content that allows each user to have different experiences with a narrative structure that is far from linearity and has no cause-effect or time-based progression relationship; this uniqueness stems from VR-specific features such as viewer guidance, freedom of movement, and the ability to take the perspective of different characters. Similarly, environmental details, audio cues, and interactive elements come together to provide the necessary technical environment for this layered narrative form. While immersion, presence, and embodiment deepen the viewer's experience and sense of empathy, agency and spatial storytelling reveal the multilayered, interactive, and reconfigurable nature of the narrative. This transformation makes VR not only a narrative tool but also an experiential space that reestablishes the individual's relationship with the world. In this context, VR narrative has the opportunity to be read not only as a form of storytelling but also as a new way of thinking, experiencing, and being.

Reality in Cinema and 'Found Story' Concept

The perception of reality in cinema has been evaluated from different perspectives since its invention. Since the formalist-realist approach distinction that emerged in the early years of cinema, many movements and genres such as réalisme poétique, cinéma vérité, documentary cinema, and mockumentary etc. are examples of this different perspective on the relationship between cinema and reality. These differences in approach were influenced not only by the artistic movements of the relevant period, but also by the production technologies used.[1]

Naturally, discussions of reality in cinema have also caused serious divisions among theorists, and at some point, most theorists have worked on the concept of 'real', just like Siegfried Kracauer, who is the subject of this study. According to Kracauer, the basic aesthetic and ontological function of cinema is to 'redeem' physical reality and mediate the direct representation of the visible world. This approach is based on a positivist understanding of reality that emphasizes cinema's original connection with photography. However, this has not prevented Kracauer from being at the center of a profound discussion of reality that continues to this day. Kracauer argues that cinema, unlike other art forms, is closer to reality on an ontological level because the camera, by overcoming the limitations of the human eye, makes visible details that are not noticed in everyday life. In this respect, cinema develops a sensitivity towards the coincidental and ordinary. Cinema not only depicts dramatic or fictional events, but also allows us to re-understand the world through direct relationships established with matter formed in the flow of time. Kracauer's realism can be evaluated not as a fixed reflection of representative reality, but as the disclosure of the constantly changing layers of the visual world through the cinematic apparatus. In this respect, Kracauer finds the aesthetic potential of cinema not in abstraction, but in the direct contact and observation-based fidelity it establishes with the external world. Cinema creates a visual map of modern life by preserving the spontaneity and chaos of the physical world. According to Kracauer, one of the most important characteristics of cinema is that objects and phenomena other than the elements deliberately placed in the frame to be seen are also recorded within that frame, which he calls temporality. The wind seen in the trees in the background of an actor telling something in his yard is a good example of temporality. The tree is permanent, but the way it moves at a given time is a temporary feature, and the idea that the cinematic camera captures this and preserves it for future generations instills the idea that cinema can capture that which is uniquely connected to physical reality. In this context, Kracauer takes as an example Walter Ruttmann's 1927 city symphony film "Berlin: Symphony of a Metropolis" in his book "Theory of Film: The Redemption of Physical Reality".

Figure 2. Berlin: Symphony of a Metropolis, Walter Ruttmann, 1927.

In one of the scenes at the beginning of the film, garbage is blown away by the wind. Kracauer has several reasons why he thinks garbage is a good example of cinema's ability to capture physical reality. He summarizes this with the following sentences;

> *Many objects remain unnoticed simply because it never occurs to us to look their way. Most people turn their backs on garbage cans, the dirt underfoot, the waste they leave behind... Ruttmann's BERLIN includes a wealth of sewer grates, gutters, and streets littered with rubbish; they offer the camera ample opportunity to satisfy its inborn curiosity and function as a rag-picker (Kracauer, 1997, p.54).*

First of all, we don't notice garbage and think about its accompanying existence. When we notice garbage in ordinary life, it is isolated to our perception when we see it on the screen, and we are confronted with it. So it has a kind of revealing effect, revealing what is dulled to our senses. But in another sense, garbage, in many ways, as an index of a world or activities that have gone before, is literally the remains of what happened in the past. The garbage that has been used and thrown away is what remains, and Kracauer is very interested in the idea that cinema documents the materials of the world that remain, because cinema documents the existence of the past, its physical reality. The ephemeral, the unstaged trash, is part of an unstaged real world, and the point is that the camera captures what is in front of it indiscriminately. Even if the filmmaker makes a series of choices with the camera, there is always an element of the camera that moves beyond the filmmaker's control, which leads us to Kracauer's concept of the "found story."

According to Kracauer, historians often construct ready-made stories about past events as if they had been progressing towards a certain goal from the beginning. However, real historical processes are mostly random, complex, like life itself, and their outcomes are not predetermined. The "found story" is the artificial arrangement that the historian makes as if the events 'naturally' formed a whole despite these random, scattered relationships between events. In this context, the historian arranges the events in a meaningful chain and later finds a 'story' for them, although this story does not already exist in the events themselves, because the events are actually disordered (Kracauer, 1997). In this way, they present a story that does not exist in the past as if it were a natural part of the past. Kracauer criticizes the idea that history progresses towards a certain end and the excessive narrativization and dramatization of history (narrative history). According to him, historical events may appear to be a whole when looked back, but this is an illusion created by historians bringing them together and organizing them. According to him, good history writing should include ambiguities, discontinuities, and coincidental connections, and should not try to organize the past with today's expectations of meaning.

Kracauer argues that the real power of cinema lies in presenting the things in the world in their raw state (natural state) - that is, the world should be shown as it is, without being narrated or dramatized. Just as the "found story" in history writing brings coincidental events into an artificial whole, according to Kracauer, classical cinema produces the same artificial whole by over-dramatizing or organizing life, and the classical Hollywood tradition can be positioned exactly against this understanding. However, real life is messy, disconnected, uncertain, and random, and a good example of cinema should preserve this 'mess'. According to him, the most valuable moments of cinema are found in places where it shows unstructured, natural things such as the flow of a crowd, the lives of ordinary people, and momentary events. Crowds are the presentation of a life that does not seek a planned story and flows freely, and when these crowds are presented without a story, the audience witnesses the organic randomness of real life. Similarly, surfaces are also very important for Kracauer; the external appearances of objects, buildings, streets, and human faces are valuable even without their stories, because they simply exist. When cinema shows these surfaces, it can only capture real existence, physical reality, without looking for a "deep meaning". If the existence of these crowds and objects in their own way is shown without loading them with deep meanings or associating them with forced metaphors, a found story is avoided. Kracauer wants objects and people to appear in their own way, thus avoiding a forced and artificially compiled story and narrative, and ensuring that the audience experiences a holistic reception process.

In this context, 360-degree VR narratives also offer an environment quite suitable for the randomly obtained physical reality that Kracauer mentions.

VR Narratives Based on Kracauer's "Found Story" Concept: 360-degree *Plastic on the Ganges* Film Series

Cinema, as a tool that 'portrays' and 'reflects' movement, establishes a close relationship with reality. Unlike other arts that convey reality in different forms, with creativity and imagination, cinema has the capacity to convey what is happening in its simplest form. This feature does not mean that the cinema technique will not shape reality or reinterpret it with its technical language. The reality of everyday life, whether in fiction or documentary, will always present a change in what is real. However, the visual language and technical features of cinema also create an endless narrative style. At this point, many theorists have expressed their views on cinema mainly through 'formalist' and 'realist' approaches. Kracauer, one of the theorists who adopts the realist approach, defines the way cinema conveys life through the concept of 'found story'. Accordingly, reality can be transformed into a narrative by transferring any everyday moment in life to the language of film. Kracauer states that the characteristics of cinema allow for this situation and underlines the transferability of physical reality. The simple transfer in this view is not a structure that keeps the film language away from aesthetics. What is important is the determination of the reality that exists in life and the processing of this reality with the language of cinema.

When it comes to aesthetics, each branch of art will have a structure that it presents in line with its technical features. However, this situation is not only the separate branches of art and the different aesthetic structures that naturally emerge. Even a single branch of art can be interpreted in an aesthetic context with different perspectives, and can also undergo a change with its temporal journey in the process. This situation is a state that does not feed art and expands its possibilities. Similar to other branches of art, cinema also finds new meaning with different perspectives in the process. Undoubtedly, this transformation is not independent of society or technological developments in society. Technology is a dynamic that strongly affects both thought and creativity. One of the ways in which today's technological axis produces thought is virtual reality. The change that virtual reality technologies bring about in the visual language begins, first of all, with the 180 or 360-degree editing of the narrative. This situation is different from the usual viewing styles. A person who is in the act of watching a movie on a wide screen in a dark hall is transitioning to the viewing stage with wearable technological devices. In fact, this is no longer called watching a movie, but experiencing a movie. In such a case, the following question is meaningful: How does reality enter the narrative with virtual technologies?

These developments, which also cause us to frequently recall McLuhan, require us to rethink the content within the framework of technical features. Therefore, it is important to explain what kind of narrative form VR technologies create in terms of visual language. VR narratives create a stronger 'as if' effect in the story, and the participants are included in an experience. VR narratives, which come across us with effects such as immersion, presence, embodiment, and being there, create a strong sense of empathy thanks to these features. At this very point, the relationship between the audience, who is included in reality and becomes a part of the narrative, and the story topic is meaningful. Because Kracauer states that physical reality will be conveyed through cinema and points to photographable reality. This also means that social reality, everyday life, the natural, and the ordinary are aestheticized through the language of film. Every day moments or effective moments of life that seem distant to most people create an area of experience, thanks to VR. Although this situation is a situation that cinema is familiar with, the VR technique adds a new dimension to this familiarity. Social realities no longer have to be viewed on a two-dimensional screen, creating a distance between the audience and the story. When the reality of daily life is combined with VR technologies, the audience is now included in this story. These moments, when the space is viewed from 360 degrees, are now moments when the audience also has a sense of presence. In this context, the study examines the 360-degree VR narrative series *Plastic on the Ganges*, produced by National Geographic and drawing attention to social reality. The series consists of three films[2]: "Generation Plastic", "Turning The Tide", and "The Living River". The series tells how plastic waste mixes with the oceans and drinking water, while emphasizing the negative effects of this situation on human health and ecosystems. The Ganges River in India is chosen as the setting in the story, and this places the audience in the midst of plastic waste, in a place in daily life. Thus, the devastating effects of plastic pollution are strikingly conveyed through the lives of real people living in that region.

- **The Representation of Social Reality and Experiential Storytelling**

The reality in which the human species lives is directly a product of humanity. For this reason, the definition of 'man who makes tools', called homo faber, has an important meaning in our culture. Because man is a living being who develops tools and shapes his environment by using them. The invention of weapons for hunting and primitive tools used in shelter construction is considered to be the beginning of this process. The domestication of wild animals and the invention of the plough are the results of significant progress in the process of domesticating nature. Because man is the one who does not have to submit to all the random conditions of nature. In other words, man is the one who can build his own world (Collin, 2012). Daily life is the world that existed long before our birth, experienced and given meaning by individuals before us. Following this organized situation, the current situation is presented to our experience and interpretation. All interpretations of this world are based on past experiences. Both our own experiences and the experiences conveyed to us by parents and teachers function as *knowledge at hand*, creating a reference scheme (Schutz, 2012). However, social reality is invisible. This structure makes the burden created by social dynamics bearable for the person. The individual tends to accept social reality directly, without questioning it, in the culture in which he/she exists. So much so that the person perceives and learns to use subjects such as cars, houses, money, restaurants, or schools, but does not think about the ontological features of any of them. In fact, he/she is not even aware that they have a special ontology (Searle, 1995).

The creation and implementation of social reality by humans does not mean that the determined realities will not change. Periodic conditions and the interaction of humans with their environment and nature bring about some changes in existing structures. First of all, humans are curious creatures who never stop their production process. Every innovation they discover and invent to better meet their daily life needs creates a new structure for themselves in the process. One of these inventions and structures is undoubtedly the means of communication. Today, the means of communication that we accept without preconditions and include in every moment and place of our lives are one of the most effective tools in the construction of social reality. Just like in others, the introduction of this innovation and its implementation in life is a development that humans do with their own hands and shape society. So much so that, media is now a powerful tool that creates its own system and shapes society in this direction. However, just as other realities are accepted by society spontaneously and applied without question, representations presented through media are often accepted as an effective type of reality.

Complex communication systems have enabled us to transcend the constraints of time and space that limited our ancestors. But this has also led to our greater dependence on others to shape our ideas about what is happening in the world (McLeod and Bonoma, 2017). Focusing on how one person can influence another is as important as examining all the basic influence mechanisms of social interaction (Tedeschi and Bonoma, 2017). However, studies of media effects encompass many other types of research. Social scientists are also interested in the persuasive aspects of mass-communicated messages, the availability of new communication technologies, the reactions elicited by frightening or disturbing media content, the effects of political communication, and more (Bryant, Thompson, and Finklea, 2013). Because the emotion that emerges as a result of media exposure is extremely interesting in its own right. However, the impact of this emotional arousal on subsequent outcomes such as interaction with the message, attitude formation, and behavior in various contexts is even more important, as these effects form the basis of personal experiences and social interactions (Nabi, 2020).

Communication studies have always been a field where new ideas, hypotheses, theories, and models are conceptualized and tested. This is all the more impressive when you consider that the object of study is always changing (Vorderer et al., 2020). In addition, the proliferation of social media has made media technologies and platforms even more central to social interaction. Even our communication with close family members and friends is now mostly mediated. Our strong relationship with information, along with the internet, reveals new ideas and behaviors. Such information is the clue that helps shape and manage social identity. The social interactions that inform our identity are now more extensive, more frequent, and immediate (Cohen et al., 2020).

One of the media tools where interaction and immediacy are most visible is cinema. Cinema is a tool intertwined with technology within this dynamic structure. Cinema, which creates a new language by incorporating current technologies into its own technical structure, stands out as a tool that tells stories. Because the language that the image reveals in order to influence the masses and convey a message is a very powerful language. However, cinema is always intertwined with technology. This situation affects the narrative structure of films and creates new possibilities in presenting the story. One of these new narrative structures of cinema is VR films, which have emerged with the inclusion of virtual technologies in the film language. VR narratives, one of the most current versions of mediated communication, present a form that includes the audience in the story. For this reason, what the film tells is perhaps more important than ever. Because the distance between the audience and the screen (or monitor) has completely disappeared. This effect is something that needs to be thought about. Stories are no longer content to be watched; they are also something that can be experienced.

The *Plastic on the Ganges* 360-degree VR narrative series, which deals with social reality and conveys it with VR technologies, is worth examining at this point. This series, consisting of three films, includes more than the usual act of watching, as it provides social awareness with virtual technologies. Because the audience takes on a role as a kind of participant and experiences the story from within the story. The damage caused to the environment and people by the plastic pollution issue discussed in the series is first presented as an introduction in the film "Generation Plastic".

In an article published by National Geographic on the subject, it is stated that "Two rivers, the Bhagirathi and the Alaknanda, converge in the western Himalaya to form the Ganges, at the Indian town of Devaprayag—Sanskrit for 'holy confluence.' The amount of plastic waste flowing out of the Ganges is estimated at more than 6,000 tons a year," and draws attention to the importance of the subject (Parker, 2022, National Geographic). All three narratives in the series address the lifestyle revealed by plastic waste in different categories. The average length of all three films is 6 and a half minutes. The films briefly show the location where the subject will take place with ambient sounds and then continue with a voice-over. This situation is the same in all three films. Information about the identities of the voice-over speakers is conveyed through texts that appear on the screen. This information: "Voice of Om Prakash Dubey – Store Owner – Kannauj-India" in the movie "Generation Plastic"; In the movie "Turning The Tide" it is "Voice of Heather Koldeway – National Geographic Society Fellow Sea to Source Expedition Co-Lead" and finally in the movie "The Living River" it is "Voice of Ganga Sahni – Fisherman – Dharni Patti-India". Therefore, the external voice is included in the narration and accompanies the real images related to the subject. This information also gives the audience preliminary information about where the subject takes place and who is narrating the issue. These narrators consist of local people and an authorized person from the National Geographic team who researches the subject. Thus, the story is presented directly through the discourse of real people, which is also a situation that increases the reality presented by the film. Creating a structure by people who live there in real time and space strengthens the social reality effect because it constructs the audience as a part of that story.

The experience effect of social reality is a situation provided by VR technologies. The experience in this series is provided by the audience being a part of the narrative. In fact, VR narratives have experience methods that can be considered stronger. Interaction and gamification are some of them. However, there is no similar dynamic in the series examined. The transformation of the social reality transferred in these films into an experience narrative is provided by the audience entering the 360-degree story space. The audience 'watches' reality among the people living there, next to them. However, this time, the act of watching does not take place in the distance between the audience and the story as in traditional narratives. It is presented through the experience directly from within the narrative. Therefore, it is seen that the transformation of social reality into an experience narrative in the series is provided by the effect of the VR technique, and no additional method is used. The audience is in the plastic piles, just like the people living there.

The film "Generation Plastic" is an introductory presentation of the narrative in the series. The film begins with real places and people, along with ambient sounds. The audience, who is included in the narrator's life together with what he conveys, first acknowledges that nothing continues as before and everything has changed. This change is intended for things that happen between the past and the present. For example, while the narrator conveys the point that this change has reached with the sentence "We used to make everything like our tools, plates and cups out of natural materials but now everything is plastic", at that moment the audience experiences the change between the past and the present with today's reality. The past is a moment conveyed by the narrative, while the present is a moment experienced by the audience. Because at that moment, the audience is among the piles of plastic, together with animals searching for food in those piles. In the next scene, this situation gives way to polluted water and the damage done to humans and animals. The transmission of the current social problem in the film diversifies with different people taking on the role of narrator. Thus, the issue of how this problem affects the people living there is represented more strongly with other views. The audience is sometimes positioned among waste, sometimes next to polluted river water. After the general transmission of the current problem, the story gradually makes this problem visible in narrower areas. Reality continues from any moment of daily life. When a woman fills a container with water and talks about how polluted the water is, how plastic waste pieces and garbage mix into the drinking water, the audience is a part of that daily moment. This daily life transmission details other problems caused by the current problem, such as the spread of bad smells in the streets, mosquitoes invading living spaces, and children getting sick. Thus, the magnitude of the problem is revealed.

The narrative of "Turning The Tide" continues from a similar point of view, but this time the subject is conveyed through the eyes of a researcher. This voice among the surrounding waste piles mentions that the materials we buy for short-term use only last for hundreds of years. Meanwhile, animals are also wandering among the waste. The participant (audience), the external voice, the animals, and the ambient sounds share the same space, that is, the chaos. In the next scene, this subject is further elaborated, and the film is conveyed directly from the voice of the researcher (narrator). This time, the focused subject is the effort to truly understand how plastic moves from land to water and how this can be stopped. Thus, attention is drawn to another dimension of the subject, so each new scene is a scene that contains information about the subject. For example, in the next scene, the narrator tells the audience with whom she shares the same environment that forty percent of the plastic produced every year is single-use plastic. However, the main striking point of the narrative is that plastics break down into very small pieces as a result of remaining in nature for a very long time, and are consumed without being noticed by every living creature in nature. After the researcher gives information about the subject as a narrator, the same subject is continued with the local people taking the position of narrator. Thus, the subject is told from different perspectives by both the researcher and the person exposed to it. Just like in "Generation Plastic", the narrator mentions that plastic consumption was not this common before, but it has become a part of life in the last 10-15 years. Thus, both films focus on a similar subject: the change in consumption in recent years. The narrator position is transferred to the researcher again, and sustainable systems are mentioned. However, this time the image is given from a general perspective to show how massive an area that the waste piles cover. Thus, a connection is established between the information given and the solemnness of the subject. The audience is among all these waste piles and within this substantial massiveness.

The narrative of "The Living River" also deals with the Ganges River dimension of the same subject in detail, and the film deals with these details through the eyes of the fisherman. The fisherman expresses the meaning that the Ganges River has for them, which meets many needs of the region, such as belief, cleaning, and nutrition. Fishing is one of the main means of livelihood in this region. The use of plastic has also included this profession, and the change has also shown itself in that regard. Just like in the other films in the series, it is also mentioned here that many handmade tools have ended up being sold in the market. However, the main issue emphasized in this film is the damage that plastic nets cause to the environment after they turn into waste, along with their fast and flimsy nature, then most of these nets are left in the river by the fishermen. Thus, people trying to survive by fishing from the river are again harmed by the plastic waste spreading from the river to the environment. In this context, all three films establish a relationship with each other because, in the film "Turning The Tide", it is mentioned that plastic waste breaks into small pieces when it remains in nature for a long time and mixes with people's daily nutrition materials. Thus, the films also draw attention to the paradoxical dimension of social reality. Another paradoxical reality is repeated at the end of the film, which is that the river has a sacred meaning for the people there, but despite that, they have to make a living by fishing from this river.

The common theme in all three narratives is the damage caused by plastic waste to nature and humans, so these damages are conveyed through real people, their voices, and living spaces. Therefore, as a *found story*, an existing reality is revealed with VR technology. It is also possible to create this reality with traditional cinema techniques, but what draws attention here is the effect and aesthetic language revealed by the VR technique. Furthermore, new techniques can uncover a new language and meaning in revealing the reality that already exists in social life. The reality here has a different meaning than watching it in a cinema or on a computer screen; the film technique points to a new stage in conveying the reality that exists in life as it is. The effect conveyed by the unique features of virtual technologies is a way of experiencing social reality.

- **Embodied Witnessing and Hyper-Identification**

There is no doubt that VR film narrative has brought innovation to cinema in terms of conveying reality as it is. This technique, together with a wearable headset, distances the person from the awareness of their physical reality and immerses them in the virtual world (immersion). The audience, who find themselves in a 360-degree space, is included in that virtual world from that moment on. The belongingness here is a result of the person's feeling of being there and their *embodiment*, that the person is a part of the narrative. Therefore, especially in VR narratives, it is also important how the person places themselves in a meaning.

The phenomena classified as narrative have a significant impact on life. In fact, the stories we watch often reflect and sustain institutional and cultural orders. However, while narratives can reveal 'truths' about social life, they can also have a function of shaking up existing power structures, depending on how these truths are reproduced or suppressed. Thinking about the social meaning of narratives means accepting that they are constructed or presented within certain social contexts (Do Nascimento, 2019). However, while humans represent social reality in different ways through narratives, they act together with social developments. In other words, technological tools that have been incorporated into society and gradually entered life also lead to the formation of new forms of thought and narrative. However, this does not always mean that any innovation contains completely original values. Technological developments also change existing narrative systems, cinema is undoubtedly one of them. VR technology, which is the subject of this study, re-aestheticizes the language of cinema.

Many sources mention that the Lumière brothers' film "L'arrivée d'un train en gare de La Ciotat", which they screened in 1895, had a great impact on the audience. So much so that, this event is referred to as the founding myth of cinema, with the audience being affected by the reality of a full-size train coming towards them and running away screaming to the back of the room. Since this 'virtual' reality of cinema was so similar to the real one that it was indistinguishable, the audience tried to escape in panic from the huge moving object that would definitely crush them. It seems that their current reality was fundamentally questioned and changed (Strutt, 2019).[3] Today, a similar effect reappears in the as-if construction of reality. VR technology defines a *hyper-reality* due to the narrative structure it presents.

Figure 3. L'arrivée d'un train en gare de La Ciotat

Figure 4. ve Evolution of Verse film visuals

The retransmission of the reality of life through the language of film is repeatedly constructed in line with the technological development of that era. The aim in this construction is always to take the viewer into that reality, and the specific nature of the language of film is effective in that regard. Because cinema, as a medium depicting movement, is already effective from the very beginning with its 'natural' form of transmitting reality. This situation also distinguishes cinema from theatre, which is one of the arts that transmits the story.

In the theater, the audience sees real people playing imaginary characters on the stage; at that time, the actors are on stage both as real people and represented characters created by the director's imagination. The aesthetic experience of the play arises from the combination of both real and imaginary elements; it reaches the audience with the collaborative effort of the actors and the entire stage crew. Reality emerges through the representation and expression of the fiction presented collaboratively (Singer, 2000). On the other hand, audiences tend to accept the events they witness on the screen as natural and think that this is how it really happened. In contrast, filmmakers know that the events seen on the screen do not develop exactly as they are shown. There is a wide range from completely fictional representations to more subtly modified ones, and ethnographic filmmakers are faced with a paradox at this point; It is known that they can only represent the reality of others, that they cannot really experience it. However, the conventions of cinema often conceal this and offer the audience the illusion of direct access to reality (Banks, 1990). The cinematic image is based on the photographic recording of successive moments of an object in time, but these moments are reconstructed as a temporal and spatial continuity by projection. Cinema offers a moving experience by recording both the development of events in time and the movement of the camera. While photography fixes a moment, cinema provides the opportunity to experience events in motion and in process. In addition, by the contribution of elements such as camera movement, sound recording, and editing, the director can shape how the events will be perceived by the audience (Allen, 1990). Many elements, such as film technique, are important at this stage. For example, while some films - especially those with intense editing or imaginative stage designs - present an illusion to the audience, other films that use long shots, depth of field, and natural locations attempt to reveal reality (Rushton, 2011). The art (and technique) of cinema, which is the moving picture, is undoubtedly very effective in that process. Especially since the close relationship between cinema and technology affects the way of telling stories, every new trend somehow establishes a connection with reality (even if the aim is sometimes to disrupt it). At this point, the relationship between VR technology and film is worth re-examining in terms of the connection it establishes with the concept of the real. In fact, films that question environmental issues, plastic waste, life, and vitality also stand out as a result of the connection they establish with reality, and Kracauer's concept of "found story" gains new meaning for 360-degree VR films.

A formal definition of CVR (Cinematic Virtual Reality) is still being developed, but the general view of this concept is still an immersive experience in which individual users can look around from a 360° perspective in synthetic worlds and hear specially designed spatial sounds (Mateer, 2017). The effect of VR technology is significantly consistent with the immersion and authenticity characteristics of film art. As a highly innovative media form, VR film has created a new aesthetic field in terms of interaction, simulation, and visual presentation. By combining art and technology, this technology offers a new film viewing experience and transforms traditional film viewing formats, providing the viewer with a more impressive visual effect (Cui et al., 2022). The visual effect carries reality to a hyper-impact dimension as the viewer enters the illusion of embodiment in the film environment. This situation, where the distance between the viewer and the story disappears, is related to the person directly experiencing the film atmosphere. For this very reason, the reality installation in documentaries is more prominent than fictional narratives in VR films. Because documentary narratives that try to convey a slice of life include the audience in this piece, with the help of the VR technique. Thus, it seems extremely interesting to be included in the spaces of people with whom we share the same universe but experience different lives. Because the "being there", "immersion", and "interaction" features revealed by the VR technique convert a story that is worth watching into an experience. This experiencing effect leads to identification, one of the basic elements of cinema, to a kind of hyper-identification, because this time, there is a new narrative style other than watching a conventional movie. *The Plastic on the Ganges* film series not only attracts attention by conveying reality as a *found story*, but also establishes a closer relationship with reality as a result of doing this with VR technology. The audience (and the participant) does not know the plastic waste problem as a problem that needs to be solved, perhaps only following the news, but tries to understand it directly from within the problem. Therefore, *understanding* is provided by *experiencing,* and the form that VR technology presents in the language of film can convey the found story more powerfully.

The audience's VR movie experience is a result of various illusions, in fact, this illusion is valid for every art form that tells a story. However, since the current features of the VR movie technique present a *participation* effect, it is useful to expand the illusion here. It is even more important to evaluate this situation, especially for stories that present a moment, a slice of real life. For example, the *Plastic on the Ganges* series not only addresses plastic waste, which is a serious problem, but it also puts the audience in the middle of this problem. The audience's participation in the story is more in the form of *witnessing*, and this is the activity of listening to and observing everything that is happening at that place, directly through the people living there. Therefore, there is nothing that will threaten the audience in the story space at that moment. The audience's physical presence consists of being there as an observer rather than directly experiencing the problems. Nevertheless, this situation does not narrow the scope of the film, because the VR technique is already powerful and creates a hyper-impact with its form that includes the audience in the story and offers a 360-degree spatial experience; this hyper-effect redefines the sense of identification of the film from a new perspective. Although the audience is a witness and observer of the story, they are often among the plastic waste, therefore, they become one of them among the piles of plastic. Finally, the witnessing effect directly identifies the conveyed problem with the person involved in the film, and similarly, the audience closely observes the animals searching for food among the piles of waste. It can transform how these wastes are integrated with the people living there into a form of empathy with the effect of embodiment and being there.

Nevertheless, Schlembach & Clewer take an analytical approach to the subject in their study titled "Feeling good: Humanitarian virtual reality film, emotional style and global citizenship". The issue that the authors emphasize in this study is that although immersive VR environments provide impressive experiences, the ethical and political effects of these experiences are open to debate. Non-fiction VR content carries the risk of creating a manipulative 'forced empathy' by activating the viewer's sensory responses before their intellectual process. VR films allow viewers to develop a deep understanding of a particular culture or social group, and this process takes place through the simulation of local specificity and intimacy. VR technology also turns into a means of satisfaction by allowing the global citizen to see the Other who is escaping from suffering and to share the experience of hope (Gruenewald and Witteborn, 2022). In such films, the viewer is presented with a problem-solution structure that promises satisfaction by sharing the suffering and creating a common sense of hope. The viewer feels that they have made a contribution to solving the pain, thus giving hope to both the suffering Other and themselves. Simulated intimacy offers the viewer of VR films a personalized experience of pain, while it carries the risk of apoliticizing the causes of this pain by decontextualizing it. With simulated intimacy, films show the viewer's body as approaching each other in a continuum in virtual space-time, with the looks and speech of the protagonists. This creates the impression of interaction with real people (Gruenewald and Witteborn, 2022). The definition of simulated intimacy mentioned in the research is also very important because, although VR films have many elements that will create empathy and hyper-identification with their unique features, this situation alone does not provide a solution. In fact, despite the fact that the viewer witnesses the existing social problem among the plastic heaps in the examined series and the striking dimension of the issue here is revealed, it is necessary to approach with distance the idea that this effect develops a solution approach for the problem. Thus, the *Plastic on the Ganges* series, which presents a slice of life with an experience effect, is both a transfer of a *found story* and an *empathy illusion*. The aim here is not to diminish the importance of VR films with a strong awareness-raising effect; the real aim is not to keep this importance away from criticism. Because the embodiment of the audience, having a hyper-identification in hyper-effect, can only mean the transfer of reality with a strong experience. In other words, the real-life story, beyond emphasizing the problematic structure of its reality, can use this emphasis to create the emotional state it will create in the audience. Therefore, it is important to take a careful approach to the empathy and embodiment effect of VR films. Is the issue the social problem that the film is about, or is it a strong experience effect provided to the audience by the combination of this problem and VR narrative features? It is definitely important for the audience to follow the social reality in the film with its bodily and experiential effects. At this point, it is impossible to think of a VR film outside of both the experience and the embodiment effect. First of all, this effect is a unique feature of the VR film; in fact, it derives its innovation and new media aesthetics from here. The important issue to emphasize in this title is not to be enchanted by the VR narrative. The series examines the plastic waste problem from a different dimension in each film. How the issue became a social problem is directly conveyed by the people living there, and it frequently touches on its negative effects on human health. At the same time, listening to this problem from the eyes and the voice of a researcher is also important in terms of creating a scientific source for the subject. All of these are about emphasizing the remarkable aspects of the subject, and it needs to be conveyed in this way. However, another important issue is that the audience 'witnesses' what is happening in the film. Because VR films, especially when they deal with 'other' subjects and people, carry a kind of 'gamification' risk due to the effect of embodiment and presence in space. It should not be forgotten that the story being told emphasizes a social reality. It is important that the priority is to draw attention to the shocking reality of the subject being conveyed, and that the narrative structure should be created accordingly. When the narrative focuses more on the audience and keeps the subject in the background, the dimension of the issue goes beyond creating a meaningful effect. Therefore, it is inevitable to a certain extent that social reality is transferred to the film as a slice of life and that the film technique is aestheticized with its own characteristics; this is exactly what Kracauer emphasizes. However, the relationship that VR technology establishes with cinema, which is already a very powerful storyteller, and the way this relationship is aestheticized should also be approached with questioning. Because the VR narrative form has new aesthetic forms of its own, outside of the traditional film style. This aesthetic form is a form that focuses on the audience.

The entire *Plastic on the Ganges* series touches upon the different dimensions of plastic waste as a social problem. The audience is in the place where this problem is intensely experienced and is included in daily life. The following time shown in the films, the lives of people living among waste, are realized before the eyes of the audience, simultaneously. However, the fact that the audience is sometimes positioned among plastic waste, sometimes on the shores of the Ganges River, and sometimes observes the gigantic dimensions of the plastic piles from a wide angle draws attention to the shocking dimensions of the problem. The body becomes a part of the problem, becoming a waste among the plastic piles. From that moment on, perhaps the definition of a comfortable area by the audience's physical reality is in the background. The effect of virtual reality, which simulates the audience's emotions in particular, is a result of establishing a time-space partnership. Throughout the film, the person is among the people there, within the narrative space.

The film also establishes temporality on a subject basis; the local people mention that they were not so intimate with the use of plastic until recently, that this use has increased in recent years, and that one-time uses in particular have become widespread. Thus, the issue is not only the size of the waste piles but also how and why it has become widespread. By these means, the audience also gains a certain idea about the reasons for the issue. The current system obliges the use of plastic and at the same time punishes the people who use it. The Ganges River, which is considered sacred by the local people, is also a source of nutrition and livelihood. Despite this, the current ecosystem resulting from the use of plastic creates a sense of entrapment and helplessness; people are both forced to use this and punished for their use. The paradox here is that the structure presented by the VR film technique also includes the audience; the audience is a witness to this entrapment.

CONCLUSION

Technological developments are significantly changing many things related to life, and one of the areas most affected by this transformation is the means of communication. Cinema, in particular, is implementing the perspective determined by technology as a storytelling tool. One of the reasons for this is undoubtedly the desire to reach the closest, even hyper-real, narrative to reality. At this point, the innovations brought about by technology can be seen as an opportunity, and the reality of life can be represented through a narrative.

Virtual reality technologies are one of the most up-to-date and striking among new media tools. Although the interest in this field does not always qualify as an upward trend, the field of virtual reality continues to develop step by step. Cinema, which creates a strong impact with both fictional and non-fictional storytelling techniques, is trying to adapt to VR technologies. In fact, VR narratives can be defined in many ways in today's post-modern era. For example, a game narrative can be cinematic, while a film narrative can become gamified with its interactive features. For this reason, it is possible to define VR narratives in more than one type according to their content. With the advent of digitalization, narrative forms have become more interactive and multi-layered, transforming the media experience by shifting viewers from passive observers to active participants. These environments, where the distance between the individual and the media is gradually narrowing, are becoming more visible with the development of virtual reality technologies. This technology, which creates the effect of experiencing a narrative content rather than merely watching it, completely eliminates the distance between the person and the media. The audience is now included in the space of reality, from near the characters by emerging within the narrative. This altenation in the occursion of the content with the consumer cannot be explained straightforward. The effect of being included in the narrative, from ethical issues to empathy, from identification to alienation, causes reinterrogation of many familiar structures.

A narrative produced at 180 or 360 degrees with virtual reality technology offers the user an area of experience with the headset it requires; this experience also qualifies as an aesthetic that the tool reflects in its own language. At first glance, VR technology, which stands out with its features such as interaction, immersion, being there, embodiment, and empathy, differs from conventional traditional narrative techniques due to the aesthetics it constructs. Thus, cinema, which already has the ability to narrate reality strongly, can reach a hyper-real effect with the VR film technique. One of the genres where this effect draws attention is documentaries. VR, which offers a strong illusion as if different times and places are the same in the hyper-effect of virtual reality, mentally transcends physical reality. In this way, many unknown, unseen, and unaware things are revealed. Discovering the reality that exists in life and aestheticizing it within the framework of the possibilities of cinema reminds us of Kracauer's concept of "found story". While the photographable reality of life can be reflected in all its normality in cinema, the answer to the question of how this reflection is shaped by VR technology is important.

Within the scope of this question, the films "Generation Plastic", "Turning The Tide", and "The Living River" from the "Plastic on the Ganges VR series" were examined in the study. The use of plastic in the Ganges and the damage it causes to humans and nature are directly conveyed through the people living there. The problem here points to a social reality, however, this reality can also be conveyed through the traditional film narrative style. What makes these films different is that they offer a 360-degree experience with VR technology. This presentation is about how the found story can be aestheticized with VR technology, which is one of the new media tools. The audience (user or participant) does not watch the plastic waste problem in the series on a cinema screen or monitor, but becomes embodied in the space with the hyper-real effect provided by VR technology. This means that the found story, that is, the reality of life, is conveyed more directly. However, this transmission is not just about creating an experience with a 360-degree camera or techniques that provide this effect. In particular, the sense of participation that the effect of embodiment and being in the space creates in the audience is important. The audience is sometimes a part of everything that happens there and sometimes just a witness. Sometimes they listen to what is happening among the people who are suffering from the situation from their own words, and sometimes they become waste among the piles of plastic. However, one of the issues that should not be forgotten at this stage is the satisfaction created by the hyper-real effect and its ethical problematic. In other words, the transition of a found reality from watching to experiencing is the result of an effect that makes the person present in the space (presence). It is possible for this embodiment to create *reality satisfaction*. Satisfaction is a result of arousing emotions. A narrative experience provided through hyper-reality carries the risk of keeping the shocking reality of the subject in the background, as it will first arouse emotions and then a sense of satisfaction. At this stage, the feeling of witnessing the life story of the other and experiencing this witnessing process with a hyper-real effect poses a meaningful question as to how the conveyed story is structured. The films that have been used as examples do not follow a clear hero, do not position themselves among them with an eye-to-eye effect, but examine the subject through different people living in the region. The audience's participatory position is more about addressing otherness with an environmental problem rather than experiencing the other person. Therefore, the audience is present in the space, participating but witnessing the events from a certain distance. This distance is occasionally broken in areas where plastic piles are shown, thus, the audience is given the impression that they are a part of that waste. This structure is important because the audience's sense of satisfaction is not about experiencing being the other but about grasping different dimensions of a social issue. Since the 3 films in the series draw attention to different dimensions of the subject, the purpose of providing information remains intact. The hyper-reality of the VR narrative is based on providing detailed information about the subject rather than providing a sense of satisfaction. However, there is, of course, no such idea as 'guaranteeing a sense of empathy' regarding VR technology. First of all, it should not be forgotten that although there are 3 films in the series, the durations of these films are quite short. The effect of 'being there' in the VR environment can eliminate this shortness; nevertheless, no hyper-effect guarantees full awareness of a certain subject under any circumstances. Nevertheless, VR technology fundamentally requires the use of a headset, which, despite all advancements, still does not offer a fully comfortable experience. Prolonged use may cause discomfort such as headaches and nausea, which undoubtedly affects the overall quality of the experience.

The aestheticization of the found story in the examined series is based on the effects of immersion, interaction, and embodiment that VR technology provides, these effects create an experience as expected. Thus, the narrative style that takes a slice of life and brings it to the screen aestheticizes VR as a new media tool with the feeling of experience and embodiment. The audience's witnessing of the story, being a close observer of the social problem, and being positioned as waste among the plastic piles is a setup that creates both aesthetics and hyper-reality. The aesthetics and reality here are also among the reasons for hyper-identification. The hyper-reality that emerges in these narratives, where the narrative is conveyed at 360 degrees and the effect of being in the space and embodiment is created, also differs in terms of identification. The audience, who sees themselves in the story by being present in the space, focuses their identification on the story together with the people. With all these, the found story creates a different aesthetic with cinematic virtual reality, and this aesthetic becomes an important part of creating the experience.

REFERENCES

Allen, R. (1993). Representation, illusion, and the cinema. *Cinema Journal, 32*(2), 21–48. DOI: 10.2307/1225603

Bal, M. (2003). Visual essentialism and the object of visual culture. *Journal of Visual Culture, 2*(1), 5–32. DOI: 10.1177/147041290300200101

Banks, M. (1990). Experience and reality in ethnographic film. *Visual Sociology, 5*(2), 30–33. DOI: 10.1080/14725869008583672

Bosman, I. D. V., Bujić, M., Cosio, L. D., Buruk, O., Jørgensen, K., & Hamari, J. (2025). Embodiment in virtual reality: An experiment on how visual and aural first- and third-person modes affect embodiment and mindfulness. *Virtual Reality (Waltham Cross), 29*(2), 49. Advance online publication. DOI: 10.1007/s10055-025-01129-w

Bryant, J., Thompson, S., & Finklea, B. W. (2013). *Fundamentals of media effects.* Waveland Press.

Burch, N. (1981). Theory of film practice. (Trans. Lane, R., H.). Princeton University Press. DOI: 10.1515/9781400853366

Cohen, J., Appel, M., & Slater, D. M. (2020). Media, Identity, and the Self. In Oliver, M. B., Raney, A., & Bryant, J. (Eds.), *Media effects* (pp. 179–194). Routledge.

Collin, F. (2012). *Social reality.* Routledge. DOI: 10.4324/9780203047927

Cui, L., Zhang, Z., Wang, J., & Meng, Z. (2022). Film effect optimization by deep learning and virtual reality technology in new media environment. *Computational Intelligence and Neuroscience, 2022*(1), 8918073. DOI: 10.1155/2022/8918073 PMID: 35634038

Do Nascimento, J. (2019). Art, cinema and society: sociological perspectives. *Global Journal of Human Social Science Research:(C). Society and Culture, 19*(5), 19–28.

Gruenewald, T., & Witteborn, S. (2022). Feeling good: Humanitarian virtual reality film, emotional style and global citizenship. *Cultural Studies, 36*(1), 141–161. DOI: 10.1080/09502386.2020.1761415

Jenkins, H. (2006). *Convergence culture: Where old and new media collide.* New York University Press.

Kittler, F. A. (1996). The history of communication media. *CTheory, Special Issues: Global Algorithm.* p. 1-18.

Kracauer, S. (1997). *Theory of film: The redemption of physical reality.* Miriam Bratu Hansen (eds). Princeton University Press.

Manovich, L. (2001). *The language of new media.* MIT Press.

Manovich, L. (2013). *Software takes command.* Bloomsbury Academic. DOI: 10.5040/9781472544988

Mateer, J. (2017). Directing for Cinematic Virtual Reality: How the traditional film director's craft applies to immersive environments and notions of presence. *Journal of Media Practice*, *18*(1), 14–25. DOI: 10.1080/14682753.2017.1305838

McLeod, J. M., & Chaffee, S. R. (2017). The construction of social reality. In Tedeschi, J. (Ed.), *The social influence processes* (pp. 50–99). Routledge. DOI: 10.4324/9781315134970-2

Mirzoeff, N. (2001). Intervisuality. In H. S. Annette W. Balkema, *Exploding Aesthetics.* Rodopi, B.V., P. 124.

Nabi, R. L. (2020). Media and emotion. In Oliver, M. B., Raney, A., & Bryant, J. (Eds.), *Media effects* (pp. 163–178). Routledge.

Parker, L. (2022). Can India clean up its holiest river? (National Geographic). https://www.nationalgeographic.com/magazine/article/can-india-clean-up-its-holiest-river-feature

Rushton, R. (2011). *The reality of film: Theories of filmic reality.* Manchester University Press.

Schlembach, R., & Clewer, N. (2021). 'Forced empathy': Manipulation, trauma and affect in virtual reality film. *International Journal of Cultural Studies*, *24*(5), 1–17. DOI: 10.1177/13678779211007863

Schutz, A. (2012). *Collected papers I. The problem of social reality* (Vol. 11). Springer Science & Business Media.

Searle, J. R. (1995). *The construction of social reality.* Simon and Schuster.

Singer, I. (2000). *Reality transformed: Film and meaning and technique.* The MIT Press.

Slater, M. (2003). A note on presence terminology. *Presence Connect, 3(3).*

Slater, M., Banakou, D., Beacco, A., Gallego, J., Macia-Varela, F., & Oliva, R. (2022). A separate reality: An update on place illusion and plausibility in virtual reality. *Frontiers in Virtual Reality*, *3*, 914392. Advance online publication. DOI: 10.3389/frvir.2022.914392

Slater, M., & Wilbur, S. (1997). A framework for immersive virtual environments (FIVE): Speculations on the role of presence in virtual environments. *Presence (Cambridge, Mass.)*, *6*(6), 603–616. DOI: 10.1162/pres.1997.6.6.603

Strutt, D. (2019). *The digital image and reality: Affect, metaphysics and post-cinema*. Amsterdam University Press.

Tedeschi, J. T., & Bonoma, T. V. (2017). Power and influence: An introduction. In Tedeschi, J. (Ed.), *The social influence processes* (pp. 1–49). Routledge. DOI: 10.4324/9781315134970-1

Vorderer, P., Park, D. W., & Lutz, S. (2020). A history of media effects research traditions. In Oliver, M. B., Raney, A., & Bryant, J. (Eds.), *Media effects* (pp. 1–15). Routledge.

KEY TERMS AND DEFINITIONS

VR Narrative: Encompasses the interactive storytelling format that spatially and emotionally immerses the user in virtual reality environments. The narrative takes on a non-linear: complex and multi-layered structure, driven by the physical movements and choices of the viewer. In this way, the viewer can become an active subject of the experience rather than a passive observer, and achieve an original experience that differs from classical narrative methods.

Immersion: Refers to the state in which the user is completely emotionally and mentally immersed in a digital or fictional world: detached from physical reality. This concept is a fundamental experience element that increases the sense of reality, especially in games, VR and new media narratives. A high level of immersion also strengthens the user's sense of 'being there' (presence).

Presence: Refers to the individual feeling as if they were physically there in a digital or virtual environment. This sentiment occurs through the senses and the strengthening of the emotional and perceptual bond between the user and the environment: especially in VR and interactive media experiences. Presence increases the perception of reality by deepening the level of immersion, and in this context, the two concepts have a directly proportional supporting effect.

User Agency: The name given to the user's ability to make decisions: direct, and influence outcomes within a digital narrative or interactive environment. This concept determines the user's level of control over the experience, especially in games and interactive stories, and this control can encompass all physical and cognitive interactions. A high sense of user agency increases participation and identification, enabling the narrative to become personal.

Hyper-Identification: Refers to the user's excessive identification with a digital character: avatar, or narrative element. This situation occurs particularly in VR, gaming, and social media environments, where the boundaries of the self are blurred and intense emotional bonds are established. Hyper-identification is a form of participation that is powerful enough to temporarily transform an individual's sense of identity, and in this respect, it creates an experientially staggering effect.

Found Story: Grounded in the reality of ordinary, everyday life. In the context of VR narratives, it refers to the participant's experience of this everyday reality through immersive, interactive storytelling structures. VR enables users not only to witness but also to inhabit and co-construct narratives, thus transforming passive observation into embodied experience.

ENDNOTES

1. The technologies mentioned are not limited to the process of recording the image; technological developments in post-production (e.g. editing phase) and distribution sectors are also evaluated within this scope.

2. In fact, it is difficult to define these narratives directly as films. Because today's narrative forms tend to establish a close relationship with each other rather than being clearly separated from each other. For this reason, a VR documentary can approach journalism, and a fictional film can turn into a game narrative. However, the explanation of Kracauer's concept of found story in the cinema technique and the fact that the narratives under examination also have film characteristics make it possible to address the subject from a cinema perspective.

3. A similar situation applies to the VR narrative of "Evolution of Verse" (Chris Milk, 2015). At the beginning of the film, there is a train that gradually approaches the audience from a distance and passes 'over' them.

Chapter 16
Television Broadcasting Shaped by Artificial Intelligence

Esennur Sirer
https://orcid.org/0000-0003-0345-4158
University of Usküdar, Turkey

ABSTRACT

Artificial intelligence algorithms, which work by taking human intelligence as an example, can be applied to every field in the "Smart Society" era. Artificial intelligence using big data is also included in autonomous applications in the media field. Artificial intelligence applications, which have recently come to the fore with personalized television examples, can be used at almost every stage of television broadcasting, including pre-production, production and post-production stages. Television broadcasting consists of multiple business components. In this context, examples of artificial intelligence appear in areas such as script writing, actor selection, set design, camera use, sound editing, music production, subtitle production, graphic design, editing processes, news production, artificial intelligence announcers, and determination of the target audience. For example, even the television content of some large broadcasting companies is designed by artificial intelligence supported by big data. This situation calls into question the future of television

INTRODUCTION

Humankind has fit centuries of functional development into a short period in the context of communication with tools. In this process, machines have taken their place in every area of life in the approximately three-century period extending

DOI: 10.4018/979-8-3373-1957-5.ch016

from the power of steam engines, the product of the first industrial revolution, to the present day. Afterwards, humanity, which had a knowledge gap, solved this by sharing it through the communication network and quickly moved from the information society to the information society. However, it seems difficult to compare this period to a logarithmic progress. Because humankind has no foresight about where it will go. However, what has happened until today has played a major role in the social, cultural and economic changes of technology in the lives of societies. "Tools constitute the essence of social relations. The individual establishes a relationship with the society he lives in by using tools that he actively dominates or passively submits to in action. To the extent that he dominates his tools, he can equip the world with his own meanings; to the extent that he submits to the tools, the form of the tool determines his thoughts and beliefs about himself" (Illich, 2018, p. 36). Artificial intelligence, which is integrated into social life in the context of human-vehicle communication, also tries to make sense of the world as the reproduction of intelligence through machines.

Famous Turkish mathematician Ord. Prof. Cahit Arf Hoca mentioned machine learning in a conference he gave in 1959 and answered the questions of whether and how a machine with adaptive capabilities could solve problems that were not considered when it was built. While the capabilities of artificial intelligence are being discussed today, Cahit Hoca stated that the real difference between the human brain and the machine was that the human brain could process aesthetic elements and felt free to do a given task or not, while the machine could not make decisions in the event of uncertainty. However, he expressed his thoughts that this situation could also be solved, and that machines that were similar to the human brain in terms of aesthetics would be able to say, "For example, they do not find such and such a piece of music beautiful."

The internet, which became a basic necessity for life very shortly after it entered the service of humanity, also opened the door to the information age. The internet has become the fastest spreading tool in history. With the emergence of the World Wide Web designed by Tim Berners-Lee in 1989, the communication order in the world has changed and a brand new and constantly moving period has begun. The World Wide Web is a bridge system that connects web pages with text, images, videos and other multimedia content accessed over the internet (Choudhury, 2014, p. 8096). In the first period of the web, called Web 1.0, easy access to information was provided via the internet. After thousands of years when those who accessed information dominated humanity, the sharing of information and ease of access were important steps for humanity. After a period of approximately ten years, the Web 2.0 period was entered in the 2000s, and the speed of the internet increased with the increase in technology and infrastructure services during this period. The fluidity called streaming has made internet users more sharing, thus diversifying production on the web, and increasing the speed of image and video production and consumption. Castells, who emphasizes that society and social life have changed with new technological developments, has named the newly emerging society as the "network society". (Atar, 2017) The communication that has taken shape within the network structure that Manuel Castells mentioned has also changed people's life-styles, and a large part of their time has now begun to be spent on social networks. Even well-known personalities have begun to use social networks that emerged in the web 2.0 era in order to increase their visibility and reduce costs (Jenkins, 2016).

With Web 3.0 (since 2010), the semantic web era has begun, and during this period, developments in the mobile internet field have created effective connection networks between web platforms. Thus, data on the internet has begun to be used in a coordinated manner between new media platforms (Dikmen, 2017:426). In the Web 3.0 period, machines have been able to better understand people, and data has been opened to sharing and use. Tim Berners-Lee first described the Semantic Web as follows: "HTML and the Web are like a big book, RDF, schema, and inference languages, all the data in the world will appear as one big database" (Choudhury, 2014).

The symbiotic network that started in 2020 is described as the highly intelligent interaction network of Web 4.0. With Web 4.0, communication systems (WebOS) that only need an internet browser to work and serve many users from a server have quickly entered daily life. WebOS is designed as a giant network consisting of intelligent interactions similar to the human brain and using artificial intelligence techniques (Choudhury, 2014). Thanks to artificial intelligence that perceives data just like a human brain, internet users can easily access the data they like and are interested in without any errors (Mediaclick, 2019). This network, which is thought to be more secure, provides access to faster and more personalized information. Web 4.0, called the Pragmatic Web, is not only about the form or meaning of information; unlike the Semantic Web, this period, called the information age, will be a period in which the ways people use information will be discussed.

In this period Artificial intelligence, as one of the most important technologies of the digital age, is reshaping both individual lifestyles and social structures. Areas with high social impact such as media and television broadcasting are also directly affected by this transformation. Technological determinism argues that this transformation is inevitable and that technology determines social structure. In this study, from a technological determinist perspective, the contributions of artificial intelligence to the media and television fields, its possible negative effects and the future potential of this technology are discussed.

ARTIFICIAL INTELLIGENCE FROM A TECHNOLOGICAL DETERMINISTIC PERSPECTIVE

The internet and the technologies that have entered our lives in the context of the internet have caused changes in our lifestyles, and the benefits of technology have come to the fore. When it comes to technological determinism, the first name that comes to mind is Marshall McLuhan. With the structural use of technology, his views have come to the fore again and have become widely talked about. In the period when the world has turned into a global village, almost everything has been determined through technology . This situation emphasizes the need to give importance to new communication tools equipped with technical equipment rather than trivializing the content of the messages. Communication tools have changed the way of life and the way of thinking of people. With the 2000s, the fact that almost everyone has started to use communication technologies has also made technology a topic of conversation. As of 2010, we have transitioned to a period where we are individually productive, and we have reached times when communication has accelerated and increased all over the world. After the 2020s, we are experiencing a period where technological transformations have increased exponentially and transformation speeds have slowed down to five-year periods. During this period, innovations such as big data, the internet of things, and artificial intelligence have been offered to the end consumer.

Technology brings many conveniences to human life. Self-learning machines offer a conformist life opportunity in the fields of education, health, engineering, defense, agriculture, trade, industry, industrial production, advertising, marketing, home life, tourism, law, communication and media. Big data and artificial intelligence applications that benefit from it and machines that talk to each other are positioned as the umbrella elements of the society 5.0, or "Super Smart Society" era, where socialization reaches its peak.

Technological determinism is the approach that sees technology as the determining force of social change. This approach argues that technological developments shape individuals' decisions, cultural structures, and social relations. In this context, artificial intelligence is not only considered a tool, but also an agent that transforms society (Brynjolfsson & McAfee, 2014). The positive effects of artificial intelligence on life include workforce efficiency, increased diagnostic speed in health services, and the spread of personalized learning opportunities in education (Marr, 2018). The fact that computer-based systems have basic skills such as learning, reasoning, self-development (learning from experience), language understanding, and problem solving can also be expressed as a simulation of human intelligence (Çakın, 2024, p. 77).

Artificial intelligence, which is described as the art of imitating and surpassing humanity, has entered a process called first productive and then productive artificial intelligence, which is thought to have started as of November 2022. This process, which is considered the beginning of a new era, is the beginning of the time when artificial intelligence exists as an intelligence, not on a singular task-based basis, proceeding on the path shown by the data. During this period, human beings will meet with the most basic dream of developers, artificial general intelligence (AGI), in 2025, and witness the efforts of inorganic beings, as the 3rd species, to exist and gain a place (Özdemir, 2025, p. 362).

However, the technological determinist perspective argues that technological developments will directly lead to social change, while assuming that human intervention is limited. This situation also paves the way for negative consequences such as unethical use, data security problems, and uncertainty in the labor market (Zuboff, 2019).

While it is widely discussed that artificial intelligence will facilitate daily life and work from a technological deterministic perspective and increase the creativity and time that humans will spend on themselves, Güven Savul, drawing attention to the fact that the age of digital capitalism has created its own form of ideology based on Christian Fuchs, mentions that the scenario in which techno-capitalism drags people, except for a handful of privileged "super-qualified workers and super-consumers", into disaster may become a reality (2019, pp. 161, 175). Harvey, who looks at the situation in the context of political economy, expresses the dynamic relationship that capitalism creates with technology as increasing production and reducing labor costs, thus seizing the surplus value produced by the worker (Durdağ, 2014, p. 31).

USE OF ARTIFICIAL INTELLIGENCE IN MEDIA

The emergence of communication tools is based on technology. The transition from wireless telephone to radio, radio being overshadowed by television with the industrialization that took place after World War II, then communication technologies mediated by the internet becoming indispensable in daily life, the age of personal production shining through social media, and the period in which artificial intelligence algorithms are included in communication has come. After this, artificial intelligence applications mediated by media have become visible in almost all communication areas .

The rate of increase in technology has decreased from 20 to 10 to 5 years. In the following period, two-year movements are expected. In other words, the integration of life with technology has accelerated considerably. Humanity seems to have become accustomed to technological innovations and inventions. This situation necessitates thinking about the political economy of the media once again. Is humankind increasing media consumption with artificial intelligence algorithms or is it a cog in the gear that feeds this huge industry? In other words, will it be the dream of thinking machines. The productive consumer is constantly producing data in the networks where they socialize. This data becomes the food of artificial intelligence.

Artificial intelligence is also changing the culture industry through media. Although this situation reminds us of dystopian movies, the rapid progress in artificial intelligence as a result of technology will bring some problems. The future development of technology will progress in line with socio-cultural goals rather than an autonomous process that will be managed only by engineers (Williams, 2013).

In the Internet 4.0 era, namely from 2020 onwards, technology-based applications have been used in content production, and in a very short time, artificial intelligence has become an auxiliary tool in the reproduction of the culture industry. Artificial intelligence has also become an effective tool in media analysis, audience segmentation and advertising targeting. With big data analytics, audience habits are analyzed in detail, and media content is shaped accordingly (Napoli, 2014).

Artificial intelligence is also transforming critical functions in the media field, especially content production, content distribution and user interaction. "Years of research on media have highlighted the view that media content is decisive in shaping society " (Akmeşe, 2020, p. 221). In modern societies, all life seems to consist of spectacle. Because consumption patterns also move away, leaving their place to a new representation (Debord, 2006, p. 35). In fact, only technique changes place. What remains is the economy-politics articulated with ideology. "With the concept of commodification of ideology, Debord emphasizes that all kinds of objects and interpersonal relationship patterns in consumer culture are produced by the system in a way articulated to the money economy" (Tutar, 2020, p. 343). Thanks to technological developments, the development, processing and management of communication and information have become easier. The increasing efficiency in the internet and information technologies has also increased the variety of media products (Kara, 2014, p. 55). However, the increasing variety is only quantitative, it is observed that similar content is put into circulation again and again.

INTELLIGENCE APPLICATIONS IN TELEVISION BROADCASTING

When it comes to large audiences, television, which uses its visual power, continues to have a privileged position in influencing and addicting the masses with the messages it presents (Bolat, 2018, p.1678). Television broadcasting, which consists of multiple work components; we come across examples of artificial intelligence in areas such as script writing, actor selection, set design, camera use, sound editing, music production, subtitle production, graphic design, editing processes, news production, artificial intelligence announcers, and target audience determination. For example, even the television content of some large broadcasting organizations is designed by artificial intelligence supported by big data. This situation questions the future of television broadcasting.

It is known that it is used in broadcasting, especially in speed-based broadcasting works such as script writing, broadcast flow and broadcast text creation, editing, and the rapid completion of stages from the editorial stage of the news to the broadcast. As a result of its integration with big data, artificial intelligence applications used in many autonomous applications in the media field are also seen in the television field. These applications, which have recently come to the fore with personalized television examples, can be used in almost every stage of television broadcasting, consisting of pre-production, production and post-production stages. In addition, artificial intelligence systems analyze user behavior, provide personalized content recommendations, and increase audience loyalty on media platforms (Gomez-Uribe & Hunt, 2016). For example; The Netflix recommendation engine is powered by AI-based machine learning algorithms, and the system constantly measures and monitors its recommendations based on interaction, offering hyper-personalized content that meets subscribers' expectations. This system, called "Meson," works like a traffic cop for multiple machine learning lines that "drive video recommendations, create, train, and validate personalization algorithms" (Zengin, 2021, pp. 710-711).

Television broadcasting also receives a significant share from the impact of artificial intelligence. Artificial intelligence is transforming both technical processes and content strategies. In terms of data-based content production, artificial intelligence can suggest content types and formats based on past audience data. However, such developments also bring ethical issues. Determining content solely based on algorithms can reduce the diversity of information and lead to commercial concerns. Therefore, the impact of artificial intelligence on television productions should be evaluated not only technically, but also in terms of sociological and ethical dimensions.

In terms of automation and production processes, it is used in functions such as control of camera movements, automatic subtitling, audio description and scenario analysis (Levy, 2020). 60% of the work is saved by using artificial intelligence for purposes such as extracting people and objects, subtitling, sound editing and enhancement, multi-camera editing, that is, editing images from many cameras at the same time, tracking the object on the color page, improving image quality, stabilizing the image, adding new light to the image, creating off-background (Akikol and Atmaca Demir, 2025, pp. 157-158).

"Artificial intelligence technology is not yet fully used effectively in the shooting phase of a television program. It has been observed that algorithmic systems with artificial intelligence technology automate workflows that require mental and labor power in the pre-production phase of a content such as script writing, content creation, actor/host selection, graphic design, or direct the editorial workforce with the suggestion-oriented outputs they provide" (Kapır, 2023, p. 28). However, in terms of interactive broadcast experience, smart televisions communicate directly with the audience with AI- supported voice command and facial recognition systems. It is thought that the effects of AI in technical and cultural film production, distribution and screening practices will occur in the viewing culture and the way of watching movies will turn into more individual experiences (Zengin, 2021, p. 723).

Program Text Generation with Artificial Intelligence

For the first time in 2016, a section of a short film's script, including dialogue script and characters, was written by artificial intelligence (Coşkuner, 2023, p. 39). Easy and fast script writing has been used in synopsis, treatment, script and dialogue script writing, story board drawings and determining the characters suitable for the script, regardless of the medium. On February 13, 2025, the TCLtv+ platform introduced the 12-minute romantic short film prepared by artificial intelligence, "Next Stop Paris", which it prepared for Valentine's Day . However, the project did not achieve the expected success. In this film, CGI and AI were used only for the creation of the environment and background effects. Although TCL used real images shot with professional cameras and various artificial intelligence applications (Midjourney, Runway ML, Nuke, Adobe After Effects and TCL tools combined) in most scenes of the film, the film was not appreciated (donanimhaber.com, 2025).

Artificial intelligence results in shifts in meaning, it can be used in objective text production that is not based on emotional basis and saves human labor. Artificial intelligence can be used especially in writing and editing news text, writing program texts and creating program flow by calculating durations.

In content production, AI - supported tools (e.g. GPT, DALL E, Runway ML) are used in areas such as news writing, video summarization, and script writing, and they speed up production processes (Diakopoulos, 2019). Artificial intelligence applications are used especially in news writing and the editorial process until the news is on the screen. Artificial intelligence, which collects, filters, and automatically provides news production, also brings a process independent of humans to the agenda in the field of journalism. "Reuters, which uses AI-supported journalism applications with the automation tool called "Lynx Insights", which it defines as a cybernetic reporter, can obtain the data that a reporter can obtain at a higher speed and size with this tool. The tool, which is thought to make great contributions to the editorial process in terms of news production or obtaining and using the data that is the subject of the news, stands out as one of the examples of robot journalism" (Erdem, 2021, pp. 868-899).

Trying to be competent in issues such as character matches and new character creation, emotion analysis, AI will also guide the process of finding actors suitable for the scenario and preparing the actor for the role. In this regard, artificial intelligence announcers who first appeared on China's national television channels have been on the screen. China's official news agency Xinhua brought an artificial intelligence announcer to the screen for the first time on November 9, 2018. "The artificial intelligence announcers who will report the news 'tirelessly' every day Wearing a red tie and striped suit, he would nod his head, wink, and slightly raise his eyebrows while emphasizing the news. "I' m not just accompanying you 24 hours a day, 365 days a year. It can be copied infinitely and I can be in different scenes to bring you the news," he said. Xinhua also introduced an English-speaking AI . The presenters, developed by Xinhua and Chinese search engine Sogou, were developed through machine learning to simulate the voice, facial movements and gestures of real-life broadcasters, according to Xinhua, creating a lifelike image instead of a cold robot (The Guardian, 2018). In addition, a female AI robot named Xin Xiaomeng, developed by Chinese search engine company Sogou, started working as a news anchor at Xinhua News Media Center, and she was officially named the world's first female robot news anchor.

Use of Artificial Intelligence in Production

The most interesting stage of a production is the production part. Because this part, which consists of multiple work components, contains a process that is difficult to manage. The triple trivet of the production consists of image, sound and light in the experience that started with cinema . The difference between television broadcasting and cinema is that this trio is watched in the comfort of home. This comfort, which we can now access on mobile, has always been remarkable as a communication area where humanity combines technology and art.

Recently, robot cameramen, robot actors, robot script writers and robot editors are also developments that pave the way for the superiority of artificial intelligence in the media sector (Erdem, 2021, p.899). The discussions that were held about the inability of artificial intelligence to be creative about 20 years ago have now been replaced by images, credits and texts made with artificial intelligence (Coşkuner, 2023, p. 38). Artificial intelligence applications used in various fields from credit design to program flow creation; It seems that in addition to image, sound and light, it will also undertake some tasks in production such as instantly processed vtr, text, graphics, animation and virtual reality applications. For example, cameramanship is one of them. Cameras that can automatically adjust color and light and sharpness according to the environment and person they are in, artificial intelligence disables camera control by matching the images of all cameras in broadcasts where more than one camera is used. "Smart robots can be used in shootings that require multi-camera systems. For example, during sports events, smart robots can monitor athletes moving on the field. Smart robots will come into play not only in sports matches, but also in shooting big shows, documentaries, and different television programs" (Ersin, 2023, p. 1219). Since 2020, drone cameras have been functioning as smart robot cameras. While these cameras could not shoot without a cameraman before, shootings have begun to be made without a cameraman with artificial intelligence and without prior design (Coşkuner, 2023, p. 39).

Artificial intelligence is taking place in the editing phase. The process of adapting Adobe Premiere Pro, which is widely used in television broadcasting, to artificial intelligence started with Adobe Firefly. With this program, unwanted images in the video can be masked and replaced with another image from the options offered with the entered command. These changes can then be added to the program working in Premiere Pro. Image masking can eliminate anything that accidentally enters the frame during shooting. This feature is used to clean brands and logos that should not be shown. In addition, if the image shot is short, artificial intelligence tools perform "generative extension" so that the clip does not distort reality. Another editing program, DaVinci Resolve, is a post-production software that allows editing, color correction, visual effects and audio editing to be performed in a single software. The latest versions of DaVinci Resolve include Neural Engine artificial intelligence tools. As a distinctive feature, this software includes advanced algorithms for complex tasks such as face recognition and object detection used to prepare smoother and more natural-looking videos. In DaVinci Resolve software, audio can also be converted to written text, and cuts made on the text are reflected on the timeline and edited instantly. In the software, effects can be used to separate the person or object in the foreground from the background, to eliminate existing objects, to blur the background, etc. In addition, noise can be cleaned by separating the sounds in audio files (Akikol and Atmaca Demir, 2025, p. 154).

In television broadcasting, color and sound adjustments that are automatically performed during live broadcasts, VTR readings, effects used during VTR transitions, music, text and graphics superimposed on the broadcast will be reshaped by artificial intelligence. In other words, artificial intelligence will now be able to write "last minute developments" on live broadcasts. At this point, the existence of editors who work in harmony with artificial intelligence is important. The training of editors who can give good commands and work in the most accurate and fastest way is an issue that needs to be emphasized.

Future predictions enable artificial intelligence applications that will perform all production in this field. While this situation provides the time of work and integration in the media, artificial intelligence also brings with it the problem of security related to information in the field of media and publishing. As seen in social media applications, data collected from unknown sources without any verification raises concerns about what is real and what is fake. Fake news and, more generally, manipulative content that leads to fake publishing can be produced with deep learning techniques inherent in artificial intelligence technology (Erdem, 2021, p. 902). This situation will also raise new ethical issues. For example, digital twins may be attempted to be commodified in virtual environments similar to the metaverse; individual behaviors in the virtual world can be widely monitored, and new forms of identity theft, abuse and deception may also be possible.

"The most popular applications of artificial intelligence today are rising from machine learning, which is considered a subset. Another subset of machine learning, deep learning, includes the imitation of nerve cells in the human brain and the reconstruction of the connections between them in a multi-layered way. Since the early 2000s, developments in technology and algorithms have paved the way for the emergence of new types of deep editing applications and the development of more efficient outputs. Today, with deep editing applications, it is possible to transfer the entire human face, part of it and facial expressions; to create a fake speech by remodeling the facial expression and mouth; and to produce a human face and a responsive face/facial expression from scratch" (Özdemir, 2021, 906, 909). Deepfake is the processing of a person's real image and voice in a virtual environment with the help of artificial intelligence. The use of the increase in video streaming speed together with "deep fake" software, which is a method of artificial intelligence and data matching, allows one-to-one copies of real people to be simulated in a digital environment. Finally, it was brought to the agenda that the videos of Donald Trump and Zelenski's fistfight, which were spread as news on social media, were produced and served using artificial intelligence technology. While a highly strategic meeting was being adapted for entertainment purposes, unfortunately, the negative social effects it could create were being overlooked (Ersöz, 04.03. 2025).

Some television productions are produced live, while others are recorded for later broadcast. Digitally recorded productions are processed and edited in the post-production stage to attract the attention of the audience. This stage includes image and sound editing, color adjustments, effects, text, graphics and animation applications. Artificial intelligence also contributes to the process of creating music and visual effects with scripts. Later, artificiality comes to the fore in the broadcast planning stage and in the organization of daily broadcast flows such as programs, advertisements and promotions. Viewer behavior is analyzed in terms of broadcast flow and broadcast planning, and more effective broadcast flows and advertising placements are created (Broussard, 2018).

Artificial intelligence applications are also seen in the reproduction of productions. Content produced for television or social media is processed with artificial intelligence and put into circulation in the form of reproduction. These applications, which are now mostly done individually, are also being handled by broadcasting organizations and production companies in this period when content is worth its weight in gold.

TRANSFORMATION AND CRITICAL PERSPECTIVES IN TELEVISION BROADCASTING

The role of artificial intelligence in broadcasting is transforming the traditional understanding of mass communication. The audience is no longer a passive recipient, but an active participant who produces data and has an indirect effect on the content. This situation enables television broadcasting to become interactive and data-driven. However, this transformation also brings with it some social effects and critical questions such as whether algorithms are impartial in content selection, the risks of leaving editorial decisions to artificial systems instead of humans, the problems that AI- supported content production will cause in terms of copyright, labor and creativity, access justice and the deepening of the digital divide. For this reason, media institutions and broadcasters need to evaluate artificial intelligence not only as a productivity tool, but also within the framework of social responsibility and to emphasize artificial intelligence literacy. Although artificial intelligence has made significant technical progress, it has not been able to replace humans. Beyond being a new designer, it is an innovative tool that increases the efficiency and effectiveness of the creative process as directed by humans. In order to fully benefit from the opportunities provided by artificial intelligence and reduce its risks, it is important to have "artificial intelligence literacy" (Kızılhan, 2025, p. 214).

On the other hand, the human being who developed artificial intelligence thinks that there should be a limit to the development of the machine and tries to implement this. They want the artificial intelligence to use its intelligence in a way that will benefit humanity, they do not want it to be rebellious. However, in this situation it contradicts the formation of artificial intelligence. Because artificial intelligence robots or computers should not pose a threat to the future and life of humans, but artificial intelligence, like every organism, will tend to mobilize all the features it has in order to live, and as its intelligence develops, the path it will instinctively follow will be to imitate the "human" and sometimes push the limits with malicious methods. In other words, dealing with artificial intelligence brings with it such a paradox. Isaac Asimov, who is considered one of the important writers of science fiction literature, created robot laws by foreseeing this situation in his work "I, Robot", where he collected 9 robot stories. Accordingly, all stories contain the "3 Laws of Robotics" created by the author: " Law 1 - A robot may not harm a human being or allow another to come to harm. Law 2 - A robot must obey orders given by human beings except those that violate the first law. Law 3 - A robot must protect its own existence, but this protection must not violate the first and second laws" (Göral, 2021, pp. 920-921).

As a thinking being, humans can take a position in the face of an event or situation they encounter, and they also bear the responsibility for it. However, no matter how advanced they are, machines do not yet have the ability to take a position in the face of an uncertain situation. Famous Turkish mathematician Ordinaryus Professor Cahit Arf said in the 1950s that machines can think and that there is no need for a devilish intelligence for this. What is important is whether artificial intelligence algorithms that use big data can be as virtuous as a human when they encounter a situation that is not recorded among the scanned data.

CONCLUSION

From a technological determinist perspective, "the medium is the message" and the future of the culture industry will be shaped by new communication technologies. A more enjoyable life awaits humanity in the future. In an era when the question of whether humans, who have gained ample free time and entertainment opportunities after the intense work tempo and obedience mechanism, will fall into the clutches of inertia and surrender their decision-making and reasoning abilities to artificial intelligence or will they continue to retain them, it seems the wisest thing for machines and humans to join forces for efficiency (Van Dijk, 2018).

In the current period, there are actually two views that are close to each other but cannot meet at a point, regarding the fact that technology is an element that works for the benefit of humanity and that life should not be reduced to technology. In fact, the dreams of a future where machines handle tasks autonomously and people have a lot of free time are being discussed through the young generation. In this sense, artificial intelligence has been met with curiosity. "The world has been dreaming of a time for a long time, but in order to truly live it, it must already have consciousness" (Debord, 2006, p. 34). The person who captures the spirit of the time is the one who truly lives it. Therefore, people need both intelligence in terms of interaction, that is, socialization, and artificial intelligence in terms of automation.

Artificial intelligence does not indicate a new production but rather a reproduction mediated by technology. During this period, individuals and institutions that read artificial intelligence well and can follow not only the editing technology but also the artificial intelligence tools will come to the fore. The media, which has played an active role in shaping the culture industry to date, seems to continue to maintain its place in the future. The media plays an active role in ensuring that people create culture and communicate. Although the channels and tools change, media mediated by technology appeals to the entire society culturally. This situation has initiated a radical transformation in the fields of artificial intelligence, media and television broadcasting. As the currently expensive artificial intelligence applications become cheaper like the technological developments before them, their areas of use will also increase.

Artificial intelligence not only supports the current systems in television broadcasting, but also paves the way for a structural transformation. However, in a period when originality is the only thing in terms of content, artificial intelligence can reduce content completely to technique. This situation can also be an obstacle to creativity. So how will the future of television, which means seeing far, take shape? Television, which can be watched from different screens at any time and place in terms of hardware and infrastructure, has a structure integrated with technology. However, although different variations are tried on television content mediated by technology with its structure that shapes the culture of the mass, it is unclear in which direction it will evolve and what kind of transformation will take place. In the light of technological developments, television will write its own story. Perhaps personal television experiences will one day end, or perhaps there will be a single television that speaks to the whole world.

At this very moment, there is a need to draw a roadmap for the use of artificial intelligence in the media field. Technological determinism defines this process as inevitable and irreversible. However, any technological move made without considering ethical, cultural and sociological contexts can disrupt the social balance. In this context, universities, media research centers and policy makers need to address the effects of artificial intelligence in the media field in a multidimensional and critical manner. The broadcasting of the future should be based not only on technical progress, but also on ethical awareness and the production of social benefit.

Another point to consider regarding the future of television broadcasting is whether productions made with artificial intelligence should be separated or should they be combined with those produced by humans and presented as collective creativity. Is collective production the success of humanity or the new truth of humanity or is it beyond truth?

REFERENCES

Akikol, R., & Atmaca Demir, B. (2025). Artificial intelligence tools used in editing and the editing profession. *Interaction, 15*(15), 150–169. DOI: 10.32739/etkilesim.2025.8.15.287

Akmeşe, Z. (2020). The effect of framing on content and meaning production in television. In E. Sirer (Ed.), *Television 4.0 society 5.0 era, new program, new audience.* (pp. 207- 222). Konya: Literatürk Publication.

Akpınar, M. (February 17, 2025). "Next Stop Paris": TCL offers a look at the future with artificial intelligence film https://www.donanimhaber.com/tcl-yapay-zeka-filmi-ile-gelecege-bir-bakis-sunuyor--187856 Access: 30.4.2025

Arf, C. (1959). *"Can a machine think and how?". Atatürk University 1958-1959 Academic Year Public Conferences I.* Emir Öngüner Private Archives.

Atar, Ö. G. (2016). Transformation of Television Viewership in the Digital Age. *Journal of Social Sciences* . Year: 4, Issue: 15, October 2017, 350-379.

Black, T. (2014). Media products within the framework of the concept of culture industry: a critical approach. *The Turkish Online Journal of Design, Art and Communication.* TOJDAC January 2014 Volume 4 Issue 1.

Bolat, N. (2018). An examination of the representation of women in the media in a male-dominated world: the example of Eşkiya Dünyakürün Olmak TV series. *Gümüşhane University e-journal of Faculty.* Volume 6, Number 2. pp. 1676-1703.

Brynjolfsson, E., & McAfee, A. (2014). *The Second Machine Age: Work, Progress, and Prosperity in a Time of Brilliant Technologies.* W. W. Norton & Company.

Çakın, Ö. (2024). Use of Artificial Intelligence in Marketing Communication of Brands. (pp. 75-100). *Brand Communication, Brand and Consumer Interaction in All Dimensions.* (Ed. Erdem and Mayadağlı). Konya: Palet

Choudhury, N. (2014). World Wide Web and Its Journey from Web 1.0 to Web 4.0. *International Journal of Computer Science and Information Technologies, 5*(6), 8096–8100.

Coşkuner, A. (2023). The Test of Cinema with Uncontrolled Technology: The Impact of Artificial Intelligence on the Film Industry. *Turkish Journal of Film Studies, 3*(1), 32–47. DOI: 10.59280/film.1284277

Debord, G. (2006). *The society of the spectacle and interpretations* (Ekmekçi, A., & Taşkent, O., Trans.). Ayrıntı Publication.

Diakopoulos, N. (2019). *Automating the News: How Algorithms Are Rewriting the Media*. Harvard University Press. DOI: 10.4159/9780674239302

Dictionary, T. D. K. (2025). Turkish Language Association Dictionary. https://sozluk.gov.tr/

Dikmen, E. Ş. (2017). Transformation of Television Broadcasting in Turkey: Social TV Broadcasting. *Gümüşhane University Faculty of Communication Electronic Journal*. Volume:5, Issue:1.

Durdağ, B. (2014). Technological Determinist Approach and Its Different Aspects in the Relationship between Technology and Social Change, *LaborComm 2014*. Ankara.

Erdem, B. K. (2021). The Impact of Artificial Intelligence on Media and Broadcasting. *TRT Academy Journal*, *VI*(13), 897–903.

Ersin, N. (2023). Television broadcasting in Turkey towards Industry 4.0: Views of media professionals. *Anadolu University Journal of Social Sciences*, *23*(4), 1211–1236.

Ersöz, E. (2025). "Trump and Zelenski fight continues in artificial intelligence". *Tercüman Journal*. https://www.tercuman.com/yorum/trump-ve-zelenski-kavgasi-yapay-zekada-devam-ediyor-618/

Gomez-Uribe, C. A., & Hunt, N. (2016). The Netflix Recommender System: Algorithms, Business Value, and Innovation. [TMIS]. *ACM Transactions on Management Information Systems*, *6*(4), 1–19. DOI: 10.1145/2843948

Göral, B. (2021). Cinema's view of artificial intelligence. *TRT Academy Journal*, *VI*(13), 919–929.

Haberler.com. (2019). "The World's First Robot Female News Anchor" https://www.haberler.com/teknoloji/dunyanin-ilk-robot-kadin-haber-sunucusu-video-11803813-haberi/ 29.04.2025

Jenkins, H. (2018). *Brave New Media* (Yeğengil, N., Trans.). Communication Publication.

Kapir, B. (2023). The use of artificial intelligence technology as a traditional media tool in the television sector. *Ufuk University 2nd International Congress on Social Sciences Artificial Intelligence and Social Sciences*. Conference Paper. May 2023.

Levy, S. (2020). *Facebook: The Inside Story*. PenguinPress.

Marr, B. (2018). *Artificial Intelligence in Practice: How 50 Successful Companies Used AI and Machine Learning to Solve Problems*. Wiley.

Mediaclick, What is Web 4.0? https://www.mediaclick.com.tr/blog/web-4-0-nedir, 30.04.2025.

Napoli, P. M. (2014). *Audience Evolution: New Technologies and the Transformation of Media Audiences*. Columbia University Press.

Noble, S. U. (2018). *Algorithms of Oppression: How Search Engines Reinforce Racism*. NYU Press. DOI: 10.18574/nyu/9781479833641.001.0001

Oxford Dictionary. (2025). https://languages.oup.com/google-dictionary-tr/

Özdemir, Ş. (2021). New Generation Threat: DeepFake. *TRT Academy Journal*, (13), 905–917.

Özdemir, Ş. (2025). From ancient legends to generative artificial intelligence: Reality, disinformation and the struggle for humanity. *TRT Academy Journal*, *X*(13), 362–369.

Savul, G. (2019). Old Debate New Discourse: Technological Development and Capitalism in the Context of Industry 4.0. *Praxis Journal*, (50), 49–178.

Susskind, D. (2020). *A World Without Work: Technology, Automation, and How We Should Respond*. Metropolitan Books. https://www.theguardian.com/world/2018/nov/09/worlds-first-ai-news-anchor-unveiled-in-china

The Guardian. (2018)." World's first AI news anchor unveiled in China". 29.04.2025.

Tutar, C., & Durukan, D. (2020). Television in the construction and transformation of gastronomy culture: The example of Masterchef Turkey and The Taste Turkey programs. *Istanbul University Sociology Journal*, *40*, 339–364. DOI: 10.26650/SJ.2020.40.1.0032

Van Dijk, J. (2018). *The network society* (Sakin, O., Trans.). Epsilon Publication.

Williams, R. (2003). *Television, technology and cultural form*. Dost Press Publication.

Zengin, F. (2021). Artificial intelligence and personalized viewing culture: Hyper-personalization of the work of art through the example of Netflix. *TRT Academy*, *6*(13), 700–727. DOI: 10.37679/trta.959576

Zuboff, S. (2019). *The Age of Surveillance Capitalism: The Fight for a Human Future at the New Frontier of Power*. PublicAffairs.

ADDITIONAL READING

Baudrillard, J. (2004). *The consumer society* (Deliceçaylı, H., & Keskin, F., Trans.). Ayrıntı Publication.

Baudrillard, J. (2014). *Simulacra and Simulation* (Adanır, O., Trans.). Doğu Batı Publication.

Berger, J. (2020). *Ways of seeing* (Salman, Y., Trans.). Metis Publication.

Bourdieu, P. (1997). *Televizyon üzerine* (Ilgaz, T., Trans.). Yapı Kredi Publications.

Burton, G. (1995). *More than meets the eye: an introduction to media analysis* (Dinç, N., Trans.). Alan Publication.

Ellul, J. (1998). *The decline of the word* (Arslan, H., Trans.). Paradigma Publication.

Floridi, L. (2020). *The Ethics of Artificial Intelligence*. Oxford University Press.

Ford, M. (2018). *Rise of the Robots* (Duran, C., Trans.). Kronik Books.

Fuchs, C. (2018). Industry 4.0: The Digital German Ideology. *TripleC, 16*(1), 280–289. https://www.triple-c.at/index.php/tripleC/article/view/1010. DOI: 10.31269/triplec.v16i1.1010

Heidegger, M. (1998). *Tekniğe ilişkin soruşturma*. Paradigma Publications.

Kızılhan, T. (2025). A comparative study on artificial intelligence and human design in communication design education. *Interaction, 15*, 196–218. DOI: 10.32739/etkilesim.2025.8.15.289

McLuhan, M. (2019). *Our Creator, the Media: A Journey of Discovery on the Effects of the Media* (Oskay, Ü., Trans.). Nora Books.

Millerson, G. (1999). *Television production*. Focal Press.

Mutlu, E. (1991). *Understanding Television*. Gündoğdu Publication.

Neuman, R. W. (2018). *Digital Difference: Digitalization and Media Effects in Everyday Life* (Metin, G., Trans.). The Book.

Postman, N. (2004). *Television: Public discourse in the age of deadly entertainment spectacle* (Akınhay, O., Trans.). Ayrıntı Publication.

KEY TERMS AND DEFINITIONS

Technology: It is the application knowledge that covers all the machines, tools, devices, methods, etc. created for the purposes of accumulating, controlling, processing and transmitting power and information in an industrial field. It is the totality of the tools and equipment developed by humans to control and change their material environment and the information related to them.

Media: The common name that encompasses all media outlets such as radio, television, newspapers and magazines that enable communication with the masses can also be defined as mass communication tools and press and publications.

Broadcast: To send out or transmit (something, such as a program) by means of radio or television or by streaming over the Internet.

Television Broadcasting: In shaping the future of television broadcasting and broadcasters, technological developments in digital video technologies and networked services, including computers and the Internet, are becoming increasingly evident. Digital video systems have become widely available for the broadcasting sector thanks to the technical capacities of systems that process and transmit information using digital methods that can be used in the production of audiovisual content. In addition, the telecommunications, informatics and broadcasting sectors have begun to intertwine.

Production: Production is a term that covers the entire production process of a content from the idea stage to the final product. It includes the technical, creative and logistical processes required to bring films, series, commercials, documentaries and digital content to life.

Machine Learning: Machine learning is a subset of artificial intelligence (AI). It focuses on teaching computers to learn from data and improving them through experience rather than being explicitly programmed to do so. In machine learning, algorithms are trained to find patterns and correlations in large data sets and make the best decisions and predictions based on that analysis. Machine learning applications improve with use and become more accurate when more data is available.

Chapter 17
Digital Television Broadcasting in Interaction With the Rhythm of Everyday Life:
The Spatial and Temporal Organization of Tele-Visual Images

Cem Tutar
https://orcid.org/0000-0002-4547-6171
Üsküdar University, Turkey

ABSTRACT

Among the thinkers who focus on everyday life within the field of sociology, the Neo-Marxist thinker Henri Lefebvre stands out from other theorists with the holistic framework he proposed. In analyzing the spatial and temporal dimensions of everyday life, Lefebvre assigned a distinctive role to mass media within these domains, which are shaped by the dynamics of the capitalist system. Emerged as a domestic medium during the modern era, the television now intersects with all facets of everyday life through its convergence with new media technologies. In the everyday life of urban living, digital television broadcasting, articulated through polyrhythmic processes, brings together tele-visual images within this new virtual topography. In this context, this book chapter aims to critically examine the capitalist organization of everyday life and television broadcasting from Henri Lefebvre's perspective, as well as to explore the relationships between the rhythms of everyday life in urban space and digital television broadcasting.

DOI: 10.4018/979-8-3373-1957-5.ch017

INTRODUCTION

The space and time, which are the structural components of the concept of everyday life, are shaped within the context of the means of production and technical possibilities of the time. In this process, the rhythm of everyday life has diversified across traditional, modern, and contemporary digital cultural spaces. The spatial and temporal organization of everyday life began systematically with the modern era, during which the capitalist system has accelerated the rhythm of daily life. According to Henri Lefebvre, this period has marked the replacement of nature's cycles with the cyclical time of capitalism. Television is a technical tool that stands out in the consumption-based organization of space and time of everyday life in modern society. While capitalism plans the flow of everyday life and television broadcasting together in the dialectical process, the rhythm of everyday life has contributed to the formation of broadcasting flow throughout the modern period. In this process, television has caused the separation of space and time from each other, not only as a technical tool but also as a socio-cultural phenomenon. Television's symbolic environment creates three types of space and time coordinates. These can be listed as the space-time coordinates of production contexts, tele-visual messages, and different reception contexts. With the modern period, the common point of this symbolic space is that it emphasizes instantaneous time emerging within an infinite present tense. Referring to the fragmentation and division of time and its integration with the system, instantaneous time has become an important component of urban life, particularly along the axis of new production processes and technological innovations of late modern society. Thus, this paved the way for a broadcasting flow and viewing practice outside the cycles of everyday life. Marking the transition from analog broadcasting to digital television broadcasting, this change emerged in the 2000s as a result of the convergence between television broadcasting and new media tools. This new broadcasting approach can be called post-television in a sense, and has content that has adapted to the new organization of space and time in domestic and work life.

Digital television broadcasting, which forms part of the digitalization of daily life, has taken on the role of a semantic interface in social life while bringing together tele-visual images in a new space and time coordinate. Digital television broadcasts accessed through mobile phones, tablets and computers have been articulated into the polyrhythmic processes of capitalist system's daily life. During this period, the media-driven day, which is characterized by the endless flow of communication and information, replaced the rituals of the past. Tele-visual images have directly intersected with everyday life, leading to a transformation in its rhythm. All these developments have also contributed to the gradual decline of physical space as a reference point in everyday life. While the digitization of space has led to its virtualization, portable technological devices have paved the way for a direct and uninterrupted relationship with the media sphere. In this context, digital television broadcasting and post-television are not merely products of technological advancements but also emerge as part of the capitalist system's dialectical process of shaping the socio-economic and cultural dimensions of social life.

A review of studies on television broadcasting reveals that this field is predominantly understood within the framework of communication tools and the dynamics of the industry. In light of evolving technological innovations, it is needed to interpret television broadcasting through diverse perspectives and paradigms at both global and local levels. Although media has been studied within the framework of communication sociology, there is a clear need for analyses that seek to make sense of the microcosm unique to each medium in practice. In this context, the present study adopts a theoretical framework that approaches digital television broadcasting through the spatial and temporal dimensions of everyday life as experienced by individuals. This study argues from a Marxist perspective that everyday life and digital television broadcasting are organized by the capitalist system in a dialectical process, and thus aims to interpret the field from a critical perspective with an attempt to explain which socio-economic and cultural dynamics shape digital television broadcasting in the process of interaction with everyday life.

SOCIOLOGICAL IMAGINARIES OF EVERYDAY LIFE

Everyday life is the setting in which people individually and collectively establish social relations and thus realize themselves. Apart from physiological needs such as nutrition, shelter and reproduction, everyday life, in which personal and interpersonal relationships are established and economic and cultural activities take place, is an area of life that is often ignored and not given enough importance. The reason for this is the given and familiar nature of everyday life for humans from birth onward. Therefore, it has not been possible for a long time for everyday life to become an object of scientific research. The science of sociology, the study of social life and structures, emerged in the first quarter of the 19th century and long focused on analyzing the systems through which social structures were formed and transformed. Although sociology and philosophy began addressing everyday life in the early 20th century through approaches like ethnomethodology and phenomenology, as well as within the scope of social theory, such as postmodern theory and cultural studies, they were unable to develop a detailed discussion on the subject. From 18th century social philosophy to the classical period of the 19th century and then to the post-war era, modernist sociology has been shaped by two main tendencies. The first of these is the systems approach, represented by Comte, Durkheim, Parsons, and Orthodox

Marxism, while the second consists of ethnomethodology, symbolic interactionism, and phenomenological approaches, which became particularly influential in the post-war period. What these two types of approaches have in common is their adherence to Cartesian and positivist perspectives (Gardiner, 2016, pp. 17–19).

With the Industrial Revolution, urban spaces became the new center of everyday life in Europe. Initially disregarded by high culture, the transformation of industrialized everyday life into a subject of research was influenced by a series of political, social, and cultural movements in the early 20th century. In the first two decades of the 20th century, two significant shifts occurred under the influence of psychoanalysis and revolutionary cultural praxis. First, in the treatment and understanding of psychic life and disorders, the interpretation of everyday conversations replaced neurological diagnosis. Second, with the Bolsheviks seizing power, the possibility of a bottom-up social and cultural transformation became evident (Roberts, 2013, pp. 31-33). The Russian Revolution of 1917 led to the emergence of everyday life as a political and socio-cultural category. Previously regarded as an insignificant domain with its mundane repetitive nature, everyday life thus became the center of collective action and transformation. The revolutionary cultural practices of those years brought Orthodox Marxism into everyday life, making it a focal point of the philosophy of praxis. In the early 20th century, the writings of Marxist theorists such as Karl Korsch, Georg Lukacs and Vladimir Lenin transformed everyday life into an active cultural category.

At the beginning of the 20th century, a series of avantgarde cultural movements that emerged alongside revolutionary cultural praxis also resisted the capitalist organization of everyday life, its enclosure by instrumental rationality, and the transformation of art into a commodity. Alongside Dada and surrealism, the Situationist International developed a revolutionary approach in both art and theory. This approach, with its subjective street ethnography of everyday urban practices, introduced the concept of psychogeography. Through this concept, the Situationist International highlighted how the city had become a "second nature" for people, countering the perception of everyday life as mundane and insignificant by emphasizing its creative and innovative potential (Wark, 2014). From a historical perspective, two key processes played a decisive role in establishing everyday life as a subject of sociological research. First, there were the revolutionary movements of the working class, which gained visibility as part of the systemic inequalities in production and labor processes within the increasingly organized capitalist system of the early 20th century. Secondly, the art and cultural movements that emerged as a part of modernist art that started during the same years and carried it forward. Both processes shifted focus from high culture to ordinary people and their everyday lives as the central concern. For these movements, everyday life stands out with its innovative and revolutionary potential that goes beyond the ordinary and familiar.

In the study of everyday life as a research subject, Bakhtin's concept of the "imagination of ordinariness" stands out as a prominent conceptualization. Bakhtin opposed positivist social science and idealist philosophy, and developed a sociological perspective based on the concrete actions of the particular. Bakhtin prioritized the dialogical relationship between subjects over the subject-object dualism in everyday life and emphasized creative processes in opposition to the homogenizing forces present in daily life (Gardiner, 2016, pp. 77-79, 85-86). Bakhtin's concept of "imagination of the ordinariness," which is based on the ordinary, has contributed to the systematic criticism of alienating practices in everyday life by centering unofficial discourses as opposed to official discourses in the theoretical explanation of everyday life. Another factor in the emergence of everyday life as a field of sociological research is the shift of the focus of critical theory in Western Marxism from Germany to France after the Second World War. Especially by the late 1950s, as French culture was being modernized under state leadership, everyday life became widely politicized in a dissident manner. This political and cultural climate, by also supporting the countercultural movements of the 1960s, brought to the fore the concept of the active cultural consumer and grassroots cultural resistance, as seen in Anglophone cultural studies. The active stance found especially in the works of Michel de Certeau stands out in the strategies and tactics of everyday life and action (Roberts, 2013, pp.117-119). In contrast to the concepts of the culture industry, mass culture, or the authoritarian personality put forward by Frankfurt School theorists Adorno and Horkheimer, Michel de Certeau focused on the liberating aspects of popular culture, and by addressing minor practices in everyday life, emphasized their liberating nature.

In the sociological imagination of everyday life, the works of Henri Lefebvre, who did a comprehensive critique of Orthodox Marxism within Marxist literature, hold a privileged position. Approaching Michel de Certeau's concept of the active cultural producer and consumer with skepticism, Lefebvre addressed the oppressive and domineering structures within everyday life while aiming for the transformation of everyday life as a revolutionary practice. According to Henri Lefebvre (2010), "everyday life has become an object of consideration and is the province of organization; the space-time of voluntary programmed self-regulation, because when properly organized it provides a closed circuit (production-consumption-production)". In Lefebvre's thought, the everyday life practices of the modern world organized within the capitalist system play a central role. Presenting a holistic perspective in the analysis of everyday life, Lefebvre criticized these structures by arguing that everyday life cannot be defined through fragmented knowledge and specialized fields.

As a relatively young discipline that emerged in the 19th century, the study of sociology reveals that efforts to define everyday life were closely tied to a series of political and socio-cultural movements in the early 20th century. In examining everyday life with its ordinary and familiar nature, theorists with differing starting points have sometimes focused on passive masses and individuals shaped by the power dynamics of their time, while at other times, they have centered their analysis on the active individual as both a producer and consumer of meaning within everyday life. However, everyday life is too complex a structure to be reduced to either of these options. Henri Lefebvre, often regarded as the founder of the sociology of everyday life, contributed to the field by striving to define everyday life holistically from a Marxist perspective.

DEFINING EVERYDAY LIFE FROM A MARXIST PERSPECTIVE

The Industrial Revolution of the 19th century played a significant role in the emergence of sociology as a scientific discipline. As industrialization spread across Europe, mass migration from rural settlements to urban centers transformed cities into new hubs of human habitation. Examining this new social order based on automation and rationalized production through a critical lens, Karl Marx and Friedrich Engels placed particular emphasis on material production and labor processes in their theoretical frameworks of social life. While considering historical materialism as their starting point, Marx and Engels criticized idealist philosophy and Hegel's thoughts. Especially in relation to the concept of alienation, they emphasized material living conditions and practical consciousness instead of the philosophical consciousness found in Hegel. In their work *The Communist Manifesto*, Marx states that in every stage of history, the economic production and exchange relations, and the social structure arising from them, form the basis of the political and intellectual history of that era, and that the entire history of humanity is the history of class struggles (2013, p. 16). In Marx's works, although everyday life is the space where relations of production take place, it is not a privileged object of study. Marx is a thinker who, within modernist sociology, primarily addresses social systems and structures from a critical perspective.

The systematic interest in everyday life in Marxism began with the works of Henri Lefebvre. Revisiting the fundamental propositions of Orthodox Marxism, Lefebvre, unlike Marx, took everyday life, the sphere in which these activities occur, as his object of study, rather than the changing nature of production and exchange relations. In the period of 1950 and afterwards, while attempting to define everyday life within the conditions of modern social existence, Lefebvre emphasized that Marx's thought is insufficient for understanding today's world, yet it remains an indispensable and essential framework for comprehending it. Lefebvre pointed out that the dominant scientific perspective of his time was shaped by neoliberals and neo-positivists, both of whom, he argued, were far from grasping the totality of social life due to their fragmented, specialized fields of study. He opposed the tendency of that era to define society through various labels, such as industrial society, technocratic society, consumer society, mass society, leisure society, and affluent society, and insisted that political economy needed to be transcended (1996, pp. 169-170, 176). According to Henri Lefebvre (1995), "the knowledge of social life cannot be explained solely by political economy, history, psychology, or philosophy. The social is often rendered invisible within the political or economic sphere or reduced to them" (p. 53). When re-examining Marxism, Lefebvre argued that it was necessary to move beyond the concept of economic man. While Marxism reduced history to relations of production, it lost sight of the total man, the individual standing in opposition to the forces of production. According to Lefebvre, overcoming alienation requires a dialectical materialist re-examination of the material products, lifestyles, myths, and fetishes generated by capitalist processes within everyday life (2006, pp. 110-113).

In his works, Henri Lefebvre critiques the rationalized and automated social life of the 20th century while addressing the formation of everyday life within the means and relations of production. From a historical perspective, in the pre-modern era, work and collective production processes in daily life were followed by times of festivity and rest. However, with the rise of bourgeois society, while individual consciousness developed on one hand, work began to take on an increasingly fragmented structure on the other. In a fragmented social life composed of work life, family and private life, and leisure time, it has become more difficult to define everyday life. Lefebvre emphasizes that the externality of these spheres to one another is both a productive domain and a source of alienation, and argues that they should be considered as a whole (2010, pp. 36-37). In his work Everyday Life in the Modern World, Henri Lefebvre explores the relationship between everyday life and philosophy. In this context, he argues that philosophy, for a long time, excluded everyday life by failing to address it as a subject, yet everyday life cannot be understood without philosophy. Defining everyday life requires a meta-philosophy that goes beyond traditional philosophy. Seeking to define everyday life from a Marxist perspective, Lefebvre aims to conduct a nuanced analysis by distinguishing between the concepts of everyday life, the everyday, and everydayness. While capitalism colonizes everyday life, it also designs it as the time and space of commodity fetishism. Everyday life is the structure that surrounds us. All human activities take place within it. Everydayness describes the life rooted in the endless repetition of capitalism within the axis of colonization. The everyday, on the other hand, contains both the cycles of this repetition and the potential to break away from it (Kardeş, 2022, p. 553). In the definitions of the neo-Marxist thinker Lefebvre, it is seen that the concept of everyday life is dealt with in much more detail than in the texts of Marx and Engels. Henri Lefebvre, who places everyday life at the center of his thought, deals with the colonizing and liberating structures of everyday life together in the social life of the modern world, which is shaped within capitalist production and consumption relations. In this context, everyday life has ontological dimensions of space and time.

While Henri Lefebvre put forward his theory of everyday life based on the dialectical method rather than empirical, he defined space and time, which are the structural components of everyday life, in detail. Therefore, he is recognized as the founder of not only the sociology of everyday life but also the sociology of space in the field of sociology. In order to make sense of today's digital television broadcasting, it is important to define space and time along with everyday life in this context.

The Concepts of Space and Time as Structural Components of Everyday Life

Humanity's life in the world takes place ontologically and practically in the dimensions of space and time. The daily life practices of each period in the historical process are a product of the established environment into which human beings are born, i.e., spatial practices and the technical possibilities brought by time. While analyzing everyday life, Henri Lefebvre analyzed in detail not only the socio-cultural description of everyday practices, but also the concepts of space and time, which can be described as the structural components of everyday life. For Lefebvre, analyzing everyday life is related to the concept of a level. In this context, everyday life is an interface in the lives of individuals and groups. The position of social groups in everyday life is related to time within an established spatial practice. While the higher social groups are independent of space and time, the lower ones continue their lives dependent on space and time. This shows that everyday life is a product of unequal development (2013a, pp. 60-66).

Lefebvre's most significant contribution to the sociology of space is his explanation of space in relation to the productive forces of the time, even though it had previously been addressed in a fragmented manner by philosophers or some sociologists. In this context, all the factors that intervene in everyday life by forming a homogenizing, fragmenting, and hierarchical scheme also intervene in space and shape it (Lefebvre, 2015, pp. 92-94). The space shaped within the processes of capitalist production and consumption is referred to as "social space." The objective and subjective aspects of social space differ from one another. On the objective level, social space encompasses power practices and planning processes, while on the subjective level, it includes the environment of the group and the individual within the group (Lefebvre, 2013a, pp. 245-246). Social space, within production processes, encompasses the power practices of the period, planners, and the ordinary people of everyday life. Especially since the early 20th century, monopoly capitalism, in organizing the social system, has begun to plan everyday life through the dimensions of mass production and consumption. The myth of social development, based on the rational planning of everyday life and the idea of efficiency, has transformed space and time in this process. This new social order, which signifies a break from traditional society, emerges as a natural outcome of the development of capitalism.

An examination of theoretical explanations of the concept of space shows that Cartesian space dominated in the West for a long time. This space is grounded in Euclidean geometry and has maintained an objective perspective since Ancient Greece. With the transcendence of the isotopic structure of Euclidean space, the concept of social space, based on a dialectical process, has emerged. In this context, three distinct spatial practices are identified. Spatial practice refers to the materialized spatial productions of a society at a given time. Representations of space are the areas designed by experts, urban planners, and technocrats. On the other hand, representational spaces are the lived and used spaces with images and symbols related to space (Lefebvre, 2014, pp. 67-68). Lefebvre emphasizes that in the historical process, the historical space emerged from religious and political absolute space, and that historical space was later replaced by abstract space. The acquisition of an abstract quality by space stems from it being a product of modernity and a result of specialized systems. Spatial practices characterize individuals' living spaces in everyday life. Among these practices, spatial practice and representations of space encompass the objective design of space, while spaces of representation involve the subjective forms of experiencing space and its symbolic meaning. As a mass communication medium, television emerged as a domestic device in modern society. In this process, the living room functioned as a space of representation, while the act of watching television encompassed a symbolic world of meaning that accompanied everyday activities. With the transition from analog to digital broadcasting, the connection between television and the living room as a space of representation has been severed. Driven by developments in communication technologies, this transformation has disrupted television's relationship with domestic space.

In the modern world, urban spaces are at the center of the areas where everyday life activities take place. With the Industrial Revolution, urban spaces emerged as new living environments for humanity. The spatial transformation that accompanied changes in production processes initiated a new era for humanity not only in a physical sense but also in a socio-cultural context. Henri Lefebvre advanced his work in the field of spatial sociology by examining urban space and everyday life practices within urban space in detail. According to Lefebvre (2020), "cities have undergone transformations not only due to the growth of material production, processes of exchange, or rationalization, that is, general processes, but also in the mode of production, in urban-rural relations, and in class and property relations" (p. 70). Lefebvre uses the words city and urban in his writings to describe two distinct processes and periods. The city refers to spaces shaped by agricultural and commercial activities before the 19th century, prior to industrialization, while urban is characterized by automated production processes and rationalized daily life activities following the Industrial Revolution. In this context, the urban spaces of advanced capitalist societies are designed around specialized domains of production and consumption processes, differing from the past. In this process, urban spaces emerge as products. The production and planning of urban space involve material, financial, and spatial/temporal elements. Capitalism creates a bureaucratic society based on guided consumption, which also enables the reproduction of production relations and social relations (Lefebvre, 2022, pp. 37-38, 50). In this process, cultural industries play a significant role in the modern era, while creative industries become prominent in the postmodern period. Particularly after the 1970s, as production processes shifted toward the service sector, industries such as marketing, advertising, cinema, and television broadcasting began to take center stage. In the everyday practices of globalizing urban spaces, these fields hold crucial roles in both production and consumption processes.

Another structural component of everyday life is the concept of time. In sociological thought, time has always stood out as a variable that is consistently taken into account. In modern sociology, time has predominantly been viewed as an independent variable in the transformation of social phenomena and events, with attempts made to explain the evolution of social occurrences in relation to time. Although time is generally accepted as a fundamental determinant in the field of sociology, conceptual and categorical analyses of time have primarily originated from the domain of philosophy. Henri Lefebvre developed a distinct perspective in the analysis of everyday life by placing the concepts of space and time at its center. Lefebvre framed his analysis of time under the heading of rhythm analysis (2017). Lefebvre approached time not as linear, as in Marx and Hegel, but based on change and cycles, as in Nietzsche, and he was influenced by music in his understanding of time. In this context, rhythm analysis addresses the interacting relationships of the world and the cosmos, beginning with the rhythm of the body. Lefebvre, in order to articulate the concept of rhythm, begins with distinctions such as repetition-difference, mechanical-organic, cyclical-linear, continuous-discontinuous, and quantitative-qualitative, and with the notion of polyrhythm, he refers to the coexistence of two or more rhythms without conflict or disharmony (2017, pp. 33-35). In Lefebvre's conception of time, cycles hold a significant place. The philosopher compares the cycles of nature with those of capitalism, emphasizing how capitalism's repetition-based cycles permeate the everyday life of the modern world. Particularly within urban life, the rhythm of daily existence consists of overlapping and interrelated polyrhythmic processes. Information and communication technologies influence the formation of polyrhythmic processes in urban spaces in two ways. First, by enabling flexible production processes, these technologies have blurred the boundaries between work life and private life. Second, they have expanded leisure activities across both space and time, transforming what were once clearly defined non-working hours into leisure activities dispersed throughout daily life. For example, thanks to the opportunities provided by new media technologies, television viewing practices are no longer limited to specific times of day or to the domestic environment, and with devices such as mobile phones, tablets, and computers, the act of watching television has extended beyond the home, taking place during commutes, break times, and sometimes even simultaneously while working.

A significant turning point in the concept of time after the 1970s is the time-space compression associated with the postmodern era, defined by the shift from Fordism to a regime of flexible accumulation. As part of the acceleration in production processes, the increased speed in exchange and consumption during this period also became a key feature of commodity production. In the postmodern era, with the advancement of information technologies, information itself gained the status of a commodity, while the dominance of fashion in mass markets accelerated the pace of consumption in lifestyles and leisure activities (Harvey, 1997, pp. 317-318). Paul Virilio characterizes this process as the end of space, emphasizing that with the acceleration of reality, tele-continents have emerged. In this new era, as cities become detached from physical location, "meta-cities" begin to form, and the space itself expands with the influence of mobile phones on metropolitan life. This general regime of visualization, which entails a simultaneous world, has given rise to a new kind of television (2003, pp. 14-18). Taking into account the explanations of Harvey and Virilio, what stands out in the postmodern world is the virtualization of everyday urban life. With digital television broadcasting, factual or fictional live broadcasts meet the ordinary person in daily life without the constraints of time and space. All these processes take form within the polyrhythmic structure of everyday life, as emphasized by Lefebvre, paving the way for a period that can be called as the post-television era.

The Construction of Mediatized Day in the Interaction of Everyday Life and Television

In the 20th century, cinema and television are the two prominent mass communication tools. Unlike cinema, television is a technical medium capable of establishing a direct relationship with large audiences with its position within the home. The development of technology after World War II played a significant role in the widespread adoption of television. Beginning in the 1950s, television rapidly became widespread, particularly in Western societies, with the United States at the top. The interaction of television with everyday life has been far more influential than that of an ordinary technical object. This is because television, as Neil Postman's (2004) stated, "has risen to the status of a meta-medium, a medium that directs not only our knowledge of the world but also our knowledge of ways of knowing" (p. 92). While television performed basic functions such as educating, entertaining and informing the public as part of public broadcasting in its early periods, it has transformed the cultural sphere into a stage of spectacle over time.

According to Guy Debord (1996), while the world of commodities emerged with the Industrial Revolution, the distinctive feature of the 20th century was the elevation of spectacle to the level of a commodity, both in propaganda activities and in the permeation of mass media into everyday life. During this period, the commodity-form began functioning as a quantifiable category, and the visible world became entirely a world of commodities, with no reality existing outside its relationship to the commodity (pp. 25-27). One consequence of this is the loss of the dialectical characteristic of daily life and social life. This is because dialectic is a category belonging to language, whereas the visual involves a linear and logical necessity based on seeing. In this context, what is seen emerges as what is constructed (Ellul, 1998, pp. 26-27). The construction of everyday life by acquiring the form of spectacle is realized in the dimensions of space and time. The modern world is filled with audio-visual mass media. In this context, these means have both provided spatial mediation and transformed the life of humanity in the dimension of time. For people, the concept of present time has a distinctive place in the individual's perception of the world by referring to the moment in which we live. As technical means that offer us the present time of other people, cinema and television impose a rhythm beyond the daily cycles of nature. The mechanized man lives in a continuously tense present (Adanır, 1986, pp. 19-23). As television, especially live television broadcasting, brings the notion of simultaneity to itself, the individual's distinction between the real and the imaginary has begun to blur. Consequently, individuals have started to experience a loss of orientation in daily life.

Henri Lefebvre, the founder of the sociology of everyday life, assigned a distinctive position to linguistic practices and mass media in analyzing the everyday life practices of the modern world. From 1950 and onwards, television played an important role in the functioning of the capitalist system in the Western world, which evolved towards individual consumption. In the distinction of images in daily life as signifier and signified, the construction of ideological meaning in the dimension of connotation takes place through television. In this process, television becomes a medium that programs daily life for consumption (2010, pp. 122, 151). Similar to Lefebvre's relationship between modernity, everyday life and television, Hartley (2008) expresses it as follows: "TV both shows and shapes contemporary life across the economic, political, social, and cultural spectrum. It plays a prominent role in producing and distributing what counts as true for many if not most people in commercial democracies". With the introduction of technical objects into everyday life, small technical devices intervene in older rhythms. The analysis of everyday life involves a "sociology of boredom." In modern societies, television has an effect similar to that of magical practices in archaic societies. In this process, as the individual's connection to everyday life is severed, mass media generalize private lives (Lefebvre, 2013a, pp. 82–84). In this context, television becomes not merely a technical device but a socio-cultural phenomenon with epistemological dimensions. Within the ordinariness of daily life, the imaginal reality presented synchronously or asynchronously influences how individuals perceive and make sense of the world.

When examining the relationship between everyday life and television, it is evident that the media-driven day is governed by the dynamics of the capitalist system. The semantic language of television shapes the fabric of everyday life, which Lefebvre (2013) refers to as the "social text." In the modern era, television's daily and weekly broadcast aligns with people's everyday routines. The most significant reason for this is that human life has been structured around regularity and repetition since primitive times. In this context, television's distinguishing feature is its capacity to function as a storytelling medium and, consequently, to produce myths (Kaplan, 1992, pp. 24, 28). The effort to make sense of the world, which is one of the basic elements of human activity in the modern and postmodern period, is mediated through the screen. Mediatized experiences that replace face-to-face relationship forms constitute the main axis of daily life. According to Jacques Ellul (1998), "the only reality the individual now encounters face-to-face is the reality they see on the TV screen. However, the reality perceived on the screen is merely a system of electronic signals composed of dots." (p. 235). This new form of experience also characterizes a virtualized life experience. According to Jean Baudrillard (2001), in contemporary societies, communication media abandon their purposes and functions, devoting all their energy to reproducing themselves. As content is lost, the number of channels, cable broadcasts, and programs increases. In this process, through mutual referencing within the media, the multimedia transforms into an intermedium (pp. 176–177).

Television serves as an interface for making sense of everyday life in different ways in both modern and postmodern culture. The reason for this is the way the capitalist system is structured. With the postmodern culture in which information technologies are used intensively, urban life has become part of a global network society. In this process, the source of productivity in the form of informational development is the technology of knowledge production, information processing, and communication with symbols. Therefore, a close relationship exists between culture and productive forces, as well as between spirit and matter (Castells, 2008, pp. 20-21). Thanks to the developing internet and new media technologies, television has come to occupy a central position in the processes of production and reproduction in the capitalist system during this period, constructing a symbolic world of meaning.

THE SPACE AND TIME COORDINATES OF TELEVISION FROM TRADITIONAL TO DIGITAL

The relationship between everyday life and television has evolved in line with the technical possibilities of the era, transitioning from traditional television broadcasting to digital television broadcasting. As a conventional medium of communication, television has brought families together in the living room throughout the modern period. With live television broadcasts, the boundaries between television and the real world have blurred, while the notion of simultaneity marks a new era in how individuals perceive the world.

In the relationship established by mass media in general and television in particular with daily life, new types of interaction emerging with the use of communication media come to the fore. Face-to-face interaction; mediated interaction that enables the transfer of information or symbolic content with individuals who are distant in space and/or time; and finally, semi-mediated interaction forms established through mass media have formed a part of everyday life with the modern period. Among the types of semi-mediated interaction, television holds a distinctive position due to the rich symbolic relationship it establishes with its audience. In this context, three types of space-time coordinates exist. The first involves production contexts, in which communicators engage in actions and interact with one another. Secondly, there are the space and time coordinates of televisual messages. Lastly, there are the coordinates of different reception contexts. The semi-mediated interaction created by television involves a process that can be defined as time-space articulation with these three coordinates. People who watch television have to suspend the time-space frames of their daily lives to a certain extent and leave themselves in different time-space coordinates (Thompson, 2008, pp. 143-145). Thompson's analysis demonstrates that throughout the modern era, television audiences engage in a complex relationship with the medium, initially accepting the interweaving of real and imagined time-space constructs while perpetually renegotiating the boundaries between them.

The transformation of traditional television broadcasting's spatial and temporal coordinates in the modern age occurred during the postmodern era. While a challenging concept to define, postmodernism serves as a process that questions the fundamental assumptions of modernism and offers alternative worlds of meaning in opposition to these assumptions (Bolat, 2019). Emerging in the Western world during the final quarter of the 20th century as a distinct movement across architecture, fine arts, philosophy, and sociology, postmodernism is characterized not only by its artistic features but more fundamentally by its rejection of modernity's universal discourses and its opposition to metanarratives (Cevizci, 1999, pp. 699-700). With postmodernism, the cultural expression of the postmodern era, speed has gained paramount importance. In this period, clock time has been partially supplanted by instantaneous time. As the future dissolves into the present, television creates a genuine time-space compression by bringing geographically distant and unrelated events into social life as a fragmented collage. This gives rise to a "three-minute culture", where viewers channel-surf rather than invest time in watching entire programs. The instantaneous time enabled by VCR technologies can be termed as video time. This development led to three significant results. First, modernity's objective time has given way to personalized subjective temporalities. Second, with the loss of faith in the future, the imperative of immediate gratification has come to the fore. As instantaneous time gains prominence, images have increasingly dominated everyday life. Finally, individuals' time-space trajectories have become desynchronized. In this process, the patterns of mass consumption are being replaced by more diverse and fragmented patterns (Uryy, 1999, pp. 37-40). Technological innovations developed with postmodern culture have suspended the notion of simultaneity in the act of watching television and paved the way for personalized viewing practices.

One of the fundamental characteristics of postmodernism is the prominence of innovations in knowledge and information technologies within social life. These advancements in information and internet technologies have also led to the emergence of a digital cultural sphere. Accordingly, both the socio-cultural framework of television and its expressive possibilities as a technical medium have diversified in traditional and digital television broadcasting. In traditional television broadcasting, the spatial and temporal coordinates of televisual images are formed within a specific set of rules. While emphasizing the flow theory of television narrative, Raymond Williams highlighted the continuous flow of daily programming rather than focusing on individual and independent programs (2003). In contrast to Williams, who emphasized a unitary structure in television broadcasting, John Ellis argued that television narrative is organized in a fragmented way. According to Ellis (1982), instead of cinema's original and independent cohesive structure, television consists of sequences that cover a maximum duration of five minutes, made up of images and sounds. These segments are grouped into either simple cumulative groups like news and advertisements, or groups that form serials and series based on some form of repetition (pp, 112, 118). In their works, Williams and Ellis analyzed the BBC's broadcast and introduced concepts related to television broadcasting. In this context, mass media takes on an ideological function in maintaining the continuity of the social system in everyday life. During the process of securing the consent of the individual, the broadcast flow and the rhythm of daily life are planned together, while television serves as a technical tool that organizes time in advanced capitalist societies (Kotaman, 2011, pp. 30-31).

The organization of broadcasting, which can be called classical television broadcasting and which lasted until the 1980s, when the phenomenon of globalization emerged, was shaped around two contrasting models that have important discursive similarities. The first model is the public service broadcasting institutionalized in Western Europe, and the second is the commercial broadcasting forms developed in the United States of America (Mutlu, 1999). In the 1950s, television shaped the tastes of large masses of people while broadcasting cultural productions such as documentaries and discussion programs with the claim of being cultural. In the 1990s, in order to reach the widest audience, television turned to productions that include sections of life and a kind of voyeurism and exhibitionism (Bourdieu, 1997, p. 54). When we consider the evolving nature of television broadcasting, it becomes evident that both the content being broadcast and television itself have undergone a transformation in their spatial and temporal coordinates. Umberto Eco (1984) conceptualized this shift through the framework of paleo (old) and neo (new) television. Paleo-television involves a broadcasting approach that accepts the audience as a passive and homogeneous part of a whole and carries the thoughts of the audience on the screen according to its own predictions. However, after the 1970s, neo-television has a broadcasting approach that accepts an active audience in parallel with the transformation in socio-cultural life, where personal preferences and identities come to the fore in the globalizing world.

Neo-television has centered on the everyday life of a globalized world, bringing forward a form of broadcasting related to urban life. In this period, where the city emerged as a vision space, reality television, in particular, has transformed into a form of relationship between the postmodern city and individuals, becoming a type of neo-television. The abundance of images in neo-television has led to television no longer being a space for representation, dreams, and analysis, but rather a mass of meaninglessness (Robins, 1999, pp. 209, 223-225). Since the second half of the 1990s, with the emergence of identity politics in everyday life on a global scale, individuals adopted different identities in the socio-cultural domain. The impact of this on the broadcasting has been the emergence of a multi-identity audience. This multi-identity refers both to the identity strategies of different individuals and to the identity practices in the daily routines of the same individual. As a result of neo-television's inability to address this audience as a representational space, a period defined by Ramonet (2001) as post-television began. The most important feature of post-television is its ability to provide an interactive appearance by integrating the viewer into the television narrative. The developments in this process can be summarized as follows: In urban spaces where digitized socio-cultural life emerged, live television broadcasts share the present moment through a notion of simultaneity. While these mediated experiences occur through screens, the time of the event, television's production time, transmission time and reception time all coincide synchronously.

In this context, live television broadcasts encompass multiple real-time mediations of global developments (Marriott, 2007, pp. 5, 104). Today, it is becoming more and more difficult to distinguish between televisions and computer screens. While their appearances are becoming more similar, the number of common functions is also increasing. As such similarities increase, today's television needs to be analyzed from a different perspective. This is because television exceeds its traditional functions today. Such changes in television are part of wider transformations that are taking place in the broader communications industry. These broader changes include the integration of the press, broadcasting, telecommunications and computers into new institutional structures; the decline in the number of individuals or institutions owning the media; changes in the range of films and television programs made available internationally; and the weakening of the various forms of regulation under which the media have traditionally functioned (Hughes, 1990, p. 170). This process is defined by Jenkins (2006) as convergence culture. This concept describes the flow of media texts into social circulation through different platforms, and programs and series produced for television have started to be consumed through video streaming sites, websites of television channels and video sharing platforms such as YouTube as a result of the proliferation of the internet. All these developments, while taking place in a digital cultural space, also diversify television viewing practices within the changing space and time organization of daily life.

Post-TV is a concept that explores the viewer's rapidly changing relationship with the visual aspect of television, film and the entertainment system. The relationship of individuals with television, also called the idiot box, has undergone a major change with the mass adoption of consumer electronics, which delivers visual content presented over the internet to global audiences. Just six years after the sudden release of YouTube, more than half of global consumer internet traffic was allocated to delivering films and television programs to online viewers. In the near future, the online delivery of films and television content will consume the vast majority of internet bandwidth. In the emerging post-television era, although commercial television will not vanish completely, it appears that old media monopolies may be replaced by new media monopolies dominated by companies such as Google and Apple, or by innovative companies that have yet to emerge (Strangelove, 2015, pp. 3-4, 231). The convergence of television with the internet has increased both technology and content production. Television continues to be viewed on other screens, contrary to the claims that it is "becoming obsolete or dead". In this process, it has integrated into the new era by strengthening its structure consisting of infrastructure, equipment and content (Sirer, 2022, p. 176). Today's television, called post-television, blurs and renders invisible the boundaries between television and daily life within the space and time organization of daily life. This new television, which is articulated to the flexible space-time organization of urban life, has a structure compatible with the multi-identity consumer life of the postmodern era.

Today, as a result of developments in the field of television broadcasting, there are views that television is coming to an end (Mikos, 2016, p. 154). The approaches that consider the end of traditional television broadcasting and its broadcast organization are divided into broadcast pessimism and digital optimism. Broadcasting pessimists emphasize that traditional television, which brought the family together in front of the screen and facilitated sharing, has come to an end with digitalization. On the other hand, digital optimists celebrate the emergence of different content in the post-broadcast era, the removal of time and space limitations, the emergence of different platforms, screens and outputs, and the diversification of forms of access to content. In this context, emphasis is placed on the satisfaction of individual needs, the viewers' demands for free choice, and the increasing control of the viewer over the television viewing experience (Tay & Turner, 2010, pp. 32-33). It is observed that rapid transformations in technology, television broadcasting industry, advertising and new business models have transformed television viewing practices. However, whether in the era of analogue or digital television broadcasting, the fact that television is one of the locomotive sectors of the capitalist system does not change. While capitalism organizes space and time at the global level, the boundaries of space and time in digital television broadcasting have expanded in the virtual topography of the network society.

The Rhythm of Everyday Life and Digital Television Broadcasting in Urban Space

Today, most of humanity lives in urban spaces. In the transition from traditional society to modern society, there has been a transformation in capitalism's relationship with space and time. In traditional societies, space and time are interrelated. However, with globalization, spatial and temporal barriers have disappeared and urban areas have become a central site for capitalism (Yırtıcı, 2009, pp. 59, 67-69). In capitalism's relationship with urban spaces, these areas constitute a part of the accumulation regime of capital. In this context, they have gained a central position in human life within production and consumption systems. Unlike the nation-state structure of the past, neoliberalism, which refers to the transformation of previous institutional frameworks, powers, divisions of labor, social relations, life styles and modes of production in a "creative destruction" project, is the concept that defines this period (Harvey, 2015, pp. 9-12). Today, two main strategies, namely neo-liberalism and neo-dirigism, shape urban space in capitalist countries. Neo-dirigism encompasses the regulations made in the urban space under the influence of experts and state capitalism and includes interventions that have an impact on the general, mixed and private levels of the urban space (Lefebvre, 2013b, pp. 76-79). When analyzed closely, while capitalism plans the spatial dimension of daily life in detail, it also constructs the temporal dimension such as production, consumption and leisure time in a coordinated way.

Although the convergence of urban space and visual technologies may appear to have begun with digital culture, it actually has a much longer historical past. Today, television content has become increasingly viral through the official websites of traditional media and video-sharing platforms. While the consumption of programs produced for television, once the most prominent mass media, has become individualized, television has moved beyond the domestic space since the mid-1970s. With the proliferation of platforms, television screens have come to occupy spaces such as shopping centers, subways, buses, trains and the exterior surfaces of buildings. Giant television screens have become part of the viewable urban space. Later, many screens became smaller and radically personalized, adapted to mobile phones, portable DVD players and car dashboards (Turner & Tay, 2009, p. 1-2). In the modern era, people's lives have started to be shaped by a phenomenon that can be called media day. On the one hand, this concept characterizes the day occupied by the media, and on the other hand, it refers to a day presented by the media in this way. The mediatized day is the occupation of time by the present by empty words and silent images in a cycle without beginning or end. In this period, imagination, a technical form of myth-making focused on the present, turns social practice into a simulation (Lefebvre, 2017, pp. 73-74). Lefebvre's remarks express a reality that started with the modern period but is now prominent in the digitalized socio-cultural field. The convergence of digital television broadcasting with individuals in urban space without any time and space limit constitutes an example of a daily life occupied by the media. In addition, the imagination, which was historically constructed in the dialectical process, was replaced by images in this period and gained a fetish position. In the 21st century, television broadcasting has become one of the important components of the digital culture domain that emerged with the articulation of internet and communication technologies with daily life. The concept of broadcast flow introduced by Raymond Williams and John Ellis in relation to the traditional television broadcasting era has evolved into the concept of digital streaming with the advent of TV IV.

In the development process of capitalism, a shift from collectivity to individuality in urban space can be observed. During the period of monopoly capitalism, the system of mass production and consumption shaped everyday life. In this context, 20th century media adopted a model of public service, information, and entertainment broadcasting that addressed a broad national and international audience. However, 21st century digital media has adopted a new form of broadcasting that successfully enhances communication facilities between producers and consumers. In this era, the concept of new media encompasses digital communication tools such as mobile phones, digital cameras, internet applications, MP3 players, and digital televisions (Laughey, 2010, pp. 157-158). With the development of new media tools, the possibilities for individual use of technology have increased. During this process, a close relationship between new media tools and digital computer technologies has come to the forefront. Thus, the audience, which has transformed from a viewer into active users, has transitioned to an environment that is vastly different from the limited presentation and one-way communication of television screens. The user decides what to watch, when to watch it, and how to watch it; by participating in discussions about the content they watch, they not only disseminate existing content but also establish a presence in this environment through their own products (Özel, 2015, pp. 28-29). All these developments are structured around the individual use of both technical devices and broadcasts. The phenomenon of individualization emerged as part of the modernizing mission and obligations in Western modernity, which are built upon the myth of constant progress. However, with the transition to the postmodern era, modern thought and the concept of the modern individual, which was once considered collective products of human reason, began to erode. Today, individualization has become less of a choice and more of a reality imposed by the system (Bauman, 2005, pp. 131-132). The emergence of the concept of the individual is associated with political liberalism, one of the social dynamics of Enlightenment thought in the 18th century. However, the concepts of the individual in the 20th and 21st centuries have often defined individuality as a product of an illusion that arises primarily in consumer preferences. In this process, the identities of individuals are also shaped within fluid living conditions. This ongoing transformation of identity is presented to individuals by the system through readily available tools and means (Bauman, 2020, pp. 16-17).

Today, the intersection point of consumption-based forms of individualization and digital television broadcasting is urban spaces. What underlies this idea is the structuring of the phenomenon of globalization through cultural practices. As Roland Robertson (1992) emphasized, a cultural perspective is necessary for social theory in the contemporary world. This perspective approaches the world through the circulation of cultural contents rather than distinctions such as global and local, universal and particular. In this process, urban spaces have also emerged as centers of the symbolic economy that rose to prominence in the post-1980 period. In this era, where urban space is shaped by the entertainment industry, art activities, media technologies, and financial markets, cultural identity emerges as a product of the global consumer society (Zukin, 1995). A reciprocal relationship exists between consumer society and mass media. The semantic world of television creates a space referred to as the smallest common culture. In traditional television broadcasting, the smallest common culture that expresses the homogeneous audience has been replaced by the smallest marginal difference that characterizes the industrial production of differences in advanced capitalist society. In this period where personality and individual preferences stand out in the cultural field, personalization, just like naturalization and functionalization, eliminates actual differences while homogenizing people and products (Baudrillard, 2013, 93-96, 117-118). Similar to the personalization in the process of presenting commodities to the market in sustaining the global capitalist system, the personalization of content also stands out in the field of digital broadcasting. In this context, the digital television viewer can be defined as an expression of homogeneously created differences in the urban space.

With globalization, which accelerated with the development of communication and information technologies in the 1980s and the integration of the internet into daily life in the 1990s, cultural differences between Western and non-Western societies began to fade. The structuring of television broadcasting in Türkiye in the new media field is closely related to developments in internet technologies and the proliferation of social media platforms. The 1990s represent a significant period in Türkiye in terms of the establishment of internet infrastructure and the emergence of private television channels for the first time. After the launch of these private television channels, websites of these channels were subsequently created. Since the late 2000s, with the widespread use of social media platforms such as Twitter and video-sharing platforms like YouTube, television channels have begun to actively use new media platforms. As the convergence between television broadcasting and internet technologies has intensified, television channels in Türkiye have started to develop new strategies in this field (Dikmen, 2017, pp. 436-437). These developments, which enable digital broadcast content to directly intersect with everyday life, are an example of cultural globalization. In Türkiye, digital broadcasting technologies play a significant role in shaping and sustaining the consumption-driven rhythm of daily life particularly in metropolitan areas.

With the entry of internet technologies into the field of broadcasting, the concept of the television viewer has also changed. Making it possible to converge with the television culture without ever touching the television device as a technological tool, the internet also allows for a more individual attitude to be exhibited. Creating a portfolio of fictional or factual content that you cannot watch on terrestrial broadcasts is one of these. In this context, there is a process that destroys the collective nature of viewership and reconstructs it in a different way (Emre Çetin, 2016, pp. 32-33). During this period, television has lost its central place in the living room and has instead become integrated into the daily practices of urban life. Today, television can be watched while working, commuting, walking, or even waiting in line at the supermarket. According to Joshua Meyrowitz (1985), television's omnipresence has transformed it into a force that binds abstract societies together. As a result, any issue can become an object of interest or concern for any member of the public.

This new spatial experience that takes place between or at the intersection of "no place" and "my place" is an indicator of the deterritorialization in the postmodern era. In this context, it is observed that with the development of electronic media, the production-consumption and leisure activities in daily practices of individuals are structurally transformed.

To summarize, in daily life activities shaped by the socio-cultural dynamics of today's global consumer society, there has been a transition from fourth-generation digital televisions, which centered on digital television broadcasting and the production and consumption of personalized content, to fifth-generation smart televisions since the 2010s. In this process, smart televisions have made watching television more interactive with internet connectivity, and as a result of the widespread adoption of resolutions such as 4K and 8K, image quality has dramatically increased. During this period, viewers use television not only to watch broadcasts but also to play games, interact with social media, and access online content. On-demand content consumption has also become widespread during this period. As a result, both the use and functions of television in domestic space have changed, and it has become possible to consume television content without time and space limitations through technical capabilities such as new media tools in public spaces. In both cases, a convergence is observed between the rhythm of daily life in urban space and the rhythm of digital television broadcasting.

CONCLUSION

Technological advancements that have developed throughout the historical process have led to changes in daily life practices. Technology primarily transforms the structure of everyday life in the context of production forces and relations, while in the second stage, it redesigns socio-cultural life. Since the last quarter of the 20th century, rapidly advancing communication and information technologies reached a new stage in the early 1990s with the integration of the internet and computer technologies into daily life. During this period, everyday life began to be shaped by technological tools far more than in the past, while the field of digital culture started to expand. On one hand, these developments structurally transformed traditional mass media tools, adapting them to the new era, while on the other hand, they gave rise to new media technologies. Particularly with the introduction of Web 2.0 in the early 2000s, second-generation internet services brought about a structural transformation in various aspects of daily life, such as production, consumption, and leisure activities.

One of the most significant outcomes of this transformation has been the changes in television broadcasting in traditional media. Since the modern era, unlike cinema, television has established a close physical and symbolic relationship with daily life. This is because television broadcasting holds an important place in the capitalist social structure in terms of production and consumption. The act of watching television initially formed part of a collective experience during times when family members were together. With developments in the field of broadcasting, television began to offer individuals a much more direct and simultaneous experience of space and time in everyday life. After the 1970s, television extended into public spaces through screens located in shopping malls, subways, and buses, moving beyond the domestic setting. Another important stage in this field has taken place with the convergence of television and portable technological devices such as mobile phones, tablets, and laptops. These developments indicate that the spatial-temporal organization of television as a technical device occurs in two areas. The first one is the spatial-temporal organization of factual or fictional productions presented on television; the second is the spatial-temporal coordinates of the television viewer in everyday life. Both, namely the processes of production as well as consumption, are shaped by the dynamics of the capitalist system in determining television's social position. With the advent of the modern era, television has become a prominent technical device in the capitalist organization of everyday life. The infinite present and the mediatized day offered by television hold structural significance in the formation and continuity of the consumer society.

The active audience theory, which emerged with the postmodern era, plays a significant role in the construction of social space and time through television. Information technologies and computers, which have been central to the rise of the postmodern period, have accelerated the digitalization of everyday life. In this era, both due to the influence of digital technologies and the structural characteristics of postmodern culture, the notions of fixed space and stable subject positions have ended. The digitalization of space has expanded television, traditionally associated with the living room, which can be considered a space of representation, across spatial and temporal dimensions. In this period, television has simultaneously become a technical device that both transcends spatial and temporal constraints within a virtual topography and integrates with everyday life, while also accompanying production, consumption and leisure activities in urban life. Such transformations are closely linked to the symbolic, cultural and aesthetic construction of space and time in the process of embedding technical devices into daily life.

The rhythm of urban spaces began to be shaped by the dynamics of the capitalist system during and after the Industrial Revolution. At the beginning of the 20th century, while monopoly capitalism programmed everyday life in urban spaces within the system of mass production and consumption, the postmodern period saw urban spaces being planned around the phenomenon of individual consumption. Post-television, which gained visibility within the scope of this process, is a concept that shows the consumption of television content and interactive interaction with television without space and time restrictions on the dimension of personal interests. Post-television encompasses a television viewing experience integrated with urban life, which is saturated with the deterritorialized images of the global consumer society. As a product of developments in digital television broadcasting, post-television both reflects television consumption synchronized with the polyrhythmic processes of urban space and constructs new television viewing rituals as part of the mediatized day.

REFERENCES

Adanır, O. (1986). *Auditory and Visual Meaning Production* [İşitsel ve Görsel Anlam Üretimi]. Transmar Publication.

Avcı, A. (2011). *Prime-Time, Time in Storytelling on Television* [Prime-Time Vakti, Televizyonda Hikâye Anlatıcılığı içinde] (A. Kotaman & A. S. Uğursoy & A. Avcı, Ed.). H_2O Book.

Baudrillard, J. (2001). *Ecran Total* [Total Ekran]. (Gülmez, B., Trans.). YKY Publication.

Baudrillard, J. (2013). *La société de consomınation* [Tüketim Toplumu]. (Deliceçaylı, H., & Keskin, F., Trans.). Ayrıntı Publication.

Bauman, Z. (2005). *The Individualized Society* [Bireyselleşmiş Toplum]. (Alogan, Y., Trans.). Ayrıntı Publication.

Bauman, Z. (2020). *Liquid Life* [Akışkan Hayat]. (Pilgir, A. E., Trans.). Ayrıntı Publication.

Bolat, N. (2019). *Modernism's New Roadmap: Post-Modernism in Communication in the Age of Posts* [Modernizmin Yeni Yol Haritası: Post-Modernizm, Postlar Çağında İletişim içinde]. Erdem, M. N., & Şener, N. K., Eds.). Literatürk Academia.

Bourdieu, P. (1997). *Surla Télévision* [Televizyon Üzerine]. (Ilgaz, T., Trans.). YKY Publication.

Castells, M. (2008). *The Information Age: Economy, Society and Culture Volume 1 The Rise of The Network Society* [Enformasyon Çağı: Ekonomi, Toplum ve Kültür 1. Cilt Ağ Toplumunun Yükselişi] (E. Kılıç, Trans.). Bilgi University Press.

Çetin, E. (2016). Who is a Television Audience? A Conceptual Discussion [Televizyon İzleyicisi Kimdir? Kavramsal Bir Tartışma]. *Erdem Dergisi*, *70*, 25–40.

Cevizci, A. (1999). *Dictionary of Philosophy* [Felsefe Sözlüğü]. Paradigma Publication.

Debord, G. (2006). *La Société du Spectacle* [Gösteri Toplumu ve Yorumlar]. (Ekmekçi, A., & Taşkent, O., Trans.). Ayrıntı Publication.

Dikmen, Ş. E. (2017). Transformation of Television Broadcasting in Turkey: Social TV Broadcasting [Türkiye'de Televizyon Yayıncılığının Dönüşümü: Sosyal TV Yayıncılığı]. *E-Gifder*, *1*(5), 425–448. DOI: 10.19145/gumuscomm.283117

Eco, U. (1984). A Guide to the Neo-Television of the 1980's. *Framework*, (25), 18–27.

Ellis, J. (1982). *Visible Fictions Cinema: Television: Video*. Routledge Publication.

Ellul, J. (1998). *La parole humiliée* [Sözün Düşüşü]. (Arslan, H., Trans.). Paradigma Publication.

Gardiner, M. (2016). *Critiques of Everyday Life: An Introduction* [Gündelik Hayat Eleştirileri]. (Özçetin, D., Taşdemir, B., & Özçetin, B., Trans.). Heretik Publication.

Hartley, J. (2008). *Television Truths*. Wiley-Blackwell. DOI: 10.1002/9780470694183

Harvey, D. (1997). *The Condition of Postmodernism* [Postmodernliğin Durumu]. (Savran, S., Trans.). Metis Publication.

Harvey, D. (2015). *A Brief History of Neoliberalism* [Neoliberalizmin Kısa Tarihi]. (Onacak, A., Trans.). Sel Publication.

Hughes, P. (1990). *Today's Television, Tomorrow's World in Understanding Television 170-187* (Goodwin, A., & Whannel, G., Eds.). Routledge.

Jenkins, H. (2006). *Convergence Culture: Where Old and New Media Collide*. New York University Press.

Kaplan, Y. (1992). *Television as a Tool for Storytelling and Myth* [Televizyon Öykü Anlatma ve Mit Üretme Aracı Olarak]. (Kaplan, G., Trans.). Ağaç Publication.

Kardeş, M. E. (2022). Moments of Freedom: Henri Lefebvre's Metaphilosophy in History of Concepts Freedom. In Öztürk, A., & Çevik, C. C. (Eds.), *History of Concepts Freedom* [Özgürlüğün Uğrakları: Henri Lefebvre'ün Metafelsefesi, Kavramlar Tarihi Özgürlük içinde]. DoğuBatı Publication.

Laughey, D. (2010). *Media Studies Theories and Approaches* [Medya Çalışmaları Teoriler ve Yaklaşımlar]. (Toprak, A., Trans.). Kalkedon Publications.

Lefebvre, H. (1995). *Conversation Avec Henri Lefebvre* [Yaşamla Söyleşi]. (Oğuz, E., Trans.). Belge Publication.

Lefebvre, H. (1996). *Sociology of Marx* [Marx'ın Sosyolojisi]. (Hilâv, S., Trans.). Sorun Publication.

Lefebvre, H. (2006). *Le matérialisme dialectique* [Diyalektik Materyalizm]. (Yıldırım, B., Trans.). Kanat Book.

Lefebvre, H. (2010). *La Vie quotidienne dans le monde moderne* [Modern Dünyada Gündelik Hayat]. (Gürbüz, I., Trans.). Metis Publication.

Lefebvre, H. (2012). *Critique de la vie quotidienne, Tome: 1, Introduction* [Gündelik Hayatın Eleştirisi I]. (Ergüden, I., Trans.). Sel Publication.

Lefebvre, H. (2013a). *Critique de la vie quotidienne, Tome: 2, Fondements d'une sociologie de la quontidienneté* [Gündelik Hayatın Eleştirisi II Gündelik Hayat Sosyolojisinin Temelleri]. (Ergüden, I., Trans.). Sel Publication.

Lefebvre, H. (2013b). *La Révolution Urbaine* [Kentsel Devrim]. (Sezer, S., Trans.). Sel Publication.

Lefebvre, H. (2014). *La production de l'espace* [Mekânın Üretimi]. (Ergüden, I., Trans.). Sel Publication.

Lefebvre, H. (2015). *Critique de la vie quotidienne, Tome: 3, De la modernite au modernisme, Pour une métaphilosophie du quotidien* [Gündelik Hayatın Eleştirisi III Moderniteden Modernizme Gündelik Hayatın Meta-Felsefesi]. (Ergüden, I., Trans.). Sel Publication.

Lefebvre, H. (2016). *Le droit â la ville I* [Şehir Hakkı I]. (Ergüden, I., Trans.). Sel Publication.

Lefebvre, H. (2017). *Eléments de rythmanalyse Introduction â la connaissance des rythmes* [Ritimanaliz Mekân, Zaman ve Gündelik Hayat]. (Batur, A. L., Trans.). Sel Publication.

Lefebvre, H. (2022). *Le droit â la ville II* [Şehir Hakkı II]. (Yetkin, M., Trans.). Sel Publication.

Marriott, S. (2007). *Live Television Time, Space and the Broadcast Event*. Sage Publications. DOI: 10.4135/9781446218273

Marx, K., & Engels, F. (2013). *Manifest der Kommunistischen Partei* [Komünist Parti Manifestosu]. (Jabban, S., Trans.). Patikakitap Book.

Meyrowitz, J. (1985). *No Sense of Place The Impact of Electronic Media on Social Behavior*. Oxford University Press.

Mikos, L. (2016). Digital Media Platforms and the Use of TV Content: Binge Watching and Video-on-Demand in Germany. *Media and Communication*, *4*(3), 154–161. DOI: 10.17645/mac.v4i3.542

Mutlu, E. (1999). *Television and Society* [Televizyon ve Toplum]. TRT Publications.

Özel, S. (2015). *The Audience in the Axis of Television and the Impact of Internet-Based Video Services on the Audience in Television in the New Media Age* [Televizyon Ekseninde İzleyici ve İnternet Üzerindeki Video Hizmetlerinin İzleyiciye Etkisi, Yeni Medya Çağında Televizyon içinde]. Özel, S., Ed.). Derin Publications.

Postman, N. (2004). *Amusing Ourselves to Death Public Discourse in the Age of Show Business* [Televizyon: Öldüren Eğlence Gösteri Çağında Kamusal Söylem]. (Akınhay, O., Trans.). Ayrıntı Publication.

Ramonet, I. (2001). *La Tyrannie de la Communication*. Editions Galilée.

Roberts, J. (2013). Philosophizing the Everyday [Gündelik Hayatın Felsefesi] [Ercan, Trans.). Doruk Publication.]. *E (Norwalk, Conn.)*, •••, C.

Robertson, R. (1992). *Globalization Social Theory and Global Culture*. Sage Publications.

Robins, K. (1999). *Into the Image Culture and Politics in the field of Vision* [İmaj, Görmenin Kültür ve Politikası]. (Türkoğlu, N., Trans.). Ayrıntı Publication.

Sirer, E. (2022). The Use of Virtual Applications in the Context of Technological Transformation of Television Broadcasting. In Molo, Ü. (Ed.), *Extended Reality and Media XR Technologies* [Televizyon Yayıncılığının Teknolojik Dönüşümü Bağlamında Sanal Uygulamaların Kullanımı, Genişletilmiş Gerçeklik ve Medya XR Teknolojileri içinde]. Nobel Publication.

Strangelove, M. (2015). *Post-TV Piracy, Cord-Cutting and the Future of Television*. University of Toronto Press. DOI: 10.3138/9781442666184

Tay, J. ve Turner. G. (2010). Not the Apocalypse: Television Futures in the Digital Age, *International Journal of Digital TV*, 1:1.

Thompson, B. J. (2008). *Media and Modernity* [Medya ve Modernite]. (Öztürk, S., Trans.). Kırmızı Publication.

Turner, G. ve Tay, J. (2009). *Introduction, in Television Studies After TV: Understanding Television in the Post-Broadcast Era* (1–7). (G. Turner & J. Tay, Ed.). Routledge.

Urry, J. (1999). *Consuming Places* [Mekânları Tüketmek]. (Öğdül, R. G., Trans.). Ayrıntı Publication.

Virilio, P. (2003). *La Bombe Informatique* [Enformasyon Bombası]. (Şahin, K., Trans.). Metis Publication.

Wark, McK. (2014). *The Beach Beneath The Street* [Kaldırım Taşlarının Altında Kumsal Var]. (Çiltepe, A., Trans.). Sel Publication.

Williams, R. (2003). *Television, Technology and Cultural Form* [Televizyon, Teknoloji ve Kültürel Biçim]. (Türkbağ, A. U., Trans.). Dost Bookstore Publishing House.

Yırtıcı, H. (2009). *Spatial Organization of Contemporary Capitalism* [Çağdaş Kapitalizmin Mekânsal Örgütlenmesi]. Bilgi University Press.

Zukin, S. (1995). *The Culture of Cities*. Blackwell Publishers.

ADDITIONAL READINGS

Elden, S. (2004). Understanding Henri Lefebvre Theory and the Possible. *Continuum*.

McQuire, S. (2008). *The Media City Media, Architecture and Urban Space*. Sage Publications. DOI: 10.4135/9781446269572

Merrifield, A. (2006). *Henri Lefebvre A Critical Introduction*. Routledge.

Moores, S. (2000). *Media and Everyday Life in Modern Society*. Edinburgh University Press.

Morley, D. (2000). *Home Territories, Media, Mobility and Identity*. Routledge.

Silverstone, R. (1994). *Television and Everyday Life*. Routledge.

Solla, G. A., & Bovino, R. G. S. (2013). *TV-Anytime, Paving the Way for Personalized TV*. Springer. DOI: 10.1007/978-3-642-36766-3

KEY TERMS AND DEFINITIONS

Marxist Critique of Everyday Life: Neo-Marxist theorist Henri Lefebvre is the founder of the Marxist critique of everyday life. From a Marxist perspective, the critique of everyday life includes the analysis of production-consumption and leisure activities. In this context, the capitalist system's organization of everyday life in space and time comes to the fore. Criticism of everyday life emphasizes the importance of mass media in the ideological construction of social life and states that individuals live within a social text. In this process, the linguistic and symbolic world of meaning of social life is evaluated from a critical perspective.

Social Space, Social Time: The central concepts of Henri Lefebvre's theory of everyday life are social space and social time. According to Lefebvre, unlike geometric, physical, biological or geographical space, there is social space. The objective dimension of social space encompasses the part of the period shaped by socio-economic and political dynamics. The subjective dimension of social space is the social environment of the group and the individual within the group. Social time is formed at the intersection of cyclical and linear time. Cyclical times involve the cycles of nature, while linear times involve processes based on knowledge, technique and reason. Everyday life is formed at the intersection of social space and time.

Rhythmanalysis: In his analysis of rhythms, Henri Lefebvre reveals the relationships between conceptions of space and time in the context of understanding everyday life. He wants to transform the concept of rhythm into a science and a new field of knowledge. In this context, the concept of rhythm is related to the phenomenon of time and repetition. The analysis of the rhythms of everyday life reveals the ideological nature of the capitalist system. Rhythmanalysis also includes the bodily existence of individuals and the disciplinary processes that the system imposes on the body. Rhythmanalysis arises in the differences between linear time and cyclical time, between clock time and lived time.

Post-TV: Post-TV is a definition that covers the period from the second half of the 1990s to the present day in studies on television. Post TV has a socio-cultural meaning based on the phenomenon of a multi-identity audience at a time when the boundaries between everyday life and television are disappearing. With the development of new communication technologies, the relationship between audience and television has become more active. In this context, Post-TV is an understanding of broadcasting in which viewers with multiple identities interact in accordance with new forms and models of consumption. Two important features of this approach to television are that viewers come together in an active participatory culture and engage directly with everyday life.

Chapter 18
Postmodernism and the Construction of Space in Digital Publishing

Can Murat Demir
https://orcid.org/0000-0002-9155-9672
Ondokuz Mayıs University, Turkey

Yeter Demir
https://orcid.org/0009-0005-8603-3536
Ondokuz Mayıs University, Turkey

ABSTRACT

At the intersection of postmodernism and cinema, digital platforms offer an innovative context that redefines the concept of space. In this way, space becomes not only a physical background but also a narrative element enriched with aesthetic, cultural and ideological elements. The Hannibal series is a powerful example of how space design is integrated with postmodern aesthetics and how it leaves an impact on the audience. The spaces used in the series are not only the movement spaces of the characters, but also metaphorical reflections of their psychological states, ideological conflicts and the narrative. The grotesque murder scenes shaped by aesthetics both disturb the viewer and prompt a deep questioning process on ethics and aesthetics. The viewer is confronted with simulations that manipulate their spatial perceptions and encourage them to get lost in the fictional world.

DOI: 10.4018/979-8-3373-1957-5.ch018

INTRODUCTION

Although postmodernism is a difficult concept to define, it stands out as a process that questions the basic assumptions of modernism and offers alternative worlds of meaning against these assumptions (Bolat, 2019). Emphasizing that meaning and identity are not fixed and can be reshaped through different discourses, this approach manifests itself in many disciplines such as art, literature, architecture and cinema. Postmodern thought invites the individual to a deep questioning process around the question "who am I?" based on decentralization, uncertainty and pluralism (Cevizci, 2020). In this context, postmodernism's understanding of space points to a multi-layered conceptual structure that transcends physical existence. Space is not only a concrete space, but also a ground for the individual's existential inquiries, aesthetic quests and ideological conflicts (İzgi, 2006).

The technological and aesthetic possibilities offered by digital platforms further stretch the boundaries of space, creating a space of cultural differentiation and experience where the physical and the intangible merge (Yılmaz, 2023). Especially on digital platforms, space gains a hyper-realistic dimension thanks to visual effects and virtual reality technologies, and is reconstructed as an environment that manipulates the viewer's perception and draws them deeper into the fictional world. As Fredric Jameson (2022) states, hyperspace based on advanced technologies constructs a world that the individual cannot fully comprehend with his/her cognitive senses and takes cognitive processes under its control. This structure not only reshapes our perceptions, but also functions as a mechanism that transforms individuals' perception of reality through technology. Especially for new generations, hyperspace has become an environment that replaces the natural environment and is accepted as a "second nature" in their perception. This situation shows that technological spaces have become more than just a tool, but a subject that radically redefines individuals' daily lives and their relationship with the environment.

The series Hannibal is a striking example of this transformation. The spaces in the series meet the audience as a reflection of the psychological states of the characters and the metaphorical depths of the narrative. Elements such as murder scenes and food scenes not only offer an aesthetic experience but also raise ethical and existential questions. This new dimension that digital technologies bring to space design reshapes the modern individual's questions about belonging, identity and the search for meaning. By blurring the boundaries between reality and fiction, these spaces reflect the individual's subjective perception of truth in a profound way. This dynamic created by the digital age, combined with postmodernism's conception of space, offers an important ground for the identity construction of both the individual and society. As a result, space design on digital platforms reflects the multi-layered approach of postmodernism, creating a hybrid space where the physical and the conceptual are intertwined. While the space constructs the individual, the individual produces the space and this mutual transformation gains new meaning especially within the boundaries of the digital age (Heidegger, 1996).

In the postmodern approach, space goes beyond being just a physical space and takes on a multi-layered structure with the meanings it carries, the experiences it offers and the images it harbors (Harvey, 2019). Every space contains an inner promise and message; this message is shaped by the interaction between the architectural structure of the space and its contents. This connection between architecture and content brings together both the substance and the essence of the space and reveals its message. It is possible for this message to be strong or weak, positive or negative; however, it is not possible for the space to be completely devoid of a message (Taşcıoğlu, 2013, cited in Kanbur, 2023). These layers of meaning that postmodernism attributes to space are reshaped with the innovative possibilities offered by digital platforms and invite the viewer to a process of both aesthetic and intellectual questioning.

The spatial reflections of postmodernism on television and digital platforms enable the transmission (Demir, 2024) and reinterpretation of culture. Television not only presents realistic or surreal stories to viewers, but also creates new layers of meaning by filtering these stories through a postmodern filter. In this context, television blends the traditional with the modern by keeping social memory up to date and offers viewers the opportunity to rebuild their identities and memories (Tutar, 2020). The postmodern process makes it possible to build a bridge between the past and the present by treating spaces as memory archives.

In the historical process, humanity has witnessed two radical stages of spatial transformation: the birth of settled life with the agricultural revolution and the acceleration of migration from rural to urban areas with the industrial revolution (Kaypak, 2014). Apartment buildings, the spatial symbols of modernity, are among the concrete indicators of these changes. However, postmodernism transforms these mechanical and functional structures into new spatial forms such as villas, mansions and mansions by blending them with the aesthetic elements of traditional architecture (Harvey, 2019). This transformation manifests itself in television series with both their remarkable designs and their reflections in everyday life. Thus, television transforms space from a mere backdrop into a dynamic narrative element that carries traces of the past, identities and cultural values.

Radical spatial transformations in human history have profoundly affected the physical and social organization of life. While the agricultural revolution initiated settled life and laid the foundations of villages and cities, the industrial revolution encouraged mass migration from rural to urban areas and paved the way for the rise of apartment buildings, one of the spatial symbols of modernity (Kaypak, 2014). With modernity, apartment buildings have become a symbol of a verticalized and dense lifestyle that emphasizes the functionality of space. However, postmodernism has reshaped this fixed understanding of space by moving it. Inspired by traditional architecture, structures such as villas, mansions and mansions have revealed a new understanding of space by enriching it with both aesthetic and historical references.

This spatial approach of postmodernism is strongly reflected in visual narratives such as television series (Harvey, 2019). In TV series universes, space is no longer just a background, but becomes a constitutive narrative element that appeals to the viewer's socio-cultural memory and psychic world. In these series, spaces are constructed as a memory archive that carries traces of the past, reflects the present and imagines the future. Enriched with visual details, these spaces are not only aesthetically pleasing, but also representational tools that contribute to the construction of social identities and values. Thus, on television and digital platforms, spaces become symbols through which both individual and social memory, and thus myths, are transformed.

In this study, space design and representations in the series Hannibal in the context of postmodernism are analyzed with the 'hypertext method'. Among the mass communication tools, television has been constantly updated thanks to the technological advances of the globalizing world and has offered many innovations to the audience with the effect of digitalization (digital media possibilities and platforms). In Turkey, private television broadcasts, which started in the 1990s, underwent a wide transformation with digital platforms in 2015. These new digital platforms have not only provided a diversity of content, but also created different genres and new methods of analyzing these genres. Hypertext is one of these methods. Hypertext, together with technology, makes it possible to convey different spatial designs and visuals in television series with a new information spiral. As a result of digitalization, it is seen that television broadcasts make it easier for the audience to access various hyperlinks at any place and time through different hyperlinks.

Postmodern space, blended with digital dynamics, offers the audience a multi-layered pluralistic experience both visually and fictionally. The extraordinary and striking space design in the Hannibal series, in accordance with the principles of ambiguity and multilayeredness of postmodernism, appear as dynamic elements that enrich the story and immerse the audience. In this context, space becomes not only a physical space but also the center of mental and emotional interactions.

WHAT IS POSTMODERNISM

Postmodernism has emerged as a synthesis of traditionalism and modernism in a chronological sense. The traditional period covers the period starting from the Classical Greek and Roman periods until the Middle Ages. According to Bingöl

(2017), traditionalism means the formation of habits by shaping people's behavior around social indicators and symbols such as values, beliefs, habits, language, which they inherited from the past and which keep people together. In traditionalism, individuality is not at the forefront, the sacred and the profane are intertwined, the only reality is God and everything takes place within the divine order. Therefore, in line with this system established by religious thought, the reflection of the sacred and the projections of human life in this order are encountered (Turan, 2011). While earthly and sacred spaces are created in this direction, structures with romanesque and gothic architecture (columns reaching towards the sky) draw attention. Emerging in the 17th century in Europe and spreading all over the world in time, modernity is referred to as the name of the break with tradition and changes in individual, political and social life (Outhwaite, 2008). Modernity has brought about social change and transformation by placing reason and humanity at the center, pushing god and the sacred into the background. Therefore, modernism emphasizes that human beings have the ability to freely make their own decisions in understanding and analyzing the universe and that they can use their reason, knowledge and free will in doing so. With modernity, the concepts of modernism and modernization emerge. Modernism refers to the artistic and cultural tendency of modern thought in the 19th century, while modernization refers to the process of moving from traditional to modern society (Giddens, 2021).

According to Smith (2007), postmodernism is the name of a philosophical and theoretical process stemming from poststructuralism that rejects the aesthetic and artistic concerns of modernism. According to Yılmaz (2014), poststructuralism, which emerged with postmodernism, is a discipline in which structuralism is handled critically and at the same time enables a break with modernism. In this context, typical reflections of postmodernism's break with modernism are seen in art, architecture, painting and literature. Arnold Toynbee was the first to use the concept. Among the main thinkers of the movement are Jean-François Lyotard, Jean Baudrillard, Jacques Derrida, Umberto Eco, Martin Heidegger, Friedrich Nietzsche, Soren Kierkegaard, Max Stirner, Jacques Lacan, Edmund Husserl, Ludwig Wittgenstein (Çağlar, 2008). Postmodernism emerged as a cultural, intellectual and artistic movement in the second half of the 20th century. Postmodernism, which started in France at the end of the 1960s, showed its influence in the United States in the 1970s and is seen to be a decentralized idea that reality is neither in God nor in thought, and that pure reality changes from person to person, from mind to mind and from society to society (Doltaş, 2004). Postmodernism deals with the removal of the boundaries between the elements of art and culture by bringing together materials from various disciplines that erode classical narrative structures, making various plays on them, in short, questioning the norms and structures of classical narrative (James, 2022). This reveals the diversity of cultural and individual interpretations of postmodernism in line with various perspectives and values. Therefore, although Smith's definition is contrary to the spirit of postmodernism, postmodernism is actually an acceptance of anti-modernist discourse (Jameson, 2022). According to Harvey (2019), postmodernism differs radically from the modernist understanding.

SOCIOLOGICAL REFLECTIONS: IDENTITY, SOCIETY AND REALITY

Postmodernism develops a critical approach against traditional sociological paradigms and modernist thought. In this framework, concepts such as culture, gender, identity, values, norms, language, social class, technology, consumption, education and power have moved away from a universal definition and gained specific and contextual meanings. The reconstruction of identities by evolving from universality to specific conceptuality is one of the most important emphases of postmodernism in the sociological context (Şen Altın, 2017). According to this understanding, social structures and individual identities are shaped in a multi-layered and variable reality that does not reflect a single truth.

Postmodernism positions sociology as a field where there is no single truth and reality must be reconstructed in social, cultural and individual terms. Bauman and May (1998) define postmodernism as a relative, pluralistic and variable understanding of reality and emphasize that ethics and morality should be interpreted according to each situation. The basic elements of society are redefined around a unique way of life shaped by concepts such as consumption, individualism and flexibility. In this context, postmodernism redesigns the symbolic connotations of modernism, allowing social structures and relations to be handled in an ever-changing, flexible and multifaceted manner (Marshall, 1999).

Psychological Reflections: Digital Space and Identity Transformation

Postmodernism, while going beyond modernism, reveals the formation of a new perception of the world. In this new understanding of the world, it is seen that human behavior has not remained indifferent and has undergone change. With postmodernism, digital media and technology isolate the individual and push him to search for a deeper "self" in his inner world. This new person appears as a self-centered, individual, consumption-oriented person who lives by internalizing information and technology (Öztürk, 2019). According to Funk (2009), the concept of "self-centeredness" of this person in the new world constitutes a structure in which the way people think, feel and act in postmodern life reinforces their self-centered feelings at the center of the world with this new character orientation.

Under the influence of postmodernism, the understanding of space is also transformed; through digitalization and media, physical spaces evolve into the virtual world, and individuals continue their existence in spaces reshaped on digital platforms. The reconstruction of space through digital and virtual environments encourages people to become isolated, to break away from their social ties and to construct meanings only in their own inner world. The transgression of the physical boundaries of space, combined with the psychological effects of digitalization, leads to the alienation of individuals not only from the outside world but also from their own inner spaces.

While radical changes and innovations are emerging in society through technology, digitalization and the media, people are becoming isolated and forced to live alone with themselves. This isolation and self-centered lifestyle is becoming increasingly evident in the "spaces" created by humans in the digital environment. Postmodernism, along with new living conditions and social changes, has had an impact on wants, needs, social and economic changes, and the diversity in the social structure has also affected the change in people's internal and external spaces (Öztürk, 2019). With these changes, human beings, who are a part of society, construct an individual and solitary "I" identity through digital media and recreate their own "reality" in virtual spaces.

Thus, the space shaped by postmodernism and digital broadcasting appears as a space where individual identity, social structure and psychological dynamics are intertwined. While these digital spaces reflect the inner world of the individual, just like traditional physical spaces, they also present the effects of individual, identity, emotional and social transformation with postmodernism.

Postmodernism and Television: Transformation of Visuality, Perception and Space

While postmodernism analyzes an important transformation process through the cultural, social and aesthetic characteristics of television, it also reshapes the relationship between the audience and television. While postmodernism emphasizes concepts such as pluralism, relativism and fragile structures of meaning instead of modernism's approaches such as universality, rationality and correctness, television has become one of the most powerful representatives of this new understanding of the world. Under the influence of postmodernism, television transforms the viewer from a passive receiver to an active interpreter by playing with genres, forms and meanings, and reconstructs the viewer's perception by fragmenting the time and space relations between artificial images, symbols, fictions and reality (İnceoğlu, 2014).

This transformation of television meets the requirements of postmodern thought and offers content in which visuality and audio are at the forefront. Television series, news, movies, game shows and discussion programs allow viewers to make sense of the events and phenomena around them, while reproducing social reality by highlighting visuals that combine these meanings in a holistic way (Çakın, 2019). In this process, while shaping people's perceptions with its visual and auditory power, television also paves the way for the cultural and social effects of postmodernism. Through television, people reproduce not only the world but also themselves, becoming consumption-oriented individuals. This form of popular culture reflected in the media shows how social identities and individual perceptions are shaped under the influence of postmodernism (Hatipler, 2017).

According to Adorno (2021), television and other mass media must be credible and serve the culture industry in order to reproduce social reality. Under the influence of postmodernism, television has become the most powerful tool of mass communication, making the viewer not only a consumer but also an active "participant" in the reconstruction of cultural meanings and social norms. In this context, television is not only a means of presenting information, but also functions to create a new space, reshaping the perception of space in postmodern society.

Postmodern and Digital Space: Allegorical Construction of Memory

Postmodernism represents a way of thinking that questions traditional perceptions of meaning and reality and offers multi-layered and multi-meaningful structures. In this context, space, as one of the fundamental elements of postmodernism, goes beyond being just a physical entity and becomes part of a symbolic, cultural and aesthetic construction process. With the impact of the digital age, the perception of space has moved beyond physical boundaries to a virtual and digital plane, and this transformation has further complicated the relationship of space with memory and its perceptual dimension.

The digitalization of space reveals new dimensions in the construction of human memory and perception. Bachelard's (2023) definition of space as an element that revitalizes time and awakens memory is echoed in digital publishing. Digital platforms go beyond traditional spatial experiences and offer a virtual "place" for readers and users. This place functions not only as a space where information and aesthetic values are shared, but also as a place of memory where individuals reconstruct their identities and cultural codes.

In digital publishing, the perception of space is largely shaped by visual and symbolic elements. Spatial elements such as visual design, color and form play a central role in making sense of the content that users experience on digital platforms. Today, digital publishing has become a metaphorical projection of the interior space, enabling the construction of a perceptual space in users' mental processes. As Ölçer (2022) states, the sense of sight has become a primary tool in perceiving and defining spatial messages. Digital environments enable users to be in a space that is not only physical but also mental and sensory.

In this process, the multi-layered structure of postmodernism manifests itself clearly in the allegorical spaces of digital publishing. Each element on digital platforms, on the one hand, provides a cultural and social context for the construction of an individual's identity, and on the other hand, contributes to the transformation of spatial perception over time. As Günal and Esin (2007) state, site-specific messages are interpreted according to the expectations and needs of the user, leading users to adapt to or conflict with the digital space.

At this point, the virtual environments offered by digital broadcasting function as "digital homeland" where fragmented time and space are integrated and individuals reconstruct their memories and identities. Postmodernism's symbolic and culturally reshaped understanding of space redefines the concept of space on both the physical and digital planes. The virtual spaces created on digital platforms present the multi-layered and meaning-laden structure of this "digital homeland" as a space where identity construction processes and cultural codes come together. In this context, postmodernist discourses and digital publishing practices deepen the perceptual and symbolic dimensions of space and reinterpret space as a means of representation and identity construction.

Psychological Extension of Space in Digital Publishing

Space has a profound impact on individuals' perceptions and behaviors. The postmodern world shaped by digital broadcasting makes the psychological traces of space more evident. People are in a constant interaction to make sense of and perceive their environment. Images presented through digital media transform individuals' perceptions of space, leading to changes in social, cultural and psychological contexts. In this context, digital publishing shapes how individuals perceive space and the social effects of these perceptions.

Space is an important factor that shapes human behavior. It transforms people by affecting behaviors at both individual and social levels. Ölçer (2022) emphasizes that space determines behaviors in social relations and changes and transforms individuals. New spaces emerging through digital broadcasting create a profound change in individuals' perceptions. This process goes beyond the mere perception of physical space and turns into a simulation that affects individuals' mental and emotional perceptions. Postmodern digital environments reshape how individuals experience and make sense of space.

The psychological perception of space is shaped by individuals' short or long-term experiences of space. These experiences transform the way individuals perceive space and differentiate over time. Aslan and Atik (2015) state that space is shaped by individuals' experiences and that these experiences create differences in the perception of space. Digital broadcasting causes individuals to perceive not the real world but the images that represent this world. While these images shape the perception of individuals by interpreting environmental information through a mental process, they simplify the complexity of the real world and make it one-dimensional (Gulec, 2017).

The contents presented on digital platforms carry individuals' perception of space to a more abstract level. These abstract perceptions reshape the connections that individuals establish with their environment and social relations. This situation becomes a powerful source of motivation that directs human behavior. Erdem (2019) states that these images simplify the complexity of the real world and create a powerful influence that affects the behavior of individuals. People have a more simplified and unidirectional perception by breaking away from the real world with the images they acquire through digital media. While this situation increases the psychological effects of space on the individual, it also causes changes at the social level.

Postmodern spaces shaped through digital broadcasting profoundly affect individuals' perception of space. While these effects lead to significant changes at the psychological level, they also reshape the social structure and individual behaviors. Simulations presented on digital platforms transform the perception of space, reconstructing individuals' relationships with their environment and their place in the social context. This process reveals the traces of postmodernism more clearly on digital platforms.

Sociological Extension of Space in Digital Publishing

While space, in a cultural and socio-economic context, separates people from their environment and allows them to continue their actions, sociology's view of space examines in depth how space interacts with concepts such as social life, culture, politics, economy, history and the meanings produced by these interactions. From a sociological perspective, space is not only a physical entity but also a social construction and indicator shaped by social structures, individual identities and cultural values (Özbey, 2018).

The modern understanding of space is described by Harvey (2019) as "a machine in which man is forced to live". Digital platforms keep viewers in a constant virtual reality, shaping their perceptions of social and cultural norms. These virtual spaces simulate not only a physical environment but also the identity formation processes, social relations and cultural practices of individuals. While the production of space in modern society constructs the social contexts of individuals, digital broadcasting leads to the reshaping of this production.

Anthony Giddens (Saygın, 2016) defines space as a product of social relations and power. According to Giddens (2016), space is a concept that affects and is affected by social structure at both physical and abstract levels. Spaces in digital publishing also affect this structure. Giddens' understanding of space enables the cultural, ideological and social meanings of the virtual spaces offered to the audience by digital media content to emerge. Since these spaces are constantly reproduced on digital platforms, the audience's acceptance of this virtual reality makes it possible for them to reproduce social norms and identities. Digital media content becomes powerful tools that shape how audiences perceive the world on both concrete and abstract levels.

In sociological terms, space includes dynamics such as inequality, conflict, change and resistance. Virtual spaces, especially those offered through digital broadcasting, constantly reproduce these dynamics and accelerate the processes of transformation in society. In Harvey's (2019) words, while modern space functions like a machine in which humans are imprisoned, digital media likewise appears as a "machine" that shapes society through media content. These contents not only reflect social structures, but also reproduce these structures and direct the social practices of the audience.

In conclusion, in line with Giddens' (2016) theories, the spaces offered by post-modern digital broadcasting play an important role in the reproduction of social structures. Digital broadcasting is becoming a powerful transmission medium that not only provides entertainment or information but also reshapes social and cultural norms (Demir, 2024).

Simulacr: The Critical Line Between Reality and Fiction

Jean Baudrillard, as one of the most prominent figures of postmodern thought, has developed important concepts to understand and criticize modern society. Simulacrum and simulation are at the forefront of these concepts. According to Baudrillard, in modern society, the boundary between reality and representation becomes increasingly blurred, leading to the emergence of a kind of artificial reality called the simulacrum. Another point that is often emphasized in Baudrillard's works is that simulacra are not reflections, substitutes or imitations of reality; on the contrary, they transform, reproduce and create their own reality without representing reality itself (Baudrillard, 1981). While the media content offered by postmodern digital broadcasting provides the viewer with a sense of reality, in fact this feeling is completely artificial and virtual.

The concept of simulacrum gains an important meaning especially in connection with the visuality of digital broadcasting. Under the influence of digital broadcasting, television and other media tools move away from reality and create a new and closed reality universe of their own. An example of this universe is television series, news programs and content on digital platforms. Baudrillard argues that such content distances society from reality and tries to influence individuals through simulacra. In an environment where the boundaries between reality and fiction are increasingly blurred, viewers no longer watch reality itself, but the reflection of these simulated realities (Baudrillard, 2024).

In Baudrillard's *Simulacra and Simulation*, simulacra are not only visual entities, but also carry social and cultural meanings. These simulacra function as a kind of cultural and social reproduction. The relationship between digital publishing and space is also discussed in this context. The content published on digital platforms not only provides entertainment, but also determines how the audience should think socially. By simulating space and time, these contents create a virtual space machine disconnected from the real world. This new space, as Baudrillard describes it, is a kind of substitute for reality; the viewer accepts this virtual space as reality itself.

Baudrillard's *The Illusion of the End* (1994) discusses the cultural and social effects of these simulations. He states that the impact of digital media on society leads to cultural homogenization. This process also plays an important role in the emergence of allegorical traces of space. The spaces offered by digital broadcasting turn into simulacra constructed with visual and audio narratives, and these spaces lose traces of reality and authenticity. These new virtual spaces, as described by Baudrillard, manipulate the way the audience experiences the world, forcing them to consume more and conform to social norms.

Spaces of Television: Digitalization and Popular Culture

Postmodernism and digitalization are two important concepts that reshape television's perception of space. While presenting spatial codes to the audience through visual media, television becomes not only a means of communication but also a center of meaning production. As Foss (1994) points out, visual elements such as editing, costumes, lighting, color and landscaping play a fundamental role in television's reconstruction of spatial perception. In this context, by reconstructing reality, television offers a new spatial experience that stimulates the viewer's imagination and emotions.

Television's process of creating the perception of space overlaps with the multi-layered, unrealistic and ironic structure of postmodernism. The reproduction of reality through visual images and imagination creates a new form of narrative that affects the world of human emotion and thought, and as Erdem (2015) emphasizes, it activates the viewer's imagination. This new spatial perception creates a short-term and consumption-oriented interaction on the audience with the influence of popular culture (Nalçakan, Canoğlu, & Özsavaş, 2017). In this context, television creates a universe of meaning that serves the purposes of the culture industry while ensuring the sustainability of everyday life (Adorno, 2021).

With the rise of digital broadcasting, the spatial transformation of television has become more evident. Postmodernism has strengthened the allegorical dimensions of spaces produced through television and transformed the viewer's perception of space into an individualized and fragmented structure. This shows that the viewer's relationship with television is not only a consumer-oriented experience, but also a process based on the construction of personal perception and memory.

Space: Sensory Perceptions and the Reconstruction of Meaning

Dr. Lecter's line "Taste and smell have made a home in the part of the mind formerly occupied by pity, and there is no room for pity at my table" (Harris, 1999) reflects an important turning point in the postmodern understanding of space. This sentence shows that space is not defined solely by physical boundaries, but has gained new meaning as a perceptual and symbolic environment. The transformation of space in Dr. Lecter's mind is structured in a way to overcome the pains and traumas of the past. Here, space is not only a physical space, but also a structure of mind where individual and collective memory, identity and emotional experiences are shaped.

In postmodernism, space ceases to be a fixed and unchanging concept and becomes a process that is reinterpreted with constant change. As in the example of Lecter's table, the association of space with senses such as taste and smell emphasizes that this space has a multi-layered and dynamic structure. While these senses bear traces of the traumas of the past, they are also connected to each other in an effort to create a new way of being. Therefore, the discourse "there is no room for pity" symbolizes the desire to construct an innovative world of meaning in the postmodern understanding of space, free from the burdens of the past.

In this context, the space of the table is considered not only as a dining area but also as a symbolic place that expresses a whole set of identity, memory and emotional experiences. The role of sensory perceptions in deepening the meaning of space has an important place in postmodernism's understanding of space. In the digital age, this transformation similarly manifests itself in digital spaces, virtual environments and media content, offering viewers the opportunity to interact at different levels of perception.

Hannibal TV Series

Hannibal (2013-2015) is a 3-season series of 13 episodes each, produced by Bryan Fuller, based on the famous Red Dragon book by Thomas Harris. The main characters of the series include Hannibal Lecter (Mads Mikkelsen), Will Graham (Hugh Dancy), Jack Crawford (Laurence Fishburne), Alana Bloom (Caroline Dhavernas), Beverly Katz (Hettienne Park), Bedelia Du Maurier (Gillian Anderson) and Freddie Lounds (Lara Jean Chorostecki).

Hannibal TV series draws attention as a psychological thriller (IMDb, 2024). The series is about the tense relationship between famous psychologist and sociopath Dr. Hannibal Lecter and trainee FBI agent Will Graham. Will Graham, who has the ability to connect with the minds of criminals, tries to cope with his own personal problems while tracking down psychopathic murders. This process, however, puts a strain on his psyche, causing him to suffer from serious psychological problems. Due to Graham's illness, the FBI chooses Hannibal Lecter as a consultant . However, Hannibal's relationship with Will quickly becomes dangerous and complicated. Over time, the two begin to manipulate each other.

Hannibal Lecter is an intelligent and intellectual person who is knowledgeable in many fields from music to art, from medicine to gastronomy (Gürbüzoğlu, 2017). But he is also a secret serial killer and a psychopath who eats human flesh. After the murders he commits, he presents the dishes he makes from human flesh as a work of art. Using French cuisine in the first season, Japanese cuisine in the second season and Italian cuisine in the third season, he presents his murders to the viewers in an elegant way. The artistic and aesthetic concerns of the series are conveyed to the audience in a postmodern style with unique camera angles and unusual space designs. When the locations and designs in each episode are analyzed, it is clear that Hannibal is much more than an ordinary murder series. Postmodern space designs lead the viewer to a hypertextual thought and transform the series into a layer of meaning.

Ted Nelson, who first used the concept of *hypertext*, defines it as a tool that enables access to other texts within large texts (Patterson, 2015). While the 'hyper' in the phrase carries the meanings of 'beyond' and 'above' in Greek, hypertext refers to a multi-layered and rich structure that transcends traditional texts (Gezginci, 2016). Hypertext can be defined as a content element that transcends borders, encompassing not only text but also visual and audio content. The *Hannibal* series is an example that embodies this definition. The fact that the series was adapted from Thomas Harris' famous Red Dragon book is a typical hypertext application. The series not only relies on the original text, but also has a structure that directs the audience to different texts by creating a rich context through characters and themes.

Lecter's character's clever murder strategies are similar to Hannibal Barca of Carthage, one of the most important figures of the Roman First Age (Kılıç, 2018). Lecter's psychological intelligence and strategic moves form a hypertext layer by reflecting Hannibal Barca's tactical genius on the battlefield. In addition, the character of Dionysus, the god of wine and ecstasy, is embodied in the wild and complex nature of Hannibal Lecter (Erhat, 2023). Dionysus' excessive, transgressive nature, which transgresses social boundaries, parallels the characteristics that push both physical and mental boundaries seen in Lecter's killing styles.

The emphasis on creativity in the character of Will Graham symbolizes an inner conflict shaped by the combination of the opposites between Apollo and Dionysus (Dürüşken, 2021). Graham embarks on a journey similar to the tragic fate of Oedipus as he tries to strike a balance between human values and his potential to turn into a monster. Oedipus, the mythological king of Thebai, fulfills his own tragic destiny by killing his father and marrying his mother (Sophocles, 2019), which parallels Will Graham's own fate by falling for Hannibal's ingenious games. Both characters face their fate by embarking on a tragic journey shaped by their internal conflicts and external influences. This is a reflection of the hypertextual structure of the series; the interwoven layers of characters and themes allow the viewer to connect each figure, event and place with different texts. In this context, *Hannibal* serves a postmodern narrative structure by guiding the viewer through different layers of text and meaning.

HYPERTEXTUAL ANALYSIS OF SPACES IN "HANNIBAL" SERIES

Under this title, the iconic murder locations in the *Hannibal* series are analyzed with a hypertextual approach. The analysis focuses on the symbolic meanings, cultural and mythological references, multi-layered structures and dynamic relationship with the audience. This analysis aims to reveal the visual and thematic effects of the scenes while deepening the narrative functions of the spaces and their connections with the psychology of the characters. The hypertextual approach makes it possible to interpret the spaces in the series as texts and to understand the audience's interaction with these texts.

Season 1, Episode 9, "Trou Normand"

Hypertext traces the connections of a particular text with other texts. In this context, the murder scene in the episode "Trou Normand" not only provides information about the murder, but also functions as a "text" that reflects the psychological states and relationships of the characters. Every detail of the murder scene, especially the atmosphere offered by the space, gives the audience clues about the subconscious of the characters. In this scene, the design of the murder scene, the color palette and the totem symbol used refer to the main themes of the series, namely balance, chaos, control and guilt. Each element of the murder scene offers another layer of meaning to the viewer. Therefore, as a metaphor, the space reflects the existential state of the victim and the philosophical thoughts about murder.

The "Trou Normand" episode, like most of Hannibal's murders, takes on a structure enriched with mythological and cultural references. From this point of view, the murder scene constitutes a rich background not only from a visual point of view but also from a textual point of view.The limbs of the murdered people, especially the arms and legs, are brought together and presented in the form of a giant totem pole rising towards the sky. The totem pole symbolizes many different meanings. It symbolizes a situation similar to the gods in ancient mythologies and their influence on people's destinies. According to Toksoy (2014), a totem pole carries many meanings such as strength, endurance and courage. This totem pole gives the impression of a work of art exhibited in an art gallery. This scene, which breaks away from physical reality and creates a visual feast in the eyes of the viewer, is a visual reflection of the concept of hypertext.

Hypertext is a structure formed by linking texts used in different contexts and meanings. The totem pole has a hypertextual feature with a new world of meaning where different people and lives are brought together. This scene, where visuality is as central as discourse, has been transformed into a television content by feeding on art, architecture and religious elements. The visual diversity designed together with the hypertextual perception of reality enriches the depth of reading and seeing of the audience.

The "hypertextual" connection here, in a way, reveals a kind of inner conflict that is also seen in Will and Hannibal's relationship. Will's process of reconstructing his own identity under Hannibal's influence offers an analysis that in a sense evokes the influence of mythological figures on human beings. Will's innate ability to "empathize" with both guilt and criminals has a similar structure to the stories of heroes who cannot escape a mythological fate.

The totem pole has a hypertextual characteristic with a new world of meaning where different people and lives are brought together. This scene, where visuality is as central as discourse, has been transformed into a television content by feeding on art, architecture, religious and mythological elements. The visual diversity designed together with the hypertextual perception of reality enriches the depth of reading and seeing of the audience.

Season 1, Episode 5, "Coquilles"

The murder scene in the episode "Coquilles" presents a world of meaning laden with deep symbolism and mythological references. According to Toksoy (2014), the representation of angels in the three Abrahamic religions (Old Testament, New Testament and Qur'an) depicts superhuman beings who mediate between God and humans as extensions of purity and benevolence. This concept appears prominently in the depiction of the murdered couple at the scene of the murder. The couple killed in the hotel room almost represents "sin". The dominant theme of sin in the scene is a natural consequence of the victims being presented as sinners. In this context, the design and visual discourse of the murder scene provides the victims with an opportunity for redemption. The appearance of the victims with angel wings emphasizes their need for divine forgiveness.

The symbolic depth of the scene also makes a strong reference to Greek mythology. Prometheus, punished by the Greek god Zeus, bestowed fire on humans and encouraged them to sin. However, this favor led to his own punishment and Prometheus was chained to a rock and left to be eaten by wolves and birds (Erhat, 2007). The victims at the murder scene in "Coquilles" are presented as sinful figures punished by God, just like Prometheus. The fact that the murderer puts himself in the place of God in the process of "cleansing sins" on behalf of humanity enables him to punish the victims in a mythological way.

This scene presents a visual presentation that subverts human psychology. The design of the murder scene creates not only a physical crime scene but also a world of meaning. The murderer's deadly creativity adds a hypertextual depth to the viewer's universe of meaning with an aesthetic adorned with mythological and religious references.

Season 2, Episode 6, "Futamono"

The depiction of the human body resembling a tree trunk in the middle of the concrete floor symbolizes the relationship between nature and humans, while the poisonous flowers placed inside the corpse symbolize the maliciousness of human nature. Both visually and semantically, this design conveys a strong message about the complex relationship between nature and humans.

As per the scenario, the identification of the corpse reveals that it is a human being who harms and disrespects nature. This can be read as a symbolism that emphasizes the corrupt relationship between man and nature. Therefore, the human corpse, which has the appearance of a tree, establishes hypertextual connections with traditional tree motifs and the representations of humans turning into trees in Greek mythology. Especially in Greek mythology, Dryope, the daughter of King Dryops, is kidnapped by fairies and transformed into a water source and a tree (Erhat, 2023), which is similar to this scene. Dryope's mythological transformation symbolizes the transformation that humans experience due to their lack of respect for nature and its forces. In this sense, the murder scene in the episode “Futamono” offers a mythological touch that describes both the crimes against nature and nature's punishment of man.

The corpse in the form of a tree presents a powerful visual narrative of human rebirth and return to nature. While this transformation reveals an understanding of existence in which nature is at the center, it draws attention to the vital importance of restoring nature to its rightful former position. While this scene symbolizes the necessity for human beings to exist in harmony with nature, it also serves as a warning that by destroying nature, human beings will also destroy themselves. In this context, the scene offers the possibility of hypertextual analysis on both visual and semantic levels, adding depth to the viewer's universe of meaning.

Season 2, Episode 4, “Takiawase”

The murder scene in this episode presents a striking visuality through the corpse whose skull has been transformed into a beehive. This scene goes beyond merely presenting a grotesque murder scene and carries deep symbolic and mythological meanings. The combination of the skull and the beehive forms a multi-layered structure that shows how human nature, death and the cycle of life are intertwined. The skull has been considered one of the most powerful symbols of death throughout history. Symbolizing the decay of the human body, leaving only bones, the skull points to the mortality of life. Here, however, the fact that the skull is turned into a hive by bees symbolizes that death is not final and that life continues. In this context, the skull becomes a place of “rebirth”.

In Greek mythology, bees were considered messengers of the gods and sacred beings. For example, during the abduction of Persephone, daughter of the goddess Demeter, into the underworld and her return to the surface, bees represented the cyclicality of life. The transformation of the skull into a beehive evokes this mythological cycle; like the sprouting of a new life after death.

In Egyptian mythology, the dismemberment of Osiris along the Nile River and the mixing of these parts with nature emphasizes that life does not end with death, but is reincarnated as a part of nature. The combination of the skull and the beehive makes this cycle of nature visible once again.

The transformation of the skull into a beehive not only creates a grotesque visuality, but also has a structure that deeply questions the relationship between life and death. Drawing on mythological narratives and cultural symbolism, this scene invites the viewer to reflect on the concepts of life cycle, return to nature and death. This space, which also reflects Hannibal's aesthetic understanding, is not only a place of crime but also a philosophical and artistic spatiality.

Season 2, Episode 3, "Hassun"

The murder scene in the chapter "Hassun" presents a hypertextual reflection of justice and measure. The metaphor of the scales is known as the symbols held by Themis and Justitia, the goddesses of justice in Greek and Roman mythology (Erhat, 2007). The scales symbolize the impartiality, balance and moderation of justice. This symbol also contains a hypertextual reference to the novel by Thomas Harris, the source of the series. In Harris' novels, the character Dr. Hannibal Lecter uses scales to weigh the organs of his victims. This symbolizes the treatment of justice as a kind of objectivity applied to the bodies of the victims.

Similar hypertextual reflections are also seen within the series. Hannibal Lecter's (Mads Mikkelsen) character's line "Justice is not the balance of a scale, but the sharpness of a knife" implies that justice is not only balanced and impartial, but can also be applied in a strong and ruthless manner. This line reveals that justice is not only an objective value, but also a concept shaped by personal interests and applied accordingly. Hannibal's understanding of justice is transformed in such a way as to legitimize all kinds of actions, revealing the conflict between different perspectives and values of justice.

The metaphor of the scales at the murder scene can be read as a visual reflection of this conflict. The scale symbolizes both a physical element of balance and the way in which the subject of justice, man, measures himself and his victims. At the same time, as a hypertext, this creates a level of meaning where different forms of justice converge in the body of the scale as an object. In this context, the crime scene is not only a place of crime, but also a representation of justice and moral values that are constantly questioned, creating a profound impact on the viewer's world of meaning.

CONCLUSION

Postmodernism radically transforms the meaning and function of space with the influence of digital broadcasting. Rejecting the functional, simple and rational approaches of the modernist understanding of space, postmodernism transforms space into a visual chaos by constructing a reality blended with quotes from the past, symbols, colors and contradictions. This process causes the space to lose its identity and meaning, and the viewer or user perceives and interprets the space as a text. This effect of digital publishing encourages a form of hypertextual reading and transforms the space into an intertextual structure.

Hypertextual reading reveals the multi-layered meaning of space in the context of digital publishing. Instead of a linear flow as in traditional texts, hypertextual space builds a network structure that offers many meanings and connections to the user. The space is no longer limited to a starting or ending point, but transforms into a system of meaning that is constantly reproduced with the active participation of users. In this context, instead of fixing space in a single reality, it is open to alternative readings and rewritings. For example, a television program or content on a digital streaming platform not only offers a visual and audio experience, but also refers to cultural and mythological narratives through symbols and references.

The transformation of postmodern space in digital publishing is deepened by mythical narratives and allegorical references. In particular, space becomes a platform where mythological texts and symbols are reproduced. Digital publishing functions as a means of knowledge and enlightenment, like the fire that Prometheus stole from the gods and offered to humans. However, this enlightenment has both a creative and destructive nature, as in the story of Prometheus. While digital media liberates knowledge, it also transforms it into an object of consumption. The visual stories offered by television and digital platforms both liberate and manipulate the viewer, creating a new kind of myth. With digital broadcasting, space is designed similar to mythological labyrinths. Just like the Minotaur's labyrinth, users face the risk of getting lost while searching for meaning in digital spaces. Related to Jean Baudrillard's concept of simulacra, digital labyrinths offer a virtual world that contains traces of reality but distances the viewer from this reality.

Hermes is known as the messenger god in mythology and symbolizes the multi-layered structure of communication. Similar to Hermes' function, space in digital broadcasting offers multiple meanings and perspectives. However, this multiplicity of meaning can also lead the viewer to a misleading perception of reality. The hypertextual structure of digital platforms offers a constant transition between symbols and narratives, putting the viewer in a continuous process of interpretation.

Television stands out as the mass media that best reflects the simulacrum understanding of postmodernism. As can be explained by Jean Baudrillard's concept of simulacrum, postmodern television draws the viewer into a virtual world by presenting not reality but the image of reality. Within the framework of a hypertextual reading, television offers a new layer of meaning in each image and narrative. The viewer is not only a consumer of content, but also an active participant in it. However, this participation often leads to what Baudrillard calls "hyperreality"; that is, the perception of reality completely replaces the fictional (Baudrillard, 1994).

The interaction of postmodernism with digital publishing offers the opportunity to treat space as a mythological text. The content produced on digital platforms reinterprets the traditional themes of mythology and reproduces these themes with the influence of consumer culture. This process transforms the viewer from a passive consumer into an active interpreter. However, these interpretations often lead the viewer to a misleading perception of reality. The combination of mythological narratives and hypertextual structure transforms the viewer from a mere consumer into a cultural actor through which meanings are created and reshaped. This transformation limits the critical thinking capacity of television and digital platforms, while at the same time creating an audience dependent on consumer culture. On the other hand, the critical approach of postmodernism offers an important perspective that encourages the re-examination of social structures and cultural norms.

REFERENCES

Adorno, T. W. (2021). *Culture Industry Culture Management* [[*Kültür Endüstrisi Kültür Yönetimi]*]. (Ülner, N., Tüzel, M., & Gen, E., Trans.). İletişim Publication.

Aslan, F., Aslan, E., & Atik, A. (2015). Perception in Interior Space [İç Mekânda Algı]. *İnönü Üniversitesi Sanat ve Tasarım Dergisi*, 5(11).

Bachelard, G. (2023). *Poetics of Space* [[*Mekânın Poetikası]*]. (Tümertekin, A., Trans.). Minotor Book.

Baudrillard, J. (1994). *The Illusion of the End*. Stanford University Press.

Baudrillard, J. (2024). *Simulacra and Simulation* [[*Simulakrlar ve Simülasyon]*]. (Adanır, O., Trans.). Doğu Batı Publication.

Bauman, Z., & May, T. (1998). *Thinking Sociologically* [[*Sosyolojik Düşünmek]*]. Ayrıntı Publication.

Bingöl, U. (2017). Postmodernism and Tradition [Postmodernizm ve Gelenek]. *Hikmet-Akademik Edebiyat Dergisi*, *3*(June), 20–33. DOI: 10.28981/hikmet.296286

Bolat, N. (2019). Modernism's New Roadmap: Post-Modernism [Modernizmin Yeni Yol Haritası: Post-Modernizm]. *Postlar Çağında İletişim*. In M. N. Erdem ve N. Kocabay Şener (Ed.), Konya: Literatürk Academia.

Çağlar, O. N. (2008). Politics and Identity in Postmodern Understanding [Postmodern Anlayışta Siyaset ve Kimlik]. *Süleyman Demirel Üniversitesi İktisadi ve İdari Bilimler Fakültesi Dergisi*, *13*(3), 369–386.

Çakın, Ö. (2019). The Power of the Reader: The Contextual Journey of Signs. [Okurun İktidarı: Göstergelerin Bağlamsal Yolculuğu]. *Postlar Çağında İletişim*. In M. N. Erdem & N. Kocabay Şener (Ed). Konya: Literatürk Academia.

Cevizci, A. (2020). *The Great Dictionary of Philosophy* [[*Büyük Felsefe Sözlüğü]*]. Say Publication.

Demir, C. M. (2024). Semiotic Analysis of Cultural Codes in Solaris Movie Poster [Solaris Film Afişinde Yer Alan Kültürel Kodların Göstergebilimsel Analizi]. *İstanbul Gelişim Üniversitesi Sosyal Bilimler Dergisi*, 11(1), 340-351. https://doi.org/.DOI: 10.17336/igusbd.1174013

Doltaş, D. (2004). *Postmodernizmin Getirdikleri ve Götürdükleri*. https://sanatokuma.blogspot.com/p/postmodernizmin-getirdikleri-ve.html. (E. T.: 17. 01. 2024).

Dürüşken, Ç. (2021). *Ancient Philosophy An Adventure of Thought from Homer to Augustine* [[*Antik Çağ Felsefesi Homeros'tan Augustinus'a Bir Düşünce Serüveni*]]. Alfa Publication.

Erdem, M. N. (2019). On the Reproduction of Reality and its Aftermath: An Overview of the Post-Reality Universe [Gerçekliğin Yeniden Üretimi ve Sonrası Üzerine: Post – Gerçeklik Evrenine Bir Bakış]. *Postlar Çağında İletişim.* Konya: Literatürk Academia.

Erdem, S. (2015). Gerçekliğin Yeniden İnşasında Görsel Efekt Kullanımı: Spartaküs Televizyon Dizisi Örneğinde Mekân Kurgusu [Usage of Visual Effects to Reconstruct the Reality: Building Space in the Frame of Spartacus TV Series]. *Gümüşhane Üniversitesi İletişim Fakültesi Elektronik Dergisi, 3*(2). Advance online publication. DOI: 10.19145/guifd.97108

Erhat, A. (2023). *Dictionary of Mythology* [[*Mitoloji Sözlüğü*]]. Remzi Publication.

Foss, B. (1994). *Narrative Techniques and Dramaturgy in Film and Television* [[*Film ve Televizyonda Anlatım Teknikleri ve Dramaturji*]]. (Gerçeker, M. K., Trans.). Türkiye Radyo Televizyon Kurumu.

Funk, R. (2013). *I and We Psychoanalysis of Postmodern Man* [[*Ben ve Biz Postmodern İnsanın Psikanalizi*]]. (Tanyeri, Ç., Trans.). Yapı Kredi Publication.

Gezginci, G. (2016). *The Problem of Hypertext Authorship in Digital Publishing* [*Dijital Yayıncılıkta Hipermetin Yazarlığı Sorunu*]. 5. Uluslararası Matbaa Teknolojileri Sempozyumu.

Giddens, A. (2021). *Consequences of Modernity* [*Modernliğin Sonuçları*]. (Kuşdil, E., Trans.). Ayrıntı Publication.

Gulec Solak, S. S. (2017). Space-Identity Interaction: A Conceptual and Theoretical Overview [Mekân-Kimlik Etkileşimi: Kavramsal ve Kuramsal Bir Bakış]. *MANAS Sosyal Araştırmalar Dergisi, 6*(1), 13–37.

Günal, B., Nur Esin (2007). Investigation of Psychosocial Quality in Housing in the Context of Human-Space Communication Model [İnsan-Mekân İletişim Modeli Bağlamında Konutta Psikososyal Kalitenin İrdelenmesi]. *İtüdergisi/a*, 6(1): 19-30.

Gürbüzoğlu, P. (2017). Ideological Constructions of Evil from Novel to Cinema: Hannibal Lecter [Romandan Sinemaya Kötülüğün İdeolojik Olarak Kurgulanması: Hannibal Lecter]. *Sosyolojik Düşün, 2*(1), 64–74.

Harris, T. (1999). *Hannibal* (Sağlam, M., Trans.). Nemesis Publication.

Harvey, D. (2019). *The State of Postmodernity* [*Postmodernliğin Durumu*]. Metis Publication.

Hatipler, M. (2017). Postmodernism, Consumption, Popular Culture and Media [Postmodernizm, Tüketim, Popüler Kültür ve Medya]. *Bilgi Sosyal Bilimler Dergisi*, (1), 32–50.

Heidegger, M. (1996). *Philosophy of the City* [*Kentin Felsefesi*]. (O. Kural, Trans.). [). İstanbul: Yapı Kredi Publication.]. *Cógito (Salvador)*, ●●●, 8.

IMDB. *Hannibal (TV Series 2013–2015)*.https://www.imdb.com/title/tt2243973/?ref_=fn_al_tt_1 (Erişim Tarihi: 20 Ocak 2024).

İnceoğlu, Y. (2014). Postmodernism and Television [Postmodernizm ve Televizyon]. *Marmara İletişim Dergisi*, *9*(9), 233–250.

İzgi, U. (2006). *Process in Architecture: Concepts, Relationships* [*Mimarlıkta Süreç: Kavramlar, İlişkiler*]. Yem Publication.

Jameson, F. (2022). *Postmodernism or the Cultural Logic of Late Capitalism* [*Postmodernizm ya da Geç Kapitalizmin Kültürel Mantığı*]. (Gönenç, C., Trans.). Alfa Publication.

Kaypak, Ş. (2014). Changing Urbanization from Modernism to Postmodernism [Modernizmden Postmodernizme Değişen Kentleşme]. *Global Journal of Economics and Business Studies*, *2*(4), 80–95.

Kılıç, M. (2018). An Overview of Hannibal's War Tactics [Hannibal'in Savaş Taktiklerine Genel Bir Bakış]. *Erzurum Teknik Üniversitesi Sosyal Bilimler Enstitüsü Dergisi*, *3*(5), 25–60.

Marshall, G. (1999). *Sociology Dictionary* [*Sosyoloji Sözlüğü*]. (Akınhay, O., & Kömürcü, D., Trans.). Bilim ve Sanat Publication.

Nalçakan, M., Canoğlu, S., & Özsavaş, N. (2017). Evaluation of Cultural Codes in Interior Design in Turkey through Television Series and Changing Housing Perception [Televizyon Dizileri Yoluyla Türkiye'de İç Mekân Tasarımında Kültürel Kodların Değerlendirilmesi ve Değişen Konut Algısı]. *Sanat ve Tasarım Dergisi*, *7*(2), 68–81.

Ölçer Kanbur, E. (2022). Investigation of the Concept of Scale in the Context of Architecture and Cinema Interaction through the Spatial Fiction of "The Bfg" Film [Mimarlık ve Sinema Etkileşimi Bağlamında Ölçek Kavramının "The Bfg" Filminin Mekân Kurgusu Üzerinden İncelenmesi]. *Turkish Online Journal of Design Art and Communication*, 12 (1), 49-70. Retrieved from https://dergipark.org.tr/tr/pub/tojdac/issue/66154/1005224

Ölçer Kanbur, E. (2023). *Changing Spatial Fictions in Istanbul City Scale in Turkish Cinema in the Context of Cinema and Architecture Interaction* [[*Sinema ve Mimarlık Etkileşimi Bağlamında Türk Sinemasında İstanbul Kent Ölçeğinde Değişen Mekân Kurguları]*]. Kocaeli Üniversitesi, Sosyal Bilimler Enstitüsü.

Outhwaite, W. (2008). *Dictionary of Modern Social Thought* [*Modern Toplumsal Düşünce Sözlüğü*]. (Pakdemir, M., Trans.). İletişim Publication.

Özbey, K. (2018). Border, Space and Memory from the Perspective of Comparative Historical Sociology: The Case of Sarp Village [Karşılaştırmalı Tarihsel Sosyoloji Perspektifinden Sınır, Mekân ve Bellek: Sarp Köyü Örneği]. *Gaziantep University Journal of Social Sciences, 17*(4), 1398–1414. DOI: 10.21547/jss.422359

Öztürk, İ. (2019). Reflection of Postmodernism on Human Behavior in Organizations [Postmodernizmin Örgütteki İnsan Davranışlarına Yansıması]. *Uluslararası Ekonomi ve Yenilik Dergisi, 5*(1), 91–100. DOI: 10.20979/ueyd.533673

Patterson, N. G. (2015). Hypertext and Changing Reader Roles [Hiper Metin ve Değişen Okuyucu Rolleri]. Ajıt-E: *Academic Journal Of Information Technology,* 6(20), 65-76. Https://Doi.Org/10.5824/1309-1581.2015.3.005.X

Saygın, A. U. (2016). Dimensions of Modernity in Anthony Giddens' Sociology [Anthony Giddens'ın Sosyolojisinde Modernliğin Boyutları]. *Abant Kültürel Araştırmalar Dergisi, 1*(2), 69–80.

Selçuk, S. S. (2012). Consecration of Difference and Fragmentation of Society in the Postmodern Era: "Other" and "Othering" [Postmodern Dönemde Farklılığın Kutsanması ve Toplumun Parçacıllaştırılması: "Öteki" ve "Ötekileştirme"]. *Sosyoloji Araştırmaları Dergisi, 15*(2), 77–99.

Şen Altın, N. (2017). Social Reality and Postmodern Novel [Toplumsal Gerçeklik ve Postmodern Roman]. *HUMANITAS- Uluslararası Sosyal Bilimler Dergisi,* 5(10), 91-109. .DOI: 10.20304/humanitas.316515

Smith, P. (2007). *Cultural Theory* [*Kültürel Kuram*]. (Güzelsarı, S., & Gündoğdu, İ., Trans.). Babil Publication.

Sophokles. (2019). *King Oedipus* [*Kral Oidipus*], (B. Tuncel, Trans.). İstanbul: Türkiye İş Bankası Kültür Publication.

Taşçıoğlu, M. (2013). *Space as a Visual Communication Platform* [*Bir Görsel İletişim Platformu Olarak Mekân*]. Yapı Endüstri Merkezi.

Toksoy, S. (2014). *Symbols & Signs with their Origins and Meanings A Visual Journey of Thousands of Years* [*Kökenleri ve Anlamlarıyla Semboller & İşaretler Binlerce Yıllık Görsel Bir Yolculuk*]. Alfa Publication.

Turan, M. (2011). *Postmodern Theory* [*Postmodern Teori*]. On İki Levha Publication.

Tutar, C. (2020). The Construction of Cultural Memory in Postmodern Urban Space: Nostalgic Tendencies Featured in Television Series [Postmodern Kentsel Mekânda Kültürel Belleğin İnşa Süreci: Televizyon Dizilerinde Öne Çıkan Nostaljik Eğilimler]. *Akdeniz Üniversitesi İletişim Fakültesi Dergisi*, (34), 102–121. DOI: 10.31123/akil.781252

Yılmaz, R. (2014). Mental Reconstruction of the World through Narrative: An Analysis on the Reception Practices of the Novels "Overcoat", "Transformation" and "Animal Farm" [Anlatı Yoluyla Dünyanın Zihinsel Yeniden Kurulumu: "Palto", "Dönüşüm" ve "Hayvan Çiftliği" Romanlarının Alımlama Pratikleri Üzerine Bir İnceleme]. Kocaeli Universty, Institute of Social Sciences, Department of Communication Sciences.

Yılmaz, R. (2023). Transfer of Oral Culture to Advertising Narrative: A Study on the Functions of Idioms [Sözlü Kültürün Reklam Anlatısına Aktarımı: Deyimlerin İşlevleri Üzerine Bir İnceleme]. *Milli Folklor*, *18*(140), 95–106. DOI: 10.58242/millifolklor.1223729

ADDITIONAL READING

Baudrillard, J. (1994). *Simulacra and Simulation* (Glaser, S. F., Trans.). University of Michigan Press.

Çetgin, Y. (2025). *Sonsuz Mekân-Formsuz Mimarlık*. İltişim Publication.

Eco, U. (1989). *The Open Work* (Cancogni, A., Trans.). Harvard University Press.

Friedberg, A. (2009). *The Virtual Window: From Alberti to Microsoft*. MIT Press.

Harvey, D. (1989). *The Condition of Postmodernity: An Enquiry İnto the Origins of Cultural Change*. Blackwell Publishing.

Heidegger, M. (1971). *Poetry, Language, Thought* (Hofstadter, A., Trans.). Harper & Row.

Jameson, F. (1992). *Postmodernism, or, the Cultural Logic of Late Capitalism*. Duke University Press. DOI: 10.1215/9780822378419

Jenkins, H. (2006). *Convergence Culture: Where Old and New Media Collide.* NYU Press.

Lyotard, J.-F. (1984). *The Postmodern Condition: A Report on Knowledge* (Bennington, G., & Massumi, B., Trans.). University of Minnesota Press.

Manovich, L. (2002). *The Language of New Media.* MIT Press. DOI: 10.22230/cjc.2002v27n1a1280

KEY TERMS AND DEFINITIONS

Digitalism: Digitalism is a cultural and philosophical orientation that emphasizes the pervasive influence of digital technologies on human life, society, and thought. It reflects how digital media reshape communication, perception, and even identity in the contemporary world.

Postmodernism: Postmodernism is a broad intellectual and artistic movement that challenges the ideals of modernism, emphasizing fragmentation, pluralism, and skepticism toward grand narratives. It often plays with metafiction, irony, and intertextuality to question objective truth and fixed meanings

Simulation: Simulation is the imitation or representation of a real-world process, system, or environment, often through digital or virtual means. It blurs the line between reality and representation, especially in postmodern contexts where simulations can replace or become more "real" than the original.

Space: Space is a conceptual and physical dimension in which events, objects, and subjects are situated and interact. In literary and cultural theory, it is not merely a backdrop but a dynamic construct shaped by perception, experience, and discourse.

Digital Publishing: Digital publishing is the process of distributing content through electronic formats such as e-books, websites, online journals, and multimedia platforms. It transforms traditional publishing by enabling immediate access, interactive features, and global dissemination of texts.

Mythology: Mythology is a system of traditional stories, beliefs, and symbols that cultures use to explain the origins of the world, natural phenomena, and human experience. It functions as a narrative framework through which societies convey values, archetypes, and collective memory.

Culture: Culture is the collective set of beliefs, practices, values, symbols, and artifacts that shape the way a group of people understand and engage with the world. It encompasses both material and immaterial aspects of human life, functioning as a dynamic system of meaning-making and identity formation.

Chapter 19
The Recreation of Space in Digital Broadcasting:
Virtual Production

Arzu Gökçen Çelik
https://orcid.org/0009-0000-5199-3901
Ondokuz Mayıs Universty, Turkey

Nursel Bolat
https://orcid.org/0000-0002-3986-7408
Ondokuz Mayıs University, Turkey

ABSTRACT

Spaces are essential elements of visual narratives and act as a supporting force for storytelling. As cinema and television broadcasting rapidly integrate with evolving technology, they are taking a leading role in creating innovative spaces. Virtual Production, a combination of virtual reality (VR), augmented reality (AR), and advanced computer graphics, offers a revolutionary method for film and television production. Virtual Production stands out as an approach that merges virtual environments with physical shooting processes, enhancing both creative freedom and production efficiency. By joining the realm of spaces created in virtual environments, Virtual Production opens up new and fascinating horizons for the cinema and television industries. Through the technological integration of footage shot at different times and locations, new virtual spaces are brought to life.

DOI: 10.4018/979-8-3373-1957-5.ch019

INTRODUCTION

Communication technologies are constantly changing in line with technological developments and the production and broadcasting process is evolving. In the context of technology, verbal, written and visual expression technologies undergo change and transformation in the process and reach the audience in different forms. Traditional broadcasting systems enter the process of digitalization with the rapid development of technology and offer an environment for the reshaping of media broadcasting and communication beyond traditional media.

As a result of technological developments in general and information and communication technologies in particular, the media has transitioned into a two-dimensional phase: traditional and new/digital. On the one hand, print and analog broadcasts (traditional media) and online and digital broadcasts (new/digital media) have come into question. The transformation has not only been in communication tools, but individuals have also moved from the reader/listener/viewer position of traditional media to the user dimension of new media (Özcan, 2017, pp. 59-60). Digital media, which is the result of technology, has been developing since the 1960s and has become an effective communication tool by appearing before the audience/reader in different fields every day (Süllü, 2018, p. 130). Digital media broadcasting has recently led to a multidimensional change in the media and broadcasting sector with the use and development of internet and computer technologies. Digital media production and consumption gives a different trajectory to the functioning of the media. Digitalization has had an impact not only on the media, but also on productions such as cinema and TV series, which have an effective language of expression like the media.

Digitalization, which has gained a place in the cinematographic universe, has increased the reality of the language of expression by combining the realistic language of cinematographic expression with technology and brought a different perception of reality to the film and series sector. By creating a form of expression beyond reality and reality, it develops the technological effects of digitalization with many techniques. Technological development in the cinematographic universe offers narratives closest to reality with many techniques since the past. The film industry has benefited from the chroma keying technique for many years, and the presence of green screens has been used in many areas, from blockbuster movies to TV series watched at home. However, in recent years, new technologies have raised the question of whether green screens will eventually become a thing of the past. The technology that will leave the green screen technique behind is beginning to show itself and the use of virtual production is becoming widespread.

Virtual Production is the digitalization of traditional production techniques. With this technology, physically built set environments are replaced by virtual set environments designed in a computer environment. Virtual set environments are created in predetermined virtual spaces. The basic components are LED walls and ceilings, unreal engine, motion capture, digital environment and 3D design.

Virtual production is developing technologically every day. With these technological advances, filmmakers are using different CG techniques to build a fantasy and realistic cinematic world and unique audiences. VP is used to describe computer-aided production and visualization filmmaking methods. It combines Virtual and Augmented Reality with CGI and game engine technologies to create shooting scenes. Theoretically, Virtual Reality (VR) is a system that offers a simulation environment where users can create and experience a virtual world (Li et al., 2022, p. 222). virtual reality is perceived as an experience environment that emerged as a result of the technological developments of the 2000s and pushes the boundaries of human-machine interaction, it is not a newly emerged concept and its technological origins date back to Ivan Sutherland's article "The Ultimate Display" published in 1965 (Erdem, 2018a). Afterwards, virtual reality applications, which first emerged with military technology, paved the way for the development of augmented reality (AR) applications and today these types have emerged as two separate fields. According to Erdem (2018b), AR technologies refer to virtual experiences in the form closest to reality, as they are applications that also need the real world. The most popular augmented reality application in recent years is the game "Pokemon Go" (Yılmaz, 2017, p. 265). This technological development then formed the basis for the establishment of virtual studios.

This study aims to examine the introduction of virtual technologies and the use of modern technology in the TV series sector. It is aimed to focus on the changes offered by the new possibilities that emerged in the context of technology as it took its place in the sector. In this context, it is tried to convey to the reader the innovations that the shift towards virtual environments has brought to the film and TV series industry. The possibilities provided by virtual production technology are evaluated in terms of program production.

Fundamentals of Virtual Production Technologies

Since the creation of moving image systems, cinema pioneers such as Eadweard and Georges Mellies have been experimenting with many illusion techniques in film productions in order to expand the visual expression of the audience. Movie veterans in the history of cinema such as Hitchcock and Kubrick have developed and used projection methods. The movie 'A Space Odyssey' directed by Kubrick in 2001 is one of the first examples of virtual production technology. The shooting of a scene set in Southwest Africa was shot by placing the images created in the studio environment in the background due to transportation problems while planning the location. This system called pre-projection is a source of inspiration for new technologies (Söğütler, 2024, p. 217).

Virtual reality technologies take place in the development technologies of the cinematographic universe. These technologies carry the perception of reality to the virtual reality created in artificial intelligence systems.

Virtual reality stands out as a medium where computer-aided environments can be created where people share their ideas and experiences and discover new things in virtual space. (Çakın ve Yaman, 2020, p.4). "Interactive designs that are increasingly deepening around virtual reality technologies, alternative worlds associated with artificial intelligence systems, and understandings that transform the audience into an active actor within the framework of the ideal of immersion, are evolving towards a different, virtual performance art with the interdisciplinary and hybrid experiments offered by the machine" (Halaçoğlu, 2021, p. 85). One of these virtual technologies is virtual production.

Virtual productions are set environments created virtually. Virtual productions have a quality that will mark a new era in the television and film industry. Virtual production technology enables the transformation of traditional production systems by creating them in a virtual environment. With this technology, effective and creative productions emerge in the cinematographic universe. In order to be successful in the application process of the technique, multiple technologies are used together. Virtual production uses many technologies including virtual sets, LED walls, real-time visualization and motion capture systems. Thanks to these technologies, flexible and creative productions emerge.

Virtual Sets and Real-Time Visualization

From past to present, human beings question their existence and create the perception of reality by combining this existence with different materials in the mind. Plato's theory of ideas and Aristotle's realism, by focusing on the concept of reality, show that the perception of reality was transmitted in different ways before generations (Ökten, 2019, p. 667).

Today, the perception of reality is shaping the new reality by moving to virtual environments in computer and communication technologies formed with the development of digital media. The perception of reality is moved to virtual environments and character, time, space designs are created in an architectural way and designed in accordance with reality. This technology has a place in the movie and series sector . This adventure, which started with computer games, opens a new area for virtual set formation in stage and space designs in movie and series sets with virtual production technique. Virtual production technologies include virtual sets.

Virtual sets are 3D spaces created in a computer environment. These sets are usually prepared using game engines unreal engine. Unreal Engine is a game engine inspired by the game called Unreal made by Epic Games. Software films that create the frame and space in the game setup are also used to create the virtual set.

In virtual sets, the progress of the set and the work in progress allows for a single shot in the set environment with real-time game engine technology and the use of LED screens. This method increases the perception of reality of the scene with a realistic narrative of the space design that needs to be created in the movie. In order for the camera to adapt the shooting range to perspective and parallax (depth), the background scene flow changes with LED walls. Motion capture devices are available to do this. The Mandalorian series is an example of this technique (Erdem, 2021, p.171).

In virtual sets, virtual set environments are set up instead of physical set environments. The set is designed in a digital environment. Thanks to the real visualization of these designs, it can be seen how the set environment is created without filming. Since the scenes can be shown before the production established in this technology, the changes in the scenes shot are made simultaneously.

Real-time visualization is the simultaneous recording of virtual spaces with camera movements. The images are not pre-positioned on the set, but are displayed simultaneously and in real time at the time of shooting. It is implemented during the production process, not during production. Most of the work that needs to be done after production is carried forward from the production process, can be applied during production, reproduced and edited. However, the decisions taken after the shooting are carried to the set during the shooting, and cinematographic elements such as correction and removal are corrected in the set environment (Kahraman, 2024, p.11).

One of the productions made with this technique is The Mandalorian. Many scenes of this series are shot with this technique. The Mandalorian was shot on LED screens in a 270 degree circular set environment. 3D images are shot on LED screens as a background. Thanks to the LED screens, the actors are rendered in this virtual environment without the need for another light source by illuminating from the line where the camera is directed in order to provide real-time brightness (depth) with the light reflected from the LED wall (Erdem, 2021, p. 171).

LED Walls and the Use of Virtual Reality

The productions used in the cinematographic universe in the developing technology technologically carry cinema and television productions to a high level of reality. Technological LED technology offers a realistic and flexible production system by making the use of time, space and visual effects that need to be created in set environments more effective and efficient.

LED walls used in virtual production are among the building blocks of virtual sets. LED walls form the entire skeleton of the set environment. These digitally created walls offer a realistic environment in the scenes created by using them together with real-time visualization.

LED walls provide real and simultaneous stage visualization in the cinema and TV series industry, and virtual scenes are created without physical installation thanks to the technology. A realistic frame is created in the set installation. The biggest impact of this is that the scenes set up in front of LED screens adapt faster to the conditions against uncontrollable situations in outdoor shooting. While larger and difficult to set up set environments are created for traditional set environments, LED walls are set up in more realistic and smaller spaces. Actors are present in real time in the scenes created around these LED walls without the need for imagination. This leads to a more realistic performance on stage (Swords & Willment, 2024, p. 12).

VR technology adds a more realistic simulation to this performance. VR technology is a technology that consists of digital data and offers a virtual space with this software. It uses the physical presence of the audience in the environment it creates virtually by creating a realistic image, sound and sensation of the audience's physical presence by creating an environment in virtual reality headsets or multiple projections (Dinç, 2022, pp. 226-227)

It allows creating an environment from every angle with videos recorded with 360-degree cameras in 3D environments. It virtualizes reality with tools with different device features and offers a more realistic image than a monitor. (Dinç, 2022, p. 227)

VR technology used with LED walls creates a digital environment. In movie and series productions, VR technology is designed and planned before the scenes. VR takes the audience into the created story and makes the audience experience the story through the eyes of the character. With the unlimited space production brought by technology, the limits of physical spaces are overcome in virtual spaces. In the scenes shot with VR, space and time are organized simultaneously in the scenes more easily during shooting.

Camera Movements and Stage Design

One of the most challenging aspects of shooting a scene is to design the scene with scene design and camera movements. The advantage of virtual production is that camera movements are created unlimitedly and quickly in the scenes created in the virtual world. Compared to other production systems, scene design and camera movement planning in virtual production is planned in a shorter time. Since this process is long in traditional productions, virtual productions are replacing traditional productions in current technology. In virtual production, the use of virtual sets and LED walls can be shot simultaneously while creating camera movements. From a technical point of view, camera movements are tested simultaneously thanks to motion sensors and computer software used during shooting, and synchronization of the shooting moment is provided by shooting the actors in real time (Wan, 2024, p. 5).

With the development of virtual production, many changes and developments have been made in stage designs. While a great deal of preparation is done before the stage design is built on traditionally built sets, in virtual productions, the stage design is prepared quickly and realistically through computer software. Thanks to this design technology, production teams save time, increase the speed of scene shooting and minimize the errors that occur during shooting. The fact that virtual productions digitally create stage designs opens a wide range of stage design in the cinematographic universe, enabling the creation of scenes that are impossible to be

Motion Capture, an important component of virtual productions, is part of this technology. Motion Capture transfers the movements of the actors during the shooting on digitally created characters. The data transferred through motion capture systems places the physical movements of the actors during the shooting on the character. Motion Capture has an important advantage in the creation of fantasy films. It gives a realistic impression by simultaneously reflecting the real movements of the actors on digital characters. This system consists of motion capture, performance capture, face capture and full body animation.

Motion Capture is a system that records the movements of the actors and the objects used during the shooting and creates the data information in digital form. This created technology comes together using different motion capture systems. Mechanical motion capture is part of this system. This motion capture system captures the movement that takes place on the exoskeleton structure of the actor. The magnetic motion capture system handles the spatial connection thanks to certain sensors placed on the joints to detect the actor's joint movements. This system is an electromagnetic system and is not preferred because it has a sensitive function. Another motion capture system is the optical motion capture system, which effectively captures facial expressions along with finger movements thanks to reflective markers monitored by multiple digital cameras. Another system among Motion

Capture motion capture systems is the inertial motion capture system. This system is minimal and realizes data transfer by utilizing inertial wireless sensors. Although it is an easy-to-use sensor with its portable feature, it records facial movements and player performance in a limited area in motion capture. Performance capture systems also have an important place in motion capture. It ensures that virtually produced characters are physically integrated into the environment. With Simulcam techniques, camera movement is simultaneously placed in real live scenes with virtually created characters. The face capture performance system, on the other hand, allows the facial expressions of the characters to be transferred in detail by defining the face of the performance capture. Full body animation, on the other hand, realizes the transfer of all the movements of the character and has been used in film productions such as Lord of the Rings and Avatar (Chanpum, 2023, p.12; Lama, 2024, pp. 22-23).

Camera movements and stage design help shape the aesthetic and narrative dimensions of film productions. Camera movements function as the basic element that draws the audience into the plot. Camera angles reinforce the narrative of the movie by giving the emotional states of the character and transfer them to the audience. Camera movements focus the audience's attention on the film production independently of the plot, creating an emotional bond between the film and the audience.

Stage design, on the other hand, physically creates the space described in the plot in film productions and consists of objects such as decor, color, lighting that must be present on the stage. In stage designs, it not only creates a background rather than physical set installations, but also increases the reality of the narrative structure in the cinematographic universe by creating a perception of time and space. Therefore, the harmony of camera and stage design becomes an important element in virtual productions to ensure visual integrity . This is how the power of visual expression and credibility in the perception of reality are created.

The Role of Virtual Production in the Publishing Industry

The process of moving image production is based on the universal rules of physical science, sensitive to technological innovations, and focused on the viewer experience. Opportunities created through new technologies in the television and cinema industry are transforming production practices by forcing production companies to be sensitive to technology. Virtual production technology is recognized as one of the important innovations in moving image production and is used by production companies in various ways.

Use in Film and Television Productions

With the development of digital media in direct proportion to technology, the broadcasting sector is undergoing a multidimensional change in terms of both production and communication with the audience. Virtual production technology, which is the pioneer of this change, appears as a mixed production system based on traditional production techniques.

As a transition to virtual production, The Mandolirian is a pioneer of TV series and movies based on the production of The Mandolirian and opens a space for the virtual production technique within the sector. By changing the perspective of producers, it eliminates the necessity of using green screen (Massad, 2023, p. 24). Since physical sets are replaced by virtual sets to create the perception of reality, different spaces are created virtually and the set environment is realized in a single space with a space design suitable for each scene.

There are many reasons why virtual production is used in TV series and movie productions. One of them is the light source required in set environments. LED walls used in virtual production provide the necessary light for the set. The computer-controlled LED walls do not need another light source regardless of time and space (Swords Willment, 2024, p. 7) As a result of this situation, LED walls used in virtual sets can change the emotion desired to be conveyed with light in space design within seconds. The lights used to convey different emotions can convey them in the same space in a single light source.

Another role of virtual production in the film industry is that instead of leaving the imagination in the set environment during the scene without the need for a green screen, it can control the actors in the created space design real and simultaneously with the relationship between the virtual camera and the environment (Li et al., 2022, p. 9) Thanks to this feature, the actor performs more effectively and convincingly in the role he plays because he sees and lives in the set environment simultaneously. Since the scenes are designed in advance, the director and cinematographer see the production process in real time before shooting, providing a fast and flexible working space during the production phase of TV series and movies.

Live Streaming and Interactive Media Applications

"Social media has become a part of society and an indispensable communication tool. The number of people who become a phenomenon by broadcasting everything they experience all day through these applications, who turn these applications into a business and earn money with the videos and advertisements they publish, is quite high. As technology develops and social media applications are updated, face-to-face communication is gradually disappearing and virtual happiness surrounds society.

As Debord said, society has now literally turned into the "Society of the Spectacle" (Yılmaz, 2017, p. 133).

In this show society, with the rapid development of technology, the media broadcasting sector is undergoing significant changes. After the movie and series sector, virtual productions started to show themselves in live broadcasting and media applications. Virtual productions provide many conveniences in live broadcasts and minimize the disruptions that may occur during shooting

Live broadcasts present events such as an event or a show to the audience in applications such as television and social media (Yılmaz, 2017, p.131)

Due to this feature, the process of simultaneous broadcasting of live broadcasts increases the disruptions that may occur during the shooting

It is very difficult to transmit an image live in live broadcasts due to the high cost and has created a broadcasting practice that we can see within the television industry. New generation communication technologies are changing and transforming the possibilities of live broadcasting (Ünal, 2017, p. 24)

In live broadcasts, traditionally created productions use multiple cameras, which creates technical difficulties. Virtual production technology minimizes these difficulties in live broadcasts

The LED walls used in technology and the accompanying virtual sets accelerate the shooting processes of live broadcasts and allow for more efficient content creation. In live broadcasts, according to the content of the programs, stage designs suitable for the content in sports and food broadcasts are created virtually in real time with LED walls. In this case, the necessity of being in a physical space in live broadcasts has been eliminated (B&H Photo Video Pro Audio, 2025).

The use of virtual production in interactive media is directly proportional to its use in live broadcasting. Interactive media provides an experience in which the audience is present on the content it creates. Examples include television shows, video games, events that are organized virtually. In virtual productions, this technology enables the audience to interact with the content produced by using interactive media and real-time visualization possibilities.

Features such as Virtual Production scene changes in live broadcasts and media interactions, and custom scene creation in television shows provide production teams with flexible workspaces to create more efficient, realistic and impressive content.

Advantages of Virtual Sets and Real-Time Production

Virtual production has become an important part of the cinematographic universe. Arkenberg predicts that with the increase in the ease of service it offers to production teams and the reduction of cost pressures in marketing, cost and time in content development, the tendency to rely on virtual production will increase and a process of intensive use of virtual production will be entered (Arkenberg, 2023, p. 4)

Virtual production offers the TV, film and TV industry many advantages over traditionally applied technologies. These advantages speed up the production stages and allow production budgets to be considered in terms of cost. Thanks to the real-time production advantage of virtual sets, unlimited scene designs are realized with fast and simultaneous production.

Time and Cost Savings

In traditionally created productions, there are factors such as the construction of physical sets, the use of different venues, and transportation and transportation operations to these venues. As a result of these, budget problems arise. Virtual production technology eliminates this problem due to its technical equipment and saves a great deal of cost and labor in the production process

The spaces created on physical sets are used with LED walls in virtual projections and outdoor and space designs are created digitally. This eliminates the need to carry equipment, i.e. labor and travel to different locations. The effect or scene designing that needs to be created in post-production on the virtual sets established during the shooting enables the creation of real and simultaneous shots with virtual production. Simultaneous shots provide the advantage of saving time as it corrects details such as reflection, light, color that need to be done during post-production during shooting (Satıcı, 2024, p. 299).

Unlimited Creativity and Flexibility

An indisputable fact of TV series and movies is that they are scenarios that start with imagination. This imagination is also reflected during shooting. While this imagination is more limited in traditional productions, in virtual productions this field reaches an unlimited power

Virtual productions create unimaginable digital worlds. Space, character and effects are transformed into high-level designs in digital environments. Therefore, it offers a flexible imagination by adding a wide-angle perspective to the stage design. Scenes that can be changed simultaneously are created in digital environments designed in the imagination with the help of LED walls and prevent disconnection in the plot. For this reason, the sets for you stand out from the real world and open the door to the existence of new worlds (Chanpun, 2023, p. 10).

As a result, production technologies in virtual productions and real-time systems contribute to the future development of the film and television industry. These technologies, which provide a great advantage to the creative process of the production stages, add speed to the virtual production system process. In addition, this situation increases the sustainability of production use environmentally by reducing the production budget. With the integration of technological development into production systems in this direction, the place of this system in the film industry contributes to this system by having a great place due to the increase in the advantage rate it provides.

Limits and Challenges of Virtual Environments

Although virtual production has a technically advantageous position compared to traditional productions, it also has limitations and technical difficulties just like traditional productions. The difficulties and limitations of virtual productions manifest themselves in technical and creative dimensions. There are problems in the adequate development of technology, the ability of human labor to adapt to the new system, and problems in computer software

When we first start from the processes of the projection stages of the creativity stage, we are confronted with digital environments where virtual production is created at an unlimited level. Set environments, which are shaped with certain restrictions in traditional production, cause confusion because they are unlimited in digital environments, and the production planning of the production is disrupted due to this orbit disorientation. The introduction of new technology into the film production sector creates a difference in the working areas of set workers and requires training for the new system. In a case study on this subject;

" The second challenge is related to the lack of multidisciplinary experts and trainers in higher education contexts. Finding a skilled Unreal Engine artist who could help us train students proved more difficult than expected. As virtual production is an emerging technology, the number of Unreal Engine-trained VFX artists and DM educators was limited during our pilot project. This problem is exacerbated by the lack of formal training in the industry itself, creating a vicious cycle that causes training to fall behind at an exponentially increasing rate" (Boutellier, Rabits, 2023, p. 78). They conclude

The limitations of the use of virtual production are reflected on the viewer beyond the technical level. This reflection negatively affects the viewer with the feeling of artificiality even in a small detail due to the high level of image quality. This situation necessitates more detailed work and work to increase the level of reality.

The need to maximize the perception of reality creates intense pressure by requiring technical competence, time constraints and cost increases. For this situation, " The first challenge relates to the cost and availability of resources and equipment. One of the biggest obstacles that higher education institutions face is the cost of resources and potentially the space needed to run a virtual production phase. This is exacerbated by the fact that the technology is still relatively new and therefore evolving rapidly, making any investment risky" (Boutellier, Rabits, 2023, p. 78). This finding in the case study is illustrative.

From a technical point of view, LED walls, Unreal Engine, camera tracking systems should have intensive equipment. In the LED walls in the set environment and in the digital set created, some problems in light, perspective and resolution settings may occur. The consequences of these problems damage the perception of reality that should be created on the audience and damage the integrity of the shooting

Another technical difficulty is the camera movements in virtual environments. When camera tracking systems are used in production, the lack of accurate timing when they do not move synchronously is a problem that crosses the boundary line of virtual production. Especially in action scenes, this technique can become inadequate (Wan, 2024, p. 4)

virtual production systems provide a flexible working opportunity, if the production system is not realized with meticulous work, it causes various difficulties.

Technical Challenges and Solutions

In recent years, traditional methods have been left behind in the film industry, opening up a huge space for virtual production technology. As in traditional productions, virtual production systems have a different technical structure. Although this technological system, which works with Unreal enginee, LED volumes, camera tracking systems, saves time and cost, it creates some technical problems.

One of the main problems of technical use is insufficient knowledge and equipment about technology in virtual production technical formation. In a study, this situation is mentioned as follows:

"This technology needs to be used properly. Some problems have already arisen because it cannot be used properly. I think that if that part is solved, many things will come by themselves. I think that since they look at the costs in terms of cost-benefit, the costs need to be brought to more affordable levels. In fact, thousands of dollars are spent blindly on a device or a platform, but the personnel is as important as the device. It is a point that is overlooked and it is actually not that costly. It is actually much cheaper and much more useful to train and educate the personnel. I think that point is overlooked, I think it escapes attention" (Apaydın, 2024, pp. 163-164). The expressions are mentioned. Another problem that comes along with this situation is the emergence of new professions that come with the lack of knowledge and equipment and the formation of a technically insufficient qualified personnel deficit. " The increase in the use of reality and virtual reality leads to the emergence of new professions and the development of professional skills in the virtual environment" (Barbaros, 2020, p. 86) Barbaros' statement proves that this gap has occurred, for this, trainings that provide technological hardware knowledge and qualified personnel should be trained for this field.

Another technical problem is the failure of virtual environments to present a real appearance. This is one of the difficult aspects of the production because, technically, the virtual and physical elements need to match when using a production and, as a result, present a real and convincing appearance. When camera movements deviate from tracking systems, they cause visual distortions and distort the perception of reality. As a solution to this, camera movement and background movement must be synchronized to achieve the desired look (Guerrero, 2024, p. 35)

Thirdly, the incompatibility of light with the background in virtual productions damages the perception of reality, the light reflected on the objects in the physical environment and the lack of balance of the light reflected in the virtual production disrupts the image integrity. In this case, the light reflected from the walls and the light coming from the physical environments should be applied in a balanced way and the light planning should be done in harmony (WeAreAnnaValley, 2023) according to the statement that light balance is the factors that create the perception of reality in virtual productions.

Reality and its Impact on the Audience Experience

Virtual reality uses blend physical and virtual environments through a certain hardware and create the feeling that elements such as event, place, time and space exist with a fictional narrative. They are audience interactive environments. Based on a technological system, these reality 3D visual narratives include five sensory organ elements such as sound, touch and hearing. Thanks to simulation technology, it provides access to the environment by breathing the digital reproduction of an event, situation and space. The Immersivenes part allows the viewer to adapt to the virtually created production in both its environmental and psychological framework. In other words, it experiences the feeling of reality in the virtual environment. Audience and space harmonization is achieved in the virtual environment. This allows the user not only to see the formation in a virtual space with the user, but to reach the reality of living in this space. Thanks to multiple digital networks and data systems, it opens the door to a sense of presence in various virtual spaces (Çankır, 2024, p. 282)

This virtual production method brings a new dimension to the concept of reality by equalizing the boundaries of the real world and the virtual world. It provides a direct transfer to the audience with set designs using real-time visualization created with LED walls, so the sets have a real integrity that is no different from a physical space. Thanks to its ability to change simultaneously, it offers reality-appropriate designs. As a result, the visual world created is built as a structure in natural and real integrity . As a result of the fact that the difference between real and virtual is indistinguishable as a result of virtual production, it can question the concept of reality on the audience by realistically designing an environment that is not physically possible.

Virtual Production in the Future

After the use of virtual production technologies increased in film production productions, LED walls started to be used in the cinema industry in 2009 with the movie Avatar. In the productions that followed, virtual production forms were developed as the use of special effects in the film and television industry and reached an important point. Many productions such as Avatar develop adaptation to virtual production in special effects and bring the production in the traditional projection process to a different structure. Apart from the film and television industry, virtual production and LED walls are spreading to many areas such as live broadcasts, studios, TV stations, online conferences and commercial shootings (Söğütler, 2024, p. 220).

The tools currently used in virtual production are very comprehensive for a growing sector such as this technology Green screen, Blue box, rear and front projection devices are widely used today. With the development of technology, it can easily produce new products with ongoing virtual production movie productions. Manufacturers are trying to design and develop a system in favor of virtual production and LED walls. The purpose of developing and organizing this software difference is to improve the technology by renewing the content production system. While the LED walls used in traditional production are based on the RGB (red, green, blue) system, the panels created in this recently developed technology are starting to form the white LED unit, the fourth of this production area. The RGBW technology developed by ROE company says that the system they created by providing color proportionality reduces the need to correct the color settings made after construction. In addition, INFILED's Infinite Colors technology, like ROE, offers the opportunity to achieve a varied, flexible and rich appearance (Lama, 2024, pp. 36-37).

These steps towards the future provide continuous change and development of the technological system in new technologies and trains. Virtual productions used in conjunction with augmented reality (AR) and virtual reality (VR) will increase the development of technology. By maximizing the perception of reality, it can bring you a revolutionary development in production. Virtual productions, which have developed so much, may become a system that we can access in the future and carry the film industry to an independent production process.

In the future, virtual production technology will have a very important place in mass communication and media. It makes a great contribution to the series, movie, television, media and game industries within these communication and media fields.

As technology develops day by day, it will open different areas of use in many areas other than these communication tools.

New Technologies and Trends

In the coming years, productions in which more real virtual environments are created by using advanced technology in the field of production continue to develop in order to save time. Artificial intelligence system will be at the forefront of virtual productions and will reduce the workforce in the use of machinery. In addition, LED walls will come to a better point in virtual reality.

When we first look at emerging LED displays, the traditional RGB (red, green, blue) system has evolved into a fourth LED technology, white LED (RGBW). Thanks to this development, RGBW panels have an unlimited color scale in color settings, making visual reality more realistic. (Lama, 2024, pp. 36-37).

Another development is mobile virtual productions. The use of these productions, which are more minimal than large productions, is increasing day by day. The most important feature of mobile productions is to make the virtual production system more accessible to independent productions.

Artificial intelligence, game engines such as Unureal Engine and Unity are the trending and emerging unit of this technology. It accelerates the shooting time in production systems. With the system and commands of artificial intelligence, the production system progresses automatically. These units, which enable unlimited scene design, affect the creativity process during the production phase.

Recent work on virtual production has seen a significant development in the technologies available to create images. Tewari and his colleagues conducted a study on the interaction between artificial intelligence and computer graphics. As a result of the investigation and for the development of VR and AR reality application systems, they looked at the (neural rendering) system. They conclude how Unreal Real Engine, Unity and Dong game engines affect the production system throughout the process and how AI and the command system facilitate the work (Silva Jasaui et al., 2024, p. 8). This study highlights the emerging trend of AI and game engines in virtual production.

Virtual Production's Role in Future Media Production

The role of Virtual Production in media production is changing day by day thanks to digital technologies. The impact it brings to the film and television industry is quickly integrated into its role in media production. The LED walls and real-time game engines in the virtual production system have a place in media production just as they have a place in the cinematographic universe. In this way, media production causes systems such as pre- and post-production and production phase to move to a flexible working area in the media.

This technology, which was created with the Covid-19 pandemic, was developed with the formation of filming bans. As this technology is integrated into the TV and film industry, it opens up areas of use to other sectors, creating new job opportunities and a new perspective (Swords & Willment, 2024, pp. 25-26).

Virtual Production's role in media production will therefore develop more comprehensively. The media can also provide production space in the advertising sector, in customized content that appeals to certain audiences. As a result, the role of this technology in media production is not only limited to the technical structure but also causes a change in the narrative structure of the media.

Virtual Production and Sustainable Publishing

Virtual production is an important innovation for sustainable broadcasting in today's film industry. Virtual productions are a good, advanced and developing system in terms of environmental and cost possibilities for sustainable broadcasting. Virtual production offers sustainable solutions to the environmental pollution caused by traditional productions and the cost overruns that occur during the installation phase of these productions. For the future of the broadcasting sector, Virtual production system is a technological production tool with an efficient system with its low resource use, environmentalist feature, fast and creative effect.

Environmental Impacts and the Contribution of Virtual Production to Sustainability

Traditionally created film productions have a carbon footprint that greatly affects the environment in the set construction process such as transportation, physical set construction, logistics. Carbon footprint is the greenhouse gas that occurs as a result of an action. Virtual production has an important place in solving this problem in the media sector. Production units such as Unreal Engine, LED volumes, digital scenes used in production create a long-term sustainability system in the virtual production process

This system reduces waste production, energy savings and logistics. Instead of collecting and transporting the décor and physical spaces created on physical sets, digitally produced space designs on virtual sets minimize resource consumption and energy use during production time. The light of the LED volumes used in the production system is sufficient during shooting, so no other light source is required. This results in energy savings (Studio Ulster, 2023, pp. 25-30)

Due to the variety of space designs created in the digital environment in virtual productions, all teams do not need to go from one place to another. All the shootings are done in a single location. This eliminates transportation and logistics problems. The limits of sustainable broadcasting do not only affect environmental factors in virtual productions. By minimizing the budget problem in film productions, the low cost of content production ensures that the structure cost gap between production companies and independent producers is closed. In conclusion, apart from the creative feature of the virtual production system, sustainability broadcasting is a useful and effective system.

CONCLUSION AND EVALUATION

Leaving traditional production systems behind, Virtual production technology has recently had a great technological use on sets in the cinematographic universe and media broadcasting. Compared to traditional production systems, it has the features of flexible working, low cost, and fast shooting. This technology, which emerged due to the film and series shooting bans during the pandemic period, is on the rise in the cinematographic universe. Features such as Unreal Enginee, Unitey, LED walls, real-time visualization used in virtual productions contribute to pre-production creativity in the film, television and advertising sectors, reducing the workload and increasing work efficiency in the production phase and post-production processes.

One of the advantages of this technology is that it eliminates the limitations of physical set construction during the production phase. Space, transportation, weather conditions and cost problems that occur in traditional production systems allow for minimum problems with Virtual production technology. Since every space created in virtual production is created with an unlimited creative power, every desired environment can be digitally created by creative teams. When the problem of changing the location is eliminated, the transportation problem is also eliminated, saving time and cost. Thanks to the real-time visualization feature used in the technology, cinematographers and the director can see the created scene live, allowing them to make creative decisions more quickly before shooting begins

The advantage of solving environmental problems, which is among the benefits of virtual production, has an important place in production systems. Problems such as the construction process of set environments in traditional production setups, time-consuming equipment transportation, and high energy consumption create problems in terms of environmental cost. In the virtual production system, this rate decreases thanks to the developing technology. Material consumption, reduced carbon footprint, and the ability to reuse the digital space created without the need for any installation allow this technology to become a more sustainable system. The fact that virtual production is a system that works independent of weather conditions also has an important place for the media broadcasting sector.

This technology has its difficulties as well as its convenience. Problems such as the cost problem in the initial installation phase, the lack of trained qualified personnel with technical knowledge, the difficulty of the system installation phase are present in the technology. The continuity of the sense of reality created in virtual production has a very important place for the audience. Each scene created must be interconnected, consistent and immersive, so that a real scene far from artificiality is created. Therefore, establishing this realistic system requires the cinematographer, editor and technical team employees to be technically equipped.

Virtual production is a great investment for the future. With the use of machines and artificial intelligence technologies, technology efficiency and creativity processes will reach incredible heights. There are major improvements in stages such as scene designs created with artificial intelligence, production of virtual environment digital characters and real-time environment creation. Thanks to simultaneous teamwork, the shooting speed will increase considerably. In the future, this technology will be used not only in the movie industry but also in many other sectors. The reality interaction opportunities provided by technology contribute on a large scale. Thus, virtual production transformation and development effect will be felt in the process.

As a result, this system creates a major change in the processes of media and broadcasting, film and television industry, content production, creativity, designing and putting what is designed into function. Beyond the limits of the traditional production system, it creates a unique space unlimited creativity while contributing to environmental impact and cost sustainability. For the correct and good use of this technology, it is necessary to give importance to technical knowledge training and infrastructure that functions properly. When these conditions are created, Virtual production technology continues to maintain its position at the top in terms of content production and leads the innovative perspective in the sector.

REFERENCES

Apaydın, C. (2024). A Research on the Use of Real-Time Visual Effects in Film Production: The Case of Extended Reality (XR) Studios [PhD thesis, Selçuk Universty, Institute of Social Sciences]. Selçuk Universty. https://hdl.handle.net/20.500.12395/54318contentReference[oaicite:1]{index=

Arkenberg, C., Loucks, J., Westcott, K., & Crossan, G. (2022). Virtual Production Gets Real: Bringing Real-Time Visual Effects Onto the Set. Deloitte Insights. https://www2.deloitte.com/content/dam/insights/articles/us175608_tmtp23-virtual-production/DI_TMTP23-virtual-production.pdf

B&H Photo Video Pro Audio. (2025, January 28). Intro to Virtual Production: The Future of Filmmaking [Video]. YouTube. https://www.youtube.com/watch?v=tyeI0oZs7cA

Boutellier, A., & Raptis, P. (2023). Teaching Virtual Production: The Challenges of Developing a Formal Curriculum. *Film Education Journal*, *6*(2), 69–81. DOI: 10.14324/FEJ.06.2.01

Çakın, Ö., & Yaman, D. (2020). Fijital (phygital) pazarlama uygulamaları üzerine bir inceleme: Amazon Go Örneği. *Middle Black Sea Journal of Communication Studies*, *5*(1), 1–10.

Çankır, M. B. (2024). Virtual Reality: Spaces Beyond the Limits of Cinema. *New Media Electronic Journal*, *8*(2), 276–292. DOI: 10.17932/IAU.EJNM.25480200.2024/ejnm_v8i2004

Chanpum, P. (2023). Virtual Production: Interactive And Real-Time Technology For Filmmakers. Humanities, *Arts and Social Sciences Studies*, 23(1), 9-17. https://doi.org/[oaicite:1]DOI: 10.14456/hasss.2023.2contentReference

Dinç, İ. D. (2022). The Future of Virtual Reality Applications in New Media Platforms and Reflections in Science Fiction Universe. *Journal of Arts*, *5*(4), 223–233. DOI: 10.31566/arts.5.4.04

Erdem, M. N. (2018a). Virtual Reality in Advertising Applications. In Çakın, Ö. (Ed.), *Traditional to Digital Advertising Media* (pp. 199–240). LiteraTürk Publications.

Erdem, M. N. (2018b). "Rethinking Corporate Social Responsibility with Transmedia Narratives and Augmented Reality", in Transmedia Storytelling, Ed. E. Aktan, Konya: LiteraTürk publications, pp. 115-158.

Erdem, S. (2021). Overview of Virtual Set Applications in Digitalizing Film Sector. *Kafkas University Journal of Institute of Social Sciences*, *27*, 159–177. DOI: 10.9775/kausbed.2021.010

Guerrero Cardoso, M. T. (2024, May). Virtual production creative process for "Crucifier" music video: A production designer's perspective [Master's thesis, University of Texas at Austin]. Texas ScholarWorks. https://repositories.lib.utexas.edu/items/c2eebb40-1664-4f79-8f9a-55d7483c03f2

Kahraman, B. (2024). Virtual Production and Cinematic Meaning as a Reversal Process in Filmmaking. *International Social Sciences and Art Research*, *3*(1), 54–65.

Lama, R. (2024). The future of virtual backgrounds in filmmaking [Master's thesis, Academy of Performing Arts in Prague, Film and Television Faculty, Department of Cinematography]. DSpace AMU. https://dspace.amu.cz/items/802d5a5a-e50e-4843-9d58-f67edb1c2615contentReference[oaicite:3]index=3

Li, H., Lo, C.-H., Smith, A., & Yu, Z. (2022). The development of virtual production in film industry in the past decade. In Kurosu, M. (Ed.), Lecture Notes in Computer Science: Vol. 13302. *Human-Computer Interaction. Theoretical Approaches and Design Methods. HCII 2022* (pp. 213–226). Springer., DOI: 10.1007/978-3-031-06047-2_16

Massand, A. (2023). A Qualitative Study into LED Volume, a Virtual Production Technology (Master's thesis). Erasmus University Thesis Repository.

Ökten, A. (2019). A Brief Review on the Perception of Reality in the Philosophies of Plato and Aristotle. *Journal of International Social Research*, *12*(65), 676–682.

Özcan, A. (2017). Digital Media Literacy: Problems, Practices and Expectations. *AJIT-E: Academic Journal of Information Technology*, 8(28), 55-66. https org://doi. /.DOI: 10.5824/1309-1581.2017.3.004.x

Satıcı, H. (2024). The Development of Simultaneous Background Technology from Projection to LED Screen and Its Effect on Film Production. *INIF E-Journal*, 9(2), 295-310. https://dergipark.org.tr/en/pub/inifedergi/issue/88296/1508298

Silva Jasaui, D., Martí-Testón, A., Muñoz, A., Moriniello, F., Solanes, J. E., & Gracia, L. (2024). Virtual Production: Real-Time Rendering Pipelines For Indie Studios And The Potential In Different Scenarios. *Applied Sciences (Basel, Switzerland)*, *14*(6), 2530. DOI: 10.3390/app14062530

Söğütlüler, T. (2024). The Future of the Moving Image: Virtual Production Technology. *Film Journal*, *4*(2), 214–234. DOI: 10.59280/film.1530664

Süllü, Z. (2018). Historical Origins of Communication and Communication Tools from Oral Culture to Digital Culture. *Kastamonu Journal of Communication Research*, (1), 119–135.

Swords, J., & Willment, N. (2024). The Emergence of Virtual Production: A Research Agenda. *Convergence (London)*, *30*(5), 1557–1574. Advance online publication. DOI: 10.1177/13548565241253903

Ulster, S. (2023). Virtual Production's Role in Carbon Reduction and Net Zero Production in the Screen Industries (Future Observatory Cultural Policy Fellowship Report). Future Observatory. https://futureobservatory.org/files/dcmsreports/futureobservatory_culturalpolicyreport_studioulster.pdf

Ünal, R. (2017). Possibilities and Limitations of the Use of Mobile Live Streaming Applications in the Context of Journalism. *Mersin University Journal of Institute of Social Sciences*, *1*(1), 24–37.

Wan, X. (2024). The Potential of Virtual Production Based on the Special Effects Of Films. *SHS Web of Conferences,* 193, 01013. DOI: 10.1051/shsconf/202419301013

WeAreAnnaValley. (2023, June 21). Virtual Production: A New Era of Content Creation [Video]. YouTube. https://youtu.be/kC9fBDCzuJU

Yılmaz, N. (2017). The Understanding of Live Broadcasting on Social Media. *New Media Electronic Journal*, *1*(1), 127–136. DOI: 10.17932/IAU.EJNM.m.25480200.2017.1/1.127-136

Yılmaz, R. (2017). Structural Transformation of Advertising Narrative in Turkey in the Digital Age. *1st International Conference on New Trends in Communication.* Istanbul Commerce Universty

ADDITIONAL READING

Alarcon, L., Diethelm, S., Rojo, O., & Calderón, R. (2008). Evaluando Los Impactos De La Implementación De Lean Construction. *Revista de Ingeniería de Construcción*, *23*(1), 26–33.

Amer, F., & Golparvar-Fard, M. 2019. “Decentralized Visual 3D Mapping Of Scattered Work Locations For High-Frequency Tracking of Indoor Construction Activities.” In Proc., Construction Research Congress 2018: Construction Information Technology, CRC 2018. Reston, VA: ASCE.

Bae, H., Golparvar-Fard, M., & White, J. (2013). High-Precision Vision-Based Mobile Augmented Reality System for Context-Aware Architectural, Engineering, Construction and Facility Management (AEC/FM) applications. *Visualization Eng.*, *1*(1), 1–3. DOI: 10.1186/2213-7459-1-3

Dodge Data and Analytics. (2017). *Optimizing Owner Organizations The Impact Of Policies And Practices On Performance For All Building Owners*. Dodge Data and Analytics.

Golparvar-Fard, M., Peña-Mora, F., Arboleda, C. A., & Lee, S. (2009a). Visualization of Construction Progress Monitoring with 4D Simulation Model Overlaid on Time-Lapsed photographs. *Journal of Computing in Civil Engineering*, *23*(6), 391–404. DOI: 10.1061/(ASCE)0887-3801(2009)23:6(391)

Hamzeh, F. R., El Samad, G., & Emdanat, S. (2019). Advanced Metrics for Construction Planning. *Journal of Construction Engineering and Management*, *145*(11), 04019063. DOI: 10.1061/(ASCE)CO.1943-7862.0001702

Karsch, K., Golparvar-Fard, M., & Forsyth, D. (2014). ConstructAide: Analyzing and Visualizing Construction Sites Through Photographs and Building Models. *ACM Transactions on Graphics*, *33*(6), 1–11. DOI: 10.1145/2661229.2661256

Leeder, M. (2017). *The Modern Supernatural and the Beginnings of Cinema*. Palgrave Macmillan., DOI: 10.1057/978-1-137-58371-0

Menache, A. (2000). *Understanding Motion Capture for Computer Animation and Video Games*. Morgan Kaufmann.

Mozar, A. 2020. What is Virtual Production in Animation and VFX Filmmaking and its Benefits. The Virtual Assist. Available at: https://thevirtualassist.net/what-is-virtual-production-vp-filmmaking-benefits/. Last access on 06/02/2022.

Russell, M. M., Hsiang, S. M., Liu, M., & Wambeke, B. (2014). Causes of Time Buffer And Duration Variation In Construction Project Tasks: Comparison of perception to reality. *Journal of Construction Engineering and Management*, *140*(6), 04014016. DOI: 10.1061/(ASCE)CO.1943-7862.0000819

Sacks, R. (2016). What Constitutes Good Production Flow in Construction? *Construction Management and Economics*, *34*(9), 641–656. DOI: 10.1080/01446193.2016.1200733

KEY TERMS AND DEFINITIONS

Digital Cinematography: The aim of Digital Cinematography is to ensure a qualified production by examining digital image production in artistic productions as in every field, both from a plastic and theoretical point of view. Especially since the beginning of the 2000s, technological developments in digital image production have encompassed the entire field of digital video production, from photography to cinema. With the opportunities that emerged with digitalization, the best simatography production process has started.

Visual Production: Since 1999, the transformation brought about by technological developments has manifested itself in the cinema industry as in every field. Visual Productions products are a combination of creative thinking, technical innovation and feedback-driven design used to meet modern market demands. Software applications and hardware devices are designed with a strong emphasis on usability, resulting in feature-rich and user-friendly lighting control products that are fast becoming the preferred choice in the market.

Chroma Keying: Chroma keying, also known as green screen technology, is a technique used in video editing to overlap or merge two images or video streams based on their color tones. This technique involves shooting the subject against a monochrome background, usually green or blue, and then replacing that background color with a different image or video in post-production . This technique is commonly used to create special effects in weather broadcasts, movies and TV shows, or to place characters in a variety of different environments. It is a powerful tool that allows video editors to create scenes that would be impossible or extremely difficult to shoot in real life.

LED Walls: LED wall panels, also known as LED display panels, are modular units with built-in LED display modules, power supply, receiving card, etc. They are used to create large and dynamic visual images. These panels are designed to be assembled together to form a seamless LED video wall or display screen. LED wall panels are available in various sizes, shapes and pixel pitches to accommodate different applications and viewing distances.

Motion Capture: Motion capture is a technology that digitizes real-world motion and has revolutionized the art world. Motion capture is a technology that measures and digitizes the real-world movements of an actor or a moving object. Using specialized cameras, sensors, processors and software, this technology captures motion data in real time and makes it animatable in a computer environment. This system captures motion data through small sensors or tracking points placed on moving objects.

Virtual Reality: It is the phenomenon of adding objects to the real world environment with computer-generated sound, image, graphics and GPS data and obtaining a physical appearance in the real world. The concept of augmented reality can also be considered as adding imaginary characters to the real world.

Unreal Engine (UE): A 3D computer graphics game engine developed by Epic Games and first showcased in the first-person shooter video game Unreal in 1998. Originally developed for PC gaming, it has been used in a variety of game genres and has been adopted by other industries, most notably the film and television industry.

About the Contributors

Nursel Bolat, Ph.D., is a professor at Ondokuz Mayis University, Department of Radio, Television and Cinema. She authored two books (Product Placement: Main Concepts and Channel, Analysing of TV Dramas), and she published numerous papers in several journals, conference proceedings, and chapters in edited books. Her majors are Broadcasting and Digital Media. She also studies Advertising. Some courses she teaches are Broadcasting, Practices in TV Prorammes, Fundamental Technics in Broadcasting, Semiotics and Editing.

***

Ayşegül Akaydın Aydın, Assoc. Prof., studied Television Journalism (B.A) in Istanbul Bilgi University and Media Management (M.A.) in Marmara University. She got her PhD degree from Radio-TV Cinema department in Istanbul University. She worked as research assistant in Istanbul Bilgi University between 2009-2017. She has been working as associate professor at Istanbul Aydin University, Journalism department, Faculty of Communication. Akaydin also lectured at Klaipeda University in Lithuania with Erasmus+ Staff Mobility Programme and she participated in summer academy programme at Thessaloniki International Media Academy both in 2019. She has published numerous articles in toptier academic journals.

Emel Ateşçi graduated from Ege University (the Department of Radio, Television and Cinema, the Faculty of Communication) in 2004. She completed her master's degree in Kocaeli University, the Institute of Social Sciences, Department of Radio and Television in 2015. She received a PhD. degree from Kocaeli University Institute of Social Sciences, Department of Communication Sciences. Her research interests are Audience Research, New Media, Communication Studies. She currently continues in her academic studies at Kocaeli University Faculty of Communication, the Department of Radio, Television and Cinema.

Abdulkadir Çabuk completed his undergraduate education in the Department of Translation and Interpreting (Arabic) at Istanbul Okan University in 2019. He received his Master's degree in 2023 from the Department of Media and Cultural Studies at Üsküdar University, with his thesis titled "Globalized Television and Culture: A Study on Arab Television Audiences Living in Turkey and Turkish TV Series." In the same year, he commenced his doctoral studies in the Department of New Media and Communication at Üsküdar University.

Volkan Çetin, who is part of the academic staff at Istanbul Bilgi University, works in fields such as 2D-3D graphic design, interface design, motion graphics, photography, and video. Additionally, he has participated in various exhibitions and short film projects.

Mert Gürer completed a master's program in Communication Sciences at the Department of Communication Sciences of the Institute of Social Sciences of Kocaeli University. In 2012, he received a PhD. degree from Istanbul University Institute of Social Sciences, Department of Radio and Television Cinema. He works on television broadcasting and programming. Currently, he is an associate professor at the Department of Radio, Film and Television at the Faculty of Communication of Kocaeli University.

Rashid Hashmi is a seasoned television journalist and academician with over 22 years of distinguished experience in broadcast journalism, combined with an impactful academic career. Currently serving as a Professor of Practice at the Sharda School of Media, Film & Entertainment, Sharda University, Prof. Hashmi is known for seamlessly integrating industry experience with academic insight, thereby fostering a dynamic learning environment. He has held senior editorial positions in prominent Indian news channels, including Executive Editor and Senior Anchor at India News, Editor-in-Chief at FM News, and Output Editor at India News, anchoring acclaimed prime-time shows such as Rajdharm, Rashid vs Rajneeti, Prime Time, and Yakshprashn. Throughout his journalistic journey, he has covered high-profile political elections, border conflicts, and national crises, producing special reports and documentaries such as "Ayodhya Tere Kitne Ram", "Shauryagatha", "Aakraman", and "Operation Meghprahahar". In academia, Prof. Hashmi has been a driving force in curriculum innovation, faculty mentorship, and industry-academia collaborations. He has facilitated numerous MoUs, spearheaded live projects, and organized news channel visits, bridging classroom theories with real-world newsroom experiences. As the head of Sharda TV and the departmental newspaper Sharda Samachar, he mentors students in live TV production, anchoring, podcasting, and content creation. His role in launching the Anchoring-Reporting Club and initiating podcasting culture at the university has significantly elevated student engagement and practical training. Prof. Hashmi is a Gold Medalist in Mass Communication and a Ph.D. Scholar at IFTM University, Moradabad, pursuing research on "Emergence of Digital Medium and AI: Navigating Challenges in a Changing Media Landscape." He also holds diplomas in News Anchoring and Video Editing. His research portfolio includes: 3 book chapters published with IGI Global 5 national book chapters 4 papers presented at international conferences in the past 10 months 2 upcoming Scopus-indexed journal publications Upcoming authored books: "Anchoring, Reporting, Paradigm Shift from Traditional to Digital Media" and "Indian Democracy in 25 Years of the New Century." Prof. Hashmi is a two-time ENBA Award winner (2022 & 2023) for his compelling news stories on the political crises in Pakistan and Sri Lanka. He has received over 20 prestigious awards in his journalism career. His exclusive interviews span key personalities including Gen. V.K. Singh, Azam Khan, Kangana Ranaut, Shahid Kapoor, and Yuvraj Singh. He has also taught at Jagannath Institute of Management Sciences (JIMS) and served as a guest or visiting faculty at several reputed institutions such as Amity University, Maharaja Agrasen College, Galgotia University, Marwah Studios, IAAN School of Mass Communication, and VIPS. Prof. Rashid Hashmi continues to shape future media professionals with a vision rooted in ethical journalism, digital innovation, and global academic standards.

Ufuk Inal has received undergraduate and master degree from Radio, Television and Cinema department in Kocaeli University. He has started PHD study in communication sciences departmant in Kocaeli University. He's currently working in Radio, Television and Cinema department in Ondokuz Mayıs University. His current research interest are Radio Broadcasting and New Media Studies.

Gözde İslamoğlu was born in Ankara in 1986. She completed a master's program in Radio Television and Cinema at the Department of Radio Television and Cinema of the Institute of Social Sciences in Kocaeli University. In 2024, she received a PhD. degree from Kocaeli University Institute of Social Sciences, Department of Communication Sciences. She works on new media, new communication technologies, communication sciences. She currently continues in her academic studies at Kocaeli University Faculty of Communication, the Department of Radio Television and Cinema.

Tuğçe Karaca Özdemir completed her high school education at Dilovası Vocational and Technical Anatolian High School. Prior to her undergraduate studies, she graduated with first place from the Vocational School of Media and Communication at Ondokuz Mayıs University. She then received her bachelor's degree from the Faculty of Communication, Department of Radio, Television and Cinema at Ondokuz Mayıs University on January 31, 2022. In 2022, she began her master's studies at Ondokuz Mayıs University Graduate School, in the Interdisciplinary Department of Communication Sciences, and graduated from the program in 2025.

Yağmur Kılıç completed her high school education at Ankara İncirli Şehit Furkan Yayla Anatolian High School. She graduated from the Department of Journalism at the Faculty of Communication, Ondokuz Mayıs University, in 2020. In 2022, she was admitted to the Master's Program in Communication Sciences at the Graduate School of Ondokuz Mayıs University and completed the program in 2025. During her graduate studies, Kılıç focused on communication theories and media discourse analysis and continues her academic work in this field. ORCID: 0000-0001-6591-5867

Rabiya Saltik Duvan was born on 28 October 1992 in Istanbul. She completed her undergraduate education at Marmara University Faculty of Communication, Department of Radio, Television and Cinema within the 30% English programme, graduating in 2015. During her education, she engaged professionally in print and digital media, working as a reporter in various newspapers and magazines, and as an editor in digital publishing platforms. With an objective to specialise in the academic domain, Saltik Duvan was admitted to the Master's programme in the Department of Radio, Television and Cinema at Marmara University in 2015, with a thesis component. In 2017, she successfully completed her master's degree, with her thesis on social media culture, and was awarded the title of “expert”. In the same year, she commenced her PhD programme at Marmara University, concurrently pursuing her academic career and assuming the role of a lecturer at Istanbul Kavram Vocational School. In 2021, Saltik Duvan was awarded the title of “doctor” by completing her doctoral dissertation on the “psychological atmosphere of the cyber world” in the context of postmodern subject experiences. In 2022, she embarked on her academic career as an Assistant Professor at Istanbul Gelişim University Faculty of Communication, where she is currently pursuing her studies. Her research focuses on various areas of the communication discipline, with a particular emphasis on new media, digital communication and media psychology. In addition to her research endeavours, she also contributes to undergraduate education through her teaching engagements, which encompass a range of undergraduate courses within the aforementioned areas of specialisation.

Esennur Sirer was born in Bursa in 1969. She graduated from Bursa Girls' High School in 1986. In 1990, he graduated from Istanbul University Journalism Faculty of Radio and Television. In 2010, she received her master's degree on Radio-TV Cinema from Istanbul University Institute of Social Sciences with her thesis titled 'The Evolving and Changing Formal Structure of Television Journalism" With her thesis titled "Football as a Popular Culture Product: Image Arrangement from the Viewpoint of the Elements of Construction in Publicity", she was awarded the title of Doctor in Radio-TV at Istanbul University Institute of Social Sciences. From 1992 to 2018, she worked as director in TRT News and Sports Publications Department in Istanbul. In addition to directing, she has been conducting her academic studies since 2007 as a faculty member in the Department of Radio, Television, Cinema and Cinema, Uskudar University, since October 2018.

Esennur Sirer completed her undergraduate education at Istanbul University, Department of Radio and Television in 1990. She completed her master's degree in 2010 at Istanbul University, Institute of Social Sciences, Department of Radio, Television and Cinema with her thesis titled "Developing and Changing Formal Structure of Television Journalism" and completed her doctorate in 2018 at Istanbul University, Institute of Social Sciences, Department of Radio, Television and Cinema with her thesis titled "Football as a Product of Popular Culture: Image Editing in Terms of Production Elements in Live Broadcasting" and received her doctorate. In the same year, she started working as an assistant professor at Üsküdar University, Department of Radio, Television and Cinema. She has been serving as the Department Head in this department since April 2020. As a result of her work during this period, she was entitled to receive the title of associate professor from the Council of Higher Education on July 28, 2021. Assoc. Prof. Dr. In addition to his theoretical studies and publications, Sirer worked at the TRT News and Sports Broadcasting Department Istanbul Directorate between 1992-2018 and served as a director and producer in many broadcasts at home and abroad.

Cem Tutar graduated from Ege University, Faculty of Communication, Department of Radio-Television and Cinema in 2006. In 2009, he received his master's degree from Dokuz Eylül University Institute of Fine Arts, Department of Cinema-TV. In 2015, he received his PhD degree from Ege University Institute of Social Sciences, Department of Radio-Television and Cinema. In 2022, he received the title of associate professor in the field of Communication Studies from the Interuniversity Council. Cem Tutar is the Head of the Department of Cartoon and Animation at Üsküdar University Faculty of Communication and is also the Head of the Department of Media and Cultural Studies Graduate Program at the Institute of Social Sciences. Cem Tutar works on media readings on the basis of everyday life and urban sociology within the field of cultural studies with an interdisciplinary perspective. In addition to his book Dynamics of Everyday Life on Television, Tutar has published book chapters, articles and papers in the academic field.

Index

A

B

C

D

F

G

H

I

K

L

M

N

O

P

R

S

T

U

V

www.ingramcontent.com/pod-product-compliance
Ingram Content Group UK Ltd.
Pitfield, Milton Keynes, MK11 3LW, UK
UKHW051028041026
15470UKWH00015B/1732

9 798337 319575